SAINT-SAËNS AND THE STAGE

The stage works of Saint-Saëns range from grand open-air pageants to one-act comic operas, and include the first composed film score. Yet, with the exception of *Samson et Dalila*, his twelve operas have lain in the shadows since the composer's death in 1921. Widely performed in his lifetime, they vanished from the repertory – never played, never recorded – until now. With four twenty-first-century revivals as a backdrop, this timely book is the first study of Saint-Saëns's operas, demonstrating the presence of the same breadth and versatility as in his better-known works. Hugh Macdonald's wide knowledge of French music in the nineteenth century gives a powerful understanding of the different conventions and expectations that governed French opera at the time. The interaction of Saint-Saëns with his contemporaries is a colourful and important part of the story.

HUGH MACDONALD's distinguished career has included appointments at the Universities of Cambridge, Oxford and Glasgow and at Washington University in St Louis. He was General Editor of the New Berlioz Edition (1967–2006) and has published books on Skryabin, Berlioz and Bizet.

CAMBRIDGE STUDIES IN OPERA
Series Editor: ARTHUR GROOS, Cornell University

Volumes for Cambridge Studies in Opera explore the cultural, political and social influences of the genre. As a cultural art form, opera is not produced in a vacuum. Rather, it is influenced, whether directly or in more subtle ways, by its social and political environment. In turn, opera leaves its mark on society and contributes to shaping the cultural climate. Studies in the series will look at these various relationships, including the politics and economics of opera, the operatic representation of women and the singers who portrayed them, the history of opera as theatre and the evolution of the opera house.

Published Titles

Opera Buffa in Mozart's Vienna
Edited by Mary Hunter and James Webster

German Opera: From the Beginnings to Wagner
John Warrack

Johann Strauss and Vienna: Operetta and the Politics of Popular Culture
Camille Crittenden

Opera and Drama in Eighteenth-Century London: The King's Theatre, Garrick and the Business of Performance
Ian Woodfield

Opera, Liberalism, and Antisemitism in Nineteenth-Century France: The Politics of Halévy's *La Juive*
Diana R. Hallman

Three Modes of Perception in Mozart: The Philosophical, Pastoral, and Comic in *Così fan tutte*
Edmund J. Goehring

Landscape and Gender in Italian Opera: The Alpine Virgin from Bellini to Puccini
Emanuele Senici

Aesthetics of Opera in the Ancien Régime, 1647–1785
Downing A. Thomas

The Puccini Problem: Opera, Nationalism, and Modernity
Alexandra Wilson

The Prima Donna and Opera, 1815–1930
Susan Rutherford

Opera and Society in Italy and France from Monteverdi to Bourdieu
Edited by Victoria Johnson, Jane F. Fulcher and Thomas Ertman

Wagner's Ring Cycle and the Greeks
Daniel H. Foster

When Opera Meets Film
Marcia J. Citron

Situating Opera: Period, Genre, Reception
Herbert Lindenberger

Rossini in Restoration Paris: The Sound of Modern Life
Benjamin Walton

Italian Opera in the Age of the American Revolution
Pierpaolo Polzonetti

Opera in the Novel from Balzac to Proust
Cormac Newark

Opera in the Age of Rousseau: Music, Confrontation, Realism
David Charlton

The Sounds of Paris in Verdi's *La traviata*
Emilio Sala

The Rival Sirens: Performance and Identity on Handel's Operatic Stage
Suzanne Aspden

Sentimental Opera: Questions of Genre in the Age of Bourgeois Drama
Stefano Castelvecchi

Verdi, Opera, Women
Susan Rutherford

Rounding Wagner's Mountain: Richard Strauss and Modern German Opera
Bryan Gilliam

Opera and Modern Spectatorship in Late Nineteenth-Century Italy
Alessandra Campana

Opera Acts: Singers and Performance in the Late Nineteenth Century
Karen Henson

Foreign Opera at the London Playhouses: From Mozart to Bellini
Christina Fuhrmann

Dance and Drama in French Baroque Opera: A History
Rebecca Harris-Warrick

Technology and the Diva: Sopranos, Opera, and Media from Romanticism to the Digital Age
Karen Henson

Female Singers on the French Stage, 1830–1848
Kimberly White

Opera in Postwar Venice: Cultural Politics and the Avant-Garde
Harriet Boyd-Bennett

Saint-Saëns and the Stage: Operas, Plays, Pageants, a Ballet and a Film
Hugh Macdonald

Camille Saint-Saëns, photograph by Dagron, early 1880s
Gunther Braam Collection, Munich

Saint-Saëns and the Stage
Operas, Plays, Pageants, a Ballet and a Film

Hugh Macdonald
Emeritus, Washington University, St Louis

CAMBRIDGE
UNIVERSITY PRESS

CAMBRIDGE
UNIVERSITY PRESS

University Printing House, Cambridge CB2 8BS, United Kingdom

One Liberty Plaza, 20th Floor, New York, NY 10006, USA

477 Williamstown Road, Port Melbourne, VIC 3207, Australia

314-321, 3rd Floor, Plot 3, Splendor Forum, Jasola District Centre, New Delhi - 110025, India

103 Penang Road, #05-06/07, Visioncrest Commercial, Singapore 238467

Cambridge University Press is part of the University of Cambridge.

It furthers the University's mission by disseminating knowledge in the pursuit of education, learning and research at the highest international levels of excellence.

www.cambridge.org
Information on this title: www.cambridge.org/9781108445092
DOI: 10.1017/9781108550925

© Hugh Macdonald 2019

This publication is in copyright. Subject to statutory exception and to the provisions of relevant collective licensing agreements, no reproduction of any part may take place without the written permission of Cambridge University Press.

First published 2019
First paperback edition 2021

A catalogue record for this publication is available from the British Library

Library of Congress Cataloging in Publication data
NAMES: Macdonald, Hugh, 1940– author.
TITLE: Saint-Saens and the stage : operas, plays, pageants, a ballet and a film / Hugh Macdonald.
DESCRIPTION: Cambridge, United Kingdom ; New York, NY : Cambridge University Press, 2019. | Series: Cambridge studies in opera | Includes bibliographical references and index.
IDENTIFIERS: LCCN 2018036665 | ISBN 9781108426381
SUBJECTS: LCSH: Saint-Saens, Camille, 1835–1921 – Criticism and interpretation. | Opera – 19th century. | Dramatic music – 19th century – History and criticism.
CLASSIFICATION: LCC ML410.S15 M3 2019 | DDC 782.1092–dc23
LC record available at https://lccn.loc.gov/2018036665

ISBN 978-1-108-42638-1 Hardback
ISBN 978-1-108-44509-2 Paperback

Cambridge University Press has no responsibility for the persistence or accuracy of URLs for external or third-party internet websites referred to in this publication, and does not guarantee that any content on such websites is, or will remain, accurate or appropriate.

For my three lifelong
confrères transatlantiques

Peter Bloom
D. Kern Holoman
Ralph P. Locke

CONTENTS

List of Illustrations | *page* x
Preface | xi

1 **Preparations for Opera:** *Le Martyre de Vivia, Le Duc de Parme* | 1
2 *Le Timbre d'argent* | 20
3 *Samson et Dalila* | 50
4 *La Princesse jaune* | 76
5 *Étienne Marcel* | 92
6 *Henry VIII* | 124
7 *Gabriella di Vergy, Proserpine* | 161
8 *Ascanio* | 188
9 *La Crampe des écrivains, Phryné* | 222
10 *Antigone, Frédégonde* | 244
11 *Javotte, Déjanire* (open air) | 263
12 *Lola, Les Barbares* | 286
13 *Parysatis, Botriocéphale, Andromaque, Le Roi Apépi, Hélène* | 311
14 *L'Ancêtre, La Foi* | 332
15 *L'Assassinat du Duc de Guise, Déjanire* (opera), *On ne badine pas avec l'amour* | 356
16 **Saint-Saëns the Dramatist** | 378

Bibliography | 394
Discography | 405
Index | 416

ILLUSTRATIONS

Frontispiece: Camille Saint-Saëns, photograph by Dagron, early 1880s
	Gunther Braam Collection, Munich | *page* iv

3.1   *Samson et Dalila*, final scene (*L'Illustration*, 8 November 1890)
	Mary Evans Picture Library | 71
4.1   Louis Gallet, photograph
	Bridgeman Images | 78
6.1   *Henry VIII*, the Synod scene, 1883
	Bibliothèque et Musée de l'Opéra/Wikimedia Commons | 151
8.1   François I, by Titian
	Musée du Louvre, Paris/Bridgeman Images | 219
9.1   Jean-Léon Gérôme, *Phryné devant l'Aréopagus*
	Kunsthalle, Hamburg/Wikimedia Commons | 230
11.1 Letter of Saint-Saëns, 16 December 1895
	Northwestern University, Evanston | 264
11.2 *Javotte*, piano score, cover
	Hugh Macdonald Collection, Norwich | 270
11.3 *Déjanire* at Béziers, 1898
	L'Univers illustré, August 1898 | 283
12.1 *Les Barbares*, mise-en-scène, Act I
	Hugh Macdonald Collection, Norwich | 298
12.2 *Les Barbares*, oxen waiting in the wings at the Opéra
	José Pons Collection, Paris | 307
14.1 *L'Ancêtre*, Act II, set by Albert Dubosq, Antwerp 1912
	FelixArchief/Stadsarchief, Antwerp | 342

PREFACE

Audiences attending performances of *Samson et Dalila* must sometimes have wondered if its composer wrote any other operas, especially if they know that he lived to the age of eighty-six. How many are there? What kind of operas are they? What happened to them? Are they any good? Not even the first of these questions can be answered clearly, since between 1864 and 1910 Saint-Saëns composed a dozen operas of a conventional kind, two satirical operettas, a number of incomplete opéras-comiques and half of Ernest Guiraud's unfinished *Frédégonde*. The variety of other dramatic works includes two full-scale open-air pageants, incidental music for half a dozen plays, a ballet and a film. The other questions are more complex, for the many hours of music that all this stage music fills represent a major slice of a composer's œuvre, surely deserving more than a rapid survey, especially when the popularity and high standing of Saint-Saëns in nineteenth-century French music is taken into account.

When I was asked to write the Saint-Saëns entries for the *New Grove Dictionary of Opera*, published in 1992, I was astonished to find almost no critical literature devoted to these works (other than *Samson et Dalila*) even though biographies and studies of Saint-Saëns's work as a whole were plentiful in many languages. It was this observation that planted in me the desire to explore Saint-Saëns as a composer for the stage and to give serious attention to an immense body of music which had escaped performance, recording and critical attention for nearly a century.

In other respects Saint-Saëns is not a neglected composer. On the contrary, his name is found frequently on concert programmes, and certain pieces are popular favourites. The *Danse macabre*, the 'Organ' Symphony, the Second Piano Concerto, the *Carnival of the Animals* and *Samson et Dalila* itself are all regularly performed everywhere. Much of his instrumental music has received full scholarly study and has been recorded, and the documentation of his life is gradually appearing in print. Yet it is easy to explain why his operas do not feature in the general consciousness of his life's work. Most of them are full-length works which are expensive and demanding to stage, and if the tradition of performing them is broken, as it was in 1921, then singers and conductors will not carry them in their repertoires. If they are not recorded, those who do not easily read scores will have no access to them. Biographers and critics have been inhibited from writing about these operas since there is no living tradition to judge them by.

Saint-Saëns's high standing among the galaxy of great composers working in France in the *belle époque* is unquestioned, and he is universally acknowledged to have been one of the most formidable musicians of his time. He was composer, virtuoso pianist, organist, conductor, poet, critic, playwright, teacher and impresario, and there was no branch of music in France in the half century between 1870 and 1920 that was not touched in some way by his presence. His vast output includes music in every genre: symphonies, concertos, chamber music, choral music, piano music, organ music, operas, ballet, incidental music, even film music. He wrote abundantly for the musical press. He travelled widely as conductor and pianist, even into his eighties. He made recordings, both live and for piano-rolls. He was a leading editor of French baroque music and a pioneer in the study of ancient music.

An œuvre as extensive as this cannot possibly all be familiar to musicians. Yet the obscurity in which the stage music has lain (always excepting *Samson et Dalila*) is too dark and too deep to be explained as fitting within a statistical norm. It is surely impossible that a composer who created one top-ranking opera and a considerable body of first-class orchestral and chamber works should somehow have failed completely in all the remaining operas. If we take into account his versatility in all genres, his high literary sensibility, his comprehensive technical skill and his close familiarity with all the music of his time, it is impossible to argue that Saint-Saëns was somehow ill-equipped to write for the stage or that he was blind to the essentials of good operatic writing. He believed in his own gifts for opera sufficiently to produce these works at regular intervals over a period of nearly fifty years, and they were all published and staged, some many times over, in his lifetime. In his biography of Saint-Saëns published in 1899, Otto Neitzel gave much more attention to the operas than to other works, assuming that they were the most important.[1]

At the moment Saint-Saëns died in 1921, taste in music (and in the arts in general) had begun to perform a somersault which condemned much of the music of the previous two generations to a spell in outer darkness. In the field of French opera both Massenet and Saint-Saëns were victims of this, and it has taken a long while for Massenet to recover. His operas are gradually re-establishing their place in the repertoire and earning the recognition they deserve, while those of Saint-Saëns have still to be given a chance to be weighed and tested. When they are recorded and revived at least occasionally on stage, I hope there will be many other evaluations besides my own on which his real achievement may be judged.

My desire to study these works in depth has not been motivated by any particular ambition to see the operas revived on stage and to claim that they are 'unjustly neglected'. Opera companies do not normally have the resources to devote to revivals of this kind. I am more specifically curious to observe the application of the composer's

---

[1] NEITZEL 1899.

high craftsmanship in a variety of dramatic genres: grand opera, comedy, fantasy, verismo, and so on, and to give these forgotten works the critical examination they have hitherto been denied. The standard critical opinion may be taken to be the summary judgment of *Grove Music Online*, the most widely read scholarly resource in English: 'Although the operas contain much agreeable and skilfully shaped music, they are deficient in theatrical effect', a judgment made without the experience of hearing them in the theatre or even, in most cases, from recording.[2]

Although my main focus is on the operas, it was impossible not to take into account the composer's lifelong interest in the spoken theatre, writing music for many stage productions of plays and even writing a handful of plays himself. His ballet *Javotte* is a gem that should never be overlooked, and his exploration of other dramatic formulæ, particularly the open-air pageants played in the arena at Béziers, was an important manifestation of his search for an ideal antique drama. His single film score, on the other hand, was no declaration of interest in a new art form, but simply a response – and a strikingly successful response – to the knock of opportunity.

My aim in this book is to provide a historical and critical account of each work with a record of its performance history, such as it is. I also raise the question of whether these works are neglected because of inherent failures in the libretto and music, or because of a lack of sympathy or comprehension on the part of those audiences and critics who have been in a position to judge them. This will be based on an assessment of the operas against the background of the complex theatrical and operatic culture of their time. If I seem to undervalue the opinions of the contemporary press, it is because, as I point out in the first chapter, I have doubts about the qualifications and reliability of critics who came, as they mostly did, from the ranks of men of letters rather than musicians. *Rezeptionsgeschichte* has the worthy aim of establishing the expectations which a composer might have to face at any time, but it cannot use contemporary criticism to replace the exercise of our own critical faculties, and I have myself long avoided reading contemporary reviews when attempting to assess the value of a French opera of this period.

The history of performances of the operas since the composer's death is in every case except that of *Samson et Dalila* a slim chronicle which can only show a better record in the next hundred years than in the last. The 2007 Australian recording of the one-act opera *Hélène* met with astonishment from many who found unexpected power and beauty in this 1904 score. A similar reaction was observed at the Bard Festival in 2012, when *Henry VIII* was heard in a fine concert performance with first-class singers. And since I began work on this book there have been, thanks to the patronage of the Palazzetto Bru Zane, first-class recordings of *Les Barbares*, *Proserpine* and *Le Timbre d'argent*, which have contributed enormously to a new understanding of these works.

[2] oxfordmusiconline.com, article 'Saint-Saëns, Camille', consulted 1.1.2018.

In 2017 alone the latter opera received an enterprising revival on the stage of the Opéra-Comique, *Frédégonde* was staged in Ho Chi Minh City and *Ascanio* was heard in concert performance in Geneva. This encourages me to believe that things are moving in the right direction.

A strong spur to my work was the Bard Festival, at Bard College, New York, in 2012, devoted entirely to Saint-Saëns's music, and in the same year there appeared two essential publications which have enormously facilitated the task. The first is the second volume of Sabina Teller Ratner's *Thematic Catalogue* of Saint-Saëns's works, devoted to the stage works.[3] She gives a full bibliographical and archival record of each work, together with copious relevant correspondence. The second is Marie-Gabrielle Soret's superbly edited collection of Saint-Saëns's voluminous writings on music.[4] To both of these scholars I acknowledge a profound debt. The documentation of Saint-Saëns's life and work is nonetheless far from complete. Most of his life he kept all correspondence he received and for many years he had a secretary who kept copies of correspondence he sent. For any active individual who lived to be over eighty in Third Republic France, this amounted to a vast exchange of letters, and in Saint-Saëns's case his fondness for travel and for staying for long periods away from Paris required a constant exchange of letters with his collaborators, associates and friends. The Médiathèque Jean-Renoir in Dieppe holds over 15,000 letters from and to Saint-Saëns, and a similar number must exist in public and private collections elsewhere, without counting the composer's constant mentions in the press: trawling the daily papers and the music journals for references to his activities in many fields would produce many more thousands of texts. In due time perhaps they will all be accessible on the internet or in print, but even then it will impose superhuman demands on scholars and researchers. I freely acknowledge that I have been able to consult only a fraction of this hoard, so there will be gaps in my discussion of the operas that other scholars will fill if, as I hope, these works come to attract more detailed critical attention than what I have attempted here. For many works, in addition, there is a variety of sketches and drafts that deserve closer scrutiny. This will be the task one day for the editors of a critical edition of the music for the stage.

Lisa Etheridge has given me essential help with the illustrations. I am further indebted to many friends and colleagues who have provided me with information and help of many kinds. Chief among them are Gunther Braam, Jeanice Brooks, David Cairns, Andrea Cawelti, Alexandre Dratwicki, Warwick Edwards, Jim Farrington, Bruno Forment, Matthew Franke, Matthieu Gerbault, Vincent Giroud, Monika

---

[3] RATNER 2012. The first volume of this publication (RATNER 2002) covers the instrumental works and the third volume, forthcoming, will cover vocal and choral music.
[4] SORET 2012.

Hennemann, Richard Langham Smith, Arnaud Laster, Gregory S. MacAyeal, Mitsuya Nakanishi, Bernard Peyrotte, José Pons, Marjorie Rycroft, Bradley Short, Marie-Gabrielle Soret, Michael Stegemann, Sabina Teller Ratner, and Tamara Thompson. I have enjoyed the continued support of Washington University, St Louis, throughout my researches. To all of these I extend my sincere thanks.

1 | Preparations for Opera: *Le Martyre de Vivia, Le Duc de Parme*

The music of the Romantic age is one of the great success stories of western culture, since the masterpieces of the nineteenth century – and innumerable compositions of lesser stature – are still the staple diet of our listening and performing today. To have been born a musician in 1835, as Saint-Saëns was, was to grow up in a world where the balance between expression, language and technical means was wonderfully well adjusted. Composers from Berlioz and Schumann to Strauss and Mahler gave the world a body of music that is passionately loved and admired, and which speaks with a strong stirring voice to listeners of every generation. Those composers were addressing their own contemporaries, of course, whose tastes and expectations were different from ours, and although we feel a strong empathy for their music, we can only envy audiences of that age who were present when works such as Chopin's preludes, Berlioz's *Roméo et Juliette*, Wagner's *Ring* cycle or Brahms's symphonies were first played and first heard.

The language of tonality – based on major and minor scales – was firmly in place, a secure harbour to which expeditions into chromatic zones always returned, the exploration itself providing individuality and piquancy without disturbing the listener's grasp of geography (to extend the metaphor) and sense of well-being at the home-coming. Music's ability to suggest things, persons, places, activities and emotions, already exploited in the baroque period, was accepted as a kind of standard glossary, so that the character of any piece could be grasped in words and its emotional content shared. A Nocturne or a Capriccio did not need to be elucidated. Tchaikovsky could respond to a request to explain the content of his Fourth Symphony by inventing a narrative that probably had little to do with his original thoughts when composing the work, but at least he recognised that some such content was taken for granted and was regarded by his audience as a help to understanding and appreciation. Once Anton Schindler had been shown up as an impostor, his tale that Beethoven told him that the opening of the Fifth Symphony represented Fate Knocking at the Door could be disbelieved, but that the motif represented *something* was never in doubt. Eduard Hanslick's tract *Vom musikalische Schön* of 1854 did cast doubt on such an assumption, but his views were shared by very few before the twentieth century. It was assumed that the stuff of poetry and painting was within the proper domain of music, and that the reader or listener could respond to one just as he or she would to the other.

Technical advances created a mighty solo instrument out of the modest forte-piano; the advent of valves enormously enlarged the relevance and potential of brass instruments; certain instruments like the harp and the bass clarinet developed carefully distinct orchestral roles. Behind such advances as these, mercantile prosperity provided big theatres and concert halls and audiences who could afford to go to them. The railways allowed musicians, especially virtuoso soloists, to travel freely and quickly from city to city. Journals devoted exclusively to music and reporting on musical news from home and abroad sprang up in every country. Lithography made printed music cheaper, allowing choral groups to expand to an extraordinary size. Orchestras and conservatoires were founded in all the major cities of Europe and America.

Music of the past was now respected and gradually allowed to infiltrate programmes in which otherwise all the music was relatively new. Beethoven was never treated as 'old' music, as his music forced itself to the centre of the repertoire, whether for pianists, chamber musicians or orchestras. Establishing the greatness of Bach was one of the nineteenth century's most important achievements. Yet new music and living composers were still the main focus of interest, and they would remain so until the middle of the twentieth century.

Within the larger picture French, German and Italian music of the nineteenth century had their distinctive lines of development. Along with her sister arts, literature and painting, music in nineteenth-century France was centralised to an extraordinary degree. In this the arts were only following the money and the politics, which since Louis XIV's time ensured that Paris projected a magnetism and drew all ambitious young men, not to mention drifters and chancers, to the capital. There were defiant provincials, of course, who insisted that money could be made and life could be enjoyed elsewhere, but the overwhelming prestige of the capital was recognised throughout Europe, feeding on itself and holding firm at least until the First World War. Being born in Paris gave Saint-Saëns, like Gounod and Bizet, a great start as a musician.

After Napoleon's defeat in 1815 France rapidly buried her reputation as a military bully and became instead an enlightened utopia for mercantile progress and artistic glory. Foreigners were welcomed to Paris and many, like Heine, Chopin and Rossini, chose to stay. Open borders offered particular advantages to musicians not dependent on language to ply their trade. From Italy, Germany and eastern Europe they came in good numbers to work with other top-class musicians and to sample the world-class wares of Pleyel and Erard. They came to attend the Conservatoire, a path-breaking institution founded in the turmoil of the Revolution, and they came, too, to attend the Opéra, about which so much was reported in the world's press. Since French was the language spoken by educated people everywhere, Paris was a city that visitors found particularly congenial and hospitable.

The prominence of opera in Parisian culture has been widely observed and studied.[1] Its roots can be traced to the superiority of French wine and cuisine, which has led to the cultivation of long, exquisite meals in which the art of conversation can only flourish. This in turn has led to the breed of French connoisseur who is familiar with all the current issues in art, literature and politics and is willing to assert his opinion on any of them. Such people read all the new novels, visit all the new exhibitions and attend all the new operas, which guarantees that the opera house will be patronised by a great number of individuals with little or no musical expertise but plenty of willingness to air their views. With opera's literary element (the libretto) and its scenic element (sets, costumes and dancing) there is still plenty for the non-musician's attention, whereas orchestral concerts offered much less scope, even though all concerts at that time included at least some vocal items.

Built in 1821 in the Rue Le Peletier, the new Paris Opéra was equipped to present large-scale spectacles with a huge stage and orchestra pit and all the latest technology. Gas lighting was introduced in 1822. This eventually allowed the house lights to be dimmed, but throughout the century the house lights were sufficient for the audience to follow the action with the printed libretto. Publishers were anxious to issue these librettos in time for the first night, so that their texts are often based on versions of the opera that were not actually staged. Vocal scores took longer to print and were not usually ready by the time an opera opened, but they are often a better record of what was sung and played. Conversation and discussion during the music was less intrusive than in the eighteenth century, but was still inescapable, with 'bravo' and 'bis' shouted or singers booed. The claque was in action throughout the first part of the century at least, noisily supporting whatever the management paid them to support. Individual artists had their personal claques too.

A major attraction at the Opéra was the magnificence and realism of the sets, sustained well into the twentieth century, though entirely lost today. If an opera was announced as in 'four acts and six tableaux' the spectator could expect six sets, some repeated as necessary, each requiring the erection in three dimensions of whatever buildings were to be seen: churches, castles, taverns, palaces, with rivers and mountains often visible in the distance. Interior settings would be fully furnished according to the style of the period. Historical accuracy in the sets and costumes was much vaunted, and a great number of expert designers were engaged. Scene changes were long and intervals many, of varying length, and in some of them an entr'acte would be played by the orchestra with the audience taking little or no notice.

The Opéra was proud of its ballet, with a large *corps* and some great dancers on its roster. Modern criticism now yawns at the idea of ballet in opera, but this was not the case in nineteenth-century Paris. It was not just the well-known interest of the rakes of

---

[1] See FULCHER 1987, JOHNSON 1995, GERHARD 1998, CHARLTON 2003 and many other studies.

the Jockey Club ogling the ballerinas with their binoculars, nor just the fact that ballet provided one of the only occasions on which even a part of a woman's legs could be seen in public. Ballet was appreciated for its scenic beauty and grace, and was intended to enhance the *couleur locale* of an opera with a setting in a particular place and time. Saint-Saëns never objected to composing ballets for his larger operas, nor did Gounod, nor did Thomas.

The standard dramaturgy of grand opera involved a love affair conducted across a tribal or religious or political barrier, with a foreground of leading singers passionately involved with each other (love, hate, jealousy, etc.), while the background was the responsibility of the chorus and the political leadership (kings, fathers, priests, etc.). The tenor voice was transformed into the heroic, stentorian instrument it has always remained, and the dramatic baritone emerged as a new type of voice, distinct from the real bass voice, which was left to impersonate kings, high priests and grandfathers. The conflict usually, but not always, ended in tragedy. Events drawn from (or imagined in) the Middle Ages or Renaissance were standard. As antiquity fell out of favour the operas of Gluck disappeared from the repertoire, while the Dark Ages and Arthurian mythology came into fashion late in the century. Everything at the Opéra was of course sung in French.

Artistic standards were inevitably variable, while social pressures maintained the prestige and showiness of grand opera. It was always the place for socially ambitious Parisians and their ladies to be seen, and evening dress was *de rigueur*. Berlioz saw in current operatic practice an opportunity for great artistry too rarely achieved and also a target of some of his most biting satire.[2] After the death of Meyerbeer in 1864, most historians suggest, the genre declined. Perhaps it lost some of its glamour with the fall of the Second Empire, but the formula remained much the same until 1914, at least as treated in their larger works by Saint-Saëns and most of his French contemporaries.

The rigidity of the Opéra's presentation was to some extent the result of Napoleon's decree of 1807, which circumscribed the roles of the capital's three opera houses. The Opéra-Comique was required to provide the lighter genre, with operas usually in one, two or three acts, often in double or triple bill. The cast was small, the chorus limited and normally no ballet included. Between separate musical numbers the plot was conducted in dialogue, sometimes very extensive, so that the entertainment was as much a play with music as an opera with speech. Emotional and political conflict was slight, always resolved happily. Public morality was not to be offended.

Saint-Saëns's operas were clearly formulated to accord with these two institutionalised genres, with minor deviations. He was no rebel in this respect. He admired but had no dealings with the third theatre in Napoleon's provision, the Théâtre-Italien,

---

[2] See especially BERLIOZ 1852, Ninth Evening.

which was exclusively devoted to Italian opera, but he was involved from time to time with the Théâtre-Lyrique, set up after the political turmoil of 1848 and prominent in the 1850s and 1860s by circumventing the rules and presenting a fresh repertoire of operas of different genres and different dimensions. After 1864 any theatre was permitted to present opera of any kind, so a raft of new ventures came and went with alarming rapidity, usually foundering for lack of funds.

The drawback of the rich artistic milieu of Parisian culture, of which Saint-Saëns was a particular victim, was the appalling inadequacy of what then passed for music criticism. Since the seventeenth century Parisian culture had always been a literary culture, which gave men of letters a privileged position as arbiters of taste. In the nineteenth century the men who wrote about books, poetry, theatre and music in newspapers and journals were normally literary men, highly cultivated and often excellent writers, but few had any musical skill or training. A review of an opera would devote as much space to the 'poème' as to the music, and the critic would often be more interested in the singers than in the music itself. Symphonic concerts attracted far less attention in the press than opera, so that a 'symphonist' was automatically assigned to a lower class of composer. The critics also exchanged faddish opinions following the hot topic of the day. The most glaring example of this is the obsession with Wagner which dominated music criticism in France for half a century.

Saint-Saëns put his finger very precisely on this problem when he wrote: 'Is it not well known that writers are inclined to judge music without knowing anything about it while musicians have no rights in the domain of literature even when they are literate?'[3] Berlioz had a similar thought in a letter to his father after the failure of *Benvenuto Cellini* in 1838: 'The French have a passion for arguing about music without having the first idea about it nor any feeling for it. It was like that in the last century, it's like that now, and it always will be.'[4]

The critics of the period were especially vulnerable to fads and fashion. Saint-Saëns analysed the problem as follows:

> In former times music criticism in France had no other aim than to reflect public opinion. One day it developed the ambition to lead the public rather than follow them. This was a noble aim, no doubt, but it manifested itself at first as bitter, blind hostility towards all innovation and all progress in art, as if it were possible to stop it! At that time – I am going back only to the Second Empire, believe it or not – Beethoven and Mozart were 'musical algebra'. The success of the *Marriage of Figaro* at the Théâtre-Lyrique was dismissively poo-pooed. Berlioz and Gounod were as good as insulted! [. . .] The lovely Prelude to *Lohengrin* was treated as a joke.
>
> Then suddenly the wind turned. Critics would acknowledge nothing that was not original and avant-garde. What was considered revolutionary until then was sneered at as reactionary. The

---

[3] Preface to Augé de Lassus 1894, p. 1; Soret 2012, p. 480.   [4] Berlioz 1975, p. 457.

Opéra, that admirable institution where poetry, drama, music, dance and miracles of staging all meet in a final product unique in the world, was scornfully repudiated. Singing was out, dancing was out; so was drama, unless that drama was the inner drama expressed by the orchestra alone. Young French composers took fright at the minefield lying ahead and dived headlong into myths and symbols.[5]

In parallel with this destructive flaw in the field of criticism, the management of opera houses, always held in the hands of the Ministry of the Interior, passed from one *fonctionnaire* to another; some of them had theatre experience as dramatists or designers, but most often they were politically acceptable managers, never a composer. An exception was Rossini as director of the Théâtre-Italien in the 1820s, but the directors of the Opéra and the Opéra-Comique were almost always men with no musical training or skill. Opera composers were thus faced with the double hurdle of winning the support of a theatre director in order to be played and of winning the support of the press in order to be applauded. Unmusical music critics were responsible for the failure to recognise Berlioz's *La Damnation de Faust* in 1846, and ill-informed theatre directors were responsible for the crime of not performing *Les Troyens* at the Opéra. Bizet had the benefit of a sympathetic director in Léon Carvalho (except in his rejection of *Ivan IV*) but the obstacle of an ignorant press who could see no virtue in *Les Pêcheurs de perles* and little good in *Carmen*. Lalo was bedevilled by being labelled a symphonist, so that his *Fiesque* was never performed at all and *Le Roi d'Ys* was played many years too late.

It is no coincidence that the best music critics of this period were themselves composers. Berlioz stands out, followed by Reyer, Joncières, Hahn and Saint-Saëns himself. The rest, non-musicians such as Scudo, Blaze de Bury, Pougin, Comettant, de Lauzières, Adolphe Jullien, Willy and dozens of others, did more harm than good.

* * * * *

If Saint-Saëns had been just a pianist, he would have been as famous and as acclaimed as Rubinstein, Leschetizky, Paderewski or any other lion of the age. His piano concertos, all of which he played himself, provide scintillating evidence of his astonishing technique both in weight and nimbleness. Yet playing the piano was only one of many activities, not all of them concerned with music, that consumed him over a very long life. He was an immensely productive composer, of course, producing music 'as an apple-tree bears apples', as he described it himself.[6] No genre of music was untouched: operas, symphonies, concertos, chamber music, songs, choral music, all in abundance; even a film score, one of the first ever composed. For many years he was organist at the Madeleine church in Paris; he conducted frequently; he wrote articles for the press and published half a dozen books; he wrote poetry and plays; he took a close interest in

---

[5] 'À propos de *La Juive*', *La Nouvelle Revue d'Égypte*, January 1904; SORET 2012, p. 582.
[6] Letter to M. Levin, 9 September 1901, DANDELOT 1930, p. 181.

astronomy, archaeology, philosophy and classical literature; he spoke many languages and travelled all over Europe giving concerts, including a series of eleven Mozart piano concertos in London; he went to Scandinavia, Russia, Indo-China and Uruguay; he was involved in the whole spectrum of music-making in France for all of his career, and was a prime mover in the Société Nationale de Musique. His tastes ranged effortlessly from Wagner to the baroque, and the composers he most admired were Mozart, Rameau, Gluck, Schumann, Berlioz and Liszt. He was a modernist and a reactionary at the same time, an atheist who composed a huge quantity of religious music, a deeply serious and thoughtful composer whose best-known work is the frivolous *Carnival of the Animals*.

His versatility and eclecticism was described by Gounod many years later:

> M. Saint-Saëns is one of the most astonishing musical personalities I know. He is a complete musician, better equipped for his profession than anyone else. He knows the repertoire by heart, he plays the orchestra as he plays the piano. He has exceptionally rare descriptive powers and a prodigious capacity for assimilation. He could write like Rossini, Verdi, Schumann, or Wagner if he wished. He has a thorough knowledge of them all, which is perhaps a guarantee that he will not imitate any of them. He is not troubled by the fear of not producing an effect (a terrible torment for the weak spirited), he never exaggerates. Furthermore he is not affected or violent or emphatic. He uses all combinations and all resources without abusing, or being a slave to, any.[7]

The early part of Saint-Saëns's long career was bedevilled by the accusation that he was a 'symphonist', and therefore not a fit person to compose operas. If ever there was a musician for whom this was the opposite of the truth, it was Saint-Saëns, since he was adept in every branch of music and showed little inclination throughout his life to specialise in one or another. As a child prodigy he exhibited his musicality as a pianist and composer of trifles for the piano and violin, but he was already studying the full score of *Don Giovanni* at the age of five. 'Every day, and without any special thought, I fed on my score with that prodigious appetite and capacity for assimilation that children have, I learned how to read a score and I learned all about voices and instruments.'[8] When he heard the opera sung in Italian a few years later, he knew it by heart. His teachers were Stamaty for piano and Boëly for organ, but their teaching and the careful nurture by his mother and his great-aunt Charlotte were not narrowly confined. At no point did they determine that he would be exclusively a great piano virtuoso. His eagerness to compose and his skill at the organ offered two alternative paths, and the boy's interest in the wider world of knowledge, especially literature and science, was evidence of his exceptional curiosity and his capacity to absorb impressions and ideas from all sources.

Opera was never excluded; it was never supposed that he would become a 'symphonist'. Throughout his life he upheld the virtues of the two characteristic genres of opera seen at the two principal opera houses during his childhood, powered

---

[7] Gounod 1896, pp. 346–47.   [8] Saint-Saëns 1894B; Soret 2012, p. 470.

by a genuine admiration for certain works and certain singers that he knew in his childhood. He started to attend the Paris Conservatoire in November 1848 when he was thirteen, and it is likely that, with *Don Giovanni* at the Théâtre-Italien behind him, he started serious opera-going at that time. The works he most clearly remembered from the Opéra-Comique date from 1849: Adam's *Le Toréador* in a double bill with Auber's *L'Ambassadrice* in repertoire since 1836, Thomas's *Le Caïd* and Halévy's *La Fée des Roses*, with Thomas's *Le Songe d'une nuit d'été* in 1850. The biggest sensation at the Opéra in 1849 was Meyerbeer's *Le Prophète*, for which Saint-Saëns always had great admiration, especially for the original leading singers, Pauline Viardot and Gustave Roger, and for the original staging, which he must have first seen at this time.

In October 1851 he joined Halévy's composition class which was exclusively directed towards the composition of vocal music and opera. Halévy himself owed his eminence to a long series of successful operas, both grand and light, and was a man of great erudition.

> My work for this class consisted of writing vocal and instrumental pieces as exercises, along with orchestration. [...] Halévy, then at the end of his career, was constantly writing operas and opéras-comiques which contributed nothing to his fame and disappeared after a respectable number of performances, never to be seen again. Absorbed in his work he neglected the class, attending only when he could find time. The students attended anyway, so we were subject to each other's teaching, a lot less indulgent than the official teacher's, whose worse fault was his excessive kindness. Even when he was there in class, he could never refuse to see singers who wanted him to listen to them. [...] When the teacher sent word that he was not coming, which was often, I used to go to the library and I completed my education there. The amount of music, both old and new, that I devoured there is beyond counting.[9]

During his student years Saint-Saëns was composing at a prodigious rate, as he was for the rest of his life. It was not focussed on any particular branch or genre. There are songs, piano pieces, chamber music, symphonies, a ballet, sacred choral music. Some of this may have been shown to his teacher, and some may have been intended for performance by his fellow-students. In 1852, at the age of sixteen, he entered for the Prix de Rome, which was awarded annually by the Institut as a scholarship to enable promising young composers to study for two or more years in Rome. There were parallel scholarships for painters, artists and architects. For musicians the prize was seen to be an avenue into the world of opera since it tested the candidate's skill at writing for voices and for the orchestra. If Rome itself was a source of inspiration for visual artists who studied antiquity or Renaissance art, for musicians there was no clear local benefit

---

[9] 'Le Vieux Conservatoire', *L'Écho de Paris*, 22 January 1911; SAINT-SAËNS 1913, pp. 42–43; SORET 2012, pp. 682–83.

other than respect for Italy as the *fons et origo* of opera, where the art of singing was cultivated more seriously than anywhere else.

It seems unlikely that Halévy took any particular interest in Saint-Saëns (or in any other student), so the drive behind competing for the Prix de Rome was probably his mother, seconded by Auber, the Conservatoire's head, who thought he should have won it. But the prize was awarded to another, for in any case he was too young to travel alone to Italy to study. Failure to win the prize would have been a setback to his career if he was not already making his mark as organist, pianist and composer with performances in all three roles already featuring regularly in Paris's concert calendar. It appears that he left the Conservatoire after the Prix de Rome result; he barely needed further instruction. He was nearly seventeen and sufficiently well connected in Paris to attract a public. Even before his student days were officially over, he was already engaged in the multifarious musical activities that he would continue to pursue to the end of his life, for another seventy years. Only the writing and the touring remained in the future. In this light it was perhaps to his advantage that he did not win the Prix de Rome; some successful prizewinners complained that they were cut off from Paris for two years when they might have been furthering their careers at home.

In this period he did not turn away from opera, even though he had more success and was more visible to the Parisian public as a composer of instrumental music. In 1854 he took the post of organist at the church of Saint-Merry, close to the Hôtel de Ville. After his First (actually second) Symphony in E♭, successfully performed by Seghers in December 1853, he wrote a piano quartet, then a piano quintet and various works for the organ. From Saint-Merry he moved up in 1858 to the highly prestigious post of organist at the Madeleine with an excellent salary. For Saint-Saëns this was a period in which he did his best to strengthen his connection with prominent older musicians, chief of whom were Gounod, Pauline Viardot, Seghers, Berlioz, Rossini and Pasdeloup.

Saint-Saëns claimed that he first met Gounod when he was ten or twelve at the house of Dr Hoffmann, whose wife was a cousin of his.[10] He would certainly have taken a close interest in the opera *Sapho*, played at the Opéra in April 1851, and when Gounod was composing the incidental music for *Ulysse* a year later, Saint-Saëns worked with the composer, playing from his sketches at the piano. Saint-Saëns considered the failure of both works a serious misjudgment on the part of the public, and he also admired parts of *La Nonne sanglante*, which also failed at the Opéra. To the end of his life Gounod remained a loyal supporter of Saint-Saëns, who later wrote, in his posthumous tribute: 'He was not too proud to take me into his confidence, young student that I was, and reveal his private artistic thoughts, saturating my ignorance with his knowledge. He discoursed with me as with an equal, and I thus became if not his pupil at least his

---

[10] 'Charles Gounod', *La Revue de Paris*, 15 June 1897; SORET 2012, p. 507. Gérard Condé suggests that the meeting took place some two years later than Saint-Saëns remembered (CONDÉ 2009, p. 74)

disciple and I completed my training in his shadow, or rather in his light.'[11] Gounod took a similarly avuncular interest in Bizet's progress at the Conservatoire, Bizet being three years younger than Saint-Saëns and a friend for life.

Pauline Viardot was one of the most prominent musicians in Paris following her success as Fidès in Meyerbeer's *Le Prophète* in 1849. Everyone wanted to be invited to her Thursday salons where, at some point, Saint-Saëns became the resident accompanist, probably introduced to her by Gounod. Her performance of Schubert's *Erlkönig* with Saint-Saëns at the piano caused a sensation. Their friendship endured until her death in 1910, and although the role of Dalila was not expressly written for her, she played an important part in the genesis of *Samson et Dalila* and was surely the model for the great mezzo and contralto roles that we find in Saint-Saëns's operas.

François Seghers was an excellent conductor who founded the Société Ste-Cécile and led it from 1849 to 1854. Saint-Saëns was the rehearsal pianist for the chorus. The First Symphony in E♭ was performed by Seghers on 18 December 1853 and dedicated to him. Seghers had withheld the composer's name when submitting the work to his committee and at the concert, knowing they would reject a seventeen-year-old composer's work. Saint-Saëns recollected with justifiable pride overhearing Gounod and Berlioz discussing his work with approval without knowing whose it was.[12]

Composers of Saint-Saëns's generation, such as Bizet, Reyer and Massenet, regarded Berlioz with veneration since they recognised his genius as well as the wall of disdain he encountered both in the press and in official circles. They saw him as a lonely figure who occasionally came into the Conservatoire library, of which he was titular head, and as a mordent critic for the *Journal des débats*, but he never had a teaching position at the Conservatoire and after the cool reception of *La Damnation de Faust* in 1846 his concerts in Paris were rare. Saint-Saëns heard the *Grande Messe des morts* in 1850 but he had no opportunity in his early years to hear *Roméo et Juliette* or *La Damnation de Faust*. The first performance of *L'Enfance du Christ* in 1854 was therefore an important event, and Saint-Saëns never ceased to advocate the revival of all Berlioz's works, not just the familiar ones. Personal contact may date from the Seghers performance of Saint-Saëns's First Symphony, but it became close in 1855 when Saint-Saëns undertook the piano reduction of *Lélio* for publication by Richault. He once accompanied Berlioz on a concert trip – he does not say which one, perhaps to Bordeaux in 1859 – and he did his best to keep the great man from too much coffee, champagne and cigars, which he believed were the cause of his death. Saint-Saëns was, with Reyer, a great comfort to Berlioz in his last days.

The oldest of these important figures, Rossini settled finally in Paris in 1855. Saint-Saëns was introduced to him soon after by the Viardots, and he became one of the regular

---

[11] SORET 2012, p. 513.
[12] Saint-Saëns's memoir about Seghers appeared in *L'Écho de Paris* on 28 May 1911 and was reprinted in SAINT-SAËNS 1913; SORET 2012, pp. 714–18.

pianists at the soirées Rossini gave every week in his large apartment at the bottom of the Rue de la Chaussée d'Antin attended by many luminaries of French society. Unlike many French musicians, Saint-Saëns suffered from no prejudice against Italian music, and he knew Rossini's works well. Rossini once asked if Saint-Saëns would allow his *Tarantelle* op. 6 for flute and piano (Ratner 183) to be played at a soirée. He naturally agreed, only to hear the great man announce the piece as something he had just composed himself. Only after the assembled company had all told Rossini what a masterpiece it was did he announce that it was actually by his young friend Saint-Saëns.

Jules-Étienne Pasdeloup was a force in Parisian music for whom Saint-Saëns actually had little respect, although they remained on good terms. Pasdeloup penetrated imperial and municipal circles which were otherwise limited in their patronage of music and enjoyed sources of money to which other conductors, notably Seghers, did not have access. From Baron Haussmann, Préfet de la Seine, Pasdeloup secured an engagement as conductor of the balls at the Hôtel de Ville and from the Comte de Nieuwerkerke a similar engagement in the Louvre. Stung by the refusal of the Société des Concerts du Conservatoire to programme any contemporary music, he started up his own orchestra, the Société des Jeunes Artistes, in 1853, drawing on Conservatoire students. Saint-Saëns blamed him for luring players away from Seghers's orchestra and causing the demise of the Société Ste-Cécile, and he also judged him (as many others did also) to be a poor conductor. With the Jeunes Artistes Pasdeloup conducted the *Marche-Scherzo* from the First Symphony in 1856 and the first performance of Saint-Saëns's third (but not numbered) symphony, known as 'Urbs Roma' (Ratner 163), on 15 February 1857. This was withdrawn by the composer and not published until 1974. The next symphony, the Second Symphony in A, op. 55 (Ratner 164), was also premiered by Pasdeloup and the Concerts des Jeunes Artistes, on 25 March 1860, and dedicated to Pasdeloup. Despite his shortcomings as a conductor he was an able and adventurous manager, and when the Société des Jeunes Artistes came to an end in 1860 he initiated the Concerts Populaires, given with an immense orchestra before a huge audience in the Cirque Napoléon. During the first decade of their existence the Concerts Populaires neglected young French composers, to Saint-Saëns's annoyance, although they occasionally played Berlioz and Gounod. Saint-Saëns's music featured twice in the 1860s, once the *Marche-Scherzo* from the First Symphony and once the Second Piano Concerto (Ratner 190) (its third performance) in 1868 with the composer as soloist.

After 1870 Pasdeloup was forced to respond to a nascent patriotism by introducing more French works and by featuring Saint-Saëns more frequently as both composer and pianist. But the latter was forever troubled by Pasdeloup's enthusiasm for Wagner and for his habitual instruction to young composers: 'Write me a symphony like

Beethoven and I'll play it.' He was also not impressed when Pasdeloup once pleaded poverty while having a new house built.

Two figures, both living far from Paris, had a profound impact on Saint-Saëns as a young man and throughout his life. These were Liszt and Wagner. Liszt, whose music and whose reputation as a formidable pianist Saint-Saëns knew in his childhood, was later to become one of his main supporters. All young pianists in those years regarded Liszt as a godlike figure, but after 1845 his visits to Paris were rare. Saint-Saëns's first opportunity to meet him was in October 1853 when, in Paris to see his three children who had not seen their father for nearly ten years, Liszt also visited Seghers's wife, a former pupil who was the children's piano teacher. It was at Seghers's house that Saint-Saëns 'saw and heard' the legendary Liszt for the first time. Liszt admired his organ playing and once said that 'the only two people left in Europe who know how to play the piano' were Saint-Saëns and himself.[13]

The figure of Wagner looms large in any account of music in the later nineteenth century, and for Saint-Saëns he represented both an inspiration and a threat. Because his hostility to Wagner was publicly and strongly expressed in his later years, he felt obliged to insist that it was never Wagner's music that he objected to, but some of its creator's actions and all the fatuous idolatry and bigotry that Wagnerism set in motion, especially after Wagner's death in 1883. When Wagner came to Paris in 1859, he was recommended to meet Saint-Saëns by both Liszt and Hans von Bülow, who had recently heard him playing Schumann symphonies on the piano. He visited Wagner several times and played *Tristan und Isolde* and *Das Rheingold* to him, with Wagner sometimes singing, sometimes with other visitors present. 'I thus learned to appreciate the skill and talent of this young musician, which was simply amazing', wrote Wagner. 'With an unparalleled sureness and rapidity in reading the most complicated orchestral score, this young man possessed a no less marvellous memory. He was not only able to play my scores, including *Tristan*, by heart, but he could also reproduce the leading or lesser themes.'[14]

Saint-Saëns attended the opening of the Bayreuth Festival in 1876 and wrote a long, thoughtful analysis of the *Ring*. But he felt that in view of Wagner's bitter hostility towards France at the time of the 1870–71 conflict, his music should not be played in France. Above all he resented the obsession for Wagner displayed by many critics who judged all music against what they regarded as the Bayreuth gold standard. It is not hard to detect the influence of Wagner in Saint-Saëns's music, and many have done so,

---

[13] *New York Times*, 17 December 1921. Liszt once said something similar about Bizet's piano playing, only including Hans von Bülow as a third equal.
[14] WAGNER 1911, vol. ii, pp. 739–40.

but that is because almost all modern tendencies of the time, particularly in the direction of chromaticism and in scene-to-scene fluidity, were too easily considered to be Wagner's patented property when they were the natural development of the musical language of the day.

* * * * *

Let us now turn to Saint-Saëns's efforts in the theatre in his early years. No young composer ever had a work staged at the Opéra, and even Gounod at thirty-two was considered too young to be so honoured with *Sapho*. Louise Bertin's *Esmeralda* was staged at the Opéra in 1836 when she was thirty-one, but that was seen to be a blatant act of political opportunism. Saint-Saëns had no expectations from that quarter, but the Opéra-Comique was much more approachable, and the boulevard theatres required stage music for operettas and plays with great frequency. No play was staged without accompanying music, and most theatres had resident musicians to perform it.

Le Martyre de Vivia
(Ratner 314)

Mystère in three acts
by
Jean Reboul

First performance: Théâtre de l'Odéon, Paris, 6 April 1850

Orchestra: piccolo, flute, 2 oboes (incl. cor anglais), 2 clarinets, 2 bassoons, 2 horns, 2 trumpets, 3 trombones, timpani, triangle, tambourine, cymbals, antique cymbals, strings.

From 1850, when Saint-Saëns was fourteen, we have nine pages of a ballet in full score, a brisk movement in 3/8, although its title and purpose are unknown (Ratner 308).[15] At the same time he wrote the music for a play *Le Martyre de Vivia* performed at the Odéon (very close to his home in the Rue du Jardinet) on 6 April 1850 (Ratner 314). The author was Jean Reboul (1796–1864), a poet much mocked in the press as the 'baker from Nîmes' since his profession was indeed baker. According to Jean Bonnerot, Saint-Saëns's secretary and first biographer, the introduction to the Odéon came from Marcellin de Fresnes, a well-connected politician who also gave Saint-Saëns free access to his box at the Société des Concerts. Saint-Saëns met de Fresnes, in turn, through Ingres, who was a friend and neighbour of his mother.

---

[15] In this chapter we identify Saint-Saëns's early stage works by Ratner numbers, as listed in RATNER 2012.

While much was made of Saint-Saëns's concert in the Salle Pleyel on 6 May 1846 when the ten-year-old played concertos by Mozart and Beethoven, no notice has ever been taken of his first appearance as a composer for the theatre; in fact Saint-Saëns seems to have forgotten about it himself. The music we have is incomplete, and consists of short movements exclusively for the orchestra without voices.[16] Like most theatre music of the time it passed unnoticed but not unheard. The final movement is a 'Danse des Corybantes', the first of many ventures in the field of exoticism. It was performed offstage by woodwind accompanied by triangle, tambourine, cymbals and antique cymbals in E and A, instruments Saint-Saëns had studied in Berlioz's orchestration treatise. It was in that treatise, too, that he found an extract of the *Harpe éolienne* in *Lélio*, the obvious inspiration for the slow movement of his First Symphony.

It was doubtless for Halévy that Saint-Saëns composed the first fragment of an opera that has survived. This is a chorus 'Près de ces charmilles', to be sung by a chorus of peasants and three characters named Aimée, Fanny and Clémency, preceded by a short introduction (Ratner 299). It is light and tuneful, as such pieces had to be. As preparation for the Prix de Rome, which required the composition of a chorus, Halévy used to set his students verses drawn from old opéras-comiques, although in this case the origin of the words is unknown. For Halévy he also composed some cantatas, one of which, *Imogine*, had been the Prix de Rome text in 1845.

In 1854 Saint-Saëns started a collaboration with Jules Barbier, librettist with Michel Carré of two of Massé's successful opéras-comiques, *Galathée* and *Les Noces de Jeannette*, and soon to become one of the best-known librettists of the time. While waiting for Barbier to deliver a libretto, Saint-Saëns composed the overture and the opening duet (Ratner 300) for a countess and a character named Gaston in which the countess wonders why Gaston does not fall for the charms of some young lady, while it is clear that Gaston prefers her, the countess: a delicate situation perfectly suited for the light touch that Saint-Saëns brings to it.[17] Barbier never delivered the rest of the libretto.

A similar relic, consisting again of an overture and one song, is once more without a title, although the author of the words, P. N. Grolier, and the intended singer, Mme Gaveau-Sabatier, both obscure figures, are named (Ratner 303). This was on a Persian subject, Saint-Saëns's first venture into those regions, and consists of an incomplete overture and an Air sung by one Saphi to his love Léila.

* * * * *

---

[16] The manuscript is at F-Pn MS 875(j); see RATNER 2012, pp. 408–10.
[17] The overture was published in 1913.

> ### *Le Duc de Parme*
> (Ratner 301)
>
> Opéra-comique in one act
>
> Libretto by Ernest de Calonne
>
> | | |
> |---|---|
> | Octave, Duc de Parme | basse |
> | Horace, son frère | ténor |
> | Pietro, serviteur | ténor |
> | Marcel | baryton |
> | Julio | ténor |
> | Antonio | ténor |
> | Léonore, Comtesse | soprano coloratura |
> | Paola, servante | soprano |
>
> Chœurs
>
> The action takes place in Parma.
>
> Orchestra: 2 flutes (piccolo), 2 oboes, 2 clarinets, 2 bassoons, 4 horns, 2 trumpets, 3 trombones, timpani, triangle, tambourine, strings.
>
> Offstage: flute, piccolo, clarinet, harp, strings.

The first opera by Saint-Saëns to have survived in almost complete form is a one-act opéra-comique without a title that survives as a complete manuscript in full score comprising an overture and seven numbers, requiring eight singers and a chorus (Ratner 301).[18] Rather than retain its clumsy identification as 'unnamed opéra-comique', I have given it the title *Le Duc de Parme* after the principal character. The libretto was by Ernest de Calonne (1822–87), a poet and minor dramatist who had been, or was still, professor of rhetoric in the Lycée in Algiers. The libretto itself, which would give us the dialogue with which to make sense of the plot, is lost. Saint-Saëns told its history in a letter to Albert Soubies in 1915:

> There is another opéra-comique, and I have all the separate numbers; the text, by M. de Calonnes, is lost, so it makes no sense any more. The overture is quite extended, but it has dated, and I don't believe it should be rescued from the oblivion to which it is forever condemned by my will, which prohibits the publication of all unpublished works. [. . .] P.S. The finale became a ballet in *Henry VIII*.[19]

Le Duc de Parme was about to go into rehearsal at the Opéra-Comique when Nestor Roqueplan, the theatre's director from 1857 to 1860, heard Saint-Saëns declare that *Le Nozze di Figaro* was a masterpiece and immediately cancelled the production.[20]

---

[18] The autograph is at F-Pn MS 2494.
[19] *Les Autographes* catalogue, n.d.; RATNER 2012, p. 345.
[20] *L'Écho de Paris*, 3 March 1912; SAINT-SAËNS 1913, p. 288; SORET 2012, p. 782.

The Overture was performed in Bordeaux in February 1860,[21] probably as a follow-up to the performance there in 1857 of the Symphony in F 'Urbs Roma'.

The Overture has a Spanish feel to it, although the opera is set in Parma, where the Duke (Monseigneur Octave) is in love with a Countess Léonore, as we learn from his gossipy servants Pietro and Paola. So is his brother Horace. To resolve the situation in the Duke's favour, the servants call on Marcel, a Figaro-like fixer, who is brought in disguised as a gypsy. He supplies a magic ring which forces the wearer to tell the truth. After various misunderstandings and mis-directed letters, the Duke and the Countess acknowledge their love, and Pietro saves Paola from the designing clutches of Marcel.

The music displays a polished opéra-comique style, with a neat comic flavour that may be gleaned from a snatch sung by Paola in the Terzettino, no. 3 (ex. 1.1):

Example 1.1 Saint-Saëns, *Le Duc de Parme*, Terzettino ('A convent, with bars and heavy bolts! For two young ladies that's not nice!')

Un cou-vent, des gril-les, et de gros ver-rous, Pour deux jeu-nes fil-les ce-la n'est pas doux!

The best music in the opera is found in no. 6, a duet for the Duke and the Countess in which the Duke, thinking that she is in love with Horace, banishes her from Parma. She is resigned to her fate, claiming that her sole crime was to love him, the Duke. There is plenty of tension in the orchestra, and it would take a great soprano to sing it. This is followed by the finale, including music from offstage and a recall of sections of the Overture, in which everything is resolved. The Andante section is what we now know as Ballet no. 6 'Scherzetto' in *Henry VIII*, and the curtain comes down on a stream of coloratura from the Countess.

* * * * *

The facetious streak that runs through Saint-Saëns's work made an appearance, perhaps its first, on 1 April 1857, as a *poisson d'avril* for his friend Madame Forgues, a singer to whom he had dedicated his song *La Feuille du peuplier*. *La Toilette de la Marquise de Présalé* (Ratner 332) is a 'scène lyrique' for soprano, female chorus with piano or harp accompaniment. The chorus impersonate chamber maids in three parts, and the middle movement is a 'Marche des crinolines'. No doubt Saint-Saëns wrote the words himself. But later, when asked if this work was his, he replied: 'Incontrovertibly! But I don't want anyone at any price to know that it's by me, the same as for the scene from *Macbeth*.'[22]

---

[21] According to a note on the clarinet part, F-Pn, MS 2494(c).
[22] In a letter from René Thorel to the director of the Dieppe museum, 14 October 1903; RATNER 2012, p. 474.

This is a reference to the music Saint-Saëns was asked to provide for another 'scène lyrique' on the sleep-walking scene in Macbeth (Ratner 324). In October 1858 Princess Metternich, wife of the Austrian ambassador, mounted a Shakespearean *tableau vivant* in honour of the Countess de Pourtalès in the Hôtel de la Monnaie. How he won access to these exalted circles is not known, but he set the Italian text by Giulio Carcano (1812–84), a moderately experienced Italian librettist, for three voices (Lady Macbeth, Dama and Medico) and orchestra, and it was evidently performed on that occasion. The only observation on this music ever made came from Saint-Saëns himself, who kept it jealously hidden. Writing the names of instruments in German and setting a text in Italian were his attempts at a disguise, no doubt, but there is no clear reason why he should have been ashamed of the music.

For the same occasion he wrote a duet based on the balcony scene of *Romeo and Juliet* (Ratner 325), a solo for Hamlet (Ratner 326) using a text from the version of *Hamlet* by Alexandre Dumas and Paul Meurice, and a duet for Antony and Cleopatra (Ratner 327) using his own words, not Shakespeare's, all with piano. By consigning the scores to the Dieppe Museum he turned his back on all these youthful efforts.

Another unpublished score from this period is the 'drame bouffon' in three acts entitled *Le Château de la Roche-Cardon, ou Les Cruautés du Sort* (Ratner 336), written for students at the École Niedermeyer, where Saint-Saëns taught from 1861 to 1865.

Saint-Saëns's biographer Jean Bonnerot describes him in the late 1850s as on the hunt for a libretto for a suitable opera and frequenting literary circles in the hope of finding a sympathetic collaborator.[23] Saint-Saëns set a scene of an opera based on Scott's *Kenilworth*, he reports (Ratner 302), but no such scene survives and no librettist is named. It was the failure to find good material that led Saint-Saëns to set a scene from Corneille's *Horace* in December 1860, according to Bonnerot, who has called it 'the first lyrical work apparently for the theatre that Saint-Saëns had performed'. The *Scène d'Horace* (Ratner 328) for soprano, baritone and orchestra is indeed a foretaste of the serious style he would bring to his major operas, and it has a real dramatic impact. Corneille's *Horace*, from 1640, reaches its climax in Act IV when Horace, having killed three Curiace brothers, his enemies, demands that his sister Camille mourn his two brothers, also killed, despite the fact that she was married to the last Curiace to die. She defies her brother, knowing that he will kill her too.

Saint-Saëns had set nothing of such dramatic intensity before, nor had he confronted the problem of setting alexandrines, with their tendency to dictate the flow of the music. This includes a rather banal snatch of march at the beginning and end, but in the rest of the piece the balance between recitative and lyrical writing and the pacing of

---

[23] BONNEROT 1922, p. 38.

the scene show no sign of immaturity. Using sequences and some urgent harmony, Saint-Saëns creates tremendous tension, especially in Camille's last speech. Notably astute is Camille's refusal to accept E♭ as her key after Horace's opening lines, and her later pleas have a tragic urgency (ex. 1.2).

Example 1.2 Saint-Saëns, *Scène d'Horace*

A vocal score was published in 1861, and it was performed at one of Pasdeloup's charity concerts on 7 March 1866 with Anne Charton-Demeur as Camille and Jules Petit as Horace. There were two more performances in Brussels in 1885. Here is a work that, like many of the operas, cries out for a strong recording.

In 1911, looking back at this early stage of his career, Saint-Saëns pinpointed the problems faced by young composers by quoting an article by Henri Blaze de Bury in the *Revue des Deux Mondes* in 1864. What to do with young composers was the problem. 'True duty, true humanity', wrote Blaze de Bury, 'would be not to encourage them but to discourage them. Where *are* these young composers, in any case? Give me some names. They should go to the theatre and listen to the *Marriage of Figaro, Oberon, Freischütz* or *Orphée*. It would do them no harm to subject themselves to models of that kind.'

The young composers who were so politely invited to take their seats were, among others, Bizet, Delibes, M. Massenet and the author of these lines. We would have been happy, M. Massenet and I, to write a ballet for the Opéra. M. Massenet proposed *The Pied Piper*, after a German story; I offered *Une Nuit de Cléopâtre*, on a story by Théophile Gautier, but we were refused the honour. When they agreed to offer a commission to Delibes, they did not dare risk giving him all of it. He got one act, and the rest went to a Hungarian composer.[24]

The situation soon changed for all of them. In 1863 Bizet received a commission from the Théâtre-Lyrique for *Les Pêcheurs de perles*; in the same year Massenet won the Prix de Rome and left for Italy; Delibes wrote a one-act opéra-comique *Le Jardinier et son seigneur* for the Théâtre-Lyrique in 1863 and a commission for (part of) the ballet *La Source* for the Opéra in 1866; and in 1864 Saint-Saëns received a commission from the Théâtre-Lyrique for what we should acknowledge as his first major opera, *Le Timbre d'argent*.

---

[24] 'Histoire d'un Opéra-Comique', *L'Écho de Paris*, 19 February 1911; SORET 2012, pp. 688–89.

2 | Le Timbre d'argent

Saint-Saëns's first complete opera is in many ways the most absorbing of all. He was still young and he composed it very quickly, and it has a remarkable libretto that belonged to an unusual genre perfected by its authors. It is a young man's opera, with a prodigal abundance of fresh musical invention, and its origins go back long before Saint-Saëns was even mentioned as its composer. Jules Barbier and Michel Carré belonged to that fertile group of playwrights and librettists that served Parisian theatre in the Second Empire and the Third Republic with an endless stream of boulevard plays, operettas, opéras-comiques and full-blown five-act operas. With the exception of serious spoken verse dramas, which were normally the work of single authors, most theatrical entertainments in Paris were written by two authors in collaboration. There were exceptions – notably Louis Gallet, who was to be an important partner for Saint-Saëns – but the excuse-me dance of writers, versifiers and dramatists who collaborated in endless permutations one with another continued to the end of the century.

In the sphere of opera, Jules Barbier and Michel Carré were the most successful of these. They wrote nearly fifty works in collaboration, from full-length spoken dramas to one-act opéras-comiques. Over thirty of these collaborations were operas of one kind or another, including some of the most successful of the age: *Faust*, *La Reine de Saba* and *Roméo et Juliette* for Gounod; *Mignon* and *Hamlet* for Thomas; *Les Contes d'Hoffmann* for Offenbach; and operas for Halévy, Meyerbeer, Bizet and a clutch of lesser names. At the start of their careers they wrote plays, including two that were to be crucial to the legacy of French opera: the three-act play *Faust et Marguerite* (by Carré alone) played in Paris in 1850; and a five-act 'drame fantastique', *Les Contes d'Hoffmann*, written by both in collaboration seven months later. These two plays fed a Parisian taste for the diabolical and the supernatural, material elements in Goethe's *Faust* and to a much greater degree in Hoffmann's stories. Both plays relate how a vulnerable hero places himself in the hands of a mysterious but powerful figure who mocks and exploits his very human failings. *Les Contes d'Hoffmann* is, furthermore, a cycle of three fantastical stories in which Hoffmann is inveigled by a Mephistophelean figure (in turn Coppelius, Miracle and Dapertutto) to betray his love for, in turn, Olympia, Antonia and Giulietta. The demons are all impersonations of Councillor Lindorf, as the women are of Stella, both being 'real' people in Hoffmann's world. In addition, his servant Andrès is transmogrified in turn as Cochenille, Franz and Pitichinaccio. Barbier and Carré came back several times to the idea of multiple personalities serving a demonic purpose.[1]

Another favourite device of theirs was the illusory transformation of the stage itself, as if the proscenium could be manipulated to frame different angles on the world. At the end of the prologue to *Les Contes d'Hoffmann* the scene dissolves into the first of the three flashbacks, only to return to the present in the epilogue. Soon after this play was staged, they presented another, *Les Marionnettes du docteur* (December 1851), which similarly gives us the real world in Acts I and V while Acts II, III and IV present an enlargement of the marionette theatre to which the doctor of the title introduces his guests at the end of Act I. They see an enactment of their various fantasies and fears, each guest transformed into a marionette and led with grotesque effrontery by the clearly demonic doctor.

A further hallmark of their work was anthropomorphic transformation, for which they drew several times, as might be expected, on Ovid's *Metamorphoses*. Their most successful operas of this kind were Massé's *Galathée* and Thomas's *Psyché*.

Their libretto *Le Timbre d'argent* was not publicly mentioned until 1864, when Saint-Saëns was proposed as its composer. But it is no surprise to read in Arnold Mortier's gossipy chronicle, *Les Soirées parisiennes de 1877 par un monsieur de l'orchestre*, under the date 24 February 1877, just after the opera's first performance, that the libretto was written twenty-five years earlier as a play intended for the Théâtre de l'Odéon, but never played there.[2] This puts its origin at 1852, at the very point when the two authors were exploiting their obsession with sinister, manipulating, Mephistophelean characters, and the theatrical conceit of seeing characters and scenes from many different angles. Although we do not have the original play in its complete form, there are copious drafts and several pages of professional copy preserved among Barbier's papers,[3] which show the principal character, Wolframb, in the clutches of someone named Argur, who transforms himself under various disguises: José, then Malhmann, then the Baron de Frohsdorf. Argur has a seductress, Niobé, to aid his plans and a magic talisman in the form of a silver bell. When this play was re-worked as a libretto, all the names were changed except those of the two principal women, Hélène and Rosa, and Wolframb was retained for a while before becoming Conrad.

In the course of its transformation and constant revision the libretto was offered, according to Bonnerot, to two composers and turned down by both, but Mortier names three: Boisselot, Litolff and Halévy.[4] Each of these wrote a few pieces, says

---

[1] For a closer study of Barbier and Carré see MACDONALD 1993. [2] MORTIER 1878, pp. 95–98.
[3] F-Po Fonds Barbier, 151 (Carton 18).
[4] The *Revue et gazette musicale* of 1 March 1877 names the third composer as Gounod, not Halévy.

Mortier, but the librettists each time found progress too slow. Boisselot, we know, was a dilatory composer, producing only three operas in a long life.

Each composer must have seen its operatic potential. Like *Faust et Marguerite* and *Les Contes d'Hoffmann*, *Le Timbre d'argent* was a play that cried out for music. The setting is eighteenth-century Vienna, with good choruses for men and women. The leading tenor is a young man wrestling with emotional conflict, the leading baritone is a sinister doctor who assumes different disguises. There are two soprano roles, and a leading part for a female dancer. There is a magic talisman (the silver bell of the title). It is a colourful story that calls for colourful music.

This libretto ended up in the hands of Léon Carvalho, director of the Théâtre-Lyrique and a leading arbiter of operatic developments in the 1860s. In 1863 he had put on Bizet's *Les Pêcheurs de perles* and Berlioz's *Les Troyens à Carthage*, and his dictatorial and eccentric management led him to take on impossible projects, present new composers, revive foreign classics and keep his public constantly on their toes, since he was not obliged by government regulation to restrict his repertoire in the way that both the Opéra and the Opéra-Comique were. He stumbled from one financial precipice to another, but always provided a hopeful arena for young French composers, even if he treated his artists and his staff with disdain and little tact.

The libretto may have come to him after Halévy's death in March 1862. It was still among his collection of unassigned operas in the summer of 1864 when Auber, Director of the Conservatoire, asked Carvalho if he had a libretto he could offer Saint-Saëns as compensation for not winning the Prix de Rome that year. Saint-Saëns's decision to compete for the Prix de Rome for the second time, having first entered in 1852 at the age of sixteen, was prompted at least in part by the principle by which Prix de Rome winners had priority when the Opéra-Comique was choosing its repertoire. Camille Doucet, the minister in charge of theatres, even told Paladilhe in 1863 that composers who had not won the Prix de Rome could not be played in state-subsidised theatres. Further handicapped by the widespread view that those who wrote symphonies were not equipped to write operas, Saint-Saëns was determined to gain a footing in the world of opera which, as everyone recognised, was the best guarantee of success as a composer. The careers of Auber, Halévy and Gounod were clear evidence of that principle, as was the career of Berlioz also, as evidence of its inverse effect.

The other four finalists for the Prix de Rome in 1864 were Danhauser, Lefèbvre, Constantin and Sieg. The seven-man jury consisted of Auber, Berlioz, Kastner, Prince Poniatowski, Elwart, Boulanger, Bazin and Duprato, only one of whom, we can now observe with hindsight, was as gifted a musician as Saint-Saëns. The prize was awarded to Victor Sieg, who at twenty-seven was a year younger than Saint-Saëns; the official report claimed that only one prize could be awarded to candidates over twenty-five. Berlioz, who had known Saint-Saëns for some years, defended his decision not to vote for him: 'I confess it pained me to vote against him, seeing that he is truly a great musician, already well known and almost famous. But the other candidate, who is still a student, has that inner fire, that inspiration; he *feels*, he can do things that cannot be learned, and he will learn the rest. [. . .] One must be fair above all.'[5] Perhaps Berlioz's judgment was warped by his wretched state of health at that time, and by the state of mind that caused him to write that very week in the Postface to his *Mémoires*: 'I say hourly to Death: "When you will." What is he waiting for?' He had not lost his wit, however, for it was on this occasion that he is said to have remarked of Saint-Saëns: 'He knows everything, he just lacks inexperience.'[6]

Sieg's career went nowhere, but Saint-Saëns gained from the powerful support of Auber, the only member of the jury to vote in his favour. In response to Auber's request, Carvalho offered Saint-Saëns the libretto of *Le Timbre d'argent*. This was the start of a fifty-year history, concluded in 1914 when Saint-Saëns completed the last of many transformations of the opera and when it was performed for the last time for over a hundred years. In 1911 he wrote an account of this history and in 1914 he issued a short brochure with a similar account, these texts enabling us to trace the course of events.[7]

His first step was to read the libretto and to ask Barbier and Carré to make some changes. This they were willing to do, so Saint-Saëns set to work immediately, going to his favourite retreat in Louveciennes, one of the western outer suburbs of Paris, to compose. The opera was drafted in two months and submitted to Carvalho, probably early in 1865. There followed two years of silence, with Carvalho so engrossed in keeping the Théâtre-Lyrique afloat that he had no time to look at Saint-Saëns's score. No doubt he had a stack of other operas claiming his attention. Eventually, pressed by the composer, Carvalho invited him to dinner, after which he played the opera through on the piano with Carvalho on one side and Mme Carvalho on the other. She was more than the Director's wife; as Caroline Miolan-Carvalho she was the leading coloratura soprano in Paris, having created the roles of Marguerite, Mireille and Juliette in Gounod's operas in her husband's theatre and taking frequent engagements elsewhere.

Both husband and wife were surprised by the quality of the music. 'Dissembling politeness turned into serious admiration and finally enthusiasm', Saint-Saëns reported. The opera would succeed, they assured him, but of course Mme Carvalho would have to sing the leading role. The problem was that the leading female role in *Le Timbre d'argent* was a dancer and the soprano part was secondary. The librettists were called in and Barbier devised a way to introduce the solo 'Le bonheur est chose légère' for the

---

[5] BERLIOZ 2001, p. 77.   [6] BONNEROT 1922, p. 43.
[7] 'Histoire d'un opéra-comique', *L'Écho de Paris*, 19 February 1911, reprinted in SAINT-SAËNS 1913 and in SORET 2012, pp. 688–93, and *Le Timbre d'argent* (Paris, 1914), reprinted in SORET 2012, pp. 871–73.

character Hélène at the end of what was then the first (later the second) act. This was not enough for the diva, especially since a strikingly beautiful and talented ballerina had been found from the Opéra named Coralie Brach. Carvalho urged composer and librettists to substitute a singer for a dancer; then he suggested having two dancers, not one. He suggested introducing animals, on the grounds that most of the action took place in a dream, and then wanted to turn the whole thing into a play, keeping only the dancer and, strangely, the chorus.

Two years passed before Carvalho was ready to put it on the stage, a period in which Saint-Saëns achieved celebrity by winning the competition for a cantata for the Exposition Universelle of 1867 with his setting of *Les Noces de Prométhée*. His success would have been much greater if the committee had performed it, as they were supposed to do. He also began to sketch out his next opera, *Samson et Dalila*. Bizet, in the only journal article he ever wrote, mentioned *Le Timbre d'argent* as awaiting production.[8] In January 1868 it finally went into rehearsal at the Théâtre-Lyrique where Bizet's *La Jolie Fille de Perth* was nearing the end of its short run. The publisher Choudens agreed to publish the opera and engaged Bizet to write the reduction for the vocal score.

Despite his perilous financial state, Carvalho was planning to stage operas also at the Salle Ventadour, the home of the Théâtre-Italien, under the title of the Théâtre de la Renaissance. *Le Timbre d'argent* was earmarked to be staged there, along with *Faust* and *Roméo et Juliette*. Thomas's *Hamlet* was in rehearsal at the Opéra, and it was because Christine Nilsson was rumoured to be playing Ophélie's death scene under water that Carvalho persuaded Saint-Saëns to add an underwater scene to his opera too. Such things were current: the libretto by Gallet and Blau for the competition about to be announced on April 1st in the same year, *La Coupe du Roi de Thulé* (which both Bizet and Massenet set), included an underwater scene.

Le Figaro informed its readers that *Le Timbre d'argent* was an 'opera-legend' in four acts with a prologue, including *féerie*, fantasy, drama and ballet.[9] There were eight to ten tableaux and plenty of scenic interest. The principal singers were to be Marie Schroeder (Carvalho's reserve soprano), Irma Marié (sister of Célestine Galli-Marié, the original Carmen), the comic baritone Eugène-Louis Troy as Spiridion, and the tenor Jules Puget as Bénédict. The mime role was now to be played by Zina Mérante. The overture was to be played between the prologue and the first act, 'which will force Mr Public to listen to it'. Particular numbers included a Neapolitan song, a dance accompanied by a fantastic bagpipe, a village waltz, a chorus of beggars, a carnival scene and an underwater ballet, 'that is to say *swum*'. The *Ménestrel* on 1 March 1868 called this scene an 'aquarium-ballet'.

---

[8] Bizet 1867. [9] As quoted in *Le Ménestrel*, 26 January 1868.

Although the opera was expected to open that month, Carvalho's fortunes were in steep decline, and the opening was postponed. At the beginning of May he was declared bankrupt and both theatres closed. Saint-Saëns was by no means the first composer to be disappointed by Carvalho's promises; Bizet had composed his largest work, the five-act *Ivan IV*, at his request in 1864, only to wait in vain for any performance. Saint-Saëns's hopes were not yet dashed, for Émile Perrin, the director of the Opéra, discussed adapting the work for his larger stage. Dialogue was not permitted at the Opéra, so the spoken interludes would have to be re-cast as verse and set to music. Librettists and composer obliged. Mme Carvalho, with no Théâtre-Lyrique to sing for, was engaged as Hélène and the great baritone Jean-Baptiste Faure, fresh from his successes in *Don Carlos* and *Hamlet*, was to be Spiridion. Perrin wanted the tenor role of Bénédict to be sung *in travesti* by the mezzo Palmyre Wertheimber simply because he wanted to offer her an engagement. Faced with the authors' refusal, Perrin yielded on this matter, even though Saint-Saëns became convinced that he really had no intention of mounting the opera at all.

Perrin's nephew, Camille du Locle, happened to be the director of the Opéra-Comique, the theatre for which the libretto had in all probability been first intended. He saw his chance and offered to put on *Le Timbre d'argent*. The dialogue would be restored, but naturally a few other revisions would be needed, and this time the librettists, Barbier and Carré, fell out. Saint-Saëns found himself playing the mediator, running back and forth between the homes of one in the country and the other in town. Eventually the two long-time partners were reconciled. Du Locle engaged an Italian dancer who turned out not to be a dancer at all and then found a real dancer for the part. 'It's unlikely that any catastrophe could intervene', Saint-Saëns said to himself, confident that he would soon see his opera on the stage. It was perhaps not a catastrophe that the tenor they approached, Léon Achard, turned it down, declaring it was too big a role for a singer of opéra-comique. Saint-Saëns sourly noted that the singer accepted an engagement at the Opéra soon after. With a dancer and no tenor, du Locle commissioned a one-act piece that needed a dancer, *Le Kobold*, from Bizet's friend Ernest Guiraud, which opened in July 1870 while crowds in the streets were singing the Marseillaise in patriotic fervour. But catastrophe did indeed intervene a few days later when Napoleon III declared war on Prussia and soon found himself a prisoner in enemy hands and his capital city under siege.

Saint-Saëns saw action as a member of the Garde-Nationale in various futile skirmishes on the outskirts of Paris when the French attempted to break out of Prussian encirclement, and the appalling suffering of the siege and the savagery of the Commune and its overthrow the following May marked him for life.[10] Yet he seized

---

[10] Melanie von Goldbeck is wrong to assert that Saint-Saëns fled Paris and went to London during the war (GOLDBECK 2015, p. 375n). The mistake stems from a false recollection by Leopold Auer in his *My Long Life in Music* (1924).

the opportunity, when the siege was lifted, to set in motion his plan for a Société Nationale de Musique, one of the most vigorous symptoms of the new cultural life that miraculously developed in Paris as the 1870s went by.

When the theatres reopened a year later, *Le Timbre d'argent* was still theoretically available to du Locle at the Opéra-Comique, but there was little prospect that he would stage it. Finally admitting that he had no plans to do so, he offered Saint-Saëns a one-act opera as compensation. This was *La Princesse jaune*, composed quite rapidly in 1871 and staged in June 1872. Also composed in 1871 was an entr'acte for *Le Timbre d'argent* which the composer almost immediately turned to a different use as the *Gavotte* op. 23 for piano (Ratner 31).[11]

There were many attempts in those years to revive old companies and start up new ones, building on the repertoire of the old Théâtre-Lyrique, whose theatre had burned down in the Commune. In November 1874 there was the short-lived 'Opéra Populaire ou Théâtre Lyrique' at the Châtelet, while at the Ventadour, Prosper Bagier, who had managed the Théâtre-Italien throughout the 1860s, set up the 'Troisième Théâtre-Lyrique Français', with a declared interest in *Le Timbre d'argent*. Saint-Saëns enlisted Barbier's help in this cause:

> If we are forced to withdraw it from the Opéra-Comique, that is clearly the way to go. But what sort of company will Bagier have for French opera? What are their general prospects? We can only so far assess the orchestra and the chorus. The orchestra is excellent, but the chorus shriek in a thoroughly unmusical way, vaguely suggesting the inhabitants of a zoo.[12]

This letter was probably written in January 1875, when the theatre had opened with *Le Freischütz*. But after six performances the government subsidy was withdrawn and the company ceased to exist. The Opéra-Comique had by then renounced its claim to the opera, and a new Théâtre-Lyrique company was formed under the directorship of Albert Vizentini, a Belgian violinist who had been Offenbach's conductor at the Théâtre de la Gaîté, recently built in the Square des Arts et Métiers.[13] Vizentini took over the lease of the theatre from Offenbach and set up the new Opéra-National Lyrique. It opened on 5 May 1876 with *Dimitri* by Victorin Joncières, followed by Massé's very successful *Paul et Virginie* (for which Barbier and Carré were the librettists) on November 15th; with the help of a financial nudge from the Ministère des Beaux-Arts, Vizentini also accepted *Le Timbre d'argent* for performance, twelve years after it was composed. By this time Saint-Saëns had completed *Samson et Dalila* and *La Princesse jaune* and had already embarked on his fourth opera, *Étienne Marcel*, while his first two operas had yet to

---

[11] See RATNER 1997, pp. 248–49. Another curious product of 1872 was *La Timbale d'argent*, an operetta by Léon Vasseur, played at the Bouffes-Parisiens on 9 April 1872.
[12] RATNER 2012, p. 82.   [13] For Vizentini's career, see PONS 2014.

be staged. He reflected bitterly on the attitudes that favoured foreign composers over young Frenchmen under the Second Empire, citing Bizet and Delibes as composers who would certainly have had their operas staged more quickly and willingly if this had not been the case.

Bringing *Le Timbre d'argent* to the stage was still not easy, and Vizentini was not easy to work with. A dancer and some singers had to be found. The dancer was Mme Théodore, but the tenor Victor Warot, whom Saint-Saëns would have liked, withdrew because he was only offered four performances, the director not expecting the piece to last any longer than that, as Saint-Saëns later found out. The replacement was a man called Ernest Blum, who had sung a secondary role in Gounod's *Roméo et Juliette*, but whose career unfolded mostly in the shadows. Golden voice, Saint-Saëns said, but no actor. The stage director, who happened to be Vizentini's father, and the ballet master, Henri Justament, refused to pay regard to the composer's wishes; some stagecraft he asked for in the Prologue (presumably a transformation) was said to be impossible, although it was later achieved in *Les Contes d'Hoffmann*, and he had to pay the stage band out of his own pocket. The orchestra was weak and needed extra rehearsals. Nonetheless Vizentini *fils* found some 'féerie' (probably equipment for flying actors in) at another theatre and was able to borrow it for the opera.

Outside the theatre things were no more encouraging. Octave Mirbeau, in the newspaper *L'Ordre*, wrote on 29 November 1876: 'So now we can't escape M. Saint-Saëns and his *Timbre*. O who will deliver us from M. Saint-Saëns?' A few days later he wrote: 'We'll definitely not be able to escape it. O well. So much the better. The public will judge this person's poor work. The performance of the *Timbre* will be his punishment and our revenge.' In the *Chronique de Paris* a few days later the same critic wrote: 'The composer is notoriously unpopular and clearly without talent. He cannot rise above an eternal mediocrity, a grotesque dwarf hoping to display his incompetence to the full light of day.' The work should be thrown like animal feed to the howling delight of the crowd, he added.[14]

Such remarks betray the level of music criticism at this time, common enough after a work had been heard, but not unknown in advance, too. Composers and authors needed thick skins. The opera opened on 23 February 1877, with Caroline Salla singing Hélène and Léon Melchissédec as Spiridion. The conductor was Jules Danbé.

* * * * *

---

[14] BONNEROT 1922, pp. 82–83.

> **Le Timbre d'argent**
> (Ratner 289)
>
> Opéra fantastique in four acts and eight tableaux
>
> Libretto by Jules Barbier and Michel Carré
>
> First performance: Théâtre-Lyrique, Paris, 23 February 1877
>
> | | |
> |---|---|
> | Circé-Fiametta | 1ère danseuse |
> | Hélène | soprano |
> | Rosa, her sister, Bénédict's fiancée | soprano |
> | Conrad | 1er ténor |
> | Bénédict | jeune tenor |
> | Spiridion | basse chantante |
> | Patrick | ténor |
> | Pierrot | ténor |
> | Frantz | ténor |
> | Rodolphe | ténor |
> | Rosenthal | basse |
> | 1er mendiant | ténor |
> | 2ème mendiant | ténor |
> | Un maître de ballet | muet |
> | Un Négrillon | muet |
> | Une habilleuse | muet |
>
> Etudiants, jeunes seigneurs, mendiants, bourgeois et gens du peuple, paysans, valets, masques, nymphes, etc., etc.
>
> The action takes place in Vienna, Austria, in costumes of the eighteenth century.
>
> | | |
> |---|---|
> | Orchestra: | 2 flutes (piccolo), 2 oboes (2 cors anglais), 2 clarinets, 2 bassoons, 4 horns, 2 trumpets, 3 trombones, contrabass trombone, timpani, bass drum, cymbals, triangle, side drum, tambourine, tambourin, bell in low F, bell in high F, harmoniflûte, harp, strings. |
> | Offstage: | 2 flutes, 2 cornets, 3 trombones, triangle, piano, harp, organ, 9 strings. |

The libretto of *Le Timbre d'argent* contains all the features we should recognise as the hallmarks of Barbier and Carré's work. Cast as an opéra-comique with dialogue, its subtitle is 'opéra fantastique', recalling the genre of 'drame fantastique' applied to *Les Contes d'Hoffmann* in 1851.

The following analysis is based on the vocal score, with Bizet's piano reduction, published, along with the libretto, in 1877. These show us the version of the opera that was heard at its first staging. It is in four acts, the second act divided into two tableaux.

Ouverture The Overture is swift but very long (641 bars), constructed from several themes from the opera. Its primary character is a presto scherzo in D major, based on the feasting scene in the finale of Act II (ex. 2.9), with a secondary theme in the dominant also to be heard several times in the opera (ex. 2.7). Also heard are ex. 2.11 and ex. 2.3, but without the dramatic significance they acquire later. The movement seems to be complete when the tempo drops to Andante sostenuto for a preview of the portrait motif (ex. 2.2), an eight-bar melody with its full extension. A frantic prestissimo closes the Overture. Later versions of the opera imposed cuts of various lengths.

ACT I

No. 1 Chœurs Scène et Prières Eighteenth-century Vienna. The painter Conrad's atelier. A door leads to the street, and opposite is a large window with small panes. At the back is a portrait of a woman costumed as Circé. A small door at the left. A chair and table at the front. Snow can be seen falling. The stage is empty.

The atmosphere is full of tension with Conrad's torment, ex. 2.1, a violent change from the carefree Overture:

Example 2.1 Saint-Saëns, *Le Timbre d'argent*, Act I, No.1

Two cors anglais colour the orchestration. The music subsides and shifts from B minor to B♭. From outside a group of young men can be heard calling for Conrad. Their 'Noël' and the snow tell us it is Christmas. The merry-makers enter from the street, some of them in masks and dominos, and meet his friend Bénédict, a musician, emerging from the door on the left.

He tells them to keep quiet since Conrad is ill. Supported by ex. 2.1 Bénédict explains that Conrad's imagination is tormenting him cruelly. Bénédict's fiancée Rosa and her sister Hélène have been trying to cheer him up. The old doctor is at his bedside. To a solemn quasi-chorale in the cellos the doctor himself then appears, with Rosa and Hélène. The doctor is named Spiridion, perhaps taking a cue from George Sand's 1839 novel of that name in which Spiridion is an aged monk with mysterious secrets. He reports that Conrad's illness is his lust for money; nothing can be done. In a forceful aside Hélène betrays her private concern for Conrad. Spiridion goes over to the portrait at the back (portrait theme, ex. 2.2), impressed that it was painted by Conrad, then leaves to the tread of his strange cello chorale, warning that there will be another crisis at midnight that will last till dawn.

Example 2.2 *Le Timbre d'argent*, Act I, No. 1

The men sing a ghostly lament, a nice example of the librettists' skill and imagination:

> Ô vain mirage !
> Mortel poison !
> Fatal naufrage
> De la raison.
> La vie est brève !
> Faut-il qu'un rêve
> Trouble le cours
> De ses beaux jours ?

Bénédict leads them to the street door. Rosa puts on her coat, while Hélène leans pensively against the door leading to Conrad's room. In prose, and therefore originally intended as dialogue, Rosa tells Bénédict that their father is expecting them back. To an echo of Hélène's private confession earlier, Rosa confides to Bénédict that Hélène's passion for Conrad is not returned. Before they leave, the two sisters sing a gentle *Prière* to the Virgin, the two voices sometimes alternating, sometimes in unison. So this opening section closes in dreamy serenity.

Dialogue Bénédict, left alone, wonders why Conrad is so distracted when he has happiness at hand. He is anxious what will happen at midnight.

No. 1bis Mélodrame Street sounds (offstage horns) bring Conrad in, in great distress. His anxiety is supported by the music heard at the opening of the curtain, with the two cors anglais again prominent.

Dialogue It's Christmas, explains Bénédict. Why aren't you with them, asks Conrad. Bénédict advises him to be as happy with Hélène as he is with Rosa.

No. 2 Mélodie Are you happy being poor, Conrad asks, as a cue for Bénédict to launch into the first lyrical solo of the opera, 'Demande à l'oiseau qui s'éveille', a perfectly crafted salon piece with a delicate high C at the final cadence and the harp in support throughout. All nature is happy, he claims, but not as happy as I am. Bénédict is milquetoast.

Dialogue Conrad mocks Bénédict for being content with virtue and poverty. He explains that the painting is his whole life, it is reality, not imagination. He is in love with the woman who was the model for his painting of Circé. Her name is Fiametta. Bénédict knows her as a ballerina who has scandalised all Germany with her affairs. Conrad curses his poverty because he needs money to woo Fiametta. When Bénédict tells him this will drive him mad, Conrad realises it is Spiridion who has told him that. Conrad, believing Spiridion is no more than a doctor, hates him and believes he brings bad luck. He wants him paid off. Bénédict takes the money and pretends he will pay him. Conrad claims to be totally in control of his senses. Bénédict leaves.

No. 3 Chœurs et Air Cornets and trombones in the wings accompany cries of 'Carnaval!' and the sounds of festivities outside, while Conrad is alone on stage. His anxiety music surges out of the depths and his torment motif (ex. 2.1) in the orchestra underlines his wretchedness. He is impervious to the laughter of others, he is out of sorts with the world, unmoved by dancing and merriment all around him. His solo, 'Dans le silence et l'ombre', makes a trenchant contrast with Bénédict's song, and he is a different kind of tenor. A strongly rhythmic motif supports the voice, unsettled in character. Conrad is full of rage and self-loathing, cursing the day he was born. As he cadences, the carnival song is again heard outside, driving him to an explosion of agony. He goes to the picture and gets the feeling it is mocking him. He draws a curtain over it and collapses in a faint.

This is a tremendous scene, putting the character of Conrad directly before us, and brimming with tension. Deranged, despairing tenors are a cliché of opera, but this is one of the best scenes of its kind. The two cors anglais are still colouring the texture.

The stage darkens and suddenly Spiridion appears behind Conrad. He is dressed as a doctor from the commedia dell'arte.

No. 4 Final Without a gap for applause the music continues directly on a Tristan chord scored for multi-divided strings. At a gesture from Spiridion the curtain over the picture opens to reveal the real Circé, smiling and motionless. The frame enlarges to show a fantastic landscape lit by the first light of dawn with a chorus of nymphs hiding in the reeds. An offstage horn plays the portrait motif (ex. 2.2) and the nymphs murmur 'Circé!' She awakes and looks around; she is a little unsure of herself.

Flutes and harp offstage start a quick movement in F♯ major, while Fiametta/Circé gradually responds to the dawn and her surroundings. She begins to dance to music that includes a foretaste of her 'bee dance' (ex. 2.5). Conrad is enraptured at the sight. Spiridion launches into a broad seductive melody in E major inviting Conrad to admit to his longing for love and riches. When he replies 'Oui ! oui ! je le veux !', Spiridion produces from his coat a little silver bell, oddly shaped and crowned with a sparkling jewel. Just strike this bell, he tells Conrad, and your wish will be answered. The bell is also an unknown person's death knell (Saint-Saëns cleverly inflects Spiridion's second verse for the dreadful price to pay), but that cannot matter since there will be gold enough to pay for the crime. All Conrad can think of is his Fiametta there before his eyes in the guise of Circé. The nymphs urge him to steal a kiss.

Speaking over a held tremolo, Spiridion tells him that if Conrad does not want the bell, someone else will; if he breaks it, it will bring his death. Conrad at first moves to reject the bell, but then Fiametta approaches him with a discreet kiss, which of course leaves him no choice but to grasp the bell.

Spiridion immediately vanishes and the scene changes back to the interior of Conrad's studio, as at the beginning of the act. Now that he has the bell, its motif can be introduced (ex. 2.3):

Example 2.3 *Le Timbre d'argent*, Act I, No. 4

The new motif alternates with the torment motif (ex. 2.1) as he debates with himself what he should do, with another threatening motif heard when he contemplates the unintended victim (ex. 2.4), also associated with Spiridion's mysterious powers. He decides to strike the bell (on a tense discord) and immediately he hears someone's dying cry. Gold coins cascade in floods at his feet to a rattle of cymbals.

Example 2.4 *Le Timbre d'argent*, Act I, No. 4

Bénédict appears at the door in great urgency with the news that Stadler, Hélène and Rosa's father, has dropped dead just outside Conrad's door. Conrad thinks the old man can be saved, but Spiridion appears behind, grasps his hand and shouts 'Inutile !' to a loud statement of the bell motif. Outside, the revellers carry on with their carnival merriment.

ACT II, TABLEAU 1

Entr'acte scored for wind and harp alone, in two parts: the music of the coming men's chorus, followed by a tune which we heard in the Overture but has not yet found its place in the opera (ex. 2.7). The curtain opens on Fiametta's dressing-room at the Royal Opera in Vienna. Her dressers are busy with her costume and some young admirers stand near. The ballet master is working out some steps, accompanying himself on a pochette.

No. 5 Chœur et Scène The chorus of twelve men, some of whom have names (Frantz, Rodolphe and Rosenthal), sing an exquisite song to Fiametta's beauty:

> Gloire à la belle des belles
> Qui pour doubler ses attraits
> De Vénus a pris les traits,
> De l'amour a pris les ailes !

Sentiment, elegance and scoring are in perfect balance here. If one longs for more, the music will return, but not in quite such a neat package.

Conrad enters with Patrick behind carrying a jewel-case. In a rather formal song Conrad sings Fiametta's praises, comparing her again to Venus (though the classically obsessed librettists now call her Cythérée). Patrick kneels and presents the jewel-case to Fiametta. As she draws out a diamond necklace, the woodwind sparkle in staccato triplets, and the young men wonder to themselves where Conrad can have found the money.

While this is going on Spiridion comes in in the form of the Marquis de Polycastre. He is followed by a liveried negro boy carrying another jewel-case. Soft trombones intone G♭. Aping Conrad's formal tone in a lower key, the Marquis explains that Fiametta's jewellery is incomplete without a diadem, which she now takes from the case held out by the kneeling negro boy. The woodwind sparkle again, and her dressers put the diadem on her head. The bystanders comment that this rivalry will exhaust the Pactolus, which, we are expected to recall, is the river in which King Midas washed his hands when everything he touched turned to gold.

Conrad's exchange with the Marquis brings back the music of the opening scene of this act, and while the onlookers wonder which of the two will win the lady's favours, the Marquis takes a pinch of snuff and idly flicks it off his lace jabot. In recitative the Marquis asks Fiametta if she will dance the 'Pas de l'abeille' which she is to dance in *Les Ruses d'amour*, the opera to be performed that night.[15] 'Oui', she nods (although the score does not tell us so). Conrad is outplayed, but he reminds himself that his turn will come.

No. 6 Pas de l'abeille A solo viola, for the ballet master's pochette, represents the buzzing of a bee with a series of tremolos. The first main tune is on the oboe, answered by the strings, in the regular four-bar phrases typical of ballet music (ex. 2.5).

She dances but the bee returns to bother her. She removes her veil, shakes it out and throws it aside; the buzzing stops. She resumes the dance to new music, but the bee comes back, requiring the full section of violas, joined in due course by cellos, flute and clarinet all madly buzzing. She takes off her belt, then unpins her hair to get rid of the bee, and finally falls into Spiridion's arms. (Saint-Saëns returned to bee music in the

---

[15] *Les Ruses d'amour* is a ballet by Marius Petipa, with music by Glazunov, first performed in 1898. It is possible that Petipa had proposed such a work when he was in Paris in the late 1840s.

Example 2.5 *Le Timbre d'argent*, Act II, Tableau 1, No. 6

opening scene of *L'Ancêtre*, composed in 1905, where the upper strings simulate the buzzing.)

Conrad leaps up to seize her. In tribute to her superb performance Conrad invites the company to his house next day (the libretto, which shows this scene as prose, i.e. dialogue, assigns the invitation to the Marquis). A new figure on the horn supports the polite rivalry between the Marquis, who offers Fiametta a palace in Florence, and Conrad, who responds by offering her a palace in Venice. The Marquis suggests a game of passe-dix to decide the issue, so Conrad sends Patrick off to fetch all the gold from his cellar (ex. 2.4 in the bass). The Marquis quietly gloats.

No. 7 Quintette The gaming scene is sung by five men (Conrad, the Marquis, Frantz, Rodolphe and Rosenthal) against animated music in C♯ minor, with an admirably tense motif running through the scene (ex. 2.6; the figure in the third bar is retrieved from behind the exchanges in the previous scene). Trumpets and trombones contribute a sinister voice to the whole scene. Saint-Saëns's model was no doubt the card scene in Act II of *La traviata*, with rising tension as Conrad plays for ever higher stakes. Every time the Marquis wins, he earns a smile from Fiametta. Since Conrad bids 200,000 ducats, he has to await Patrick's return with his gold. A bell rings to signal the start of the ballet performance in the theatre, so, promising to return to the table later, the Marquis leads Fiametta off, followed by the group of young men.

Example 2.6 *Le Timbre d'argent*, Act II, Tableau 1, No. 7

Dialogue Conrad is about to follow (ex. 2.1) when Bénédict comes in from the other side carrying his violin. He tells Conrad that he is engaged to Rosa. The wedding is to be tomorrow in Stuckradt, in a house which Conrad gave for orphans. Impossible, says Conrad, he has promised to give a fête for Fiametta. Annoyed, Bénédict upbraids him for his cupidity. Conrad admits that Fiametta is a vulgar Danaé. You will be missed, says Bénédict, hinting that someone has been weeping for him. You mean Hélène, says Conrad. He remembers an old tune which Bénédict used to play on his violin.

No. 8 Romance This one? asks Bénédict, leading off with a simple melody in G major. Conrad closes his eyes and imagines he hears Hélène singing. It is indeed her, for she has entered the room silently, and she now gives the complete song, 'Le bonheur est chose légère', about the frailty of love. Accompanied at first just by Bénédict's solo violin, the rest of the strings (except the double basses) gradually join in, muted. The solo violin part becomes more and more elaborate, and two episodes in the minor add a touch of pathos to this supremely well-crafted song.

The simplicity and charm of this song gave it a life of its own outside the context of the opera. It was for a long time the only part of the opera to be recorded. The scene was a later insertion, revealed by its awkward intrusion between the gaming scene and the theatre scene. But the music is of high quality, and it gives Hélène a stronger presence in the opera.

Conrad is lulled into a dreamy nostalgia, but wakes suddenly at the end, while Hélène hides. Bénédict offers to produce Hélène as if by magic, but Conrad violently rejects the idea. 'My thoughts are elsewhere', he cries to a figure that has already figured in the Overture and the Entr'acte, but which is now for the first time supporting words (ex. 2.7):

Example 2.7 *Le Timbre d'argent*, Act II, Tableau 1, No. 8

To a phrase from his violin melody Bénédict makes an embarrassed exit, and Hélène leaves too. As soon as they are gone, the bell theme ex. 2.3 is heard, and that gives place to the theme of Conrad's torment (ex. 2.1) in the bass. He is determined to win Fiametta, whatever the cost.

ACT II, TABLEAU 2

Entr'acte Continuous music covers the scene change to Tableau 2. After a long B major chord the closing music of the *Pas de l'abeille* is heard from offstage on strings and brass, followed by the sound of applause.

No. 9 Chœur et Scène The applause is explained when the curtain rises to show a theatre stage as seen from the back, with a conductor beyond and the audience in the distance. Fiametta has just finished her solo dance on a vaguely oriental set, and is taking her bow with her back to the real audience. Two large curtains close off the stage, then open to allow Fiametta to receive a shower of bouquets, then close again. The dancers pick up her flowers and a dresser throws a coat over her shoulders. After a reprise of the Circé music from Act I, the usual coterie of male admirers appears and sings a ravishing chorus in her praise, 'Séduisante almée'. Only twelve bars long, it cries out to be repeated, but that is not to be.

Conrad is there too, and thinking the field is clear he offers his hand to Fiametta, although soft trombone chords (ex. 2.8) warn us that danger lurks.

Example 2.8 *Le Timbre d'argent*, Act I, Tableau 2, No. 9

A strange figure, bearded and wearing the costume of an Italian ballad-singer, intervenes. He carries a guitar. It is of course Spiridion again, and to introduce himself he has a song.

No. 10 Chanson napolitaine With triangle and tambourine in support, Spiridion's main set piece (a counterpart to Mephistopheles's 'Le Veau d'or') is an appealing crowd-pleaser, identifying himself as Caméléone, who will sing whatever his listeners would like to hear. A chameleon is an apt image for Spiridion.

No. 11 Scène et Chant bachique Fiametta and the young men applaud, and Conrad invites this Italian entertainer to the fête he is to give next day. Spiridion, with a laugh, says 'I am a magician too', and the scene changes instantly to the interior of a magnificent Florentine palace. The floor opens and a table, laden with delicacies, rises up; a chandelier comes down. Lackeys appear in the background. The music is grand and classical.

Example 2.8 underlines Conrad's discomfort as Fiametta mimes her admiration for the Marquis's brilliant creation. The Marquis is anxious to return to the gaming table, but meanwhile a feast is laid out for all to enjoy, and Spiridion launches into a drinking song, 'Dans le bruit et dans l'ivresse', which the men repeat in hearty unison. Offbeat string chords drive the pulse.

No. 12 Final Marked *Presto con fuoco* in waltz time, this scene sets off exactly as we heard it at the beginning of the Overture with great orchestral energy (ex. 2.9). Women

Example 2.9 *Le Timbre d'argent*, Act II, Tableau 2, No. 12

now join the chorus of men, and the words rhyme *vin* and *divin*, *désir* and *plaisir*, *jeunesse* and *ivresse*, as a thousand other drinking choruses had done before it, many of them penned by Barbier and Carré.

Solo exchanges are conducted over a constant interplay of ex. 2.9 and ex. 2.7. Conrad is unsure what part he is to play in this when Patrick arrives to tell him that his hoard of gold has been stolen (ex. 2.4 in the trombones). The Marquis enrages Conrad by noticing his pallor. The appearance of his torment motif (ex. 2.1) and the bell motif (ex. 2.3) in quick succession tell us what is on his mind. But he holds firm and refuses to commit another murder just to get money. The rapid music resumes. Everyone thinks Conrad is losing his mind with all this talk of murder, especially when he turns his rage on everyone present, drawing his sword and cursing them all as 'valets et bandits'. He is especially fierce to Fiametta, and the curtain falls on a fast and furious B♭ minor as Conrad forces his way out.

ACT III

No. 13 Entr'acte et Chœur The Entr'acte draws on music which we are about to hear in the third act. The first half pairs an agitated figure from the duet for Hélène and Rosa, no. 14 (ex. 2.10), followed by a preview of the gentle chorus heard when the curtain opens. The scene is a German ivy-clad cottage shaded by trees with, in the distance, a view of the Danube. It is now summer, and a group of poor people have gathered at the cottage where, every week, Rosa, now about to be married to Bénédict, gives out alms. They sing a very beautiful chorale in simple homophony and in pastoral F major, each line separated by the figure which made up the second part of the Entr'acte.

Example 2.10 *Le Timbre d'argent*, Act III, No. 14

Rosa appears at the door in her wedding dress with her sister Hélène. In response to their compliments she invites them all to attend her wedding later that day, and they leave. The scene has a refreshing sense of calm and placid beauty after the frantic atmosphere of the preceding act.

No. 14 Duo A short exchange in which Rosa worries about Hélène's state of mind leads directly into recitative starting with ex. 2.10. Hélène responds that she cannot be unhappy to see her on her wedding day. There follows a long duet in which Hélène reveals that she loves Conrad, which Rosa knew already. Fate keeps them apart, while

Rosa is happy in her love. The music flows well, with constant underlying agitation provided by ex. 2.10. In the first part of the duet Hélène sings below Rosa's pitch as if she were a mezzo, but after the central part, where she confesses her love and names Conrad as its object, she takes over the upper line, rising to high D: she knows her love has no future, but she can share her despair with her sister without restraint.

Dialogue Hélène recounts the episode (no. 8 in Act II) when she was about to speak to Conrad but he didn't want to see her. She is sure it's all over. Bénédict comes in with the news that Conrad is following just behind. He tells Hélène that Conrad needs her to cure himself of his obsession. Hélène is overjoyed and they go into the house to prepare for his arrival.

No. 15 Récit et Cavatine Conrad appears and has the stage to himself. He is in a thoughtful mood. This, he realises, is where he hid his treasure. In the previous act Patrick reported that his gold had been stolen, but now Conrad apparently has another hoard in the country. This suggests that the authors originally intended Conrad to strike the bell at the end of the previous act, as at the end of Act I, when he was desperate for money. In fact they have him drawing back from the brink at that point.

Conrad's agitation increases and he violently turns his back on his impulses and false hopes. In calmer mood he sings his *Cavatine* 'Nature souriante et douce'. Limpid and elegant, it is framed as a pair of *couplets* in D♭ major, perfect for a lyric tenor and free of all tension.

No. 16 Scène et Duo Hélène comes out of the cottage and they greet each other a little hesitantly. Hélène is obviously nervous (ex. 2.10). The bell motif draws a sigh of regret from Conrad, and they embark on their main duet in the opera, both holding back. The whole of the opening part of the duet is to be sung *à part*, Hélène full of anxiety, Conrad reminding himself that happiness is right in front of him and 'over there' is all vain delusion. When the tempo changes from a lilting 9/8 to 3/4 they finally address each other and are soon duetting with true passion. The final part, at 'Bienheureuse journée !' has the *élan* of a cabaletta, but instead of closing at full throttle, the last few pages are to be sung mostly *pianissimo*, calling for a show of tenderness and delicacy from both singers.

Dialogue Spiridion appears, this time disguised as the coachman Pippo. He is conducting a young lady in a carriage which has broken down nearby. When the lady appears at the back in travelling costume, it is of course Fiametta. Conrad is alarmed and at first tries to hurry with Hélène away to the wedding, but then, after catching Fiametta's eye, sends her on ahead. Hélène is troubled, but nevertheless goes. Spiridion hides behind a tree leaving the stage to Conrad and Fiametta.

No. 17 Scène Their exchanges are conducted on his side in recitative and on her side in mime. The vocal score helpfully indicates Fiametta's gestures and responses, identifying her as Circé. It is certainly a most unusual operatic scene. Conrad inevitably falls under Fiametta's spell, mysteriously seconded by Spiridion/Pippo standing near and occasionally inserting a dark insinuation. At first Conrad is firm in his determination not to be drawn back into Fiametta's world. He explains that he has lost everything gambling. Fiametta's response is an amorous melody on the flute (ex. 2.11) which undermines his resolve:

Example 2.11 *Le Timbre d'argent*, Act III, No. 17

He feels he is in the grip of a dream (while Pippo, still hiding, joins in) and collapses on a bench. 'No, it is not a dream,' mimes Fiametta, 'I love you, let's go away!' Conrad is caught in her trap, and they 'sing' an urgent love duet, Fiametta leading off as high violins, Conrad responding *propria voce*. As it ends, Fiametta falls into his arms and he tells her of his buried treasure nearby. He rushes off to find it.

Dialogue Pippo emerges from the trees, laughing. He congratulates Fiametta on her work. Violin and bagpipes are heard, coming from the wedding party. Pippo suggests they join the festivities, but Fiametta feels she is dressed wrong. He touches her with his finger and transforms her into a gypsy girl. He draws her aside as the wedding party enters.

No. 18 Chœur et Chanson The rustic music is all in four-bar phrases with plenty of drones and heavy barline beats and the chorus joins in the conclusion. Bénédict offers to sing a song, so everyone listens. 'L'humble papillon de nuit' is a charming three-verse song about a moth and a star falling in love. Bénédict sings the first verse (the moth) and the sopranos echo his last line; then Rosa sings the second verse (in the minor) and the tenors do the echo; they share the third verse and the full chorus conclude. The superbly delicate orchestration requires a 'harmoniflûte', essentially an accordion.[16] Marked 'voix céleste', it sustains high notes during Bénédict's verse, not Rosa's, and returns for the third verse, which is supported by high tremolo muted strings. The moth could have been represented by a single flute, busy throughout, but then Saint-Saëns changed it to two flutes alternating and sharing the work. The melody and shape of the phrases are faultless. This would make a lovely concert piece.

---

[16] The 'harmoniflûte' is described in an advertisement by Mayer-Marix in the *Revue et gazette musicale* of 9 November 1856, p. 364, and illustrated in the same journal on 2 August 1857, p. 256.

No. 19 Scène, Danse bohémienne et Final Holding a pair of bagpipes and no longer a coachman, Spiridion emerges from hiding with Fiametta holding a tambourine. They introduce themselves over seemingly random chords on horns and bassoons. Bénédict welcomes them and the chorus admire Fiametta's beauty. Punctuated by trumpets and trombones, Spiridion proposes that Fiametta should dance for them. Spiridion warms up his bagpipes (woodwind, including bass clarinet) and climbs on a barrel. Bénédict and Rosa are alarmed that Conrad and Hélène are not there.

The gypsy dance is heavy-footed music. Oboe and cor anglais imitate the bagpipe with mostly woodwind support, ending noisily. Fiametta dances and rattles her tambourine (notated) while the chorus sing and dance around her.

Spiridion hangs his bagpipes on a branch and jumps down, but they keep playing. This of course is only suggested since the orchestra is providing its sound anyway. The dance gathers momentum with lots of exotic augmented seconds with sharpened fourth in a minor key and peasant drones. Suddenly, over a sinister rising chromatic scale in the bass and a bass drum roll, Spiridion, shouting over the music, sees Conrad coming with the silver bell in his hand. The peasants think Spiridion must be the devil.

Still unseen, Conrad strikes the bell. Bénédict clutches his heart and falls dying into Rosa's arms. The bagpipe stops and the dancing stops. Conrad and Hélène appear, Conrad appalled to find Bénédict dead, Hélène supporting Rosa. Spiridion tells Fiametta to go. She leads Conrad away, followed by a grinning Spiridion.

ACT IV

No. 20 Entr'acte, Chœur et Scène A moonlit street, back in Vienna, with the house of Hélène and Rosa on the right. At the back a bridge with statues. Snow has fallen. It is still carnival time, presumably leading up to Lent, even though the previous act took place 'beneath the summer sun'. There is no Entr'acte in effect since the same boisterous carnival music that was heard in Act I brings on the maskers from all directions in a 'German masquerade'. It has more charm and more tunes than before, and sets up lively stage movement for the entrance of Conrad pursued by maskers, whom he takes to be demons coming to torment him.

No. 21 Scène et Chœur The maskers fall silent, while from her house Hélène can be heard singing a melancholy song. Her voice rouses Conrad from his befuddlement. The chorus reminds him that it is Hélène at her window. Like Faust revived by the presence of Marguerite, Conrad feels himself saved by her divine presence.

Dialogue (The text in the printed libretto is in verse, intended for music, although no music exists for it.) Inevitably the sudden appearance of Spiridion wrecks his elation. The doctor is now shamelessly costumed as the devil. He tells Conrad to go into Hélène's house and confess to her all about the silver bell.

No. 22 Ballade Over a diabolic augmented chord the chorus want to know more about the silver bell. Conrad begs Spiridion not to tell, but the latter is eager to do so. His *Ballade* is a strong movement in G minor for the main melody of which the bell motif (ex. 2.3) provides the opening phrase over a gale of chromatics in the strings. The tone is sinister and bewitching, and the chorus are drawn in with curiosity. The end of the first verse reminds us: 'One more rich man means one more dead'. The tale continues of the silver bell lying beneath the waves enticing one victim after another to plunge after it. The Sirens' song lures passers-by who stare into the water and can count the dead.

The latter part of the *Ballade* tells us that Conrad has thrown the bell into a lake, and in the 1913 version the act would have begun with a scene showing Conrad trying to retrieve it. This piece is one of the best scenes in the opera, a great number for a dramatic baritone.

Dialogue Spiridion tells Conrad to knock on Hélène's door, but Conrad draws a dagger and stabs Spiridion. The maskers intervene. Spiridion reassures them that he is unscathed.

No. 23 Chœur, Scène et Ballet Their suspicion that he is the devil is confirmed when he calls on his 'daughters of hell', namely Circé and a group of nymphs all wearing white satin masks who appear on the bridge at the back. An elegant dance in 6/8 originally placed here was recycled nearly twenty years later as the *Entrée de l'Amour* in the Divertissement in Tableau 5 of *Ascanio*.[17] So there is only a waltz as a pure ballet scene for Fiametta/Circé and her *corps*. In the course of the movement Circé and the nymphs surround Conrad, who tries to escape their seduction but is finally led down to the front of the stage where she signs to him that he should strike an imaginary bell. Moonlight gives the scene a sense of mystery and magic.

The melody is a 3/4 version of ex. 2.11. Secondary themes are heard in the dominant and the subdominant as in most conventional ballet movements of this type, and the music works up to a strong close with full orchestra.

No. 24 Final Conrad tries to free himself from their clutches. Spiridion steps in and unmasks Circé. The nymphs unmask too. The orchestra launches into a reprise of their amorous duet (in no. 17), but they are interrupted by Hélène, who comes out of her house. 'This is her', he tells her, pointing to Fiametta. 'Always her', Hélène replies.

---

[17] See F-Pn MS 686.

Cries of 'Carnaval!' distract them, followed by the Angelus bell, but then Hélène takes control of the situation, determined to save Conrad from the devil as a mother would defend her child. A great flow of coloratura confirms her strength of will while Conrad can only feebly echo Spiridion's *Ballade* about the silver bell.

The maskers leave at Hélène's wish. In a dramatic recitative Hélène confronts Fiametta with a challenge to leave Conrad alone. Let Fiametta work with the devil; she herself has heaven on her side. The scene is tilted in Hélène's favour since Fiametta's replies are expressed in defiant gestures while Hélène has some powerful driving music to sing with strong orchestral support. Conrad steps forward, begging Hélène's forgiveness. This turns into a trio, with Spiridion telling Fiametta that Conrad is lost to her while Hélène and Conrad rejoice in each other's love, ending in a full-blooded unison.

If you thought this would be the happy ending for the opera, there is more in store. Heavy trombone E♭s interrupt the trio. In a powerful recitative with much dissonance and prominent trombones, Conrad pulls suddenly away, ashamed that he has caused the deaths of Bénédict and of Rosa's father. He curses the talisman and wishes he could destroy both it and the ubiquitous Fiametta/Circé, even though he knows that to destroy the bell is to bring his own death.

The tempo slows to Poco adagio. To a steady tread of unison strings the ghost of Bénédict appears on the bridge, holding the bell. He advances towards Conrad. Circé runs to Spiridion's side. Bénédict advances, hands the bell to Conrad who curses it (its motif on two trombones answered by two horns) and crushes it beneath his feet to a heavy blow on the tamtam.

The orchestra erupts with *fortissimo* diminished sevenths and chromatic scales. Spiridion seizes Conrad's arm with a Mephisthophelean cry of 'Il est à moi!' The stage darkens and when we see it again we are back at the start of the opera, in Conrad's atelier. The portrait motif (ex. 2.2) and Fiametta's waltz (ex. 2.9) cover the transformation and point to the portrait of Circé on its easel. Conrad is stretched out in a chair with Spiridion looking over him, Bénédict standing near. Hélène and Rosa are kneeling. It is full daylight.

In dialogue over the music, Spiridion tells Bénédict that the fever will pass. Conrad wakes and looks around in confusion. Rosa tells Conrad that her father awaits him at the church. Conrad replies that he does not expect the doctor to cure him, but asks Hélène and her father if they will consent to their marriage. He sees a silver bell on the table.

Everyone is happy: Spiridion slyly concludes, 'Work and love: all happiness is there.' Outside, people are gathered on the church steps to bless the couple. Noël! Alleluia!

* * * * *

It was all a dream. Many a fine fantasy has been written within the framework of a dream, and the more convincing the fantasy the more disappointing is the revelation that it was not real. Hoffmann's stories do not resort to that device, nor did Goethe in *Faust*, but Barbier and Carré nonetheless succeeded in *Le Timbre d'argent* in gathering together all their favourite themes and stage illusions in a libretto with strong tenor and baritone roles, two contrasting sopranos, a secondary tenor, and plenty for the chorus. With the exception of Rosa, they all get strong solo numbers, sometimes two.

In addition, the libretto calls for a dancer in a principal role. Mime is thus a primary story-teller, and ballet plays a more important part than it does in many a five-act grand opera in which ballet is the obligatory *divertissement*, whether relevant or not. Opéra-ballet had a long ancestry in France since the beginning of the seventeenth century. As elsewhere in Barbier and Carré's stories, the character of Spiridion in *Le Timbre d'argent* explicitly identifies the devil with the doctor. We never learn why Conrad is so dissatisfied with life, but unspecified yearning is a common theme in Romantic literature. Conrad's distress in his first big solo 'Dans le silence et l'ombre' is sufficient to mark him out as the devil's next victim.

The portrait/sculpture theme also recurs in Barbier and Carré's first opera libretto, *Galathée*, written for Massé in 1852, although here in *Le Timbre d'argent* the artist does not fall in love with his creation, as did Pygmalion with his statue of Galatea, but the portrait is seen to come to life, as does Oscar Wilde's Dorian Grey and the picture galleries in Sullivan's *Ruddigore* and Britten's *Owen Wingrave*. The multiple personalities that Spiridion assumes recur in the character of Mercure in their libretto *Psyché* for Ambroise Thomas (1857) and most strikingly in *Les Contes d'Hoffmann*.

The libretto is also contemporary with Adolphe Adam's one-act opéra-comique *La Poupée de Nuremberg*, played at the Opéra-National in February 1852, with a libretto by Adolphe de Leuven and Arthur de Beauplan. This is based on the same story as the Olympie story in *Les Contes d'Hoffmann*, with a doll that mimes and does not sing, like Fenella in the *Muette de Portici* of Auber, regularly staged at the Opéra since 1828.

The action of the silver bell in bringing wealth at the price of a life may be derived from Balzac's *Peau de chagrin* (1831), an immensely popular novel, in which the ass's skin fulfils its possessor's wish but only at the price of his gradual physical decline. A silver bell is also used as a message of death in Hugo's play *Lucrèce Borgia* (1833).[18]

The stagecraft of *Le Timbre d'argent* is exceptionally ambitious. In Act I the scene of Conrad's atelier dissolves into a nymph-filled landscape and back again. In Act II the first tableau shows Fiametta's dressing-room at the theatre, with a scene change to the

---

[18] In his paper 'Palimpsestes littéraires et musicaux du *Timbre d'argent*', read to the conference 'Saint-Saëns à pleine voix' (Opéra-Comique, 12–14 June 2017), Stéphane Lelièvre proposed *Victorine* by T.-M. Dumersan (1831) and *Les Mémoires du Diable* by Frédéric Soulié (1838) as further sources of this theme.

stage itself, seen from the back. This transforms into a banquet scene, which in turn is dissolved into a Florentine palace. The third act is set outside a country cottage, without any scene changes, and the fourth opens underwater (in the final version) and changes to a street scene that dissolves back to the opening scene in Conrad's atelier. With all this to devise, the stage staff at any theatre would have an unusual challenge. This is a remarkable libretto, very clearly reflecting some of the theatrical obsessions and technical advances in French opera in the Second Empire. The composers who turned it down were perhaps unable to accept that it could work on stage, or were unwilling to take the risks involved. Saint-Saëns at twenty-nine was keen to accept the challenge; he had the technique and the imagination to tackle it and he composed it quickly.

The score may not command the wizardry that Berlioz or Rimsky-Korsakov might have brought to the story, but it displays a remarkable range both of styles and of feeling. It may not satisfy twenty-first-century opera audiences, who find the combination of ballet and opera and the combination of speech and song broadly unacceptable, but no singer would be disappointed with the principal roles of Spiridion, Conrad or Hélène, who all have magnificent numbers in solo or in ensemble. The network of motifs is applied helpfully, with good judgment, Saint-Saëns's fluent gift of modulation is not over-used, and the orchestration is masterly throughout. He does not linger over prayer scenes, as Gounod might, and his vocal declamation is faultless. It is a brilliant first opera, much more original than anything by Halévy, Massé or Auber, and a match for the music which his friends Gounod and Bizet were writing in the same years.

Bizet was thrilled to observe not a trace of Wagner and not a trace of Berlioz.[19] Saint-Saëns himself summed up the opera many years later:

> *Le Timbre d'argent* does not claim to be anything other than a light work [...] There's no intrigue, and the opera will be of no interest to anyone who does not see that its real subject is simply the struggle of an artist's soul against life's vulgarities, its inability to live or think like the rest of the world, whatever its desires and urges. The artist's ideal is in his art; his human nature forces him to look for it outside art, but he'll never find it because art based on Nature is not Nature and because if the artist looks for his ideal in Nature everything he finds will be illusory. Conrad at first thinks his ideal is embodied in Fiametta, without seeing that the Circé his brush created is that ideal and that Fiametta is merely its shadow. Lured by the dancer into a life of luxury he finds only disappointment, crime and madness. [...] Cured of this fatal passion and restored to his senses, he thinks he has found happiness in the love of the chaste, affectionate Hélène. But he doesn't find it there either, and a sequel might show us Conrad wearying of Hélène's virtuousness as he did of Fiametta's vices, while Hélène despairs of her inability to satisfy an insatiable soul for whom ordinary life is without interest.

---

[19] Letter to Guiraud, 1867, published in *Le Ménestrel*, 18 July 1875.

Saint-Saëns's misogyny then peeps out:

> Conrad succumbs. While driving him to commit a crime, the enchantress has also made him abandon his artistic convictions. And that's very human. Don't we see that every day: well educated, normally perfectly honourable men sinking to the worst degradation under the influence of the most vulgar women?[20]

* * * * *

Reactions to the opera after opening night on 23 February 1877 were, as usual, contradictory, as the critics wrestled with whether it was Wagnerian or not and whether it was tuneful or not, offering widely different answers. They also raised the old grumble that Saint-Saëns was a symphonist and therefore unsuited to the theatre, which irritated him intensely.[21] The public's response was to sustain it for eighteen performances, which was neither success nor failure. Both of Bizet's operas, *Les Pêcheurs de perles* and *La Jolie Fille de Perth*, survived the same number of performances a decade earlier. The performances might have continued if Vizentini's management had not become bankrupt at the end of the year.

Two performers were outstanding: Léon Melchissédec as Spiridion, and Adeline Théodore as Fiametta/Circé. Caroline Salla was good as Hélène, although her voice was heavier and more dramatic than that of Madame Carvalho for whom the part was written. Choudens issued a long catalogue of extracts and arrangements from the opera.

It is hard to determine whether Offenbach attended any of these performances, although the likelihood is great. He had conducted the stage band for the performances of Barbier and Carré's play *Les Contes d'Hoffmann* in 1851, and the idea of writing an opera on the same material is said to have come to him on the train to Chicago in the summer of 1876.[22] Carré being no longer alive, the libretto was reshaped by Barbier alone, but how far the project had reached by early 1877 is unclear. Barbier could not have failed to ensure that Offenbach saw such a similar exercise in multifaceted demonism. When Offenbach died in 1881 before his opera had reached the stage, Saint-Saëns wrote an obituary that recognised his extraordinary gifts.[23]

The first revival of *Le Timbre d'argent* took place in Brussels two years later. At that time the Théâtre de la Monnaie served as an alternative house for many French operas refused by Parisian houses or in need of revival. Saint-Saëns spent a few days there to rehearse, but left before the first night on 10 February 1879. It was successful with twenty performances.

---

[20] *Le Timbre d'argent* (1914), in SORET 2012, pp. 871–72.
[21] He gave some samples of such criticism in his *Causerie musicale* of October 1879. See SORET 2012, pp. 232 and 235–36.
[22] *L'Avant-Scène Opéra*, no. 25 (1980), p. 13.   [23] SORET 2012, pp. 278–81.

Of all Saint-Saëns's operas, this one was revised the most; there had already been many revisions between its first completion in 1864 and first publication in 1877, and the vocal score was eventually issued in six different versions. The libretto was issued several times unchanged but it matches none of the vocal scores. Some of Saint-Saëns's revisions as late as 1913 involved excavating music he had written over forty years before. A vast collection of manuscript material relating to the opera is preserved at the Bibliothèque nationale de France, at the Bibliothèque-Musée de l'Opéra and in the publisher Choudens's residual archive, so in the absence of a critical edition a summary of the different forms the opera took must suffice.

The original plan was an opéra-comique in four acts with prologue and epilogue, like the original play. This closely matches the plan of *Les Contes d'Hoffmann* and the 1851 play *Les Marionnettes du docteur*. The scenes in the real world, in Conrad's atelier, are presented as prologue and epilogue, while the dream sequence is enacted in Acts I to IV. The prologue would have consisted of the present Act I. Similarly, the epilogue would begin half way through the present no. 24, when the scene changes back to Conrad's atelier. When the opera was in rehearsal at the Opéra-Comique in 1868 the overture was to be played between the prologue and Act I.[24] Spiridion's name was originally Wolframb. The underwater scene proposed by Carvalho and the recitatives required by Perrin were written in the 1860s, although they were not adopted until 1913.

The 1877 version, as narrated above, put the overture at the beginning and divided the opera into four acts, the prologue and epilogue being absorbed in the first and last acts. Some passages originally intended as dialogue (printed as prose in the libretto) were set to music as recitative. These included the section in no. 1 between the men's 'Ô vain mirage !' and the *Prière* for Hélène and Rosa.

Dialogue and *parlé* over music were retained for the revival in Brussels in 1879, but a number of revisions were applied and the vocal score was issued in its new form. Substantial cuts were made in the overture. The orchestral introduction to no. 1, introducing Conrad's torment motif, was cut. As soon as Spiridion has given him the bell (in no. 4), instead of agonising over its fearful power, which he does in the 1877 version, he strikes it at once. The exchanges between the *Pas de l'abeille* (no. 6) and the gaming scene (no. 7) were removed from the score, but probably performed as dialogue, as shown in the printed libretto. The second verse of Hélène's 'Le bonheur est chose légère' (no. 8) was cut, and the exchanges that followed were evidently restored as dialogue, with Conrad singing his final lines 'Démon de l'or'. Part of the exchanges in no. 11 before the *Chant bachique* were cut.

In Act III the 1879 version shows an optional cut of the tiny part for Second Beggar in no. 13. The introduction to no. 14, the *Duo* for Hélène and Rosa, was cut too, or perhaps

---

[24] *Le Ménestrel*, 26 January 1868.

The new scene at the start of Act IV is set by moonlight beside a lake. Seeking to recover the silver bell which he has thrown into the water, Conrad encounters a group of Sirens who tease him with pre-echoes of 'Sur le sable brille', Spiridion's *Ballade*, yet to be heard, with its derivation from the bell's motto theme. Lured by their seduction, he is about to plunge into the depths when he recovers his senses and runs off. Saint-Saëns was perfectly aware that the scene closely resembles the opening scene of *Das Rheingold*, but he wrote it before he had heard that opera and no doubt felt in 1913 that he was no longer afraid of the competition. He was also concerned that yet another scene change would require an entr'acte; in fact the music runs directly into the return of 'Carnaval!', which has a good stretch of music before the curtain has to rise. The ending preserved the shorter version worked out for the first Brussels performances in 1879.

The three performances in Brussels in March 1914 were a great success and Saint-Saëns was very satisfied. He wrote a brochure about the opera to accompany the performances.[30] This was the last time he heard the opera, in fact the last time anyone heard the opera for over a century, a long silence in which the two airs 'Demande à l'oiseau qui s'éveille' and 'Le bonheur est chose légère' enjoyed some currency as solo songs. Then in June 2017 it was very successfully staged at the Opéra-Comique under the patronage of the Palazzetto Bru Zane, directed by Guillaume Vincent and conducted by François-Xavier Roth. This was issued as a CD-book in 2019.

---

[30] SORET 2012, pp. 871–73.

3 | *Samson et Dalila*

Saint-Saëns left two full accounts of the genesis of *Samson et Dalila*: one in a letter to Henri Collet;[1] the other in an article published shortly before his death.[2] The latter reads:

> An elderly music-lover who used to visit me often had drawn my attention to the subject of Samson as an idea for an oratorio, since that form was much in favour at the time. [...]
> I knew a charming young man then related to my family by marriage, Fernand Lemaire, who wrote a little poetry. I had set some of his verses to music. I mentioned the oratorio idea to him. 'An oratorio!' he said, 'No! Let's do an opera!' So we settled on an opera. As soon as we spoke about it there was an outcry. A biblical opera! Yet, since legendary operas were then in vogue, I was not discouraged. My poet had written the first two acts. I'd made a few rough drafts of the first act myself, for my own eyes only, and done the whole of the second.
> The barely credible fact is that apart from the sketch of the Prelude, it existed only *in my head*; in the desire to give my friends an idea of it all at home, I wrote the three roles without a note of the orchestration.

The letter to Collet tells us that the elderly music-lover was an admirer of Voltaire's libretto *Samson*, set by Rameau in 1734. No music on this libretto survives, but it has been described as 'the best [libretto] that Rameau was ever to set'[3] and was surely consulted by Saint-Saëns. A letter of 1901 to Jules Combarieu provides a few more details:

> [The score] consisted only of some illegible sketches and the parts for the three singers in Act II [...] clearly written with cues and bars' rest indicated, while the orchestration existed only in my head. [...] Apart from the theme for the treadmill Act III was not even begun.[4]

The 1921 reminiscence continues:

> I forget the names of the three singers, whom I accompanied naturally from memory, since apart from the vocal parts *nothing was written down*. The small select audience (which included Anton Rubinstein) were icy. The composer received not a single compliment, not even out of courtesy.

There is surprisingly little evidence from the 1860s, over forty years earlier, to confirm this account: no tell-tale sketches, no letters and no mentions in the press. According to

---

[1] COLLET 1922, pp. 31–32. [2] *La Revue universelle*, VI/9 (1 August 1921); SORET 2012, p. 1061.
[3] GIRDLESTONE 1969, p. 196. [4] *Revue d'histoire et de critique musicales*, 1901, p. 392.

Bonnerot, the librettist Lemaire (his first name is given as either Fernand or Ferdinand) was a creole from Martinique, born in 1832, three years before Saint-Saëns, who married one of Saint-Saëns's wife's cousins. He died in 1879. Saint-Saëns set two of his poems as songs, 'Souvenances' and 'Tristesse', but it is remarkable that the librettist of one of the most successful operas never wrote another libretto, never published any poetry and is otherwise lost to history.

The libretto is certainly very accomplished work for someone who had not ventured into this field before. Saint-Saëns confirmed that although he habitually contributed a good deal himself to the librettos of his operas, and in this case the 'scenario is almost entirely by me',[5] he contributed only a single line to the libretto of *Samson et Dalila*, Dalila's 'Lâche! Cœur sans amour! Je te méprise, adieu!' (in Act II), which testifies warmly to Lemaire's skill.[6] He goes on to say, 'But the whole canvas of the piece was by me, even the smallest detail', from which we may deduce that having been alerted to the subject of Samson by his elderly friend, and having decided with Lemaire that the work should be an opera, not an oratorio, Saint-Saëns outlined the characters and worked out the sequence of acts and scenes before passing it to Lemaire to versify.

When did all this take place? Bonnerot places the first play-through, which took place at one of Saint-Saëns's Monday at-homes in the Rue Monsieur-le-Prince, in 1867, although since Anton Rubinstein was present it was more probably between March and May 1868 when Rubinstein was in Paris concluding a series of concerts of his own music; he conducted the orchestra when Saint-Saëns gave the first performance of his Second Piano Concerto on May 13th.

It is unlikely that Saint-Saëns would have wanted to embark on another opera immediately after *Le Timbre d'argent* was written and while it was awaiting performance at the Théâtre-Lyrique, but after two years, with the performance still an uncertain event, a very different opera might suggest itself as a good move. There was rarely any gap in Saint-Saëns's productivity, so there are no obvious months when other music was not being written in abundance, and he was busy throughout this period with concerts and with his duties as organist at the Madeleine.

If these preliminary efforts belong to 1867–68, the origins of the opera go back much further, since it is mentioned as 'notre oratorio' in a letter of 11 August 1859,[7] and an autograph full score of the opening Prelude bears the date '26 7bre [September] 1859'.[8] This explains Saint-Saëns's mention of the Prelude as the only part of Act I written down. It is most unlikely that Saint-Saëns imagined this as part of an opera at that time; headed simply '1. Chœur', it was probably one of a series of sacred choral works that he produced during his early tenure of the organist's post at the Madeleine. Bonnerot

---

[5] Letter of 25 June 1909; RATNER 2012, p. 43.
[6] *Les Annales politiques et littéraires*, 9 January 1921, p. 28; SORET 2012, p. 1054.
[7] See Fabien Guilloux, Critical Edition of the libretto, forthcoming. [8] F-Pn MS 545(b).

mentions eighteen *cantiques* in French or Latin composed in 1859.[9] The piece is incomplete, breaking off before the choral entry 'Quoi ! veux-tu donc'; as a prayer to the God of Israel it implies no more than a sacred choral work, with no suggestion of a theatrical or dramatic context.

Many questions remain. Were these few lines of verse written by Lemaire? If not, by whom? At what point did Saint-Saëns associate this piece with the Samson story? Also unexplained is his apparent enthusiasm for treating the subject as an opera rather than as an oratorio, a decision that may have been taken much later than he suggests. He was right to recall that oratorios were somewhat in favour at that time, with choral singing an ever stronger feature of Parisian music, and with works like David's *odesymphonies*, Berlioz's *L'Enfance du Christ* and Franck's *Rédemption* finding favour with the public. Massenet's *Marie-Magdeleine* and *Ève* were to exploit this taste very successfully in 1873 and 1875. Saint-Saëns had himself composed a choral setting of Psalm 17 in 1865. The plentiful participation of the chorus in the finished opera *Samson et Dalila* suggests that an oratorio could have suited the subject well, and there was Handel's *Samson* (which Saint-Saëns knew) to prove it.

He had to confront two factors: first, biblical operas had always had a troubled history in the face of censorship from the church and of widespread disapproval of treating the scriptures as drama; and second, a common view of Saint-Saëns as an instrumental composer, a brilliant pianist and composer of symphonies who had never won the Prix de Rome and was therefore ill-equipped to compose opera. Saint-Saëns embarked on *Samson et Dalila* in blatant and courageous defiance of these two forces, which he greatly resented and which did, as he had every reason to expect, delay the performance of the opera for many years.

His unusual approach to writing the work – doing it mostly in his head – suggests that he had doubts about the enterprise from the start. In his 1921 reminiscence Saint-Saëns implies that he had drafted the Prelude and sketched out parts of Act I and the whole of Act II, but it is hard to know what that means if nothing was written down. It is clearer to understand his desire to run through parts of Act II at his home, for which occasion he wrote out vocal parts for the Grand Prêtre, Dalila and Samson, filling in the accompaniment at the piano. We cannot know why that small private audience reacted so coldly, but clearly the singers were too undistinguished to lodge in the composer's memory and were hobbled by sight-reading from an incomplete copy of the music.

A second run-through was arranged soon after. This time the singers were the composer Augusta Holmès singing Dalila, Henri Regnault singing Samson, and Romain Bussine in the role of the Grand Prêtre. Regnault, a painter, had won the Prix de Rome in 1866 with a painting, 'Thetis Bringing Achilles's Arms Forged by

---

[9] BONNEROT 1922, p. 38.

Vulcan', for which the nineteen-year-old Augusta Holmès had posed topless. She and Regnault may have been lovers, with more enthusiasm for each other than Dalila had for Samson. A gap in Regnault's Rome studies enabled him to be in Paris for this soirée, but his career was brought to a tragic end by the war of 1870–71 in which he was killed, greatly lamented by his many friends, including Saint-Saëns.

This second performance was again greeted with little enthusiasm, with the result that Saint-Saëns took no steps towards drafting, let alone completing, his opera/oratorio. Of Act III only the opening had been set to music. Thus it rested until June 1870, when Saint-Saëns attended the celebrations organised by Liszt in Weimar for the centenary of Beethoven's birth. In conversation with Liszt as he was leaving he mentioned the unwritten *Dalila*, evidently identified as an opera. 'Finish your opera,' said Liszt, 'and I'll get it played here.'[10]

War with Prussia was declared almost immediately after, and in the aftermath Saint-Saëns was kept busy by his unceasing schedule of concert appearances and by the foundation and first activities of the Société Nationale. For this organisation he composed a series of orchestral works: *Le Rouet d'Omphale* and *Marche héroïque* in 1871 (the former dedicated to Augusta Holmès and the latter to the memory of Henri Regnault), *Phaëton* in 1873 and *Danse macabre* in 1874. The Cello Concerto in A minor was written in 1872. In 1871, to compensate for his failure to mount *Le Timbre d'argent*, du Locle at the Opéra-Comique offered Saint-Saëns a commission for a one-act opera, at the same time introducing him to Louis Gallet, the librettist with whom Saint-Saëns would collaborate on many projects in future years.

Saint-Saëns's third opera, *La Princesse jaune*, was thus his first opera to be performed, appearing at the Opéra-Comique on 12 June 1872. *Le Timbre d'argent* had already been composed and revised more than once, though still not staged, while *Samson et Dalila* remained in the form of a Prelude, some completed vocal lines for Act II, some ideas for Act I still in the composer's head, and a single theme for Act III. Even so, he found working with Gallet so congenial that they embarked on a much larger project, the grand opera *Étienne Marcel*, which was under way by August 1873.

On 19 October 1873 the *Revue et Gazette musicale* announced that Saint-Saëns had just completed his oratorio *Dalila* and that it would be performed by the Concert National du Châtelet, which was run by Édouard Colonne. With this promise of a performance Saint-Saëns had to set to work at once to complete it, postponing *Étienne Marcel* until later. At that point, in October and November 1873, on his doctor's advice, Saint-Saëns took a holiday in Bologhine (then called Saint-Eugène) in Algeria – a country he was to go back to many times and where he died – which may have helped in suggesting a biblical setting.

---

[10] COLLET 1922, pp. 31–32.

When he returned to Paris he probably had the first two acts composed, if not scored. The Châtelet performance was then postponed for a year, perhaps because the score was not ready. At this point Pauline Viardot, the greatest mezzo-soprano of her time, aged fifty-three but still in good voice, enters the picture. Every Thursday in the summer months she would invite friends to her house in Bougival, one of Paris's western suburbs, for music-making. Three undated letters to her leave a trail of confusion.[11] The first, dated 'London, May' (presumably 1871, since Saint-Saëns took refuge there from the Commune in May of that year): 'We will have a tenor, the pearl of tenors, Vergnet! He and Auguez will be ready for Thursday and you'll be able to Dalila away'. Numa Auguez was a bass (Grand Prêtre) and Edmond Vergnet was a tenor with a great career ahead, including the first Samson at the Paris Opéra in 1892, although in May 1871 he was only twenty and almost unknown.

The second letter reads: 'You can shine at our Thursday soirée, I'll prepare a fine Bach fugue to open the ball on the organ. I'll send Auguez the part so that he can look at it again.' Then in a mixture of German and French: 'Ich bin ganz delectirt à l'idée de vous réentendre chanter *Dalila* dans saisons (!!!!)' The third letter reads: 'I have written to Vergnet; he replied that he'd come on Saturday. Try to be there! I'd love to hear my big duet at last before I die!'

These texts cannot be easily reconciled with the only documented occasion on which Pauline Viardot sang the role of Dalila. This was on 20 August 1874, a Thursday, not *chez elle* in Bougival, but on an outdoor stage at Croissy-sur-Seine, nearby. Act II was sung with Saint-Saëns at the piano and Viardot costumed in sumptuous oriental dress. Auguez sang the Grand Prêtre, but the Samson was not Vergnet; the role was sung by Charles-Auguste Nicot from the Opéra-Comique. In her recollection of this event Viardot claimed that Saint-Saëns had never heard this music before.[12] Bonnerot reports that the evening was a surprise for Saint-Saëns, which, if true, precludes the preparations mentioned in the three letters, but in Viardot's recollection the only surprise was the singers' appearance in costume. If Auguez needed to look at his part 'again', there must have been another read-through with Viardot and Vergnet, though no such event has been traced. But how could Saint-Saëns tell her he longed to hear 'my great duet at last before I die' when he had heard it at least twice before?

The Director of the Opéra, Halanzier, was present at this 1874 soirée, but he declined to consider *Dalila* for the Opéra, which at that time had no theatre, its famous home in the Rue Le Peletier having burned down in 1873. In any case, the music was not yet written. Viardot's singing so impressed Saint-Saëns (not for the first time) that he thereupon determined to complete his fragmentary opera. 'It was for her that I wrote

---

[11] RATNER 2012, p. 30. The originals are at F-Pn n. acq. fr. 16723 and 16277.
[12] Pauline Viardot, 'La jeunesse de Saint-Saëns', *Musica* (1907), p. 83, cited in COLLET 1922, p. 37.

the role of Dalila,' he claimed later,[13] even though the plan of the work had been in his mind for several years. Undoubtedly she spurred him on to finish the work, for which she eventually received its dedication.

Act I was finished in 1874 or early 1875 and given in concert at the Concert National du Châtelet on Good Friday, March 26th, of the latter year under the title *Samson, drame biblique*. Emilia Bruant sang Dalila, Victor Caisso was Samson, Théophile-Adolphe Manoury was the Grand Prêtre and Colonne conducted. It was not well received; in fact Henri Cohen's review in the *Chronique musicale* described it as totally lacking in melody, but with over-audacious harmony.[14] The Intendant of the Vienna Opera, Franz Jauner, who attended the concert, was, in contrast, enthusiastic about it and promised Saint-Saëns to see it staged in his theatre.[15] Two 'airs de ballet', presumably the *Danse des prêtresses de Dagon* and the *Bacchanale*, were played at the Châtelet on 16 January 1876.

The full score of Act II is dated 1875 and the full score of Act III is dated January 1876. Liszt kept his promise, and although he no longer had an official position in Weimar he spent a part of every year there and had friends there he could canvass. In the last months of 1875 he wrote a number of letters to the Baroness Olga von Meyendorff, widow of the Russian ambassador to Weimar, to Hans von Bülow and to Grand Duke Carl Alexander urging them to arrange for the opera's staging there. Without any favourable response, he turned to Vienna, where in October 1876 he believed *Samson et Dalila* would be staged the following Easter.[16] This plan failed to materialise, while in Weimar it was eventually agreed to mount the first performance. Liszt had meanwhile arranged for his disciple Richard Pohl, an experienced translator, to provide the German translation for the singers.

Samson et Dalila was first performed complete, and on the stage of the Weimar Hoftheater, on 2 December 1877, only ten months after the first performance of *Le Timbre d'argent* in Paris, and eight months after Massenet made his debut at the Opéra (to Saint-Saëns's chagrin) in the new Palais Garnier with *Le Roi de Lahore*. It was conducted by Eduard Lassen, who had taken over as conductor after Liszt's resignation nearly twenty years before, and was sung in German under the title *Simson und Delila*. The singers, all from the Weimar roster, were: Samson, Franz Ferenczy; Dalila, Augusta von Müller; and the Grand Prêtre, Hans von Milde, the original Telramund in *Lohengrin*. With Saint-Saëns on the trip to Weimar were Romain Bussine, Auguste Durand (his publisher), two journalists, Armand Gouzien and Charles Tardieu, and Gabriel Fauré, always a close friend. Liszt himself was not there, spending his winters, as he regularly did, in Budapest. The opera was heartily applauded, with the composer

---

[13] SORET 2012, p. 1062. The same words are found in the letter to Collet (COLLET 1922, p. 33).
[14] BONNEROT 1922, p. 75; COLLET 1922, p. 39.
[15] Georges Servières, in *Le Figaro*, 3 March 1890.   [16] *La Revue musicale*, May 1928, p. 64.

repeatedly called on stage by an enthusiastic audience, which included the Grand Duke Carl Alexander and his family. It was performed five times.

After the performance there was a dinner at the Erbprinz hotel at which Saint-Saëns made a speech: 'All my thanks are due to the man who is the heart and soul of music today, the man whose generosity is without equal, the man who has led us all out of obscurity.' He did not identify Liszt by name. 'To our astonishment,' wrote Fauré later, 'no one applauded. Our German neighbours were shooting furious glances at us. A *Doktor* rose to his feet, scarlet with indignation. "We are surprised," he exclaimed, "that it should not have occurred to M. Saint-Saëns to thank Father Liszt." The Germans had missed the point. Saint-Saëns was obliged to make a second speech to explain his first one.'[17]

The second performance on December 8th started badly but picked up in the second act to the point where Saint-Saëns thought the performance incomparably better than on the first night. Since the chorus director was ill, Saint-Saëns himself conducted the offstage chorus, played the castanets and lit the torches, feeling 'like a fish in water'.[18] Three more performances were given that winter, and although the main Parisian music journals had not sent reviewers, they mostly reported the opera's success from the lengthy review which Charles Tardieu wrote in the *Indépendance belge*.

* * * * *

Samson et Dalila
(Ratner 288)

Opéra in three acts and four tableaux

Libretto by Ferdinand Lemaire
after the Book of Judges, Chapter 16

First performance: Hoftheater, Weimar, 2 December 1877

Dalila	mezzo-soprano
Samson	ténor
Le Grand Prêtre de Dagon	baryton
Abimélech, Satrape de Gaza	1ère basse
Un vieillard hébreu	2ème basse
Un messager philistin	ténor
Premier Philistin	ténor
Deuxième Philistin	basse

Hébreux, Philistins

Orchestra: 3 flutes (piccolo), 2 oboes, cor anglais, 2 clarinets, bass clarinet, 2 bassoons, contrabassoon, 4 horns, 2 trumpets, 2 cornets, 3 trombones, tuba, 2 ophicleides, timpani, bass drum, cymbals, triangle, glockenspiel, crotales, castanets, tambourine, tamtam, 2 harps, strings.

---

[17] *Candide*, 9 December 1937, p. 19, cited in Nectoux 2008, p. 94.
[18] Letter to Auguste Durand, 7 December 1877; Ratner 2012, p. 31.

Unlike *Le Timbre d'argent*, Saint-Saëns's next opera, once complete, underwent almost no changes from its original form. Durand, Schœnewerk et Cie published the vocal score a year ahead of the 1877 Weimar performances with Pohl's German translation alongside the French, and the theatre printed the libretto, and in these sources we see the same opera as that performed ever since, in almost every detail. This reflects well on Lemaire's skill as a librettist. If it was to be an opera rather than an oratorio, it would need theatrical elements of decor, movement and dance to justify its action on stage. The biblical setting allowed ragged costumes for the imprisoned Hebrews and vulgarly ostentatious costumes for the Philistines, and the spectacular dénouement, when after an exotic ballet the Philistines' temple is brought down on everyone below, including Samson himself, is nothing if not theatrical. In the balance of the three principal characters, too, Lemaire exercised fine judgment, and the opposition of two tribes required a contrast of musical styles, drawing Saint-Saëns into the field of exotic music from which he always drew great inspiration.

Samson's story is recounted in the Book of Judges, beginning with his birth in Chapter 13, his marriage to a Philistine woman and the story of the swarm of bees in the lion's carcase in Chapter 14, tying torches to foxes' tails and killing a thousand Philistines with the jawbone of an ass in Chapter 15. In Chapter 16 he is enticed by the Philistine Delilah, whose personal feelings are of no concern to the chronicler of Judges, to reveal the source of his strength. He is shorn and blinded by the Philistines and made to grind corn. He is brought to their festivities 'to make them sport', and set between the pillars which he then pulls over, causing the house to collapse and to kill 'more than they which he slew in his life', as well as himself.

This story had been told in the form of oratorio and opera before. There were operas by Graupner (Hamburg, 1709) and Tuczek (Vienna, 1808), and the libretto by Voltaire set by Rameau (1734).[19] In the mid 1850s Liszt's disciple Joachim Raff, after writing a doctoral dissertation for the University of Jena on the subject of Samson, composed a five-act opera *Samson* to his own libretto which was never published or performed. Handel's oratorio *Samson* (1743), based on Milton's poem *Samson Agonistes*, was a popular success in England. Both Milton (and hence Newburgh Hamilton, Handel's librettist) and Voltaire treat only the end of the story, as recounted in Chapter 16, beginning with Samson in captivity, shorn and blind. Milton's introduction of a chorus was naturally adopted and extended by Handel, and both introduce Manoah, Samson's father, who pleads with his son to let himself be ransomed. They also have a Philistine giant Harapha, who challenges Samson. The destruction of the temple is recounted by a Hebrew (in Milton) or a messenger (in Handel), followed by

---

[19] The editor of the 1792 edition of Voltaire's works compared the last act of *Samson* to 'that in the libretto by Quinault' although no Samson libretto by Quinault is known. *Œuvres de Voltaire*, tome IX, Paris, 1892, p. 169.

scenes of lamentation by the chorus and, in Handel, the brilliant aria 'Let the bright Seraphim' at the close, sung by an Israelitish woman. It is possible that Saint-Saëns's first efforts were prompted by the performance in Paris in October 1857 of a concert work *Samson*, probably an oratorio, by the great tenor Gilbert Duprez.

Voltaire's libretto is full of allegorical figures such as War, Pleasure and Love, almost disguising the Hebrew origin of the story. Bacchus and Hercules appear in a Prologue. Dalila falls in love with Samson, who works a miracle by making water gush out of a rock. The last act closes with the destruction of the temple and Samson's death. This libretto was the starting point for Lemaire's, for although the latter included none of Voltaire's baroque allegory, he adopts Voltaire's Grand Prêtre as a leading character and begins Act I, like Voltaire, with a chorus of Hebrews lamenting their suffering in captivity. He introduces a character Abimélech in Act I, killed by Samson, equivalent to Voltaire's scene where Samson overturns the Philistines' altars.

Lemaire's (or Saint-Saëns's) central idea was to treat the relationship between Samson and Dalila neither as a mighty hero resisting the passionate advances of an enemy seductress nor as a symbolic game between War and Love, but as a romantic encounter in which Samson and Dalila are playing out the after-effects of their earlier relationship, not part of the biblical narrative, before the action of the opera begins. We are to suppose that Samson had moved on, kindling Dalila's enduring rage. She is a woman scorned. While he is lured back into her arms by her seductiveness, she is now motivated solely by the desire for revenge and to save the Philistines from Samson's destructive might. Strong though this dramatic confrontation is, Lemaire and Saint-Saëns deprived themselves of alternative scenarios, one of which would have been a Dalila genuinely in love with Samson and forced into betraying him by the Grand Prêtre; the other, which Verdi would surely have preferred, is a Dalila torn between her love for Samson and her duty to her tribe. In the opera as we have it, we may accept her amorous behaviour in Act I to be authentic (it may be interpreted either way), but by the time she is confronted by the Grand Prêtre in Act II there is no love left; she resists neither her overlord nor her conscience. From that point on her passion is wholly feigned.

Music cannot easily do irony. As in *Così fan tutte*, where the men feign love to the most convincingly amorous music, Dalila's music here, like her words, has all the warmth of the real thing. In his *Grand Traité d'instrumentation*, which Saint-Saëns knew well, Berlioz cites Gluck's *Iphigénie en Tauride* and explains how in Oreste's air 'Le calme rentre dans mon cœur', the agitated viola line gives the lie to the sentiment of the words: his heart is not calm at all. But in a scene as extended and intense as Act II of *Samson et Dalila* no such subtle subtext would have been possible.

The score is not divided into numbers, as had been the practice of Meyerbeer and Berlioz in their grand operas (and of all opéras-comiques) but into scenes, most of which flow into the next scene. The implication is that dramatic continuity is the goal, a natural development at that point of musical history of which Wagner by no means had the monopoly. The entrance of a new character does not necessarily imply a new scene (as had been the practice of earlier librettos and classical theatre), although often that may be the case. Scenes usually sustain a single key, but there is no evidence that Saint-Saëns had an overall tonal plan for this or any of his operas. Motifs, on the other hand, are very often attached to a particular key. Saint-Saëns was not dogmatic about this.

* * * * *

ACT I

Scene 1 The opening scene in B minor is one of the finest parts of the opera, a sustained cry for pity from an oppressed people. The plain simplicity of the choral writing, the eternal pleading figure in the violins and the deep boom on the first beat of every bar give the movement a powerfully oppressive sense. After the mysteriously plaintive F♯ from a bassoon in the first bar, the low B in bar 7 (especially when the double basses provide the lowest octave) strikes the ear as the age-old lament of the Hebrew people, now in the twentieth year of captivity by the Philistines. The first five minutes are to be sung before the curtain rises, which reinforces the sense that this might equally be an oratorio.

A new figure in the strings supports the women's two brief lines on their own and the build-up to the opening of the curtain (ex. 3.1):

Example 3.1 *Samson et Dalila*, Act I, Scene 1

The tempo doubles for a vocal fugue, 'Nous avons vu nos cités renversés', on the theme just now prefigured by the women. It inevitably recalls Handel, and eventually settles on a long Neapolitan C major without ever cadencing in the tonic B minor.

The switch to E♭ major for Samson's opening lines is unreasonably shocking since he is emerging from the crowd, not appearing from elsewhere, and his message of hope is entirely at variance with everyone's gloomy acceptance of their fate. The chorale-like theme given out softly on the horn that launches him on his exhortation (ex. 3.2) begins, furthermore, as an inversion of the fugal subject: his message, full of manly vigour, is the opposite of their dismal instincts.

Example 3.2 *Samson et Dalila*, Act I, Scene 1

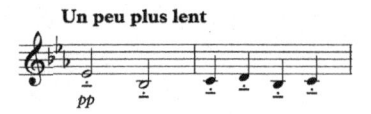

The chorus respond in their own key with their own theme. 'Hélas! paroles vaines!' they lament. The scene shows Samson winning the Israelites bit by bit to his view of their situation, to his key and to his theme. His second attempt has a flexible dotted figure in support, and his third is irrefutable once the harps join in. The gradual transformation of the popular mood, ending on a great cry of 'Jehovah' in E♭ major, is superbly engineered.

Scene 2 Then in comes Abimélech, satrap of Gaza, supported by a troop of soldiers. He is an invention of the authors, for the name belongs to other characters from the Old Testament. The likely source was Chapter 9 of Judges, just before the Samson episodes, where Abimelech is the king of the Philistines who slew seventy of his brothers and was in turn felled by a millstone thrown by a woman. Here in the opera he represents Philistine authority, like the king in the Voltaire version, and he has a motif that defines his brutal behaviour (ex. 3.3):

Example 3.3 *Samson et Dalila*, Act I, Scene 2

After taunting his helpless captives, he turns to mocking their God, and for this Saint-Saëns draws on the tasteless orchestration of two ophicleides answered by piccolo and upper woodwind with cymbals marking the barline. The source was probably the *Dies iræ* episode in the finale of Berlioz's *Symphonie fantastique*, where a similarly grotesque effect is called for. Bernard Shaw was not impressed by this passage, describing it as 'brusque measures and grim orchestral clinkings and whistlings'.[20] Samson is infuriated too, and Lemaire's excellent verse has the orchestra boiling with the hero's rage:

---

[20] SHAW 1932, vol. iii, p. 55.

> Je vois aux mains des anges
> Briller l'arme de feu,
> Et du ciel les phalanges
> Accourent venger Dieu.
> Oui, l'ange des ténèbres,
> En passant devant eux,
> Pousse des cris funèbres
> Qui font frémir les cieux !
>
> In the hands of the angels
> I see the shining fiery sword,
> And the hosts of heaven
> Assemble to avenge the Lord.
> Yes, the angel of darkness
> Passes before them
> And utters funereal cries
> That fill the heavens with terror!

Abimélech is enraged too, all the more when Samson and the Israelites launch into a great battle-hymn, 'Israël, romps ta chaîne ! Ô peuple, lève-toi !', at the climax of which Abimélech hurls himself at Samson, brandishing his sword. As palpable demonstration of his supernatural strength and God-given power, Samson simply snatches the sword and turns it on Abimélech himself, killing him with a single blow. The Philistine soldiers draw back, while Samson leads the Israelites away. We are to assume that their bonds are broken and that they are free to run off and wreak havoc.

Scene 3 There is very little time for their exit, for the Grand Prêtre enters immediately from the temple of Dagon and finds only the satrap's corpse and some scared soldiers. Two of them claim over a rumbling, surging bass line to have been disabled by some supernatural force, earning the Grand Prêtre's scorn.

Scene 4 The passing of time is telescoped, with operatic licence, for a Philistine messenger comes in to report that the Israelites have ravaged the harvest, and the two frightened soldiers join him in urging flight. But the Grand Prêtre is made of sterner stuff, as with considerable backbone in the orchestration he curses Samson, the Israelites and their God, and in his fury he hopes that 'une compagne infâme trahisse son amour' – that a shameless companion will betray her love. It is critically important to catch this line in interpreting the end of the act.

Scene 5 Meanwhile the Philistines leave and some elderly Israelites enter, men and women. Pace and tension drop out of the music as dawn breaks, expressed by long slow chords in the orchestra. The men then chant, at considerable length, about their faith in salvation, over deliberately simple music, a scene that contrasts strongly with what has gone before, suggesting the monastic modality of plainchant. Samson and the other Israelites enter silently in the middle, their destructive foray completed.

Scene 6 A complete change of key and colour introduces a group of Philistine women who enter, with Dalila, from the temple. As if everything was peace and happiness, the women sing of the spring, the flowers, the birds, all things bright and beautiful, and the music has marvellous delicacy (ex. 3.4). This is the most ravishing moment in the opera.

Example 3.4 *Samson et Dalila*, Act I, Scene 6

très doux

Voi - ci   le prin - temps nous por - tant des   fleurs,

Dalila immediately addresses Samson as the hero who has conquered her heart. Her character and her actions can only be understood if we know that they have been lovers before and that she is bitter about his infidelity. This is not the Bible's version, but it is supported by her mention of 'memory' at the start of Act II as the force that will bring him back into her power. At this point she is still hoping to win him back, and her music is irresistibly alluring (ex. 3.5); the Grand Prêtre has not yet put into action his plan to find a 'shameless companion'. Samson prays that he may resist her and an old Hebrew warns him in the plainest language to avoid the trap. This becomes a trio whose tone is clearly amorous, on Dalila's terms, despite the two men's separate responses.

Example 3.5 *Samson et Dalila*, Act I, Scene 6

dolce espressivo

O mon bienaimé suis mes pas   Vers So - reck,   la dou - ce val - lé - e,   Dans

cet - te de-meure i - so - lé - e   Où Da - li - la   t'ou - vre ses bras!

A dance is offered, performed by the priestesses of Dagon. This is a movement of exquisite delicacy in which the marking 'sempre pianissimo' means what it says. The only other instruction is to play even softer. Touches of harp and tambourine lend exotic colour, a distraction from the impulses stirring in Samson's mind which he cannot disguise, as he watches Dalila's every movement. Some darker moments at the end cast a brief shadow.[21]

The act closes with an air for Dalila in E major, 'Printemps qui commence', in which she hopes that love will return for her and bring the same joys that spring brings to the world of nature. The first section is thinly scored with the second violins sustaining an inner pedal on the note B; the middle part is more richly textured for Dalila's lines:

> En vain je suis belle !
> Mon cœur plein d'amour,
> Pleurant l'infidèle,
> Attend son retour !
>
> I am beautiful in vain!
> My heart filled with love
> Weeps for the unfaithful one
> And awaits his return!

The old Hebrew warns Samson once again, but he is silent, wrestling with his feelings.

ACT II

It is easy to see why this act was the first to be completed and performed. The seduction of Samson has been set in motion, and at the climax of their encounter disaster intervenes in the shape of Samson's capture and humiliation. There is a certain parallel to the second act of *Tristan und Isolde*, where a similar (but assuredly more erotic) scene of passion is violently interrupted. Saint-Saëns models the shape of the act and controls the build-up with extraordinary skill, and draws on rich resources of invention throughout. With thoughtful staging the act can be amazingly effective.

Prélude The Prelude is a small tone-picture of a serene landscape with rumbling basses and chromatic scales that foreshadow the storm that will break later, and this is in turn preceded by eight bars of uncertain tonality reminiscent of the brief improvisation that nineteenth-century pianists would insert before longer items in a recital. Saint-Saëns later reported that he had the idea of the storm running through the action of this act after hearing the last act of Rossini's *Otello*, where the final scene is accompanied by a storm offstage, at the Conservatoire.[22]

---

[21] The autograph at F-Pn 545 provides a four-bar concert ending in A minor instead of the four bars preceding the change of key.

[22] SORET 2012, p. 684. Possibly a performance with piano at the Conservatoire on 4 August 1863, sung by Mme Sousterelle.

Scene 1 The curtain rises to show Dalila's house in the Valley of Soreck veiled in luxuriant creepers and exotic plants, with Dalila herself seated on a rock before the door. Night is falling progressively throughout the act. She has now been cast in the Judas role she has to play, and in quest of vengeance she is eager to carry out the plan of seduction which will rob Samson of his strength once she has prised his secret from him. She knows what she has to do and has no more qualms about it. Her monologue at the start of this act confirms her determination to bring him to his knees. In 'Amour ! viens aider ma faiblesse !' love is invoked only as an instrument of treachery, not to satisfy any longing of her own. Two figures shape the aria, both to be heard again later (a and b in ex. 3.6):

Example 3.6 *Samson et Dalila*, Act II, Scene 1

The mention of love brings tenderness to her voice, but not to her thoughts, and in the middle section she trusts that his memories of their former love will bring him back to her. The aria is superbly scored, with even warmer support for the return of her opening bars, and the coda closes with the voice taken down to low A♭.

The uncertain tonality and rumbling basses return as lightning is seen in the distance (ex. 3.7):

Example 3.7 *Samson et Dalila*, Act II, Scene 1

Scene 2 The arrival of the Grand Prêtre, who now has his own motif (ex. 3.8), is marked by square rhythms and forceful counterpoint to introduce a long scene for the two characters:

Example 3.8 *Samson et Dalila*, Act II, Scene 2

Both are on the same page as far as defeating Samson and the Hebrews is concerned, but the Grand Prêtre needs to reinforce Dalila's resolve. Unlike in the equivalent scene for Amonasro and Aida in Act III of *Aida*, the Grand Prêtre has only to confirm Dalila's determination, not to persuade her to act. It is finally clear from this scene that Dalila's bitterness goes back to an earlier relationship with Samson, of which the Grand Prêtre is fully aware. The scene is in four sections, the first three of which are each defined by a 'scene-motif' present only in the orchestra, not in the voice, and used only here, not as a leitmotif throughout the opera. This is a technique employed also by Berlioz, Gounod and Massenet. The Grand Prêtre dominates the first section with a motif that expresses something of the urgency of the Grand Prêtre's presence (ex. 3.9):

Example 3.9 *Samson et Dalila*, Act II, Scene 2

Following two furious verses of this, outlining the threat of Samson's superhuman strength, he explains that Samson's earlier love for her betrayed a weakness and that she has only to rekindle the flame for him to be vulnerable again. Dalila responds with echoes of ex. 3.6a, confident in her power to use love as a weapon of war.

The next scene-motif supports her longing for vengeance, ex. 3.10, and a third scene-motif, ex. 3.11, combines with this as she recounts her earlier attempts to lure Samson into giving away his secret, the first time she has mentioned the secret of his strength as the object of her seduction. This refers to verses 6 to 14 of the biblical account, which report these episodes. This time, she claims, he is in her power, and a sly reference to ex. 3.6a glosses her line 'J'ai préparé mes armes'. The scene concludes with a vigorous duet in F minor on ex. 3.12, promising death and destruction to the Hebrews.

Example 3.10 *Samson et Dalila*, Act II, Scene 2

Example 3.11 *Samson et Dalila*, Act II, Scene 2

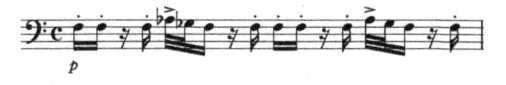

Example 3.12 *Samson et Dalila*, Act II, Scene 2

Dalila is even offered a horrifying low F for the word 'mort'. The Grand Prêtre exits to a quick review of the preceding motifs, then the music resumes the rumbling basses and chromatic scales from the opening of the act.

Left alone, Dalila has misgivings, against music from the opening of the act which suggests unease and calm at the same time, fearing either that her seduction will fail or that Samson will not come.

Scene 3 He does of course appear, in a state of great nervousness expressed by a halting version of ex. 3.6b and accompanied by hints of lightning, ex. 3.7. At first he does not see Dalila, who suddenly steps forward with words of sweet welcome. His nerves need to be soothed, a task she undertakes with a song of plain, unemphatic affection in a pure B♭, 'Samson! ô toi! mon bien-aimé'. A phrase in the orchestra (ex. 3.13) is important throughout this scene:

Example 3.13 *Samson et Dalila*, Act II, Scene 3

His replies, full of regret, follow a descending chromatic bass in the manner of Berlioz, and the second reply forces the music into E♭ for a reprise of his heroic exhortations in Act I, ex. 3.2. His mission is to save the Hebrews, a defiant declaration, from the heights of which his coming fall is all the more disgraceful.

With a new bitterness in her tone, Dalila, now in B minor, upbraids Samson for his broken promises, 'and I drank only poison in the ecstasy of your kisses'. With ex. 3.2 in the bass, Samson pleads that he was subject to a higher power and then softly confesses that he loves her. Distant thunder (ex. 3.7) marks the moment.

Recalling ex. 3.6a, she still reproaches him for ever having left her, knowing that she has him at her mercy. At his now passionate declaration of love the orchestra introduces the unusual texture of repeated chords that will anchor the duet when it finally arrives, ex. 3.14. The scoring of this pattern varies, sometimes involving woodwind, sometimes divided strings.

Example 3.14 *Samson et Dalila*, Act II, Scene 3

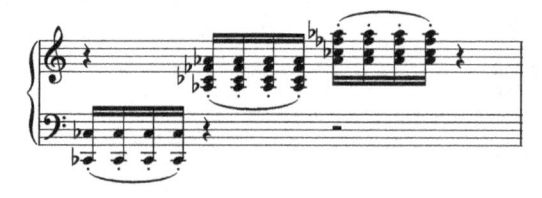

Dalila leads the duet with 'Mon cœur s'ouvre à ta voix', for although this has all the appearance of a solo aria, its dramatic strength lies in Samson's inability to remain silent in the face of a seductive melody so powerful that he intrudes on the link between the verses with a soft 'Dalila ! Dalila ! je t'aime !' The melody of the refrain is marvellously sculpted (ex. 3.15):

Example 3.15 *Samson et Dalila*, Act II, Scene 3

When she sings the second verse, 'Ainsi qu'on voit des blés', intensified with chromatic sextuplets falling from the first two beats of every bar to illustrate the corn waving in the wind, he does not wait for her to conclude but turns the closing bars into an intense duet. In the four-bar close, he rises to a soft, high B♭, the last time Samson and Dalila are on tender terms.

Dalila now plays the game by which she will unman her adorer. Her duty is to extract from him the secret of his strength, and so she proceeds to cast doubt once again on the sincerity of his love. Thunder is heard. Because Samson had deceived her before, she cannot trust his word now. With constantly increasing intensity, supported by a turbulent orchestra full of chromatic scales bubbling out of the depths, the scene is one of the most powerful in French opera. Saint-Saëns is not trying to imitate Wagner, as many of his critics accused him, but it has the same boiling fury and the same driving tonality as certain pages from *Der fliegende Holländer* or *Die Walküre*.

Dalila insists she cannot love him fully without knowing his secret; Samson insists that his loyalty is to his God and his people. He continues to refuse to disclose his secret. The dramatic crux comes when, over a heaving roll on the timpani and bass drum (swelling in alternation), Dalila hurls the insult at him 'Lâche ! cœur sans amour !' ('Coward! Heart without love!') and tears off into her dwelling. This final provocation works, for Samson lifts his arms to heaven, hesitates, but then rushes after her into the hut.

Symbolically her seduction is complete, but her power over Samson is not achieved until he tells her, in the words of the Bible, 'There hath not come a razor upon mine head; for I have been a Nazarite unto God from my mother's womb: if I be shaven, then my strength will go from me, and I shall become weak, and be like any other man.'

The libretto passes this by. A furious orchestra depicts neither love-making nor argument within the hut but the menace of Philistines who have been watching all along (ex. 3.8), rising to a cataclysmic diminished seventh and a crash from the tamtam. Dalila appears at the door summoning the Philistine soldiers to come in and seize Samson. His secret, clearly, is out.

ACT III, TABLEAU 1

Scene 1 The first tableau of Act III shows Samson in chains in a Philistine prison in Gaza. His hair is shorn, his eyes are blinded, and he has been set to work in the treadmill. The wheel turns to the steady, painful murmurings of the strings. An oboe gives out a desolate version of ex. 3.1, originally in Act I a defiant call by the Hebrews, 'Nous avons vu nos cités renversés', but now a despairing lamentation. Saint-Saëns does not make the mistake that Gounod made in *Polyeucte* and elsewhere of portraying the Hebrews (Christians in Gounod's case) with sanctimonious, churchy music. Samson sustains a dejected recitative throughout the first scene, imploring his God for mercy while knowing he does not deserve it. In the distance the Hebrews can be heard full of resentment at Samson's betrayal of their cause. The whole scene has a welcome penitential atmosphere after the raging emotions of the previous act. As Philistine guards enter to take Samson away, the curtain falls.

ACT III, TABLEAU 2

Scene 2 The uncivilised tread of soldiers gives way to luminous chords and copious harp arpeggios as the new scene reveals the interior of the Philistines' temple. The building is filled with the priests and grandees, as well as Dalila, her attendant girls and the general populace. The roof is supported by two pillars, and a statue of the god Dagon stands at the centre. A spectacular decor is definitely required, and while we adjust to its splendour the full chorus sings a second version of the women's chorus in Act I, ex. 3.4. The words are now 'L'aube qui blanchit déjà les coteaux', greeting the dawn now, not the spring. Saint-Saëns should not be upbraided for repeating a piece as ravishing as this when he could naturally have composed something new.

There follows one of the composer's best-known pieces, the *Bacchanale*, a ballet sequence. If the opera was ever to be played at the Paris Opéra or the Vienna Opera, as Saint-Saëns hoped, it would need a ballet. In this case the occasion for a ballet is aptly provided by a scene of public festivity and its idiom determined by the pagan character of the celebration. Not all grand operas offered any reason at all for a ballet, but here it is fully justified, and it contributes to the dramatic effect of what follows. The success of the *Bacchanale* is due to its flagrant exoticism with 'Arabic' augmented seconds and diminished thirds. It is also constructed as a single movement, not a series of ballets of deliberately various types grouped as a *divertissement* (as in Gounod's *Faust* or Thomas's *Hamlet*). It has a slower central section which is languorous and sensual (as such tales as the *1001 Nights* were seen to be) and then returns to the main tempo in order to generate a barbarous frenzy in keeping with the Philistines' coarse triumph over the Hebrews. The final pages are furiously noisy, bereft of all taste and manners as the Hebrews' enemies are bound to be.

The wailing tune on oboe, cor anglais and harp (ex. 3.16) has since become the standard model for all quasi-Arabic tunes in the public imagination. Saint-Saëns reported that this tune had been given him by General Yussuf, an adventurous character born Joseph Vantini on the island of Elba in 1808, who played a considerable part in the French conquest of Algeria in the 1830s, rising to the rank of general in the French army.[23] Since he died in 1866, Saint-Saëns must have noted down the theme some years before he found a use for it.

Example 3.16 *Samson et Dalila*, Act III, Scene 2

Scene 3 Supported by his theme (ex. 3.8) the Grand Prêtre advances towards Samson, whose blinded steps are guided by a child, and taunts him as Dalila's 'lover'. Dalila is told to bring him a cup of mead in which to toast his seducer. The Philistines, no doubt looking forward to witnessing his execution or at least his conversion to their faith, will drink with him. Samson quietly prays. Woodwind in the orchestra mock him with a frivolous version of ex. 3.15; Dalila mocks him with the exact phrases of their duet, revealing that she was always dissembling. Recalling their journey into the mountains and their passionate embraces, she gloatingly tells him that it was all deceit, all vengeance for his earlier betrayal, all paid for in advance.

Samson quietly admits his fatal weakness, and the Grand Prêtre taunts him with the promise that if Jehovah restores his sight, he will himself bow down to the Hebrews' god; meanwhile he will continue to mock him and hate him. Samson is roused to fury. How can this heathen impostor be allowed to defile the name of Jehovah! Will God not restore his sight and his strength just for one instant to allow him to take vengeance? The music has immense vigour here, to match the intensity of Samson's plea, and it gives way to further mockery from the crowd.

The Grand Prêtre calls upon Dalila to initiate the invocation to their god Dagon. They go to the altar and pour a libation from sacred cups on to the flame burning on the altar. The flame flares up and vanishes. This ceremonial action is supported by a banal theme in B major appearing in almost every bar (ex. 3.17). The crudity of the

Example 3.17 *Samson et Dalila*, Act III, Scene 3

---

[23] *L'Écho de Paris*, 17 March 1912; SORET 2012, p. 796.

theme, its repetitive rhythm and the plainness of the vocal writing exactly portray the barbarity of the Philistines' cult, and at the words 'Dagon se révèle', the Grand Prêtre breaks into an idiotic tune over a trivialising oompah accompaniment. Dalila takes off with coloratura scales and the crowd enthusiastically echo their jollity.

The Grand Prêtre invites Samson to offer a libation to Dagon and instructs the boy to lead him to the centre of the temple so that he can be seen by all. With great passion Samson prays for the Almighty's aid and whispers to the boy to guide him to the temple's marble columns. The chorus resume their vulgar chant with help from the glockenspiel, but when the tempo increases they shout to their god over swirling strings and leave banality behind, as if the sheer intensity of their faith permitted them to build a powerful climax with *real* music. Saint-Saëns's skill here is exemplary, for the most dramatic moment of all has arrived.

Samson's rage, once aroused, knows no bounds, as we saw in Act I when he felt the sting of Abimélech's insults. Now, when the Philistines yell 'Gloire!' at him, we hear the same music again: furious tremolandos from the inner strings, soaring scales from the first violins, downward chromatic scales from the trombones. With a final plea to God to restore his strength, the music resolves its long, tense cadence on a colossal B♭. Samson, the Bible tells us, 'took hold of the two middle pillars on which the house stood', 'bowed himself with all his might', and the whole edifice collapses on everyone below. The victims have time only for a desperate 'Ah!' before the curtain falls. Even if the curtain is delayed until the end of the music, there are barely fifteen seconds available for some spectacular stagecraft. It is not practical for Samson in full sight to grasp two pillars since they would need to be relatively slender and rather close together. The usual solution is for the two pillars to be close but, in Milton's term, 'massy', so that Samson can push, not pull. If his wrists were chained to the two pillars he could pull, but then his ruse of asking the little boy to lead him to the pillars loses its force.

* * * * *

Knowing that Vaucorbeil, the new director of the Paris Opéra, was not prepared to consider mounting *Samson et Dalila*, despite their personal friendship, Saint-Saëns regarded the successful premiere in Weimar in December 1877 as only the first step on a long road. In London, for example, biblical operas were forbidden; this was bound to be a problem almost anywhere. It was little help to point to all the biblical operas that had been successfully staged without inciting the wrath of God. Montéclair's *Jephté* (1732) was revived for years at the Opéra and Méhul's *Joseph* (1807) was successful everywhere, especially in Germany. Rossini's *Moïse* and Gounod's *La Reine de Saba* were no longer played, but not forgotten. Having seen his opera staged, Saint-Saëns was convinced it should never be regarded as an oratorio. Yet he permitted two concert performances to take place in Brussels, just a few months after the Weimar

Act III, Tableau 2 | 71

Figure 3.1 *Samson et Dalila*, final scene (*L'Illustration*, 8 November 1890)
Mary Evans Picture Library

performances, largely, one suspects, to snub the directors of Brussels's chief opera house, the Monnaie, who had stubbornly resisted all suggestions of staging the opera. The final tableau of the opera was played at the Châtelet, in Paris, conducted by Saint-Saëns, on 26 and 28 March 1880, without attracting much notice. In that same month Saint-Saëns gave a concert in Paris entirely devoted to the music of Liszt as a gesture of thanks.

The second stage production was given in March 1882 in Hamburg. Hans von Bülow, visiting Hamburg to conduct a performance of Brahms's *Requiem*, saw the opera and wrote to a friend in a delighted mixture of English and French: 'Saint-Saëns here, conducts to-morrow night 3rd performance of his Samson. Great success! Il est si gentil, si charmant, si fiévreux!'[24] Two days later he was still enraptured by the music, though horrified to find that Saint-Saëns did not know how to conduct. His later judgment was that it was the most important musical drama to have been composed in the last twenty years and that Saint-Saëns was the only composer who could learn a salutary lesson from Wagner's theories without getting carried away by them.[25]

Meanwhile, in February 1879, Saint-Saëns's fourth opera, *Étienne Marcel*, had been performed in Lyon and he had embarked on the composition of his fifth, *Henry VIII*. This was staged at the Opéra in March 1883, his first work to be played there. There followed a work for the Opéra-Comique, *Proserpine*, in March 1887, and another one for the Opéra, *Ascanio*, in March 1890. For eight years, in effect, *Samson et Dalila* was forgotten while Saint-Saëns continued his extraordinarily active career as composer, conductor and pianist, travelling constantly. There was talk of a production in Wiesbaden which did not take place. The conductor Lamoureux included Dalila's Act II air 'Amour, viens aider ma faiblesse' in his concert on 6 April 1884, sung by Mme Brunet-Lafleur.[26] In a letter of 2 March 1888 Saint-Saëns speaks of the success of *Dalila* in Liège,[27] although no other source mentions a performance there. A letter of 23 August 1890 recalls the second act being done by Colonne 'three years ago', again without confirmation.[28]

With the death of his mother at the end of 1888 and the constant postponements inflicted on *Ascanio* by the Opéra despite having accepted it for performance, Saint-Saëns reached a low point in his life. This caused him to dispose of his apartment and everything in it except his music, to compose almost no music for a lengthy period, and to go abroad, as it seemed, indefinitely. In October 1889 he left for Spain, and two months later embarked at Cadiz for the Canary Islands. Three days before sailing he read in a newspaper that Henri Verdhurt, director of the Théâtre des Arts in Rouen, was establishing a 'Nouveau-Théâtre-Lyrique-Français' to be classed as the leading opera

---

[24] BÜLOW 1907, p. 147. [25] COLLET 1922, p. 42. [26] Servières, *Le Figaro*, 3 March 1890.
[27] Letter to Auguste Durand; RATNER 2012, p. 32.
[28] Letter to Auguste Durand; RATNER 2012, p. 33.

house outside Paris, and that *Samson et Dalila* was his choice for its inauguration. This theatre had already proved itself to be ahead of Paris in 1883 when it was the first French theatre to revive Bizet's *La Jolie Fille de Perth* since his death, and it had staged Saint-Saëns's *Étienne Marcel* in 1885. The choice of *Samson et Dalila* was certainly encouraged by Saint-Saëns's friends in Paris, especially Fauré and Chabrier, and it would be a pointed insult to the Opéra to be giving the opera in France and in French for the first time.

The performance on 3 March 1890 was a breakthrough for Saint-Saëns, yet his determination to stay abroad, living a quiet life incognito in Las Palmas, held firm. He did not attend, nor did he return to Paris for the premiere of *Ascanio* three weeks later, but he had the satisfaction of reading a series of favourable reviews since the proximity of Rouen to Paris meant that the press was fully represented. The conductor was Gabriel Marie. Verdhurt was persuaded by the opera's success to transfer the production to Paris, knowing it had never been heard there. He rented the Théâtre de l'Eden, an ornate theatre on the Rue Boudreau very close to the Opéra which had opened in 1883. He commissioned new sets and engaged Parisian singers. The conductor Gabriel Marie remained, with Saint-Saëns (having returned to Paris in May) to guide him in rehearsal. It opened on 31 October 1890 with Rosine Bloch as Dalila and Talazac, the original Hoffmann, as Samson. Bouhy, the original Escamillo, was the Grand Prêtre. Saint-Saëns was delighted with the casting and with the performance as a whole, knowing that it was a stepping-stone to the Opéra itself.

The Rouen performances mark the start of *Samson et Dalila*'s elevation to the status of world fame. From then on, it was to be heard all over the world, never out of the select list of operas familiar to opera-goers, never again condemned to years of silence. The Opéra was finally persuaded to stage it, but even before that happened there were performances in Barcelona, Bordeaux, Geneva, Toulouse, Nantes, Dijon, Montpellier, Monte Carlo, New York, Florence and Algiers. Before the century was out, it was heard also in New Orleans, Milan, Cairo, Antwerp, Moscow, St Petersburg, Saratov, Montreal, Buenos Aires, Lisbon, Rio de Janeiro and Amsterdam. Other cities followed in close succession. In London it was first done only in concert form, in 1893, to be staged there for the first time at Covent Garden in 1909. This popularity has lasted to this day.

It is worth listing these cities if only to emphasise the opera's sudden rise to fame and the sad contrast with Saint-Saëns's other operas, most of which were played in several cities during his lifetime but all condemned to obscurity after his death in 1921. *Samson et Dalila*, in contrast, has never fallen out of favour. The composer wrote to his publisher Durand: 'Don't forget that you paid me 15,000 francs for the worldwide rights and that *Samson* has made a fortune – for you.' In his later years he conducted it frequently as guest. The last performance he attended was in the open-air amphitheatre in Verona in July 1921.

The first Opéra staging took place on 23 November 1892, twenty years after the music had been written. It was conducted by Edouard Colonne and rapturously received. In retrospect Saint-Saëns attributed the shortcomings of the production to the Opéra's preference for Wagner:

> When, after years of hesitation, the Opéra decided to stage *Samson et Dalila*, I was promised a magnificent production. I was shown a projector that would show storm clouds crossing the sky in Act II. But they decided almost immediately to follow *Samson* with *Die Walküre*, and all at once my splendid production was robbed. My opera was done with the miserable sets they still have, using bits of [Massenet's] *Le Roi de Lahore* with Hindu gods in Act I. I had to devote all my energy to getting a thin red strip to show the dwindling twilight at the start of Act II. They didn't want to preempt the great twilight effects in Act III of *Die Walküre*.[29]

The hundredth performance at the Opéra was reached in 1897 and by 1976 it had been played 965 times in that theatre, outnumbered only by *Faust* and *Rigoletto*. The Opéra traditionally required an important contribution from the corps de ballet, and so for their production Saint-Saëns wrote an extra movement named *Réveil des princesses*, to be danced immediately before the *Bacchanale* in Act III. It is a graceful movement, fifty-seven bars long, and it was included in a new edition of the vocal score that Durand brought out at this time (268 pages), but it was not included in the printed full score nor in the definitive vocal score (285 pages).[30] The latter has an extended passage to cover the scene change between the two tableaux of Act III, an obvious improvement in view of the importance of the set for the final scene. Thus after the Philistine soldiers have taken Samson off, there is an additional passage of thirty-one bars with some expressive writing for the wind and some bold key-shifts leading to the entry of the harp and the opening of the curtain. These additional bars, recalling Dalila's 'Printemps qui commence' in Act I, allowed Saint-Saëns to remind us of her tender side (whether feigned or real) between the anti-tonal tread of the Philistines and the early daylight illuminating the interior of the Philistine temple.

On 13 April 1878 Saint-Saëns wrote to Durand: '*Dalila* is and will always be my masterpiece.'[31] Many people will agree with this judgment, and certainly by common consent it is the greatest of his operas. In view of his inexperience when he first embarked on it and the even starker inexperience of his librettist, it is an extraordinary achievement. Saint-Saëns defied prejudices about biblical subjects and about his own gifts, and proved that he understood the nature of dramatic music, the needs of the voice, the implications of stage action and the opera composer's craft in all its varied aspects.

---

[29] 'Germanophilie', 19 November 1914; SORET 2012, p. 911.
[30] The full score of *Réveil des princesses* is found only in the autograph, F-Pn MS 545 (10).
[31] RATNER 2012, p. 31.

Like Wilde and Strauss with Salome, Saint-Saëns took a plain Bible narrative and created a female character of evil depth, not simply the tool of the Philistine clergy. She is driven by her desire for vengeance, having once given herself to Samson and then been rejected. She is not troubled by remorse, although a scene in which the tenderness she once felt returns to nibble at her determination might have been dramatically effective. Saint-Saëns prefers to present her as unwavering and to leave all feelings of remorse to Samson. While this could be seen as Saint-Saëns the misogynist showing us a woman who is both a liar and a whore, Dalila is at the centre of the action throughout, if not the object of anyone's sympathy. It is one of the great mezzo roles to be found in nineteenth-century French opera. Samson is unquestionably heroic, in the mould of some great tenor roles from Florestan to Radames, but Dalila provides the central focus.

To represent this with music Saint-Saëns drew on extraordinarily rich resources. The final scene of Act II is one of the greatest things he ever did, and certainly one of the supreme scenes of nineteenth-century opera, even in competition with Verdi and Wagner. Dalila's relentless sugary sweetness and Samson's fatally flawed resistance are conveyed in music of increasing power and intensity all the way to the central catastrophe. The final scene, where Samson recovers his strength by a supreme effort of will, is no less strong, and the choral writing throughout is always apt: deeply moving in the opening scene for the Hebrews, fanatically vulgar in the closing scenes for the Philistines. If it is the familiarity of the *Bacchanale* in the last act, now regarded as the very epitome of the nineteenth-century conception of Middle Eastern music, that assures *Samson et Dalila*'s popularity in the concert hall, the opera itself is in little danger of falling into the pitiful obscurity that envelops Saint-Saëns's other operas.

4 | La Princesse jaune

At the moment in 1871 when *La Princesse jaune* was commissioned, Saint-Saëns already had one opera, *Le Timbre d'argent*, composed and awaiting performance, and a second opera, *Samson et Dalila*, planned and partially composed. Well known in Paris as organist of the Madeleine church and as a virtuoso pianist, he was widely presumed to be unfit to write operas, especially since he had never won the Prix de Rome, which laid great emphasis on the training of composers for the theatre. Theatre directors took more notice of gossip and the tendentious opinions of the press than of actual talent and potential, which they were in most cases ill-equipped to judge.

The violent disruption caused by the Prussian siege of Paris in the winter of 1870–71 was no sooner over than Saint-Saëns set about the formation of a society for the promotion of French music, propelled by the nationalist sentiment inflamed by recent events. The founding group, which included (besides Saint-Saëns) Franck, Bussine, Guiraud, Massenet, Fauré, Dubois and Duparc, met in February 1871 (Bizet was away from Paris that week). The political situation very soon became much worse when the Commune took over the city, and calm was not restored, after fearful destruction and slaughter, until the end of May. Nonetheless the Société Nationale de Musique was able to give its first concerts before the end of the year, beginning on November 17th. In the years that followed, the Société gave prominence to a remarkable number of young and not-so-young French composers, especially Bizet, Lalo, Guiraud, Godard and Franck. Saint-Saëns himself contributed a series of important orchestral and chamber works. *Le Rouet d'Omphale* was heard on 14 April 1872, the Cello Concerto and *Phaëton* in 1873, and the *Danse macabre* in 1875. The composition of *La Princesse jaune* and the completion of *Samson et Dalila* both fall within this very active period of his life.

Camille du Locle, director of the Opéra-Comique, had on his conscience the fact that both his uncle Émile Perrin, director of the Opéra, and he himself had earlier agreed to stage *Le Timbre d'argent* in their respective theatres; he himself had even settled questions of casting and production when the war broke out. Now, with the restoration of peace, the urgent task of rebuilding Paris's cultural activity called for works which could be mounted swiftly and cheaply. Long complicated operas were impossible, although Offenbach's three-act *Fantasio* was accepted in January 1872 as an exception. One-act operas had always been staple fare at the Opéra-Comique, but now, in July 1871, they were more than ever the answer to the theatre's immediate needs. Four young composers were signed up: Paladilhe, Bizet, Saint-Saëns and Massenet.

Saint-Saëns and Bizet were both being compensated for the Opéra-Comique's failure to stage larger works, *Le Timbre d'argent* in Saint-Saëns's case, *Grisélidis* in Bizet's. The librettist assigned to both composers was Louis Gallet, a relative newcomer on the operatic scene. Gallet had won the prize for a libretto to be set in the Opéra competition in 1867–68 with *La Coupe du Roi de Thulé*, written in partnership with Édouard Blau, another aspiring *littérateur* also working at the Assistance Publique. Bizet and Massenet both set this libretto (and both subsequently dismembered their scores), while the winner was Eugène Diaz, son of the painter Narcisse Diaz. Gallet then on his own – he was out of line at this period in preferring to write librettos on his own – wrote *Le Kobold* for Bizet's friend Ernest Guiraud, performed just before war was declared in 1870. Now he suggested an oriental tale for Bizet based loosely on de Musset's poem *Namouna* (the title was changed to *Djamileh*), while for Saint-Saëns Gallet proposed a story on a Japanese theme: *La Princesse jaune*, the Yellow Princess. 'Being by chance neighbours, both living at the upper end of the Faubourg St-Honoré, we quickly became friends', Saint-Saëns recalled in a tribute to Gallet after his death in 1898.[1]

Since this was the first of many collaborations with Gallet, Saint-Saëns's recollections of his character should be offered here.

> He had a penetrating, open-minded intelligence, much common sense, a natural sense of humour, talent, and erudition without pedantry, which made him an ideal partner, the one I'd always dreamed of meeting without ever expecting to do so. He knew how to adopt my ideas without abdicating his own personality. Drawing on a depth of knowledge of astonishing richness, he filled out my imagined fantasies with solid elements without which they would have been nothing. [. . .] Although not a musician, Gallet had a fine judgment for music; in literature and in painting we had the same tastes; we both loved to escape from serious work and fool around like children. We bombarded each other with fantastic sonnets, with baroque verse and wild drawings, a contest in which he surpassed me both in poetry and painting, for there was a painter in him which could easily have been developed with a little work. Without any claim to distinction he painted landscapes and seascapes from nature, of excellent taste and tone. He occasionally helped out with theatre decor. The excellent desert in Massenet's *Le Roi de Lahore*, the lovely convent in my *Proserpine*, among others, were based on his drawings. [. . .]
>
> His capacity for work was prodigious. He was never without a pen in his hand, scribbling out some papers for the Assistance Publique, where he had a senior position, drawing up reports, writing novels, articles for journals, comedies, plays, librettos, and a colossal correspondence too. Then he wrote sonnets as relaxation. There were speeches in prose and

---

[1] SORET 2012, p. 543.

Figure 4.1 Louis Gallet, photograph Bridgeman Images

verse for the inauguration of statues and for literary dinners; advice or even assistance for beginners too weak to get on without help. How can one survive such toil? One doesn't, one collapses. Over and over again I urged him to slow down and leave aside work which didn't need to be done at once. But for Gallet work was a passion, and nothing could tear him away from it.[2]

Following *La Princesse jaune*, Gallet collaborated with Saint-Saëns on a number of works, mainly the operas *Étienne Marcel*, *Proserpine*, *Ascanio*, *Déjanire* (originally a play, then an opera) and *Frédégonde*, composed by Guiraud but left unfinished at his death. Gallet also wrote the texts for two choral works, *Le Déluge* in 1875 and *Les Soldats de Gédéon* in 1876. For Massenet he provided the texts of *Le Roi de Lahore*, *Le Cid* and *Thaïs*, and of the oratorios *Marie-Magdeleine* and *Ève*. Since the craze for Wagner

---

[2] *Revue de l'art ancien et moderne*, II, 10 December 1898; SORET 2012, pp. 543–44.

took off in the mid 1880s, Saint-Saëns was glad to have a partner who shared his views:

> Cool-headed and independent, Gallet could never howl with the wolves; he fought them, but not wanting to give offence he did so with discretion and tact. It did no good since they took no notice; without giving him credit for a literary skill that few librettists possessed, they reacted to each of his works with pure hostility, quite lacking in indulgence or justice. This hostility pained him. He knew he did not deserve it, having put so much care into his work and so much courtesy into his criticism.[3]

Gallet's memoirs, *Notes d'un librettiste*, written in 1891 while Saint-Saëns was still alive, are relatively silent about their working relationship compared to the generous portrait he painted of Bizet, although there is no reason to suspect that they were ever on anything but the most congenial terms.

The choice of Japan as the setting for the new opera was guided by the craze for *japonaiserie* that had seized France since Japan opened up to western influences in the 1860s. At the Exposition Universelle of 1867 Parisians had gazed with astonishment at costumes and prints in the Japanese pavilion, being seen in Europe for the first time. The Japanese presence at the Exposition was small, but it made a big impression. Saint-Saëns never went to Japan, but he included a short, delicate poem on his imagined Japan in his collection of verses, *Rimes familières*, in 1891. When Saint-Saëns and Gallet suggested a Japanese subject to du Locle he was alarmed. 'He insisted that we modify it, and it was he, I think, who had the idea of a half Dutch, half Japanese setting in which this little work called *La Princesse jaune* was to take place.'[4] The choice of Holland was not entirely random, since Dutch traders had maintained links with Japan during the long years when Japan was otherwise inaccessible to foreigners, so the Dutch had at least some familiarity with the culture, unlike all other Europeans.

Saint-Saëns saw the first outline of the libretto on 19 September 1871,[5] although he probably did not begin to work on the score until the end of the year, after the opening concerts of the Société Nationale and his completion of *Le Rouet d'Omphale*. His draft of the opera in short score (without the overture) is dated 5 February 1872, to be followed by the task of orchestration. The overture, composed last, is dated 22 May 1872, the day that Bizet's *Djamileh* opened at the Opéra-Comique. Meanwhile Paladilhe's *Le Passant* had already, as the wits observed, *passed*, after only three performances.

For Paladilhe, the youngest of the four, who had won the Prix de Rome at the age of sixteen, this was his first opera to be staged, even though he had four previous operas awaiting performance. He was well known for a song, *La Mandolinata*, which he sensibly included in the new opera, whose libretto was an adaptation of a play by

---

[3] *L'Écho de Paris*, 12 November 1911; SORET 2012, pp. 753–54.   [4] *Ibid.*, p. 751.
[5] Gallet's letter to Saint-Saëns, 18 September 1871, F-DI Dossier 1.

François Coppée. Its opening on April 24th was unfortunately part of a long evening with contributions from various theatres and by various instrumentalists, and a guest appearance by Jean-Baptiste Chollet, now seventy-three, who attempted to sing scenes from Hérold's *Zampa*, originally written for him in 1831. Another veteran tenor, Gustave Roger, sang bits of *La Dame blanche*.

Le Passant had a strong cast, with leading ladies Célestine Galli-Marié (Paladilhe's mistress and later the creator of Carmen) and Margaret Priola, but it could not survive the accusations of Wagnerism that the press threw at it, accusations of which Paladilhe was certainly innocent. The libretto was disliked too, being judged anti-lyrical. Nor were the public taken by the work.

Bizet's *Djamileh* came next on a triple bill with Deffès's *Le Café du Roi* and Gounod's *Le Médecin malgré lui*. Saint-Saëns wrote Bizet a sonnet of admiration, suggesting that playing the opera at the Opéra-Comique was casting pearls before swine. The press were mostly approving, and it ran for eleven performances, never to be revived in Bizet's lifetime.

One of those eleven performances was on the same bill as *La Princesse jaune*, being played for the first time on 12 June 1872, Saint-Saëns's first experience of seeing an opera of his own on stage. He had excellent singers for his two roles: Alice Ducasse as Léna and Paul Lhérie as Kornélis. She had made her debut at the Théâtre-Lyrique in 1867 and sang for many years at the Opéra-Comique, always admired by Saint-Saëns in his reviews of her in other roles. Lhérie similarly appeared at the Opéra-Comique in a number of roles, extended in his case by descending to baritone roles later in his career; he thus created the role of Don José in *Carmen* in 1875 and later appeared as Escamillo. The Dutch set for *La Princesse jaune* was designed by Rubé and Chaperon, and the conductor was the tireless Deloffre, always at the podium at the Opéra-Comique after long service at the Théâtre-Lyrique in the previous decade. Hartmann issued the vocal score (71 pages) which bore a dedication to the art historian Frédéric Villot, a curator at the Louvre, an appropriate choice for an opera about (in a remote sense) Japanese and Dutch art.

But the opera ran for only five performances, effectively killed by a hostile press who were convinced that Saint-Saëns was a performer not a composer: 'algebraic formulations' said Arthur Pougin; 'incomprehensible music of the future' wrote Albert de Lassalle; 'not a trace of inspiration' thought Adolphe Jullien. The one critic to see virtue and charm in the opera was Ernest Reyer. But this was the level of music criticism in France at that time against which all composers, especially young composers, had to battle. When we contemplate Saint-Saëns's score today it is hard to grasp how such bizarre prejudices infused these so-called men of letters, for it is by any standards that we would accept today a charming, skilful and touching little opera.

* * * * *

> *La Princesse jaune*
> (Ratner 287)
>
> Opéra-comique in one act
>
> Libretto by Louis Gallet
>
> First performance: Opéra-Comique, Paris, 12 June 1872
>
> | | |
> |---|---|
> | Léna | soprano |
> | Kornélis | ténor |
>
> Chœur dans les coulisses
>
> Orchestra: 2 flutes (incl. piccolo), 2 oboes (incl. cor anglais), 2 clarinets, 2 bassoons, contrabassoon, 4 horns, 2 trumpets, 3 trombones, timpani, gong in G, triangle, harp, strings.
>
> Offstage: chime in E, small bells, gong in E. In no. 6 (from main orchestra): flute, clarinet, 2 horns, 3 trombones, triangle, bass drum.

Ouverture Being a one-act opéra-comique, *La Princesse jaune* consists of an overture followed by half a dozen numbers interspersed with dialogue. The two characters each have two solo scenes and the opera concludes with two duets. The Overture, composed last, is made up of extracts from the music to be heard after curtain-up and fashioned into a tuneful, cheerful orchestral apéritif entirely in G minor or G major. The emphasis is on the exotic music, starting with Kornélis's Air (No. 2) with its unusual scoring (see ex. 4.1), transposed to G minor. It then takes in the Allegro section from No. 5, when Kornélis reacts with excitement to the Japanese scene he sees before him, strongly pentatonic, with triangle and piccolo for extra colour. After a gentler quasi-pentatonic tune, the lively music returns to close the Overture.

The opera's setting is the house of Léna's parents in Holland, at an unnamed date. Through a large window at the back can be seen some snow-covered Dutch houses, while the interior is a large work-room with a table covered in papers and books. Strongly in evidence is a panel painted with the image of a Japanese woman, and near it are some steps and a table with paints and brushes. Beneath it is a rotating stool carrying some Delft pottery with the flower painting unfinished. Other unfinished pots are lying around. There are doors at either side of the stage. A clock tells us it is morning.

Dialogue The first scene is a monologue for Léna, who calls to Kornélis from outside one of the doors but gets no reply, so she comes in and looks around. She looks through the opposite door but is surprised to find no one there. 'He didn't say where he was going', she tells us and notices that his lamp is out of oil, so he has been working all night. She is troubled by his obsession with the image of a Japanese woman, wondering how such a figure can so seduce a young intelligent man. 'What's your secret?' she asks the picture. 'Is it your exotic grace?' She loves Kornélis, her adoptive cousin, and admits that jealousy is creeping up on her. She is consoled to think that the woman has been dead for three or four hundred years. Kornélis is a 'docteur', a scholar, and there are abundant books and papers to prove it. He and she both dabble in painting and pottery, although at no point is it suggested that he painted the portrait of Ming himself. It must be an old portrait he has found.

She straightens up the room, reflecting how happy they are. She marvels at his interest in Chinese, Persian, Japanese and Sanskrit, and picks up a large book, *The History of Japan*, and two others called *Japan Revealed* and *Marvels of Japan*. He must be crazy, she concludes, thinking they were happy when they both made pottery with flowers painted on it.

She finds a loose note in one of the books. The ink is not dry. A poem! His night's work! She reads the title: *Homage to the beauty of whom I have only an image and by whom I am eternally bewitched*, and scrumples up the sheet in a rage.

No. 1 Récit et Ariette She straightens out the paper and reads the two texts, one in Japanese, the other in (one supposes) Dutch. The Japanese is a poem in classical Japanese from the ancient anthology 'Manyoushuu', the 'Anthology of Ten Thousand Leaves' which Gallet must have researched with the help of a Japanese speaker. It means:

> In this current life, the god does not allow me to be near your body. You are far away.
> I despair waking up in the morning, longing for you. If you are a bead I will carry you in my hand; if you are a garment, I will always wear you. Your soul only appears in my dreams.[6]

The Japanese she reads line by line in jerky syllables on notes from a pentatonic scale, alternating with French on a monotone, whose meaning is:

> O Ming, if my body is enslaved and cannot break its fetters with dreams of cradled love, my thoughts fly to you. In the humble nest of my affection you reign alone, O my mistress!

No literal translation this, but the sentiments are the same, with the added benefit of learning that her rival's name is Ming and that the author is passionately in love with her. After each verse Léna breaks out in (spoken) fury, and yet she determines not to give away her discovery.

Her short Ariette is a burst of spleen directed at the image on the panel, wondering what its secret can be. If only I was made like that, she sings bitterly, perhaps he would love me too. I hate you! The piece is more rage than melody.

---

[6] I am indebted to Mayuko Kataoka for identifying and translating the Japanese poem.

Dialogue Kornélis comes in without noticing Léna. He takes off his snow-covered coat and takes various pots and bottles out of his pockets.

'It was Kokha', he says, from which we are to believe that he has been enjoying a drug supplied, he goes on to say, by a Professor Paulus, whom we never see, clearly another Dr Spiridion. His mention of 'charme' is picked up by Léna. She calls to him. He is surprised to see her in tears. She asks him what he meant by 'charme'. Did he go early to a witches' sabbath, or are you ill, she asks. Still speaking *à part*, he wonders if she has guessed his secret, and, aloud, tells her he is happy, especially with his work.

'I have my good Léna, whom I love, and your parents.'

'Your eyes tell me that's not true', she says. 'You speak your dreams aloud sometimes, without realising it. You dream of other countries, China, Japan . . .' 'There's nothing wrong in that', he replies.

No. 2 Air Here Saint-Saëns goes back to a song he had written the year before during his brief stay in England, 'Désir de l'Orient', on his own poem evoking Chinese and Middle Eastern delights:[7]

> Là-bas, dans un ciel de turquoise,
> Brille un soleil d'or ;
> Là-bas, sur la terre chinoise,
> L'art fleurit encor.
>
> Là-bas, dans la brise embaumée,
> Les chants amoureux
> S'éteignent, comme d'une almée
> Les yeux langoureux.
>
> Là-bas, dans les eaux du Bosphore
> Les blancs minarets
> Regardent leurs long cous d'amphore
> Parmi les cyprès.
>
> Là-bas, la sultane enivrée
> De parfums amers
> Mêle à sa chevelure ambrée
> La perle des mers.
>
> Mais ici, ciel morose
> Et nuit sans réveil !
> Sur sa tige languit la rose
> Rêvant du soleil !

---

[7] The song was published as no. 2 in the second set of *Vingt Mélodies et Duos*, published by Durand.

> Ah! que ne puis-je à tire d'aile,
> Orient sacré,
> Atteindre ton azur fidèle,
> Ton beau ciel nacré!

Gallet replaced this with eight verses, so that the song is now longer, and with a different ending. The sonority of the music is very unusual, to match Kornélis's far-fetched fantasy: the basis of the song is an open-fifth ostinato to suggest an exotic drone, with an up-and-down melody given out by violins in four-part close harmony, while behind this the harp has a rapid four-note figure endlessly repeated, ex. 4.1:

Example 4.1 *La Princesse jaune*, No. 2

Kornélis's vocal melody introduces a modal D♯ from time to time, and a new flowing theme is supported by flute and two clarinets spread over three octaves. Having evoked a life of luxurious exotic delights, Kornélis allows himself to reflect on life here in the real world (Gallet here picking up a hint from Saint-Saëns's poem): nothing but a humdrum life under clouded skies, and for a bar or two the music lapses, with delicious irony, into modern chromatic harmony, only to return to the drone ostinato and modal melody for a reprise of the first verse.

Dialogue 'You don't need much to make you happy', says Léna. She picks up a couple of porcelain bottles he has brought in. This annoys him, so he gathers up some of his things and goes off to his room with an angry glance in Léna's direction. Left alone, she reflects on how quickly her happy prospects have vanished. She must go and leave this all behind.

No. 3 Air Her Air is a lament for lost love, a beautifully crafted song in D minor without any vocal histrionics. A middle section picks up speed and intensity and the reprise is gently enriched. Gallet reversed the first four lines at the end, perhaps hoping the composer could provide a similar palindrome, but the melody is basically the same, each phrase fitted to different words. Most expressive of all is the play-out in the orchestra, the oboe taking the melody to represent Léna's painful distress, and fading away on solitary violins. She goes slowly out.

Dialogue Kornélis runs back in with a small cup of lacquer and a bottle, delighted to be alone. Thanking Professor Paulus for the magic talisman, the 'mysterious word', he addresses Ming, promising to bring her alive. He reads in a book: 'Drink this potion and it can bring all you could desire!' He pours the contents of the bottle drop by drop into the cup, then makes a long speech about the thrill of the philtre, and finally drinks it. Perhaps it means death! Then he puts down the cup and approaches the image of Ming, arms wide open.

No. 4 Scène The scene begins at this moment with a rising two-octave chromatic scale. Soft trombone chords introduce a continuous flow of triplets designed to charm the image to life. Kornélis is full of eager anticipation, convinced that Ming will come alive. 'Anime-toi' he repeats, gazing at her deep black eyes. The song is in two verses and as the horn and clarinet play out the melody, he draws back from the picture never taking his eyes off the image. He falls into his chair in a state of ecstasy, muttering to himself. A clock strikes ten.

Dialogue Léna comes in but at first does not notice Kornélis splayed out in his chair. She arranges her painting stool and starts to paint. Her rage has calmed a little and she is determined to play her part and hold her own. Catching sight of him she calls out 'Cousin', but he doesn't hear her.

No. 5 Scène, Chœur, Chanson et Duo The longest stretch of continuous music in the opera starts with murmuring strings rising to a big C major chord marked by the trumpets' first entry with trombones in support. Kornélis is dreaming of fantastic palaces upon golden clouds. To the accompaniment of little bells an invisible chorus of women sing a pentatonic song (E major) in Japanese in nine-bar phrases. The Japanese means 'What's the matter with you? Good afternoon, today is a fine day', by which Gallet is betrayed picking sentences at random from a phrase-book for travellers! Then Léna, still painting (although the vocal score has her singing from the wings) sings the same song in her own version: 'My April has passed, I'll go no more to the ball', the accompaniment repetitive and plain.

This sequence was revised in the second edition, probably worked out with Gallet in 1896 and incorporated in the vocal score of 1906. In the new version at the height of Kornélis's vision Léna sings a plaintive song in E minor in folksong style, with string accompaniment. The words are the same as those for her song in the earlier version, but now to expressive western, as opposed to oriental, music. This is followed by the entry of the little bells and the offstage 'Japanese' chorus. This sequence makes more sense of Kornélis's reaction: 'Strange music!' as he leaps up, imagining that he has entered the gates of paradise. As if at his bidding, the set is gradually transformed into 'an interior and a Japanese landscape', presumably a Japanese interior with countryside visible in the distance.

Kornélis is overjoyed. The music is vigorous, pentatonic and repetitive, unreal in effect. He is deluded into thinking he is looking at the perfect Japanese garden. There's everything there except his idol: he sees a crowd of merchants, fields, pagodas, painted houses, silk fabrics and brass monsters on guard; he catches the aroma of tea. But where is she? At this moment his eye falls on Léna, who is dressed in the same Japanese costume as Ming and forms part of the tableau he has been looking at. Where the portrait of Ming used to be there is now an image of a Dutch girl in Léna's clothes. Kornélis's heart is captured and he addresses Léna in a burst of wonderful lyricism (ex. 4.2):

Example 4.2 *La Princesse jaune*, No. 5

Léna's response is an agitated and enigmatic aside: 'Il sait donc le secret de mes vœux !' ('So he knows the secret of my wishes!') At all events she does not for a moment believe his declaration 'Je t'adore', and blames lack of sleep for his derangement. She, on the contrary, is asleep, he asserts, and in fact his insistence that he loves her gradually undermines her doubts, and a fine passage of duetting ensues. With a sudden diminished seventh she pulls back and accuses him of loving only the painted image. 'That image?' he cries, without looking at the picture which now, of course, shows only a girl in Dutch costume, 'I detest her'.

Kornélis tries to convince her by singing a song she probably knows. Its start is almost entirely pentatonic in F major with a very regular setting of the words, like a folksong, 'Sur l'eau claire et sans ride'. Saint-Saëns seems to be trying to capture the tone of a nursery rhyme or long-remembered song. Its imagery of skies and clouds and stars serves to explain Kornélis's love for Ming as a mirror reflection of his real love for Léna.

She can make no sense of this. Why can we not speak to each other like normal people, she asks. He manages to wring a reluctant 'Je t'aime !' out of her and goes on to ask for a kiss with which to prove it. This is too much for her and she runs off. He pursues her. She is actually frightened. He grabs her and won't let her go. They sing a strongly agitated ensemble at the end of which she manages to run off. Everything resumes its former arrangement. He still calls on Ming. He seems to be losing his senses and he falls into a chair, while the little bells from the beginning of the scene are heard offstage.

No. 5bis Mélodrame follows immediately, with the alternation of speech and music so characteristic of opéra-comique. Léna comes back in, and after some dialogue in which Kornélis seems to be remote from reality, she sings back to him his song about gazing at the clouds and the sky. In dialogue she explains to him that he was hallucinating, and there beside him is the potion that was the cause. She drags him to the picture and tells him to speak to it: 'She's alive! I'm the one who's mad!' He looks at the image and realises it is Léna's beauty that he is looking at.

No. 6 Récit et Duo His 'Je t'aime' launches the final number. He begs her to tell him again that she loves him. How fickle, she replies, turning like a windmill! She still thinks he's lying when he calls her his only love, while the music recalls her first Air and her jealousy of Ming. If not her, then who is your new love, she asks. She taunts him in an Allegro molto, accompanied almost entirely by full orchestra chords, telling him to go and find a beautiful Indian, or Ethiopian, or whatever. After this little *tour de force* she bows low, sarcastically, and prepares to go.

'The devil take Japan!' he cries, protesting that he wants to rediscover earlier happier days. A waltz is heard from the fair in the street outside, played by an offstage oom-pah band. She hesitates to accept his invitation to dance, but his ardour is too much for her, and they are soon singing the same amorous phrases back and forth, and some truly warm duetting, always within the emotional bounds of opéra-comique, takes the opera to its happy end:

> L'amour chasse le doute
> Et nous montre la route
> Du Paradis perdu!

> For love drives doubt away
> And leads us on the way
> To the Paradise we lost!

* * * * *

The libretto of *La Princesse jaune* may be criticised for its playful dabbling in the field of hallucination and illusion, complicated by the desire to introduce miraculous transformations of the stage-set in the manner of Barbier and Carré's stories. With Kornélis falling in love with an image he has painted under the influence of an unseen Dr Paulus/Spiridion, the comparison with Conrad's fateful passion in *Le Timbre d'argent* is irresistible, to the point where we may guess that Gallet was familiar with that still unperformed opera and that Saint-Saëns himself wanted to exploit that vein of fantasy again. He was clearly happy to introduce 'Japanese' music, identifiable by pentatonic scales which had served to suggest the orient, specifically the Chinese, since the eighteenth century and would reappear in *The Mikado* and *Madama Butterfly* to flesh out the Japanese. The story is slight in that all that happens is that Kornélis recovers from his hallucinatory passion for the painted Ming and returns to what we may assume was his pre-existing love for his cousin Léna. A one-act opera could scarcely attempt more. There is an element of satire in showing an individual so obsessed by an exotic culture that he loses all sense of reality. The mysterious unseen Professor Paulus provides the drug that turns Kornélis's brain. Kornélis appears to be both potter and painter, so the choice of Holland for the action makes a certain sense, as well as sharpening the distinction between the real present and the exotic elsewhere, or perhaps between two exotic elsewheres, one more exotic than the other.

Saint-Saëns is mindful throughout that opéra-comique was not a genre for music of too great a sophistication. The critic who declared the opera had 'no melody'[8] was expecting the kind of opéra-comique tunes produced in abundance a generation earlier by Hérold and Adam, unaware that times had changed. Neither Bizet nor Massenet were likely to satisfy those tastes. In order to retain his audience's attention it was sufficient for Saint-Saëns to include some exotic music, in quotation marks as it were, with a folk-like flavour from time to time. With only two characters there is little ensemble writing, and the moments of dramatic intensity are carefully chosen. The lyrical richness exhibited by ex. 4.2 reveals Saint-Saëns's ability to generate real feeling in a character like Kornélis who, until he realises the error of his ways, arouses little sympathy, while Léna has, in her Air (no. 3), a touching solo that shows the master's hand.

At the Opéra-Comique in 1872 *La Princesse jaune* was played only five times, better than *Le Passant*, but not as good as *Djamileh*. The fourth opéra-comique by a young French composer to be staged that year was Massenet's *Don César de Bazan*, played in November. This was in three acts, not one. It ran for thirteen performances. Massenet was building his career at that time more on concert works and oratorios than on opera, a strategy that led to his next opera being performed at the Opéra in 1877: *Le Roi de Lahore*. Bizet's *Djamileh* was successful abroad in the 1890s but was not revived in France until 1938. *La Princesse jaune* did better than that, for Saint-Saëns lived to see it re-enter the repertoire of the Opéra-Comique with occasional performances in the provinces and abroad, the first of which took place in Stuttgart in 1880. This was a private court performance with the text translated by A. von Loën. The first stage revival was given on 7 February 1885 in the town of Angers, where Saint-Saëns had conducted his choral work *Le Déluge* a year before. Out of admiration for the piece, Gabriel Fauré arranged the overture both for four hands and for eight hands at two pianos, and in this latter form it was played at a concert of the Société Nationale on 19 February 1887, with d'Indy, Fauré, Messager and Raymond Blanc at the two keyboards. This arrangement was played again in 1899 by Fauré, Saint-Saëns, Cortot and Diémer in aid of raising a monument to Louis Gallet, who died in 1898.[9]

---

[8] Cited without source in REES 1999, p. 169.   [9] REES 1999, p. 339.

A revival in Boulogne-sur-mer in 1890 caused Saint-Saëns to reflect to his publisher Durand: 'You know, between us two, the music of *La Princesse jaune* is ravishing.'[10] Perhaps it was the experience of playing the overture in 1887 that encouraged Messager to compose his own Japanese opera. While his *Madame Chrysanthème*, based on the novel by Pierre Loti and performed in 1893, was not a success, a later opera on a play derived from Loti's novel, *Madama Butterfly*, a disaster in 1904 but soon to be a triumph, has cornered the market in operas with a Japanese setting.

It was at the possibility of a revival of *La Princesse jaune* in Brussels in 1896 that Saint-Saëns, with Gallet's help, revised no. 5 so that Léna's song comes before the Japanese song with bells, not after it, and this change was incorporated in a new vocal score issued by Durand in 1906 (88 pages) when the opera was played in Dieppe (24 August 1906) and finally revived for nine performances by the Opéra-Comique (16 October 1906).[11] Then a 1909 revival ran for twenty-eight performances, with two more in 1914, a satisfying record for the composer in his old age. Albert Wolff, chief conductor at the Opéra-Comique between the wars, revived it there in 1935 and again in 1946 and he was the first to record the Overture. Its most recent reappearance at its Opéra-Comique home was in 2004. Other recent revivals have been New York (2001) and London (2004), both concert performances, with stage performances in Lucca (2004), Berlin (2005), Siena (2010), Buxton (2013) and Melbourne (2017). The Overture was sufficiently familiar in the 1920s to be recommended as music to accompany silent films in the categories 'Comedy Pictures' and 'Overtures'.[12]

The Overture has been recorded many times, and the complete opera has three commercial recordings to date: the first from French Radio in 1957 conducted by Tony Aubin, with Nadine Sautereau and Jean Mollien; the second from the BBC in 1999 conducted by Peter Robinson with Janis Kelly and John Graham-Hall, sung in English with a connecting commentary; the third from Chandos Records in 2000 conducted by Francis Travis with Maria Costanza Nocentini and Carlo Allemano. None of these recordings include the dialogue. Of all Saint-Saëns's operas other than *Samson et Dalila*, *La Princesse jaune* has enjoyed the most favour in recent times in both recording and performance, despite the difficulty that one-act operas face in finding a niche in the modern repertoire. This is not a new problem. In 1913 Saint-Saëns wrote to Pierre-Barthélémy Gheusi, librettist of *Les Barbares*:

> I'd like to see the Opéra-Comique return to the days when one-act works were staged and played with care, when the performance of a two-act work was as important as that of a work in three or four acts. For administrative reasons theatre directors don't want to run things

---

[10] Letter of 23 August 1890 to Auguste Durand; RATNER 2012, p. 8.
[11] The modern reprint of this score by Eroïca Music Publications includes the spoken dialogue.
[12] Erno Rapée, *Encyclopedia of Music for Pictures*, New York, 1924, cited in PASLER 2012, p. 368.

that way, claiming they are responding to public taste. That's completely wrong. The public have rejected short operas because they have been badly staged.[13]

Saint-Saëns was also aware that dialogue operas were being squeezed out, a situation which is much more acute today than in 1913 when he wrote:

> I would like to see the end of this war on dialogue which has been waged for too long. The result is that young singers no longer learn to speak dialogue or to act. This combination of spoken dialogue and singing goes back to the Greeks. It's not anti-aesthetic, as people claim. And don't tell me that it's not done any more when three pillars of the repertoire, *Mignon*, *Carmen* and *Manon* all belong to that genre.[14]

Dialogue had already played an important part in his conception of *Le Timbre d'argent*. He was to return to dialogue opera with *Phryné* in 1893 and to the one-act form with *Hélène* in 1903.

---

[13] Letter of 27 November 1913 to Gheusi; RATNER 2012, p. 10; SORET 2012, p. 879.   [14] *Ibid.*

5 | Étienne Marcel

The poor showing of *La Princesse jaune* at the Opéra-Comique in June 1872 might have left Saint-Saëns wondering if opera was worth both the labour involved in writing such a work and the frustration of dealing with theatre directors and impresarios. *Le Timbre d'argent* was apparently without a future, having rung its silver bell at the door of all the Parisian theatres likely to accept it. *Samson et Dalila* remained a fragment in need of many months of work before it was ready to be hawked to the same gentlemen who had turned down his first opera. The deafening chorus of critics stereotyping him as a pianist and an organist deepened his discouragement.

At the same time the regeneration of French music which the Société Nationale was designed to nourish had its focus on instrumental music, attempting to achieve for modern French composers what the Société des Concerts du Conservatoire had long been doing for the German classics, also in the orchestral and instrumental sphere. The Société Nationale's concerts alternated orchestral and chamber music with some vocal items in the mix. Even though the Opéra's grand new building was slowly but surely approaching completion, the burgeoning of non-operatic music in the public arena was an unmistakable element of 1870s concert life. The Concerts Danbé, the Concerts Colonne, the Orphéon, Pasdeloup's Concerts Populaires (already flourishing in the 1860s) and new enterprises from such men as Hartmann and Lamoureux were all enriching the scene while bringing forward a new generation of French composers including Lalo, Duparc, Castillon and Delibes, while continuing to foster the music of Gounod, Thomas, Franck and the older gang.

For a few years, therefore, it is not surprising that from the public's point of view Saint-Saëns was principally involved in concert music, while still devoting himself keenly to his organist's duties at the Madeleine. He also branched out into almost the only musical activity he had not thitherto mastered: that of music criticism. In 1872 began the appearance of that remarkable body of writing on music which continued unabated until his death and fills a thousand pages in Marie-Gabrielle Soret's admirable edition.[1] For a new review aptly entitled *La Renaissance littéraire et artistique* he wrote thirty articles over a period of twenty months between 1872 and 1874.

[1] SORET 2012.

In January 1873 Auguste Tolbecque gave the first performance of Saint-Saëns's Cello Concerto in A minor, a brilliant one-movement work that has been played by all cellists great and small ever since. This was part, unusually, of a concert given by the Société des Concerts, reaching out – which they rarely did – to French composers. His first Cello Sonata appeared at this time too. He inaugurated new Cavaillé-Coll organs in Versailles and Sheffield. He gave two-piano recitals with Fauré. Following the success of *Le Rouet d'Omphale* in January 1872, he composed a second symphonic poem, *Phaëton*, in 1873, to be followed in 1875 by *Danse macabre*, based on a song also entitled *Danse macabre* on a poem by Henri Cazalis written in 1872.

Saint-Saëns could have been forgiven if in this hectic period of diverse activities he turned his back on the stage, but he did not. It has generally been assumed that *Étienne Marcel* was not composed until 1877, yet Gallet was already working on his next libretto for him, while fully engaged writing texts for Massenet's religious works: *Marie-Magdeleine* (first performed 1873) and *Ève* (1875), as well as the grand opera *Le Roi de Lahore*, composed in 1875 and staged at the Opéra in 1877. Saint-Saëns described their collaboration in a tribute to Gallet published in 1911:

> We were dreaming of a historical opera, not being as prejudiced against this genre as younger composers already were. But I was not by a long chalk *persona grata* with theatre directors, in fact I was their *bête noir*. I did not know which door to knock on when Aimé Gros, who had taken on the management of the Grand-Théâtre in Lyon, asked me for an opera. It was a fine opportunity, so we seized it and put together, with considerable pleasure, the historical opera *Étienne Marcel*.[2]

In 1919 Saint-Saëns wrote: 'Aimé Gros was one of my best friends and to him I am indebted for having written the score of *Étienne Marcel* at his request. He staged it with a brilliance that has never been matched.'[3]

The truth is, however, that Gallet and Saint-Saëns began to plan *Étienne Marcel* many years before there was any prospect of a performance in Lyon. For the first surviving manuscript, a preliminary draft of the opera in short score bears the date, written in minuscule lettering on the first page, 21 Août MDCCCLXXIII.[4] If this date was inserted after the manuscript's 200 pages had been drafted, librettist and composer had indeed been unusually busy in the year since the performances of *La Princesse jaune*. If this was the date when work began, it was soon broken off, since the last few months of 1873 were devoted, as we have seen, to the completion of Act III of *Samson et Dalila*. On the advice of his doctor Saint-Saëns spent October and November in Algeria, the first of many happy visits to that country, where he found he could work well undisturbed.

[2] 'Louis Gallet', *L'Écho de Paris*, 12 November 1911; SORET 2012, p. 752.
[3] Letter to Antoine Sallès of 11 September 1919; RATNER 2012, p. 109.
[4] F-Pn MS 931; see RATNER 2012, p. 97.

Having resumed work on *Samson et Dalila*, it is unlikely that he would pay any attention to *Étienne Marcel* until the earlier work was finished, which was not until January 1876. This gap in the composition of the new opera would not have been possible had there been a theatre in Lyon (or anywhere else) ready and willing to mount it. But enough of *Étienne Marcel* was done for Saint-Saëns to write in February 1875 to Oscar Stoumon, director of the Théâtre de la Monnaie in Brussels: 'I much regret that I was not informed about your visit to Paris. With great difficulty I had arranged a performance of some extracts from *Étienne Marcel* which I would have liked you to hear.'[5] Saint-Saëns goes on to try to interest Stoumon in the still unperformed *Timbre d'argent*.

From this letter we learn that certain parts of the opera were ready for performance with piano, and that no other theatre was in the running for its production. Whether Saint-Saëns had completed a substantial part of the opera before August 1873 and whether he continued to work on it between 1874 and 1876 remain open questions. If he did, it was always in parallel with new instrumental works. The *Variations on a Theme of Beethoven* for two pianos, which he used frequently on his concert tours, was first heard in 1874, followed by his fourth Piano Concerto in 1875, and in 1876 the collaboration with Gallet produced a fine choral work, *Le Déluge*, which is still very little known.

Knowing that Halanzier would not accept *Samson et Dalila* for the Opéra because of its biblical source, it was worth completing the historical, Paris-centred drama of *Étienne Marcel* in the hope that it would have more appeal for the director to offer in his new building as a new work in a traditional genre. When this grand building, the Palais Garnier, opened in January 1875, its repertoire was mostly the tried and true works of Halévy and Meyerbeer, with Thomas's recent successful *Hamlet*. We have no record of Saint-Saëns offering his new opera to Halanzier, but it is likely that he did, especially since he knew that Massenet was also at work on a grand opera with a Gallet libretto, *Le Roi de Lahore*. The course of events was dictated by the fact that Massenet was keenly supported by his publisher, Georges Hartmann, a powerful force in Parisian music, while Saint-Saëns was drawn away from Hartmann's stable to another new publisher, Auguste Durand, whom he had known as a student at the Conservatoire. Hartmann had published *La Princesse jaune*, the first two piano concertos, and a number of smaller pieces, but starting with the *Marche héroïque* for orchestra (composed in memory of Henri Regnault), published in 1873, Durand became Saint-Saëns's publisher, followed in due course by Auguste's son Jacques. Hartmann ceded all his Saint-Saëns works to Durand.

Whatever hidden forces were at work, on 26 July 1876 Massenet was told that the Opéra would stage *Le Roi de Lahore*, and on the same day was awarded the Légion

---

[5] Letter of 1 February 1875; RATNER 2012, p. 103.

d'Honneur. Saint-Saëns's thinly disguised envy of Massenet's success may be said to take root at this point and to provide both a spur and an irritant throughout his many years of dedication to the art of opera.[6] At least *Le Timbre d'argent* made it to a Parisian stage in January 1877 before the premiere of *Le Roi de Lahore* in April.

1876 was also the year of Bayreuth, for Saint-Saëns attended the second performance of the *Ring* cycle there and wrote a series of seven articles for the journal *L'Estafette*. His attitude to Wagner was of great public interest, so he was anxious to distance himself from the ill-informed polemics that the French press delighted in: 'I have studied the works of Richard Wagner in depth', he declared.

> This study has given me the purest pleasure and the performance of those works which I attended have left a profound impression on me and given me thrills which all the theories in the world could never make me forget or deny. Because of that I have been accused of Wagnerism, and for a while I considered myself to be a Wagnerian. How wrong I was! I have met Wagnerians, and I know that I am not one and never will be one.

Saint-Saëns's attitude to Wagner and his debt to Wagner are complex topics which we will take up later. For the moment it is sufficient to observe that there was never a Damascene moment for Saint-Saëns and that he never felt the decisive impact of Wagner, as Chabrier, Chausson and Debussy did. Nothing in his music suffered any abrupt or even gradual change. He had come to know Wagner personally as early as 1860 and had impressed him by playing his scores with great fluency. Everything that Saint-Saëns wrote thereafter emerged from a background in which an intimate knowledge of Wagner's music (which very few Parisians possessed) played its part.

When Saint-Saëns returned home from the successful premiere of *Samson et Dalila* in Weimar in December 1877, it was still not clear that *Étienne Marcel* would find a theatre. In the following January Vizentini's Opéra-National-Lyrique at the Théâtre de la Gaîté, where *Le Timbre d'argent* had been played a year before, came to an end and a new version of the Théâtre-Lyrique was revived at the Salle Ventadour under the management of the music publisher Léon Escudier. Saint-Saëns tried to interest him in *Samson et Dalila*, still at that time unknown in Paris. When Escudier argued that it would be impossible to find a suitable singer for the role of Dalila, Saint-Saëns offered him *Étienne Marcel* instead, which, although unfinished, could be ready for rehearsal by the beginning of May 1878 and for performance in July during the Exposition Universelle of that year.[7] 'It is a real grand opera, in the strict meaning of the term. It has a large role for a baritone, which you could give to Melchissédec.' This singer, it will be recalled, had recently sung the role of Spiridion in *Le Timbre d'argent*. 'The first two acts are

---

[6] See Jean-Christophe Branger, 'Rivals and Friends: Saint-Saëns, Massenet, and *Thaïs*', in PASLER 2012, pp. 33–39.
[7] Letters to Escudier and Durand cited in RATNER 2012, p. 103.

orchestrated, the third is three-quarters sketched out, the fourth will be short.' Escudier was unmoved.

Halanzier, at the Opéra, suddenly changed his opinion of Saint-Saëns and told him that since Thomas was not satisfied with the casting of his *Françoise de Rimini* (it was not performed until 1882) and Gounod could not find the right tenor for his *Polyeucte*, there was an opening for *Étienne Marcel*. When Gounod heard about this, he suddenly found a tenor, Marius Salomon, so *Polyeucte* went into rehearsal and opened on 7 October 1878.

It is possible that Saint-Saëns had had the option of a Lyon production since the beginning of 1877 when Aimé Gros took on a two-year appointment as manager of the Grand-Théâtre. Now, with all options of a Paris theatre eliminated, Saint-Saëns was fortunate that Gros's offer to mount *Étienne Marcel* at the Grand-Théâtre in Lyon was still good. They knew each other well. Gros met Saint-Saëns as a violin student at the Conservatoire in the 1850s, and they had played together in three concerts Saint-Saëns gave in Lyon in March 1865. Saint-Saëns was back in Lyon in March 1867 and again in February 1869, March 1873 and March 1876.

Saint-Saëns completed work on the opera in October 1878 after a year of many successes in the concert hall for his orchestral and choral works but a period of intense domestic disaster. At the age of thirty-nine in 1875 he had married Marie-Laure Truffot and they had two sons. In March 1878 the elder boy, André, aged two, fell from a window of their fourth-floor apartment to the ground. His baby brother, Jean-François, died, too, from pneumonia very soon after. A stronger marriage might have survived this double blow, but theirs was fragile; although husband and wife remained together three more years, a permanent separation followed in 1881.

It is unlikely that in these circumstances Saint-Saëns could take much cheer from composing the finale for five characters for an opéra-comique called *Nina Zombi* (Ratner 334)[8] which was put on by the Cercle Volney on 17 May 1878 with nine other composers contributing one number each. Some of the lines he had to set were, ironically:

> Le mariage
> Est la société
> Par laquelle s'engage
> À perpétuité
> Le couple fol ou sage.

There was also the blow to his amour-propre Saint-Saëns suffered when Massenet was elected to the Institut after a head-to-head election in which Saint-Saëns won the first

---

[8] The manuscript of Saint-Saëns's contribution is incomplete (F-Pn MS 875q).

ballot, but was defeated in the second round when only he and Massenet remained as candidates. Massenet was also appointed by his former teacher Thomas to take on the prestigious composition class at the Conservatoire. To absorb himself then in the production of *Étienne Marcel* was naturally a compensation of incalculable value. Things moved swiftly, for the opera was staged in Lyon on 8 February 1879. Far from being the originating stimulus for the opera, as Saint-Saëns and his biographers have maintained, therefore, Gros was its rescuer long after the libretto had been written and the score all but orchestrated. Gros's tenure as director was for only the two years 1877 to 1879 in any case. It is nonetheless much to his credit that he ventured to introduce Saint-Saëns's music to a public that knew him only as a pianist. The successful premieres in 1877 of *Le Timbre d'argent* in Paris and of *Samson et Dalila* in Weimar undoubtedly helped persuade the Lyon management to take the risk.

The Grand-Théâtre, which still stands today, much transformed by a large semicylindrical superstructure, was built in 1831. Its repertoire was equally divided between French and Italian operas, very few of which were given for the first time. The resident conductor was Alexandre Luigini, the set designer Jean-Baptiste Genivet and Gros himself directed the staging. The singers were members of the theatre's troupe, none of them yet of national celebrity: the three main roles were sung by Michel Delrat (Étienne Marcel), Théodore Stéphanne (Robert de Loris) and Reine Mézeray, one of three singing daughters of Bordeaux's theatre conductor Louis Mézeray (Béatrix). The baritone part of Eustache was sung by Pol Plançon, later to be a notable exponent of Faust at the Opéra and a popular star at both Covent Garden and the Met; he came back to sing in the revival of *Ascanio* shortly before Saint-Saëns's death. A vocal score with a reduction by André Messager and a dedication to the composer's mother was published by Durand (365 pages), and the libretto with a dedication to Aimé Gros was published by Calmann-Lévy.

The opera was unquestionably a success with the Lyon public, eventually attaining forty performances (according to Saint-Saëns's memory in 1920[9]). Fearing the opera's revolutionary theme, Lyon's aristocracy stayed away from the first night,[10] but the city's dignitaries all attended the premiere and the press from both Lyon and Paris were there in force. An audience who had booed the garden scene in *Faust* were attentive and enthusiastic, and applause at the ballet in the scene in front of Notre-Dame was so noisy that the dancers could barely hear the orchestra.[11] Saint-Saëns later described Lamy, the choreographer, as the best *maître de ballet* he had ever known,[12] and as we have seen, he later looked back at this first production as the best he ever saw.

* * * * *

[9] Letter of 13 September 1920 to Gaillard; RATNER 2012, p. 110.
[10] *Le National*, 10 February 1879, cited in PASLER 2009, p. 305 note 12.
[11] BONNEROT 1922, p. 95.   [12] Letter of 7 September 1881; RATNER 2012, p. 105.

Étienne Marcel
(Ratner 290)

Opéra in four acts

Libretto by Louis Gallet

First performed: Grand-Théâtre, Lyon, 8 February 1879

Étienne Marcel, prévôt des marchands	1er baryton
Robert de Loris, écuyer du Dauphin	ténor
Eustache	2ème baryton
R. de Clermont, maréchal de Normandie	basse chantante
Jehan Maillard	basse
Pierre, jeune seigneur, ami de Robert	2ème ténor
L'Hôtelier	trial
Béatrix Marcel, fille du prévôt	soprano falcon
Le Dauphin Charles	contralto
Marguerite, mère de Béatrix	mezzo-soprano
Un héraut	ténor
Un artisan	baryton
Denis, serviteur de Marcel	ténor
Une sentinelle	ténor
Josseran de Mâcon, trésorier du Roi de Navarre	coryphée
Lecoq, Évêque de Laon	coryphée
Un échevin	coryphée
Marion, suivante de Béatrix	coryphée
Rousselette, ribaude	muette
Simonne, ribaude	muette

Seigneurs, échevins, artisans, bourgeois, pages, écuyers, soldats, clercs, écoliers, ribaudes, bohémiens, filles d'Egypte, etc.

Orchestra: piccolo, 2 flutes, 2 oboes (incl. cor anglais), 2 clarinets, 3 bassoons (incl. contrabassoon), 4 horns, 2 trumpets, 3 trombones, tuba, timpani, bass drum, cymbals, triangle, crotales in C♯, tambourine, strings.

Offstage: 2 trumpets, 2 bass trumpets, tamtam, bells in C, B♭ and F, organ (two players).

The Battle of Poitiers in 1356 was a resounding defeat for France at the hands of the English. King Jean II of France was captured by the Black Prince and taken to London, leaving his son Charles the Dauphin as regent. In the countryside the aftermath of battle was extreme lawlessness as mercenary mobs freely pillaged every town and village. In Paris the Third Estate, comprising all the population apart from the nobility and the clergy, had formed a powerful body under the leadership of Étienne Marcel, whose title Provost of Merchants gave him the equivalent status of mayor of the city.

A tense stand-off between the Dauphin and Marcel, representing the nobility and the wealthy bourgeoisie of Paris respectively, would have been recipe enough for trouble even without two other factors: the violent peasant uprising, known as the 'Jacquerie', that erupted in the summer of 1358; and the intrusion of Charles of Navarre, a claimant to the French throne as grandson of Louis X.

The bourgeoisie pressed for reform, led by Marcel and supported by the city aldermen and magistrates, and by Robert Lecoq, bishop of Laon. The Dauphin rejected their proposals. A young clerk, Perrin Marc, sold two horses to the Dauphin, but Jean Baillet, the treasurer, refused to pay. Marc killed Baillet with a knife and took sanctuary in the church of St-Merry (predecessor of the building where Saint-Saëns had himself been organist at the beginning of his career). The Maréchal de Clermont disregarded the right of sanctuary, breaking into the church and having Marc hanged. This stirred up the church against the Dauphin. The bishop of Paris, Jean de Meulan, excommunicated Robert de Clermont.

On 22 January 1358 a popular assembly resolved to break with the Dauphin's advisers. An armed crowd escorted Marcel to the palace where the Dauphin had his two advisers with him. After a heated exchange Marcel's supporters attacked two marshals and killed them. Marcel told the Dauphin he had nothing to fear and took his brown/black bonnet and attached it to his own red and blue hood, colours adopted by the Parisians.

The Dauphin fled by night and sought help from the nobility of the provinces. His army set up at Vincennes, on the eastern edge of Paris, at the confluence of the Seine and the Marne. Marcel fortified the city, making an alliance with Charles the Bad, King of Navarre, whom he named head of the Parisian troops. But when, in an encounter with the royal forces, he ordered his men to pull back, it was clear that he had made a deal with the Dauphin. Accused of betraying the Parisians' cause he withdrew to St-Denis with his troops.

Meanwhile the Dauphin was stirring up trouble against the Paris commune. Marcel was blamed for the suffering of the city. Jean Maillard, an alderman, led the protest against Marcel even though he had originally been one of his partisans. Charles of Navarre sent Josseran de Mâcon, his treasurer, to persuade Marcel to open the gates at the Porte St-Denis to him. Marcel agreed, feeling betrayed by his own supporters. When on the night of 31 July/1 August 1358 he gave the order to open the gates, the guards refused, and scuffles broke out. Marcel escaped to the Porte St-Antoine, where the same scene was enacted, this time leading to Marcel's death, struck down by Jean Maillard or one of his companions. The provost's death was the signal for a massacre of his followers.

When he entered the city the Dauphin saw Marcel's body laid out on the steps of the church of Ste-Catherine du Val des Ecoliers. Close associates of Marcel and Navarre were executed, but for the citizens of Paris a general amnesty was proclaimed.

This blood-soaked episode from French history is recounted by Gallet in a lengthy preface to the libretto, printed in 1879. He acknowledged his sources as Froissart's well-known *Chronicles*, several histories of France and an immense book by F.-T. Perrens, *Étienne Marcel, prévot des Marchands*, published in 1874 after work on the opera had begun. Perrens, who taught at the École Polytechnique, had also written a study of Marcel in 1860, *Étienne Marcel et le gouvernement de la bourgeoisie au quatorzième siècle : 1356–1358*, which Gallet must have known.

Gallet's task was to fashion a workable libretto around these events. With all that civil strife as background, he created foreground interest with the Romeo-and-Juliet formula also found in Meyerbeer's *Les Huguenots* by supposing that Marcel's daughter Béatrix is in love with Robert de Loris (a historical figure), the exiled king's chamberlain and thus an enemy. Gallet also invented the character Eustache, a Judas-like figure. The Dauphin, Maillard, Clermont, Lecoq, Josseran de Mâcon and Marguerite Marcel were historical. In the earliest drafts Béatrix was called Jehanne and Marguerite was Jacqueline.

These turbulent events provided great opportunities for the chorus in public scenes, and in Act III there was excellent scope for the mandatory ballet. The three principal roles are soprano, tenor and baritone, and the usual supporting characters have small parts.

For Saint-Saëns and Gallet, searching for suitable episodes in their plan for an opera, or perhaps a series of operas, based on the history of France, the events of 1358 were a suitable choice since the sufferings of Paris under siege and Commune were still vivid in everyone's mind. It is hard to see any particular political message in the opera, beyond a warning of the perils of insurrection and of treachery. Saint-Saëns had no patience with popular insurrection and would hardly have included the final tableau, with the Dauphin entering Paris in triumph, if he would not himself have welcomed the return of the monarchy. The theory put forward by Jean Gallois that the opera was inspired by the political events of May 1877,[13] when republican interests overcame President MacMahon's royalist intentions, is untenable since the opera had been in existence for some years before that. Saint-Saëns always hoped, in vain, that the Parisian theme would strengthen the case for a performance at the Paris Opéra, especially since Marcel was regarded as a Parisian hero with a splendid equestrian statue of him erected in front of the new Hôtel de Ville, which was being rebuilt just as the opera was being composed, and with a nearby street given his name in 1881.

* * * * *

ACT I

Prélude The opera opens with a clear straightforward statement of Étienne Marcel's motif, with its descending series of fifths, ex. 5.1:

---

[13] GALLOIS 2004, pp. 219–20, and PASLER 2009, p. 305 note 13.

Example 5.1 *Étienne Marcel*, Prelude

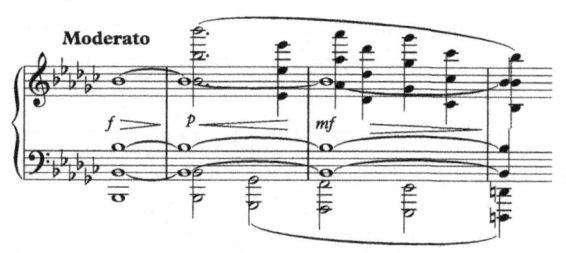

[musical notation: Moderato]

The short sombre Prelude also includes the trumpet call from the Herald's pronouncement in the first scene and some busy chromatic figures from the final scene of the opera, but returns soon to the descending fifths (or diminished fifths, as they become in the major mode).

Scene 1 Once the curtain opens, the mood is completely different. We see the interior of the mediaeval Les Halles, with pillared arcades crowded with people. Beneath the pillars are taverns occupied by soldiers, bourgeois and artisans in separate groups. Robert de Loris, equerry to the Dauphin, and his young friend Pierre, both tenors, are alone at a separate table in discreet conversation. Crowds of people coming and going at the back make a very lively scene epitomised by the opening tune, ex. 5.2:

Example 5.2 *Étienne Marcel*, Act I, Scene 1

[musical notation: Vivace, (wind)]

With minimal originality, Gallet has the soldiers call out 'À boire', answered from across the stage by the group of artisans out-shouting them with their own 'À boire', all to the accompaniment of highly animated music. The innkeeper does his best to cater for both groups. As the metre changes from 2/4 to 3/4, Pierre toasts Robert, while Robert toasts the Dauphin, cautiously looking round. A strangely dressed character, Eustache, a baritone, who has been banging on the table and drinking freely, is prevailed upon to sing a song, which he willingly does, being well primed in claret.

Such songs early in the action were a regular feature of grand opera, conventionally a pair of *couplets*, but here three verses, in 6/8 and in F major. In a song which demands some aptitude for comedy, Eustache tells of the Seneschal of Poitiers who had three equerries and a page who were all in love with his wife. One day he went away on his great horse, so the suitors all vied for her attention. But she had other ideas and received a lover of her own choosing. Was he a prince or a grand lord? No, no, he was a poor man. And I won't tell you who it was, adds Eustache. 'It was you', the artisans cry; Eustache says nothing.

Gallet's seven stanzas in a tight rhyme scheme suggest that the poem may have been written for some other purpose. Saint-Saëns solved the problem by elongating the second *couplet* to accommodate three stanzas of the poem, with two in each of the others. Even then he varies the beginning of his third *couplet*, and the orchestration, with horns alluding to the Seneschal's ride, is varied too. Saint-Saëns seems to have Berlioz's Song of the Rat and Song of the Flea (in *La Damnation de Faust*) in mind as his models.

The music allows for no applause at the end since it runs directly into an exchange between Robert and Pierre, supported by a gently flowing figure in the violins (ex. 5.3), from which we learn that Robert is in love with Béatrix, daughter of their enemy, the provost Étienne Marcel. This music represents his tender feelings for her.

Example 5.3 *Étienne Marcel*, Act I, Scene 1

Pierre is alarmed. The tempo quickens as Pierre calls the innkeeper over and gives him some money. The innkeeper reacts violently, accusing him of passing clipped coinage. Pierre claims the protection of a royal edict, but this is scorned by the innkeeper, who soon has all the artisans behind him. We work hard and pay our taxes and this is how the nobility treats us, hiding behind royal edicts, he moans. The soldiers, implicitly royalist, lurk in the background. Robert curses the bourgeoisie, and brushes aside a sly comment from Eustache.

Scene 2 A fight is avoided by the arrival of Béatrix and her confidante Marion. They are being harassed by a group of soldiers, but the new key (D) and a delicate tone presents their four-part harassment as light-hearted, even charming, one of the most fetching episodes in the opera. But Robert is mercifully on hand to rescue her, while the soldiers shamefacedly retreat when they see who he is. His intervention does not go unnoticed by the crowd: 'C'est un brave seigneur', they agree.

Scene 3 Example 5.1 announces the entry of the provost, Étienne Marcel himself, who disapproves of his daughter going out and about. We were going to church, she protests, when we were surrounded by the king's soldiers: This young lord, she goes on, saved me. There is an uneasy handshake as a solo cello introduces an expressive figure that weaves in and out of the texture, ex. 5.4:

Example 5.4 *Étienne Marcel*, Act I, Scene 3

[musical example: Moderato]

The quartet that grows around this theme is full of tension, for when Marcel learns that his daughter's rescuer is Robert de Loris, equerry to the Dauphin, he lets go his hand, suspecting he is her lover. Béatrix and Pierre have anxieties of their own. The ladies go on their way while Robert and Pierre have duties at the palace. Example 5.3 gives us Robert's thoughts as he leaves.

Scene 4 Artisans and bourgeois now crowd around Marcel to hear what he is planning to do in his struggle against the Dauphin. Eustache is with them, since a tune he sings later is heard. Their discontent dominates the rest of the act, coming to the boil with alarming suddenness. In a rapid conspiratorial whisper they assert their readiness to back the provost (ex. 5.5). Turmoil from outside is explained by Eustache: 'A herald is about to pronounce sentence on one of our men!'

Example 5.5 *Étienne Marcel*, Act I, Scene 4

[musical example: Allegro — Que soit pro-chai-ne L'heure où la chaî - ne se bri-se - ra!]

Scene 5 With trumpets in support, the herald, on a monotone, reports that Perrin Marc, condemned for murder and resistance to the law, is to be taken at once to the place of execution. Gallet's libretto has the name of Perrin Marc revealed by Eustache and by angry shouts from outside before the herald's proclamation. Marcel comments: 'Perrin Marc! I had guessed it. An innocent man struck down for defending his own life.' In the score, though, we do not hear Perrin's name until the Herald sings it, and his crime is not explained. The fact that the sanctuary of a church was violated by the king's marshal is a powerful factor in stirring up Marcel and his supporters as well as the clergy.

Scene 6 They all now gather at Marcel's bidding in a grand processional scene, a familiar feature of grand opera from *La Juive* to *Aida*. The music is a formal march in E♭, as one by one we see the entrance of the 'Maîtrises de Paris' (apprentices), the 'échevins' (magistrates), the guilds, bishop Lecoq and the clergy of Notre-Dame. Each delegation carries its banner, most of them wearing clothes in red and blue as their Parisian insignia. Marcel welcomes each group. It is now dark so the artisans and bourgeois are carrying torches.

The March's eighty-eight bars in a gradual *crescendo* imply that more and more people are to fill the stage. The men formally declare their allegiance to Marcel in their desire for liberty and freedom from oppression, followed by a reprise of the conspiratorial chorus heard before the herald's intrusion (ex. 5.5), this time sung loud. There follows a sequence of three scenes in which the separate groups come forward: first the magistrates (to a busy figure in the strings in C minor that strikingly anticipates the first Allegro of the Third Symphony), then the clergy (hymn-like music), who state their grievances against the Dauphin; then finally Eustache steps forward as representative of 'the people' who will rise in revolt when the time comes.

The original plan seems to have been for an individual to represent each group, with his last line echoed by the chorus.[14] Thus the C minor music was planned to be sung by Eustache and the churchy music by the bishop, with echoes from the artisans and the clergy respectively. In order to include the magistrates, the C minor music was given to them, singing in chorus, and the churchy music to the clergy, with no reponses to the last line; the artisans are then represented by Eustache, who does get an echo from his group. The second edition of the vocal score revised the clergy's section so that the bishop alone sings it, with a refrain from the clergy, but the magistrates' section was unchanged. The reasoning must have been that the magistrates' representative would have been Jehan Maillard, whose more dramatic intervention is saved for a few pages later.

Announced by ex. 5.1 Marcel addresses the assembly in gestural recitative. He reports that the English are invading and that the Dauphin and his venal councillors are incapable of protecting the country. He rouses his audience with powerful oratory leading to the climax:

> Ah ! tu récolteras, Prince, ce que tu sèmes,
> Et ton peuple abattu se révolte à la fin !
>
> Ah, Prince! You will reap what you sow,
> And your oppressed people will rise in revolt!

This releases another yet more furious reprise of the chorus of ex. 5.5, to which the women's voices are now joined. A new figure appears, representing the turmoil of the streets, ex. 5.6.

Example 5.6 *Étienne Marcel*, Act I, Scene 6

A new voice intrudes, that of Jehan Maillard (bass), identified as a magistrate by the busy C minor music heard before. Although he does not introduce himself, he is

---

[14] Some of this is visible in the early draft, F-Pn MS 931.

a draper and a supporter of Marcel, but he issues a dark warning, like Caesar's soothsayer, that the passions he arouses may ricochet back against him. Marcel brusquely dismisses the suggestion and goes on to call the crowd to arms. 'To the palace!' they all shout. The rest of the scene is a thunderous roar of popular rebellious frenzy, with unstoppable music to match.

ACT II, TABLEAU 1

Scene 1 The violence that the first act has threatened is now unleashed. As if there had been no break, we hear the closing shouts of Act I and the surge of ex. 5.6, but from a distance, a masterly dramaturgical touch. For we are now within the royal palace, from which viewpoint the gathering of the crowds can be heard as an ugly low-pitched roar while clarinets and bassoons echo the clamour of the crowd. Gallet set the scene with great precision: it is a vast candle-lit hall supported by clusters of gothic columns with a blue ceiling decorated with stars and fleurs-de-lys in gilded metal. Beneath a canopy the royal throne is empty. The Dauphin is seated, with Robert de Loris standing next to him. The Marshal, Robert de Clermont, is working on a pile of documents at a table, with pages standing ready to take his orders. On the right, in front of an immense window stands a group of lords looking out on to the street, muttering with a certain alarm about the goings-on outside. Other lords are seen at the back.

The Marshal (a basse chantante), who was responsible for the attack on the church where Perrin Marc was in sanctuary, is confident that the bourgeoisie is docile and presents no threat. As long as they pay their taxes, they are free to be rowdy in the streets.

The twenty-year-old Dauphin (played by a contralto) is not so sure, knowing that the palace is vulnerable to an attack by the crowd. When the Marshal reassures him that all will be well and goes over to join the lords, the Dauphin turns to Robert, who has been boasting, as lovers do, about his new conquest. The Dauphin is envious, singing a brief Air 'Parfois je songe en ma tristesse', which touches on the age-old distress of kings who long for the tranquillity and peace of mind which kingship never gives. Perhaps Saint-Saëns was thinking of Herod in Berlioz's *L'Enfance du Christ*, a work he greatly admired.

The Air has some lovely phrases but is over all too soon. The noise from outside is increasing and, as knocking is heard on the outer doors, a group of royal archers enter over agitated music and report to the Marshal that the palace is threatened. The Dauphin caustically asks Clermont to explain. Keep the doors firmly closed, is his instruction, and strike down the people if they resist. Hearing that the people are led by Marcel, the Marshal scornfully orders his arrest.

'The Dauphin! The Dauphin! Death to traitors!' come the shouts from outside. The Marshal bitterly recognises his own vulnerability but calls the lords and archers cowards when they urge the Dauphin to flee. But the Dauphin steps forward and gives the order to open the gates. It is too late. The gates have already yielded to the onslaught of the crowd. The Dauphin urges Robert to stay close to him and, seating himself on the throne, claims he is ready to die.

Scene 2 With no let-up in the fury of the orchestra the assailants enter. They are led by Marcel himself, accompanied by the clergy of Notre-Dame, the guilds, the artisans, including Eustache, and an armed rabble. They are wearing blue and red hoods and ornamental clasps in gold and blue porcelain to proclaim their cause. 'Death to Clermont!' is their cry, but before they do the deed, Marcel imposes silence and addresses the Dauphin. To the strains of the processional march from Act I he insists that they have no quarrel with him, but only with those who ruin the country and divide the nation, namely the Marshal of Normandy, Robert de Clermont. The Marshal accuses Marcel of stirring up discord when the English are invading. 'One day you will answer for France's suffering!' he claims, to which Marcel's riposte is '*Our* suffering!'

The key of E♭ minor and a feverish figure in the strings support Marcel's direct accusations of bankrupting the nation on the backs of the people. His call for the Marshal to resign is drowned out by the crowd clamouring for his death. Marcel pleads with the Dauphin to dismiss his councillors. 'Never!' insists the Dauphin, unleashing the full fury of the mob. They fall in a rage upon the Marshal, who falls dead in a pool of blood on the steps of the throne (the Marshal's final desperate 'À moi!' is incorrectly given to Marcel in the vocal and orchestral scores). Robert de Loris stands to protect the Dauphin. At the Marshal's death Marcel declares their work is done, but Robert attacks him with raised sword. Eustache intervenes to save Marcel, who tells Robert to go on his way, muttering a warning to him not to get in his way again. The Marshal's body is carried off.

Marcel then addresses the Dauphin with words of peace. He removes his brown and gold cap and places on his head the red and blue bonnet of the revolt, a gesture with some historical authenticity. The Dauphin and Robert mutter what little consolation they can find and silently shake hands. The triumphal march concludes the tableau.

ACT II, TABLEAU 2

Scene 1 It is time for an indoor scene of greater intimacy. Example 5.4, suggesting Béatrix's anxiety, prepares the next tableau, which shows the Marcel family parlour with its heavy furniture and symbols of municipal grandeur. A high-backed chair is prominent at the front of the stage. Béatrix and her mother Marguerite (mezzo-soprano) are sitting together, clasping each others' hands. Their servant Denis is seated at the back by the door, polishing a sword. The curfew bell tolls twice. Example 5.6

rumbles in the distance. Marguerite goes to the window. Béatrix's thoughts are for Robert's safety. Denis suddenly gets up to announce the arrival of Marcel.

Scene 2 Solemnly entering to ex. 5.1, Marcel seems unaware of his wife and daughter. He throws off his bonnet, his sword and his coat, which Denis picks up and takes away. The women watch Marcel nervously as he settles into the big chair. Noticing their presence, he reports that Paris is free; with the same chromatic chords that accompanied the removal of Clermont's body in the previous scene he declares that 'those who plotted to destroy it are dead!' (That scene showed only one victim, but the historical Clermont was murdered along with Jean de Conflans, the Dauphin's other marshal.) Marguerite reminds her husband that divine justice punishes the spillers of blood, while Béatrix more urgently asks him who died.

'Clermont', he replies.

'Did no one go to his aid?'

'No-one.'

Then, probing Béatrix's curiosity over threads of ex. 5.4, he tells her that Robert de Loris was the only one to resist and that he is dead. The old trick works, for she cries out in grief and her father grabs her, accusing her of being in love with him. Against the rise and fall of ex. 5.7, he turns in fury on his daughter for loving a man who only wants her for his mistress. 'I am mad to have spared his life!'

Example 5.7 *Étienne Marcel*, Act II, Tableau 2, Scene 2

It is Béatrix's turn to be furious with her father for having deceived her. A fast ensemble opens up, Marcel determined to kill Robert, while the women plead with him to be merciful. Béatrix taking the blame for herself does nothing to soften his thirst for vengeance. A great deal of musical excitement, including a long held high A♭ for Béatrix, is generated in a short time before Marcel storms out in rage.

Scene 3 Example 5.7 and then ex. 5.4 support a brief scene in which Béatrix begs her mother to let her be alone for a while. Marguerite embraces her and goes out.

Scene 4 Béatrix's solo Air begins at once, 'Ô beaux rêves évanouis !' With no vocal histrionics she calmly laments her shattered dream in a shapely sixteen-bar melody sensitively scored. After a middle section which recalls the bright hopes she once nourished, the melody returns intact; and as the coda softly echoes the middle part, the curfew bell is heard once again, tolling three times.

This should be a signal for sleep, but she is too agitated to sleep and the music hints at a coming cabaletta. Instead, in order to breathe the night air, she goes to the window, where (to no one's surprise but hers, given this genre of opera) Robert himself appears, having scaled the balcony.

Scene 5 Their scene together is necessarily full of tension but also full of tenderness. Béatrix tells him that her father has learned the truth and has sworn to kill him. In a series of highly expressive phrases, Robert reassures her that he is not alarmed and has prepared for their flight, provided that she truly loves him. Béatrix's reply could not be more touching, ex. 5.8:

Example 5.8 *Étienne Marcel*, Act II, Tableau 2, Scene 5

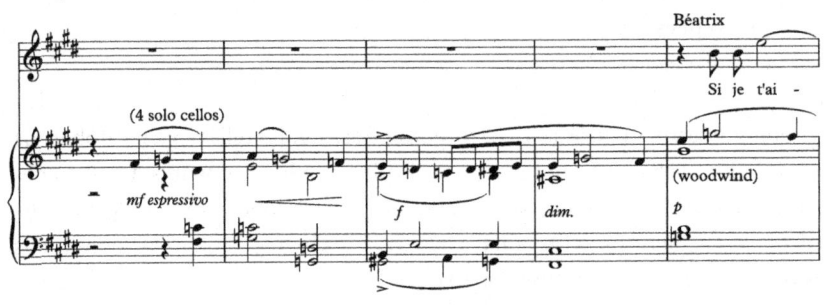

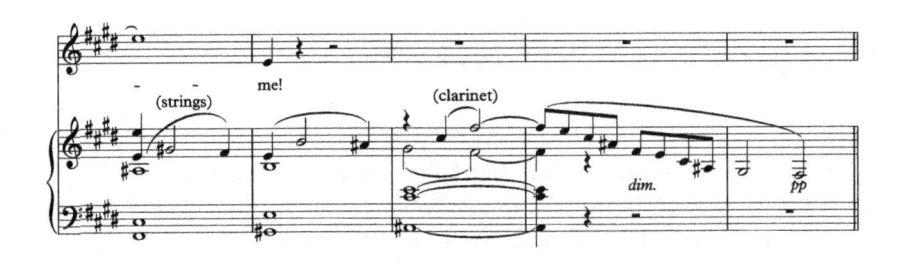

The text of the lovely Adagio in B major that follows echoes Ophelia's reply to Hamlet in Thomas's opera (libretto by Barbier and Carré):

Barbier and Carré:

> Doute de la lumière,
> Doute du soleil et du jour,
> Doute des cieux et de la terre,
> Mais ne doute jamais de mon amour !

Gallet:

> Interroge les astres d'or,
> La terre, l'air que je respire,
> Tout s'animera pour te dire,
> Si tu peux en douter encor
> Que je bénis mon doux martyre,
> Que ton amour est mon trésor !

For the last two lines the music speeds up and her solo quickly becomes a duet, albeit short, perhaps as a trailer for the more extended love duet that follows.

It is introduced by Robert's music (from the opening scene of the opera) and settles into E major Andante, ex. 5.9:

Example 5.9 *Étienne Marcel*, Act II, Tableau 2, Scene 5

dolcissimo
Ô pure ex - ta - se,

The lovers are happy in their cocoon of love, but reality interposes with a shift to G major and some speedy music in which Robert urges Béatrix to flee the city with him and the Dauphin, who also plans to escape. Go if you must, she says, but how can I leave my home? With even speedier music Robert accuses her of not loving him, making her all the more distraught and torn. How can I leave my mother and my home, she asks. As the violins' semiquavers get ever more hectic, she yields, knowing she will be accursed. They return to E major for a heated version of ex. 5.9, committed one to another, and ending in a hushed 'Ah ! viens !'[15]

They are about to rush from the house when violent knocking is heard. Shouts of 'Marcel !' rise from the street. After a few hurried exchanges she urges him to flee through a side door. He wants her to go with him, but she refuses.

Scene 6 He is about to leave when Marcel himself appears in that very door. Marcel calls in his supporters from the street and, pointing to Robert, calls out 'À mort le traître !' But Robert draws his sword and, with some swift swashbuckling, fights his way to the window and leaps out. The room empties, leaving Marcel dumbfounded and Béatrix in a lifeless heap on the floor. The orchestra closes the act hammering out ex. 5.9.

---

[15] In the third edition of the vocal score the act ends at this point.

ACT III

Scene 1 Scenes of noisy celebration in public places were a standard element of grand opera, for they displayed the sets, the chorus and the theatre's corps de ballet to their full advantage. Such scenes have fallen out of favour partly because of their expense, with many extras needed in the chorus and in on-stage bands, partly because the function of ballet in opera has been questioned on dramaturgical grounds. In nineteenth-century Paris, however, such qualms were unknown, and the costs involved in filling the stage with people were considerably less than they are today. Gallet and Saint-Saëns would not hesitate to include such a scene in their opera, for the public would demand it. Gounod in *Faust* and Thomas in *Hamlet* provided extensive ballets, following the standard practice evolved by Meyerbeer and Halévy. It was helpful if the ballet could serve some narrative purpose in the opera, but that was by no means necessary.

In *Étienne Marcel* the ballet is occasioned by the action being placed at midsummer, so that the celebration of St John the Baptist's Day would bring the populace out on to the square in front of Notre-Dame in festive mood. With historical accuracy, Gallet describes the scene with the Hôtel-Dieu, the oldest hospital in Paris, next to the cathedral. He would know, since the building was demolished and a new one built some distance away in 1877 under the management of the Assistance Publique, the organisation by which Gallet was employed.

Between the two buildings the Seine with its grassy banks can be seen. In the middle of the stage stands a pole garlanded with ribbons; at the back is a low platform, and in front of the Hôtel-Dieu a stone bench. A great crowd of people has gathered to watch the popular dances. The people sing a plain song about their release from oppression since the Dauphin and his court have left Paris. For a merry scene of this kind one might expect the composer to produce a routine piece of no special interest, but Saint-Saëns never composes with his eyes shut. Details in the scoring and harmony show the hand of someone alert to every possibility, inventive down to the last detail.

With a change of key and metre, Eustache emerges from the throng with a girl on either arm. The music echoes his comedy song from the opening scene. He is in love with his two beauties and needs to find them a good place to watch the dancing. 'What a merry fellow!' they call out, to which he replies, 'That's the way I am!' – which will prove in the course of the act to be not entirely true. He exhorts everyone to enjoy the holiday and they reply with a reprise of their opening song.

Ballet Various instrumentalists assemble on the platform, and beneath the decorated pole around which the dancers perform people begin to build a bonfire.

There are five ballets, altogether filling fifteen minutes or more. First is the dance for students and their girls, an ebullient movement in E♭ developing ex. 5.2, all in two-bar phrases, orchestrated with panache. Then a *Musette guerrière* over a series of drones is given principally to the wind, but its relaxed charm is far from warlike. The anomaly is explained in the autograph full score, where the dancers are given as 'four acrobats in *travesti* with swords and little bucklers, accompanied by a bagpiper'.

The *Pavane* was a deliberate archaism, but with no attempt to evoke the fourteenth century, let alone the sixteenth. The tune is plain and timeless, the scoring filigree modern. An earlier version of this dance, perhaps from Saint-Saëns's youth, is headed simply 'Air de ballet'. The *Valse* is the longest of the dances, challenging Tchaikovsky with a wealth of themes and colourful orchestration. At one point Saint-Saëns treats one of the themes in close canon. Although he marks no acceleration in the score, the movement clearly works up to a brilliant close.[16]

The fifth dance is a gypsy dance with crotales and tambourine. The main section is written in the Dorian mode over an unusual bass line provided by double basses and timpani, and the last section is brisk and uninhibited. The final dance is in a rabble-rousing mood, turning from minor to major for the coda, which turns out to be an accelerated reprise of the opening music of the act.

Scene 2 After such a festive ballet, the opera has to resume the ominous tone that the action so far has generated. The principal conflict, between the Dauphin and the bourgeoisie under Marcel's leadership, has left the latter in charge of Paris while the Dauphin is mustering his forces elsewhere. But new elements are about to make themselves felt, as we learn when Jehan Maillard enters with a group of his bourgeois friends. He is troubled by the popular spirit of rejoicing when the English are threatening and when Charles, King of Navarre, is waiting for a moment when the city's defences look weak. Marcel and his forces are now placed in a position where any alliance is dangerous and treachery is a constant source of fear.

The traitor that Maillard suspects is Eustache, who hitherto has seemed a harmless bon viveur, fond of wine and women. This new side of his character requires a new motif, ex. 5.10, unusually Wagnerian in character:

Example 5.10 *Étienne Marcel*, Act III, Scene 2

---

[16] At the end of his life Gallet wrote to Saint-Saëns: 'I didn't remember that I was the *author* of the Valse in *Étienne Marcel*! Thankyou for reminding me about that' (F-DI Gallet Dossier 10, letter of 26 November 1897). 'Auteur' would normally mean 'composer', but presumably not here.

Assuming his cheerful persona by recalling the drinking music from Act I, Eustache wonders why Maillard is looking at him in that strange fashion.

'Go on your way', says Maillard.

'Clearly you don't like me. Come along, princesses!' And he would have led his companions off if Maillard had not laid his hand on his shoulder and forced him to listen.

'What were you going to do at the Porte St-Denis this evening?' he asks, to the sound of ex. 5.10 on clarinet and bassoons.

'Enjoying the moonlight', answers Eustache, clearly uncomfortable.

Here Maillard introduces a motif for Charles of Navarre, ex. 5.11:

Example 5.11 *Étienne Marcel*, Act III, Scene 2

Saint De-nis ap-par-tient à Charles de Na-var-re;

With this enemy encamped in St-Denis, just north of Paris, the Porte St-Denis would be his point of attack, no place therefore for someone like you to hang out, Maillard sneers, before moving on with his supporters.

Over a restless accompaniment full of fragments of ex. 5.11, Eustache reasons with himself. The Dauphin is not defeated, in fact his forces are strong, and Marcel seems to have lost control of the city. A new leader is needed and Charles of Navarre is the one. The gates will open for him.

The bells of Notre-Dame ring out and the groups of people who were on stage throughout this exchange move to one side as a formal procession arrives for a victory celebration in the cathedral. Marcel leads the magistrates and the clergy to a richly scored hymn which grows in a great crescendo until the organ comes in at full strength and the triple west doors of the cathedral open, allowing a view of the nave.[17] The procession is received by Bishop Lecoq. Most of the crowd remain outside in the square.

Scene 3 Soon a Te Deum can be heard from inside the cathedral, reminding French opera-goers of Halévy's *La Juive*, which opens with a Te Deum heard from within a church in the city square of Constance in the year 1414, while the action of

---

[17] The final entry of the organ in this scene requires two players.

the opera gets under way in the square itself. Wagner's *Die Meistersinger* opens in a similar fashion, but it is unlikely that Saint-Saëns knew it when *Étienne Marcel* was first sketched out.

Against intermittent interruptions from the Te Deum (marked *forte* because it is sung offstage), Béatrix enters on her own and moves towards the Hôtel-Dieu. She mutters to herself that she has received a rendez-vous. A raggedly dressed pauper lying on the Hôtel-Dieu steps begs for alms, staring at Béatrix, who recognises him at once: it is Robert. While she pretends to look for some coins in her purse, he urges her to flee with him; he can also save her father from the fate that threatens him; he will collect her at curfew. 'Heaven preserve you!' he says aloud, picking up the coin she has thrown down.

Scene 4 But Eustache has seen them and is suspicious about the man in rags. He offers to help him collect money, but Robert turns away. As ex. 5.2 is heard, Eustache addresses him aloud as Messire Robert de Loris and attempts to arrest him as a spy for the Dauphin. The crowd joins in, denouncing him as a spy.

Scene 5 Eustache sends for Marcel. As the rapid music continues, Marcel emerges from the cathedral and is confronted by Eustache holding Robert. Marcel rejoices to have him in his clutches while Robert submits to his fate. Seizing the chance of a sympathetic audience, Marcel declares the Dauphin to be still a formidable enemy, having gathered his forces outside Paris. But, he goes on, he still needs cowardly spies.

'Enough!' cries Robert. 'Take your revenge, but don't degrade me.'

Scene 6 He is about to be led off when Maillard appears, taunting Marcel: 'Another victim! Another crime, is it not?' Marcel, stung by this reproach, insists that Robert is the Dauphin's spy. Since neither he nor the assembled crowd had any particular reason to believe it, Maillard suggests that Robert's only crime was to be loyal to his master.

The scene is set for the big ensemble that grand opera always offered when the plot's tensions have reached a point where all the principal characters are torn in the face of conflicting loyalties, complicating news or threats from outside. A broad 3/4 tempo and a rich key (D♭ major) now support a long section in which Robert, Marcel, Eustache, Maillard and the people all take part, while Béatrix, who has been watching unseen from the side, adds her troubled voice.

Maillard tells the archers to release Robert, immediately countermanded by Marcel. The people are on Maillard's side, and now they want Robert freed. Marcel is supported by Eustache and some artisans. The ensemble settles down when Maillard leads off with ex. 5.12:

Example 5.12 *Étienne Marcel*, Act III, Scene 6

[Musical score: Maestoso. Vocal line (Maillard): "É - cou - te la voix de la fou - le, El - le dé-fend que le sang cou - le, El - le n'en a que trop ver - sé!"]

Soon Béatrix's voice is heard soaring high over the rest, as in Verdi's great ensembles, joined by Robert in octaves, and the shuddering accompaniment persists until a thrilling grand cadence is eventually reached. The archers and the crowd are still squabbling over the prisoner Robert, and eventually Marcel signals to his archers to give way. Maillard urges Robert to flee and Béatrix goes into the Hôtel-Dieu. Marcel collapses on to the stone bench in despair. This is the turning-point of the drama, when Marcel realises that he no longer has the support of the people.

The ceremony being now over, the procession comes out of the cathedral and moves out of sight.

Scene 7 Eustache pretends to leave, but lingers as Marcel pours out his feelings in a magnificently restrained monologue. His followers have deserted him, and no one came to his aid. Thinly accompanied (with an important contribution from the contrabassoon) and expressive to the last syllable, Marcel's Air (in E♭ minor) is a searching portrayal of a man who has tasted success and power and now sees them drifting away.

Scene 8 Example 5.10 brings Eustache out from the shadows to confront Marcel. He has a plan to outfox Maillard and his friends with the aid of a powerful prince. Example 5.11 tells us that the prince is Charles of Navarre before Eustache reveals his plan to open the Porte St-Denis to allow Charles to take Paris and thus overcome the Dauphin. Marcel is appalled at the suggestion, as if Eustache is urging him to sell his honour. But Eustache persuades him that he has lost the support of the people and lives in danger of his life; Navarre is his only hope.

After a pause they launch into a rapid duet, 'Ah ! quelle pensée infernale !' in which Marcel sees himself on the brink of a fatal decision, while Eustache assures him this is the right path to save himself. In the middle section Marcel wonders how Eustache can change his allegiance from the voice of the people to this new intrigue. 'You are a lion, and I am a fox', Eustache replies, assuring him that if he goes that night to the Porte St-Denis, he will be there to support him. Navarre's theme is briefly heard, then the duet is reprised and they go out.

Scene 9 The square is now invaded by people carrying torches, preparing to light the bonfire. The act closes with the music with which it opened, the crowd singing their hymn of triumph and dancing round the bonfire as the flames rise up.

ACT IV

Prélude The grim atmosphere of the final act is well captured by a restless theme presented on violins and cellos in octaves, ex. 5.13:

Example 5.13 *Étienne Marcel*, Act IV, Prelude

Scene 1 The set represents the Porte St-Martin seen from the inside, the gate being fortified with towers and forming part of the city walls. On the left is a guardroom with a lantern and on the right a small house, dimly lit. Maillard, knowing that the action at this gate is critical, approaches the guardhouse with his usual bodyguard. He has a few words with the duty guard, warning them to be on the lookout for treachery: no one is to be admitted to the city.

He leaves. A sentry takes up his position by the gate and a detachment of soldiers goes on patrol to a lively little march that belies the atmosphere of the scene so far. While this music continues, Eustache appears leading a man whose face is hidden in his cape and hood. It is Josseran de Mâcon, treasurer to Charles of Navarre, a silent role. Eustache promises him he will soon be meeting the Provost of Paris in the little house to which he leads him. Josseran hands Eustache a bag of money, to the latter's undisguised delight, and goes in.

Marcel arrives almost immediately, greeted by Eustache in an irritating bantering manner. Tonight, he tells him, if you do what Josseran tells you, you will be governor of Paris; if you don't, you will be the Dauphin's prisoner. Almost without a word Marcel goes into the house, leaving Eustache to gloat over his money and his scorn for the world's idiotic values. After his departure the patrol returns and silently enters the guardroom.

Scene 2 Next to arrive is Robert, who has followed Marcel, suspecting that something was up. He now sings the solo Air he has so far not been granted, and it has the energy and urgency that the situation forces on him: 'Je crois, j'attends, j'espère'. It is a pity that the vocal line lapses into regular crotchets after a fine opening phrase for these words, so that the orchestra seizes the guiding hand with its constant syncopation and driving bass. Like the other Airs in this opera, it is ternary, with a middle section in which he affirms his determination to win Béatrix, no matter what. It is essential that it be sung at maximum speed.

Scene 3 When Marcel and Josseran emerge from the house, Robert hides. Marcel steps forward, ignoring Josseran, and over the themes attached to Charles of Navarre and himself (ex. 5.11 and ex. 5.1) he has a final brief monologue in which to reflect miserably on the crime of handing Paris over to the invader. But with sudden vigour he addresses the people of Paris: 'You, whom I so loved, it is your hatred that drove me to this. My vengeance is sweet.'

With a determined step and a rising motif which we have not heard since the Prelude to Act I, he addresses the sentry, who calls out the guard. They recognise him, but when he calls for the keys of the gate, they consult each other briefly and give a defiant 'Non!' These are Maillard's orders, they tell him. The confraternity of Notre-Dame will come to his aid, he assures himself, telling Josseran his promise will hold.

Scene 4 Before he can go back into the little house he is confronted by Robert, who has seen what Marcel is up to. As a rebel against the Dauphin, he urges, you could expect clemency, but as a traitor to your people you stand condemned.

Scene 5 Desperate to win him back, Robert calls in Béatrix and her mother, who rush to Marcel and embrace him. The quartet that follows, built on ex. 5.13, has a superb urgency. But all their pleas, including an offer of safe conduct from Robert, are futile. Marcel's pride will not allow him to be deflected, not even by Béatrix's last desperate plea. The approach of an angry crowd is signalled by ex. 5.5 and ex. 5.6. Marcel now knows that all is lost. With a final reprise of ex. 5.1 he bitterly admits that Maillard knew of his plans, and in a touching farewell he takes Robert's hand, begging him to take care of Béatrix. He refuses to stay but goes defiantly to his death, rushing off to meet the crowd. The arrival of the confraternity is too late to help him.

Scene 6 Over the clamour of the tocsin and the insistence of ex. 5.5, Béatrix urges Robert to save her father. But it is too late; the noise suddenly subsides, and he can only lead Béatrix and her mother to one side as the confraternity return bearing

Marcel's bloodstained body. It is a moment for the most powerful harmony, and Saint-Saëns does not disappoint us. Maillard (waving a victorious axe), Eustache and the crowd press on to the stage crying Hail to the Dauphin and prosperity for the people of Paris.

Scene 7 That might seem to be the end of the opera, but Gallet and Saint-Saëns added a brief tableau, whose only words are 'Noël!' ('Hail!' with no reference to Christmas) sung by the chorus. They did not specify a change of scene from the gloom of the Porte St-Denis except to say that the Dauphin enters 'the streets of Paris' on horseback, surrounded by his equerries throwing money to the people. The music is an extended fanfare in E♭.

* * * * *

Saint-Saëns later recalled:

> Gallet forced himself to respect the historical facts, as far as that is possible in a work for the theatre. In spite of some well-known examples he felt it was wrong to attribute purely invented deeds and feelings to people who had actually lived. In this, as in so much else, I was entirely in agreement with him. I would even go further in saying that I cannot get used to the strange sauces that are applied to legendary characters. In my view it's the legend that's interesting, not the character, who loses all validity if you take away the legend that enfolds him. But everyone knows that I'm just an idiot.[18]

Clearly, though, it would have been impossible to retain the full historical facts in an opera libretto, especially one dealing with such complex events as these. The real Étienne Marcel's intricate relations with the nobility and the people of Paris make it hard to comprehend his attachment to Charles of Navarre, so the character of Eustache, Gallet's creation, provides the element of treachery needed to set up the scene at the Porte St-Denis and Marcel's death. The real Eustache d'Aubrecicourt was equally amoral but was not the model for Gallet's Eustache, whose playful nature encompassed a disdain for normal rules of behaviour and for loyalties of any kind. It was also necessary to remodel the character of Robert de Loris, and to invent his passion for Marcel's daughter. Unusually for an opera of this kind the soprano does not meet the tragic end that Marcel suffers, and her future with Robert is left for all to guess.

Neither Gallet nor Saint-Saëns had any scruple about the length and grandeur of this work. In the 1870s grand opera was affordable and popular; without four or five acts (the four acts contain six tableaux, with a separate set for each), a full cast of characters, plenty of ballet, processional scenes with a variety of colourful costumes and sets which reproduced historic architecture in every detail, the public would be disappointed and

---

[18] 'Louis Gallet', *L'Écho de Paris*, 12 November 1911; SORET 2012, p. 752.

critical. Such works presume big theatres, experienced designers and stage crew, full orchestras with some novelties in the pit, and big voices.

Étienne Marcel has five principal characters – soprano, tenor and two baritones, 'basse chantante' and bass – eight small parts and a handful of non-singing characters. Four of the five have solos, amounting to Airs, as does the Dauphin, who only appears twice, silently at the end. There are two duets, one trio, two quartets and one big ensemble. For Eustache, whose personality is so much of a chameleon, his solo utterances are random in length and character, with the exception of the song he offers to a drunken audience in the first scene. The chorus is exceptionally well served. This is an opera about the people, after all. They appear in every scene, dressed as lords, artisans, magistrates, clergy, soldiers and the populace itself. The musical distribution has been carefully worked out, in other words, and the opera is not divided into numbers, not quite as seamless as Wagner, but without formal breaks except between tableaux. The motifs are used in the conventional way, so that the later parts of the opera relate more frequently to earlier themes than the rest.

As for Saint-Saëns's musical invention, that was never his problem, for the variety of moods and character in the music is formidable. The only charge one might bring is against his vocal writing, which can be formulaic, especially in comparison with the orchestration, but it is doubtful if that would be noticed in a good performance with sensitive singers. To assess the opera against others of the same repertoire is hard, but it is significant that Steven Huebner has concluded that 'it is not at all certain that Saint-Saëns's historical operas are theatrically, vocally or compositionally inferior to those of Meyerbeer.'[19] *Étienne Marcel* is a better opera, too, than *Les Vêpres siciliennes* and *Simon Boccanegra*, even if Verdians would be loath to admit it. After Tchaikovsky's death Saint-Saëns discovered that in a letter to a friend he 'was dreadfully scornful of *Étienne Marcel*. He only knew it from reading the vocal score. I remember writing some ill-considered things about *Manon* long ago in the same conditions. But when I saw *Manon*, I completely changed my opinion. It think it would have been the same for Tchaikovsky if he'd heard it, all the more since on the piano my work is like a bird without its feathers.'[20]

* * * * *

Étienne Marcel underwent several minor revisions after the Lyon premiere. A second edition of the vocal score (357 pages) appeared in about 1885 with five changes, perhaps reflecting the revival at the Château d'Eau.

1) Act I:[21] When the separate groups enter, the magistrates' brief words are followed by a hymn-like entry from the bishop alone, without the support of the cathedral

---

[19] CHARLTON 2003, p. 311.   [20] Letter to Auguste Durand, 30 June 1906, RATNER 2012, p. 106.
[21] Pages 64–66 in all vocal scores.

clergy. They echo his last line, 'Pour lui nous serons sans merci!' in the three-bar gap before Eustache sings.

2) Act III:[22] After the grand cadence in D♭ major at the end of the full ensemble, the chorus sing in unison

> Que notre volonté l'emporte!
> Elle doit être la plus forte,
> Le temps de la tienne est passé!

In the original version there followed seventeen bars in which Maillard secures the release of Robert over the squabbles of the archers and the populace. Marcel is humiliated. In the new version the curtain falls for the end of the act. The linking passage which accompanied the exit of everyone except Eustache and Marcel became the introduction to the first tableau of Act IV (without Eustache), and Marcel's monologue 'Tous sont partis' is the opening scene of the new act set 'in a street in old Paris'. The original Act IV is now Act IV, Tableau 1.

There is definitely a dramatic loss in cutting the squabble after the ensemble in which Marcel loses control of the people, but to start a new act with his monologue is clearly an advantage.

3) Act III (first version), Act IV, Tableau 1 (second version):[23] The scene for Eustache and Marcel following Marcel's monologue concludes with a ternary duet. The middle section and reprise of the duet are now permitted, in a footnote, to be cut, a reduction of sixty bars.

4) Act III (first version), Act IV, Tableau 1 (second version):[24] This same scene for Eustache and Marcel concludes with their exit. Six extra bars are now added to modulate from B♭ major to C major as dominant of F minor. The following scene, in which the chorus reprise their hymn of triumph and dance around the bonfire, is cut, since the action is no longer in the space in front of Notre-Dame. This is a cut of 103 bars, with no musical loss.

5) Act IV (first version), Act IV, Tableau 2 (second version):[25] This scene, in which, before attempting to get the gate opened, Marcel confesses his crime in delivering Paris to the enemy, is extended in the new version. Where, before, he sang three bars of recitative, 'La vengeance me reste et la vengeance est douce!', he now has seventeen bars in which he sings:

> Du moins pour ton salut j'accomplirai ma tâche,
> S'il en est temps encor, oui, je te sauverai,

---

[22] Page 278 in the 365-page and 357-page scores; p. 271 in the 343-page score.
[23] Page 297 in the 365-page score, p. 295 in the 357-page score.
[24] Page 303 in the 365-page score, p. 300 in the 357-page score.
[25] Page 331 in the 365-page score, p. 322 in the 357-page score.

> Malgré tout je t'arrêterai,
> Toi qui veux retomber sous le joug de ton maître !
> S'il en est temps encor ! Peut-être !

The full score helpfully prints both the first and the second versions of this passage. The 357-page vocal score shows half of the new version only.

After the successful performances in Prague in 1887 Saint-Saëns reported that Gallet had some new ideas for the fourth act based on newly discovered historical documents. 'This would make our work into a monument', he wrote,[26] although no major revisions were carried out.

Not long afterwards he wrote: '[*Étienne Marcel*] is extremely good just as it is, and the last act, leaving out the tenor's pointless Air, is very effective, finishing in grandiose fashion with the entry of the Dauphin, which must be kept, along with the quartet and the nocturnal march. [. . .] The third act, as you know, now ends with the big ensemble, and Marcel's Air opens the first tableau of the last act.'[27]

The full score, printed by Durand, matches this version, as given in the 357-page score.

A third edition of the vocal score (343 pages) appeared before 1891, with three further changes that were perhaps put in place for the Lyon revival that year.

1) Act II:[28] At the end of the love duet for Béatrix and Robert, instead of the entry of Marcel and a confrontation from which Robert narrowly escapes by jumping out of the window, there are now simply the few bars of orchestral peroration that close the act. There is a considerable loss here, hard to explain, unless it was deemed necessary to allow some strong high notes for the lovers and an opportunity for applause.
2) Act IV (first version), Act IV, Tableau 2 (second version):[29] the full seventeen bars are given in their final version.
3) Act IV (first version), Act IV, Tableau 2 (second version):[30] Robert's entire solo scene is cut. There is no doubt that a solo scene holds up the action so late in a drama of this kind. It was unusual for the tenor to have no solo number earlier in the opera, and Saint-Saëns, as we saw just now, regarded it as 'pointless'.

In 1891, after this last edition was printed, Saint-Saëns wrote to his publisher:

> Gallet has written me a long letter, asking to revise the last act. I am not against that, but I recall that this very act when carefully staged was very effective. Gallet is unhappy with all his characters, with the exception of Jehan Maillard. He seems to attach little significance to Eustache. Now Eustache is the picturesque element in the work, especially in the last act,

---

[26] Letter to Gouzien, RATNER 2012, p. 104.   [27] US-NYpm, cited in RATNER 2012, p. 104.
[28] Page 174 in all vocal scores.
[29] Page 331 in the 365-page score, p. 322 in the 357-page score, p. 315 in the 343-page score.
[30] Page 323 in the 365-page score, p. 313 in the 357-page score, p. 306 in the 343-page score.

where he has a substantial part. His duet with Marcel is, in my humble opinion, one of the best things I have done in the theatre. But it is difficult to sing and to act. Just getting the notes is not enough, however well done.

In 1913 Saint-Saëns told Durand he would like to make a new edition with the last act restored to its original state and the opera divided into five acts, not four, the two tableaux of Act II becoming Act II and Act III. This was not done, and no further changes in the last act were made.

* * * * *

Saint-Saëns had good reason to expect that after the success of *Étienne Marcel* in Lyon and the impact of *Samson et Dalila* in Weimar the new opera would find its way to Paris. The Opéra was its obvious destination there, and the director who took over from Halanzier in 1879, Emmanuel Vaucorbeil, was by no means opposed to Saint-Saëns's work. Saint-Saëns wrote him a persuasive letter arguing the case of *Étienne Marcel*, ending, '*Étienne Marcel* will be played this winter in Amsterdam and the Hague; it will go round the world and the Opéra will end up having to play it. Wouldn't it be better to play it now?'[31]

There were indeed performances in Holland in February 1880, which Saint-Saëns attended; in Brussels on the same tour he encountered Ernest Gye, manager of the Royal Opera House, Covent Garden, who promised to consider *Étienne Marcel* for his next season. More pressure in that direction was exerted by Queen Victoria herself, having heard Béatrix's Air from Act III, 'Ô beaux rêves évanouis !' sung 'with great purity of style and pronunciation'[32] by her youngest daughter Princess Beatrice accompanied by Saint-Saëns on a visit to Windsor Castle in July of the same year. Nothing came of that.

Despite Saint-Saëns's forecast, the opera did not exactly go round the world, and the Opéra never played it, which caused him great bitterness. To be fair to Vaucorbeil, his early productions included Verdi's *Aida* in 1880, Gounod's *Le Tribut de Zamora* in 1881 and Thomas's *Françoise de Rimini* in 1882. By that time he had commissioned *Henry VIII*, so there could be no question of *Étienne Marcel* there for a while.

The first revival in France took place in Rouen on 26 March 1885 in a theatre that specialised in mounting French operas that had not been heard in Paris. It had nine performances. Since 1879 a theatre on the Rue de Malte, Paris, near the Place de la République, originally built as a hippodrome but now redesigned, had been giving opera along with other types of spectacle. In 1885 it was occupied by a group calling themselves the Théâtre-Lyrique-Populaire, run by the tenor Gustave Garnier. He accepted *Étienne Marcel* for performance and although he was desperately short of funds, he opened on 24 October 1885, himself singing the role of Robert. Numa Auguez, who had sung in *Le Roi de Lahore* at the Opéra, was Marcel, and Edith Ploux was Béatrix. The conductor was

---

[31] Letter of 19 September 1879, RATNER 2012, p. 104.   [32] SORET 2012, p. 793.

A. Steck. It is doubtful that the theatre can have afforded any of the opera's splendour, for after four performances[33] the show closed for lack of money. Perhaps the splendour was there, which would equally explain the shortage of money. There were a few notices in the Parisian press, but not enough to give the work much chance of revival.

That was the last time that *Étienne Marcel* was heard in Paris, for Saint-Saëns was wrong to believe that the Opéra would eventually have to play it. It never did, a matter of acute pain for the composer, nor has it, to this day. But it cannot be said that the opera disappeared from view. During Saint-Saëns's lifetime it was the subject of revivals in different cities at various intervals, enough to hold its head far above the thousands of operas that were never revived at all. He was particularly pleased with the performances in Toulouse and Bordeaux, and negotiations were at least begun with a number of other cities and other theatres. The long list of arrangements and transcriptions of scenes from the opera given in Ratner's *Catalogue*[34] (including an arrangement of the ballets for two pianos by Debussy in 1890) shows that the opera enjoyed considerable currency on domestic pianos. The *Pavane* and Béatrix's Air were particularly favoured. Saint-Saëns himself had performed the ballets in a piano duet version in Vienna in 1886, and in 1890, when he was travelling incognito on a ship to Egypt, a passenger played a fragment from the opera on the piano, unaware that the composer was his fellow-passenger.

The record of performances of *Étienne Marcel* is as follows:

Lyon, 8 February 1879
Amsterdam, February 1880
Prague, 19 March 1887
Lyon, 7 December 1891
Algiers, March 1895
Toulouse, 22 December 1899[35]
Bordeaux, 26 March 1912[36]
Lyon, 1914
Monte Carlo, 7 March 1918
Montpellier, 11 July 1994

This list shows only two productions abroad, Algiers being part of France at that time. There was talk of a production in Brussels in 1900 which did not take place. *Étienne Marcel* has never been performed in Germany, England or the United States, perhaps because few people outside France know anything of the country's troubled fourteenth-century history, let alone the name of Étienne Marcel – other than as that of a Metro station. Lyon remained loyal to the work, with revivals in 1891 and 1914.

---

[33] According to RATNER 2012, p. 102, there were eleven. [34] RATNER 2012, pp. 100–01.
[35] Saint-Saëns's full report of the Toulouse production is given in RATNER 2012, pp. 105–06.
[36] Saint-Saëns's full report of the Bordeaux production is given in RATNER 2012, pp. 107–08.

The opera did not quite die with its composer, for it has had one revival in recent times. On 11 July 1994 it was given in a concert performance at the Montpellier Festival, conducted by Hubert Soudant, and relayed on French radio. The Marcel, Alain Fondary, has a fine voice, but the performance is marred by extensive cuts, including the ballet and the final tableau. Meanwhile, the ballets have been well recorded by Melba Recordings, with Orchestra Victoria conducted by Guillaume Tourniaire. *Étienne Marcel* is perhaps the one Saint-Saëns opera that would most benefit from a first-class modern recording.

6 | Henry VIII

A few months after the opening of *Étienne Marcel* in Lyon on 8 February 1879, Halanzier, director of the Paris Opéra, came to the end of his term of office after eight eventful years. He had successfully steered the institution through recuperation after the Commune of 1871, the fire that destroyed the theatre in the Rue Le Peletier in 1873, the company's temporary stay at the Théâtre Ventadour, and the opening of the new Garnier opera house in 1875. His strength was efficient management rather than artistic flair, and he had always accepted the general view that a master of instrumental music and a brilliant pianist such as Saint-Saëns could not be seriously considered as a composer of opera.

He was replaced by Emmanuel Vaucorbeil, a minor composer with some experience in government administration, who was much more sympathetic to Saint-Saëns and was prepared to widen the Opéra's repertoire. One of his first actions was to go to Sant'Agata to persuade Verdi to allow *Aida* to be played at the Opéra, where it appeared in March 1880. It was not its first performance in Paris, since the Théâtre-Italien had staged it in 1876, but it was a coup for the new management and an encouraging sign for the future.

Saint-Saëns was now in the position of having at last seen all his four operas staged, albeit two of them far from Paris, and having a supporter in the director's chair at the Opéra. He interpreted this as a prospect that *Étienne Marcel* would be played there and, as we have seen at the end of the last chapter, he wrote to Vaucorbeil in September 1879 to urge this course of action. There is an undated letter from Saint-Saëns to an unknown correspondent declaring: 'What is certain is that I shall never write anything for the Opéra so long as they have not played *Étienne Marcel*.'[1] We therefore have to record that at some point in the next two years this vow was broken when he agreed to compose *Henry VIII*, destined to be the first of his operas to be played in France's leading opera house.

Apart from *Étienne Marcel*, heard in Holland, and the last scene of *Samson et Dalila*, played at the Châtelet early in 1880, Saint-Saëns was not engaged in the production or performance of any operas in this period, however much his mind strayed over possible projects. He was touring a great deal, with concerts in Germany, Austria and Switzerland in February and March 1879. From there he went to Milan, where the publisher Ricordi offered him a libretto by Angelo Zanardini based on Alexander the

---

[1] RATNER 2012, p. 104.

Great, *Il Macedone*. Perhaps clinging to his plan to compose historical operas only about France, he turned the offer down. Then he had an engagement to write a work for the Birmingham Festival that year, which was at first rumoured to be a Breton opera[2] but which was in fact the choral work *La Lyre et la Harpe* on Victor Hugo's poem contrasting pagan philosophy with Christian morality.

Since his long essays on the *Ring* in 1876, Saint-Saëns had not been writing music criticism, but in July 1879 he began a series of contributions to a new journal, *Le Voltaire*, which he kept up at a steep pace until the end of 1881, with nearly forty articles of considerable substance. He appeared regularly as soloist, composer, conductor or all three, with all Paris's principal concert bodies and at all the best concert venues: the Conservatoire, the Société Nationale, the Concerts Populaires, the Salle Pleyel, the Trocadéro and the Salle Érard. The main composition to emerge during this period is the *Suite algérienne* for orchestra, inspired by his visits to that country (with many more to come), but composed mostly in France and on the road. It was first performed in Paris on 19 December 1880. Two similar exercises in local colour followed, both for orchestra: the *Nuit à Lisbonne* and the *Jota Aragonese*, echoes of his visit to Spain and Portugal in October 1880.

That trip was the third foreign engagement of the year, concerts having already called him to Baden-Baden in May and London in June. The origins of *Henry VIII* may be pinpointed to the visit to Madrid since it was there that he met, probably not for the first time, Léonce Détroyat, one of the opera's librettists. According to Bonnerot,[3] Saint-Saëns had been pondering an opera based on the memoirs of an actress at the Russian court in legendary times, with a story that turned out to be too close to that of *Samson et Dalila*. Vaucorbeil had offered him a ballet, which he refused, hoping to hold out for *Étienne Marcel*. Another idea that fitted the requirement as an episode in French national history was the story of Vercingetorix, the Gauls' heroic leader against Julius Caesar. Saint-Saëns was perhaps looking at one of the four librettos on this popular subject submitted to the 1867 opera competition, or perhaps at the one that had been offered to Bizet in 1869.

Like Ferdinand Lemaire, librettist of *Samson et Dalila*, Détroyat had not written a libretto before; in fact his career differed sharply from the Parisian *literati* regularly employed in that sphere. Born in 1829, he served in the French navy for twenty-two years, in the Crimean War, in Indo-China and especially in Mexico, where he was appointed to the Emperor Maximilian's cabinet as director of military affairs. He was able to extricate himself from that office before the disaster that overcame Maximilian in 1867, and he later reported to the French government on the Mexican débacle.

---

[2] BONNEROT 1922, p. 97. There was perhaps confusion with Lalo's *Le Roi d'Ys*, written but not performed at that point.

[3] BONNEROT 1922, p. 103.

He left the navy soon after and went into journalism. In 1870 he inherited the proprietorship of *La Liberté*, a liberal newspaper founded by his uncle-by-marriage, Émile de Girardin, and he later added other publications to his stable, including *L'Estafette*, to which Saint-Saëns had contributed in 1876. He was familiar with the prominent politicians of his time and was also on friendly terms with musicians. Keen to write for the stage (as many journalists were), he wrote or drafted a libretto about the English King Henry VIII based on a play by Calderón, *La cisma de Inglaterra* (Détroyat was fluent in Spanish), working with Armand Silvestre, a Parnassian poet whose verse was set by nearly all the composers of the day. Silvestre's main duty was versification.

With the support of Halanzier, Détroyat invited Gounod to a reading of the libretto which took place in de Girardin's salon soon after the failure of *Polyeucte* at the Opéra in October 1878.[4] Gounod liked it and must have composed some music for it, since he suggested a play-through of certain scenes with Faure singing Henry and the tenor Capoul the part of the fool (later removed). Two years later, on 19 June 1880, Gounod renounced the libretto, saying he was depressed and that it was his fault, not the libretto's, that he couldn't undertake it. Three days later he put it more bluntly, saying that the drama aroused in him no 'impulsions', only repulsions. In fact he had already undertaken to compose *Le Tribut de Zamora* (a libretto earlier offered to Verdi and turned down) before he saw *Henry VIII*, and was busy with that opera throughout this period.

Détroyat next offered *Henry VIII* to Victorin Joncières who, like Gounod, turned it down. There followed the meeting in Madrid with Saint-Saëns who was at first, he tells us,[5] unhappy with it, since it did not fit his plan for a series of operas on French history. He was evidently unhappy, too, with the rather too strident Catholic bias of the play on which it was based. He suggested writing an opera on Voltaire's *Un Orphelin de la Chine*, which has no connections with French history whatever, but Détroyat showed no interest in that.

Halanzier's approval of Détroyat's libretto was shared by Vaucorbeil, who, in his desire to mount an opera by Saint-Saëns, must have preferred the prospect of an unwritten *Henry VIII* to a revival of *Étienne Marcel*. Saint-Saëns had already turned down Vaucorbeil's offer of a ballet, as we have seen. Gounod, no stranger to operatic failures, backed the plan for *Henry VIII*, telling Vaucorbeil: 'Saint-Saëns is entitled to a flop at the Opéra'. Vaucorbeil called both Détroyat and Saint-Saëns to his office. 'There'll be no opera,' he said to Détroyat, 'unless it's by Saint-Saëns'; he then turned to Saint-Saëns

---

[4] The fullest account of the genesis of *Henry VIII* is found in THOREL 1903 using correspondence supplied by Détroyat's widow (she was the granddaughter of Sophie Gay, who held a celebrated salon some fifty years earlier). Saint-Saëns's own account, in *L'Écho de Paris*, 10 June 1909 (SORET 2012, pp. 647–48) is much less informative, with more than a hint of bitterness.

[5] *L'Écho de Paris*, 10 June 1909; SORET 2012, pp. 647–48.

(with an unspoken allusion to *Étienne Marcel*) and said: 'There'll be no opera unless it's with Détroyat.'

If Saint-Saëns was unwilling to compose *Henry VIII*, Détroyat was ready to offer him a different libretto, a work also written in collaboration with Silvestre entitled *Inès de Castro*, based in part on Camões's Portuguese epic *The Lusiads* and in part on a Spanish play by Lope de Vega, a historical subject that had cropped up regularly in operatic history. This, too, had been offered to Verdi and turned down. Vaucorbeil urged Saint-Saëns to undertake it, evidently in preference to *Henry VIII*, and the issue came to a head in March 1881 when Saint-Saëns was staying in Nice. The local paper there announced on 11 March that the composer was working on a grand opera in five acts entitled *Inès de Castro*. Alarmed, Saint-Saëns wrote to Vaucorbeil to assure him that 'a good genie who visits me often is advising me to go for *Henry VIII* rather than *Inès*.' He wrote to Détroyat's wife: 'Détroyat writes in some distress since he read in the newspapers that I was writing an opera with Silvestre with no mention of your husband. Like Socrates I have a guiding demon whom I always obey and who speaks to me when I'm alone. The demon has spoken and I am ready to do *Henry VIII* and I will never do *Inès*.' On 27 March he told Silvestre: 'It's a fact that music comes to mind of its own accord when I think of *Henry VIII* and does not come to mind at all when I think of *Inès de Castro*.'[6]

Vaucorbeil, Régnier (the Opéra's director of productions), Saint-Saëns and the two librettists then undertook a major revision of the *Henry VIII* libretto. Vaucorbeil preferred to give the part of the Queen, originally intended for Rosine Bloch, a mezzo-soprano, to Gabrielle Krauss, a soprano who had taken the leading roles in Gounod's two recent operas, *Polyeucte* and *Le Tribut de Zamora*. This reversed the usual distribution which would give the lower voice to the older Queen and the higher voice to the beautiful young Anne Boleyn.[7] As a soprano the Queen naturally draws the main dramatic interest, especially since it is her fate at the end which holds our attention.

Vaucorbeil also argued for including some elements from Shakespeare's *Henry VIII*, a major shift in the shape of the work. Assent to all these changes was hard to achieve, but the availability of singers and the necessities of the drama forced compromises on them all. Saint-Saëns was strengthened by his election in January 1881 to the Institut chair vacated by the death of Henri Reber, an indication of official recognition that he greatly valued. In May, Silvestre was telling his partner:

---

[6] BONNEROT 1922, p. 106, has the main account of *Inès de Castro*; the letter to Mme Détroyat is in RATNER 2012, p. 138. Détroyat and Silvestre's libretto *Pedro de Zalamea* was set by Benjamin Godard and performed in Antwerp in January 1884.

[7] A similar distribution is found in Donizetti's *Roberto Devereux* (1837), with the elderly Queen Elizabeth a high soprano and the younger Sara, her rival, a mezzo. In the last act of that opera Essex is heard being led to execution offstage, as Buckingham is in the first act of *Henry VIII*.

You have to accept several capital scenes from Shakespeare, then our libretto will be accepted. Shakespeare is solid reassurance for us. If you don't agree, Saint-Saëns doesn't want to miss his chance, he'll do a different libretto.

Silvestre was perhaps not aware that Saint-Saëns had already stated his definite preference for *Henry VIII*. Détroyat conceded, and the press announced that Saint-Saëns had promised to deliver the score in September and that the premiere would take place in February 1882, an unusually optimistic schedule for a big opera such as this, especially since the libretto was not finally ready until late July. The whole process by which creative artists and management had to reach a consensus on the content of the opera Saint-Saëns later described with pain in his voice: 'Both the subject and the librettists were imposed on me. Not a single scene escaped miscroscopic examination. I tell you in perfect honesty that if I had to climb once again that Calvary that was *Henry VIII* I would simply prefer not to be played at the Opéra. I will never again submit to such humiliation.'[8] Four years after he wrote these words, *Ascanio* was premiered at the Opéra.

During the year, Saint-Saëns had composed a *Hymne à Victor Hugo* intended to accompany the erection of a statue of the poet, but the work remained unplayed for three years when the public subscription failed to meet its target. To add to the tension during the period when wrangling over the text of the opera was at its height, his domestic situation was steadily deteriorating, and in July 1881 he took his wife to the health spa La Bourboule, in the Auvergne, where one day the composer disappeared without warning, leaving his wife to search for him in vain in the surroundings and to resign herself to the fact that he no longer proposed to live with her. She left the apartment in the Rue Monsieur-le-Prince while he continued to live there with ever longer and more frequent absences from Paris. There was never a divorce and he lived alone for the rest of his life, closer now to his elderly mother.

At all events, the composition of the score began in earnest in August 1881. His first move after skipping out of La Bourboule was to visit London in search of English music of the period to provide a little authenticity for the score. He visited the Royal Library in Buckingham Palace.[9]

> The librarian,[10] whom I knew, granted me access. In a large manuscript volume from the sixteenth century I found a theme of such character that it is like a skeleton of the opera [. . .] Arranged for the harpsichord, the theme was buried beneath thickets of pointless ornamentation.[11]

---

[8] Letter of 28 August 1886, cited in FAURE 1985, p. 96.
[9] The visit to Buckingham Palace was thought by Bonnerot to have taken place immediately after the Madrid meeting with Détroyat in October 1880. Rees put it even earlier, after the audience with Queen Victoria at Windsor Castle in July 1880 (REES 1999, p. 234).
[10] William G. Cusins, Master of the Queen's Music.
[11] *L'Écho de Paris*, 17 March 1912; SAINT-SAËNS 1913, p. 13; SORET 2012, p. 794.

Saint-Saëns was shown at least two manuscript collections of keyboard music from the early seventeenth century: Will Forster's Virginal Book; and Benjamin Cosyn's Virginal Book, both now in the British Library.[12] From these he copied four extracts on a bifolium, all reduced to the basic outline.[13] Two were from Will Forster's book, the first a passage from a *Grounde* (the 'Carman's Whistle') by William Byrd on f. 70 r, which he used for the scene in Anne Boleyn's quarters at the start of Act IV. The second was a part of the piece named 'The New Medley' on f. 74 r, which begins as in ex. 6.1:

Example 6.1 Anon., *The New Medley*

He copied this, adding the name 'W. Bird' (which no source of this tune provides). 'I freed it from affected ornamentation like a statuette found covered in fungus and moss', he wrote.[14] This became the opening of the opera's Prelude, ex. 6.2:

Example 6.2 *Henry VIII*, Prelude

After two four-bar passages, the virginal piece ends with the following (as copied by Saint-Saëns), which provides the second strain of the Prelude (ex. 6.3):

Example 6.3 Anon., *The New Medley*

---

[12] GB-Lbl R.M. 24.d.3 and GB-Lbl R.M. 24.l.4.   [13] F-Pn MS 823(7).
[14] Letter to Auguste Durand, 27 February 1888; RATNER 2012, p. 141.

He used this theme (ex. 6.2) again in the *Marche du Couronnement*, op. 117, composed for the coronation of Edward VII in 1902, and as an *Offertoire* for organ in 1913.

The other two passages he copied came from Cosyn's Virginal Book. The first is the opening of 'Mr Beauins Service' on f. 111v, which is the Venite from the 'Dorian Service' by Elway Bevin. The second, headed 'Te Deum', is from Thomas Tallis's 'Dorian' Service on f. 119r. Neither tune was used in the score of *Henry VIII*.

From London he went on to Edinburgh, where he might have got the idea of basing the ballets on Scottish tunes. He later copied ten Scottish tunes and one English tune from an 'old collection of Irish and Scottish music' belonging to Détroyat's wife.[15] He wrote to Détroyat from Edinburgh on 10 August:

> Don't bully our charming collaborator, let him do his good work. We're not in that much of a hurry. I didn't begin working until 4 August. It's now the 10th. Of these six days I had to give up two because I was in no condition to work. In the other four days I did the *Prélude* and the first three scenes very calmly without any haste. I stop as soon as I feel at all tired, as I always do. Taking into consideration the very difficult circumstances in which I find myself [a reference to his separation], I hope to finish the first three acts by the end of September. You can begin rehearsals then if you like, but I don't think they're planning to mount *Henry VIII* as soon as that. When I give my score to the Opéra on January 1st as a New Year's gift, it will have all it needs with nine months to go before the next season begins, time enough to make a nice little child!
>
> In Henry VIII's time they danced passepieds, gigues, gavottes and sarabandes. I don't know what they want at the Opéra, but I don't think there is any point in racking our brains about it; they will just want what 'they' get.[16]

The rest of the score followed at a steady pace, since other obligations pressed upon him as usual. No doubt he could compose on tour. In October he was in Liverpool for two concerts conducted by Max Bruch; in December he went to Brussels to review the premiere of Massenet's *Hérodiade*; in January and February 1882 he undertook an immense tour that included concerts in Leipzig, Berlin, Prague, Mulhouse, Strasbourg (the latter two cities being then German cities) and Lille. From there he went to Hamburg to conduct the first three performances of *Samson et Dalila*, the first since the Weimar performances of 1877.

A complete draft of the opera was ready by 26 May 1882, when there was a reading in Vaucorbeil's office at which Saint-Saëns would have played the work through. Singers were assigned to the various roles and the sets were ordered. All the costumes had to be freshly made. Saint-Saëns still had the task ahead of orchestrating his score, and for this purpose he rented a house at Le Tréport on the Normandy coast. He was not isolated

---

[15] Soret 2012, p. 648. His copies are on a bifolio at F-Po A640b (VI). [16] Thorel 1903, p. 2.

there, since he was near the holiday home of his publisher Auguste Durand, whose son later recalled that he was in an usually high-spirited mood, perhaps enjoying his liberation from an unhappy marriage. He had his desk set in a large bay window where he could look out over the beach.

Rehearsals began in September but the projected opening date was several times postponed. Revisions and adjustments were constant. Louis Mérante, the balletmaster, presented Saint-Saëns with a scenario for the ballets before they had even been composed. An aria had to be written for Queen Catherine to build up her part. The quartet in the final scene was added despite Saint-Saëns's initial resistance. Stage rehearsals began on December 2nd, even though the last act was not yet finalised. The autograph full score is dated 'December 1882' at the end.

The opera might then have opened in January, but a further delay was caused by Saint-Saëns's long-standing engagement to give concerts in Berlin and elsewhere in Germany. Opening was announced for 22 February 1883, then March 5th, the date which finally presented an eager audience with the work which had been widely anticipated and discussed, as major operatic events in Paris always are.

The opera was well cast. King Henry himself was played by Jean-Louis Lassalle, later to sing the roles of Benvenuto Cellini in *Ascanio* and the Grand Prêtre in *Samson et Dalila*, both at the Opéra. He was particularly tiresome in rehearsal, getting Saint-Saëns to add a high F♯ to his aria 'Qui donc commande quand il aime' and complaining to Vaucorbeil that the composer had followed 'that route where symphony reigns to the detriment of the art of singing'.[17] Queen Catherine was Gabrielle Krauss, Austrian by birth, who sang for twenty years on Parisian stages, and had starred in Gounod's *Le Tribut de Zamora* in 1881. She was triumphant in her new role and acknowledged by Saint-Saëns for her superb impersonation of the Queen. Anne de Boleyn was Renée Richard, also admired by the composer, and Don Gomez was Étienne Dereims. On the podium was the Opéra's chief conductor Ernest Altès. The stage direction was by François-Joseph Régnier de la Brière, now seventy-five, after a career as actor and director at the Comédie-Française. Saint-Saëns found him 'excellent and charming':

> What precious advice he gave me! What delightful conversation we had after those exhausting rehearsals! His refinement, his integrity, the fruit of his experience, the charm of his friendship, these are all impossible to forget.[18]

For Mérante, the choreographer:

> Choreography was a real art. I had been led to be nervous of him and he of me. He claimed to know nothing about music, and I, as a symphonist who scorned ballet, was thought to be

---

[17] Frédéric Patureau, *Le Palais Garnier dans la société parisienne 1875–1914*, Liège, 1991, cited in HUEBNER 1999, p. 221.
[18] *L'Écho de Paris*, 10 June 1909; SORET 2012, p. 648.

impossible to work with. We got on like a house on fire; working with him was a real pleasure.[19]

A five-man team of two Lavastres, Carpezat, Rubé and Chaperon were responsible for the sets, and Eugène Lacoste designed the costumes. The visual aspect presented a particular challenge, since the Tudor court had not been represented at the Opéra before, and just as Saint-Saëns had researched the music in England, so Lacoste, who declared that his work was 'primarily historical research', went over at his own expense to consult portraits and costume histories at the British Museum, the Tower of London, Hampton Court and Windsor Castle, where he was assisted by the Prince of Wales.[20]

At the second performance a few cuts were made, including the Legate's Air in Act III, Tableau 1. Further cuts were made in the course of the twenty-six performances in that season, the last on June 5th, and there were eight more performances in the winter of 1883–84. It was an undoubted success, and Saint-Saëns looked back on the production after seeing it staged many times elsewhere as one of the most satisfying of his career. The press were out in force, finally recognising that Saint-Saëns should be considered seriously as an opera composer. Few critics knew *Samson et Dalila*, so a major production at the Opéra by a Member of the Institut demanded something more searching than the glib accusations of Wagnerism and the frivolous gibes about Saint-Saëns's facility that had been their standard reaction in the past. The favourable press was reinforced by success at the box office and the general awareness that here was a great new opera to represent the French school. Edmond Hippeau's review in the *Renaissance musicale* was published as a 79-page brochure. In *Le Gaulois* on September 21st Maupassant published a story, *Une Soirée*, which tells of Maître Saval, a lawyer from Vernon, north-west of Paris, who comes to Paris to see *Henry VIII*. Falling in with a group of *bons viveurs*, he gets diverted from the purpose of his visit to a night of drinking, and he misses the last train home. This tale is enough to tell us that this was the kind of opera that provincial lawyers were anxious to see and that Maupassant did not need to name the composer. '*Henry VIII*' was sufficient for his readers.

* * * * *

La cisma de Inglaterra, by Pedro Calderón de la Barca (1600–1681), was probably written about 1627 in Madrid at a time when Spain was at war with England following the political crisis in 1623 over the issue of a Spanish bride for the future Charles I. The complications of the marriage between Henry VIII, Charles I's ancestor, to Catherine of Aragon, the Infanta María's ancestor, would have carried considerable topical resonance. Henry's decision to break with the Catholic church was forced on him when the Pope refused to accept his argument that his marriage to Catherine of

---

[19] *Ibid.* [20] See WILD 1997, pp. 214–32. The costume designs are preserved at F-Po.

Aragon was nullified by her earlier marriage, at the age of fifteen, to his elder brother Arthur, who died five months later. Having married Henry in 1509, she produced a daughter, Mary, but no son. Henry's desire to marry Anne Boleyn, one of the Queen's ladies-in-waiting, was driven by infatuation and by his determination to father a son and heir. Unable to obtain the Pope's authorisation for a divorce, since the Pope was in the power of Charles V of Spain, Catherine's uncle, he broke away from Rome, declared himself head of the Church of England, divorced Catherine and married Anne. His counsellors Wolsey, Cranmer and Cromwell played variously devious parts in these events.

Unlike Shakespeare, who in his *Henry VIII* showed no particular sympathy for the Queen, Calderón wrote from the Spanish point of view, putting the Queen closer to the centre of the drama and at the same time following Anne Boleyn's story as far as her execution. Using as his sole source the *Historia eclesiástica del cisma del reino de Inglaterra* by the fervently Catholic Padre Pedro de Ribadeneyra, he depicts Anne Boleyn as a wicked schemer and even allows Henry to feel sympathy for the Queen he has deposed. Cardinal Wolsey plays an important part siding with Anne in order to further his own aspirations to the papacy, but Cranmer and Cromwell do not appear.

The play traces Wolsey's eventual fall from power after attempting to use Anne's influence as Queen for his own advancement; it also recounts Anne's sudden fall from favour when the King discovers, by means of some letters, that Charles, the French ambassador, was once her lover. It closes with Henry's acknowledgement of Princess Mary as his heir and her refusal to promise religious tolerance, which the King rather weakly recommends, with barely a mention of the breach with Rome and the establishment of the Church of England. The King is portrayed as capricious and quick to anger, with little understanding of the manipulations of court life. Neither Wolsey nor Thomas Boleyn nor Princess Mary appear in the libretto, at least in its final form.

From Shakespeare came a number of characters and incidents. The Duke of Norfolk, the Duke of Suffolk, the Earl of Surrey, the Papal Legate Cardinal Campeius (Campeggio), Archbishop Cranmer and Garter King of Arms[21] all come from Shakespeare, not Calderón. The breach with Rome is an important element in the narrative, critical for the plot of the opera. The death of the Duke of Buckingham is directly taken from Shakespeare; so is Anne Boleyn's elevation as lady-in-waiting to the Queen. The letter that Anne has received from Don Gomez, which in Calderón is the cause of Henry's immediate repudiation of her, is cleverly turned in the libretto into a source of strength for the Queen, who has the letter in her possession and is thereby able to defy her husband to the end.

As first drafted, the libretto was based on Calderón with no input from Shakespeare. The origin of the opera was undoubtedly Détroyat's interest in Spanish literature and

---

[21] The authors appear to have thought that 'Garter' was the official's name, not his office.

theatre, and the distance the libretto came from its first form is a convincing explanation of the arduous and argumentative hours the authors, the composer and the Opéra management devoted to fashioning a viable opera libretto.

Queen Elizabeth was a familiar character in opera, having appeared in a Rossini opera in 1815, in three Donizetti operas and, more recently, in Ambroise Thomas's *Le Songe d'une nuit d'été* (in which she is wooed by Shakespeare), while her parents, Henry VIII and Anne Boleyn, were leading characters in Donizetti's *Anna Bolena* of 1830, which Saint-Saëns evidently saw with Marietta Alboni in the title role.[22] This opera treats the tension between Henry VIII's present and future queen, in that case Anne Boleyn and Jane Seymour, with Henry cast as a bass.

At first Saint-Saëns called the work of Détroyat and Silvestre an 'extravagant' libretto. A comic figure Pasquín, a *gracioso* or fool, whose interventions in the play resemble those of Shakespeare's fools, was excised, to Saint-Saëns's regret, to prevent direct comparison with *Rigoletto*. He survives in the stage directions for the ballet at the end of Act II, where 'un bouffon' informs the King that the entertainment is ready. Unlike the spoken theatre, grand opera demands public ceremonial scenes, the nearest to this in Calderón being the closing part of Act II where, before parliament, the King formally claims the invalidity of his marriage. (He also takes a swipe at 'that monster Luther'.) The Queen with great eloquence affirms her faith in the sacrament of marriage and in the Pope's authority. She refuses to leave the country, as Henry urges her to do. This is expanded in the libretto as the synod scene, Act III, Tableau 2, with the proclamation of the establishment of the Church of England, which Calderón barely mentions (except in his title).

We know from Victorin Joncières' review of the first performance[23] that a second grand scene was originally envisaged for the last, fifth act, which reflected Calderón's third act in recording the King's marriage to Anne, her fall from grace and her execution, perhaps even the King's presentation of Princess Mary as his heir (Joncières knew this from having been offered the libretto to set before Saint-Saëns saw it). All this was abandoned, so that the opera goes no further than the Queen's death, and the funeral march for Anne was put back to Act I and adopted as a funeral march for the Duke of Buckingham, whose death spreads a general fear of the King's capricious brutality.

In sum, the opera is more nearly based on Shakespeare's play than on Calderón's, and although neither author is credited in the printed librettos and scores, the opera was generally believed, at least in 1903,[24] to be based on Shakespeare. The prominence of Wolsey in both plays and his absence from the opera might invalidate a claim of either play to be the origin of the libretto, but only historians would be likely to complain that the opera needs his intervention.

---

[22] SORET 2012, p. 875.   [23] *La Liberté*, 12 March 1883, cited by HUEBNER 1999, pp. 219–20.
[24] See THOREL 1903, p. 1.

Such a thing, as understood at the Opéra at that time, required strong roles for the principal singers, opportunities for the chorus, a justification for ballet, varied and colourful, preferably exotic, decor, and a strongly emotional ending. The historical time and place were excellent for sets and costumes, and court ceremonial was always accepted as an opportunity for dancing. The libretto has two strong and well-contrasted female roles, a central baritone role for the King with a secondary tenor role for Don Gomez, who replaces Calderón's Charles, the French envoy, as the Spanish Ambassador and Anne's lover. If Wolsey had been retained, he would have been a bass or another baritone; no doubt Verdi could have handled the extra complexity, but Saint-Saëns chose not to. Above all, the Queen's fate becomes the central dramatic issue, as it was in the first two acts of Calderón's play.

* * * * *

Henry VIII
(Ratner 291)

Opéra in four acts

Libretto by Léonce Détroyat and Armand Silvestre

First performance: Opéra, Paris, 5 March 1883

Henry VIII, roi d'Angleterre	baryton
Don Gomez de Féria, ambassadeur d'Espagne	ténor
Le Cardinal Campeggio, légat du pape	basse
Le Comte de Surrey	ténor
Le Duc de Norfolk	basse
Cranmer, archevêque de Cantorbéry	basse
Catherine d'Aragon	soprano
Anne de Boleyn	mezzo-soprano
Lady Clarence, dame d'honneur de Catherine	soprano
Garter, roi d'armes	ténor
Quatre seigneurs	2 ténors, 2 basses
Un huissier de la cour	basse
Un officier	ténor

Seigneurs, juges, membres du parlement, officiers et soldats, pages, dames d'honneur, hommes et femmes du peuple, etc.

Orchestra: 3 flutes (incl. piccolo), 2 oboes, cor anglais, 2 clarinets (incl. alto clarinet), bass clarinet, contrabass clarinet (ad lib), 2 bassoons, contrabassoon, 4 horns, 3 trumpets, 2 cornets, 3 trombones, tuba, timpani, bass drum, cymbals, triangle, tambourine, tamtam, 2 harps, strings.

Offstage: Orchestre militaire.

Prélude It was rare for an opera composer to write its overture first, but in this case the Prelude was the first music to be written, based on the anonymous 'New Medley' which Saint-Saëns found in the Royal Library at Buckingham Palace, ex. 6.1. The music was not strictly appropriate for Henry VIII's time, but it suggests an earlier age in keeping with the delight in *musique ancienne* shared by a number of French composers at the time. In *Le Roi l'a dit* of 1873, Delibes introduced a gavotte and a minuet, and his music for Hugo's *Le Roi s'amuse* in 1882 consists of six dances 'dans le style ancien'. Saint-Saëns himself had composed gavottes and minuets, and in *Étienne Marcel* he included a *Pavane* to suggest a historical context. The opening strain of ex. 6.2 recalls the Gabrieli brass sound, but its repeat on strings in octaves with harp accompaniment jars with a true pre-baroque style.[25] Example 6.3 provides a balancing phrase, and the two are developed into a modern-sounding climax, out of which fragments of the theme ease the key from F to B♭ and towards the melodic outline of the first music to be heard as the curtain opens.

ACT I

Scene 1 The scene is a room in the royal palace with two large windows overlooking the public square. This is the first of six tableaux spread over the four acts, requiring different scenery for each. Act II in Richmond Park provides a broad outdoor setting, and the synod scene in Act III, Tableau 2 is intended for grandeur. The other settings are private royal apartments, with for the final tableau an interior at Kimbolton Castle where the Queen was confined.

The scene between the Duke of Norfolk and Don Gomez sows the seeds of the opera's plot. The Duke had served a similar purpose in the first scene of Shakespeare's *Henry VIII* in conversation with the Duke of Buckingham, and here in the opera he learns that Don Gomez, having met Anne Boleyn in France, is in love with her, and believes his love to be returned. Norfolk warns him that the King, who has already had Anne's sister Margaret (*recte* Mary) as his mistress, now has his eye on Anne herself; Don Gomez feels sure that Anne's love is true, and to prove it he has a letter she wrote him, now placed for safe keeping in the hands of the Queen, the Don's compatriot and patron. Norfolk warns Don Gomez that the King is not to be trifled with and, for proof, he mentions the Duke of Buckingham, whose unmerited condemnation for treason is a certainty.

The first scene introduces a number of musical motifs that will be heard later, in some cases throughout the opera. The exchanges are conducted over smoothly flowing orchestral groups, and when the Don tells of his love, he is carried away

---

[25] A different version of the scoring includes saxhorns, which were readily available at the Opéra. F-Pn MS 823(2).

on a lyrical breeze, 'La beauté que je sers est telle'. One phrase is particularly touching, ex. 6.4:

Example 6.4 *Henry VIII*, Act I, Scene 1

His *chant d'amour* has a second verse, with the Duke joining him in a coda. With new agitation and a repetitive pithy figure (ex. 6.5) in the orchestra, the Don hastens to hint that he met his love at Blois; the Duke easily guesses that Anne Boleyn is the lady in question. This is her motif:

Example 6.5 *Henry VIII*, Act I, Scene 1

Mention of the crucial love letter sends the strings into agitated dissonance with another new motif, ex. 6.6, certainly Wagnerian in character:

Example 6.6 *Henry VIII*, Act I, Scene 1

Norfolk is pleased to think that Anne's love is not available for the King to plunder, since Henry is not to be taken lightly, and definitely not as a rival in love. He needs to warn Don Gomez about Henry's character, and in doing so introduces a series of motifs to be heard throughout the opera, ex. 6.7.

Five motifs here (marked A–E) may be identified as brief indicators of Henry's character, all to be heard throughout the opera. A is surprisingly bland, perhaps for the King's charming exterior, while B is decidedly menacing. C and D betray deceit and shiftiness, and E ought to make Gomez feel uncomfortable, suggesting the King's disdain for the law.

Example 6.7 *Henry VIII*, Act I, Scene 1

Scene 2 Norfolk's warning is borne out almost at once by the sounds of unrest outside with the alto and bass clarinets generating a restless background. A number of Lords and other men enter, bringing news that Buckingham has been condemned to death, as

Norfolk had anticipated. Not one of them is in sympathy with this action, but they are nervous of their disaffection being known to the King. What might have been a murky conspirators' scene, agitated and threatening, Saint-Saëns treats more as a shocked meditation on the horror of the court's judgment. Four of the Lords have separate lines and the rest sing in subdued hymn-like homophony, and the dynamic only once briefly reaches *forte*. With his gift for apt invention, Saint-Saëns has a memorably desolate phrase circling round the Lords' thoughts, ex. 6.8:

Example 6.8 *Henry VIII*, Act I, Scene 2

and motifs B and D from ex. 6.7 are woven into the accompaniment.

Solemn brass announce the entry of the King with the Earl of Surrey. The Lords greet him with obsequious expressions of submissiveness and withdraw.

Scene 3 Norfolk introduces Don Gomez to the King. In his reply the King displays none of the severity which is so far all we know of him. He is gracious (motif A), acknowledging Don Gomez as Ambassador recommended by the Queen, at the mention of whom motif D is heard. She has told him that the Don has a fiancée in London (ex. 6.5) and that she, the Queen, has a letter the fiancée had written to the Don as proof of their love. The letter motif (ex. 6.6) would be too unsettling for Henry in this ingratiating manner, so we hear only motif A, with motifs D, C and E entering the texture. Motif A certainly suggests his dignity and beneficence, even if feigned.

Seemingly unaware that she is the Don's paramour, Henry announces that Anne is to be lady-in-waiting to the Queen. The scene passes in a gentle lilt, but the conversion of ex. 6.5 into a legato melody behind Henry's words tells us that he knows her identity all too well.

Scene 4 Don Gomez and the Duke of Norfolk then exit, leaving the King with the Earl of Surrey. In real life the Earl was the Duke of Norfolk's young son and Anne Boleyn's cousin; in Shakespeare he was the Duke of Buckingham's son-in-law working to bring down Cardinal Wolsey; in the opera he is a confidant of the King with information that the Pope is against the King's divorce and a willing audience for the King in self-pitying mood. Without the Earl present this would be a monologue, the King's main aria in the opera, in which he laments the inability of a monarch's unlimited power to control his heart, 'Qui donc commande quand il aime'. This is not quite the lament of a lonely ruler, isolated by his power, longing for the simple life, such as Berlioz had created in Herod in *L'Enfance du Christ* echoing Henry VI:

> O God! methinks it were a happy life,
> To be no better than a homely swain.[26]

This Henry is unable to command the woman he loves to return his passion, driving him to a forceful expression of despair and agitation in the middle section, but coolly contemplative of his weakness in the beautiful opening and closing sections. The end of the aria is where the singer Lassalle bullied Saint-Saëns into allowing him an extra high F♯ at the end when the composer had preferred his calmer, resigned cadence.

Scene 5 The Queen enters and Surrey leaves. The Queen is represented by a new suave phrase led by clarinets, ex. 6.9:

Example 6.9 *Henry VIII*, Act I, Scene 4

An important scene now unfolds in which the King and Queen search out weakness one in the other, concluding with the Queen's desperate admission of her vulnerability and the King's confident advancement of his plan. In Shakespeare the King and Queen confront each other twice, both times in public. Nor do they have any scene alone together in Calderón. The advantage of dispensing with Wolsey and allowing the Queen to question the King in private is here seen to give the libretto great dramatic strength.

He informs her, first, that she is offered a new lady-in-waiting, sent by the French. Catherine breaks excitedly in with 'Anne Boleyn!' He is alarmed that she seems to know her already. Repressing in an aside her possession of the letter to Don Gomez (whose mention brings a recall of ex. 6.4), she replies that the fame of Anne's beauty precedes her and accepts the offer.

In return she asks for a reprieve for the Duke of Buckingham, following Shakespeare's Act I, Scene 2. Her lines are smooth and melodious, his replies jumpy and nervous, and he becomes angry while she pours out her pleading with more and more passion until brought up short by an interrupted cadence and a dark outline of motif A on two low clarinets and a bassoon. He tells her that Buckingham was always

---

[26] *Henry VI, Part III*, Act II, Scene 5.

her enemy, which was never true. The Queen then calmly claims, over ex. 6.9, that he no longer loves her. He denies it and with the lines

> Domptant jusqu'à ma conscience
> Pour rester toujours votre époux!

obscurely implies that he would even act against his conscience in order to remain her husband. The orchestra supports this with ex. 6.10, which was first briefly heard in the opening scene when Norfolk hinted to Don Gomez that the King is in love with Anne.

Example 6.10 *Henry VIII*, Act I, Scene 4

This opens up a tense exchange over dark chromatics in which the King explains that their marriage is invalid since she was his brother's widow. But the Pope blessed our union, she insists. Despite papal infallibility, he replies 'avec hypocrisie', the book of Leviticus is clear, an argument omitted by Calderón in his desire to stress the King's respect for the Pope.

A return of motif A in its gentlest form brings honeyed words from Henry, pleading how difficult it is to respect his vows, however much he respects her, when there is no son and heir. The rest of the scene is a real duet under cover of which Henry can mention Anne by name in justifying his pursuit of her, while Catherine despairs of ever retaining his love. The conclusion is magnificent, with both singers in the grip of powerful emotions.

Scene 6 The room then gradually fills for the formal installation of Anne Boleyn as lady-in-waiting to the Queen. She is led in by Surrey, followed by Norfolk, Gomez and the lords and ladies of the court. Things get off to a delicate start when Anne and Don Gomez catch sight of each other, which Henry notices: 'So you two know each other?' he disingenuously remarks. Her motif ex. 6.5 punctuates the King's presentation. The ladies of the court salute her and the alliance with France. Catherine consoles herself that Anne's love of Don Gomez will protect her own position as Queen. The music continues its steady elegant support as the King then announces that he has named Anne Marchioness of Pembroke.

Henry and Anne continue their exchange, he declaring his passion in an undertone (originally *parlé*), she nursing the impossible dream. They seem not to notice that by superb dramatic irony the music has already announced the grim procession that will take the Duke of Buckingham to the scaffold. Everyone else crowds to the windows to see the procession pass, while Henry and Anne hang back unheard by the others. A solemn rhythm is set up by the offstage band, a rhythm that will ominously recur later in the action, ex. 6.11:

Example 6.11 *Henry VIII*, Act I, Scene 6

A complete band is required offstage, although Saint-Saëns did not specify its constitution, notating its music in the printed full score simply on two staves.[27] Its effect may be judged from the layout of this soaring theme which recurs throughout the ensemble, ex. 6.12:

Example 6.12 *Henry VIII*, Act I, Scene 6

At the start Saint-Saëns sets down a firmly rhythmic figure in slow march time, while approaching from a distance is heard a chorus of monks intoning 'De profundis'. In reply to Anne's asking what the mournful singing is about, Henry tells her that a traitor is to die, which turns her dream of happiness into a horrified vision of the axe and the block. Henry, blinded by love, cannot see the irony of her own future thus foretold. His passion has a new theme, ex. 6.13:

Example 6.13 *Henry VIII*, Act I, Scene 6

Si tu sa-vais com-me je t'ai-me! Com-me je t'ai - me!

[27] A score of the first eight bars in Saint-Saëns's hand survives at F-Po A640b(VI) requiring an immense band that the Paris Opéra could apparently provide: 2 E♭ clarinets, sopranino saxhorn, 2 cornets, soprano saxophone, alto saxophone, tenor saxophone, baritone saxophone, 2 trumpets, 3 trombones, alto saxhorn, 2 E♭ saxtrombas, 2 B♭ saxtrombas, bass saxhorn, contrabass saxhorn, side drum, bass drum, cymbals. These numbers are surprising in view of Saint-Saëns's criticism of the wearisome sound of excessive trumpets in Massenet's *Hérodiade* (SORET 2012, p. 327).

One of the highlights of the opera follows in a steadily expanding ensemble based on ex. 6.12, in which everyone laments and fears the awesome caprice of the King's power. Anne fears it too, and her phrases link with those of Don Gomez, while Henry insists that the price of treason is death. Inexorably the music accumulates towards a colossal cadence in F minor, after which the curtain falls on a frantic burst of orchestral energy.

The fact that the reason for Buckingham's death is not explained (he was a thorn in Wolsey's side) does not reduce the impact of this ensemble. Steven Huebner has argued that it has only the effect of a patchwork, pointing out that the scene's original purpose was in a final act when it would be Anne's execution taking place while Henry courts Jane Seymour in the foreground.[28] On the contrary, in its new position as the culmination of the first act, this powerful and highly operatic scene forces everyone to recognise the capricious nature of royal power and their own collective vulnerability. It is one of Saint-Saëns's finest achievements.

ACT II

The second act was the part of the opera most subjected to revision in the period leading up to the first performance. A great number of passages were cut, including the Septet with which the act was originally intended to end. Here we will discuss the opera as it was performed in 1883 and published in the 444-page vocal score.

Entr'acte An *Entr'acte* prepares the listener for the gentler milieu of Richmond Park, and its E major is a refreshing change from the flat keys that accommodate almost all of Act I. Some introductory gestures include reminders of the finale of Act I. The main section is a flute solo with harp chords in a graceful style later to represent the King and Anne's love, ex. 6.14, alternating with chant-like music, a favourite mannerism for Saint-Saëns, and leading directly into Scene 1.

Example 6.14 *Henry VIII*, Act II, Entr'acte

Scene 1 The court has moved up the river to the Tudors' favourite place of recreation, Richmond Park. The effect is similar to the change of scene from Act I to Act II of *Les Huguenots*, when dark male Parisian conspiracy gives place to open-air feminine amusements in the park at the Château de Chenonceaux. Watched by ladies and gentlemen of the court, some pages are fencing, and the song that comments on

[28] HUEBNER 1999, pp. 220–21.

their play is for a few sopranos and a few tenors, not unlike some of Meyerbeer's duets, neatly orchestrated and delicate in effect. This is one of those perfectly shaped pieces of which Saint-Saëns was a master, yet because it does not further the plot in any way it is an easy target for those who are impervious to charm for its own sake. This scene was cut in later revivals at the Opéra, and was restored when Saint-Saëns suggested that the pages could be playing ball, not fencing. He also pointed out that it made an effective contrast with the grim finale to the previous act.

Scene 2 The pages run off before the piece is over, followed by their companions, leaving the stage for Don Gomez. He is now convinced that he no longer has Anne's affections. In London she evaded his attempts to see her, and now when plague has begun to spread in the city, Henry has brought her out to Richmond, leaving the Queen behind. There was scope for a full aria here, but Saint-Saëns has given Gomez a bizarre succession of angry phrases, including a reminiscence of ex. 6.4, but the music is broken up and thin, and the shorter version that replaced it introduces the wrong mood and concludes in the wrong key.[29] This was an opportunity missed.

Scene 3 Anne Boleyn appears at the back with her ladies, who sing a charming little song in her praise, and she returns the compliment, full of images of the birds and flowers that surround them. In this act she is the central character, confronting in turn Gomez, Henry and the Queen.

Scene 4 She dismisses her companions on seeing Don Gomez, who asks bluntly what insulting treatment he is to expect from her. Still in serene mood, Anne tells him she is pleased to see him. His music is much more edgy, accusing her of rebuffing him in London. Her excuse that she was busy serving the Queen fails to convince him, and when he mentions their earlier vows of love she insists, over ex. 6.4, that she loves him still.

The published version of this duet omits over 150 bars which are found in the autograph. These prolong the furious rancour between Anne and Gomez, concluding with the conviction that their destiny is to be apart.

Scene 5 With ex. 6.5 reappearing in the orchestra, the King appears. 'You here!' he says ('cheerfully' in the first libretto, 'severely, with astonishment' in the second edition), 'paying court to the lovely Marchioness?' Don Gomez explains himself by reminding the King that he knew Anne in France, then makes a hasty exit.

Here, too, the autograph shows a prolongation of Henry taunting Don Gomez, this time seventeen bars, probably cut before the first performances.

Scene 6 Henry and Anne now have their first scene alone together, based loosely on a scene in Calderón, and the immediate appearance of ex. 6.13 in the key of E sets the

---

[29] The shorter version is printed as a supplement to the 444-page vocal score and as the main text in others. The original is in the 444-page score only.

amorous tone. Anne is firm at first, telling him to expect nothing of her. Even when you accept the honours I bestow? he asks. She explains that she feels sullied by Henry's affair with her sister. The music generates more tension as Henry piles on the argument and the ardour, while Anne can only ask him to be patient. For a brief moment they exchange lines in a caressing D♭ major, in which she admits she is touched (which may be intended as an aside, since Henry is singing too).

There follows a more formal song for Henry which Saint-Saëns himself inserted here, devising his own text:

> De tes beaux yeux, le feu brûle et m'enivre.
> De mes tourments ton amour me délivre.
> Ô ma beauté, viens ! sois à moi !
> Pour esclave, prends ton roi !

He also claimed to be the author of the lines that replaced them:[30]

> De ton regard la douceur me pénètre !
> De doux frissons il emplit tout mon être,
> Ô mon amour, crois donc en moi !
> Ton esclave c'est ton Roi !

The melody is Henry's opportunity to produce a honeyed baritone legato as the smooth-talking suitor joins the violas in ex. 6.15:

Example 6.15 *Henry VIII*, Act II, Scene 6

He sings a second verse in which Anne is unable to prevent herself joining in, just as Samson cannot hold back from joining in the second verse of Dalila's 'Mon cœur s'ouvre à ta voix'. Her intervention suggests she is weakening, even though she is begging Henry to rein in his passion.

With an abrupt recall of ex. 6.7 motif A in its agitated form, the King presses his suit (as old-fashioned opera synopses used to say). Decisively Anne insists she will not be his mistress. Example 6.7 motif D is then called in to support the King's strong reaction: 'Not my mistress! My wife!' 'But you have a queen!' she replies. Example 6.10 returns, expressing nothing less than his devious plan to replace one queen with another. Anne's transformation as she begins to take in the implications of being queen is the

---

[30] The first version is reported by THOREL 1903, p. 2; Saint-Saëns claimed the second version in a letter written in June 1909 (RATNER 2012, p. 152).

King's victory. Over soft harp chords she mumbles 'Reine! Je serais Reine!' and as the King intensifies his wooing the music slips back into E major for a reprise of the elegant music of the Entr'acte (ex. 6.14), marking the moment when she yields. The amorous duet ends with whispered vows of fidelity on both sides.

Three abandoned sections of this duet are found in the autograph.

Scene 7 The King leaves Anne alone to sing a monologue in which she can confess the naked ambition which is driving her. Although she begins in a calm tone, the prospect of the throne quickly forces the music into an Allegro more spirited and exciting than anything we have heard in the opera so far. Being Queen would be for Anne the supreme pleasure and she is not ashamed to admit it. Whether it is compatible with love is a question that fleetingly crosses her mind, but not for long.

Scene 8 She is clearly unprepared for the real Queen to appear at that moment. So are we, since Don Gomez believed she had been left in plague-ridden London. Laying a hand on Anne's shoulder, Catherine seems to have overheard the previous scene since she firmly assures her that she herself is the Queen of England. She is dignified throughout, and Anne reacts with humility, protesting that at first she tried to avoid the King. The Queen scathingly replies 'You poor child, enduring all the favours the King bestowed on you! You thought I was taken in?'

When she tars Anne with the same infamy as her sister, Anne is provoked to furious defiance. With the orchestra returning to the themes of her recent duet with Henry, she casts at her rival what might be the final stone: 'Your husband is mine!' Catherine keeps her temper by reprising her dignified music and explaining that her faith in God assures her justice in the world to come.

Although found in neither Calderón nor Shakespeare, this confrontation is excellent opera, particularly as the Queen's soprano raises her character and integrity above the mezzo's guilty intrigue. The balance of rectitude in the Queen's favour clearly stems from Détroyat's Spanish angle on the story.

Scene 9 Henry enters, furiously asking the Queen what she is doing. He clearly believed she was in London.

'I am here to remind my King that I am Queen!'
'Why? I have not yet said she is not.'
'Not yet!'
'You will be Queen, I agree, until removed by law. Rome will decide.'

The Duke of Norfolk, who is accompanying the King with a group of courtiers, announces the arrival of the Papal Legate. Catherine feels reassured. The Legate (bass) solemnly declares that in response to the King's dubious plans, he has brought an 'austere response'. He has his own theme, ex. 6.16:

Example 6.16 *Henry VIII*, Act II, Scene 9

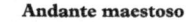

The series of scenes for one or two characters at a time that has taken the act to this point clearly needs an ensemble here to round off the act. Only the threat of the plague in London explains the Legate's unexpected appearance in Richmond Park, but clearly the announcement of the Pope's decree has to be delivered formally indoors, in the following act. So the act, as originally planned, concluded with a Septet, which survived until the rehearsal period when Gabrielle Krauss, in the role of the Queen, anxious to preserve her voice for her later scenes, sang it without conviction and it was dropped.[31] It proved too difficult to assemble all seven singers in one place for rehearsal. It survives in the autograph sources, in the Opéra *matériel* and in the layout of the vocal score, revealing that although it was always referred to as a Septet, there are eight singers taking part: Catherine, Lady Clarence, Anne, Gomez, Surrey, Henry, Norfolk and the Legate.

Without the Septet, Henry's contrived reply that tomorrow they would have time to hear him at leisure and that what they now need is entertainment is critically weak dramaturgy. The Septet does not resolve that problem, but it magnificently brings together the emotions building in the course of the act. For modern taste it provides a far better conclusion to the act than the ballets. 'The true end of the act would always be the ensemble,' Saint-Saëns wrote in 1895, 'of that there cannot be the shadow of a doubt.'[32] It appears to have been done in Moscow in that year and was tried in Milan the same year, although it remains unpublished. The ballet, which was always demanded of an opera of this kind, thus follows here.

Ballet

The *Ballet-Divertissement* consists of seven dance movements, like the ballet in Thomas's *Hamlet*. They incorporate five Scottish tunes and one English tune taken from the 'old collection' mentioned above. The seven numbers are:

1 *Introduction – Entrée des clans*
2 *Idylle écossaise*
3 *La Fête du houblon*

---

[31] Letter to Auguste Durand of 28 February 1888, RATNER 2012, p. 141.
[32] Letter to Auguste Durand, 24 December 1895, RATNER 2012, p. 145.

4 *Danse de la Gipsy*
5 *Pas des Highlanders*
6 *Scherzetto*
7 *Sarabande, Gigue et Finale*[33]

Such ballets were designed to show off not only the prowess (and the legs) of the dancers, it was the composer's opportunity to display his skill in writing for the orchestra, with some exotic colour if possible. Saint-Saëns's striking *coup* here was to announce the ballets with a brilliant passage which would, in, say, Rimsky-Korsakov, be given to a solo violin. But he has the entire violin body play, both firsts and seconds, with tremendous élan, an inimitable effect which would make any audience sit up and pay attention.

The *Entrée des clans*, presumably intended to be Scottish, begins with a well-known minor-mode English folksong, 'The Miller of Dee', treated in fantasy-style in C minor until suddenly interrupted by trumpets (onstage according to the vocal score, but not so in the full score) with a martial theme, the Scottish melody 'For the lack of gold she left me'. The folksong resumes, until the martial music in the major provides a sturdy conclusion.

The *Idylle écossaise* uses the tune 'Auld Rob Morris', also quoted in Max Bruch's *Scottish Fantasy* of 1880.

The *Fête du houblon* is the celebration of the hop-picking season, but instead of riotous beery music, Saint-Saëns represents this with a slow, elegant melody which loses its elegance towards the end when the horns and cymbals restate it with, perhaps, a few jugs of ale in their bellies.

The *Danse de la Gipsy* introduces an augmented second in the melody and a tambourine in the accompaniment, recalling the *Bacchanale* from *Samson et Dalila*. Its second half is a straightforward minor-key waltz in standard ballet style with eight-bar phrases.

The *Pas des Highlanders* is another Scottish scene, to be danced in kilts, no doubt, even if there were never any highlanders at Henry VIII's court. The themes are 'Peggy, I must love thee', heard at the beginning and the 'Duke of Richmond's March', heard at the end, with a brisk Allegro in between.

The *Scherzetto*, written for the dancer Mlle Subra, is the shortest and neatest of the ballets, with more fun and games for the violins at the end. It was originally part of the finale of the opéra-comique *Le Duc de Parme* composed in the 1850s.[34]

The *Sarabande* is pompous, unlike most baroque examples of the dance, and it leads directly into the *Gigue*, based on a vigorous Irish tune. A brief section in the middle offers a contrasting tune, probably Irish too.

---

[33] The *Pas des Highlanders* and the *Sarabande* are missing from the printed full score.
[34] Letter of 10 November 1915 to Soubies, RATNER 2012, p. 345.

ACT III, TABLEAU 1

Scene 1 The first Tableau, whose series of short scenes was cut in all subsequent versions of the opera after 1883, having already been shortened in many scenes, is set in the King's apartments. The first scene alternates angrily between A minor and F minor while the King tells the Earl of Surrey that he has no wish to see the Papal Legate, who has asked for an audience, and dismisses him.

Scene 2 In disjointed recitative the King then rages against the power of Rome. A king's duty should be his power, the law should be his conscience and God should be his Pope, and for the first time since the Prelude the Tudor tune ex. 6.2 is heard. This scene was a replacement for a monologue in which Henry confesses his passion for Anne, and as such it emphasises Henry's tough political determination instead of his amorous weakness.

Scene 3 Anne has requested a meeting to ask him to release her from her promises since it poses great dangers for him. She sees him losing his throne because of her and then blaming her. The music is broken up and agitated. The king responds by reasserting his desire for her and accusing her of having another lover (while ex. 6.6 reminds us of the perilous letter she wrote to Gomez). She appeals against such a charge with ex. 6.14 and declares that she loves only him. The ominous pulse of ex. 6.11 reveals his icy disbelief.

Scene 4 The Duke of Norfolk enters to inform the King that the Legate insists on seeing him. Using ex. 6.7 motif D to hint that he trusts his diplomatic skills in confronting the visitor, he consents.

Scene 5 The Legate enters and bows, supported by his theme, ex. 6.16. Resigned to the Legate's verdict going against him, Henry sends Norfolk to warn the Queen that judgment is near, and promises Anne a future happiness which he cannot offer now. Anne leaves with Norfolk, as ex. 6.14 sounds softly in the background.

Scene 6 The scene for Henry and the Legate is full of tension, even though the Legate's threats of dire consequences fail to break Henry's intransigeance. Kings in the past who defied Rome had been forced to seek pardon: Philippe Auguste of France, for example, and Otto of Germany. When the Legate, understanding that Henry is intent on schism (he can barely bring himself to utter the word), is then informed that a synod has been called to decide the issue of his marriage, he breaks out in rage and more threats, none of which cause the King to give an inch. The Legate is supported by ex. 6.16 throughout, and Henry by adaptations of his themes, ex. 6.7 motifs A, D and E.

Scene 7 To close the Tableau the Legate has a scene on his own in the severe key of E♭ minor. It is a prayer on behalf of the Queen and the people who will suffer from the King's intemperate action. For the Legate it is unthinkable to turn against God's will, and he will do his duty to the end, even if it means casting an anathema on the evil-doers.

ACT III, TABLEAU 2

Grand opera had set a taste for scenes in which large assemblies gather to enact critical issues of political, religious or legal business. The spoken theatre provided little precedent here, for these scenes are often dominated by the chorus. Examples of such scenes were the arrival of the Holy Roman Emperor at the Council of Konstanz in Act I of Halévy's *La Juive*, the coronation scene in Meyerbeer's *Le Prophète*, the Carthaginian festival in Act III of Berlioz's *Les Troyens*, the Wartburg scene in Wagner's *Tannhäuser*, the auto-da-fé in Verdi's *Don Carlos*, and the triumphal scene in *Aida*. There were many others. Paris audiences would not have been disappointed to find a similar scene at this point in *Henry VIII*, knowing the king's reputation for magnificence and political grandstanding.

The Synod Scene, designed to meet this very taste, is set in a large public room in Parliament where the court is assembled. The 1883 set was clearly modelled on Westminster Hall. Fanfares offstage precede a long *Marche* which allows for the processional entry of the main dignitaries. First come ushers and mace-bearers, then the Archbishop of Canterbury, then the King, then the Queen, then the judges. Anne Boleyn is not present. The music is anything but banal, treating two themes in imaginative ways and moving in a controlled crescendo to the point where the chorus take over.

The judges, sufficient in number to form a sturdy four-part men's choir, remind the public that the case in hand is serious and solemn, namely whether to break a vow of marriage blessed by the Pope. The people duly respond in agreement. Garter King of Arms declares the Synod open. Archbishop Cranmer, who is presiding, sets down the broad 9/8 pulse which is commonly called upon for such solemn moments, and leads a prayer which grows magnificently with everyone joining in, including Garter King of Arms and Lady Clarence, and the Queen's voice soars superbly over the ensemble.

Henry is summoned to step forward, then the Queen. Against a wheedling motif already heard in his private dialogue with the Legate, he addresses the court, ex. 6.17:

Example 6.17 *Henry VIII*, Act III, Tableau 2

Figure 6.1 *Henry VIII*, the Synod scene, 1883
Bibliothèque et Musée de l'Opéra/Wikimedia Commons

He demands on the authority of Leviticus to be freed from the marriage which he contracted with his brother's widow and trusts in the judges' good judgment. This speech was originally delivered by Archbishop Cranmer with ex. 6.17 active in every bar of the accompaniment, then it was later adapted for Henry's higher voice and the orchestral part thinned out.

The Queen then pleads in turn. She is very disturbed, addressing not the court but the King, with the tonality constantly shifting. But a return of ex. 6.9 settles the key and calms her mind. Her aria 'Car je ne suis qu'une étrangère' is extraordinarily beautiful, of a disarming simplicity, and for the first time drawing our full sympathy to her plight and the rightness of her claim. A harp and a solo viola at first underline the innocence of her plea, then the orchestra, still light, supports her ravishing closing phrases. The whole assembly is moved to mutter in sympathy. A more animated middle section appeals to the rectitude of King Henry VII in arranging their marriage and of the Pope in blessing it, to which the company (excluding Don Gomez and Henry) respond in a warm ensemble which continues under the reprise of her main melody.

The Queen has so powerfully and so sincerely (and so musically) made her case that the King leaps to his feet in fury, rage in his eyes. The Queen knows she is lost, unless some unknown protector can come to her aid. Don Gomez steps forward in protest at what is proposed, speaking on behalf of the King of Spain and threatening war. This has precisely the opposite effect to what he had intended. The English lords are outraged that a foreigner should threaten them, and the King seizes his chance to appeal to 'England's noble sons' to side with their sovereign. After such a show of sympathy for the Queen, this noisy outburst registers the offended loyalty of every person present.

Calmer music is provided for the judges, who have been deliberating during the hubbub, to prepare their verdict. Their spokesman the Archbishop borrows Henry's wheedling motif ex. 6.17, perhaps to remind us of Leviticus, for without any discussion or summary, to a chilling alternation of C$\sharp$ major and G major chords on the lower woodwind, he pronounces the King's marriage null and illegitimate.

The Queen's protest is angry, heartfelt and unheard. The courtiers whom she accuses of betraying her are silent. She leaves the court, followed by Don Gomez and Lady Clarence.

The proceedings are not over, for the Papal Legate is yet to be heard. It was a clever move on Henry's part to postpone the Legate's formal appearance until after the Synod had declared its judgment. Even before the exchange between the Legate and Henry in the previous tableau, in which neither gave an inch in argument, Henry had fully made up his mind. The Legate solemnly enters bearing the papal bull and supported by some cardinals. His theme, ex. 6.16, is heard in magnificent counterpoint with the march that opened the Synod.

The bull sent from Pope Clement VII upholds the validity of Henry's marriage, of course, and annuls all contrary acts. Henry defiantly informs the Legate that the people will answer for him, and the doors are thrown open to admit a rabble whom he addresses in language which might still be heard today: 'Children of England, free sons of a free country, are you willing to accept laws from a foreigner?' 'No, never!' they shout. 'Do you agree that a man based in Rome [think Brussels] should usurp my authority?' 'No, never!' Saint-Saëns wanted a supplementary chorus to crowd on stage at this point, but was never able to get it at the Opéra.

They will follow him to the ends of the earth, it seems. Demagoguery at its most powerful and effective launches a loud, fast ensemble during which Henry declares himself to be the head of the Church of England and announces that he will marry Anne Boleyn, Marchioness of Pembroke. The culmination is a full-blooded choral statement of the Tudor melody from Buckingham Palace, ex. 6.2. Just before its close the Legate, who has waited for his moment, excommunicates Henry, who remains defiantly content to let history be the judge.

ACT IV, TABLEAU 1

The mood of the music that precedes the opening of the curtain is dark and unsettled, recalling ex. 6.7 motifs B and C and ex. 6.12, while a new figure, ex. 6.18, prefigures the coming scene. The end is ominous, for the motif of Henry's passion, ex. 6.13, is swiftly followed by the dotted figure in the timpani that led Buckingham to the scaffold, ex. 6.11.

Example 6.18 *Henry VIII*, Act IV, Tableau 1

Scene 1 In Anne Boleyn's private quarters a group of lords and ladies are rehearsing a ballet in honour of the King. Anne is seated, watching them. The music is the extract from Byrd's *Carman's Whistle* which Saint-Saëns had gleaned at Buckingham Palace, played on oboe, harp and muted strings.[35] He called it a 'petit passepied'. It serves as background to a secretive conversation between Norfolk and Surrey who have observed the King's sullen and unfriendly moods since his marriage to Anne, and she, they say, now weeps a lot and is in fear of her husband. Ex-Queen Catherine has been confined to Kimbolton Castle (some sixty miles north of London) where she is in failing health. They report that the King asks after her, perhaps following Calderón's suggestion that he never really loved Anne.

---

[35] Saint-Saëns does not indicate that these players are on stage, but he would have liked them to be. See his letter to Auguste Durand of 23 February 1894, RATNER 2012, p. 144.

Scene 2 The music is cut short by the announcement of the Spanish Ambassador, Don Gomez. Anne is alarmed. The Don greets the company with ex. 6.5. He is hoping to see the King in order to give him a message from Catherine. This alarms Anne further, for fear that the fateful letter might find its way to the King.

Scene 3 Norfolk, Surrey and the dancers withdraw, so that over ex. 6.7 motifs B and C Don Gomez can explain that Catherine's message contains her vow of loyalty and love to the King.

A second motif, even more disturbed, ex. 6.18, reveals Anne's deepest fear that Don Gomez or Catherine will reveal to the King any love letter that once passed between them.

The melody that saw off the Duke of Buckingham, ex. 6.12, sounds ominously in the background. Gomez assures her that he has burned them all, including those with broken promises, he slyly mentions. One letter, though (ex. 6.6), is still in Catherine's hands, enough to cause Anne's outburst of terror.

Scene 4 Henry enters. He wishes to speak to Gomez alone. Anne, clinging to Henry's love, ex. 6.13, as a last hope, withdraws.

Scene 5 Henry needs Gomez for one thing only: to find out the truth about him and Anne. Gomez remains in England for one purpose only: to be Catherine's only remaining friend and supporter. A tender passage from the Queen's aria in the Synod scene recalls her plight. Gomez conveys the message she asked him to deliver (her lifelong devotion and love) in a brief aria of surpassing simplicity and beauty 'Ô mon Roi, bien qu'étant par vous délaissée' – E minor moving to E major – which has all the hallmarks of the Queen's phrasing and of her passion.

The King decides to go to Kimbolton, determined to wrest the secret from Catherine, who he hopes will want to be avenged on Anne. Don Gomez is fearful that the King plans 'a new crime' against his friend and compatriot. This is conveyed in a hasty duet, both singing *à part*.

ACT IV, TABLEAU 2

Catherine's quarters in Kimbolton Castle. Saint-Saëns wanted faded green, autumnal colours in the scenery, with dark-coloured furniture. As if to confirm that it was her music all along, Don Gomez's aria from the previous scene reappears now in E♭ minor as a prelude to the final tableau of the opera, followed by an echo of her aria in the Synod scene.

Scene 1 Catherine is seated by a large fireplace, while outside people can be heard celebrating the King's birthday to the Tudor tune ex. 6.2, which may now be considered a kind of royal anthem.

An interrupted cadence brings the focus indoors to the ex-Queen nursing her memories. As she sings nostalgically of her beloved Spain, Saint-Saëns resists the temptation to write Spanish music. He does the very opposite, with a solo scene of almost unbearable pathos using a recurrent 5/4 bar and the alternation of E minor and C minor harmony to convey a profound sense of sadness and loss, ex. 6.19:

Example 6.19 *Henry VIII*, Act IV, Tableau 2

[Musical notation with text: "Je ne te re-ver-rai ja - mais, Ô dou-ce terre où je suis née,"]

The aria calls for singing of perfect poise and expression, for although it is not technically demanding, it conveys the essence of the Queen's dignified suffering throughout the opera. This is where the drama has been leading, exactly as Calderón intended. Saint-Saëns disregards the two balanced stanzas of the poem with a middle section and some additional words about 'foggy England', returning to ex. 6.19 to close.

Feeling death to be near, she calls in her ladies and proceeds to give them mementos: a ring to one, a cross to another, to others jewels. She intends her Book of Hours to go to Don Gomez, and she places between its pages the letter given him by the woman who stole her husband and 'embittered his soul'. She dismisses them in order to receive a veiled lady, announced by Lady Clarence.

Scene 2 It is of course the new Queen, although Catherine is surprised to see her. This scene is superbly handled, both in text and music, rising to a bitter exchange between the two queens over music never free of tension. Anne at first surprises Catherine by asking her as a Christian for forgiveness; she is full of remorse, she was carried away by the glamour of the throne, she turned her back on her previous love. Yes, replies Catherine, I am not your only victim; the other one loves you, but you never loved him.

This is the turning point, for Anne is stung to challenge Catherine to produce the letter that proves her love for Don Gomez. It is clear to Catherine at once that this is Anne's real purpose in paying her a visit; she wants the letter back to save her own neck (ex. 6.6). The music rushes headlong forward as Anne resorts to begging for the letter. Catherine goes to the Book of Hours and withdraws the letter. She defiantly refuses to hand it over, hinting that she might pass it to the King.

Scene 3 At that moment the King suddenly appears, with Gomez. Catherine hurriedly scrumples the letter. Henry addresses both women politely, forming a melody out of ex. 6.7 motif A. Turning to Catherine, he explains that he was wrong to remove her from the throne and wrong to replace her with someone who would betray him, anger rising in his throat. He has come for the letter (ex. 6.6). In a ferocious aside over low chords on cellos and basses, he reveals that he expects jealousy and pain to make her talk. Feigning sweetness, he tells Catherine over a melody that belonged in Act II to his love for Anne that he is sure his wife is innocent; another of their love themes, ex. 6.14, joins the pretence, as he assures Anne of his love, and she, nervously, of hers. He takes her in his arms while from outside well-wishers celebrate the King's birthday.

The scene is designed to arouse Catherine's jealousy to the point where she will reveal the letter which will seal Anne's fate. Henry's song, 'Anne ma bien-aimée' (of which Saint-Saëns himself wrote the verse) is too saccharine to be real, but it stretches Catherine's forbearance to the limit. Catherine, Anne and Gomez join in, none of them reassured by the King's blandishments. It devolves into a quartet in which Henry is sure that his trick has worked, Anne and Gomez are terrified that Catherine will yield, while Catherine herself can only pray to the Almighty for guidance. When Henry repeats yet again that he has only ever loved Anne, Catherine's heart gives out. She collapses with a shriek, casts the letter into the fire, utters a few muttered prayers and dies.

Henry of course has the last word. Infuriated at failure, he has no resort but bluster and menace. 'If I ever learn that I am mocked, there always remains the axe.' As the curtain falls, Anne surely recognises the ominous timpani figure that took Buckingham to the block.

* * * * *

The strength of the opera lies in its magnificent portrayal of a tragic Queen, the model of innocence and controlled defiance. Against a forceful adversary who recognises no rein on his personal power she was always bound to be discarded, but she pleads with unwavering faith in the rightness of her cause. Centuries of belief that God would stand for those who put their faith in Him come up against the new law of Realpolitik, with its trail of destructive acts. Saint-Saëns later said that if he set the dying Catherine's despair with conviction it was because he was himself in a moribund state when he wrote it. 'I felt I was myself saying farewell to life, which is why it was done with such sincerity.'[36]

Détroyat's instinct was right to draw on Calderón for the main focus of the libretto, while Vaucorbeil was right to insist on introducing some of the lighter and more colourful elements from Shakespeare. They were all right to remove Cardinal Wolsey from the intricacies of the story. They might have called their opera *Catherine of Aragon* if her name had carried as much recognition as her husband's.

---

[36] Letter to Camille Bellaigue, 20 July 1909, RATNER 2012, p. 152.

The story is not simply the messy resolution of a love triangle. There is a tragic element to Anne Boleyn's story too, already made plain in the final scene of the opera when she sees Henry's venom beginning to turn on her. She is after all best known to history as Henry's tragic victim. Casting her as a mezzo gives her a sultry side, and showing her take the fatal steps from uneasy resistance to enthusiastic compliance gives the role depth and nuance. Greed and ambition emerge in a young girl whom we see at the start as a lady-in-waiting in love with a harmless tenor.

As for Henry himself, he knows how to turn on the charm; he almost persuades us in his first act aria that kingship is burdensome to him. He is genuinely in love, too. But his dominant trait is ruthlessness, and there must always be iron in the voice. His only selfless thought is the desire to leave his kingdom in the hands of a son and heir, since so much of Europe's ills in previous centuries arose from disputed succession. But he will stop at nothing to achieve his ends, including taking the unthinkable step of schism with Rome.

The detail of the letter which the Queen holds brings tension to the final scenes and assures her moral triumph over the other two. All three principals have great solo moments and good duets, while the grand ensembles are magnificent, especially the Synod scene, the close of Act I as the Duke of Buckingham is paraded past the window, the abandoned Septet in Act II, and the final Quartet.

An unresolved problem lies in the character of the Papal Legate, whose only purpose is to transmit the Pope's refusal to countenance Henry's divorce. More of the background is provided by his appearance with a solo aria in the first tableau of Act III, but the removal of that tableau in most versions of the opera reduces the Legate to little more than a messenger and renders his appearance in Richmond Park in Act II quaintly improbable.

Saint-Saëns relies more than before on a substantial list of motifs, most of them attached to individuals but without any special nuance. The opera is divided into scenes which run continuously. They are based on the traditional theatre practice of defining a scene by the entrance or exit of characters, but most of the scenes have a musical identity, sometimes with 'scene-motifs' that appear in the orchestral accompaniment and serve as the binding material for the scene, unlike motifs which appear throughout the opera. As in Wagner, the method is not rigorous, for motifs can appear without obvious reason. Most are apposite to their purpose, although ex. 6.7A is surely too bland a figure for such a sturdy figure as the King. The Queen has ex. 6.9 attached to some of her entries, and fleeting attachments to other motifs. The opera as a whole is an excellent example of Saint-Saëns's unfailing level of craftsmanship and taste. If he cannot engender the emotional heat that Verdi or Tchaikovsky were capable of, he is proof against banality of any kind, even in the ballets. His portrayal of the two queens is apt and sensitive throughout, and even the smaller parts of Don Gomez and the Papal Legate are well provided for.

* * * * *

A problem that was recognised from the beginning was the opera's excessive length. We have seen that many sections of Acts II, III and IV, including the Septet, were removed before the opera opened, and all revisions that were later imposed on the opera were cuts from Acts II and III, some of which may be judged beneficial for the dramatic flow.[37] The second editions of the vocal score and the libretto lack the following passages:

1) Act II, Scene 1: the very pretty song of lords and ladies while the pages play at fencing. Long operas, alas, can rarely afford such charming scenes that do not propel the action at all.
2) Act II, Scene 2: the second half of Don Gomez's scene was replaced with a smoother, less defiant, shorter passage. This revision must be early, since it was printed as a three-page supplement to the first edition of the vocal score (444 pages).
3) Act II, Scene 7: Anne's solo, ecstatic at the thought of being queen, lost its main Allegro, from 'Je vais donc enfin te connaître'.
4) Act II, Ballet 5: the *Pas des Highlanders* was cut.
5) Act II, Ballet 7: the *Sarabande* was cut, leaving *Gigue et Final*.
6) Act III, Tableau 1: the entire Tableau was cut, eighteen minutes of music.
7) Act III, Tableau 2: the judges' chorus at the opening of the Synod Scene was cut.
8) Act III, Tableau 3: Archbishop Cranmer's pronouncement of the judges' verdict and Catherine's embittered reaction were cut.

The last of these is inexplicable, since this is a crucial moment in the proceedings of the Synod. Saint-Saëns can never have agreed to it. The loss of Act III, Tableau 1 is regrettable, but despite the serious diminution of the Legate's role, the drama can accommodate it. It is a fact of opera that basses can rarely grab their audience's attention as other voices can, especially when they have no influence on the eventual outcome of the action.

A second edition of the vocal score (390 pages) and a full score were both printed quite soon after the first performances. Vaucorbeil having died in 1884, his successors at the Opéra, Eugène Ritt and Pierre Gailhard, suggested omitting Act III altogether, which Saint-Saëns naturally resisted. Finally they agreed in February 1888 to reinstate the full opera, although certain cuts seem to have remained. Saint-Saëns suggested setting the Synod Scene, which now comprised the whole of Act III, in a chapel, for which purpose he would add an organ part. In 1894 he suggested at the Opéra setting the scene in the chapel at Hampton Court instead of 'that immense set which hampered the work so badly'.

---

[37] The complexity and abundance of the sources of *Henry VIII* deserve a full textual study.

It was not many years before it became clear that this opera would find a ready audience in other cities and other countries. It eventually became of all Saint-Saëns's operas the one most frequently performed, after *Samson et Dalila*, at least during his lifetime. Liszt made several attempts to get it performed in Germany and Hungary. Translated into German, Italian and Russian, it appeared in many of the major cities of Europe. Saint-Saëns attended a great many of these, occasionally conducting and coaching the singers whenever possible. In 1895 it was staged at La Scala, Milan, with great fanfare as the opening opera of the season. In 1909 it was doing so well that Saint-Saëns wrote to his publisher: 'I fail to understand why such a work isn't in the repertoire everywhere.'[38] His original Catherine, Gabrielle Krauss, remained the touchstone for how the part should be interpreted, but her successor in the role at the Opéra, Félia Litvinne, a great Wagnerian in her day, ran her close.

The record of performances is as follows:

1883	Opéra
1884	Toulouse
	Prague
1886, 88, 89, 91, 92	Revivals at the Opéra
1887	Frankfurt (in German)
	Marseille
1889	Ghent
1895	La Scala, Milan (in Italian)
1897	Moscow (in Russian)
1898	Madrid
	Lyon
	Covent Garden, London
	Ghent
	The Hague
1900	Antwerp
	Prague (in German)
1904	Toulouse
1906	Bordeaux
1907	Cairo
	Madrid
	Barcelona
1908	Monte Carlo
	Aix-les-Bains
1909	Revival at the Opéra
1910	Covent Garden, London

---

[38] RATNER 2012, p 153.

1911	Algiers
1917	Monte Carlo
	Revival at the Opéra
1919	Bordeaux
1920	Vichy
1935	Brussels
1974	New York (with piano)
1983	San Diego
1988	Montpellier (concert)
1991	Compiègne
2002	Barcelona
2012	Bard College (concert)

In March 1884 Saint-Saëns wrote a virtuoso transcription for piano solo of the Quartet in the last scene, which he played to great applause in San Francisco in 1915.

The decline of performances after Saint-Saëns's death is very striking and the absence of the opera in the post-war period is more striking still. Barcelona's recent revival reflects the Spanish element in the story, no doubt, but Covent Garden's neglect of a sturdy masterpiece based on a central episode in English history is truly sad. The state of recordings is sadder still, since although there have been four recordings of the opera, all are incomplete, and most of them inadequately sung. Of all Saint-Saëns's operas, the urgent need of a good, complete recording of *Henry VIII* is the most glaring.

7 | Gabriella di Vergy, Proserpine

Gabriella di Vergy
(Ratner 335)

Drama lirico in one act

Libretto by Camille Saint-Saëns

First public performance: La Trompette, Paris, 14 March 1885

Alfredo	ténor
Il Conte di Vergi [sic]	baryton
Gabriella di Vergi [sic]	mezzo-soprano

piano, harp

Sometime in 1884, the year after *Henry VIII*'s successful run at the Opéra, Jules Barbier, librettist of *Le Timbre d'argent*, hosted a performance of *Gabriella di Vergy*, a 'drama lirico' for which Saint-Saëns wrote both the words and the music. This work belongs to the large body of facetious pieces that Saint-Saëns could never resist writing, and which remained mostly unpublished at his death. Of this one, the libretto was printed but not the music.[1] It originated much earlier, since Saint-Saëns wrote to Barbier in the period 1868–70, when *Le Timbre d'argent* was under consideration at the Opéra-Comique, since there was a question of performing *Gabriella di Vergy* in Pauline Viardot's salon at that time.[2] This is also the title of operas by Carafa (1816), Mercadante (1828) and Donizetti, whose opera received its first performance in Naples in 1869, after the composer's death, so it may have been news of that posthumous event that supplied Saint-Saëns with the material for his spoof. Ratner gives 1883 as the date of composition in view of the private soirée given by Barbier,[3] but it was probably put together by Barbier or Viardot and Saint-Saëns in 1869 and perhaps performed then. Its first public airing was in 1885 at the Trompette, an informal chamber music society that had been in existence since 1860 and at which Saint-Saëns was a frequent performer. It met in the Société d'Horticulture's building in the Rue de Grenelle. The piano part was played by Pauline Viardot, with a repeat three weeks later with Saint-Saëns at the piano. It was performed in private in 1893 and twice more at the Trompette in 1900 and 1905.

---

[1] The libretto may be consulted on Gallica (gallica.bnf.fr).   [2] Ratner 2012, p. 480.
[3] Ratner 2012, p. 477.

The printed libretto describes *Gabriella di Vergy* as 'a carnivalesque sketch parodying Italian opera and composed, words and music, by an elderly organist – a work of his youth'. In Donizetti's version the heroine, believing her lover Raoul to have been killed in the Crusades, marries the Count of Vergy. Raoul of course returns, with tragic consequences. The Count murders him and presents his heart to Gabriella in an urn. She dies of grief and horror.

Saint-Saëns's version for three voices with piano and harp is contained in six short, light pieces in jocular style, yet the story is inevitably gruesome. The text is Italian, with snatches of French thrown in ('Ma femme m'a trompato' sings the Count). He sings gleefully about killing Alfredo (his wife's lover's name in this version) and cutting him up. He then serves his heart up for Gabriella to eat. In horror she kills herself. As Bonnerot commented, this was an 'amusement with no pretensions and no purpose other than to provoke laughter one day and be forgotten the next'.[4]

It is, certainly, poles apart from Saint-Saëns's next operatic project, *Proserpine*, which is, of all his operas, the one that has fallen deepest into the abyss of neglect. In the near-century between 1919 and 2016, after being one of Saint-Saëns's most successful operas, not a note of it was heard except on the occasional adventurer's piano. The recent concert performances and recording have revealed it to be a work of Saint-Saëns's maturity, with a carefully crafted libretto and enough good music to excite any receptive listener. Saint-Saëns's biographers relate its history, naturally, but few have ventured to study the music and assess its achievement.[5]

It is conceived on a smaller scale than *Étienne Marcel* and *Henry VIII*, since it was not intended for the Paris Opéra. Its destination was to be the Opéra-Comique, which no longer required the cosy domestic entertainment of earlier years; the regulation requiring spoken dialogue had lapsed, and the happy ending was no longer *de rigueur*, especially not after *Carmen* and its successful revival in 1883. Recent productions at the Opéra-Comique included Offenbach's *Les Contes d'Hoffmann*, put together after the composer's death, and Delibes's *Lakmé*, both being launched on successful careers. With its four acts and its full cast of characters, *Proserpine* was nonetheless ready for any major opera house, and the two leading characters offer magnificent roles for singers prepared to accept the challenge.

Jean Bonnerot, Saint-Saëns's secretary and biographer, placed the origins of *Proserpine* in 1883, the year of *Henry VIII*'s first performance, when Saint-Saëns came

---

[4] BONNEROT 1922, p. 119.
[5] Badge of obscurity: no contributing author or sub-editor noticed that in Jann Pasler's two important books on Saint-Saëns (see Bibliography), the opera is mis-spelled *Prosperine* throughout.

across a volume of poetry by Auguste Vacquerie (1819–1895) entitled *Mes premières années de Paris*, published in 1872.[6] A close friend of Victor Hugo, Vacquerie wrote plays and poetry and worked as a journalist, including acting as one of Alexandre Dumas's many ghost-writers. He had little contact with music. This volume contained a verse drama *Proserpine* about a sixteenth-century Italian courtesan, Proserpine, so named because the Greek goddess Proserpina was Queen of the Underworld, living in darkness.

Saint-Saëns had in fact encountered the play at least three years earlier. He had had some discussion with Carl Rosa, founder of the Carl Rosa Opera Company, in London in the summer of 1880 during the same visit in which he had hoped, with Queen Victoria's support, to get *Étienne Marcel* accepted by Covent Garden. Saint-Saëns suggested to Carl Rosa the subject of *Proserpine*, but it fell on stony ground.[7] In 1913, when Saint-Saëns reprinted Bonnerot's narrative, he could plausibly have forgotten when he first read Vacquerie's play; the visit to London took place when he had not yet encountered Détroyat's *Henry VIII* and was looking around for his next libretto. He could also have forgotten what was discussed with Carl Rosa, but he would surely not have thought Gallet was involved so early, since Bonnerot explains how Gallet was brought in later. The composition of *Henry VIII* intervened. But when the baritone Victor Maurel and two Corti brothers from La Scala opened a season of opera in Paris in December 1883 as an attempt to revive the old Théâtre-Italien, they advertised for French works to be sung in Italian to alternate with Italian ones.

Remembering *Proserpine*, he put the idea to Vacquerie, who agreed. They submitted the plan to Maurel, who did not accept it for his season.[8] Early in 1884 Saint-Saëns had the opportunity to perform a work of his that had been waiting three years to be heard. This was his *Hymne à Victor Hugo*, intended to accompany the erection of a statue to the great man for which the necessary funds failed to materialise. Now he was asked by the impresario Louis Bruneau (the composer's father) if he had a work that could feature in his 'Concerts de Printemps' at the Trocadéro. The *Hymne à Victor Hugo* was performed with great splendour on 15 March 1884 in the presence of the eighty-two-year-old poet, who made only rare public appearances.

Saint-Saëns had been avoiding Hugo for some years ever since he, Hugo, suggested Saint-Saëns might set the libretto for *Esmeralda*, based on his novel *Notre-Dame de Paris* and previously set by Louise Bertin in 1837. Saint-Saëns thought little of the

---

[6] Bonnerot's account of the genesis of *Proserpine* appeared in *L'Écho de Paris* on 6 November 1911 and was reprinted in Saint-Saëns's book *École buissonnière* in 1913, pp. 63–65. Vacquerie's book is accessible on Gallica.

[7] REES 1999, p. 269; Marie-Gabrielle Soret, 'De la genèse à la réception', PROSERPINE 2016, p. 11.

[8] The operas that Maurel accepted were Salvayre's *Richard III*, Jonçières's *Le Chevalier Jean*, Eugénie Legoux's *Joël*, Diaz's *Benvenuto Cellini* and Dubois's *Aben Hamet*. In fact none of these were staged.

libretto and feigned incomprehension.[9] His *Hymne à Victor Hugo* contained a veiled mockery of Hugo's ignorance of music by quoting a popular tune for which Hugo had once provided words believing the tune to be by Beethoven.[10] This embarrassing fact was either not revealed or it was forgiven, for the concert vastly pleased the honoree, who invited Saint-Saëns to dine with him forthwith. Saint-Saëns thereafter dined 'often' with Hugo in select company that included Hugo's close friends Vacquerie and Paul Meurice (one of whose plays was to provide Saint-Saëns with the material for *Ascanio*). At one of these dinners, according to Bonnerot, Vacquerie suggested that it would be worth making a French (not Italian) libretto from his verse drama *Proserpine*. Saint-Saëns thought of his favourite collaborator Louis Gallet (author of *La Princesse jaune*, *Étienne Marcel* and *Le Déluge*), who accepted at once. There is no evidence that Saint-Saëns was thinking of another work for the Opéra. *Henry VIII* had dispelled any resentment he felt that neither *Samson et Dalila* nor *Étienne Marcel* had been played there, and although Vacquerie's poem lacked the domestic charm that Opéra-Comique audiences were assumed to prefer, it was suitable for the new conditions there.

So the plan of *Proserpine* was put to Léon Carvalho, who had been in charge of the Opéra-Comique since 1876, along with the idea of a two-act opéra-comique on Guillery, a bandit from French folklore as represented in an 1855 play by Edmond About. Having been the first to steer Saint-Saëns towards opera in 1864 by giving him the libretto of *Le Timbre d'argent* but never staging it, Carvalho might well have felt a certain obligation towards him now. He actually preferred the plan for *Guillery*, but was persuaded, perhaps by Saint-Saëns himself, to accept Gallet's outline of *Proserpine* for the Opéra-Comique in February 1885.

Gallet was at that time preoccupied with writing *Le Cid* for Massenet, not to mention *Patrie!* for Paladilhe and *Michel Columb* for Bourgault-Ducoudray, all done in his spare time from his job as a hospital administrator. An unmentioned spur behind Saint-Saëns's urge to get his next opera on the stage was Massenet's unstoppable success, with *Manon* opening at the Opéra-Comique in January 1884 and *Hérodiade* (earlier staged in Brussels) at the Théâtre-Italien (in Italian) a few days later. The Opéra put on *Le Cid* in November 1885. It had been an unsettling year. No major compositions emerged in 1885; there was a violin sonata written for Marsick and the *Rapsodie d'Auvergne* for piano and orchestra for Diémer, which Saint-Saëns played frequently in his last years, sometimes in an arrangement for piano solo.

March 1885 is the date appended to the Introduction Saint-Saëns wrote for a collection of miscellaneous essays he was preparing for the publisher Calmann-

---

[9] Saint-Saëns, 'Victor Hugo', *L'Écho de Paris*, 16 April 1911; SORET 2012, p. 704.
[10] Saint-Saëns, 'Les Faux Chefs-d'œuvre de la musique', *La Nouvelle Revue d'Égypte*, February 1903; SORET 2012, p. 574.

Lévy under the title *Harmonie et Mélodie*. The first essay in the book, written in 1879, attempts to answer the question 'What is Music?', while the second is his report on the Bayreuth Festival of 1876. Including this essay is his excuse for devoting almost the entire Introduction to the Wagner question, which in 1885 had risen to a peak of polemical warfare in the French press. Wagner's death in 1883 brought into the open an army of Wagner idolators who had previously been smarting from the ignominious rejection of *Tannhäuser* in 1861 at the Paris Opéra, but were numerous enough to force independent critics to judge every new opera on whether it conformed or not to Wagner's principles. Wagnerism was crudely reduced to four processes: the abolition of separate numbers in opera in favour of continuous music; the application of leitmotifs; the avoidance of balanced melody; and chromaticism. All four features had been evident in varying degrees in French opera for a generation or more, yet their occurrence was often attributed to Wagner's influence. We will return to Saint-Saëns's debt to Wagner in more detail in the final chapter, since all his operas were subjected to the debate to some degree. At this point in his career, just when he at last felt justified in calling himself a serious composer of opera, he was heartily sick of being at one turn accused of Wagnerism and at the next taken to task for rejecting it. His new Introduction explained that he admired Wagner profoundly, but still felt free to object to certain passages and certain features of the operas which troubled him. He sums it up as follows: 'I admire the works of Richard Wagner profoundly, in spite of their bizarrerie. They are superior and powerful, that is enough for me. But I have never been, I am not, and will never be a devotee of the Wagnerian religion.'

Harmonie et Mélodie came out in August 1885, by which time he had added a 'Conclusion' which drew attention to the closing scene of *Die Meistersinger* and its blessing of 'holy German art'. 'For those who understand the symbols,' he wrote, 'this is a call for Pan-Germanism and for war on the Latin races.' With the French press split, as one might expect, between those who applauded his courageous stand against the Wagnerians and those who felt it was unchivalrous to say such things with Wagner only recently dead, Saint-Saëns set off on a series of concert tours. In November he was touring with the violinist Raphaël-Diaz Albertini in north-east France, then in Brittany. Then he went to London to give a concert with the Sacred Harmonic Society.

In January of the new year, 1886, he was in Berlin, where on January 22nd he performed with the Philharmonic Society. The German press were ready to stir up trouble, using the publication of *Harmonie et Mélodie* to justify their belief that Saint-Saëns 'over the question of *Lohengrin* in Paris had displayed his hostility to art and to the music of the fatherland'. He was nonetheless warmly applauded by the audience, and again the next day at the Singakademie. But German impresarios began to shut their doors against him and his concerts were cancelled in Kassel and Dresden; the planned production of *Henry VIII* in Prague was postponed (until 1900). 'Now there is a Saint-Saëns question here, as there is a Wagner question in Paris,' he wrote, seeing the potential benefit of such publicity. Many German musicians who had their own reasons for disliking Wagnermania felt that he had spoken up for them too, and his future tours in Germany were barely diminished in number or less successful in acclaim. He gave well-received concerts in both Prague and Vienna on that trip.

Meanwhile he was composing two works of diametrically different dimensions. The first was a symphony, commissioned by the Royal Philharmonic Society in London; the second was another humorous piece, eventually to spread his fame to corners of the globe where none of his other works could reach. This was the *Carnival of the Animals*, a 'zoological fantasy' for two pianos and small orchestra written for a Shrove Tuesday concert at the Trompette. Themes by Berlioz and Offenbach are gently satirised, and the xylophone brings old bones to life, as in the *Danse macabre*. But humour does not exclude beauty, for amid the jokes and nudges, one of the animals, the swan, glides serenely over the water in the most perfectly crafted short piece for cello and piano that man could conceive.

Liszt, arriving in Paris soon after to prepare a performance of his oratorio *The Legend of St Elizabeth*, requested a private performance of the *Carnival* in Pauline Viardot's salon, which Saint-Saëns was only too happy to arrange. He also showed Liszt the score of his new symphony which he had decided to dedicate to the great man. Liszt died in Bayreuth a few months later.

The symphony, eventually known as his Third, or by popular assimilation the 'Organ' Symphony, was his most formidable work since *Henry VIII*. He had not written a symphony since 1859, but the Société Nationale had purposefully encouraged French composers to pay more attention to instrumental forms (ironically drawing on German models). Saint-Saëns's new symphony is unmistakably indebted to Beethoven and Schubert, yet it forms part of the sequence of French symphonies that were appearing in those years: Bizet in 1871; Messager in 1877; Debussy in 1880; Fauré in 1884; Lalo in 1885; d'Indy in 1886; and Franck in 1887. After the performance in London in May 1886 – the reception was only lukewarm – it was gradually adopted in the symphonic repertoire and has been a particular favourite for twentieth-century audiences in blatant contrast with the fate of his operas.

Early in 1886 Gallet worked on *Proserpine*, 'forgetting as much as possible that I was working for a musician. It's very amusing. It allows me to borrow large extracts from the original poem. You will let me know what you think. I must be able to tell Vacquerie that we are in agreement about this when I take him the first act.'[11]

The libretto of the first act of *Proserpine* was eventually finished, copied and approved by Vacquerie in May 1886, and the rest was delivered by July, so the composer could set to work. His first action was to go to Florence to capture a sense of the city where the opera's intrigue was to take place, although not actually identified by name. Perhaps he

---

[11] Gallet to Saint-Saëns, 14 March 1886, F-DI Dossier 1.

knew that in 1882, while composing *Manon*, Massenet had stayed in the very house in the Hague where Prévost, author of the novel *Manon Lescaut*, had lived. After a short visit Saint-Saëns settled into a house in Chaville on the outskirts of Paris in the direction of Versailles to compose the score, whose first draft bears the dates July 10 at the beginning and September 27 at the end. Gallet and Saint-Saëns were in constant correspondence, discussing details. Bonnerot paints a charming picture of the composer at work:

> It was a simple little studio at the far end of a courtyard with a garden full of irregular paths and overgrown grass, and on one side an old broken-down cemetery wall. The graves nearby made the silence the more affecting. The composer's only companion was a young cat that liked to be fondled. One day when someone brought along a three-month-old puppy for him to admire and embrace, the cat took umbrage, rolled its eyes, and fled. It didn't come back for three days.[12]

In early November Saint-Saëns played the opera through to Carvalho, and the Opéra-Comique began at once to prepare for its performance. The full score was finished on 22 January 1887 and the first performance took place on March 16th.

These preoccupations shielded Saint-Saëns to some degree from a humiliating series of events at the Société Nationale, in whose founding in 1871 he had played the major part. The society was always supposed to confine its performances to French music, but the movement to broaden the repertoire had gathered strength to the point where a vote to include foreign music in November 1886 forced Saint-Saëns to resign from his central position in the organisation. He remained as President but artistic control was taken over by César Franck, whose disciple Vincent d'Indy had been a forceful advocate of the change of statute. The issue was broader than the more specific debate about Wagner, for Brahms and others were writing symphonies and quartets that some Frenchmen (not many) were curious to hear, but the setback challenged Saint-Saëns's dedication to the future of French music and intensified his already profound dissatisfaction with Parisian musical life.

The musical director of the Opéra-Comique, Jules Danbé, conducted the performances of *Proserpine*. Charles Ponchard was in charge of the mise-en-scène, Jean-Baptiste Lavastre (who had worked on *Henry VIII*) of the decor, with Gallet himself helping with the setting of Act II. The title role was sung by Caroline Salla, who had sung Hélène in the premiere of *Le Timbre d'argent* in 1877 and whose 'magnificent voice' (in Saint-Saëns's words) was much better suited to the more dramatic part of Proserpine. Cécile Simonnet, who sang the role of Angiola, was described by Chabrier as 'gniang-nian', i.e. flabby or spineless.[13] Albert Lubert was Sabatino, and Émile-Alexandre Taskin was Squarocca.

---

[12] SAINT-SAËNS 1913, pp. 62–63.   [13] CHABRIER 1994, p. 425.

The press were, as usual, divided, with the balance of approval in Saint-Saëns's favour. Gounod's paean of praise was published two days later in *La France*, and Reyer's on March 27th in the *Journal des débats*. By other critics the libretto was harshly treated, being ridiculed as 'clumsy', 'boring', 'antimusical', even 'immoral'. The music was lifted from *Die Walküre*, one critic claimed. In *Le Gaulois* Louis de Fourcaud damned the opera with faint praise, calling the music 'grey' and 'dry', yet acknowledging the composer's skill. Saint-Saëns never forgave him for this, especially since his long review appeared the day after the performance: he had not heard the opera.[14] Saint-Saëns summed up the reception of *Proserpine* in a letter to *Le Ménestrel* written a month after the opera's opening:

> The press were unanimous that I have much talent. That's more than enough to earn my gratitude. What more could one want? That *Proserpine* should be acknowledged as possessing every quality, that all with one voice should declare it to be melodious, clever, easily understood, scenic, dramatic, moving and entertaining? That would have alarmed me. I would have been reminded of the proverb 'Children with too much spirit don't live long'.
>
> Will *Proserpine* live long? I have no idea. But it will not have passed unnoticed, and I ask no more than that.
>
> A single note of agreement has surprised me in this array of notices. It surprises me all the more since I have heard it every time I have produced works in the theatre. When my music is not symphonic or declamatory, or when it is frankly melodic, critics accuse me of giving in to public taste and being untrue to my principles and my most cherished theories.
>
> Now nobody knows what these theories and these principles are, since I have never stated them. They have been attributed to me, which is not at all the same thing.[15]

Durand & Schœnewerk published the vocal score (245 pages). After ten performances the box office was doing well, and the opera might have had a long run were it not for the calamitous fire that destroyed the Opéra-Comique on the night of May 25th during a performance of Thomas's *Mignon*; 131 lives were lost. With great presence of mind Danbé saved the score of *Proserpine*, but the choral and orchestral material was lost. Taskin was decorated for his life-saving actions, but Carvalho was found guilty of negligence, along with his chief fire officer, sentenced to prison and then acquitted. Within four years he was back in charge of the rebuilt Opéra-Comique. Although the company moved into temporary premises at the Châtelet, *Proserpine*'s scenery was lost and its run of performances was over. It came briefly to life on 9 May 1889 when the Act II finale was revived for a special gala at the Exposition Universelle.

* * * * *

---

[14] Letter to Jacques Durand, 9 March 1910; RATNER 2012, p. 179.
[15] *Le Ménestrel*, 17 April 1887; SORET 2012, pp. 376–77.

> *Proserpine*
> (Ratner 292)
>
> Drame lyrique en four acts
>
> Libretto by Louis Gallet
> after a poem by Auguste Vacquerie
>
> First performance: Opéra-Comique, Paris, 16 March 1887
>
> | | |
> |---|---|
> | Proserpine | soprano |
> | Angiola, sœur de Renzo | soprano |
> | Sabatino | ténor |
> | Squarocca | baryton |
> | Renzo | basse |
> | Orlando | ténor |
> | Ercole | baryton |
> | Filippo | 2^d ténor |
> | Gil | 2^d ténor |
> | une religieuse | |
> | trois jeunes filles | |
> | trois novices | |
>
> Seigneurs, mendiants, religieuses, soldats
>
> The action takes place in Italy in the sixteenth century.
>
> Orchestra: piccolo, 2 flutes, 2 oboes, cor anglais, 2 clarinets, 2 bassoons, contrabassoon, 4 horns, 2 cornets, 3 trombones, tuba, timpani, bass drum, cymbals, triangle, tambourine, harp, strings.
>
> Offstage: flute, viola, cello, harp, organ, bell in B♭.

'I have been accused,' wrote Saint-Saëns in 1911,

> of thinking Vacquerie was a genius. Genius! That would be saying too much, but he had considerable ability. His prose was classically pure and his verse was sonorous metal, despite oddities that were hard to admire. It was precious, unusual and always very personal. What attracted me to *Proserpine* was the degree of interior action in the drama, which is so well suited to music. By expressing what the characters themselves cannot say and by stressing and elaborating the picturesque elements of the play, music successfully presents what would not be possible without it.[16]

From a writer close to Hugo and Dumas it is not surprising to find a historical drama full of strong action, sexual intrigue and sharply painted characters. Vacquerie's *Proserpine* might be compared to Hugo's *Le Roi s'amuse* (better known to opera-goers as *Rigoletto*).

---

[16] *L'Écho de Paris*, 12 November 1911; SAINT-SAËNS 1913, pp. 65–66; SORET 2012, p. 753.

Courtesans and assassinations at the Medici court have provided material for innumerable blood-and-thunder tales, and if this story enticed Saint-Saëns nearer to what was later classed as verismo, he was ready to face the challenge of violent emotions and action. The Opéra-Comique had moved into much more serious territory, partly to distance itself from operetta, and partly in response to new ideas in the theatre; the requirements of dialogue, tunefulness and moral uplift had all been abandoned. At all events, writing *Proserpine* was a very different task to writing *La Princesse jaune* for the same theatre fifteen years earlier. This is a drame-lyrique, not an opéra-comique.

Vacquerie's drama is set in sixteenth-century Italy in order to accommodate the blunt sexual mores assumed to have been the norm at that time and place. Otherwise only the names of the characters tell us they are Italian. Gypsies could be found anywhere in Europe. Proserpine is a twenty-two-year-old woman with an insatiable appetite for sex, jewellery, wealth and so on, and strong emotional reactions to go with it. When it comes to men, she is said to refuse no one; a lord is as welcome as a fisherman.

> Oui, tous, jeune ou vieux, laid ou beau,
> Sont égaux dans son lit comme dans le tombeau.
>
> Yes, young or old, ugly or beautiful,
> All are equal in her bed, as in the grave.

Wishing to marry off his sister Angiola[17] to the young man Sabatino, Renzo imposes the extraordinary condition that although the couple are in love, Sabatino may not marry her until he has bedded Proserpine, which, surprisingly, he has thitherto failed to do, despite many attempts. Renzo believes that a young man should be 'saturé de débauche' in order to be ready for marriage and he needs to have made the most alluring catch of all. If Proserpine is so indiscriminate in her choice of lovers, Renzo wonders, why has she turned Sabatino down? Her vanity and pride, Sabatino explains, have led her to hate him. Eventually Sabatino accepts the challenge.

Alone with Sabatino, Proserpine explains that he offered to love her, the one thing that would make her turn him down. If she ever loved a man, she would kill him. When Sabatino accuses her of thinking him too poor, she is furious and throws him out. She then encounters a petty criminal, Squarocca, and offers him great rewards to do her bidding. Informed by Orlando that Renzo has gone to Turin to fetch Angiola from her convent and that Sabatino has been in love with her for two years, Proserpine's jealousy is aroused.

Near a gypsy encampment Squarocca has devised a plan for abducting Angiola while Renzo is bringing her back from her convent. Briefly in Proserpine's power before Renzo rescues her, Angiola believes Proserpine to be a gypsy who can read her palm.

---

[17] Gallet admitted he didn't like the name Angiola. 'Is it three syllables or four? How about Gelsomina, Maddalena, Margarita, or Pasqua-Rosa?' Letter to Saint-Saëns, 29 September 1886, F-DI Dossier 1.

Misfortune will come to the man you love, she warns, and to your brother too. Throwing off her disguise, Proserpine tells her that Sabatino belongs to herself. Angiola is saved by Renzo, but Proserpine hurries back to the city to find Sabatino and confesses that she has always loved him. Sabatino rejects her and when Angiola arrives, telling of her escape, they fall into each other's arms. Proserpine appears from hiding and stabs Angiola. Sabatino grabs the dagger and stabs Proserpine.

All dramatic interest in this play must reside in the character of Proserpine, who explains in the last scene the reason she had always rejected Sabatino's advances when she was always, she claims, in love with him: she never wanted him to be one of the crowd. Yet earlier she told him that love was what she was afraid of. 'If I loved you, I'd kill you' she said, revealing a bizarre psychotic condition which in the end manifested itself as jealousy of the girl that Sabatino had chosen to marry. With Proserpine ignorant of Renzo's conditions for Sabatino to marry his sister, Vacquerie fails to enmesh the behaviour of Renzo with that of Proserpine in such a way as to create a strong dramatic issue.

Saint-Saëns was drawn, as he said, to the 'interior action' of the drama and felt that music could contribute an element that enhanced the effect of the drama. With five principal characters, scope for a chorus and a complete act set in Angiola's convent that was not in the play, it makes a medium-scale opera with a strong central soprano role to represent a woman with overmastering passions and a hint of madness. Except in Act II, which Gallet wrote entirely himself, his libretto draws frequently on Vacquerie's lines, including some extended scenes.

* * * * *

ACT I

Prélude Like *Henry VIII*, the opera is divided into scenes, not numbers, each of the four acts having a prelude or entr'acte to introduce it. The first act's prelude is short, presenting at once a strange angular unison theme that will accompany Proserpine throughout (ex. 7.1). The distorted intervals will sometimes be straightened out in the course of the opera and sometimes left as they are. The string sound is blended with alternating wind colours.

The theme is left undeveloped, raw and charmless, for the moment. It is followed by some sombre chords which will serve for the opera's tragic ending and occasionally in between.

Scene 1 The curtain rises quickly on the gardens of Proserpine's palace, with statues visible between the trees, where she is entertaining a group of citizens. Before she comes in, the men have the opportunity to chatter (and inform us) about their hostess's racy way of life, a familiar theatrical device for presenting a leading figure, darkly parallelled by Hofmannsthal and Strauss when their serving women gossip about Elektra before she comes on stage. To Vacquerie's Orlando, Filippo and Ercole is added a group of eight men. The libretto includes women in the party, but they do not sing. The music is *vivacissimo* for their gossip, as they wonder who will be Proserpine's partner for the night. Since she has not been seen for a month they wonder if she is in love. 'What a grotesque suggestion!' is the reply.

Scene 2 Proserpine (soprano) enters to her theme, ex. 7.1, already sweetened with harmony and with some of its sharp edges smoothed. But she is not the lively hostess we expect. All she says is: 'Sabatino hasn't come . . .' Her words are 'parlé' but assigned to notes in the score. The gossip music resumes as the men beg her to make her selection for the evening, but she makes no reply. Orlando (tenor) and Ercole (baritone) pay formal court to her with a lovely Siciliano, classically scored for flute (Orlando) or oboe (Ercole) and harp with pizzicato strings. Proserpine's response is another dry 'Sabatino hasn't come . . .' while flutes and clarinets weave ravishing garlands around the Siciliano's tune.

Example 7.1 *Proserpine*, Act I, Prelude

Scene 3 They all follow Proserpine away into the gardens, while Renzo (baritone) and Sabatino (tenor) come forward. Their scene is held together by a skittish figure, ex. 7.2, as Sabatino's motif:

Example 7.2 *Proserpine*, Act I, Scene 3

Renzo wants to be sure that Sabatino has renounced his philandering days before he will allow him to marry his sister Angiola, currently in a convent. Renzo is puzzled that Proserpine has never been one of his conquests, doubting that Sabatino can be truly reformed until she is. While Renzo presses him hard, Sabatino protests that he is done with all that, breaking out in warmly lyrical lines (ex. 7.3):

Example 7.3 *Proserpine*, Act I, Scene 3

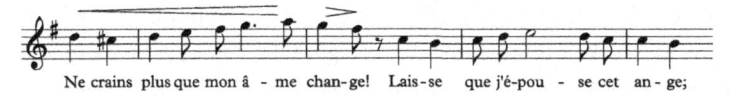

Ne crains plus que mon â - me chan - ge! Lais - se que j'é-pou - se cet an - ge;

Renzo's instructions are to 'make a proposition' to Proserpine, no more than that. Gallet avoids Vacquerie's explicit language requiring Sabatino to seduce her.

Scene 4 Proserpine returns with her admirers and her motif (ex. 7.1), and although she is privately delighted to see Sabatino, it is Renzo that she warmly greets. She has held the entertainment for his arrival. Sabatino is confused by her coldness. With reminders of ex. 7.1, the party music of the opening scene has continued to be heard until now. Having laid on a concert inside the palace, Proserpine herds her guests indoors in order to be alone. From inside we hear the strains of a Pavane, played by flute, viola, cello, harp and organ. Like the Pavane in *Étienne Marcel*, this one is in D minor and is hardly intended to be a pastiche of sixteenth-century Italian music. It is soon over, and we are to imagine it carrying on indoors while the focus is turned on Proserpine, who has the stage to herself.

Scene 5 Her monologue is a short but painful quest for the love that eludes her. Rather than compose a big aria for her, for which Vacquerie's play provided plentiful material, Saint-Saëns decided to give her a simple line supported by chromatic harmony with an occasional touch of whole-tone sound, played entirely (except for a single wind chord) by divided strings. Her words are the following:

> True love, pure source I longed to drink from,
> Will you offer yourself to my burning lips?
> Ecstatic dreams lingering in the memory,
> Hopes of a day, must it be goodbye?

But Proserpine is more than a woman searching for elusive love. She does not use this moment to explain her free-and-easy ways, nor is there any suggestion that she harbours a deep-seated desire for Sabatino or that he had ever offered her the very love she says she craves. Nor is there any hint of the murderous jealousy that will drive her later. Gallet and Saint-Saëns may have missed an opportunity here to explore the complexity of Proserpine's dark soul, preferring her to confront Sabatino at once.

Scene 6 He appears, unseen, and calls her name. Her excited response 'Lui! lui!' is unguarded, but then she remembers to behave coldly, telling him she wanted to be alone. He presses her to explain why his advances have always been refused, and what could possibly make her love him. The mention of love prompts her to explain, using Vacquerie's lines almost entirely, that the courtesan offers beauty and pleasure in return for money, horses, palaces and material things. Love needs none of those things, love needs only love in return. If she offered her soul, she would get only money in return, not love. 'You love me, you say. Take care that one day I might take you at your word.'

For a moment she resembles Carmen warning Don José to take care not to love her. But Proserpine's reason is not that she is fickle and will move on. The courtesan's life brings her the things she wants and needs; she is afraid of loving someone for fear that she would never be taken seriously. When Sabatino, missing the point, assures her he is rich, she is bitterly insulted. She may, deep down, be in love with Sabatino, but she cannot trust his feelings for her, and she is right, since, however ardently expressed, we know that Sabatino is dissembling.

Their exchanges are supported by ex. 7.1, which Proserpine sings, in its original bare form to start with, and then adapted to different harmony. Her description of the courtesan's world recalls the lively music of the opening scene. Sabatino's lines are backed by occasional recurrences of ex. 7.2, and the climax is reached when she yells 'Sortez!' at him for suggesting she is only interested in money. In an aside she swears vengeance for the insult. Meanwhile Sabatino finds Renzo, saying 'I did as you wished', leading him away. He has indeed made a proposition, ignorant of the damage it has done.

Scene 7 Proserpine has another short scene alone. This exactly reproduces the music of the Prelude with ex. 7.1 and its sombre attachment weaving under the voice. She feels a demonic rage within herself, particularly at his claim to be rich. 'If he were a beggar, I'd be a beggar too.'

Scene 8 A fearful rumbling in the bassoons heralds the entry of Gil (tenor), one of Proserpine's friends, with two others dragging in a ruffian named Squarocca. This is his motif, ex. 7.4:

Example 7.4 *Proserpine*, Act I, Scene 8

Gil had caught him breaking into Proserpine's private quarters with plans to steal her jewellery. After a short silence Proserpine tells Gil to withdraw with the two others, to their obvious surprise.

Scene 9 Proserpine has hatched a plan and sees in Squarocca her chance to put it into action. Would he prefer gaol or money? The music is a scherzo, as if Proserpine were just playing a game. Would he prefer a cell or the arms of a woman looking like her? He cheerfully chooses the latter. But she is not playing a game. Summoning Gil to untie his cords, she leads him off to join the party.

Scene 10 The light-hearted flavour of the Act I finale is caught by its principal motif, ex. 7.5:

Example 7.5 *Proserpine*, Act I, Scene 10

The formal entertainment being over, guests pour out into the garden complaining that Proserpine has deserted them. She is spotted with the ill-dressed Squarocca, whom they take to be just another of her unusual partners. Under busy light-hearted violins they wonder why Sabatino isn't there. Orlando reveals, to Proserpine's horror, that Sabatino is engaged to Renzo's sister Angiola, currently in a convent in Turin, and has been in love with her for two years. Enraged, Proserpine exhorts everyone to enjoy the fun while calling Squarocca over to instruct him in her evil design. 'If murder is what you want, my steel is ready', he assures her. Beneath the jollity and fun which Proserpine actively encourages, we can only guess what her instructions for Squarocca are to be. She leads the big tune of the closing section in which all enthusiastically join. If there are women present, they still do not sing in the chorus.

ACT II

Prélude Act II is entirely the invention of Gallet. Vacquerie's poem proceeds directly to the trap laid for Angiola on the highway, but the opera greatly profits from presenting her earlier in her convent, with the benefit of female voices in support. The Prelude is a short single statement of a broad, quiet theme, perfectly shaped, and accompanied by a constant flow of triplets in 9/8 time. The melody is confined to the woodwind, while the watery underpinning is shared by strings and murmuring horns. The tranquillity of the convent is beautifully prepared.

Scene 1 Having designed the set for this act, Gallet set out his directions precisely, as many operatic settings at that period were:

> The interior of a convent. On the left-hand side is a wall shutting off a garden with a large iron gate with ornamental grill. On the right is the cloister's arcade. Within the cloister is the entry to the chapel and the refectory. Between these two elements the space is filled in the middle by pots of shrubs. At the back a row of pomegranate trees in bloom. Beyond the shrubs, which have gaps through which can be seen alleys with hedges clipped in the sixteenth-century manner, are the trees of a great garden. Here and there can be seen the

continuation of the convent buildings. It looks bright and sunny. Only the cloister is in a soft shadow. On that side the branches of some tall plane trees overshadow a table and some stone seats. The iron gate on the left is available for entrances. It leads into the convent's entry courtyard.

Angiola is surrounded by novices in white wearing red scapulars and by inmates of the convent, while nuns in white wearing black coats come and go through the iron gate into the cloister.

From the chapel can be heard the Ave Maria being sung in three parts with organ accompaniment while the swaying figures from the Prelude provide anchorage between the lines of the chant. A chant-like theme is then heard, seeming to represent Angiola in her convent surroundings, ex. 7.6.

Example 7.6 *Proserpine*, Act II, Scene 1

In fact we have heard this melody before, in the previous act, when Sabatino carelessly suggested to Proserpine that love was something too chaste for them to be discussing. He had Angiola in mind without daring to mention her.

Three young girls (inevitably reminiscent of the three boys in *Die Zauberflöte*) tell Angiola that a blue-eyed knight with a dark moustache is to be her husband. Three novices join them asking Angiola if she loves him?

Angiola (soprano) replies with naïve sweetness that it may be a mirage that vanishes. Her brother, she believes, does not want her to marry. The six girls find that hard to believe and urge her not to give up hope, all sung in a ravishing flow of six parts. A distant bell rings the noon angelus, calling them all away. A nun takes Angiola aside to tell her that her brother Renzo is on his way. Angiola's pulse quickens with a mixture of anticipation and anxiety.

Scene 2 Renzo embraces his sister and assures her that she will not be condemned to the cloister. Example 7.2 is heard, to remind us of Sabatino. What would her many suitors think? He has in fact brought one, a 'sinner cleansed' by Angiola's goodness.

Scene 3 He gives the word and, to Angiola's undisguised delight, Sabatino appears at the grilled gate with ex. 7.7 prominently heard in the orchestra.

He may have been in love with her for two years and she with him, but they have evidently not yet acknowledged their love. Their greeting is rather formulaic. Renzo assures her that Sabatino has 'seen the devil face to face and returned unscathed'.

Example 7.7 *Proserpine*, Act II, Scene 2

Sabatino addresses her in an aria in E♭ major 'Comment dire bien'. The aria depicts the blameless exterior Sabatino is now required to present, with special touches from solo viola and solo oboe.

Angiola replies demurely, and Sabatino at last reveals a little ardour. To ex. 7.6 Renzo instructs him to give her the ring. Saint-Saëns ignored Gallet's request, in the libretto, for a 'symphonie brève' and a 'scène muette' here. It is too soon for a love duet, so Renzo leads into an ensemble in which Sabatino and Angiola are close in sentiment and harmony, generating some real warmth and allowing each of the lovers a top B♭. The trio is short, but no longer than it needs to be.

Renzo instructs Sabatino to return and prepare for their arrival in town. A brief snatch represents the carriage that will take them there, ex. 7.8:

Example 7.8 *Proserpine*, Act II, Scene 3

He and Angiola are to stay three days more. A bell tolls. Angiola explains that this is to summon poor people for their daily alms of food.

Scene 4 All the inhabitants of the convent appear with food and wine and set it out on the table. Beggars and pilgrims of all ages come through the grill gate and line up for the distribution. Among them is Squarocca, who on Proserpine's orders has passed himself off as a pilgrim of Saint-Jacques. The bustle of the scene is well represented by a busy cello figure under the repetitive woodwind, ex. 7.9:

Example 7.9 *Proserpine*, Act II, Scene 4

Novices, nuns and Angiola as givers and the poor as recipients make up a many-voiced ensemble in which ex. 7.9 is constantly active. On turning to the major a new Verdian theme is heard, ex. 7.10:

Example 7.10 *Proserpine*, Act II, Scene 4

A middle section gives respite to the cellos by recruiting the violas for the lower element of ex. 7.9. Sabatino is in raptures watching Angiola serve the needy. Squarocca has spotted her, appreciating her beauty as good reason for Proserpine's jealousy. He addresses her with admiration and a blessing, and Angiola replies by asking him to pray to St-Jacques for them. Renzo leads the swooning Sabatino away and the ensemble resumes its proper key with the cellos back on duty. A page of elegant counterpoint makes a suitably sacred close to a superb ensemble which lingers happily in the memory.

ACT III

Act III was remodelled four years after the first performances, but we will consider its second version later. As originally composed, it is set in the mountains where Squarocca plans to kidnap Angiola on her way from the convent in Turin to the unnamed city where the action takes place. The set shows the interior of a broken-down hut used by smugglers and herdsmen. A stormy sky can be seen through a gash in the wall.

Prélude The Prelude sets the tone with agitated strings providing backing for a wild flute figure, ex. 7.11, answered by grumblings in the cellos and basses.

Example 7.11 *Proserpine*, Act III, Prelude

Scene 1 Proserpine is revealed crouching by the fireplace. She is dressed as a gypsy with a heavy hood to hide her face. Squarocca, still dressed as a pilgrim, appears with news of his visit to the convent, and in reporting that Angiola is beautiful beyond words, his own temptations are clearly implied, especially as ex. 7.10 backs his report. He continues with ex. 7.12, always associated with Proserpine's jealousy:

Example 7.12 *Proserpine*, Act III, Scene 1

Squarocca: Un doux regard voilé d'ombre, mais où l'on sent que le feu de l'a-mour

That is not what Proserpine wants to hear; she is more concerned with the plan for the girl's abduction. Squarocca explains that the coachman bringing Renzo and Angiola is one of his friends who will arrange for the carriage (ex. 7.8) to suffer a broken trace nearby while two more of his friends offer to help. In the dark the travellers will take refuge in this very hut, and thus fall into their hands. As the music builds up with ex. 7.11, rushing chromatic scales and a storm outside, Proserpine interrupts to imagine Renzo captured and tied to a tree on the highway, to be rescued by passers-by, while Angiola remains her captive. Example 7.12 underlines her jealousy. The moment has arrived, so Squarocca leaves a lamp by the window and goes off.

Scene 2 Proserpine finally has a full-length scene to herself. Since her instincts are the central motivation of the opera, we need to consider the text here. It also explains the choice of name for the opera's central character.

> Oh, I used to have only love. Now it is burning jealousy! Was I not tormented enough before? Must I suffer every single pain one by one? My destiny is fixed. What does it matter whether Angiola marries him or not? If she were dead, would I not still be a girl? No, no. It kills me to think of him giving her his name and marrying her. Perhaps it is only spite. He would love me if he could know me. No, I will give myself to him, he alone will possess me! Could he not be mine instead without sharing? A curse on whoever comes between us! I will be avenged! I want to be the only one in his heart!
>
> O goddess of the underworld, whose name I share, my dark royalty is twinned with yours. O my sister, we are two queens away from the sunlight. You are far from the daylight, I am far from love, mine is a similar suffering!

Example 7.12 provides support to begin with. Proserpine's disordered state of mind is clearly represented by the scene's rapid changes of key and time-signature, not settling, as an aria might, into any firm material or idea until she invokes Proserpina, goddess of the underworld, when ex. 7.11 and some powerful syncopations bring the scene to an end. Saint-Saëns has no doubt intentionally avoided extending this scene any longer than minimally necessary, perhaps to move the action forward.

Scene 3 Squarocca's return is sooner than she expected. The carriage has stopped on the road nearby, so now they wait for the travellers to knock. To give signs of life and guide them in, he sets up the light and launches into a boisterous drinking song, in the spirit of the Song of the Flea in *La Damnation de Faust*, which might be compared to Eustache's boozy song in the opening scene of *Étienne Marcel*. Here, though, Squarocca is not given the opportunity to sing a second verse since he hears Renzo and Angiola approaching.

Scene 4 Proserpine reacts to the sight of Angiola with admiration loaded with jealousy (ex. 7.12). Her face is concealed. Squarocca has thrown off his pilgrim's cloak and is not recognised by Renzo or Angiola. Picking up some straps and ropes he takes Renzo out to repair the carriage leaving Angiola to have her fortune told by Proserpine, who explains that her face is hidden since she is the 'Unknown, the future that never shows its face'. Angiola's curiosity about gypsies is aroused.

Scene 5 Proserpine takes Angiola's hand and pretends to read in it that she is coming from a convent and that an important event, changing her name and a charming young man await her, facts she already knows. Sinister alternations of augmented and minor triads over soft drumrolls do not alarm the innocent Angiola, but Proserpine's sudden outburst 'If he loves you, beware!' terrifies her. A fiery new theme conveys Proserpine's outburst, ex. 7.13:

Example 7.13 *Proserpine*, Act III, Scene 5

Allegro non troppo

Le ciel dit a - na - thème à vo - tre ma - ri - a - ge!

'Go back to the convent, renounce your marriage', Proserpine yells, threatening harm to both Sabatino and Renzo. Angiola recovers her strength and defiantly accuses Proserpine of being no fortune-teller. When Angiola proclaims 'Il m'aime', Proserpine, having thrown off her gypsy disguise, promises blood and misery (ex. 7.13) for both her and Sabatino. This is a splendid high-octane duet.

Scene 6 Angiola calls out for Renzo for help, but it is Squarocca who comes in, while ex. 7.13 continues over a rumbling bass. Proserpine instructs him to deliver Angiola to her the next day and leaves precipitately, intending to get back before her captive gets there.

Scene 7 Shots are heard, and Renzo rushes in. Squarocca breaks out of the hut, leaving the fainting Angiola to be revived by her brother. But Renzo's soldiers apprehend

Squarocca and drag him back in (in the libretto the soldiers enter with Renzo and seize Squarocca inside the hut). Squarocca switches to the comic tone and the jumpy phrases he had adopted in his drinking song, pleading that he is just an ignorant fool and even flattering Angiola with honeyed words and with the advice to beware of the woman who addressed her earlier. Who is she, demands Renzo. 'La Proserpine!' Squarocca replies, escaping with a leap as the curtain falls.

ACT IV

Entr'acte The Entr'acte is a four-minute orchestral movement of a strongly agitated character which vividly describes Proserpine's haste to get back to town. The main idea is an original galloping figure that persists until a return of ex. 7.1 on flute and clarinet brings a measure of calm, at least until the thunderous timpani return. The music moves restlessly from key to key but begins and ends in a fiery A minor. It was intended to cover the scene change without an interval. Saint-Saëns tellingly reported that the entr'acte failed in its effect in 1887 since it was played after an interval and thus became a prelude which felt too long.[18] This lends support to the notion that an entr'acte in nineteenth-century French opera is usually intended to cover a scene change without an interval. Saint-Saëns is certainly careful to distinguish between 'entr'acte' and 'prélude'.

Scene 1 The curtain opens on Sabatino's modest quarters in the city prepared for a celebration or reception of some kind. He has the scene to himself, gazing out of the window and reflecting on the joy of his impending marriage to Angiola, 'that virginal soul', after all those 'damaged hearts'. He is turning his back on the life of indulgence for a purer, chaster love. This is a short aria with each vocal phrase lovingly shaped and designed for a lyric tenor with superb control.

Scene 2 The first four notes of ex. 7.1 announce both Proserpine and trouble. She loved him once, she now explains, but rejected him for fear that she would herself be rejected. 'I suffered from imagining that on that dreadful day when you would possess me, I would be for you, as for everyone else, nothing but an unclean vessel to be tasted and thrown away.' She has come in a last attempt to convince him that she loves him. But Sabatino is adamant, insisting that she leave. 'We have to live or die together,' she warns him, as he shows her the door, all the more urgently since Angiola's carriage is heard arriving. A scene which started with a certain tenderness in the music becomes gradually more heated and tense. Proserpine at one point recalls her moment of fury in Act I when she felt insulted by Sabatino. This time she is hurt because he refuses to believe her assertion of love.

[18] Letter to Auguste Durand of 26 December 1891, RATNER 2012, p. 174.

Once he has gone from the room, Proserpine hurries back in, takes a quick look from the balcony and then hides in the window curtains.

Scene 3 Coming in with Sabatino, Angiola breathlessly explains that she had been lucky to escape, as Renzo will explain. For the moment the lovers are absorbed in each other, building towards a duet in which Proserpine, audible from her hiding place, contributes a third voice full of menace. The lovers meet in octaves and rise to a high B at the cadence, at which moment Proserpine emerges from behind the curtain and stabs Angiola, who falls lifeless to the ground. Sabatino grabs the dagger and stabs Proserpine in turn. She still has some breath in her, begging Sabatino for a word of pity, which he refuses. As a stupefied Renzo hurries in, Proserpine enigmatically tells him: 'It is I who killed her – and I who killed myself.'

* * * * *

As early as August 1887 Gallet was proposing to enlarge Act III, and this led eventually to an important revision of the text. Both Vacquerie and Gallet were involved in the discussion. Saint-Saëns's later operas all survive in one basic version, but *Proserpine* exists in two distinct versions, of which the second was clearly preferred by the composer, since after 1895 it was adopted in all revivals during his lifetime, most especially when the opera was revived at the Opéra-Comique in 1899. Perhaps the prospect of Carvalho's return to the helm of that theatre encouraged Saint-Saëns to think that *Proserpine* might be revived there. The fact that the choral and orchestral material, lost in the fire, would have to be made again may have supported Saint-Saëns's urge to make a new version, especially if he felt it needed major repair. When he said he undertook the work 'par acquit de conscience',[19] he had clearly been harbouring concerns about the viability of the opera in its original version.

He started the revisions in Ceylon on his long eastern travels at the beginning of 1891, presumably after discussions with Vacquerie and Gallet before he left Paris. By March 19th, writing from Cairo, Saint-Saëns reported that the revisions were done, with only orchestration still required. He made the necessary modifications for the vocal score which was issued by Durand as a 'nouvelle édition' in August 1892 (234 pages). Having resumed direction of the Opéra-Comique in May 1891, Carvalho did not take the opera back into his repertoire, so Saint-Saëns hoped it might be taken up by the Opéra instead, offering to add some extra ballet. Since he was already in discussion with them in advance of their performances of *Samson et Dalila* in November 1892, the prospect of a revival of *Proserpine* there was not good. Lyon showed some interest but did not take it up. It was in Toulouse in December 1894 that *Proserpine* was first heard in its new form. He had an excellent cast there, Lemotte as Proserpine, Galand as Sabatino and an unnamed baritone as Squarocca, 'a true bandit, a Hercules who could knock

---

[19] Letter to Auguste Durand of 1 April 1891, RATNER 2012, p. 174.

policemen over'. Durand now printed the full score to match the new version of the vocal score.

It was mainly Act III that was affected by the revision, although there were changes in Act IV, including, importantly, the end. Act III is now set outdoors in a gypsy encampment in the mountains, so it is the exterior of the hut that is visible to the audience. At curtain-up gypsies are dancing a spirited tarantella in F♯ minor (Scene 1). Squarocca appears, greeted in familiar fashion by the gypsies. Although both men and women are present, only the men sing. 'On te croyait perdu, on te croyait pendu' ('We thought you lost, we thought you hanged'), they say, but he has no time to recount any recent escapade since he needs their aid in support of a woman, a princess ('as I am a marquis') who pays well. They respond eagerly and move off. The tarantella returns and concludes in F♯ major. 'Poor Franck being no more of this world,' Saint-Saëns wrote, 'I felt I could venture into that key, which was respectfully reserved for him during his lifetime.'[20]

A letter to Durand from December 1891 reveals that Saint-Saëns would have been willing to add a ballet at this point, in addition to the tarantella, if the Opéra were to show any interest in mounting *Proserpine* (which they weren't).[21]

Proserpine appears in gypsy costume and the existing music for the beginning of this act is adapted for a new exchange with Squarocca, including ex. 7.11, the recall of ex. 7.10 and ex. 7.12 (Scene 2). The scene is shorter than before, since Squarocca agrees to deliver Angiola to her without spelling out his plan for holding up her carriage and without any mention of Renzo. He goes off leaving Proserpine alone (Scene 3). The words of her solo scene are now:

> Why did I come? What can I expect? To separate them? If I could do that and even if she were to disappear would I get him to love me? Would I be any nearer to my crazy dream? Would it efface the past? O, if he had loved me, what treasure he would have found in my submissive heart! What a pure, gentle, heavenly home I would have made for this long dreamed-of love! In my misery I often thought of accepting him as he offered himself to me. I am at the limit, I have suffered too much, and faced with inexorable fate my pride is near to giving in . . . I have no more strength . . . To be young, to be beautiful, their queen they call me, and yet not to be able to love!

The passage from 'Ah ! s'il m'avait aimée' to 'Leur reine, disent-ils, et ne pouvoir aimer !' is twice as long as before and better constructed, since it moves from an Andante to an Allegro molto, and, in parallel, from B major to B minor. The Andante is particularly beautiful, ex. 7.14:

---

[20] Letter to Auguste Durand of 19 March 1891, RATNER 2012, p. 173.
[21] Letter to Auguste Durand of 26 December 1891, RATNER 2012, p. 174.

Example 7.14 *Proserpine*, Act III, Scene 3 (version 2)

[Musical example: Andante, dolce molto espressivo, with vocal line and piano accompaniment. Text: "Ah! s'il m'a-vait ai-mé-e, Quel tré-sor en mon cœur sou--mis il eût trou-vé! Quel-le re-trai-te pure, et douce, et par-fu-mé-e, J'au-rais faite à l'a-mour si lon-gue-ment rê-vé!" Markings include (strings) ppp, dolce, (fl.), ppp.]

Her scene ends with the invocation to Proserpina goddess of the underworld as before. This version spells out more clearly Proserpine's frustration at having long loved Sabatino yet never believing that he could love her.

The act continues as before, except that Proserpine has to go into the hut to fix a lantern to the door. Squarocca sings his drinking song, and Renzo appears with Angiola, whose palm Proserpine pretends to read (Scenes 4 and 5). The end of the act (Scene 6) was revised so that when Angiola calls out for Renzo to rescue her, Squarocca appears (Scene 7) and is instructed by Proserpine to hold Angiola captive and deliver her to her tomorrow. Proserpine rushes off. Over a final orchestral tutti shots are heard outside, Renzo rushes in with some soldiers, Squarocca is arrested and Angiola is freed. The earlier, faintly frivolous ending was dropped.

The entr'acte before Act IV was omitted in the revised version, and so, being omitted from the printed full score of the opera, was published separately as an orchestral work in 1909. In the confrontation between Proserpine and Sabatino (Scene 2) the crucial admission 'I suffered from imagining that on that dreadful day when you would possess me, I would be for you, as for everyone else, nothing but an unclean vessel to be tasted and thrown away' is effectively strengthened. A little later her elaborate declaration of love is reduced by some fifty bars to a simple but brutally frontal 'Je t'aime!'

Perhaps the most important change in the revised version concerns the ending. Emerging from her hiding place, Proserpine is prevented from stabbing Angiola by Sabatino. Renzo comes in at that moment. But she manages to stab herself and to hold on to life long enough to sing 'My misfortunes are over; with grim vividness I can feel death put my troubled heart to sleep. Be happy . . .'

This is certainly an improvement on Vacquerie's dénouement and on the first version of the opera where Proserpine gratuitously kills Angiola, and then claims to have killed herself, even though it was Sabatino who stabbed her. On balance the revision may be judged an improvement throughout, although the addition of a gypsy tarantella in Act III barely makes up for losing the unusual entr'acte before Act IV. The excellent Palazzetto Bru Zane recording of 2017 adopts the revised version but includes both tarantella and entr'acte.

* * * * *

The Toulouse performances of 1894 were followed by more in Nantes in 1895 and Lyon in 1896. The most significant revival was at the Opéra-Comique, the opera's original home, in November 1899, the management of that theatre having by then passed from Carvalho to Albert Carré, nephew of *Le Timbre d'argent*'s librettist Michel Carré. The building had been recently rebuilt. During the remainder of Saint-Saëns's life *Proserpine* was regularly played both in France and abroad. In the years leading up to the First World War it was being staged frequently enough for Saint-Saëns to think that it had finally reached the status of a successful opera. In Paris it was staged at the Trianon-Lyrique in 1911 and at the Gaîté in 1914 and again in 1919; in the provinces: Monte Carlo and Aix-les-Bains in 1910, Marseille in 1912; abroad: Cologne in 1903, Milan in 1900, Berlin in 1914, Alexandria in 1902, Cairo in 1903, Brussels in 1913, Lisbon in 1914. Never yet, it appears, in Britain or the United States. And the silence since 1919 lasted almost a century, until the concert performances in Munich in October 2016 (issued as a recording by Palazzetto Bru Zane in 2017) revealed the great vitality of the opera.

* * * * *

The impact of the opera rests largely on the personality of Proserpine, who is revealed in the course of the opera to have a heart, in fact a wounded heart, even though there is little in the first two acts to suggest that she is anything other than a courtesan with a reputation for indiscriminate sexual affairs. Such women were known as 'horizontales', while Renzo refers to her as 'cette universelle'. Her two solo scenes in Act I give no warning of what truly drives her. But elsewhere there are a few hints of her obsession with Sabatino and it is important that they make their mark. In the first scene her friends wonder why she has not been seen for a month and ridicule the idea that she might be in love, which of course she is. In the second scene her only words are 'Sabatino n'est pas venu', spoken twice, while she ignores everyone else, and in Scene 6 she responds to his arrival with an ardent 'Lui! lui!', after which she 'immediately affects an icy tone'. Careful stage management can ensure that these moments are not lost, otherwise her behaviour in the last two acts will seem arbitrary and unmotivated.

With excellent judgment Gallet and Saint-Saëns altered the conditions Renzo imposes on Sabatino in order to allow him to marry Angiola. Vacquerie's Renzo has the far-fetched idea that Sabatino must be completely versed in debauchery in order to turn his back on it and be fit for marriage, while the opera's Renzo requires Sabatino merely to show, from a last attempt, that Proserpine will never yield to him. In that way he can declare that his days of promiscuity are over.

The invention of Act II set in Angiola's convent, not part of Vacquerie's drama, contributes much to the variety of colour the opera needs, introducing women's voices, an attractive set and an atmosphere of solemnity that throws Squarocca's dark dealings into sharp relief. Squarocca himself is an assassin in the mould of Sparafucile, with a jovial side that comes out in his drinking song. We may question his competence, since although he does manage to deliver Angiola into Proserpine's hands, he is immediately arrested by Renzo's men and then disappears from the opera.

It is hard to measure Sabatino and Renzo as in any way distinct from other operatic tenors and supporting baritones, but Angiola, otherwise an innocent young soubrette, shows a steely and surprising resistance to Proserpine in their confrontion in Act IV. Proserpine herself stands out as a role that needs superb acting and singing as well as an understanding of the complexities of her behaviour. She has the stage to herself several times in the course of the opera, but only in Scene 2 (revised as Scene 3) of Act III does she fully unburden herself of her obsessive love for Sabatino and hint at the violence that lies not very deep beneath the surface. In confrontation with Sabatino she dissembles, allowing anger and later jealousy to replace what should have been tender passion. There is no tenderness in her since her deep-seated feeling for Sabatino knows no half measures. This is a tale where all might have been well if only she had made her feelings known to Sabatino earlier, but that, as she explains herself, was impossible so long as she could not trust him to love her in return.

In the music Saint-Saëns does not depart from his now well-established style and technique. It is fluently chromatic while still firmly based in a tonal language, as his music would remain until his last days. The division of the opera into scenes corresponds as before to the entries and exits of main characters, and is sometimes treated as a musical unit. More often material from one scene will overflow into another, since the themes are recurrent. They are motifs with or without clear illustrative function, although Destranges in 1895 identified eleven motifs with names in the manner of Wagner's analysts in the 1890s. He thus named separate motifs for 'aspiration to love', 'conjugal love', 'rejected love' and 'true love'.[22] Most of the motifs are heard in the

---

[22] DESTRANGES 1895, p. 40.

orchestra, seldom in the voices. Destranges judged *Proserpine* to be a Wagnerian work because of the presence of leitmotifs and because of 'the fusion of music and drama'. But it can hardly be said too often that all operas present 'the fusion of music and drama' to some degree and that leitmotifs had been a linking technique in almost all nineteenth-century opera. 'Whereas Wagner brings leitmotifs to the forefront,' Saint-Saëns wrote, 'I make them the background, giving the foreground to the vocal parts, treated *vocally* as far as stage realism will allow. In *Proserpine* especially this system is taken to an extreme. That's what no one has yet deigned to notice.'[23] Saint-Saëns worked in total independence from Wagner despite his critics' determination to draw Wagner into the discussion. Would that it were no longer necessary to do so today.

Proserpine has had strong admirers. Destranges put it on a level with *Carmen*. Charles Koechlin, a faithful admirer of Saint-Saëns, singled out *Proserpine* as one of his best operas.[24] Reynaldo Hahn, writing in 1911, considered the second act to be 'a perfect masterpiece, one of the most polished and exquisite scenes in music of any time' and singled out a number of scenes elsewhere in the opera as especially successful and moving.[25] Saint-Saëns himself believed that its future could be as bright as that of *Samson et Dalila*, and that its vitality would sooner or later become clear.[26] He later said that the opera was 'dramatic, melodious, (highly) symphonic, moving, amusing and unusually literary.'[27] 'I am more convinced than ever of the quality of *Proserpine*. In a large theatre with a full opera company, the small roles taken by proper artists, a strong orchestra, and a sumptuous and accurate production, it would be *very beautiful*. But will we ever see that?'[28]

---

[23] Letter to Camille Bellaigue, 18 November 1910, RATNER 2012, p. 181.
[24] Michel Duchesneau in PASLER 2012, p. 329.   [25] *Le Journal*, 12 November 1911.
[26] Letter to Auguste Durand of 1 December 1894, RATNER 2012, p. 175.
[27] Letter to Jacques Durand of 5 February 1910, RATNER 2012, p. 179. The wording is suspiciously similar to his letter to *Le Ménestrel* written after the premiere and quoted earlier.
[28] Letter to Auguste Durand of 6 January 1903, RATNER 2012, p. 177.

8 | *Ascanio*

Saint-Saëns was as quick to move on to his next opera after *Proserpine* as he had been after the premiere of *Henry VIII*. He was now over fifty years old and the composer of six operas, all of which had been staged, none of which could be called a failure. Common gossip could no longer keep representing him as a 'symphonist' with no right to be composing for the stage. If anything, it was symphonic music that he was neglecting. The first four operas were dormant, it is true, but *Henry VIII* had been performed at the Opéra in three of the previous four seasons and *Proserpine*'s run at the Opéra-Comique was cut short not by lack of public support but by the calamity of the theatre's destruction.

The Opéra needed new repertoire, as always, since their recent French novelties – Reyer's *Sigurd*, Massenet's *Le Cid* and Paladilhe's *Patrie* – were not sufficiently successful to be revived every season. The coming centenary of the Revolution in 1889 was in everyone's mind as a year of special celebration, with another Exposition Universelle planned on an even bigger scale than before and the mighty wrought-iron limbs of the Tour d'Eiffel already beginning to take shape on the Champ de Mars.

A new director was in place at the Opéra. Having presided over the premiere of *Henry VIII*, Vaucorbeil, the director, died in office in December 1884 to be succeeded by the partnership of Pierre Gailhard and Eugène Ritt. Gailhard, a bass-baritone who had sung such roles as Mephistopheles and Leporello at the Opéra, was to occupy this position with various partners until 1907. He mostly took charge of artistic matters while Ritt looked after personnel and the books. As before, all composers with a claim to performance at the Opéra needed the good will of these men, since the theatre's prestige remained high and its state-funded resources were enormous, even if its artistic record in the last years of the century was not particularly distinguished.

Following concert tours to Russia and to London in early 1887, Saint-Saëns composed a series of smaller works: a *Morceau de Concert* for horn and orchestra; a part-song *Les Guerriers*, full of patriotic energy; and a remarkable song for soprano and orchestra, *La Fiancée du timbalier*, on a poem by Victor Hugo. This moving piece reveals Saint-Saëns's instinctive feeling for dramatic irony as the drummer's fiancée watches the parade of returning troops with her fiancé not among them.

At the same time he was in discussion with the Opéra about *Henry VIII*, since the directors wanted him to reduce the four acts to three to allow them to mount it with an independent ballet. He refused to revise the opera, but gave permission for performances of Acts I, II and IV in their original state. At the same time the question of a new opera was raised. The ink was scarcely dry on the score of *Proserpine* before the ever-productive Gallet was hawking new ideas to his obedient composer: Soulié's 1837 novel *Sathaniel*, perhaps, or Dumas's 1856 novel *Orestie*? Another idea was called *Brunehilda*. This could not possibly have been considered, not so much because of Wagner, whose *Ring* had already been performed and published, but because of Reyer's *Sigurd*, well known to Brussels and Paris audiences, in which Brunehild is the leading character. Gallet persuaded Ernest Guiraud to accept it instead, and it came into the world in 1895 as *Frédégonde*, a substantial part of which was composed after Guiraud's death by Saint-Saëns himself.

Another libretto was called *Dourgha*, taken from a Breton legend of Arthurian provenance. Rather than risk the Wagnerian label by taking on a legend of doubtful origin, Saint-Saëns was still hoping to create a series of operas on the history of France, which made a third subject, *Agnès de Méranie*, a possibility. Her story was touching and dramatic, for she was married to Philippe-Auguste of France in 1196 and had three children by him. But Philippe had repudiated his previous wife, and although Pope Celestine III turned a blind eye, his successor Innocent III, two years later, placed France under an interdict, eventually forcing Philippe to take back his first wife. Agnès died soon after.

This story, involving a rejected older queen, a young, beautiful, new queen and papal intervention, was too similar to that of *Henry VIII*, even though in this case it is the young queen who is the tragic figure. It was at least French. It had already provided some background for Bellini's *La Straniera* in 1829 and for a play *Agnès de Mélanie* by François Ponsard in 1846. The story which Gallet and Saint-Saëns did decide on in July 1887 was of a similar caste, since it was based on a play by a contemporary of Ponsard, Paul Meurice (1818–1905), staged at the Théâtre de la Porte St-Martin on 1 April 1852 and called *Benvenuto Cellini*. Saint-Saëns had known Meurice since childhood, as Meurice's first wife was a friend of Saint-Saëns's mother; he never said he saw the play, but he had been thinking about it for some time. He knew that the actor Mélingue made a big impression by sculpting a statue himself every night on stage.

This was to be Saint-Saëns's third successive opera set in the sixteenth century, and it provided again, as in *Henry VIII*, opportunities for colourful costumes and decor, scenes of royal magnificence, a ballet divertissement and some strong roles: three leading women and two leading men, with two kings and an assortment of minor figures and incidents. The principal dilemma is created by a love-chain in which a woman loves a man who loves another woman who loves (and is loved by) another man who is loved by a third woman. Saint-Saëns was intrigued by the idea of four different kinds of love. The action follows some sections of Cellini's autobiography later than those depicted in Berlioz's opera *Benvenuto Cellini*, which had been a failure at the Opéra in 1838 and not seen in France since. In Meurice's play Cellini and his apprentice Ascanio are working for François I at the French court in 1539. Playwright, librettist and composer corresponded through the summer months before submitting a scenario to Gailhard and Ritt, who accepted this proposal.[1] A contract was signed on 26 September 1887 requiring the finished score to be submitted by 1 August 1888 in order to be staged during the Exposition Universelle of 1889.

Preferring now to distance himself from Paris when he had a major work on hand, Saint-Saëns left for Algiers in November 1887 and set to work at once. The first draft of Act I begins with the date 17 November 1887. 'I began my big work today,' he wrote. 'I've found a very quiet spot which is perfect, and it's very hot.'[2] He found the task 'terribly difficult'.[3] The libretto is in seven scenes, or 'tableaux', so for the purposes of providing a five-act opera as required at the Opéra, the last four scenes were paired as Acts IV and V. By the time the opera was orchestrated, it was the first four scenes that were paired as Acts I and II, so in our analysis we will for convenience's sake refer to Tableaux and not to Acts (see Table 8.1).

Table 8.1 Ascanio: Acts and Tableaux

Tableau	Draft		First version		Second version	
1	Act I		Act I	Tab 1	Act I	Tab 1
2	Act II			Tab 2		Tab 2
3	Act III		Act II	Tab 1	Act II	
4	Act IV	Tab 1		Tab 2	Act III	
5	Act IV	Tab 2	Act III			
6	Act V	Tab 1	Act IV		Act IV	
7	Act V	Tab 2	Act V		Act V	

The first tableau was finished in twelve days and the second on December 14th. In the new year, 1888, Saint-Saëns returned, after a brief visit to Paris, to Algiers to resume work. He took a villa on a hill overlooking the city and devoted himself exclusively to the opera, leaving only to listen to local café musicians in the evenings. 'I still had a voice then,' he later remembered, 'and I recall the pleasure I took in singing the aria Benvenuto sings while carving the statue of Hebe! I put my heart into it, drawing on all the resources of an organ which was the best I had at my disposal.'[4] He orchestrated the first tableau and then pressed on with the draft, composing the third tableau between the 3rd and 18th of March. He then jumped to Tableau 6, finishing it on April 18th.

---

[1] In a tribute to Gallet written in 1911, Saint-Saëns singled out Ritt as the one who specifically asked for a new work (*L'Écho de Paris*, 12 November 1911; SORET 2012, p. 752).
[2] Adolphe Jullien, *Musiciens d'aujourd'hui*, Paris, Librairie de l'art, 1892, p. 322.
[3] Letter to Gallet of 17 November 1887; DANDELOT 1930, p. 117.
[4] *Excelsior*, 26 October 1921; SORET 2012, p. 1073.

Before tackling the final scene the crucial issue of the casting had to be resolved. In Cellini's memoirs he tells how he cast his statue of Perseus, throwing everything he could find into the furnace, including his own finished treasures, when metal ran short. Both Meurice and Gallet were keen to adapt this for a different statue, but in the end Saint-Saëns decided against it, partly because it was one of the most effective scenes in Berlioz's opera, partly because Cellini's role was already long enough, and partly because he feared the audience would leave after it, missing the final action of the opera. So the final tableau, without the casting, was finished on May 6th. He then went back and finished Tableaux 4 and 5 on May 12th. The ballets were, as usual, left for later. Saint-Saëns and Gallet were in steady correspondence throughout this period.[5]

Saint-Saëns returned to Paris (via Toulouse) at the end of May 1888 and finished the piano reduction of the opera in order to have it ready for rehearsals and for Durand to engrave. He then returned to the orchestration: Tableau 2 in July; Tableau 3 in August; and the rest was finished on September 28th. The title of the opera was now changed to *Ascanio*, to avoid confusion with Berlioz's opera. In order to write the ballets he took a room in the Allée de l'Observatoire, near the Luxembourg. He would go there every day from his apartment in the Rue Monsieur-le-Prince, taking with him some carrot soup with a meat extract and 'un petit appareil à l'alcool' for his lunch. Saint-Saëns and Gallet made a trip to Fontainebleau to plan the setting for the divertissement, selecting the 'Jardin des Buis', the box garden, as the best spot. Saint-Saëns also searched for sixteenth-century tunes in the Bibliothèque Nationale. He completed his draft for the ballets on 16 November 1888.

Rehearsals had already begun in August, and in October it was announced that Jean de Reszke would sing the part of Ascanio and the American soprano Ada Adini would be the Duchesse d'Étampes, a part for which Saint-Saëns would have preferred Emma Calvé. There were some concerns about Adini's pronunciation of French. Jean-Louis Lassalle, one of the leading baritones of the time, who had sung the role of Henry VIII, was always cast as Benvenuto Cellini.[6] Saint-Saëns had secured Renée Richard, who sang Anne Boleyn in *Henry VIII*, for the mezzo-soprano part of Scozzone. Rehearsals at the Opéra ran in parallel with Gounod's *Roméo et Juliette*, originally staged at the Théâtre-Lyrique in 1867 and then transferred to the Opéra-Comique in 1873. The management had persuaded Gounod to revise his score for the bigger house and conduct the performances himself. But while Jean de Reszke was signed up as Roméo, no satisfactory Juliette could be found despite a search that went on for months. In October the great Adelina Patti, like de Reske at the height of a starry international career, became available and was immediately assigned the role of

---

[5] The discussion of *Ascanio* in this correspondence (held at F-DI) is more detailed than that surviving for the genesis of any of the other operas. It deserves a more detailed study than is possible here.

[6] In 1902 Lassalle made a recording of 'Enfants, je ne vous en veux pas' from Act IV.

Juliette. It opened on November 28th to rapturous applause. Saint-Saëns wrote an enthusiastic review in *La France* with particular praise for its two principal singers.[7] It was immediately decided to present this as the Opéra's contribution to the 1889 festivites and pass it off as a 'new' opera.

On January 13th of the new year, 1889, the *Ménestrel* reported that *Ascanio* rehearsals were continuing and that the opera could be staged soon, but Renée Richard became ill and her putative replacement, the Belgian Rosa Bosman, had just had a baby; and since de Reszke's contract ended on May 1st, it would be too late to open in April. A week later it was announced that because of casting difficulties *Ascanio*, once earmarked as the new opera for the Exposition, was indefinitely postponed. It was on occasions like this that Durand, Saint-Saëns's publisher, seems to have been less aware of his role of promoter than he should have been. His rivals Heugel, Choudens and Hartmann were all more active in support of their own composers.

These alarms registered only feebly in Saint-Saëns's mind, since on 18 December 1888 his mother died, aged seventy-nine. Despite his long absences and constant travelling in recent years, he was deeply attached to her, and her passing had the effect of alienating him yet further from Paris and from its tribe of professional musicians, many of whom he disliked. He was now less often to be seen at the Opéra or on the boulevards. He left his apartment in the Rue Monsieur-le-Prince and went to La Seyne-sur-mer and Tamaris, both on the Mediterranean coast near Toulon, for a couple of months. From there he went to Algiers in March 1889. Bonnerot describes this period as 'long months of forgetfulness, drained of thought, during which he struggled to revive, all work being impossible. His only occupations were walking, siestas in the sun, reading old copies of *La Revue des deux mondes*, and especially his correspondence with Gallet.'[8] The only work he could manage was the orchestration of the *Ascanio* ballets.

In the composer's absence the Opéra directors were in no hurry to bring the opera forward. When the Exposition opened on May 7th, Saint-Saëns was still away. He was not there a week later when the Opéra-Comique opened its special offering in the company's temporary home in the Place du Châtelet: Massenet's *Esclarmonde*, written for and featuring the American star Sybil Sanderson. With its splendid Byzantine costumes and the dazzling coloratura of the soprano, this was one of the Opéra-Comique's most elaborate efforts, and it attracted audiences in thousands. It ran for ninety-nine performances before the end of the year with a few more in 1890 to reach a hundred performances, with Sanderson singing in every one.

By June Saint-Saëns was back in Paris to attend the resumption of rehearsals of *Ascanio*. Mmes Adini and Richard took part, along with Martapoura, who sang the Mendiant, and Muratet, who perhaps sang one of the kings. Lassalle was

---

[7] *La France*, 30 November 1888; SORET 2012, pp. 393–96. [8] BONNEROT 1922, p. 136.

absent.[9] Saint-Saëns would not have minded missing the first performance of César Franck's Symphony in D minor given by the Société des Concerts on February 17th nor, for different reasons, the three performances of his own Third Symphony in March and April. But he was there on June 20th when his symphony opened the first main concert of the Exposition conducted by Jules Garcin. On September 5th the Opéra-Comique offered excerpts from a dozen different operas, including the second act finale of *Proserpine*. His music was performed, too, by a number of choral societies and wind bands. Perhaps he heard the Russian music presented by Rimsky-Korsakov in two concerts in June. He studied the musical instruments on display at the Exposition, including the Javanese gamelan so admired by Debussy, and wrote three long articles on them for *Le Rappel*, a journal edited by Auguste Vacquerie. For the November issue of *L'Artiste* he wrote an even longer article on 'Drame Lyrique et Drame Musical'.

One of the leading events of the Exposition was the competition for a cantata to be staged with a painted decor and some dancing in the Palais de l'Industrie three times in September when awards were to be given out. The winner was Saint-Saëns's friend Augusta Holmès with her *Ôde triomphale en l'honneur du centenaire de 1789*. It was performed by 900 singers and an orchestra of 300, conducted by Colonne. Throughout her career Holmès had to contend with criticism which either put her music down as inherently feminine or accused her of assumed, and thus false, virility. Her *Ôde* was roughly handled in the press, as usual, while Saint-Saëns applauded the work for its skill and integrity, and wrote her a short poem which contained the lines:

> La haine est le plus grand hommage ; soyez fière
> De l'avoir mérité.

> Hatred is the highest tribute; be proud
> To have earned it.

The Opéra was staging *Roméo et Juliette*, but without Adelina Patti. Her place was taken by Emma Eames and, at the end of the run, Nellie Melba, who had made her European debut in Brussels the year before singing Gilda in *Rigoletto*. The Opéra's repertoire, perhaps intended to be a retrospective of the previous half century, consisted otherwise of revivals of *Guillaume Tell*, *Les Huguenots*, *Le Prophète*, *L'Africaine*, *La Juive*, *Rigoletto*, *Aida*, Paladilhe's *Patrie*, and *Le Cid*. Saint-Saëns could at least take comfort that *Henry VIII* received eight performances during the Exposition in its revised form, always coupled with a ballet. There was no effort to present a new work other than Ambroise Thomas's ballet on Shakespeare's *Tempest*. Throughout the year the press were keen to know what had happened to *Ascanio* and why rehearsals kept being interrupted. After June Saint-Saëns was given nothing but vague promises. In July he went off to the south of France and in September Renée Richard left the company to work in Russia. At the

---

[9] *Le Ménestrel*, 9 June 1889.

end of December the *Ménestrel* published a furious article directed at the management of the Opéra who had contracted to stage *Ascanio* in 1888 and were now complaining that Gallet and Saint-Saëns were impatient to see the work come to life.

Saint-Saëns devoted a good deal of time at this period to closing up the apartment in the Rue Monsieur-le-Prince and divesting himself of many of his possessions. He gave them to the city of Dieppe, where his father's family came from, whose municipal authorities placed it in the city's castle museum, the origin of the present-day Saint-Saëns archive kept there. He kept his music library and left it on deposit at the offices of the piano- and harp-maker Erard. For the immediate future he had no plans for a permanent home in Paris or anywhere else. As winter approached, furthermore, he felt his usual hunger for a warm climate for the sake of his ever-delicate health.

In October 1889 he therefore left for Spain, visiting Malaga, Granada and Cadiz, where he finished one of the few compositions of the period, the *Scherzo* for two pianos, with its main theme based on a whole-tone scale, a piece which he played on many occasions in later years. On November 30th he wrote to Gallet to tell him that in the year since his mother's death he had not been able to find the peace of mind he sought; he was going to disappear without leaving any address and cut himself off from all but his closest friends. He sent Gailhard and Ritt his instructions for the staging of *Ascanio*, which they were to obey without making any changes at all. He reviewed possible names for the singers to be engaged with Gallet's approval, and he entrusted the supervision of rehearsals to Guiraud. *Lohengrin*, he pointed out, had been first staged in Weimar without Wagner, and *Aida* in Cairo without Verdi. *Ascanio* could be staged in Paris without Saint-Saëns.

And it was. For five months he lived quietly in Las Palmas in the Canary Islands under the name of Charles Sannois, 'business man'. He was at pains to keep his identity secret, pretending to be not very good at the piano. He read a lot, and spent more time writing poetry than music. This helped him clear his mind on metaphysical matters which had become more troubling since his mother's death. In the Canaries, he later said, 'I found the complete calm which I absolutely needed.'[10] Anecdotes about his stay in the Canaries are abundant, but insights into his state of mind are hard to come by beyond what can be gleaned from a volume of poetry, *Rimes familières*, which he published soon after. He also wrote a 'bouffonnerie antique', *Botriocéphalus* ('Tapeworm'), a one-act comic dialogue between a faun and a fury which was published in a later edition of *Rimes familières* and was performed in Ismailia in 1891, at the Odéon in Paris in 1902, also in Béziers in that year.

Eventually he was bound to be recognised by the islanders, since his picture appeared in the French press, and eventually he was bound to resume his professional life, half in Paris, half elsewhere. His absence from Paris was not itself worthy of note, but the fact that almost no one knew where he was encouraged wild speculation. Some even said he was dead.

---

[10] *Excelsior*, 26 October 1921; SORET 2012, p. 1073.

Saint-Saëns's absence was particularly mystifying when, first, *Samson et Dalila* appeared for the first time in France thanks to Henri Verdhurt, director of the Théâtre des Arts in Rouen, and second, *Ascanio* received its first performance at the Opéra three weeks later, on 21 March 1890. It suggests either that he was indifferent to the reception and even to the quality of the performances, which he could have supervised in rehearsal, or that he was perfectly confident that both operas would be properly done and well received. With so little correspondence despatched from the Canary Islands, even to Durand or Gallet, we have few ways to judge his feelings.

The many Parisians who attended the performances in Rouen were given incontrovertible evidence that Saint-Saëns was to be taken seriously as an opera composer, if they had not thought so before. Its success persuaded Verdhurt to take *Samson et Dalila* to Paris, for a production at the Théâtre de l'Eden on 31 October 1890, which thus gave Parisians the chance to see *Ascanio*, *Henry VIII* and *Samson et Dalila* all within the year.

Saint-Saëns could scarcely expect that his instruction that *Ascanio* be performed without any alterations would be respected, in view of his absence, even though Guiraud did what he could. Decor, costumes, choreography, orchestra and chorus were all prepared in good order; it was only, not surprisingly, the singers who created difficulties, as they had a year earlier when the opera was first taken up by the management.

Stage direction was by Gailhard, the conductor was Augusto Vianesi, the chorus master Jules Cohen. The costumes were by Charles Bianchini, the choreography by Joseph Hansen. The team of set designers was the same as for *Henry VIII*, with strong input from Gallet. Of the singers, the baritone Jean-Louis Lassalle had sung the role of Henry VIII since its debut and was well known to Saint-Saëns. The tenor Cossira (Ascanio) had recently replaced Jean de Reszke as Romeo; Plançon (François I) had been singing principal bass roles at the Opéra since 1883, most recently as Friar Laurence; the tenor Téqui (D'Orbec) was the Opéra's Tybalt; Ada Adini (La Duchesse d'Étampes – Saint-Saëns called her 'la belle Madame Adiny') was a recent acquisition by the Opéra, who went on to sing Brünnhilde in La Scala's first *Walküre*. The mezzo role of Scozzone had been a problem from the start, since Saint-Saëns had always wanted Renée Richard, his Anne Boleyn. When this singer left the company, the part was given in Saint-Saëns's absence and without his permission to Rosa Bosman, a soprano. Guiraud was instructed to adjust the role for a higher voice, and it is the higher version that appears in the first vocal score, published by Durand the same year.[11] Emma Eames, who sang Juliette to replace Adelina Patti, sang the role of Colombe. Saint-Saëns called this a 'splendid cast'.

The dress rehearsal went poorly, but the first night went very well. The press were admitted to the dress rehearsal as well as the performance, but their bad grace was once again evident in their reviews. One critic found the opera to be full of 'Italianisms';

---

[11] Scozzone's song in Act II, Tableau 3 is given at two pitches in the vocal score, the higher pitch in a supplement. The full score gives it in the lower key only.

another opined that the composer 'has a mediocre sense of drama [. . .] all his operas veer between the old operatic conventions and the invariably logical principles of Wagnerian dogma'. Another wrote that the music 'is admirably written, but lacks not only originality but also personality, even feeling'. Charles Malherbe wrote a sympathetic analytical booklet on the opera, and the ever-loyal Gounod wrote a long article which praised the composer for being true to his art. 'The great composer is there in every note.'

The public, as before, liked the opera very much. It was played regularly until the end of May, when Lassalle had to leave for an engagement in London. Saint-Saëns presumably missed it, but was there to see it when it returned for more performances in September. All in all there were thirty-one performances in 1890, with three more in 1891.

* * * * *

Ascanio
(Ratner 293)

Opéra in five acts and seven tableaux

Libretto by Louis Gallet
after the play *Benvenuto Cellini* by Paul Meurice

First performance: Opéra, Paris, 21 March 1890

Benvenuto Cellini	baryton
Ascanio	ténor
François 1er	basse
Un mendiant	baryton
Charles-Quint	basse
Pagolo	basse
D'Estourville	ténor
D'Orbec	ténor
La Duchesse d'Étampes	soprano dramatique
Colombe d'Estourville	soprano
Scozzone	contralto/mezzo-soprano
Une Ursuline	soprano
Dame Périne	mime

Ouvriers, apprentis, élèves de Benvenuto
Seigneurs et dames de la cour de François 1er
Gardes, hommes et femmes du peuple

The action takes place in Paris in 1539.

Orchestra: 3 flutes (incl. piccolo), 2 oboes, 2 clarinets, 2 bassoons, contrabassoon, 4 horns, 3 trumpets, 2 cornets, 3 trombones, tuba, timpani, bass drum, cymbals, triangle, side drum, castanets, harmonica, 2 harps, strings.

Offstage: 2 piccolos, 2 flutes, 2 oboes, 2 clarinets, 2 horns, 4 trumpets, 4 trombones, crotales, cymbals, anvils, side drum, tambourine, triangle.

In 1844 Alexandre Dumas *père* published a five-volume novel entitled *Ascanio*, drawing on the section of Benvenuto Cellini's *Vita* covering the years 1540–44 which he spent in France in the employ of François I. Cellini's account mentions his two assistants Ascanio and Pagolo, and reports his constantly shifting relationship with his employer and his almost completely antagonistic relationship with the King's mistress Madame d'Étampes. Cellini also mentions in passing a fifteen-year-old girl named Scorzone and records that Ascanio was in love with an unnamed girl.

Dumas added a number of characters and invented endless intrigues and confrontations in the manner of his other historical novels. Although Benvenuto Cellini is the central character of the story, he probably called it *Ascanio* since Berlioz's opera *Benvenuto Cellini* had been played at the Opéra as recently as 1838. It was common knowledge that Dumas employed assistants, and in this case most of the writing was the work of Paul Meurice.[12] In 1852 Meurice re-wrote the story as a play in five acts and eight tableaux and gave it the title *Benvenuto Cellini* to show that this was his work and not Dumas's. In his Preface he acknowledged *Ascanio* as his source but did not mention Dumas by name. Staged at the Théâtre de la Porte St-Martin, Paris, on 1 April 1852, with music supplied by Adolphe de Groot, the play was very successful.

The action of the play takes place in 1540. At the centre of the plot is Cellini himself, proud and reckless, confident of his genius, and prepared to defy the French nobility and even the King himself. Many of his works in gold, silver, bronze, marble and so on are seen on stage, and his first preoccupation is always to complete his current work and win the world's admiration. One scene shows the famous episode, also represented in Berlioz's opera, when Cellini, in casting a big bronze (in this case his *Jupiter*, not his *Perseus*) has to throw all his finished artefacts into the cauldron in a desperate effort to provide enough metal.

Working against him are one of his own workmen, Pagolo, the powerful Duchesse d'Étampes (the King's mistress) and her half-sister Scozzone, whose love for Cellini is rejected. A divisive issue, taken from the original narrative by Cellini, is the Grand Nesle, an imposing building across the river from the Louvre, which the King has assigned to Cellini as his studio and workshop, thereby dispossessing the powerful mayor of Paris, D'Estourville, whose beautiful daughter Colombe is the object of Ascanio's youthful passion and also the summit of female perfection in the eyes of the sculptor Cellini. D'Estourville, with the connivance of Madame d'Étampes, is determined that neither Cellini nor Ascanio should have any contact with his daughter. The latter pair plan to secrete her in a large reliquary chest that Cellini has made and to deliver it to a convent nearby. Moved by Cellini's generosity in giving up his love for Colombe in favour of Ascanio, Scozzone offers her own life by taking Colombe's place

---

[12] Meurice told Saint-Saëns that he wrote the whole novel himself. *L'Écho de Paris*, 12 November 1911; SORET 2012, p. 752.

in the chest, knowing that she would be confined for two days by the Duchesse. This note of tragedy impairs Cellini's winning of the King's favour and precipitates his return to Italy.

Gallet's task in converting this long, wordy play into an opera libretto involved removing a number of episodes and smaller characters, providing opportunities for set numbers such as arias, duets and choruses, managing a ballet sequence, and writing the whole thing as verse, not prose. A perfect occasion for the ballet divertissement was provided by the ceremonial meeting of the two Kings François I and Charles V in Act III of the play. Meurice wanted Cellini's squabble with the Duchesse d'Étampes to be at the centre of the action, but Gallet considered that anti-lyrical, preferring a story with more love interest. A critical question arose with the foundry scene, which Gallet and Saint-Saëns eventually decided to omit, bearing in mind the already heavy demands on Cellini's vocal stamina. They were perhaps, too, mindful of Berlioz having already composed such a scene and also of the Opéra's unfortunate experience with the foundry scene in Gounod's *La Reine de Saba* in 1862, when a kiln exploded, showering the stage with sparks and debris. As for Gallet's verse, he composed lines of every possible metre, including alexandrines, with rhyme always present, if not always close enough to be audible.

*****

TABLEAU 1

Scene 1 A scene of bustle and activity is presented at once, since the opera has no overture, and the spectator is greeted by a workshop full of men and boys, Cellini's workers and apprentices, finished and half-finished pieces of sculpture, moulds, patterns, sketches, jewellery, ornaments, and vessels of all shapes, sizes and materials. Hammering adds to the racket, hushed only by the entry of Benvenuto Cellini (baritone), who points to Ascanio's drawing of an angel as a model of excellence, to be copied by all. Looking next at Pagolo's effort, Cellini treats it as worthless. Pagolo (bass) angrily tears it up, full of jealousy and rage, and determined to get back at both Ascanio and his master. Pagolo tells Cellini that Ascanio has received a letter which he went off to read in private.

From the first bar the music presents a number of motifs that persist throughout the opera, the first three always accompanying Cellini's team of workers or the sculptor's métier, ex. 8.1a–c. Upper and lower elements of ex. 8.1a are used both separately and on their own, and the bass element is sometimes inverted. Example 8.1c is scored for two anvils.

Example 8.1 *Ascanio*, Tableau 1, Scene 1

[musical example with parts (a), (b), (c); (a) marked Allegro molto moderato, (3 times), f; (b) marked f, triplets; (c) marked "2 anvils"]

When Cellini admires Ascanio's work, this phrase is heard, ex. 8.2:

Example 8.2 *Ascanio*, Tableau 1, Scene 1

[musical example]

And a motif for Ascanio suggests youthful high spirits, ex. 8.3.

Example 8.3 *Ascanio*, Tableau 1, Scene 1

[musical example marked f, dim., p]

A clock strikes noon and the apprentices and workers tidy up to leave for their meal. Cellini reminds them that they are expecting an important visitor, the King no less, and so they are to be back in good order.

Scene 2 Ascanio (tenor) appears and moves off with the men, but Cellini restrains him. The music moves from F to B♭, guided by some elegant wind solos and a recall of ex. 8.2, for Cellini's admiration of Ascanio. In an arioso Cellini affirms his fatherly affection for him and then hesitantly enquires what the letter might be. The letter has its own motif, ex. 8.4:

Example 8.4 *Ascanio*, Tableau 1, Scene 2

Ascanio is delighted to tell him, thinking it is from his new-found love, though he is not willing to name her. It is an assignation, unsigned. Cellini wants to know more. Ascanio's little song 'Si loin et si haut' is charming, full of adolescent adoration, ex. 8.5:

Example 8.5 *Ascanio*, Tableau 1, Scene 2

But he is not willing to reveal the name of his *bien-aimée*, and Cellini with a good grace tells him that a new happiness is worth more than an old friendship, with a warning that in such affairs perils always lurk. The scene closes with echoes of ex. 8.2 and ex. 8.3.

Scene 3 As Ascanio leaves, an abrupt change of key and tempo announces the appearance of a new figure, Scozzone (contralto), who has stepped through a different doorway. The original Scorzone in Cellini's *Vita* was a girl of fifteen whom he chose as a model for some statuary he was working on at Fontainebleau. 'The young thing was pure and virginal, and I got her with child', he wrote. In Meurice's play and in the opera Scozzone, as she is now named, is older and a much more complicated character. She has been Cellini's mistress and his model for statues of Juno, Venus and Diana, and she loves him still. But he is now looking for the perfect model for his statue of Hebe. She feels rejected, failing to understand that the artist in Cellini puts the needs of his art above the needs of his heart. She came with Cellini from Florence. This low-voice role may be compared with that of Anne Boleyn, although it was performed in 1890 by a mezzo-soprano, with some of the tessitura adjusted.

The music of her first scene has a certain grandeur, with a broad new theme in D♭ major, ex. 8.6.

Example 8.6 *Ascanio*, Tableau 1, Scene 3

In expansive mood, Cellini explains to her that he loves her still, even though she is acute enough to know that that now means something different. A lighter scherzando middle section, with a new motif (ex. 8.7), explains how he named her 'Scozzone', or 'Casse-cou', for her carefree, reckless nature.

Example 8.7 *Ascanio*, Tableau 1, Scene 3

For Cellini art is sacred, with a richly scored motif to reinforce its divine status, ex. 8.8. When his art becomes intertwined with his love for his model, real or imaginary, the motif is attached to her. This plays an important role in the opera.

Example 8.8 *Ascanio*, Tableau 1, Scene 3

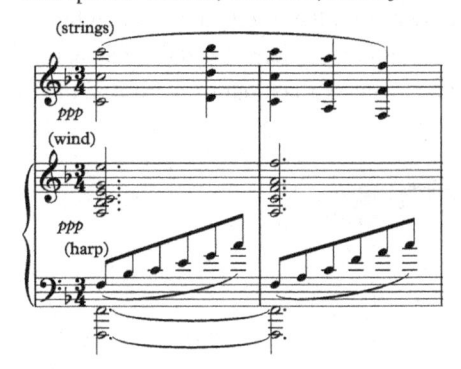

Scozzone should only be jealous of art, he rather priggishly tells her, and wins from her an assurance that she will accept her lot since she will always retain a place in his heart, all to a richly harmonised statement of ex. 8.6.

To a new motif (ex. 8.9) in reply to Cellini's questions, Scozzone reveals that Ascanio is in danger since he has caught the eye of the Duchesse d'Étampes, the King's mistress.

Example 8.9 *Ascanio*, Tableau 1, Scene 3

With a recall of ex. 8.2 Cellini at once grasps the dire implications of this news, since the Duchesse's previous lovers have all faced the King's brutal punishment. Now he guesses the origin of the mysterious letter Ascanio has received (ex. 8.4). He is resolved to protect him.

Scene 4 A great bustle erupts (ex. 8.1) as Pagolo comes in with news that the King is approaching. Workers and apprentices rush in to open up cupboards and put all their work on display with very little time before the King comes in accompanied by the Duchesse d'Étampes and his suite.

The King addresses Cellini with the most refined orchestration in support: solo flute and harp with divided violas and cellos providing background harmony. He sings his sculptor's lavish praises, comparing him to Archimedes and Praxiteles. The Duchesse has been poking through some jewellery on display in a bowl and has picked out a bracelet. It is Ascanio's work.

While Cellini shows the King samples of medallions and other work with the courtiers following behind, the Duchesse accosts Ascanio and asks him to fit the bracelet on her arm. Brazenly flirting, she decides to buy it, then asks him to make a lily for her with some of her diamonds. Scozzone is watching. She warns the Duchesse that the King might notice, which only encourages the Duchesse to a burst of coloratura and a defiant 'Je l'aime !' A number of themes emerge from this scene, the most important being ex. 8.10, representing the Duchesse's fascination with Ascanio.

Example 8.10 *Ascanio*, Tableau 1, Scene 4

The King has now completed his inspection and arrived at a table where the clay model for the bust of Jupiter stands, represented by the key of C major and solid support from the brass. This is the King's commission and intended to be Cellini's supreme masterpiece. The King desires it to be cast in bronze within the month. The problem, Cellini points out, is lack of space, pointing out that the Grand Nesle would serve his purpose perfectly. 'It's yours,' says the King without hesitation, only to be told by the Duchesse that the building is assigned to d'Estourville, mayor of Paris and one of her supporters. Undeterred, the King gives the order to assign the Grand Nesle to Cellini.

Three cornets and a triangle evoke the coming ceremonial when the King is to receive his old enemy Charles V, who was both King of the Spanish empire (including the Netherlands) and Holy Roman Emperor. King François had been his prisoner in Spain in 1525–26. Cellini is instructed to plan the celebrations to be held at Fontainebleau and then to cast the statue for him, the King, alone. As the King retires,

Ascanio muses that he will now be close to the object of his passion, Colombe, d'Estourville's daughter (ex. 8.5), while Scozzone warns Cellini that the Duchesse has her eye on Ascanio.

TABLEAU 2

One of Saint-Saëns's strongest gifts is his ability to generate lively street scenes. The open space in front of the Cloître des Augustins, like Les Halles at the opening of *Étienne Marcel*, is now the scene of great vitality and movement, fully represented in the music. The stage directions are hard to reconcile with the known geography of that part of the left bank in the sixteenth century, but Gallet's setting, reproduced almost exactly from Meurice's, requires the spectator to see the two Nesles, Grand and Petit, the Tour de Nesle in the distance, the Seine, and the Louvre across the river, as well as a door into the cloister chapel and a tavern.

Scene 1 A group of full-throated students is singing a pair of verses full of boisterous nonsense, teasing the barmaids, while townsfolk and children move freely around.

Scene 2 This exhilarating music has to give way to something more sober since people are heading for the chapel, including Colombe and her maid. Convinced that the unsigned letter was from her, Ascanio is waiting for her with a version of ex. 8.5 in his thoughts. It must have been another woman, replies Colombe. Or a hoax, he thinks, but then realising that the service is about to begin, he withdraws, mentioning to Colombe that with the move into the Grand Nesle they will be neighbours (ex. 8.3). (Although unexplained in the text, d'Estourville, Colombe's father, has to vacate the Grand Nesle but retains the Petit Nesle.) Their exchanges start as dialogue and develop into a duet, fluently and melodiously unfolding. Example 8.5 completely conveys the warmth that will bind the two of them.

They are accosted by a beggar, who is given a more prominent part in the opera than in Meurice's play, and it scarcely advances the action. Saint-Saëns was fond of this scene, and it explores the growing bond between Ascanio and Colombe. Bare modal woodwind convey the beggar's sorry condition, for when Ascanio and Colombe respond they are allowed more comfortable harmony. The beggar is touched that although they are not married they seem to belong to one another, as if the beggar had an illumination about their future. Turning eventually into a Trio, the scene overextends itself, but was never cut in later revisions. The beggar moves away and the others go into the chapel.

Scene 3 Enter d'Estourville and his sidekick the Comte d'Orbec (both tenors) with a group of 'showy, noisy gentlemen', all shocked that the mayor has been ordered to give up the Grand Nesle to this 'locksmith', as d'Estourville calls Cellini. Pithy, jumpy music gives them the right scornful tone, and d'Estourville is characterised as a dyspeptic nuisance such as Dr Caius in *Falstaff* or sometimes Beckmesser in *Die Meistersinger*. D'Orbec has to remind his friend that it is the King who has ordered and signed the deal. Two recurrent phrases characterise this group, ex. 8.11a–b.

Example 8.11 *Ascanio*, Tableau 2, Scene 3

(a) Non! non! mille fois non!

(b)

Scene 4 Example 8.1 brings in Cellini who asks politely how to enter the Nesle, holding out his authorisation. D'Estourville puts it in his pocket without reading it. Cellini leaves to search for the perfect model for his bust of Hebe, which, unlike the bust of Jupiter, is the work that really inspires him.

Scene 5 The Duchesse d'Étampes appears, masked, carried in a litter. She promises to help d'Estourville, who leads his followers off.

Scene 6 Shortly after Scozzone too arrives, disguised in a heavy cape. She is intent on discouraging the Duchesse's interest in Ascanio.

Scene 7 Thereupon Ascanio emerges from the chapel reading the mysterious letter (ex. 8.4). No sooner has the Duchesse told Ascanio that it is she who made the assignation than Cellini appears from behind them and forcefully interrupts their conversation. Since Ascanio admits he does not know the woman he is with, Cellini suggests he should decide whom to follow. When the Duchesse says 'Go!' Ascanio leaves, accompanied by ex. 8.2.

Scene 8 Knowing perfectly well to whom he is speaking, Cellini explains that there are two people whom he loves: Ascanio and the King. A certain woman loves one while being mistress of the other. In something like a short formal aria, Cellini's defiance rises to a huge cadence in C major, revealing his strength of feeling when it comes to protecting Ascanio. With some heat the Duchesse challenges his right to tell her what to do. 'Is it war, then?' he asks, launching into a shorter second verse of his aria, boldly challenging his own standing with the King against hers.

She explodes again, and the urgency and intensity of what follows is unlike anything heard before in Saint-Saëns's operas except in the second act of *Samson et Dalila*. A great rage rises in the orchestra as the Duchesse declares unremitting war, to which Cellini responds with enormous dignity and a slightly slower tempo, telling her to leave

Ascanio alone. 'I am not afraid of you, Duchesse d'Étampes', he declares, forcing her to throw off her mask. She calls for d'Estourville to help, and Scozzone rushes forward to warn Cellini that the Duchesse never forgets an insult.

Scene 9 The chapel doors open and the organ is heard from within. At that moment, as if he had nothing on his mind, Cellini catches a first glimpse of Colombe coming out with the people. His total absorption is expressed with the exclamation 'La divine enfant!' and the Hebe theme ex. 8.8 (now in 4/4) heard at different registers. Scozzone senses at once that this is the one who will supplant her in Cellini's affections. The Duchesse tells d'Estourville at his door that she will support him in holding on to the Grand Nesle, and d'Estourville calls his daughter back inside. 'His daughter!' exclaims Cellini, delighted to think she will be a neighbour (as Ascanio had also reflected). By tearing up the King's order for occupancy of the Grand Nesle (ex. 8.11a), d'Estourville infuriates Cellini, who is prevented from drawing blood by Colombe stepping between them, allowing D'Estourville to enter the building. Devastated by what she has seen, Scozzone vows to separate Cellini from his new prize no matter the cost.

Scene 10 The foundrymen's music from the opening of the opera (ex. 8.1) shows Cellini's little army arriving from the back with waggonloads of the tools of their trade, ready to set up in the Grand Nesle. Cellini tells them they have to take their new quarters by force, which they are very ready to do. In town-crier style Ascanio formally calls on d'Estourville to admit them. The response is a defiant shot from an arquebus. This precipitates a clamorous outburst from Cellini's men, leading shortly to a Presto finale which charges at breakneck speed to the curtain as the men join in the assault from all sides.

TABLEAU 3

Scene 1 Like Tableau 1, Tableau 3 opens with a view of Cellini's workshop and of his men hard at work, only now they are in their new premises in the Grand Nesle. Its garden and the Petit Nesle are visible in the background. The orchestral support is accordingly new, based on a busy heaving string figure, and lifelike blows of hammer on anvil conveyed by percussion, harp and upper wind. The vocal score can give little sense of its effectiveness. A clay bust – the Jupiter ordered by the King – stands at one side carefully wrapped; at the other is a large 'châsse' or reliquary chest made of silver and gold, commissioned by the Ursuline nuns. It has a separate panel on the side and a hinged lid. The men are working on this object since it has to be finished the next day. Pagolo is actually inside it, attaching ornaments.

Scozzone comes in and although Pagolo urges them to pay her no attention, they stop work to listen to her. She has a song to sing brought from her home, 'Bella Fiorentina', based, according to a note in the vocal score, on a sixteenth-century song. Saint-Saëns originally had her sing Palestrina's madrigal 'Alla riva del Tebro', but then decided it was too refined and not amusing enough, so he set some new words, presumably by Gallet, to a tune that resembles the Palestrina, hence the attribution in the vocal score.[13] She accompanies herself on a guitar, and the song rather quickly loses its folk-like quality when it keeps shifting key and when each verse ends in a flurry of coloratura spread over more than two octaves. According to the libretto, she sings with excessive jollity in order to hide her preoccupation with the faithless Cellini.

The song and applause over, the apprentices want her to sing more. Her singing reminds them of Italy, and briefly she joins them in a charming Neapolitan-sounding sing-song, all too brief. They then play a prank on Pagolo by shutting him into the reliquary and singing a *De profundis* in jocular manner; then they release him, with Scozzone looking on, just as he thought he was entombed forever. This episode is found neither in the play nor in the libretto and it was removed from the second version of the opera, but it is dramatically significant in the light of what happens later, and it has its own startling motif, ex. 8.12:

Example 8.12 *Ascanio*, Tableau 3, Scene 1

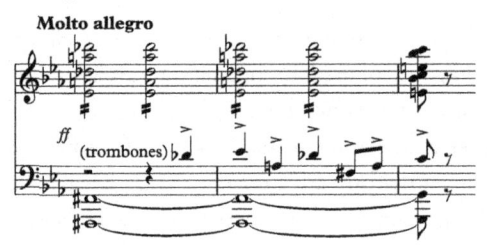

Benvenuto Cellini now comes in with an official 'in severe Spanish dress' and takes a look around, neither of them speaking. Some elegant four-part music for strings is given a solemn tint by treating all the violins as one section and separating the cellos from the basses. This is a curious way, to say the least, to indicate Cellini taking official possession of his new quarters.

They then leave, followed by all the apprentices and Scozzone, leaving Ascanio alone. He has been present throughout this scene but without taking part. He can think of nothing but his love, in whose praise he now sings a gently lyrical aria, 'À l'ombre des noires tours', maddeningly reticent for the principal tenor's chief solo. It rises to a certain degree of passion in the middle of the tripartite scheme, and ends as quietly as it began. Almost any other composer would have taken the opportunity – a tenor alone on stage – to raise the roof, but Saint-Saëns treats Ascanio always as little more than a boy on the verge of manhood; Cellini and Scozzone are the real victims of emotional torment.

[13] F-Pn MS 530 (Saint-Saëns's draft) shows the original version, rejected in his letter to Auguste Durand of 17 June 1888 (RATNER 2012, p. 209). Saint-Saëns published a setting of 'Alla riva del Tebro' as a song in 1869 and an arrangement of the Palestrina as a song in 1898.

Scene 2 Cellini re-enters with his students, to announce that the Emperor Charles V has summoned him. But his loyalty is to the King. They have finished the reliquary, so they now have to prepare the metal for casting the Jupiter. It is his turn to be alone, so he commands them all to leave.

Scene 3 It is odd to present Cellini's encomium to Colombe so soon after Ascanio's tribute to the same young girl. But he is not yet aware that Colombe is the object of Ascanio's love. For him she is his long-sought Hebe, always suggested by ex. 8.8. Like Pygmalion, he is obsessed with his own creation, for the Hebe is a much more personal work than the Jupiter or the reliquary, both commissioned. Colombe is still a 'vision', and when she appears at the back of the stage leaning lightly on a balustrade, he goes eagerly to work on his statue. This is the scene in which the actor Mélingue, who was also a painter and a sculptor, shaped the Hebe every night on stage in the 1852 production. In the opera the stage directions simply require Cellini to set to work. He does so as Colombe, from her distant spot, sings a melancholy ballad 'Mon cœur est sous la pierre' without accompaniment. Perhaps this mildly modal ballad was in Debussy's mind when he wrote the unaccompanied song for Mélisande 'Mes longs cheveux descendent' a year or two later.

Cellini replies with ardent passion addressing his 'douce Hébé' as the 'idéale maîtresse', and begging her, with full orchestral support, to emerge, alive, from humble clay. The big cadence here in F major does not justify the cut (which was done at the Opéra) of the second half of his aria, since it has to return to D major, and in any case this is stirring music in which Cellini begs his 'chaste goddess' to raise him to the status of a god, no less. The music should also tell us that Cellini is as much in love with Colombe as with his clay model.

Scene 4 Colombe disappears. At that moment Scozzone comes in, causing Cellini to put a hasty cover over his model. The musical texture changes completely, giving way to a long elegant solo for the first violins in B major (ex. 8.13) lightly accompanied, against which Scozzone, the woman scorned, at first asks Cellini if she may sit and watch him working.

Example 8.13 *Ascanio*, Tableau 3, Scene 4

She knows he has found his 'nymph', his 'goddess', and the temperature rises as she accuses him more and more bitterly of betraying her. The tempo increases too, and the exchanges reach a point of fury where Scozzone threatens to be avenged on him, implicitly threatening Colombe herself. She understands better than he does the complexity of his feelings for his new model who has not even posed for him. She goes off, leaving Cellini to reflect over ex. 8.6 that he might have spared her suffering. 'O how sad that human happiness is always built on the suffering of others!'

Scene 5 Ascanio comes in with a sealed message from the King. Cellini puts it down without reading it, since he is anxious to tell Ascanio that he has found his perfect muse. The music rolls fluently forward as Cellini explains against constant reminders of ex. 8.8 that the Hebe he has found has won not only his admiration but his love. Ascanio is happy for him and for her. Against a strong 6/4 chord of C major, Cellini unveils his statuette, causing Ascanio to cry out 'Colombe! The mayor's daughter!' While Cellini is carried away at the thought of his artistic triumph, Ascanio in an aside gives way to a powerful howl of grief, knowing he can only weep and keep silent.

Scene 6 Offstage music is heard, coming from the Petit Nesle. The score describes it as 'grotesque', the libretto as 'discordant', so presumably, although the notes are plain enough, the players are to play them badly, and no doubt out of tune. Cellini's students come in with Scozzone, who brings news which she delights in telling Cellini to his face: the Comte d'Orbec, d'Estourville's friend, is to marry Colombe, his daughter, within a week. Cellini's outrage confirms Scozzone's suspicions, and Ascanio too reacts with passion. Cellini is determined to appeal to the King, and then remembers the letter. He opens it and reads it (spoken in the first version, sung in the revised version): 'Cellini may remain in France in my service. But for a grave offence which has wounded me deeply, he is banished from my presence.'

The Duchesse d'Étampes is clearly behind this move. The orchestra boils and Cellini rages, affirming that he is no subject of the King. 'Where will you go?' ask Ascanio and Pagolo. 'To the Emperor Charles V!'

TABLEAU 4

Scene 1 The tension throughout the previous Tableau was at such a level that some respite is badly needed. Across the river, in the Louvre, the King and his *maîtresse-en-titre* the Duchesse d'Étampes are in a relaxed mood, while a group of courtiers, including d'Estourville and d'Orbec, are seen in the gallery a little further away. The King's music from the first tableau is heard again. To the Duchesse he sings a song full of old-fashioned gallantry over a delicate waltz rhythm. Strings provide the lightest of accompaniments with an occasional comment from a bassoon. Gallet's verses dictate the alternation of six-bar and five-bar phrases of which it is made up.

The Duchesse responds but in a different metre and a different tone, although she is expressing her affection for the King, and they come together in a duet. The scene is full of charm, betraying nothing of the tension beneath the surface.

She proposes that when Charles V arrives in three days' time, having been given free passage of French territory, he should be held prisoner as a strong political move, counsel which the King accepts without a murmur. As the courtiers come down from the gallery he informs them that there will be great celebrations at Fontainebleau with ballet and jousting on the water. They all leave.

Scene 2 Ascanio enters with some hesitation, nervous about seeing the Duchesse, for whom he has brought the lily made of diamonds.

Scene 3 She enters and receives the jewel with flattering compliments. In her most seductive manner (aided by a solo cello and solo violin) she asks him what he would like in payment. Ascanio replies with a little two-verse song in G minor about his elusive dream of love. Thinking she is the object of his hidden passion, the Duchesse urges him to say more with a song of her own (cut in the later edition of the score) that brings out a tender side of her, not seen before.

Groups of courtiers have been gathering in the gallery at the side, including Colombe and her father. 'I adore a pure and lovely angel', sings Ascanio, on seeing her: 'Colombe!' The Duchesse is now alarmed, with a new motif to show it, ex. 8.14:

Example 8.14 *Ascanio*, Tableau 4, Scene 3

Scene 4 As Colombe comes down to join them the Duchesse is all smiles. She presents Colombe with the lily so that she can wear it on her wedding day. She takes the bouquet that Colombe is wearing instead and asks Ascanio to judge between the flowers. For him the flower made by the sun is finer than the flower made by a man, and the flower he prefers is . . . you. As he gives Colombe the real flower, the Duchesse grabs it, enraged, and tears the petals out.

As the pace quickens Ascanio makes a full declaration of his love for Colombe, and the rest of the scene is a strong love duet in octaves, the lovers deaf to the furious coloratura invective of the Duchesse. If the tableau at least began at a lower temperature, it closes, like the previous one, at a high pitch of excitement. In the second version of the opera the first three scenes of this tableau were attached to the following tableau and rather awkwardly located at Fontainebleau.

TABLEAU 5

Scene 1 The scene is the formal garden of the palace of Fontainebleau. With his keen eye for decor, Gallet describes the scene in minute detail. Every level, every tree, every statue, every decoration is spelled out in the libretto. There are two temporary arches, one bearing the royal F, the other the imperial K. A cascade is seen at the back and forests in the distance, and at the centre in front is the space where the ballet is to be performed. The Opéra had a long-standing reputation for magnificence in scenes of this kind, going back two hundred years.

Over solid pompous music the two groups, French and Spanish, approach from separate sides through their respective arches. The two kings embrace as the chorus acclaim them and a row of trumpets and trombones on stage spell out a fanfare. The Duchesse d'Étampes notices that Cellini is having a merry time in the Emperor's entourage, with Ascanio near him.

Saint-Saëns's sketches show the following scene to have caused him trouble, with many revisions. The rather stiff exchanges of the two kings are supported by a scene-motif, ex. 8.15.

Example 8.15 *Ascanio*, Tableau 5, Scene 1

François, dissembling, says he is happy to allow Charles to traverse his country, but notices that he has a 'rebel' in his entourage. Charles is proud of his acquisition, while François hints that he could easily hold on to Cellini by making Charles his prisoner. Cellini steps between them and insists that he should not be the cause of a quarrel, let alone a war, between them. He did not rebel, he insists, he was sacked, but he undertakes nonetheless to finish the Jupiter within three days. His reply, when François offers him a free choice of his reward if he succeeds, hints at Colombe; at least that is what the Duchesse assumes in thereupon asking the King's permission for her to sponsor the marriage of Colombe d'Estourville to the Comte d'Orbec. Cellini privately assures Ascanio that he will not let that happen. The marriage is set for tomorrow.

To the music that accompanied his mention of the Emperor in the first tableau, François pays tribute to his imperial guest and the people reprise their noisy acclamation with the surprising adjunct of a rapid ensemble in D minor for everyone present. Inaudibly (inevitably in such a clamour) they all give voice to their various concerns. Gallet may well have sighed, after composing seven different stanzas with cleverly matching rhyme schemes, that not a single word can be heard. It is time for the entertainment.

Ballet The divertissement is a series of twelve ballet movements lasting twenty-five minutes. These were designed as a feast for the eye with costumes and outdoor setting fully representing the Renaissance French court at its most magnificent, and a feast for the ear since Saint-Saëns refused to treat ballet music as in any way inferior or routine.

In fact some of the opera's best music is found here, and furthermore there was a conscious attempt, as there had been for *Henry VIII*, to evoke historically authentic music. He told Durand that he wanted natural trumpets in the orchestra since there were no modern instruments at the court of François I.[14] In the Bibliothèque nationale he searched for some suitable music. He was looking for a choral piece which could be danced to, and he found

> a little printed collection, very rare and luxuriously printed, with ornamental decorations. It was a collection of choral pieces with amorous words; this high-quality printing suggested that they were to be sung in elegant society. It would be hard to describe the vulgarity of the words and the elegance of the edition and of the music. One would hardly utter such rude words in male company, and these are choruses for mixed voices in four parts, for men and women![15]

At least four of the melodies in the ballets were taken from this collection, probably one of Pierre Attaingnant's many publications of chansons in partbooks, all of which have obscene songs mixed in with courtly love poetry. One tune, that of no. 5, Saint-Saëns acknowledged he found in Arbeau's dance manual of 1588, *Orchésographie*. He had a better knowledge of French early music than most of his contemporaries, especially of Rameau, whose music he edited for Durand, beginning in 1895, at least in a supervisory capacity. Like Massenet he was never averse to including period pastiche in his operas.

The Maître des Jeux acknowledges the two sovereigns to formal *maestoso* music (no. 1). A curtain of flowers and plants is raised by eight children dressed as clowns revealing the Fontainebleau Nymph asleep. She awakes to the delicate sound of harp and woodwind, bows to the King, and prepares to evoke his favourite gods and goddesses.

No. 2 is an elegant baroque dance in which the three goddesses Venus, Juno and Athene appear. In no. 3 Diana is next to appear accompanied by twelve dryads and twelve naiads. Being a huntress she is heralded by a distant horn. Their dance is a gavotte. The next god (no. 4) is Bacchus with his twenty female Bacchantes who thump drums and stamp around while an oboe takes on a wickedly tiring stream of notes, joined in turn by a second oboe, a pair of flutes, then a pair of clarinets.

Phoebus-Apollo and the nine Muses (no. 5) are introduced by a dignified rising phrase as preface to a dance tune in minor mode. Whatever its origin, the tune appeared in Arbeau's dance treatise *Orchésographie* of 1588 and hence is familiar as the *Basse-danse* from Warlock's *Capriol Suite* of 1927. Phoebus then takes his lyre (no. 6) with which to announce the entry of Amour (Cupid), danced by a female dancer. Leaving the Renaissance behind, Amour leads off with some contemporary ballet music in the

---

[14] Letter to Auguste Durand, 30 November 1889, PASLER 2012, p. 28.
[15] *Annales du théâtre et de la musique*, 1905; SORET 2012, p. 610.

style of Delibes. This piece was originally composed some twenty years earlier for the ballet at the end of *Le Timbre d'argent*, to precede the *Valse des nymphes d'enfer*. All the gods and goddesses join with more complicated music for more complicated action: Amour is pursued but never caught, laughing at the gods and playing with Phoebus whose light (the sun) she snuffs out. In the ensuing night Phoebus convinces the King that Amour has a beautiful soul as well as a beautiful body.

In no. 7 Amour introduces Psyche, whispers to her under cover of the dark and seduces her with sweet words, the wooing conducted by a flute with gentle harp accompaniment. Amour goes to sleep, gazed upon by Psyche, then goes off, leaving Psyche in distress.

No. 8 is a lively dance with a Neapolitan rhythm and some brilliant orchestration. The full ensemble of gods with all their supporters join in.[16] When a solo flute takes over with some virtuoso runs and figures (no. 9), Amour returns with a variation of his own.

One of the King's pages dressed as the dragon from the garden of the Hesperides brings in the golden apple (no. 10). To a repetitive rhythm on a firm string unison Venus, Juno and Pallas Athene contend for the award of the apple. The Fontainebleau Nymph awards it to Venus, who refuses it, passing the award for beauty instead to the Duchesse d'Étampes sitting at the King's side.

The finale (no. 11) brings all the gods, goddesses, bacchantes, dryads and naiads – over fifty dancers – together in a waltz that veers between ancient and modern styles. It speeds up with great excitement at the end. No. 12 is the triumphant apotheosis, with the Fontainebleau Nymph at the centre and the stage band adding its brilliant fanfares.

Nothing more is said or sung about the treacherous capture of Charles V.

TABLEAU 6

Scene 1 Tableau 6 is back in Cellini's workshop in the Grand Nesle. The reliquary chest is now ready, placed in a bay behind a curtain. The music that introduced us to this scene in Tableau 3 is heard in an inactive version, since the workers are not there. Only Pagolo is present, watching Ascanio slip across the balustrade at the back towards the Petit Nesle. A knock on the door brings in Scozzone, who discards her mantilla-like cape, and the Duchesse d'Étampes, who keeps on her cape but removes her mask.

Pagolo tells the Duchesse what he has already told Scozzone: that Cellini and Ascanio are planning to rescue Colombe from marriage to d'Orbec by hiding her in the chest. It has to be delivered to the Ursuline nuns who have commissioned it and she would be safe there, since her godmother is the Mother Superior. The Duchesse has a murderous plan. In a scene which builds in dark intensity throughout thanks to the

---

[16] An earlier version of this ballet movement is found at F-Pn MS 689.

sinister motif (ex. 8.12) that might be described as 'chest as grave', Pagolo tells her that a person could only survive a few hours in the chest, certainly less than a day, and that it cannot be opened from inside. She dismisses him and confides to the horrified Scozzone that she will insist that the chest be delivered to the Louvre first, so that the King can admire it. She intends to hold it there for three days. After only a brief hesitation Scozzone is enthusiastic. 'Death to the hated rival!' they both cry, Scozzone's cry following behind the Duchesse's and a semitone higher.

Scene 2 The Duchesse goes out leaving Scozzone in a state of high agitation, alone for only half a minute, but long enough to swear to win Cellini back, even at the price of this crime. Gallet and Saint-Saëns, following the single line when Scozzone is alone in Meurice's play, should really have allowed themselves a more developed aria at this point if only to explore Scozzone's divided passions and loyalties.

Scene 3 For she now confronts Cellini again to a pedestrian version of the motif that supported their last scene together, ex. 8.13. He teases her about keeping company with the Duchesse, but she opts for a more hostile approach. She tells him she knows about his plan to abduct Colombe in the reliquary, which angers him, and she then rubs salt in the wound by revealing that Colombe's real lover is Ascanio.

Scene 4 To prove it, she draws Cellini into the shadows while Ascanio helps Colombe over the low wall that marks off the Petit Nesle. This is a critical scene in the opera. An important new theme is introduced, ex. 8.16, perhaps reminiscent of a famous theme in the overture to *Prince Igor* (in the opera it is Igor's aria) and borrowing a harmonic alternation beloved by the Russians.

Example 8.16 *Ascanio*, Tableau 6, Scene 4

Colombe is relieved to have escaped from the clutches of the Duchesse and feels such gratitude to Cellini for arranging her abduction to the care of the Ursulines that she feels she could love him. 'No, don't love him!' replies Ascanio anxiously, going on to warn her that Cellini loves her in the same way that he does. Colombe is alarmed since she did not realise this before. Cellini, meanwhile, exclaims (from his concealment) on realising that Ascanio loves her too. Their two secrets are out.

The scene is both a love duet and a tormented quartet since it settles eventually into a luxurious 12/8 tempo in A♭ in which Ascanio and Colombe share a ravishing ascending line while Cellini and Scozzone insert their own agonies, the whole making one of those pulsing ensembles that are the glory of nineteenth-century opera, coming to rest on a final cadence in which it may be imagined that all problems are resolved. The composition of this quartet gave Saint-Saëns, he reported, 'un mal de chien'.[17]

Ascanio shakes himself out of the delirious dream and decides he is too weak ever to outdo his master. At this Cellini steps forward, to the lovers' horror, and to brief hints of ex. 8.8 recalling a love that he now denies, he tells them in a short aria 'Enfants, je ne vous en veux pas', to love each other as they clearly do. When the Jupiter is cast he intends to ask the King for the hand of Colombe as his reward, not for himself but for Ascanio. All three, including Scozzone, who has also emerged from hiding, are overwhelmed by Cellini's nobility of mind, sealed in a brief quartet.

Scozzone might have thought that Cellini's renunciation of Colombe would open the way for her to claim him for herself. Instead, she expresses the wish to die for him as the only comparable renunciation she could make. But Cellini needs her to accompany Colombe to the convent and sits down to write a letter to the Mother Superior. This gives the stage to Scozzone, whose monologue is brief but highly expressive, wishing that Cellini would always have something to remember her by. Exactly what's in her mind we do not yet know.

A knock on the door means that Colombe must be hidden. Scozzone is given her instructions and a letter, and although Cellini now asks her to come back once Colombe is safe, her whispered aside ('Ah! jamais!') tells us that she will not. 'May he weep for me as much as I have loved him' are her words as she leads Colombe into the bay where the reliquary stands and closes the curtain behind them.

Scene 5 Some soldiers led by d'Orbec charge in, followed by Cellini's workmen curious to see what's going on. Colombe is nowhere to be seen. Arrested and confined to his workshop, Cellini insists that he must deliver the reliquary to the Ursulines at the Queen's request, to be carried by his men and escorted by Scozzone. The curtain opens and eight men are assigned to lift the chest. They carry it out accompanied by a woman in Scozzone's clothing who never looks back, causing Cellini to feel abandoned.

But he has a pressing obligation to cast the Jupiter, so a sudden energy invades the music, mostly using ex. 8.1. There is work to be done, and as a door opens revealing the foundry beyond, the workmen join Cellini and Ascanio in the thrill of creating a masterpiece out of clay and sand. A great clamour from the orchestra brings the curtain down. If the authors had insisted on including a foundry scene, it would have followed here.

TABLEAU 7

Scene 1 Unbeknownst to Cellini and Ascanio, the reliquary chest has been taken not to the convent of the Ursulines but to the Louvre, where it now stands in front of

---

[17] Letter to Philippe Bellenot of 25 April 1888; RATNER 2012, p. 209.

a window in an oratory adjoining one of the large palace rooms. It is shrouded in darkness and only moonlight reveals its rich ornamentation. The slow-moving music includes a moving re-hearing of Scozzone's theme ex. 8.6.

The Duchesse d'Étampes comes in with a lamp and gazes at the chest, gloating at the thought of her victim already dead inside it and at the prospect of Cellini's horror when he finds her. Anxious to be sure that there is someone inside, she summons up the courage, with some recalls of ex. 8.12, to release the clasp. She feels inside with her hand and withdraws it in horror.

Scene 2 At that moment an eight-part choir is heard singing the praises of the God of Kings and of the King of Gods, supported by a trumpet solo and the full orchestra. Curtains are drawn back to reveal a large gathering of the court, splendidly lit, with the statue of Jupiter in pride of place, its bronze gleaming. Cellini and Ascanio accompany the King. The Duchesse slips out of a side door and then joins the company unnoticed.

Without any ado the King offers Cellini whatever he wishes, and Cellini, as promised, asks for the hand of Colombe not for himself, but for Ascanio. Seeking the Duchesse's approval, the King asks where she is. Right on cue Colombe appears in the crowd accompanied by an Ursuline nun. Example 8.8 is heard as she greets the King, then her father, then Ascanio. The Duchesse mutters to herself in confusion and horror and even joins in the noisy ensemble that pours praise on Cellini and his work. As it closes she asks Cellini, 'If Colombe is alive, who's in there, dead?' Cellini sees the reliquary where he did not expect to find it, rushes over to it, forces it open and cries out Scozzone's name. In a torrent of self-mortification he drops to his knees as the curtain falls.

* * * * *

In the process of composition, as we have seen, many changes were made, the most significant being the abandonment of the foundry scene, instead of which the opening up of the foundry was stitched on to the end of Tableau 6. If the vocal score that Durand published in March 1890 (391 pages) represents the version presented at the first performance, the changes embodied in the second edition of the vocal score (363 pages) were adopted during that run of thirty-four performances, since Saint-Saëns was correcting proofs soon after they ended. There was also a full score which quite closely matches the second edition of the vocal score, issued in 1893. The first version could have been reduced by cutting the Fontainebleau scene entirely or the beggar's scene in Tableau 2, or by reducing the intrigue in the early scenes. In fact Saint-Saëns preferred to make a dozen relatively short cuts, as set out in Table 8.2.

In the case of Tableau 4, Scene 4, the scene between the Duchesse and Ascanio with the lily, the only one that shows a softer side of her character, Saint-Saëns said that although it was essential for the action, it was dropped because it did not suit Mme

Table 8.2 *Ascanio*, the second version

	Tableau	Scene	Vocal score page	
1)	2	8	106	32 bars were cut, abbreviating Cellini's defiant duet with the Duchesse, from her 'Assez!'
2)	3	1	154	41 bars were cut, removing Pagolo's playful confinement in the reliquary chest.
3)	3	3	166	Cellini sings through four bars earlier left to the orchestra.
4)	3	3	169	Although not cut in the second edition, a footnote indicates that 29 bars were cut, beginning at 'Brûle-moi!'
5)	3	6	195	Cellini reads the letter on given pitches, adding one bar.
6)	4–5		199	This tableau (lacking Scene 4) and the next were combined as Act III, not Act II, Tableau 2 and Act III. The decor of Act III (Fontainebleau) served for the first part of the new Act also, instead of the Louvre.
7)	4	3	217	24 bars were cut, from 'On saura vous comprendre!'
8)	4	4	220	The whole of Scene 4 was cut.
9)	5	Ballet	292	8 bars were cut from no. 9, the flute solo.
10)	5	Ballet	295	A footnote indicates that Ballet no. 10 was cut at the Opéra.
11)	6	4	344	Instead of voices from outside, Ascanio reports the arrival of the King's men. Outside voices are heard at the opening of Scene 5 instead.
12)	7	2	378	52 bars of the chorus 'O force immense' were replaced by 21 bars in which the chorus sing the same words and end with the same climax and cadence. No soloists sing.

Adini's interpretation of the role.[18] The revision in the final scene came about because Gailhard, in 1890, revised this himself in a manner which Saint-Saëns found detestable, so he wrote yet another version himself.[19]

The thirty-four performances that *Ascanio* received at the Opéra between March 1890 and April 1891 represent real success as the institution saw it. Saint-Saëns naturally hoped that *Ascanio* would remain in the Opéra's repertoire; one of the directors, Ritt, told him that he was keen that this should happen. Lassalle was willing to sing Cellini and Saint-Saëns wanted Blanche Deschamps to sing Scozzone. She was currently much applauded in contralto roles in *Le Prophète*, *Le Roi d'Ys* and *Hérodiade* and was soon to sing Dalila at the Opéra. She had already sung Scozzone's song 'La Fiorentinelle' in concert. But by November 1891 Saint-Saëns was convinced that a revival at the Opéra was not a good idea.

He had hopes for the opera's eventual success elsewhere. Toulouse had shown an interest as early as 1888, Covent Garden in 1891. The Metropolitan Opera engaged the

---

[18] Letter to Auguste Durand, 19 February 1898; RATNER 2012, p. 211.
[19] Letter to Rouché, 1 December 1913; RATNER 2012, p. 213.

leading Opéra singers to play *Ascanio* in New York, but a fire in August 1892 destroyed the auditorium and put an end to those plans. The director of the Algiers Théâtre Municipal hoped to put it on in the spring of 1893 but did not do so. Saint-Saëns was ready to admit that it was not in excessive demand: 'It's a work that will carry on quietly underground, like *Samson*, and one day emerge triumphantly from incubation. Get the Trio, the Duet for the King and the Duchesse, and the Quartet sung in concerts and soon after you'll see. I don't include the Florentine song because its reputation is already made.'[20]

The appearance of *Samson et Dalila* at the Opéra in November 1892 secured a foothold for Saint-Saëns in that institution that lasts to the present day, but it did nothing to further the prospects of his other large operas, perhaps the reverse. In 1894 there was a fire at the Rue Richer warehouse which destroyed the sets of both *Henry VIII* and *Ascanio*, and although the government contributed to the cost of replacements, these two operas were left off the list. *Henry VIII* was revived in 1909, but *Ascanio* not until 1921.

In 1897 there were discussions with Covent Garden which got nowhere. In 1898 Saint-Saëns proposed to Durand that they withdraw *Ascanio* from the Opéra and offer it to the Opéra-Comique, where it could be staged by cutting all but the last of the ballets. 'We would be played three times a week and we'll have a great success, I'm convinced, because the work has done its time underground and is ready to emerge.'[21]

In 1904 there was some discussion about mounting *Ascanio* in Monte Carlo, but it was too long for members of the audience who came in from Nice and had late trains to catch. Saint-Saëns would particularly have liked to see the great baritone Maurice Renaud take the part of Cellini. But it was not played there then, nor in 1912 when the Monte Carlo director, Raoul Gunsbourg, had contemplated a revival.

Good news finally came from the Grand Théâtre, Bordeaux, where *Ascanio* was revived on 31 March 1911. That theatre had already staged *Samson et Dalila*, *Phryné* and *Henry VIII*. Saint-Saëns coached the conductor Montagné and approved of the singers. He described the performance as a 'bonne affaire'.[22]

In November 1913 Jacques Rouché was named the new director of the Opéra, an appointment that would eventually bring *Ascanio* back to the stage where it was first played. Saint-Saëns immediately wrote to Rouché from Algeria with suggestions for casting and an explanation of the confusion that had affected the final scene when it was originally staged in his absence. Although Rouché was an enterprising director who introduced some remarkable works to the stage of the Opéra during his thirty years' tenure, he also felt an obligation to earlier French works that deserved a hearing. *Ascanio* fell into this category, along with *Les Troyens*, both of which were staged in 1921. If this revival was a long time coming, it at least took place during Saint-Saëns's lifetime,

---

[20] Letter to Auguste Durand, 20 April 1892; RATNER 2012, p. 211.
[21] Letter to Auguste Durand, 11 February 1898; RATNER 2012, p. 211.
[22] Letter to Jacques Durand, 2 April 1911; RATNER 2012, p. 212.

with seven performances in November and December 1921. Despite his eighty-six years, Saint-Saëns gave Rouché detailed instructions how to stage the opera[23] and took a close interest in the rehearsals, and his admiration of the conductor Reynaldo Hahn was mutual. He made a cut in the duet for the King and the Duchesse in Tableau 4, Scene 1 and it is possible that he allowed a number of other cuts which never found their way into a printed score. He had an excellent cast, with Marcel Journet as Cellini, Marcelle Demougeot as the Duchesse d'Étampes and, finally, a true contralto in Lyse Charny as Scozzone. On December 4th he left for Algiers, where he died twelve days later. The last performance took place three days after that, and although there is no suggestion that the Opéra felt no obligation to continue the revival with the composer gone, *Ascanio* was not to be heard again for nearly a hundred years.

* * * * *

Like *Henry VIII*, *Ascanio* is a thoroughly rewarding opera from many points of view. Unless it were set in a timeless mythological background of the Wagnerian ilk, a grand opera in 1890 invariably required a historical setting, and the setting of *Ascanio* was particularly attractive since it presented scenes from old Paris as well as the gardens at Fontainebleau. Ceremonial and state occasions – the meeting of two kings, no less – were perfect for choreographers and costumiers, and Saint-Saëns hoped that the King's role would be sung by someone who resembled François I in Titian's famous portrait in the Louvre. No doubt he would have liked the Charles V to bear his extraordinary profile too. The opera's seven tableaux required six different sets from the workshops, but the Opéra could always afford extravagance of this kind, and was proud to do so.

The story is well told, as any by-product of a Dumas novel should be, and the tensions between characters are carefully worked out. Gallet must take credit here, although he followed Meurice's play closely. The intrigue may have been manufactured out of the slender information provided by Cellini's *Vita*, but it holds together well, and the finding of the wrong corpse at the end has the same powerful impact as when Rigoletto finds that of his daughter Gilda. The dramatic situation of the quartet in Tableau 6 – a pair of lovers being watched by a second pair in concealment – resembles that of the quartet in *Rigoletto* too.

The plot has the additional value of celebrating Cellini as an artist and the divine nature of art itself. The historical Cellini pressed the point, and so does the operatic Cellini in Berlioz's opera. Here in Saint-Saëns's hands Cellini is first and foremost a supreme artist, therefore the equal of kings and emperors, and if he is human enough to fall in love with his models, first Scozzone then Colombe, he is always ready to sacrifice love on the altar of art. He is thus cruel to Scozzone and willing to renounce

---

[23] Letter to Rouché, 5 July 1921; RATNER 2012, pp. 214–15.

Figure 8.1 François I, by Titian
Musée du Louvre, Paris/Bridgeman Images

Colombe. Cellini also loves Ascanio, as a father might, and will do anything for him, including protecting him from the dangerous Duchesse and giving up Colombe to him. Cellini's is the central role in the opera, so it is a pity that the opera could not bear his name. Any baritone would enjoy the challenge of the wide range of moods, from leader of his workmen, to far-from-servile royal employee, from passionate admiration to steaming anger, from love to jealousy to self-sacrifice. His confrontations with the Duchesse in Tableau 2 and with Scozzone in Tableau 6 are particularly strong, and he is hardly less impressive everywhere else.

Ascanio is not at the centre of the story despite giving his name to the opera. He is young and vulnerable and therefore an easy victim of the Duchesse's infatuation if Cellini had not interposed himself. He is wholly loyal, and his love for Colombe has all the naïveté of first love. The part should be sung by a light tenor, not a heroic tenor who mistakenly believes that the title role must be a big role. Colombe, too, is very young, so her voice should pair with Ascanio's and contrast with that of the Duchesse, who, as chief villain, requires the hard edge of a dramatic soprano, inclined to coloratura effusions from time to time. She has a tender side, but it shows only once, in Tableau 4, in the scene of the lily with Colombe and Ascanio. She pays for her villainy by finding that her victim is not the innocent Colombe, as she supposes, but her friend and co-conspirator Scozzone.

Saint-Saëns cared deeply for Scozzone, insisting on many occasions that she be a real contralto. In *Henry VIII* a similar voice is that of Anne de Boleyn, portrayed as attractive, ambitious and unscrupulous. Scozzone is attractive and easily influenced, but her love for Cellini is deep. She is hurt first by his coolness and then by his declared passion for Colombe, and she would have been glad to connive in Colombe's murder until the moment when Cellini, seeing the sincerity of Ascanio and Colombe's love for one another, renounces his feelings for Colombe. This noble gesture persuades Scozzone that she must pay for her involvement in the conspiracy to murder Colombe by taking her place in the reliquary chest, knowing that the Duchesse would make sure that whoever was inside would not survive. Unfortunately she has no opportunity to convey these extraordinary feelings, and we are left to think of her self-sacrifice as that of Sydney Carton going to his death in place of the innocent Charles Darnay.

The score of *Ascanio* is a magnificent achievement. Saint-Saëns never allows his invention to flag or routine to take over. The constant alertness of his orchestration and his harmony makes new points in every bar, and although the opera lacks grand solo scenes and arias that opera-goers might crave, the tension and pace of the action is superbly controlled, so that as dramatic forces pile up one upon another, the music can generate equal excitement and intensity, creating that sensation experienced at the end of certain acts in all the best operas, including *Samson et Dalila* and *Henry VIII*, that we have been driven to a point of tension where the music simply has to stop.

Chromaticism is everywhere because that was Saint-Saëns's natural language at this point in his life, colouring the tonality and not controlling it. Motifs are abundant, some persisting throughout the opera, some recurring just a few times, some confined to scenes and acting as 'scene-motifs'. The motifs I have cited in the text here are only the most readily observable and the most pertinent.

As for continuity, that element of Wagnerian opera that was much discussed at the time, Saint-Saëns identifies 'Scenes' (not very systematically) where new characters enter, as he did in his earlier operas, and the music usually runs on from one Scene to the next without a break. But there are sometimes full breaks, even opportunities for applause, and a direct change of tempo and key can occur without any pretence at modulation. A valid criticism of the opera is that there is too much action, and that more of the novel and the play should have been discarded. It is strange, that librettist and composer prized the beggar's scene in Tableau 2, which could easily be cut. In other respects it is not that the action is obscure or unnecessarily complicated; it simply means that the composer was left without opportunities for big solos and ensembles which might have added to the opera's attractions. There is a sense throughout that the story still has some way to go and the action must move on.

The viability of *Ascanio* was demonstrated with great éclat on 24 November 2017 when Guillaume Tourniaire, who had already recorded the twelve ballet movements in 2012, conducted a concert performance in the Opéra des Nations, Geneva, with a strong cast of French singers and the orchestra of the Haute École de Musique de Genève. The performance was later issued as a set of CDs. The opera, which had been resting unheard for ninety-six years, sprang into life. On the day before it was previously performed, 18 December 1921, the conductor of that revival, Reynaldo Hahn, wrote:

> How can one not admire the precision, the accuracy and the taste with which he presents his characters and makes them speak? In this respect *Ascanio* is truly marvellous. In character, colour and ornamentation it is like a Renaissance work of art, and it offers an incomparable example of vocal declamation, the accentuation being so right, the psychology of each character being so complete and well drawn. Saint-Saëns is the last great classic of music.[24]

---

[24] *Excelsior*, 18 December 1921.

9 | La Crampe des écrivains, Phryné

Ascanio was receiving regular performances at the Opéra when *Samson et Dalila* finally arrived on a Parisian stage. On 31 October 1890, thirteen years after its first performance and over twenty years since the music was begun, *Samson et Dalila* was played at the Théâtre Lyrique de l'Eden on the Rue Boudreau, a stone's throw from the Opéra itself. The cast was excellent, with Bloch as Dalila, Talazac as Samson and Bouhy as the Grand Prêtre. Saint-Saëns was greatly impressed by the conductor Gabriel Marie, and the directors of the Opéra, equally impressed, could hardly now argue that Saint-Saëns was not an opera composer or that a biblical opera was unacceptable on the stage. They may even have been encouraged by the failure of Verdhurt, who had brought the production from Rouen, to exploit the box office in ways Parisians understood, so the run was short with only five performances.

Saint-Saëns left soon after for his winter retreat, this year to Spain and Ceylon, his first visit to Egypt and the Suez Canal. Already thinking about a new opera, he took with him a libretto on the story of Éviradnus, one of the *Chevaliers errants* in the first book of Victor Hugo's immense series of poems, *La Légende des siècles*. This is a grim story about two kings, Ladislas of Poland and Sigismond of Germany, who are in league with the devil. They intend to prey upon the Marquise of Mahaut. Having put her to sleep with a potion, they cast lots which assign her property to Sigismond and her person to Ladislas. In order to avoid strife with Sigismond, who also desires her, Ladislas decides to cast her into the castle dungeon, but is prevented by Éviradnus, an old Knight Errant, who is hidden in a suit of armour from which he emerges to strangle Ladislas and lay Sigismond low.

This libretto, by the journalist Alphonse Pagès, was set as an opera in 1899 by Nedje Xanilef. It was certainly wise of Saint-Saëns not to take it on. The useful work he did do on that trip was the revision of *Proserpine*. He was also reminded of *Étienne Marcel*, since he travelled on the steamer incognito under his earlier pseudonym Charles Sannois, and a lady fellow-traveller happened one day to play a fragment from that opera on the piano, unaware that its composer was listening. Before journey's end she recognised him from photographs. As for new works, the year 1891 saw the composition of *Africa*, for piano and orchestra, and the transformation of his *Mélodies persanes*, written in 1870, into a major work for soloists, chorus and orchestra under the title *Nuit persane*.

Of the original six songs, Saint-Saëns kept five and added two new ones. He then divided them into four groups and composed a Prelude for each group and orchestrated the whole thing. Each Prelude requires a Récitant, as the 'Voice of the Dream', to declaim verses which must have been provided by Armand Renaud, the author of the song verses and a fellow Parnassian. The resulting work is closer to the *ode-symphonie* than to a song cycle or dramatic cantata, recalling such works as Félicien David's *Le Désert* and Bizet's *Vasco de Gama*, for it has dramatic continuity and a consistently exotic colour. Music with a Mediterranean or Middle Eastern flavour was now almost an obsession with French composers, Saint-Saëns leading the flock and expertly demonstrating in *Nuit persane* how it should be done. The pedal basses, modal scales, pitchless drumming and dark-coloured woodwind were perhaps something of a cliché, but it was a cliché on which Saint-Saëns played with infinite skill. The two newly composed songs, *La Fuite* and *Les Cygnes*, not having originated as songs with piano, show a particular richness of orchestration, and the songs for contralto – *La Solitaire*, *Les Cygnes* and the Prelude to Part IV – display Saint-Saëns's strongly sympathetic treatment of that voice, as in the roles of Anne Boleyn and Scozzone.

* * * * *

> ### *La Crampe des écrivains*
>
> Comedy in one act
>
> La Baronne
> Zénobia
> Fanny
> Gontran
>
> The action takes place in Paris at the Baronne's house.

Another product of the year was a play entitled *La Crampe des écrivains* ('Writer's Cramp'), written in Algiers for an amateur theatrical company. It is short, clever and amusing, with a plot in which Zénobia appears to be taking advantage of her friend the Baronne by entertaining a gentleman in her, the Baronne's apartment. The gentleman turns out to be the Baronne's estranged husband, who is reconciled to his wife by mistaking Zénobia's amorous thoughts to be hers. Because of Zénobia's writer's cramp, they were written under dictation in the Baronne's hand.

As if living in a completely different world, Saint-Saëns revised Lully's music for Molière's comedy *Le Sicilien*, a play which Bizet had once planned to turn into an opera. Insisting that a harpsichord be used for the performance (at the Opéra in May 1892), Saint-Saëns was already recognised as an expert in French baroque music. As a sequel he was then invited to reconstruct Marc-Antoine Charpentier's music for Molière's *Le Malade imaginaire*, played at the Théâtre Lyrique de l'Eden just a few days after *Samson et Dalila* was heard at the Opéra in November 1892.

Then, moving to yet another different world, his next composition was the Second Piano Trio in E minor in five movements, started in Algiers and finished in Geneva in June 1892. It contains no trace of exoticism or pastiche but displays Saint-Saëns's proven accomplishment in modern chamber music and also his vast piano technique.

Triggered by successful performances in Rouen and Paris in 1890, *Samson et Dalila* was staged in 1891 in Lyon, Marseille and Geneva, and in 1892 in Nantes, Toulouse, Bordeaux, Aix-les-Bains, Dijon, Montpellier, Monte Carlo and Nice. Saint-Saëns attended the performance in Marseille but showed little interest in the other cities, apart from confirming the satisfaction of seeing the work finally take off. In contrast, he was exceedingly exercised by the prospect of *Samson et Dalila* at the Opéra. *Ascanio* was still being played there, but a number of new works were competing for that stage. Massenet's *Le Mage*, with a Persian setting, opened at the Opéra in March 1891 but lasted only thirty-one performances, a poor number by that composer's standards. In September *Lohengrin* broke the prohibition on Wagner's operas that had been in place at the Opéra since the scandalous *Tannhäuser* of 1861. A Gallet libretto, *Thamara*, set by Louis Bourgault-Ducoudray, was heard in December. With its Islamic setting this opera was stuffed with exotic music and much admired by Debussy. Reyer's *Salammbo*, set in ancient Carthage and staged on 16 May 1892, had a strong following. *Aida* had set the standard for reviving ancient Egypt.

Exoticism in a non-European setting had taken a firm hold, in short, making *Samson et Dalila* a perfect choice. Convinced that Massenet's *Hérodiade*, first performed in Brussels ten years before, was being promoted for performance at the Opéra, Saint-Saëns would only allow his opera to be staged if no other biblical opera was in the repertoire. In fact Massenet himself was preoccupied with the premiere of *Werther* in Vienna and seems to have made no moves in regard to *Hérodiade*, which by a curious irony was not performed at the Opéra until a few days after Saint-Saëns's death.

So he felt finally vindicated when on 23 November 1892 *Samson et Dalila* was performed at the Opéra, the first of over a thousand performances running with few breaks until the present day. The stage set for Act I was borrowed from Massenet's *Le Roi de Lahore*, but the Act III sets were new, including machinery for bringing down the temple that never worked properly. Cast and dancers were strong, and the conductor was the reliable Édouard Colonne. The press finally acknowledged Saint-Saëns's mastery, and a profitable box office was assured. There have been new productions at regular intervals, with the latest staging seen on 1 October 2016.

Within a fortnight France lost two of her leading musicians, Édouard Lalo in April 1892 and Ernest Guiraud in May, both of them composers that Saint-Saëns had energetically promoted in the Société Nationale de Musique in the 1870s. He was on good terms with both. Lalo, at the age of sixty-nine, left his opera *La Jacquerie* unfinished, to be completed by Arthur Coquard. Guiraud, dying younger, at fifty-four, also left an opera unfinished: *Frédégonde*, with a libretto by Gallet. Within a few days of his death, Saint-Saëns told Durand that he would undertake the completion of this opera, however hazardous the attempt might be.[1]

Whether Saint-Saëns was actively seeking a new opera libretto for himself in this period is an open question. He discouraged Gallet from sending him any ideas for long operas that would require endless hours of work. He was approached by Mme Détroyat, wife of the librettist of *Henry VIII*, whose husband Léonce was about to take over management of the Théâtre de la Renaissance on the Boulevard Saint-Martin and who intended to put on opera there. Having worked happily and productively with him ten years earlier, Saint-Saëns was keen to find a piece to offer him. The urgency meant that only a shorter work could be considered, and his mind turned to a comic play he had been given a few years earlier by Lucien Augé de Lassus (1841–1914), a dramatist, traveller and writer who had written at least one opera libretto, *L'Amour vengé*, set to music by Léon de Maupéou and played at the Opéra-Comique in 1890. He had travelled widely around the Mediterranean and had a particular interest in Greco-Roman antiquities, while nourishing ambitions as a playwright and dramatist which were never fulfilled, except in his collaborations with Saint-Saëns.[2] He wrote the poems for setting by Prix de Rome candidates in 1885 and 1887, the first entitled *Endymion*, the second *Didon*, whose winning composer was Gustave Charpentier. It was this task that introduced him to Saint-Saëns. His book titles reveal his interest: *Thèbes, Hymne et Chanson* (1877), *Routes et Étapes* (1877), *Voyage aux Sept Merveilles du Monde* (1878), *Chez le Bey de Tunis* (1881) and *Le Forum* (1892). In 1888 he published *Les Spectacles antiques* with a generous dedication to Saint-Saëns, undoubtedly in homage to the essay *Notes sur les décors de théâtre dans l'antiquité romaine* which Saint-Saëns published shortly after his visit to Pompeii in July 1886. Their friendship yielded two operas and an affectionate book on Saint-Saëns written by Augé de Lassus at the end of his life and published in 1914.

Knowing both Saint-Saëns's interest in antiquity and his recent operas, Augé de Lassus took his drama *Phryné*, a comedy set in ancient Greece, to the composer in his apartment in the Rue Monsieur-le-Prince, probably around 1888. Originally a one-act comedy in verse, it had grown into an opéra-comique libretto in three acts. Augé de Lassus's account of the libretto's fate is irresistibly fanciful:

> One day, dreaming of a perfect marriage, *Phryné* knocked at Saint-Saëns's door. Mutual attraction was immediate. They were made for one another. It was more than a meeting, it was a betrothal. Saint-Saëns has a need for bright, open gaiety, also for mockery, even if it stings. As a child at the Paris Guignol he had seen policemen being beaten up to the accompaniment of a squeaky fiddle, so it could only amuse him to flout the Athenian areopagus and give justice a rough ride. He knows the character of the ancient world. He has his humanities, as they used to say. Evoking Athens, inviting the muse to sit for a moment on the steps of the Parthenon, that's what attracts him and amuses him: to catch a glimpse of

---

[1] RATNER 2012, p. 503.   [2] Augé de Lassus's career is recounted in YON 2007.

that marvellous alliance of grace and beauty and the gods' brilliant marriage of joy and the divine city, all to be summed up and captured in the glorious word 'Greece'. Saint-Saëns possessed that vision to some extent already; it needed only to be set free. Elegant and pretty, the bird took wing. With its golden eyes it catches sight at once of its prey. It seizes it, not to tear it to pieces, but to make it its own and to bring it back to us still quivering, defeated, and deliciously ready to do service.

But being scrupulous and stubborn, Saint-Saëns can get sudden changes of wind, like squalls, once the work is finally taken on and begun. He bears wounds, still unhealed, from certain injustices and villainies, mainly serious misapprehensions, which he seems to bear with magnificent stoicism. Despite his courage, he has experienced discouragement. On the brink of a long hoped-for setting, *Phryné* is set aside. One day to the original author's house there comes a stranger. He gives no name and disappears at once, a mysterious messenger sent by a secret tribunal to which there is no appeal. The messenger's message is a scroll held out, returned and left, that's all. Alas, *Phryné* has returned home, and the scroll, opened with considerable apprehension, delivers the waif manuscript to its author, mourning for its shattered hopes. Poor *Phryné*, so longing for sunshine and a playful love affair, there she is, back in the darkness and silence of a drawer, like the grave.

Years pass, and *Phryné* is not a woman to give in to the ravages of time. She thinks always of her lost love; how is she to know if that faithless man still thinks about her? She doesn't even know where in his wanderings her lost fiancé indulges his caprices. But the world is smaller than you think. Divorced before they were ever joined, the partners meet by chance. The special setting is a *terrasse* on the Boulevard St-Germain. One walks by, the other spots him. They greet one another and talk. Not a word about *Phryné*. One of them is thinking about her a lot, but *tacet*, as they say in music. Poor girl! The mere mention of her name might bring a disastrous rebuff. [. . .] Yet this chance meeting perhaps brought the inconsolable exile back from limbo, to which she was not at all resigned. The place to find Saint-Saëns is precisely where you least expect to, at a moment when you're thinking of something else. I was crossing the Pont des Arts, not far, it's true, from the kind of house that she inhabited, but my mind was full of anything but the splendours and miseries of courtesans. And here comes Saint-Saëns, as if coming from another world. Meeting, greeting, talking. Saint-Saëns was the first to speak:

'And *Phryné*?'

'She's there for you.'

'Good. Bring her round tomorrow morning.'

So for the second time, with light rapid steps and her heart beating with emotion like her parent's, *Phryné* ascended the stairs of no. 14 Rue Monsieur-le-Prince. And thus what was once a mad dalliance became real love.[3]

How long this process took is not clear. Bonnerot assigns Saint-Saëns's first sight of the libretto to around 1888, which is plausible. In February 1892 Saint-Saëns mentions *Phryné* as a possible ballet, and implies that Carvalho had asked him to consider it for

---

[3] Augé de Lassus 1914, pp. 163–67.

the Opéra-Comique. 'But in view of his attitude I have no desire to do so,' he wrote.[4] He preferred to work with Détroyat, and his decision to set the opera definitely belongs to the end of 1892 when he had already begun work on completing Guiraud's *Frédégonde*. Détroyat planned to include it in his new opera season in 1893, for which Augé de Lassus agreed to reduce the three acts to two. Setting *Frédégonde* aside, Saint-Saëns began to draft *Phryné* in Algiers on 12 January 1893.[5] It was the speediest of all Saint-Saëns's operas to be written, being completed within three months, even allowing for the fact that the orchestration of Act I was consigned to André Messager, who had himself provided the opening opera for Détroyat's season. His *Madame Chrysanthème*, a forerunner of *Madama Butterfly*, was first performed on 26 January 1893.

Act I was drafted by the end of January and sent off to Paris for Messager to work on. Act II took a little longer but was drafted by March 6th. By this time there was a radical change of plan in Paris. Détroyat's season at the Renaissance closed at the end of February, having offered Messager's *Madame Chrysanthème* and Offenbach's *Les Contes d'Hoffmann* in alternation for a month. Clearly his money had run out, and the theatre was soon taken over by Sarah Bernhardt. Into the breach stepped the ever-opportunistic Carvalho, offering to put on *Phryné* at the Opéra-Comique. Saint-Saëns was wary of Carvalho's methods and intentions. 'Make sure Carvalho knows the piece, if you can,' he wrote to Augé de Lassus. 'It's not enough for him just to read the libretto. He imagines the action according to his own ideas and fits the staging to this hypothetical opera, leading to endless battles.'[6]

For the title role Carvalho had Emma Calvé in mind, fresh from her first international successes in New York and London. With her return to London he decided to postpone it until the autumn season, to which Saint-Saëns responded with some firmness, knowing it was perfectly possible to have the opera ready in May. He had always imagined that Cécile Simonnet, his Angiola in *Proserpine*, would sing the role. It is surprising that someone who had said of the role 'What woman will ever be able to match such an ideal?'[7] would be content with a singer of, it seems, only moderate distinction.

On March 12th Saint-Saëns took a five-day holiday in Blida, a town of orchards and gardens at the base of the Atlas mountains beautifully evoked in the third movement of the *Suite algérienne* of 1879, and returned to Algiers to orchestrate Act II. Messager had meanwhile finished the orchestration of Act I. Then came the news from Carvalho that he had secured Sybil Sanderson for the role of Phryné. Sanderson had wowed *tout Paris* with her singing and her physical appeal in *Esclarmonde* in 1889. Since then she had been singing *Manon* in Brussels, in London and at the Opéra-Comique, and she was widely

---

[4] Letter to Auguste Durand, 27 February 1892, RATNER 2012, p. 226.
[5] The letter to Durand saying he had started Act II, cited by Ratner (RATNER 2012, p. 226) as dated February 1892, must belong correctly to 1893.
[6] Letter to Augé de Lassus, 26 February 1893, RATNER 2012, p. 231.
[7] Letter to Augé de Lassus, 12 January 1893, RATNER 2012, p. 227.

assumed to sing only in Massenet's operas. She was already in the composer's mind for the main role in *Thaïs*, to be performed at the Opéra in 1894.

The prospect of such a popular diva appearing in the highly seductive role of Phryné guaranteed the success of the opera, but Saint-Saëns was more alarmed than excited, jealous, as ever, of Massenet. 'I'm afraid of this American woman. In the background there's someone who has an interest in her *not* playing Phryné. There could be objections, indispositions, who knows? And we'd be delayed until kingdom come. With Simonnet there would be no trouble. Beware! Anything can happen around a theatre's trapdoors. Beware!'[8] Saint-Saëns was also worried that Sanderson's American accent would be disturbing in verse dialogue.

She was engaged, however, and with her a fine baritone Lucien Fugère for the part of Dicéphile. Fugère's long career covered a vast range of opera, from Offenbach as a young man to Bartolo (in *Il barbiere di Siviglia*) at the age of eighty-five. He was to be closely associated with the baritone roles in Massenet's later operas. The score was finished by April 1st. Saint-Saëns arrived back in Paris in the middle of the month to oversee rehearsals, which went smoothly, it seems, under Jules Danbé, the Opéra-Comique's conductor. He had to check Messager's orchestration of Act I and perhaps he added some coloratura with Sybil Sanderson's special agility in mind.

Phryné opened at the Opéra-Comique on 24 May 1893 and ran for fifty performances in its first year, an unequivocal success. The stage set was designed by Rubé and Chaperon, the same partnership that had designed the interior of Détroyat's Théâtre de la Renaissance. The costumes were by Théodore Thomas, although Saint-Saëns particularly wanted them to be designed by Léon Heuzey, an archaeologist who had written a study of ancient Greek costume. 'Our characters need to be dressed as they were dressed in Phryné's time, not like picturesque carnival characters.'[9]

The statue of Aphrodite unveiled at the end of the opera was the work of the sculptor Daniel Campagne, who made a plaster version for the stage in 1893 and a marble version in 1894.[10] The latter work, or a copy of it, came into Saint-Saëns's possession and can be seen in the background of photographs of him taken at his home. The pose is unapologetic with both arms held away from the body. The frontispiece to the vocal score (by F. Marcotte) shows the final scene of the opera with the statue of Aphrodite life-size, but her hands are placed across the body with conventional modesty. *Le Figaro*, on the day of the opera's opening, fatuously suggested that the statue was introduced into the story because Sybil Sanderson was unwilling to bare all.

Reviews in the press accepted the piece for what it was, a light opéra-comique in the traditional form of individual numbers separated by dialogue, with comic elements and

---

[8] Letter to Augé de Lassus, 18 March 1893, RATNER 2012, p. 234.
[9] Letter to Augé de Lassus, 22 February 1893, RATNER 2012, p. 231.
[10] It may be seen at www.anticstore.art/60728P#gallery-1.

a satirical strain in raising the issue, if not the reality, of nudity in an era when the female body was more thoroughly concealed in public than ever before. Wagnerism was finally irrelevant, and the fact that the Opéra had played *Die Walküre* only two weeks earlier must have given pause to those who had insisted for years that Saint-Saëns was tarred with the Bayreuth brush. Some of the critics were doubtless hearing mature Wagner for the first time. Gounod, on his deathbed, wrote to Saint-Saëns: 'Thankyou for [the score of] your exquisite *Phryné*. I shall listen to it with my eyes, the musician's second pair of ears.'[11] He had earlier attended the opera and found in it 'all the perfect originality of colouring so clear when it's needed and always in good taste. You once said I'd never suspect which of my works taught you most about orchestration for the theatre. The fact is I have no idea, but what I do know is that you should now be teaching it to me.'[12]

Durand issued a vocal score (145 pages) to accompany the performances and a full score (175 pages) later in the year. Neither score includes the dialogue. Individual numbers were as usual available for sale, as well as the libretto.

* * * * *

Phryné
(Ratner 294)

Opéra-comique in two acts

Libretto by Lucien Augé de Lassus

First performance: Opéra-Comique, Paris, 24 May 1893

Phryné	soprano
Lampito, esclave de Phryné	soprano
Dicéphile, archonte	basse-chantante
Nicias, neveu de Dicéphile	ténor
Cynalopex, démarque	2ème ténor
Agoragine, démarque	basse
Un héraut	

Peuple, esclaves, chanteurs, danseurs, joueurs de flûte et de tambourin, soldats scythes

The action takes places in Athens, fourth century BCE.

Orchestra:	2 flutes, 2 oboes, 2 clarinets, 2 bassoons, 4 horns, 2 trumpets or cornets, 3 trombones, timpani, bass drum, cymbals, triangle, tambourine, harp, strings.
Offstage:	triangle, sistra, harmonium, harp.

---

[11] Letter of 12 October 1893, BONNEROT 1922, p. 158.
[12] Letter of 4 June 1893, RATNER 2012, p. 235.

Figure 9.1 Jean-Léon Gérôme, *Phryné devant l'Aréopagus*
Kunsthalle, Hamburg/Wikimedia Commons

The original Phryné was a celebrated Athenian courtesan who flourished about 328 BCE. She was said to be the mistress of the great sculptor Praxiteles and the model for his famous statue of Aphrodite, widely copied in the ancient world. This was said to be the first life-size representation of the nude female form and was unusually shocking since it was placed in a temple. Athenaeus relates that when Phryné was accused of impiety she would have been condemned had she not stood in the courtroom and unveiled her bosom, a display which immediately persuaded her judges to acquit her.

This story inspired the artist Jean-Léon Gérôme to paint his spectacular painting *Phryné devant l'Aréopagus* in 1861, a work which caused a sensation and was much discussed. It was certainly known by Augé de Lassus and probably by Saint-Saëns too, since he and Gérôme were well acquainted. It depicts some two dozen men in scarlet robes in a state of collective shock and fascination while a fully frontal Phryné stands boldly naked in the centre, her robe having been swept from her by her advocate Hyperides. She covers her face, not her body, with her hands. The dealer Goupil commissioned the sculptor Alexandre Falguière to make a rendering of Phryné based on the painting. This was issued as a tiny ivory, a bronze statuette and half life-size in marble.

Phryné had already appeared on the Parisian stage. Henri Meilhac, one of Offenbach's (and Bizet's) librettists, wrote a three-act comedy *Phryné* which was played at the Gymnase on 14 February 1881, and an anonymous *Phryné* presented by the Chat Noir in January 1891 'drew in the whole of Paris'.[13]

Nudity on stage being unthinkable at that time, Augé de Lassus had the idea of making a play out of the nudity of Aphrodite, as a statue, while Phryné remains fully dressed. His instincts as both dramatist and antiquarian combined in presenting a comic story which drew an audience on the mere suggestion that the famously sensual Sybil Sanderson might be the one to be unveiled. At the same time he used the familiar comic trope of an older man with absurd pretensions with regard to an attractive younger woman. This is Dicéphile, the self-important 'archon', or chief Athenian magistrate, whose record in upholding morality and the law is celebrated with a bust whose unveiling at the beginning of the opera neatly counterpoints the unveiling of Aphrodite at the end. He is a 'basse-chantante' or baritone, while the tenor is his penniless nephew Nicias, who is in love with Phryné, although her standing as a courtesan precludes her admission that she might be in love with him. Minor characters include Lampito, Phryné's personal slave, sung by a soprano, and two comic characters Cynalopex and Agoragine, both 'démarques' or junior magistrates on Dicéphile's bench. As a comic pair they are descendants of Beppo and Giacomo in Auber's *Fra Diavolo* of 1830 and cousins of Pistol and Bardolph in Verdi's *Falstaff*, whose premiere in Milan took place only two months before the premiere of *Phryné*.

Originally this was a three-act verse play, reduced to two acts when made into a libretto for Saint-Saëns. It is in verse throughout, even in the dialogue, which would normally be in prose for an opéra-comique. As usual, the dialogue is found only in the printed libretto, not in the vocal score. The action is slight since it is necessary only to overcome Dicéphile's tight-fisted disapproval of his nephew, to prick his pomposity and for Phryné to humiliate him by leading him on to believe that he might see the unveiling for which he lusts, when of course he gets to see only a nude statue, albeit the famously sensual masterpiece by Praxiteles.

* * * * *

ACT I

Introduction The scene is a street in Athens with Phryné's large house on the left. A bust of Dicéphile, still covered, stands at the back. A variety of ideas, most of which will be heard later, make up a short prelude in the key of E♭, the key with which the opera will also end.

---

[13] Cited in BROOKS 2008, p. 240.

Dialogue A crowd of people are milling around Dicéphile (baritone), Athens's chief magistrate, who is to be honoured with a public bust in gratitude for his success in upholding law and order. Agoragine (bass) and Cynalopex (tenor), both junior magistrates, stand apart, offering cynical comments on their boss's self-importance.

A herald lists the services that Dicéphile has provided, unveils the bust and lays a wreath at its foot. Exhorting the people to sing their magistrate's praise, the herald leaves the stage with his escort.

No. 1 Chœur et Ensemble The men obediently sing Dicéphile's praise and the false modesty of his acknowledgement is neatly revealed in ex. 9.1. Agoragine and Cynalopex question his worthiness. The key moves up from E♭ to E♮ as a group of young slaves arrives with garlands to be laid at Phryné's door, repeating the music of the Introduction. As Agoragine points out, to Dicéphile's obvious embarrassment, their masters are her clients. (Saint-Saëns here omitted to set a pair of Augé de Lassus's lines which rhyme 'aux dieux' with 'odieux'.)

Example 9.1 *Phryné*, Act I, No. 1

Phryné (soprano) herself appears, drawing all attention away from Dicéphile. In a solemn lilting 6/8 in F♯ major the chorus sing her praises. Against dense harmony in the strings they sing in unison, which, as Erin Brooks has pointed out, was to represent the pagan world in Saint-Saëns's 'ancient' works.[14] In 1912 Saint-Saëns told Camille Bellaigue that the melody is in the 'second plainchant mode' (Dorian). 'You will be as surprised as I was that it was not deliberate. I only noticed it later.'[15] The grace of Phryné's movement as she crosses the stage is conveyed in an elegant phrase on two flutes, ex. 9.2:

Example 9.2 *Phryné*, Act I, No. 1

---

[14] BROOKS 2008, p. 241.   [15] Letter of 27 February 1912, RATNER 2012, p. 240.

'What's going on?' she asks her slave Lampito (soprano), whose reply leads Phryné (again to ex. 9.2) to move across to Dicéphile and pay her respects ('modestly' received by ex. 9.1), quietly acknowledging that her own virtue was not above reproof. Agoragine mutters that she is going a bit far, but the chorus reprise their opening adulation, to which Phryné adds another flattering compliment. Dicéphile grins and bows to ex. 9.1. Taking Lampito's arm, she starts laughing at her own hypocrisy, and as they pass the bust her little group breaks into laughter. Meanwhile the chorus repeat their song in praise of Phryné, this time with harmony. Dicéphile joins in, acknowledging his own fascination with her.

Dialogue Dicéphile is left alone with Agoragine and Cynalopex for a little male banter about Phryné. Dicéphile admits both that he is taken with her and that she makes fun of him. Agoragine tells us that Praxiteles has used her as the model for his statue of Aphrodite, which prompts Dicéphile to complain that Praxiteles offends modern taste by leaving his statues insufficiently clothed.

He changes the subject to his nephew Nicias. Cynalopex has investigated the extent of Nicias's debts to his uncle which make him liable to imprisonment. Agoragine warns Dicéphile that his status as guardian makes him susceptible to a plea. The two démarques are instructed to apprehend him.

Seeing Nicias (tenor) approach, Dicéphile (surprisingly) tells the pair to make themselves scarce. Nicias congratulates his uncle on the bust recently unveiled and immediately asks for a loan of two talents (or twelve thousand drachmas), adding that a magistrate's office is surely profitable. Refusing his request, he adds, would amount to stealing from him, forcing him to starve. Dicéphile suspects that a woman is behind his insistent behaviour, perhaps even Phryné ('How did he know?' the young man asks himself). Let me give you some advice, says Dicéphile.

No. 2 Duo The bassoon's gift for comic mockery was never put to better use than here in supporting Dicéphile's avuncular boast that clean living and cold reason are the secrets of his success, the latter illustrated by a few bars of Handelian counterpoint. Nicias's first sung phrases would be the envy of any tenor wishing to make an immediate impression. 'Rien sur la terre / N'est solitaire' he sings *appassionato*, while Déciphile is too busy repeating his creed, softly and staccato, to notice.

The sequence is repeated, with Nicias given the introductory lines (no bassoon) and Dicéphile allowed to boast that he has never loved anyone but himself, with Nicias's 'Quel goût!' and ex. 9.1 in response. The duet refrain is now a semitone higher than before with high B instead of high B♭ for Nicias and a crafty modulation inserted to bring the tonality back to B♭ and the bassoon's bottom note as the last word.

Dialogue With a nod in the direction of his bust, Dicéphile leaves the stage. Nicias turns the tone from comedy to serious drama with a monologue in which he laments his dependence on a mean-spirited uncle, his lack of family and friends, his debts, and above all his failure to win Phryné's response to his adoration. She sends him occasional encouraging glances, but he is convinced they are false.

No. 3 Cantabile et Chœur Nicias's solo is a tender and shapely verse, the phrasing dictated by the alternation of long and short lines, beginning with ex. 9.3:

Example 9.3 *Phryné*, Act I, No. 3

Ô ma Phry-né___ c'est trop peu que je t'ai-me, Il faut m'ai-mer.___

The modulation into and out of G major is particularly well handled.

He sits down on a bench lost in thought. A group of dancers and singers then appear, playing flutes, citharas and tambourines.[16] The cithara, represented here by a harp, was a Greek lyre in which Saint-Saëns took a particular interest, ever since his visits to Pompeii. He published two essays on the subject.[17] Such a spectacle of song and dance was familiar from Greek vase-painting, which Augé de Lassus and Saint-Saëns clearly hoped to reproduce. Their song is energetic, catchy and scarcely ethnic at all save in its solid rhythm and noisy percussion, which includes tambourine, triangle and 'sistres', instruments from the ancient world known to Saint-Saëns from Kastner's and Berlioz's treatises and from the score of *Les Troyens*. The player shakes a metal frame in which a loose metal bar jangles against the sides. As local colour the group serves extremely well, better than in cheering up Nicias, who declines to join in their merriment. The music executes a neat disappearance as the singers and dancers leave the stage.

Dialogue Inconsolable, Nicias decides he should beat someone up before making away with himself. Agoragine and Cynalopex approach and debate nervously and urgently how best to apprehend him. Announcing their intention to take him to prison on the orders of Dicéphile, they are met by a hail of blows from a stick which Nicias has conveniently found.

---

[16] 'Tambourin' in the libretto and vocal score would normally indicate the small provençal hand-held drum. But the full score calls for 'tambour de basque', a tambourine.
[17] 'Note sur la lyre antique', *Le Monde artiste*, 23 October 1892, SORET 2012, pp. 447–48; 'Essai sur les lyres et cithares antiques', *Institut de France, séance publique du 25 octobre 1902*, SORET 2012, pp. 565–68.

No. 4 Final Against an orchestral uproar the unfortunate démarques cry for help as Nicias's blows continue to fall. Who should appear at that instant but Phryné, emerging from her door with her slave Lampito. The music cools as Nicias explains that he has no particular taste for prison. With unmistakably tender support from the strings (ex.9.4) and appalled at the mere suggestion of prison, Phryné calls on all her slaves to come out and defend him, which renews the uproar as they mercilessly thrash the unfortunate officials and send them on their way. The scene recalls a similar scene in *Falstaff* Act I, when Sir John chases Pistol and Bardolph out of the Garter Inn with a broom.

Example 9.4 *Phryné*, Act I, No. 4

A lone oboe brings peace back to the scene. Nicias thanks Phryné, who responds over variations of ex. 9.4. He plans to flee the city as a last resort, if only it didn't mean moving far from her. She immediately offers him the hospitality of her home, allowing her a little ariette 'Si, le front couronné de lierre', in which her essential simplicity and tenderness emerge, since she can overlook (with a hint to Nicias) the lies of those who claim to love her. He is content to accept her hospitality 'for the present'.

Seeing the bust of Dicéphile (and hearing the bassoon's antics transferred to heavy horns and strings), he has a sudden urge to get back at the source of all his troubles. The singers and dancers conveniently reappear, so he interrupts their song since this time they can do something for him. He throws his last remaining coins at them. He grabs a goatskin water bottle from one of the singers and hands it to Lampito with instructions to place it on the head of the bust. Lampito does so, setting it ludicrously askew.

Gales of laughter introduce the main section of the finale, a swift 6/8 in E major, very close to Offenbach's style with a facile tune and regular phrase-lengths. Saint-Saëns was fully aware that sinking so low was dangerous. 'This finale took more guts and more disregard for what people would think than when I wrote the *Danse macabre* as a young man', he later wrote.[18] Phryné joins in, and soon her coloratura takes off while the chorus hammer home the refrain 'Dicéphile est un fripon', an unkind but not actually libellous name to call him. Everyone, including Nicias and the dancers and singers, pile into Phryné's house while the music and the daylight both fade.

---

[18] 'À propos d'*Orphée*, l'opinion de C. Saint-Saëns', *Le Figaro*, 4 December 1907, SORET 2012, p. 641.

When it is dark Dicéphile emerges with a lantern, proud that thanks to his policing policies, the streets are quiet and safe. He is undeceived by singing coming from Phryné's house. Hearing only his name he thinks the citizens are celebrating his great day. But then his lantern falls upon the bust, with its idiotic coiffure. Furious, he shakes his fist at Phryné's house and swears vengeance. Phryné and Lampito are heard from the wings still arpeggiating with joy.

ACT II

No. 5 Introduction et Duo Some elegant three-part writing for the upper strings suggests the civilised interior to which the action will now move. The Introduction continues with a full statement of Nicias's Cantabile, no. 3 (see ex. 9.3), which grows to a full climax at the height of which the curtain opens. The scene is Phryné's boudoir, 'rich, elegant and Greek'. Furnishings consist of a couch and a table, on which are scattered jewellery, 'objets de toilette' and a mirror.

Phryné is seated at her mirror in which she espies the approach of Nicias. Accompanied only by the first violins in a meandering counterpoint, he thanks her for having protected him the day before, and acknowledges that this is a debt he regrets not being able to repay. He now comes to say goodbye and leave her for good.

Her response is to set up a breezy waltz tempo, leading into a full duet. Augé de Lassus may have intended this scene as dialogue, since it has none of the usual layout of sung duets with balanced verses for each singer. Nonetheless Saint-Saëns has shaped it into a scene that progresses from Nicias's determination to leave Athens to a full acknowledgement of mutual love. The critical passage is the exchange where Nicias accuses Phryné of never loving anyone. She protests, claiming 'secret tensions' in her heart, and on hearing that he has lost everything admits that she loves him and has done so for a long time. Here, more than anywhere, Saint-Saëns is writing in a romantic language but keeping passion reined in. There is great warmth in the music, but no neurotic excess.

Dialogue Lampito enters to report that Dicéphile is furious and determined to bring to justice those who so ill-treated his staff. Nicias is similarly determined to treat his uncle in the same way as yesterday's victims if he gets a chance. Phryné wisely offers to find a peaceful solution. Perhaps Aphrodite will be sympathetic to a couple in love.

No. 6 Air et Trio In Algiers Saint-Saëns used to visit a park which 'led gently down to a small hidden beach, shaded by date trees, where the sea dies in amorous contentment. I used to go there to listen to its murmur and to reproduce it in the accompaniment to Phryné's air « Un soir, j'errais sur le rivage ».[19] Saint-Saëns's scoring is

---

[19] 'Algérie', *L'Écho de Paris*, 24 December 1911, SORET 2012, p. 761. See also Saint-Saëns's letters to Augé de Lassus, [21 February] 1893, RATNER 2012, p. 227, and to Bellaigue of 2 January 1891, RATNER 2012, p. 244.

wonderfully suggestive of the steady breaking of waves on the shore, each bar coming to a whoosh of extra sound at mid-point. A low clarinet, harp, timpani and shuddering strings achieve this with remarkable realism. There were two precedents in French opera which Saint-Saëns may have had in mind. In Gounod's *Sapho* (1851) the poet's final air 'Ô ma lyre immortelle' is sung on the cliff-top as Aegean waves are heard breaking far below. Berlioz particularly admired this piece and created his own impression of waves breaking on the shore, this time in Carthage (not so far from Algiers) in the Septet in Act IV of *Les Troyens* (1857).

One evening by the seashore near the temple of Aphrodite Phryné felt she was in the goddess's presence as she plunged naked into the water. Suddenly she heard the name 'Aphrodite' called out. It was a group of fishermen who had mistaken her for the goddess who famously emerged from the waves at birth. Saint-Saëns has moved well away from opéra-comique in this number, composing with a complexity and resourcefulness required for scenes of religious severity. Little wonder that he spoke of it, before he began to write it, with awe and anxiety. It is certainly the most powerful page in the opera, scored with great skill, and it leads into a grand orchestral peroration in G major while the three of them 'stand in ecstatic contemplation of Venus emerging from the waves.'

Picking up the devotional tone, Lampito and Nicias join Phryné in a hymn to Aphrodite, sung almost entirely in unison and octaves against a high pedal D and occasional figures in the flute winding their way upwards.

Dialogue Lampito starts to go but sees Dicéphile approaching. Phryné tells Nicias to remove himself smartly, but he only goes through one of the doors with the plan to stay close. She then instructs Lampito to admit Dicéphile and make him wait, since she intends to appear in her own good time. She goes into her apartments.

Lampito brings in Dicéphile who is in a hurry to see his mistress. 'She will be with you shortly', is the reply, and when Dicéphile says he is intrigued to see where this woman lives who 'sets every heart aflame', Lampito is ready to show him round.

No. 7 Ariette There has to be a solo number for the soubrette Lampito. Augé de Lassus had not provided this in his version of the libretto, so Saint-Saëns had to ask for something, partly because Lampito has little to sing in Act I apart from some quite difficult entries in the finale. It was Saint-Saëns's idea to insert an Ariette on the cue of Dicéphile's curiosity about the house. What Augé supplied was too short, so Saint-Saëns composed the verse about jewellery, 'Bijoux choisis par elle', for the reprise of the tune, and was very pleased with the whole piece when it was done.

'C'est ici qu'habite Phryné' is a neat little song, lightly scored, which makes no special demands on the singer but offers an opportunity for comic action as he shows first the mirror (whose purpose is to make its mistress smile), then the bed (perfect for stolen kisses), then the jewels (whose purpose is to make their mistress more beautiful).

The bed is a 'lit de repos', for we are only in Phryné's antechamber, but its music is deftly languorous. It is instructive to recall that only nine years later the mention of a bed at the Opéra-Comique, in *Pelléas et Mélisande*, had to be removed in early performances for fear of giving offence.

Dialogue Lampito exits, leaving Dicéphile alone to take a closer look. He likes the feel of the place and observes that his own lodgings are inferior. It all suggests a state of happiness 'often shared'. The mirror reminds him of the hours women spend in front of it, whereas he gets no pleasure from looking at himself. Men are fools, he adds, ever since his ancestors went to war against Troy just over a woman. (Did Saint-Saëns have any suspicion he would himself compose an opera on this story?)

No. 8 Couplets Dicéphile's song is, like Lampito's Ariette, short and neat, and completely within the tradition of opéra-comique. The alternation of long and short lines in the verse is clearly audible in the music, and humorous in effect. The first couplet takes the old male adage 'Women are nothing but trouble', and the second takes Orpheus to task for getting so upset over Euridice. 'If I was him,' Dicéphile concludes, 'I'd have said to Cerberus: that's my Euridice you have there. Keep her!'

Saint-Saëns had to get Augé de Lassus to rewrite the first couplet. He suggested a few lines as replacement, but both versions were replaced in the final version.[20]

Dialogue Phryné appears and the scene begins with a series of asides, she and Dicéphile taking turns to confide in the audience. Although the obvious malefactor is Nicias, she knows that the magistrature can call her before the Areopagus on various charges of immorality, real or trumped up. She is determined to prevent this at any price. At any price? Perhaps not, if she's clever, which she is. Dicéphile, for his part, thinks she's off her guard.

With great solemnity he tells her that the Areopagus is in session to consider her crimes. Facing him squarely she asks 'Do you believe the Areopagus will find Phryné guilty?'

'I'm sure they will. Yet, perhaps it would be a shame . . .'

'Wouldn't it.'

Dicéphile now raises the matter of the vandalised bust, for which he thinks Phryné is responsible. As she invites him to sit close to her on the couch, he admits to himself that the siren is beautiful and that her song is dangerous.

No. 9 Duo et Scène de l'Apparition It was clear to Saint-Saëns that this was the most important scene in the opera. An older man falling for the seductive wiles of a younger woman had been a stock scene in comedy for centuries, but Saint-Saëns chose to set it

---

[20] These drafts are given in the letter to Augé de Lassus of 14 February 1893, RATNER 2012, p. 229.

as coolly as possible, especially in Phryné's part, while allowing Dicéphile some staccato entries that guarantee his loss of dignity.

Phryné begins by pretending, supported by the strings, that they are already in court. He should state the indictment and begin the interrogation. Before he can do so she leaps to her feet and declares her innocence and her beauty, as if one confirmed the other. Returning to the courtroom illusion, she calmly asks him to proceed with the charges. Augé de Lassus had marked her line 'Poursuivez l'interrogation' as 'lively and direct', but Saint-Saëns explained in their correspondence that he deliberately kept a seductive quality in her music 'so as not to spoil the effect of her increasing magnetism and of a spider's web in which the grotesque Dicéphile will get himself caught'.[21]

Breaking the illusion, she asks for an adjournment while she completes her toilette. The pretence that she is emotionally disturbed by his presence brings on a burst of coloratura, and the accompaniment settles into a steady tread in the bass with off-beat chords in the upper strings moving sometimes in strange harmonic steps. She draws him into her web by asking him to pass her her mirror, then piece by piece she orders him to get her jewellery, her necklace, her ring, a ribbon ... As her orders become more imperious he is rapidly overcome. He loses his head and attempts to kiss her, but she pushes him off since she still has a gold bracelet for him to put on her arm. He drops it so she picks it up and puts it on herself. The poor man is completely in her thrall. As the music speeds up, Phryné calls upon Aphrodite to help her complete her victory.

Coming up for air, as it were, he begs her to give him a break, but she has one more request to ask. Would he fetch a rose for her which is behind the curtain that hangs across an alcove at the back of the stage? As he approaches the curtain the stage is plunged in darkness, to Dicéphile's alarm. Just a storm somewhere, she says, urging him on. The curtain opens to reveal a full-length marble statue of a nude Aphrodite on a pedestal decked with myrtles and roses. The statue reproduces Phryné's features and is lit with a mysterious Erda-like blue light (electricity at the Opéra-Comique was very new).

Soft trombone chords and juddering muted strings set the atmosphere for this scene. A descending sequence of minor chords provides ghostly harmony, then divided strings trace a similar sequence upwards to reach the extreme key C♯ major, where distant voices are heard. Tenors and contraltos in unison sing the song 'C'est Phryné quand elle passe' from the opening scene of the opera accompanied by a harmonium and a tracery of muted strings. They confirm Dicéphile's deluded belief that he is looking at Phryné in all her glory, and a fragmented version of ex. 9.2 brings the key back from the heights to the E major where the scene began. Against soft choral chords and the kind

---

[21] Letter to Augé de Lassus, 2 March 1893, RATNER 2012, p. 232.

of orchestration that would be apt for describing paradise, Dicéphile confesses his adoration for the 'goddess'. Flutes repeat the upward winding figures which earlier represented Aphrodite arising from the water.

Dialogue Dicéphile steps forward to take the statue in his arms but the curtain falls and the statue disappears. As the lights come on he turns to find Phryné lounging on the couch. He is confused and deranged, but she is calm. He throws himself at her feet, begging her to make his dream a reality. 'You forget I am in court', she replies.

'You will be acquitted, I am sure', he answers, reaching in vain for her hand to kiss.

At this moment Nicias, Lampito, Agoragine, Cynalopex, with slaves and others, come in to find Dicéphile on his knees. He insists he is in charge, but Nicias reminds him of his proven fallibility. Dicéphile concedes Nicias's claim on his money in return for which all is forgiven, so when Phryné says

> Votre fête d'hier vous est ici rendue
> Yesterday's celebration does you honour after all

Dicéphile can reply

> Et tout cela pour voir une statue!
> And all just to see a statue!

No. 10 Final All join in singing Dicéphile's praises, first with a reprise of the opening chorus, no. 1, and then with the merry tune of the first act finale. Lampito presents Dicéphile with a cup, while Phryné and Nicias stand in a tight embrace.

* * * * *

Phryné was second only to *Samson et Dalila* in popularity in Saint-Saëns's lifetime. Following fifty performances in its first year at the Opéra-Comique, it was revived there in 1899, 1901, 1910, 1916 and 1935, despite the hostility that developed between Saint-Saëns and Albert Carré, who took over the theatre after the death of Carvalho in 1897. Saint-Saëns was convinced that Carré was entrenched against him, yet both *Phryné* and *La Princesse jaune* were regularly revived under his management. In 1910 Saint-Saëns suspected that the management was treating *Phryné* as a secondary pairing with *Pagliacci* but observed that it proved to be the more popular of the two.[22]

In France *Phryné* was performed in Lyon (1894), Aix-en-Provence (1896), Bordeaux (1900), Nice (1902), Paris Trianon (1909), Marseille (1909), Nîmes (1910), Algiers (1911), Cannes (1911), Aix-les-Bains (1911), Vichy (1913), Paris Gaîté (1914), Monte Carlo (1919), Paris Théâtre-Lyrique (1919), Deauville (1920) and Rouen (1920). Saint-Saëns took an active interest in all of these and often helped in rehearsal.

---

[22] Letter of 26 January 1910 to Caroline de Serres, RATNER 2012, p. 239.

Abroad it was staged in The Hague (1893), Stockholm (1894), Ghent (1894), Geneva (1895), St Petersburg (1895), Milan (1896), Brussels (1896), Antwerp (1896), Cairo (1896), Elberfeld (1900) and New Orleans (1914).

Part of the opera's success was undoubtedly due to the star quality of the 'unforgettable' Sybil Sanderson, to whose artistry Saint-Saëns warmed considerably as the run went on. At the end of October 1893 she moved to the Opéra to rehearse Massenet's *Thaïs*, which opened on 16 March 1894, while her part in *Phryné* was taken by Jane Harding, a good soprano by all accounts but whose debut was met with violent protests in the theatre on the night of 22 February 1894. Perhaps they were partisans of Sybil Sanderson who blew a fanfare on whistles when Harding first appeared and threw a live and bewildered rabbit on to the stage at the end of the first act. Carrots, onions and cauliflower, according to *Le Ménestrel* three days later, rained down from the upper gallery at the end.

At the end of 1894 the next Phryné was the Countess de Gimel, who was, according to Saint-Saëns, 'very pretty with a pretty voice, a bit small, and playing like a salon actress'.[23] Sanderson only sang the role later in Milan in November and December 1896, for which she must have had to learn Messager's recitatives and the whole role in Italian. Jane Harding later sang it in St Petersburg and Brussels. A good number of sopranos sang the role in the French provinces and once, in Algiers, the statue was played by a girl wearing a bathing costume.[24]

Nellie Melba took an interest in the role and hoped to sing it at Covent Garden in 1895, but this did not happen. She did eventually sing it in New Orleans in 1914.

For the Milan performances in 1896 the dialogue was set to music as recitative by André Messager and the libretto translated into Italian by Amintore Galli. Having orchestrated Act I and assisted at rehearsals, Messager was ideally placed for this purpose, and his recitatives use snatches of the opera's music in a perfectly functional way to link the separate numbers. Durand put out a new vocal score of this version (197 pages). Somewhat mysteriously Saint-Saëns told Augé de Lassus in 1908 that the Italian version could be used in a proposed performance at the Liceu, Barcelona. 'I believe this version has never been used; it's time it began its career.'[25] In 1909 the version with recitatives was issued with a German translation.

In contrast to this record of uninterrupted success, remarkable for a one-act opéra-comique, only three revivals have been traced since Saint-Saëns's death in 1921: at the Opéra-Comique in 1935; in Cairo in April 1938; and in a concert performance given by French radio in 1960. With Denise Duval in the title role and Jules Gressier conducting, this was released as a CD in 2013. A narration replaces the dialogue.

---

[23] Letter of 2 October 1894, RATNER 2012, p. 236.
[24] Letter to Philippe Bellenot of 3 March 1921, RATNER 2012, p. 245.
[25] Letter of 24 November 1908, RATNER 2012, p. 237.

Present-day opera-going habits have made *Phryné* doubly resistant to revival, since singers and audiences no longer tolerate dialogue, especially in a foreign language, and market experts claim that one-act operas are hard to sell at the box office (it has two acts, true, but less than one hour of music with perhaps ten minutes of dialogue). In Saint-Saëns's lifetime it was never paired with either of his other short operas, *La Princesse jaune* or *Hélène*, but an enterprising impresario should surely be bold enough to try that for the first time.

* * * * *

The variety of styles in this short opera is remarkable. A recognisably traditional opéra-comique style marks the two short solos in Act II, Lampito's Ariette no. 7 'C'est ici qu'habite Phryné', and Dicéphile's Couplets no. 8 'L'homme n'est pas sans défaut'. These are direct, tuneful and amusing. The end of the first act finale is, as Saint-Saëns was fully aware, a page from Offenbach's dangerously vulgar book. Then there are imagined evocations of ancient Greek music, in the citharas and sistra played on stage in the Chœur no. 3 and the modal song they sing in mock-ancient unison. Another unison tune is given to Phryné, Lampito and Nicias at the end of no. 6, chanting a hymn to Venus against a single sustained high D.

Most important, *Phryné* displays Saint-Saëns's wealth of musical expression, from the street fight that opens the Act I finale no. 4 to Nicias's melodious response to his curmudgeonly uncle in the duo no. 2, and to Phryné's ravishing recollection of waves breaking on the seashore in no. 6. He may have been cautious about including obscure classical references in the text (he cited Paphos and Cnidos) that an Opéra-Comique audience might not know, but he does not write down to them when rich musical expression is called for.

The presence of statuary in this opera and the suggestion that cold marble might magically come alive continues to explore the theme presented by Conrad and his adored painting in *Le Timbre d'argent*, by Kornélis and his adored painting in *La Princesse jaune*, the Philistines' idols in *Samson et Dalila*, and Benvenuto Cellini's adored statue of Hebe. Saint-Saëns could hardly forget the occasion in 1875 when he had himself played the part of the statue Galatea in a performance of the ballet *Galatea and Pygmalion*, in which Pygmalion was danced by none other than Tchaikovsky. According to Tchaikovsky's brother Modest, Saint-Saëns danced with considerable skill. Furthermore, this was a period when placing statues in public places in Paris was something of a craze.[26]

Classical sculpture represented for Saint-Saëns the ideal of formal perfection, which he consciously aspired to attain in his music without ever wishing to exclude emotional and dramatic elements without which it would be dry and dead. At a further remove he

---

[26] See Gustave Pessard, *Statuomanie parisienne*, Paris, 1912.

saw Hellenic culture in general, as many others did, as a useful counterpoise to the Nordic influence to which it was thought most Germans (and many French) had succumbed. The more time he spent near the Mediterranean, the more convinced he became that southern skies presided over a lost cultural purity. Greek mythology had already left its mark on his music, for example in *Le Rouet d'Omphale*, *Phaéton* and *La Jeunesse d'Hercule*, but the composition of *Phryné* marks a significant moment when antiquity begins to be a major magnetic force in his creative consciousness.

10 | Antigone, Frédégonde

Saint-Saëns undertook to complete Guiraud's *Frédégonde* in 1892, soon after his friend's death in May of that year. The opera was still called *Brunehilda* or *Brunhilda* and was well known to Saint-Saëns, since it was to him that Gallet had first suggested the subject in 1879 and had again attempted to interest him in it in 1887. Saint-Saëns had many reasons for not undertaking it at those times, so it passed to Guiraud, whose energies were largely taken up by teaching at the Conservatoire and by acting as editor for Choudens in such tasks as the completion of Offenbach's *Les Contes d'Hoffmann*, writing recitatives for his friend Bizet's *Carmen* and overseeing the series of posthumous publications of Bizet's music which Choudens put out as soon as *Carmen*'s popularity began to spread. One of Guiraud's last labours, ironically, was the completion of *Kassya*, the opera that Delibes left unfinished at his death in 1891. Just as Rimsky-Korsakov and Glazunov gave a lot of time to completing unfinished works by their Russian colleagues Mussorgsky and Borodin, it was a similarly fraternal spirit that drove French composers to do the same. Guiraud thus completed works by Offenbach, Bizet and Delibes; Bizet completed Halévy's *Noé*; Arthur Coquard completed Lalo's *La Jacquerie*; Saint-Saëns and Dukas completed *Frédégonde*; and Franck's *Ghiselle* was completed by a team of no less than five of his pupils: Coquard, Bréville, Chausson, Rousseau and d'Indy.

On the day that Saint-Saëns began the composition of *Phryné*, 12 January 1893, he wrote from Algiers to get Gallet to send him what existed of *Brunhilda*. He found that Guiraud had drafted, in vocal score, three out of six tableaux, more than he expected, and that the task of completion would not be too arduous. He suggested that Paul Dukas, as Guiraud's pupil, could orchestrate the three finished tableaux, and he also decided to reduce the three remaining tableaux to two. He and Gallet exchanged a few thoughts on how to improve the libretto.

But in his preoccupation with *Phryné* he decided he could not work on *Brunhilda* for at least a year. Carvalho wanted him to write something to follow *Phryné* at the Opéra-Comique, suggesting *Grisélidis* and *La Vivandière*. A libretto by Sardou, *Grisélidis*, based on Boccaccio, Chaucer and Perrault, had occupied Bizet in 1870, although it never progressed beyond sketches. Another libretto on the same subject by Armand Silvestre and Eugène Morand was now in Carvalho's hands. Turned down by Saint-Saëns, it was offered to Massenet, who accepted it at once, although the opera was not played until 1901, after Carvalho's death. *La Vivandière* was a libretto by Henri Cain about revolutionary soldiers in 1794, which Saint-Saëns also rejected, so it was set by Benjamin Godard, who died in January 1895 without completing its orchestration. Once again, fraternal duty called on Paul Vidal to complete the opera, which opened at the Opéra-Comique in 1895 and enjoyed considerable success.

Soon after the opening of *Phryné* in May 1893 Saint-Saëns was invited to London by the Philharmonic Society to give a concert in which he played his Second Piano Concerto and conducted *Le Rouet d'Omphale*. Honours were shared with Tchaikovsky, who conducted his Fourth Symphony. For some reason the two composers had never been able to revive the friendship they enjoyed on Saint-Saëns's first visit to Russia in 1875. Tchaikovsky, now in the last year of his life, was not well, and for some time now he had shown little desire to mix with other musicians on his travels. They had both to remain in London for over a week before going on to Cambridge, where they were to receive the honorary degree of Doctor of Music, along with other distinguished European musicians. This famous occasion was masterminded by C. V. Stanford, Cambridge's Professor of Music, as a celebration of the fiftieth anniversary of the university's Musical Society. The plan was to invite the leading musicians from five countries. Verdi and Brahms having turned it down, their places were taken by Boito and Bruch. Grieg, the token Scandinavian, accepted but was not well enough to attend. Tchaikovsky and Saint-Saëns were there to represent their countries, and they both appreciated the special nature of the occasion, but they seem to have remained aloof one from another. Perhaps they had too much in common, not too little. In September Saint-Saëns was back in London for the first performance there of *Samson et Dalila*, played as an oratorio, since stage performances of biblical works were prohibited. The performance was lamentable.[1]

He returned to Paris and very quickly wrote some music for a very different kind of stage work. This was a play by Edmond Cottinet, journalist and dramatist, who achieved fame by founding holiday camps for schoolchildren. His play *Vercingétorix* took a favourite subject for arousing French nationalist feeling, and it seems likely that Saint-Saëns helped out at the last moment by supplying two short pieces of music, perhaps to supplement whatever music Cottinet had already put in place. For Act I of the play he wrote twenty bars of 'Arabic' music scored for cor anglais, two clarinets, two darbukas, two small drums and one large drum, and for Act III he wrote an eight-bar fanfare for two trumpets. The interest of this piece resides entirely in the scoring for Arab drums, a kind of music with which Saint-Saëns was very familiar from North Africa. Fifteen performances were given at the Odéon, beginning on 7 October 1893.

---

[1] The full horror is described by STUDD 1999, p. 196.

> **_Antigone_**
> (Ratner 317)
>
> Tragedy by Sophocles
>
> Translation by Paul Meurice and Auguste Vacquerie
>
> Incidental music
>
> First performance: Comédie-Française, Paris, 21 November 1893
>
> Bass solo, double men's chorus
>
> Orchestra: 4 flutes, 2 oboes, 2 clarinets, harps, strings.

At the same time a new theatrical project aroused Saint-Saëns's enthusiasm. The two writers whose works formed the basis of, respectively, *Ascanio* and *Proserpine*, Paul Meurice and Auguste Vacquerie, were planning to revive Sophocles's *Antigone* which they had put on at the Second Théâtre-Français in 1844. Now, almost fifty years later, they planned to stage it at the Comédie-Française, and instead of Mendelssohn's music, composed for the Berlin Schauspielhaus in 1842, which they had used before, they wanted something less contemporary, with a stronger suggestion of antiquity. For Saint-Saëns this was a perfect opportunity to work out some of his theories about ancient Greek music which had played a part in the composition of *Phryné* earlier in the year.

Strangely enough, Saint-Saëns had already composed some music for *Antigone* at the age of fifteen, which survives as a sixty-five-page full score covering five scenes from the play.[2] The new score, which came rapidly into being in October 1893, was very different, in fact different from anything he had ever composed before, even considering the antique features included in *Phryné*. Wisely he explained what he was trying to do in a preface to the printed score and in an article published by *Le Figaro* a week after the performances opened.[3] The preface reads:

> In order to reproduce the effect of a Greek chorus as closely as possible, the chorus all sing in unison, using not modern major and minor scale but the Greek modes, as still found in plainsong. Melodies have been strictly matched to the rhythm of the poetry so that the words can be easily heard by the audience.[4]
>
> Whenever characters speak in lyric verse (when they were probably sung by the actors), they are supported by incidental music written in more elaborate scales than those mentioned above, and which, according to M. Gevaert's research, were applied by the

---

[2] F-Pn MS 864 (RATNER 2012, p. 407).
[3] *Le Figaro*, 28 November 1893; SORET 2012, pp. 476–77.
[4] For a discussion of the modes in *Antigone* see BROOKS 2008, p. 247.

Greeks principally to instrumental music, although vocal music used them sometimes too. The music for the exit of queen Eurydice is borrowed from *The Trojan Women* by Euripides. It is not by Euripides himself, but by a musician who worked with him, Euripides being evidently the first tragedian who did not write his own music. The final chorus is an imitation of a hymn by Pindar.

The hymn to Eros is based on a Greek popular song collected in Athens by M. Bourgault-Ducoudray.

The instrumental interludes between choruses are borrowed from M. Gevaert's book on ancient music.

Under the name 'flutes' the Greeks used actual flutes and some instruments with single or double reeds, ancestors of our oboes and clarinets. We have used these three kinds of instruments, also harps treated simply and almost always melodically, as lyres must have been. Some strings complete the ensemble. The instruments support unison voices or play a decoration over the melody. According to M. Gevaert this rudimentary polyphony was practised by the Greeks. You will not hear any of the glittering effects of modern music. It is like a line-drawing, supported by plain colours, whose charm comes entirely from its simplicity. In this union of poetry and music poetry takes first place, with music serving simply as its auxiliary.

François-Auguste Gevaert was a Belgian composer and scholar who had been prominent in Paris, and certainly known to Saint-Saëns, until 1870 when he returned to Brussels to head the Conservatoire there. His *Histoire et théorie de la musique de l'Antiquité* (1875–81) was an immense study of ancient music, taking this very recalcitrant topic much further than anyone had attempted before. Bourgault-Ducoudray was also a composer/scholar who took an interest in folk music of different lands. Saint-Saëns's use of a modern Greek folk tune was legitimised by the current belief that folksong had survived unchanged from ancient times.

Here is Euridice's exit, supposedly from the time of Euripides (ex. 10.1). The modal scale used here, with its augmented seconds, is not found in plainsong, and the austerity of the texture, maintained almost throughout this music, can give a good idea of Saint-Saëns's radical approach at a time when lush, complex orchestral textures were everywhere adopted, even in the spoken theatre.

Example 10.1 *Antigone*, Part 3, No. 13

Of the fifteen short sections of music for *Antigone*, much of it is monodic. The first chorus for Theban elders is accompanied in unison throughout, which would certainly have surprised an audience in 1893. The chorus that responds has a line of counterpoint running above it, which, though still austere, brings a little modern musical colour into the mix for the first time. The chorus never sing in harmony. Typical of the simplicity and austerity of this music is the introduction to the second Stasimon, ex. 10.2, which would persuasively convey a sense of antiquity to a late-nineteenth-century audience.

Example 10.2 *Antigone*, Part 2, No. 6

The harp's occasional arpeggios provide a more modern sense of harmony. Saint-Saëns is not suggesting that this is music that could have been heard in fifth-century BCE Greece, for there are themes and phrases that belong entirely to his own time, but it is as radical as anything that Debussy or Satie were doing at the same time. 'My task was nothing other than to offer the public music which lacked all the resources of the present day, which are so entrancing and so familiar.'[5] Saint-Saëns's attempt to recreate Greek music is in retrospect more audacious than Stravinsky's in *Œdipus Rex* thirty-four years later. In *Antigone* he found the right opportunity for a stage work of this sort, since he could never have extended this approach to a whole opera.

Antigone ran at the Comédie-Française for several weeks and was revived there in 1894, 1897 and 1909. Part of its success may be attributed to the great actor Mounet-Sully, already famous for his performances of Sophocles's *Œdipus Rex*, who played Creon (his brother Paul played Tiresias). Mounet-Sully also took it to Lyon in 1894. In later years the play was revived in the outdoor arenas in southern France in which Saint-Saëns took a close interest. In 1894, 1897 and 1909 it was staged in the Roman theatre in Orange, presumably, if the dates are a guide, played by the cast on tour from the Comédie-Française. To introduce the performances in Orange in 1894, Saint-Saëns composed a *Hymne à Pallas-Athéné* for soprano and orchestra, sung by Lucienne Bréval, fresh from her triumph as Brünhilde in *Les Valkyries* at the Opéra. In 1912 *Antigone* was played in the Roman arena in Nîmes, and in 1921 in the outdoor theatre at Béziers. From there, right at the end of his life, he wrote: 'They tell me again and again that the music is very successful; it struck me as quite the opposite, but never mind. Madeleine

---

[5] *Le Figaro*, 28 November 1893; Soret 2012, pp. 476–77.

Roch [playing Antigone] was admirable and her powerful voice filled the arena. But this tragedy is really too depressing. And then the verse is often very weak, despite all the effort Meurice and Vacquerie put into it. Sophocles's lines must be better.'[6]

* * * * *

During rehearsals for *Antigone* the death of Gounod was announced, and his funeral took place at the Madeleine on October 27th. Saint-Saëns shared organ duties with Théodore Dubois, who had succeeded him as organist there in 1868 and was still in charge. Nearly all French composers of Saint-Saëns's generation owed much to Gounod, not only as the master of a fluent lyrical language which they all adopted, but also as a mentor to the young, prepared to encourage and promote anyone in whom he saw talent. Although they had not been personally close in recent years, Saint-Saëns was definitely in this category and he wrote a brief tribute in *Le Journal* on the day Gounod died and a longer memoir, under the title 'Charles Gounod et le Don Juan de Mozart', in *La Vie contemporaine* two weeks later.[7] Gounod's religiosity was certainly not to Saint-Saëns's taste, whereas Massenet, though no *dévôte*, assimilated that side of Gounod more easily. Just a week before his death Gounod wrote Saint-Saëns a charming note of admiration for the score of *Phryné*.

Although the year 1894 began without any pressing obligations, he was not thinking about opera, not even about music. He devoted his winter retreat at Las Palmas in the Canary Islands to writing a short book entitled *Problèmes et Mystères*, entirely devoted to questions of science and religion, mostly in support of his incurable scepticism. Perhaps it was Gounod's death that led him to set down his thoughts on paper, although the book honestly concludes that his problems and mysteries have no clear solutions.

Gallet begged him to get to work on *Brunhilda*, but he was in no hurry to do so. His compositions at this time were all for keyboard: a *Caprice arabe* for two pianos, which resumes the sound of Arab drumming he had put into *Vercingétorix*; a *Thème varié* for piano, deliberately virtuosic for the Conservatoire students who were required to study it; and *Three Preludes and Fugues* for organ which are no pot-boilers but majestic works for the king of instruments that organists unaccountably neglect.

Saint-Saëns was not back in Paris for the premiere of Massenet's *Thaïs* in March, but he saw it as soon as he could and wrote Massenet an extravagant letter of admiration.[8] He admired Gallet's skill in devising 'poésie mélique' as a kind of prose suitable for singing, and he was enchanted, like everyone else, by Sybil Sanderson's singing. We do

---

[6] Letter to Jacques Durand of 22 August 1921, RATNER 2012, p. 418.
[7] The first is in SORET 2012, pp. 467–68; the second was published as a separate brochure in 1894 and is reprinted in SORET 2012, pp. 469–76.
[8] MASSENET 2001, p. 125.

not know if he went to see Massenet's *Portrait de Manon* at the Opéra-Comique in May. On Verdi's *Falstaff*, on the other hand, which arrived at the Opéra-Comique in April that year, we do have his thoughts:

> In *Falstaff* Verdi exceeded his own target of competing with *Die Meistersinger* while preserving his own style, by giving the words precedence over the music and creating the mood of a musical 'conversation'. But either because the orchestra is at fault from an excess of sound, or because the volubility of Italian makes the words hard to hear, the listener often misses them and it casts a shadow over the work. I have only fully enjoyed it when following the text in the libretto. It is asking too much of the comprehension of the public who do not find the music sufficiently interesting in itself, as they do with the great Saxon. Yet there are pearls in this jewel-box, and the finest is the final ensemble, with its brilliant impact and its masterly writing. It ought to be heard in concerts.[9]

In June Gallet submitted a proposal for *Brunhilda* to the Opéra, now in the charge of Gailhard with his new partner Bertrand, and in September Saint-Saëns visited Gallet in his summer home at Wimereux, near Boulogne on the Channel coast. Gallet had recently lost his wife, and they worked there on the definitive libretto of their opera. In November Bertrand signalled that it would be staged at the Opéra the following November, insisting that a ballet be included. Saint-Saëns had first to attend rehearsals for the revised version of *Proserpine* in Toulouse, although he left before the first performance to take a short break in Spain, where he confessed he was a 'little afraid' of beginning work on *Brunhilda*; he immersed himself in zarzuelas, seguidillas and malaguenas instead.[10] He then boarded the 4000-ton steamship *Saghalien* sailing from Marseilles to the Far East via the Suez Canal and Singapore, leaving behind a country plagued by anarchist attacks and about to explode in controversy with the conviction of Alfred Dreyfus in December 1894.

What he wrote first on this trip was not the opera but a virtuoso piano piece, *Souvenir d'Ismaïlia*, which he sent back from Ismailia on the Suez Canal to his pupil Isidor Philipp, who played it at a Trompette concert in April. Then, as the ship crossed the Indian Ocean further than Saint-Saëns had ever travelled before, he worked steadily at the two tableaux of the opera. By the time he reached Saigon, in French Indo-China, on 13 February 1895, he had completed the draft. A month later, during which he attended a spectacular Chinese festival, the new governor-general of Indo-China arrived in Saigon, Armand Rousseau, who had been Saint-Saëns's neighbour in the Rue Monsieur-le-Prince. The two immediately left for the island of Côn Son, notorious for the prison of Poulo-Condor, but celebrated also for its rare vegetation and strange fauna, which interested the composer greatly. They had for guide Louis Jacquet, director of the Saigon botanical garden, whom Saint-Saëns had met on his voyage to Ceylon in the winter of 1890–91.

[9] *L'Écho de Paris*, 12 October 1913; SORET 2012, p. 844. [10] DANDELOT 1930, p. 133.

This was where the orchestration of *Brunhilda* was mostly done, to be finished on the journey home. He was back in Paris in May 1895. The principal operatic event he had missed was the staging at the Opéra in February of *La Montagne noire* by Augusta Holmès, her first opera to be staged and alas a failure. The opera is set in the war-torn Balkans in the seventeenth century with some similarities to *Aida* and Massenet's *Le Mage*. An exotic Turkish slavegirl bewitches a Montenegran soldier and somehow survives at the end of the opera while the men come to grief. Holmès wrote her own libretto. Saint-Saëns was much less close to her than in earlier years, yet his admiration for her work was all the more persuasive because it reached her not in a letter but through a third party.

For *Brunhilda* there were still ballets to write and Dukas's work on the orchestration of the first three tableaux to be overseen.[11] Saint-Saëns felt free to make certain revisions to Guiraud's work which he felt his friend would have supported. The last page of the score is dated 13 September 1895, when the opera was ready to go into rehearsal, with no obstruction whatever from the management of the Opéra except to change the title to *Frédégonde* with one eye on the *Ring* and the other on Reyer's *Sigurd*, even though their Brunhilda was drawn from Nordic myths and was not the Brunhilda of history that Gallet put at the centre of his opera.

Saint-Saëns had always had Lucienne Bréval in mind for the part of Brunhilda, but after a long break her singing was 'deplorable' in a revival of *Aida* just at that time, which did not bode well. Two days before opening night she had to be replaced by Marie Lafargue, who had recently made her debut as Desdemona in Verdi's *Otello* at the Opéra. Bréval sang a few performances later. The Frédégonde was the Belgian contralto Meyrianne Héglon, who was later to sing both Anne Boleyn and Dalila at the Opéra also. The tenor, Mérowig, was sung by Albert Alvarez, the current Radames in *Aida* and Nicias in *Thaïs*, who would later sing Samson and a number of Wagner roles. The conductor was Paul Taffanel, former flautist, who also conducted the Société des Concerts. The elaborate historical sets were the work of six different designers, act by act: Chaperon *père et fils* (Act I); Carpezat (Act II); Jambon and Bailly (Act IV); and Amable (Acts IV and V).

Opening night was 18 December 1895. Saint-Saëns, who hated to be in Paris in the winter and who had just passed his sixtieth birthday, was present, perhaps feeling that he had to be there for the sake of Guiraud's memory. The work was well received, Saint-Saëns's part in it especially, with Guiraud's share inevitably treated with less respect. It was perhaps too much of a hybrid – half horse, half cow – to win permanent favour in competition with Verdi, Massenet and *Samson et Dalila* itself, and it lasted only

---

[11] Dukas gave an account of the completion of *Frédégonde* in the *Revue hebdomadaire* in December 1895. See DUKAS 1948, pp. 529–30.

eight performances. Saint-Saëns was hurt by this on Guiraud's behalf but was probably not surprised.

* * * * *

Frédégonde
(Ratner 340)

Drame lyrique in five acts

Libretto by Louis Gallet

Music by Ernest Guiraud and Camille Saint-Saëns

First performance: Opéra, Paris, 18 December 1895

Brunhilda, reine d'Austrasie	soprano
Frédégonde, reine de Neustrie	mezzo-soprano
Mérowig	ténor
Hilpéric, roi de Neustrie, son père	baryton
L'Évêque Prétextat	basse
Fortunatus	ténor
Landéric	1ère basse
Un serviteur	baryton
Quatre seigneurs Goths	
Quatre clercs	

Leudes Austrasiens, seigneurs Goths, nobles Gallo-Romains, peuple

Orchestra: 2 flutes, piccolo, 2 oboes, cor anglais, 2 clarinets, bass clarinet, 2 bassoons, sarrusophone, contrabassoon, 4 horns, 4 trumpets, 3 trombones, tuba, timpani, bass drum, cymbals, triangle, side drum, harps, strings.

Gallet found the material for *Frédégonde* in *Récits des temps mérovingiens* by the historian Augustin Thierry, a work based on the writings of Gregory of Tours, the principal contemporary source. He also read Venantius Fortunatus, chief Latin poet of the time, who, as bishop, married Sigibert and Brunhilda, and who plays a part in the opera.[12] Of the sixth-century Merovingian dynasty, it has been said that their 'repulsive annals are, on the whole, the most hopeless and depressing page in the history of Europe. From generation to generation their story reeks with blood; there is nothing that can be compared to it for horror in the records of any nation on this side of the Mediterranean.'[13]

---

[12] Two lines from Fortunatus's *Epithalamium* for their marriage appear at the head of Act I in the libretto.
[13] Charles Oman, *The Dark Ages 476–918*, London, 1905, p. 159.

Gallet was not so much interested in the horrific aspect of their history as in the operatic potential of the conflict between love and loyalty within a family of powerful rulers. Not many stories from the Dark Ages had been seen on the French stage. Hervé presented an operetta *Chilpéric* in 1868, and *Merowig*, an opera by Franck's pupil Samuel Rousseau, was played at the Théâtre de l'Eden in 1892, but it was more often legendary figures like Amadis the Gaul or King Arthur, with Wagnerian overtones, that attracted librettists and composers.[14] An element of *Frédégonde* that undoubtedly appealed to Saint-Saëns was its historical basis, going back to the origins of the French nation.

When Clothar, the last King of the Franks, died in 561, his lands, which comprised most of modern France and much of modern Germany, were divided between his four quarrelsome sons. War was particularly intense between Sigibert, King of Austrasia (the eastern sector), and Hilpéric, King of Neustria (north and west), whose wives were sisters. Hilpéric had his wife murdered in order to replace her with the wicked Frédégonde, causing Brunhilda, the other sister, to swear vengeance. After Sigibert's death Brunhilda, his widow, having been captured and imprisoned by Hilpéric, fell in love with Hilpéric's son, her nephew Mérowig. Mérowig freed her from prison and persuaded Bishop Prétextat to marry them in Rouen Cathedral. Hilpéric forced Mérowig to become a monk, but he was murdered in 577 by Frédégonde's agents, while Brunhilda fled.

This is the historical outline which Gallet fashioned into a libretto. He created scenes of clamour and revelry for the purposes of the opera, with space for a ballet at the end of Act III. It is not known what was lost when the original last three acts were compressed into two, but without a sub-plot much was probably gained. Brunhilda being certainly at the dramatic centre of the story, it is a pity that Frédégonde had to usurp the opera's title. What was a handicap in 1895 might have aroused some useful curiosity in later years.

Guiraud's reputation as a composer has been compromised by having described Debussy's work as 'clumsy' (although Debussy liked him a lot) and by his well-meaning interference with Bizet's and Offenbach's legacy. Marmontel described him as 'incurably indolent', but his music, though not extensive in range, is sophisticated and inventive, not unlike that of his close friend Bizet. It is a pity that we do not have recordings of his two first-class orchestral suites instead of the innumerable recordings of the *Arlésienne* and *Carmen* suites that bear his name as arranger. His music modulates freely and often, and the density of his harmony, much more evident than that of Saint-Saëns, sometimes approaches a Wagnerian sound. He is particularly fond of enharmonic modulations to a key a major or minor third away, a mannerism which Saint-Saëns seems to have adopted in his share of Act III of the opera, while Acts IV and V represent the real Saint-Saëns and offer something of a relief after the constant harmonic sidestepping in Guiraud's part. Those three acts of *Frédégonde* are nonetheless the work of

---

[14] *Frédégonde*, a five-act verse drama by Alfred Dubout, was played at the Comédie-Française in May 1897.

a thoroughly professional composer. They contain some stirring, finely wrought music, good enough at least for Saint-Saëns to attach his name to it in this collaboration. Our purpose is to study Saint-Saëns's contribution to this opera, but it would be altogether wrong to dismiss Guiraud's share as not deserving serious attention too. Guiraud had written over an hour's music, to which Saint-Saëns added another hour.

* * * * *

Prélude This is by Saint-Saëns, not Guiraud. It is a compressed movement that includes a military summons to start and end, and, after a preview of the sacrilege motif ex. 10.8, a more lyrical central section based on Fortunatus's music from the beginning of Act V. This generates a climax of great warmth.

ACT I

Scene 1 Act I is set at the Austrasian court of Queen Brunhilda in the Gallo-Roman Palais des Thermes in Paris (of which just a few fragments of wall remain today). A gathering of Gothic nobles and rudely dressed vassals and populace acclaim their queen. The poet Fortunatus, who is portrayed not as a churchman but as a fop, his arms and fingers covered in rings, welcomes her arrival, which is marked by an expressive Andante, ex. 10.3:

Example 10.3 *Frédégonde*, Act I, Scene 1

The melody is deftly extended for over thirty bars as she reclines on a couch deep in cushions, to be followed by an even longer melody for Fortunatus singing the praises of Brunhilda, revealing Guiraud's considerable harmonic skill and invention.

Scene 2 Fortunatus then reports that Hilpéric and Frédégonde are being held captive in Tournai. Brunhilda rejoices that now she will have vengeance for the murder of her sister, whose memory she tenderly recalls. Everyone calls out for Hilpéric's death, yet Brunhilda puts that matter on hold in order to celebrate their new-found peace with light music and draughts of mead. A pretty dance movement follows.

Scene 3 Trumpets are heard offstage and four men run in with the news that the Neustrians have entered Paris with Hilpéric and Frédégonde at their head. The Austrasians were fed fake news and the colossal clamour that ensues covers their immediate defeat by their enemies.

Scene 4 With noisy fanfares in C major, Hilpéric emerges triumphant. Frédégonde is at his side and his son by his former wife, Mérowig, hovers in the background. 'With perfidious charm' Hilpéric promises to treat Brunhilda with the respect due to a queen, but she replies that she should be spared the outrage of seeing her palace occupied by 'debauchery and crime' in the person of Frédégonde. While Brunhilda quietly reaffirms her determination to be avenged, Hilpéric orders her to be taken to a convent in Rouen, with his son Mérowig as escort. His orders are accompanied by a slippery motif, ex. 10.4:

Example 10.4 *Frédégonde*, Act I, Scene 4

With gross insolence, Hilpéric orders Brunhilda's diadem to be removed and placed on the head of Frédégonde. While Mérowig quietly admires Brunhilda's pale expression, like that of a dying flower, Hilpéric and Frédégonde are consumed with each other, and the whole ensemble takes shape as a flowing quartet in D♭ major, growing out of an expressive theme, ex. 10.5:

Example 10.5 *Frédégonde*, Act I, Scene 4

Hilpéric instructs his men to pillage the palace and strip it of its treasures, which they do with relish. With Frédégonde exulting in her triumph and Mérowig lost in quiet thought, the curtain falls.

ACT II

Introduction The Introduction recalls ex. 10.5 as a reminder of Brunhilda's downfall, while Hilpéric's triumph is represented by ex. 10.4 in the bass. The scene is still the Palais des Thermes in Paris, but now in the gardens, with the Seine visible in the background.

Scene 1 Brunhilda is seen amid the flowers, while Mérowig watches her from a distance. As she moves out of sight he confesses he is hesitant to approach her for fear of her repressed rage. But there is passion in his admission that 'she is my captive and I am in her power!' This is a passage of twenty-four bars which Saint-Saëns composed, replacing whatever Giraud had written earlier.

With ex. 10.5 still supporting the voices Brunhilda appears, lost in contemplation. When Mérowig addresses her she thanks him for arranging for her to be still in Paris, though captive, with gardens around her. The forty bars she sings here, beginning 'C'est à vous que je dois ces retraites fleuries' (pages 87–89 of the vocal score), too long to quote, might be taken as a perfect example of Guiraud's special gift of extended melody over resourceful expressive harmony. Still nervous of addressing her directly, Mérowig sings *à part* of his submission to the charm of her voice.

Scene 2 One of his father's vassals, Landéric, comes in to inform Mérowig that Hilpéric is wondering why he has not taken Brunhilda (who has withdrawn out of sight) to the convent in Rouen. When Mérowig replies that he will obey the order at once, Landéric departs.

Scene 3 Brunhilda has overheard him and is distressed that the peace she enjoys in Paris must end. She knows also that once inside the convent Frédégonde will be able to arrange her death. This brings out Mérowig's hatred of his stepmother, who could equally have him killed in order that her own sons may succeed to the throne.

Fury turns to passion as he declares his love, which she too confesses. Their love duet concludes the act with a new stirring tune in B♭, in the middle of which she tells him of her plan to link up with Austrasian forces near Rouen. A triumphant ex. 10.5 brings down the curtain.

ACT III

Scene 1 A noisy series of fanfares introduces a scene near Rouen where, by a village church, Austrasians and some Neustrians loyal to Mérowig are encamped. Both groups confirm their new alliance under Mérowig and his queen-bride Brunhilda.

Scene 2 The poet Fortunatus appears, dressed in a simple white tunic and with a forlorn look.[15] He reports merely that he has decided to enter the cloister. He has a message for Brunhilda and Mérowig who are then seen approaching to a recall of ex. 10.3. His mission to secure the Bishop's consent to their marriage has produced only the Bishop's promise to visit them there.

---

[15] At this point the libretto indicates a *divertissement* in which a group of girls wave branches and blossom. Its misplacement here is indicated by its instruction for Prétextat, whom we have not yet seen, to reappear and bless the assembly. Saint-Saëns placed it at the end of the act, with two more dance movements.

Scene 3 Mérowig reminds Brunhilda that the Bishop has reason to fear Hilpéric and Frédégonde, and everyone is aware that there are struggles ahead, but they sing out defiantly, men and women together, with lots of fanfares and panache.

Scene 4 The Bishop then enters on a white mule, followed by clerics bearing his episcopal insignia. All bow low. The Bishop's opening lines are set to another of Guiraud's finely crafted long melodies, richly harmonised in the key of G♭ major. Then the music turns sour as he declares his loyalty to king Hilpéric and condemns Mérowig's sin in resisting his father's will. He deplores their 'profane love' not as incestuous, as he might, but as disobedient. Mérowig replies that his fight is not with his father but with Frédégonde, and Brunhilda takes up the argument. In stirring octaves they plead that their love may be pardoned by heaven. The vassals join in urging the Bishop to relent. He foresees death and disaster, but Mérowig is defiant and Brunhilda pleads for Frédégonde to be punished, not her. The ensemble that builds up is powerful enough to force the Bishop to relent.

This is the point where Guiraud's draft came to an end, or at least where Saint-Saëns's own sketches begin (page 168 of the vocal score). To a 'Marche religieuse' the Bishop joins their hands and leads them into the church. Children's voices are heard from within singing the Pangue Lingua (the words of which are, historically, by Fortunatus). While the ceremony proceeds, Fortunatus and some clergy emerge from the church distributing alms to the people. There follows a passage of considerable tension as the people observe fires in the distance with alarm, while the serene Pangue Lingua continues to be heard from inside the church. The newly-weds then come out, passing under an arcade of the vassals' swords to the roar of trumpets and drums. Distant sentries are heard calling a warning, and Mérowig acknowledges the approach of Landéric and his troops. Nonetheless a wedding calls for festivities, so the tumultuous cries of 'Amrah!' and calls for dice, drink and feasting take no heed for the morrow. In any case the Opéra demanded a ballet, and this was the best occasion for it.

Ballet From here on the music is all by Saint-Saëns. Three ballet movements close the third act, of which the first is for young girls waving branches of apple blossom. According to Ratner the theme in a gentle 6/8 pulse in D minor is by Guiraud, but whether it was drafted for this purpose or taken from an earlier work she does not say.[16] It rises to quite a strong climax before ending in the major. The second ballet is an Allegro dominated by trills applied to almost every note of the melody; and the third is a Presto lurching between bars of three beats and bars of two, with a brief recall of the first ballet before the end.

---

[16] RATNER 2012, p. 498.

This last ballet is interrupted by the tolling of a bell. The Bishop reappears with his clergy and passes through the crowd dispensing his blessing. They all leave off their frolics and bow down in fealty.

ACT IV

Scene 1

The scene is the same as in Act I: Brunhilda's palace in Paris now occupied by the usurpers Hilpéric and Frédégonde. Hilpéric is absorbed in thought conveyed by some twisted harmony, ex. 10.6, which is later more precisely used to convey Frédégonde's machinations.

Example 10.6 *Frédégonde*, Act IV, Scene 1

Frédégonde enters and kneels beside him. Distant trumpets arouse him and he addresses her tenderly. Her style is anything but tender, and throughout this act she is seen more and more as Lady to Hilpéric's Macbeth. She reports that Mérowig's forces have been defeated and that he and Brunhilda have taken refuge in the church of St Martin in Rouen.

Their long duet begins with Hilpéric confessing his love for her in a relaxed but sensuous aria, as if he would gladly forget wars and feuds in order to be alone with her. His accompaniment relies a good deal on ex. 10.7:

Example 10.7 *Frédégonde*, Act IV, Scene 1

This is not to Frédégonde's taste at all. For one thing she doubts the sincerity of his love. She is also concerned that despite Mérowig's desertion, Hilpéric still favours him as his successor above the sons that she has borne him. To ex. 10.6 she accuses Mérowig of conspiring to take over Clothar's entire empire.

With the aid of ex. 10.7, Hilpéric implores her to forget their sons and the world. But Frédégonde is all the more enraged, convinced that her sons mean nothing to him. In that case, she replies, with a careful display of tears, I will leave you and suffer in the shadows. Hilpéric is forced to insist that he loves her and to swear to do her will. Example 10.6 with its harmonies straightened out reports her satisfaction.

What she demands is the capture of Mérowig in his sanctuary and his perpetual imprisonment in a monastery. Hilpéric is outraged but powerless, ex. 10.8:

Example 10.8 *Frédégonde*, Act IV, Scene 1

[musical notation: "Sa-cri-lè - - ge!"]

The duet closes with an exultant hymn of satisfaction from Frédégonde and desperate admissions of love from Hilpéric.

ACT V

Scene 1 A statue of St Martin marks the boundary of the churchyard of St Martin in Rouen. Gallet's eye for detail specifies: 'The church is like those early wooden basilicas then common all over Gaul whose soaring construction with pillars made of several tree-trunks lashed together and pointed bays with wooden buttresses betrays the origins of the ogival style.' A small garden and a shelter for refugees border the apse of the church. To music of ecclesiastical modesty, Fortunatus, in monk's habit, is tending the garden. To a melody already heard in the Prelude, he rejoices in the peace and serenity of his surroundings, shared by Brunhilda and Mérowig, who are duetting lusciously in G♭ major. Fortunatus's voice joins them in a brief, lovely trio.

Fortunatus warns them that they have stepped beyond the limits of the sanctuary where anyone would be free to arrest them; better to stay in the church garden, he advises.

Scene 2 Bishop Prétextat appears and announces that King Hilpéric is coming to confirm peace with Mérowig, who is visibly suspicious. The Bishop assures him that at St Martin's he is protected by God. Mérowig and Brunhilda go into the church, while the Bishop remains, apparently praying.

Scene 3 Frédégonde approaches with an alternation of conspiratorial chords that pursue her in the coming scene, ex. 10.9:

Example 10.9 *Frédégonde*, Act V, Scene 3

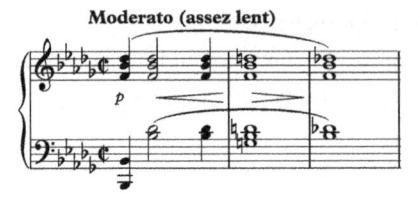

She accuses the Bishop of being her enemy, to which he protests that he has no enemies. He regards her as the subject of the King and the King as subject of God. 'What insolence', she hisses under her breath. She wants Mérowig removed from sanctuary, but the Bishop insists that that would be of his own free will, and leaves. The safety of sanctuary is supported by a motif, ex. 10.10:

Example 10.10 *Frédégonde*, Act V, Scene 3

Scene 4 Her plan is to remove Mérowig to a monastery where he would not be protected and to see Brunhilda her slave.

Scene 5 The final scene sees the entry of the King and a train of bishops, clerics and vassals from one side and of Brunhilda and Mérowig from the other, within the church boundary, with the Bishop and Fortunatus between the two groups. The King demands that Mérowig repent, which he does. He then asks him to come out of sanctuary and entrust himself to the King. This is not so straightforward, and ex. 10.9 reinforces Mérowig's suspicions. Example 10.10 and ex. 10.8 tell us that Mérowig is grateful for sanctuary while the King is fearful of sacrilege. Frédégonde whispers to Hilpéric not to falter; Brunhilda whispers to Mérowig not to obey. The King pursues his blandishments while the women scream insults at each other. Mérowig eventually yields, stepping across the boundary into his father's arms. Fortunatus and Brunhilda are horrified, and a strong ensemble anxiously awaits the King's reaction.

Example 10.8 introduces his deeply conflicted reply, King and father being at war within himself. For Mérowig should be condemned, yet he loves him. He passes the decision to God, as interpreted by the assembled bishops: pardon or the cloister? Frédégonde shamelessly threatens them if they go against her wishes. Their internal debate is tortuous, ex. 10.11, with Prétextat opting for pardon, the others for the cloister.

Example 10.11 *Frédégonde*, Act V, Scene 5

Brunhilda is rightly appalled at 'God's' verdict. With a dark solemnity reminiscent of the priests in *Aida*, the bishops condemn Mérowig to confinement in a cloister, to be tonsured and removed from the world. There follows a throbbing 12/8 rhythm, hallmark of grand ensembles in French opera since *Guillaume Tell* and harbinger of the final action. Sides are drawn, with Brunhilda and Fortunatus denouncing the verdict, Frédégonde and her supporters applauding it. Under Frédégonde's watchful eye the King has to support her.

Bishop Prétextat steps angrily forward to denounce the bishops as wolves in sheep's clothing and the King and Queen as liars and criminals, with a ringing anathema on all of them. The throbbing 12/8 resumes with more intensity than before. Such music is static but tensely dramatic since explosive emotions rise gradually to the surface just as the harmony winds towards the huge final cadence.

The people shout for pity for Mérowig. With the King's violent 'Jamais!' Frédégonde knows that victory is hers and that her sons will one day reign. Mérowig knows his cause is lost. Accusing Frédégonde directly of stealing his father, his love and his liberty, he draws his sword and kills himself to the emphatic chords of ex. 10.9. He throws the blooded sword at Frédégonde's feet as he falls. Villainy has triumphed.

* * * * *

Villainy triumphed in real life as well. The historical Mérowig was sent to a monastery, from which he escaped only to be murdered by Frédégonde's agents in 577 as he crossed the border. Hilpéric was murdered in 584 by an unknown hand; Prétextat was murdered in 586 on Frédégonde's orders. Brunhilda escaped but was captured and barbarously put to death by Frédégonde's son as an old woman in 614. Frédégonde alone, whose crimes 'fill many pages in the gloomy annals of Gregory of Tours', died in her bed.

Frédégonde is certainly one of the most unsavoury villains in opera, suitably cast as a mezzo, and never given a solo scene in which to vaunt her savagery. Her husband Hilpéric is a villain too, but with enough of a conscience and paternal feeling to suffer remorse, although he too is denied a spacious opportunity to explore these feelings. Mérowig is a heroic and attractive character, while Brunhilda holds centre stage as a wronged woman, with passionate feelings of both anger and love. The balance of two good characters (higher voices) and two bad (lower voices) invites comparison with *Euryanthe* and *Lohengrin*. Both Prétextat and Fortunatus have very satisfying secondary roles.

Frédégonde received eight performances at the Opéra in the winter of 1895–96 and then sank without trace until it was unexpectedly revived by the Municipal Theatre in Ho Chi Minh City, Vietnam, where Saint-Saëns had completed the draft score, on 20 October 2017. The opera was conducted by Patrick Souillot and directed by Caroline Blanpied.

The vocal score came out in 1896, with the usual vocal excerpts separately available. It was published not by Saint-Saëns's usual publisher, Durand, but by Paul Dupont, a firm that issued mainly operetta and had little influence in the field of grand opera, even if they had the will to further the opera's chances when one of the composers was dead. The ballets were published as score and parts, and Saint-Saëns put together a *Souvenirs de Frédégonde* for virtuoso cello and piano (treating Guiraud's themes as fairly as his own), but the opera's full score and parts were never printed.

The voices of the two composers are inevitably distinct. Saint-Saëns did not try to imitate Guiraud's style, except perhaps in the closing bars of Act III, and he created his own motifs. His music is less dense than Guiraud's, both in texture and in rhythm, and his skill at handling the shifting tension of individual scenes is far greater. Guiraud seeks more to maintain a constant pressure on the ear without responding to the dramatic flow, especially in Act III, and he lacks the classical skills of balance and clarity that always distinguish Saint-Saëns's work. His music is nonetheless an excellent example, along with Franck and Chausson, of a direction in French music which grows out of Gounod and moves towards Wagner, and which might have developed into a more personal voice if he had composed more music and lived beyond his fifty-four years.

11 | *Javotte, Déjanire* (open air)

On 16 December 1895, not long after passing his sixtieth birthday and two days before *Frédégonde* opened at the Opéra, Saint-Saëns wrote to a magazine editor with a revealing summary of his state of mind which has not, as far as I know, appeared in English before:

> I must tell you that I am neither a mathematician nor an astronomer nor an illustrator, and if I have my little follies, like many other people, I don't suffer from a desire to pass for what I am not. Fauré and Joncières do wonderful drawings, while I cannot draw, much to my regret. I also regret my total ignorance of mathematics, which has been an impassable barrier in my desire to study astronomy. Berlioz spoke somewhere about a man who *would have liked to be* a famous geologist. Me too. I *would have liked to be* a great scholar and a great painter. That's as far as my talent and my knowledge has got me. The doodles and scrawled landscapes in my letters are simply proof of my friendship for certain people, and of the recipients' appreciation of their true worth.
>
> I have written some poetry, though it was perhaps a mistake to publish it. I get sent, alas, many printed volumes of poetry which go some way to excusing my weakness. I do not regard myself as a poet even so. I know too well what I lack, namely the abundance and unstoppable flow which once allowed me, when improvising at the organ, to hold an audience's attention for two hours or more without the least fatigue or anxiety, with no more effort than a river needs to flow along its course. Chipping away at my poems I have learned to appreciate real poets, and for that reason I am not ashamed to have written them.
>
> Since my earliest years I have had only one ambition as a musician, and that is to be a musician in the broadest sense of the term, and I have only one regret, which is that life is not long enough to achieve that. I have been a pianist and an organist and I have composed something in nearly all genres. But erudition and a profound knowledge of the history of music has escaped me, and as composer I will have realised only a small part of my dream. That is why I would not want to write any more for the stage, which can manage without me very well in any case. I would like to go back to chamber music, symphonic music, organ music, and purely vocal music. Will I live long enough to accomplish my goal? I don't think I will, and I don't think, to tell the truth, that I would want to.[1]

The remark about lacking a profound knowledge of the history of music was prompted by his recent involvement with the monumental edition of Rameau's music, conceived in 1894 by Durand and entrusted to Saint-Saëns as General

---

[1] The letter is held by Northwestern University, Evanston, and is cited in RATNER 2012, p. 506.

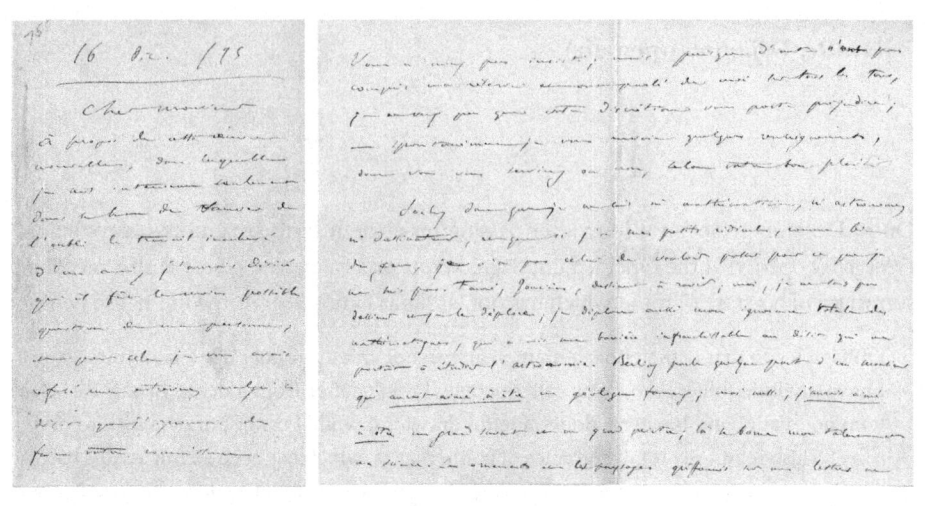

Figure 11.1 Letter of Saint-Saëns, 16 December 1895
Northwestern University, Evanston

Editor. For the rest of his life he was overseeing the steady production of impressive volumes, carefully edited and beautifully printed, beginning with the *Pièces de Clavecin* in 1895. By the time the edition came to an end in 1924 eighteen volumes had been published. Saint-Saëns's assistant Charles Malherbe, librarian at the Opéra, probably did the detailed work, and later d'Indy was brought in to edit the operas *Hippolyte et Aricie*, *Dardanus* and *Zaïs*. In the face of endless *Gesamtausgaben* of German composers coming out of Leipzig, there was a nationalist motive behind this publication, but Saint-Saëns and his colleagues felt strongly that Rameau was a major composer who had been allowed to fall into neglect and who deserved to be made accessible in a practical form. Saint-Saëns had of course been composing keyboard pieces and ballets with titles like *Gavotte* and *Rigaudon* for some time, in the operas as a reinforcement of a historical background. Whether the forms and manners of French baroque opera influenced his writing for the stage is another question, probably to be answered in the negative, although he always felt ballet to be a legitimate, in fact important, element of modern opera.

He was not, furthermore, unfamiliar with the problems of editing eighteenth-century music, since he had been collaborating on the series of Gluck editions instituted by Fanny Pelletan in 1873. The editions of *Alceste* (1875), *Orphée* (1889) and *Écho et Narcisse* (1902) were largely his work.

In his final remarks Saint-Saëns was wrong not to expect a long life, since he still had a quarter of a century ahead of him, as it turned out. But since childhood he had been haunted by his father's early death from consumption and was always treated as a delicate child. He was more troubled by his health than he need have been, for although bronchial problems recurred with some frequency, they never lasted long and his endless engagements and commitments were scarcely ever interrupted by ill health; he never cancelled a concert. There were some severe occurrences, for example in 1873, when he first went to Algiers to recuperate, and in 1883 after the production of *Henry VIII*, and especially in 1906 on his first crossing to North America, when he was seriously ill; but in reality he was robust rather than sickly. He disliked cold, damp weather and believed that it did him no good (like most of us) and so made a habit of going to north Africa or somewhere else in the sun in the winter. He was fortunate to be prosperous enough and free enough of domestic ties to indulge that preference. Although he dreaded the Russian snows, his tour there in the winter of 1874–75 gave him no special trouble.

In the passage quoted above there is one thought that concerns us most particularly since he is confessing to an inclination not to write any more for the stage. This was clearly a reaction against the work that he had put into *Frédégonde* and a hint that his heart was not in it. The next opera was indeed some five years in the future, but the interim saw some dramatic works of a new kind, and it would have been contrary to his aim to be a 'musician in the broadest sense of the term' if he had confined himself to other genres. The letter in effect announces that his forthcoming trip would be devoted to chamber and orchestral music, as in fact it was.

Immediately after the premiere of *Frédégonde* (late December 1895) Saint-Saëns left for Milan, where *Henry VIII* was being staged for the first time at La Scala and where he lodged in the apartment habitually occupied by Verdi. A full-length portrait of the maestro hung on the wall. Finding that the company had little idea how to perform his music, he was able to sort out some problems in time for the final rehearsal, and he was pleased with the performance, especially with Félia Litvinne as Catherine and Mario Sammarco as Henry. The opera, sung in Italian, did not please the Italian public, however, and the opening night was restive at least until the third act, which Saint-Saëns had shortened and which won warm applause.[2] The second performance was much more enthusiastically received, but by that time Saint-Saëns was on his way south to Naples, where he took ship to Egypt. He stayed this time in Luxor and in Cairo and, after composing some songs, he worked, as he had promised, on chamber and orchestral music.

The Second Violin Sonata was done first and despatched to Durand in March. Its carefree tone and two scherzos might suggest that Saint-Saëns was in a skittish mood, and certainly his muse was fecund. Then he took a trip by boat up the Nile to Aswan

---

[2] This was Saint-Saëns's recollection. In her *Ma Vie et son Art* (Paris, Plon, 1933, pp. 68–69), Litvinne said that Saint-Saëns appeared on stage with the singers and was loudly applauded.

and the island of Philae to see its temples and ancient monuments.[3] He returned to Cairo to compose a piano concerto which he imagined would be a suitable novelty for the concert forming in his mind to take place fifty years after his remarkable first concert in 1846, when, at the age of ten, he had played pieces by Handel and Kalkbrenner, a sonata by Hummel, a Prelude and Fugue by Bach, and two concertos, one by Mozart and one (no. 4) by Beethoven. He had made some sketches for the new concerto in the Canary Islands two years before, and now he worked them out at great speed, the whole work, his Fifth Concerto, being completed in little more than three weeks.

The unusual feature of this work is the middle movement, which is unlike anything else by Saint-Saëns or anyone else and has earned the concerto the nickname 'the Egyptian'. It is not simply that many of the themes have a Middle Eastern character, based on modal intervals; it proceeds strangely from one episode to another without any apparent direction, like a dramatic improvisation, although the balance of the movement is carefully controlled. There are diatonic and pentatonic themes in the mix, and two curious passages that stand out. In one, the left hand plays a series of notes which are coloured by the right hand with soft chords that give it the sound of an organ mixture stop, a device later used by Ravel in his *Boléro*. The other is a strange chirruping in the distant key of F♯ major, beneath which a Chinese melody is heard against soft blows on the tamtam. Was Saint-Saëns recalling his journey to the Far East in 1894 or just being playful?

On this visit Saint-Saëns met the Egyptologist Émile Amelineau, who was studying the early Coptic Christians and who suggested the plot of an opera, *Isis*, which he had devised. Saint-Saëns declined the offer, perhaps mindful of his plan to stay away from the stage, and perhaps thinking of Massenet's recent *Thaïs* which had the same setting in Coptic Egypt. Only a few months earlier Saint-Saëns had written a 'concert paraphrase' of the closing scene of Massenet's opera and dedicated it to Mme Massenet.

He returned to Paris in May 1896, and the concert marking fifty years since his debut in the same hall, the Salle Pleyel, took place on June 2nd. He again played the Mozart B♭ concerto that he had played when he was ten. The sold-out concert also included his new works: the *Thaïs* paraphrase, the Second Violin Sonata, played by Sarasate, and the Fifth Piano Concerto, with the composer naturally as soloist. Paul Taffanel conducted.

Before he was back in France, nonetheless, he had already embarked on a stage work. From Milan in May he wrote that he was 'working on his ballet'.[4] This may have belied his renunciation of the stage, but it accorded with his ambition to cover

---

[3] These were removed in 1970 when the building of the Aswan dam submerged the island. They were re-erected on the nearby island of Aguilkia which was then, somewhat deceptively, renamed Philae.
[4] Letter to Auguste Durand, 6 May 1896, RATNER 2012, p. 361.

all genres; he had composed plenty of ballet music for his operas and always enjoyed doing so, but he had not written a full ballet before. In the culture of the day, ballet and opera shared the most prestigious stages on an even footing and there was less of a barrier between ballet-goers and opera-goers than there is today. It is true that most ballet music was shaped in regular phrases, to assist the dancers, and it rarely achieved the sophistication that Tchaikovsky brought to it, but in France the art of the dance was held in the highest regard, as it had been since Louis XIV's time and especially since the codification of classical ballet by Jean-Georges Noverre in the mid eighteenth century.

The plan for the new work came from Jean-Louis Croze, Gallet's godson, who had provided poems for two earlier songs and the text for his *Hymne à Pallas-Athéné*, composed to accompany the performances of *Antigone* in the Roman theatre in Orange in 1894. Croze was on the staff of the Théâtre-Marigny on the Champs-Élysées. He proposed a ballet named *Magali* set in Provence, but, with Dubois's 1883 ballet *La Farandole* still current at the Opéra, Saint-Saëns instead suggested a story, apparently from Boccaccio, to be named *Aliboron*, in which two lovers shut a donkey in their room in order to deceive an elderly marquis ('maître Aliboron' being derived from La Fontaine's fable in Book I, *Les Voleurs et l'âne*). In the end a quite different story was devised.

When the Théâtre-Marigny temporarily ran out of money, the Monnaie in Brussels and the Grand-Théâtre in Lyon both took up the new idea, named *Javotte*. The score was mostly written in Aix-les-Bains and in Paris, finished in September, held up for a while by the composer's eye strain. In fact, the Lyon theatre was first in the field, directed by Albert Vizentini, to whom Saint-Saëns felt indebted for having been the first to bring *Le Timbre d'argent* to the stage twenty years before. The ballet opened in Lyon on 3 December 1896 and in Brussels fifteen days later. Lyon's claim for the first night won out because *Javotte* shared a double bill there with a revival of *Proserpine*. Saint-Saëns rehearsed the company for three weeks and conducted the first night. The choreography was by 'Madame Mariquita' (as she was known) and Javotte was danced by Elisa Damiani, of whom Saint-Saëns said, 'I embraced the little Javotte, and it felt as if I was burying my nose in a rose.'[5] The next day he wrote:

> This little ballet will give pleasure because it is essentially good-humoured; most ballets are too pretentious and not very amusing, except *Coppélia*, which is a masterpiece of light ballet. Otherwise they tend to be too artistic, like *Giselle* and *Sylvia*; these are not played any more in Paris, but they are played still abroad. In France these are thought to be too long; ballet is just an hors-d'œuvre, but those ballets have to be the most important part of the evening, against

---

[5] Letter of 6 December 1896, RATNER 2012, p. 361.

the current trend. Nothing can be done about that. The result is that *Javotte* is in a good situation, having been designed for these very conditions.[6]

* * * * *

Javotte
(Ratner 306)

Ballet in one act and three tableaux
by
Jean-Louis Croze

First performance: Grand Théâtre, Lyon, 3 December 1896

Javotte
Hélène, sa mère
Jean, amoureux de Javotte
Brisquet, garde champêtre
Le Père François, père de Javotte

Danseurs et danseuses, paysans et paysannes

The action takes place in the Nivernais.

Orchestra:	2 flutes, piccolo, 2 oboes, 2 clarinets, 2 bassoons, 4 horns, 4 cornets, 3 trombones, tuba, timpani, bass drum, cymbals, triangle, mirlitons, bell, harps, strings.
Offstage:	flutes, clarinets, brass, cymbals, bass drum, side drum.

Javotte is divided into thirty-one short numbers in three tableaux, which run continuously and last about an hour. The action is a story of peasant life in a village in the Nivernais, roughly the modern département of Nièvre, west of Burgundy.

Tableau 1 At curtain-up a village *fête* is in full swing, with the stage full of dancing couples. A church is visible at the back. The young man Jean is sitting apart on his own, anxious because his sweetheart has not come. His four-note motif (ex. 11.1) pops up from time to time in the orchestral texture.

Example 11.1 *Javotte*, Tableau 1

---

[6] Letter to Durand of 10 December 1896, RATNER 2012, pp. 361–62.

The other girls offer to dance with him, but he refuses. Saint-Saëns's representation of offer and refusal is charmingly picturesque (ex. 11.2):

Example 11.2 *Javotte*, Tableau 1

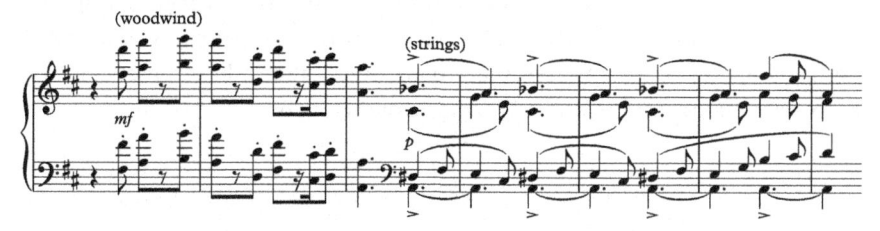

This illustrates very well Saint-Saëns's desire to reflect the action in the music when he can. The girls, rebuffed, make fun of him, so he moves away to wait somewhere else, and the general dancing resumes.

An elderly couple approaches, wearing clogs and cursing and swearing. To the fine-looking village policeman in his new blue uniform they explain that their daughter Javotte has left home and has probably joined her sweetheart at the dance. They anxiously ask if anyone has seen her, to music which could have been sung (ex. 11.3):

Example 11.3 *Javotte*, Tableau 1

(Avez - vous vu Ja - vot - te?)

The horns speak for the determination of the law to find the lost girl, and the three leave the scene.

When Jean comes back the girls are still making fun of him, when Javotte herself appears, out of breath and all smiles, and the lovers fall into each other's arms. The *Pas de deux* that follows is short, wistful and very elegant, making much use of ex. 11.1, and it is followed by a *Bourrée* for the company in which Jean and Javotte soon join. This is not the baroque courtly dance that Saint-Saëns might have learned from Rameau, but a simulation of folk music with stolid orchestration and modal touches. Whereas Saint-Saëns's interest in ancient Greek music was scientific and intellectual, he never took an ethnological interest in French folk music but simply supplied what any audience would recognise as folksy in spirit.

The church bell is heard, supported by strings in open fourths and fifths. This was an idea Saint-Saëns picked up from Rossini's *Guillaume Tell*, to give the effect of a bell not unlike the experimental overtones recently introduced in the Fifth Piano Concerto.[7] The young folk move off to attend Vespers, leaving Jean, Javotte and a table of drinkers at the back.

---

[7] 'L'Harmonie moderne', *Le Monde musical*, 30 November 1912; SORET 2012, p. 828.

The music passes imperceptibly to a very moving passage for strings as Javotte weeps with regret and shame that she has disobeyed her parents and that they are not in church.

Javotte's parents clomp on stage, and her father is ready to strike her, but she takes refuge in the more sympathetic arms of her mother, the strings again voicing her feelings. They take her off home, leaving Jean disconsolate and again prey to the jeers of his companions, who are now resuming their frolics after a brief observance of Vespers, to a resumption of the boisterous music of the opening.

Figure 11.2 *Javotte*, piano score, cover
Hugh Macdonald Collection, Norwich

Tableau 2 This is set indoors in Javotte's humble village home with a spinning wheel in the centre. The family enters and Javotte discards her festive dress in order to set to work, like Cinderella, on the cleaning, scrubbing and spinning. Her parents are now going out to the *fête* while she, as punishment for her earlier escapade, must stay home and work. They address her in basic unisons and then leave, carefully shutting the doors and windows.

She sets to work on the dishes but immediately drops one. An oboe reminds her that she was wrong to disobey, but as the oboe and flute remind her of ex. 11.1 she remembers that she and Jean love each other, and in no time at all she is dancing the Bourrée again. Remorse again intervenes, so she sits down to spin. The spinning goes well (two clarinets) to start with, but the thread soon gets tangled and breaks. She throws down the distaff and decides to knit instead. Saint-Saëns's kntting music is perfect (ex. 11.4):

Example 11.4 *Javotte*, Tableau 2

But this cannot keep her from leaping to her feet and dancing a full-blooded waltz. Next it's time to sweep the floor, but before she has begun there is a knock, not at the door, which she cannot open, but at the window. It is of course Jean, and after eager embraces she shows him round the premises as if he were a distinguished guest. There's a suggestion of baroque formality here.

Suddenly she decides to wreck the place and throw everything she can to the floor, with the orchestra's enthusiastic support. Now they have a long duet, with a slow waltz to begin the *Pas de deux*. Its second part is a light presto in traditional ballet style. Their duet over, they decide to leave by the window and disappear.

The parents now stagger back from the party, both the worse for wear. They find the house in chaos, no Javotte and the window open, and so come to the right conclusion. A knock on the door brings in the village constable, in even worse shape. Proudly announcing that he has caught the fugitives he leads in a young couple. 'Mais ce n'est pas eux !' Noisy demonstrations of exasperation bring down the curtain.

Tableau 3 The third tableau is back on the village green at night, the venue set for a ball. Folksy fiddles lead off a general gathering of the villagers, some of whom, divided into men and children, are playing kazoos ('mirlitons'). Saint-Saëns hoped that members of the theatre's chorus could be brought on for this, provided that they learned their parts properly and stood near the front of the stage. In the crowd are the notables whose function is to name the girl who dances the best as Ball Queen. Four girls step forward in turn, the plot nicely supporting the aim of presenting the widest possible variety of dancers and dancing.

The first girl has a delicate Allegretto, a trap for unwary string players, lightly scored. The judges are not impressed. The second has a lilting *Siciliano*, the third a brisk and noisy movement, and the fourth a beautiful *grazioso* for wind alone. The judges display some dissatisfaction and disagreement after each one and end up discouraged. Right on time Jean and Javotte appear, to the delight of everyone, who seem to have made up their minds in advance who is to be Ball Queen. Javotte eclipses her rivals at once, and it only takes a short, rapid dance to convince the judges that she is the star. Her four rivals are happy to return to their beaux and join in the general dance.

Javotte's parents, still enraged at their disobedient daughter, arrive with the constable. 'Where is she?' (ex. 11.3) they ask, and the villagers pretend to look for them, to a soft pizzicato *tempo di marcia*. Inevitably they are found. The constable restrains her father from striking them both and delivers a harangue, articulated by trombones and horns. Jean has resort to a timid version of ex. 11.1 to plead for mercy, declaring that they are in love and (clarinet solo) want to get married. 'In that case,' reply the parents after the briefest reflection, 'we give our consent.'

A happy ending is clearly in sight, but there is more action yet. A band is heard approaching with a procession of lords and squires of the village. Javotte and Jean are presented to the Mayor, and the lovers dance a *Grand Pas de Deux*. Saint-Saëns was clearly determined to surpass himself for this movement, and he did. Scored for four solo cellos and a double bass in another echo from *Guillaume Tell*, this piece in B major 9/8 reaches far above the familiar habitation of 'ballet music' into symphonic territory with ravishing results, as the full orchestra takes up the sweep of melody. How could such a piece lie so long unheard, even by those who hold Saint-Saëns in high regard?

Two more dances bring the festivities to a close, the first in a rather self-conscious 5/4 rhythm, and the second an animated finale in which the band merrily joins. Neither can quite restore the marvellous sense of elevation produced by the *Grand Pas de Deux*. From the start Saint-Saëns himself recognised that the final scene needed to be tightened up. He felt the four dances by rival contestants were too long, although a lesser number weakened the story. He suggested cutting the second and third dances, and the second edition of the vocal score (121 pages) lacks these movements. It has the first dance danced by two contestants, so that there are at least three dancers altogether, but the idea came from Vizentini and seemed unsatisfactory to the composer.

He also suggested cutting the *Grand Pas de Deux*, when the orchestra was likely to blanch at double-sharps, and the 5/4 dance which follows it. But although no one would shed a tear over the latter, no performance without the *Grand Pas de Deux* would convey the masterly imagination that Saint-Saëns can rise to even in a work where no such miracle is expected.

Javotte was a success, as it deserved to be, especially in the French provinces. In 1898 Saint-Saëns made an orchestral suite for concert use, drawing on the first and third tableaux. The ballet was played in Brussels, Berlin, Barcelona, Milan and St Petersburg, and for Saint-Saëns it was a satisfaction that both the Opéra-Comique and the Opéra took it into their repertoires. At the Opéra-Comique in 1899 he discovered how difficult Carvalho's successor as the theatre's director, Albert Carré, could be; among other things Carré had a woman dancing the part of Jean, against Saint-Saëns's wishes. Ten years later the ballet was performed to great acclaim at the Opéra, in contrast to which a visit to Dieppe a month later to rehearse the same work there was all the more painful. 'I left the rehearsal, preferring to take the air and look at the boats rather than argue pointlessly with a rude, foolish woman with no talent.'[8] The Opéra mounted the ballet again in 1935 for the Saint-Saëns centenary, and it remained in repertoire until 1962. But today it is not even talked about in the ballet world, let alone performed, a sad fate for an enchanting and exhilarating score. There are, however, two excellent recordings of the music, so the ballet is not quite dead.

* * * * *

One reason why Saint-Saëns was disinclined to write more operas during this period was the fact that at least five of the eight operas he had already composed were doing well, although he rarely attended performances in widely scattered cities unless they happened to be where he wanted to go. In the same month that *Javotte* was first performed in Lyon, for example, there were performances of *Samson et Dalila* in St Petersburg, *Javotte* itself in Brussels, *Henry VIII* and *Phryné* in Milan, *Phryné* in Brussels, *Phryné* in Antwerp, and *Proserpine* in Madrid. Both *Henry VIII* and *Ascanio* would have been revived at the Opéra if their sets, destroyed by a warehouse fire in 1894, had been rebuilt. New sets were built for *Henry VIII* in 1909, but none for *Ascanio*.

Reports of performances of his operas far and wide would come in steadily until the end of his life, leaving no doubt that he was now, with Massenet and Puccini, one of Europe's leading opera composers. There were voices already beginning to wonder whether and when French music would change direction, for Charpentier's realist *Louise* and Debussy's mystifying *Pelléas et Mélisande* were both composed, but not yet heard: both were lying in wait.

The winter and early months of 1897 were spent in the Canaries, where habitually he preferred to write prose rather than music. For a composer as fertile as Saint-Saëns, this was truly a fallow period. But the seed of a major new project was planted immediately after the premiere of *Javotte* when Saint-Saëns gave an organ recital in the cathedral at Béziers, near Montpellier, on his journey towards Spain and the port of Cadiz. His visit was arranged by a prosperous wine-grower aged thirty-six named Fernand Castelbon

---

[8] Letter of 17 August 1909, RATNER 2012, p. 365.

de Beauxhostes, who dabbled in music and directed a local choral society. After performing in the amphitheatre at Valence (on the Rhône south of Lyon), Castelbon became passionately involved in the idea of open-air performances on a large scale which would draw in all ranks of the populace and thus expose them to the best in art. The philanthropic social movement of which this was a part had its spokesman in Romain Rolland, while for Saint-Saëns it opened up further opportunities for exploring ancient Greek drama as a by-product of the Mediterranean climate.[9]

The town of Béziers had the remains of a Roman amphitheatre, and also a wooden bullring which burned down in 1896. The half-finished brick arena being built on the site suggested to Castelbon the possibility of establishing a festival there, so he invited Saint-Saëns to try out the acoustics and, if he was satisfied, take on the role of musical director. This no doubt provided food for thought during his long hibernation in the Canaries, so when he returned he went directly to Béziers in May 1897 en route to Toulouse, where he needed to discuss a revival of *Étienne Marcel*. He agreed to compose a new work for the 1898 Béziers festival and to engage the faithful Gallet to write the spoken and sung text. His experience with *Antigone* was in his mind, since it had been played in the open air at Orange in 1894 and was due to be revived there this year, 1897.[10]

Consultations with Gallet during the summer in Paris and Wimereux produced the plan for *Déjanire*, a subject which had been in Gallet's teeming mind for some time. He had wondered whether to write it as a play or as an opera, so the Béziers proposal made a neat mélange of both. He was now in poor health, but he worked with Saint-Saëns with enthusiasm, drawing on two classical plays, *The Trachiniae* by Sophocles (Greek) and *Hercules Œtaeus* by Seneca (Latin), to tell the story of the death of Hercules brought about by the poisoned tunic of Nessus, the same story as that of Handel's oratorio *Hercules*. It is a story of strong emotions and violent death painted in the broad strokes that both Gallet and Saint-Saëns felt were appropriate for outdoor performance in front of a large audience. They also supposed they were recreating the democratic spirit that lay behind ancient Greek theatre.

'All the dialogue would be declaimed,' Gallet wrote to Saint-Saëns on November 15th, 'only the choruses would be sung. There would be a full ballet in the last act. With an introduction, a march, etc, it would make up a work that would be broad and impressive, and I think of fine character.'[11] Following the 'prose mélique' which he wrote for *Thaïs*, Gallet wrote what he called 'prose rythmique' for the principals who

---

[9] See NECTOUX 1991.
[10] Saint-Saëns recounted the background of the Béziers festival on several occasions, including: 'À propos de Déjanire' in *Le Théâtre, la vie mondaine* of 25 February 1911; 'Les deux *Déjanire*', in *Musica*, November 1911; 'Les Arènes de Béziers', *L'Écho de Paris*, 7 July 1912; these are reprinted in SORET 2012, pp. 694–95, 748–50 and 819–23.
[11] F-DI Fonds Saint-Saëns, Gallet dossier 10.

were going to have to declaim it to a vast amphitheatre, with mostly conventional verse for the chorus. At the end of the month Gallet sent Saint-Saëns a draft of the play (for it was not a libretto, as Saint-Saëns insisted) in three acts and four tableaux. Castelbon and the mayor of Béziers went to Paris to assure Gallet that no expense would be spared and that the people of the town were entirely behind this extravagant project. Saint-Saëns was meanwhile in Spain, entertaining the royal family and overseeing a revival of *Samson et Dalila*, before moving on to Las Palmas for the 1897–98 winter. His own contribution to *Déjanire* was clearly going to be less arduous than for a normal opera, and he did not begin to compose the music until March 15th of the new year.

He returned to Béziers in April to check the logistics of the space, then continued to compose the score in Lyon and London, where, in both cities, *Henry VIII* was in rehearsal. At Covent Garden it opened on Bastille Day and was sung in French. Meanwhile an ailing Gallet rehearsed the actors for *Déjanire* in Paris while the choruses and bands were assembled in Béziers. Most of the dancers came from Paris. The music for bands was scored by Charles Eustace, director of the military music school at Montpellier. Early in August Saint-Saëns was back in Béziers with the task of coordinating the enormous number of participants. Between rehearsals he began rescoring the work for a normal theatre, since plans were already laid for later taking the work to the Odéon in Paris, which had supplied the actors.

The performance finally took place on 28 August 1898, with a second performance the following day. There is no question that the aim of presenting serious art to the populace was achieved, and reverberations of the event echoed far and wide in the press, both in France and abroad. It was generally felt, whether true or not, that nothing like it had been attempted since antiquity. A sure sign of its success in the eyes of Castelbon and the citizenry of Béziers is that the festival continued, with breaks, until the 1920s.

Just how many people took part and how many attended is hard to calculate, but it seems that there were around 250 instrumentalists made up of two military bands and a large string orchestra, plus eighteen harps and twenty-five trumpets. The Barcelona Municipal Band was brought in to supplement the local military band. The chorus numbered around two hundred, which is actually rather few in relation to many choral gatherings of the later nineteenth century, and there were sixty dancers. The audience is given as ten thousand, many of whom had come from Paris or equally far. The set was provided by the arena building itself, with a large arcade added to provide the suggestion of an interior in Act II. Behind the stage could be seen a hill rising with various antique temples on its slopes, a construction so skilfully painted by the artist Marcel Jambon that many people thought it was a real hill in the distance.

* * * * *

> ### *Déjanire*
> (Ratner 311)
>
> Tragédie in four acts by Louis Gallet
>
> First performance: Les Arènes, Béziers, 28 August 1898
>
> La Muse
> Hercule
> Philoctète
> Iole
> Déjanire
> Phénice
> Lichas, Chef des Héraclides
>
> Coryphée   soprano
> Coryphée   ténor
> Les Héraclides, compagnons d'Hercule
> Les Œchaliennes, compagnes d'Iole
> Les Étoliennes de la suite de Déjanire
>
> Orchestra: strings, harps, trumpets.
>
> 1er orchestre militaire: piccolo in D♭, flute, 2 oboes, clarinet in E♭, 2 clarinets, bass clarinet, 4 saxophones, bassoon, 2 cornets, 2 trumpets, 2 horns, 4 trombones, 9 saxhorns, string bass, timpani, bass drum, cymbals (these numbers to be augmented).
>
> 2ème orchestre militaire: piccolo in D♭, flute, 2 oboes, clarinet in E♭, 2 clarinets, bass clarinet, 4 saxophones, bassoon, 2 cornets, 2 trumpets, 2 horns, 4 trombones, 9 saxhorns, string bass, timpani, bass drum, cymbals (these numbers to be augmented).

ACT I

The play begins at the point when Hercules, having completed his twelve labours and having married Deianira, daughter of Œneus, has fallen in love with Iole, daughter of his latest victim Eurytus, tyrant of Œchalia. Gallet supposes that Iole is in love with Philoctetes, Hercules's supporter and friend, creating a chain of passion and jealousy that can only end in tragedy.

Prologue Saint-Saëns asked for a bell to be struck three times, followed by a flourish from all the harps. This silenced the audience, to allow a Muse to step forward and declaim the praises of Béziers, in a remote descendance from Lullyan operas with their prologues that glorified the king.[12] The Muse's lines are interspersed by flourishes from all the harps.

---

[12] The Prologue was not included in the vocal score, but is found at F-Pn MS 510.

The audience can see see the acropolis of Œchalia, with buildings at both sides of the vast stage, one of them the gynaeceum, or women's quarters, and in the gap between them a huge nuptial pyre being erected for the wedding of Iole and Hercule.[13]

Prélude This is taken bodily from the first part of Saint-Saëns's symphonic poem *La Jeunesse d'Hercule*, which he composed in 1877, except that at its first hearing the theme is bare of any accompaniment, in keeping with the breadth and simplicity that Saint-Saëns was trying to convey in the new work (ex. 11.5).

Example 11.5 *Déjanire*, Act I, Prelude

No. 1 The men's chorus, almost entirely in unison, sing the praises of the great Hercule, and they are joined by a tenor coryphée celebrating the forthcoming marriage. The military bands accompany the chorus, the strings the coryphées.

In contrast the female chorus takes Iole's part, and the music becomes at once less pompous and more intimate. Their coryphée is even more impassioned, foretelling disaster for the city. Before any of the protagonists have appeared we are aware of fierce dramatic tension (ex. 11.6):

Example 11.6 *Déjanire*, Act I, No. 1

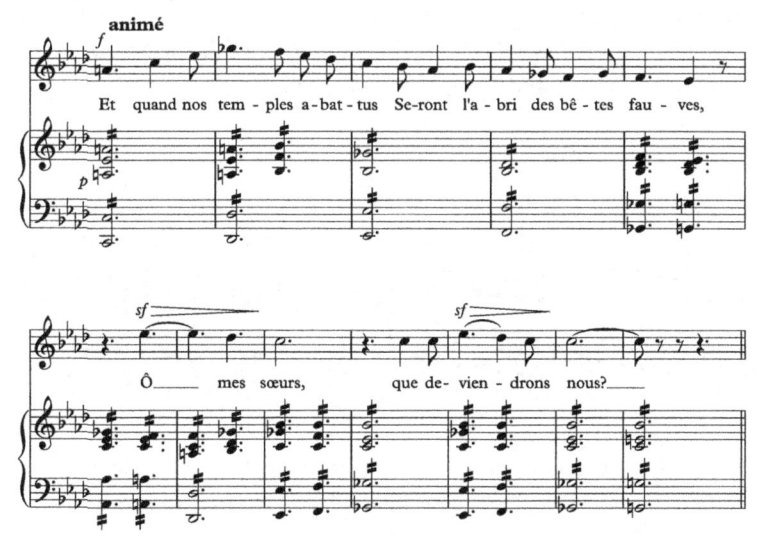

---

[13] I give the French form of proper names in the context of the play itself.

The scene closes with the men's chorus singing Hercule's praises as before, unmoved by the women's woes.

Dialogue The arrival of Hercule and Philoctète is announced, and the massed brass have their chance to fill the arena with sound. In dialogue Hercule informs Philoctète that he intends to marry Iole, whose father he has just killed, information that alarms Philoctète since he and Iole are in love. Furthermore, Hercule requires Philoctète to tell Iole himself of this plan. Hercule plans to go to Calydon to inform Déjanire, his wife.

Phénice, Déjanire's nurse, who is also a sorceress (a character evidently invented by Gallet), enters with two maidservants with the news that Déjanire is tired of weeping at home and longing for Hercule's return. So she is coming here to find him. Hercule tells Phénice that Destiny will separate him and his wife forever. Phénice must return to Calydon to tell her. She leaves, uttering warnings of dreadful consequences.

Philoctète is told now to go to Iole with his assignment, then Hercule leaves. A gentle modal melody on violins in octaves, said to be a modern Greek melody, is heard as Iole herself then appears, begging protection against her conqueror, as if she knew what was in store. She had been tipped off by the construction of the wedding pyre. Iole asks Philoctète to tell Hercule that he must give up any idea of marrying her, confessing her love for Philoctète.

No. 2 Some agitated music starts up in the orchestra, and the men's chorus announce the arrival of Déjanire in a stormy mood. 'The hunter is less scared of an Armenian tigress than of her', they declare, and her horse-drawn chariot makes a splendid entrance into the arena. Saint-Saëns was proud that the figure of Déjanire standing boldly in her chariot was wholly in the spirit of Greek theatre, echoing scenes from Aeschylus's *Oresteia* and Euripides's *Iphigenia*.[14] Her motif is disturbingly chromatic (ex. 11.7):

Example 11.7 *Déjanire*, Act I, No. 2

Phénice is with her. She gets down from her chariot and invokes Juno to avenge the outrage she has suffered. She insists on seeing Iole before Hercule, so she leads her party into the gynaeceum, where Iole resides.

---

[14] 'Causerie sur l'art du théâtre', published in Stoullig's *Annales du théâtre et de la musique* for 1905; SORET 2012, p. 606.

ACT II

Prélude Act II takes place within the gynaeceum, suggested by a pillared structure moved in from one side. Saint-Saëns must have been confident that the Prelude to this act could be heard clearly, even though it is marked *piano* and very lightly scored. It is written in a deliberately unsophisticated style, with a suggestion of modality, perhaps intended to evoke a timeless antiquity, but in reality leaving an impression of emptiness and naïveté. As characterisation of Iole, it surely does her less than justice.

No. 1 Iole is appalled at fate for delivering her into the hands of her father's murderer. The doors open to admit Déjanire and her companions to very different music (ex 11.7). She addresses Iole accusingly and, despite Iole's protests, treats her as if she had stolen Hercule from her.

No. 2 Hercule enters to a strident and threatening whole-tone fanfare. He orders everyone but Déjanire to leave. He asserts his right as hero and husband to be obeyed, to which Déjanire gradually succumbs. She begs for a return to the love that united them before. Unmoved, he insists on pursuing his destiny which will separate them forever. She must return to Calydon. She agrees, but asks to take Iole with her, which Hercule of course refuses. At this she breaks out in a rage, threatening him with the fury of the gods. She leaves with a harsh reminder of ex. 11.7.

Hercule sends for Philoctète, who tells him that Iole insists that an unmovable barrier exists between her and Hercule. Philoctète is sent to watch over Déjanire. Iole herself then enters, only to be confronted by a passionate declaration of love from Hercule. She is unmoved, at which Hercule suspects that she has another lover and insists that she name him. She refuses. When Philoctète returns, Iole lets slip a gasp and a desperate glance in his direction. Hercule guesses that she loves Philoctète and subjects the two of them to violent verbal abuse.

No. 3 He orders his soldier Lichas to arrest Philoctète as a traitor, as a new stretch of strongly dramatic music covers the entry of the chorus. Hercule swears he will shock the world with the intensity of his vengeance, and the act ends with the most extended music of the work so far. The chorus sing Gallet's non-rhyming verses recording the moment when Hercule's destiny finally turns. The accompaniment is agitated, and by no means all the choral writing is unison. The tenor coryphée is fearful for yet more blood that may be spilled; the soprano coryphée begs the Furies to stay their hand. The music settles into a more celestial mood as women's voices and harps call upon Pallas Athene to bring calm to the land. The men remind us that it was long ago predicted that Hercule would meet his end in this place, and the scene fades with Hercule's theme (ex. 11.5) softly recalled in the bass.

ACT III

No. 1 Act III, still set in the gynaeceum, begins with a *Symphonie* played with the full chorus singing a mournful verse of foreboding and a strongly chromatic idiom in support.

No. 1bis Déjanire enters with Phénice, who offers to win Hercule back using her enchantments, but Déjanire remembers a talisman she has never used for fear that it might have fatal effects. In an extended *mélodrame* (the eighteenth-century type, in which lines of speech alternate with music but do not compete with it) she recounts how once when she and Hercule were crossing the river Erynus she was taken across by the centaur Nessus, who then attempted to carry her off. Hercule shot Nessus with an arrow, and Nessus, as he died, gave her a tunic which he had pressed into his blood, ambiguously assuring her that it would ensure that she would never again have to worry about her husband's infidelity. Iole comes in with her women. She confesses she loves Philoctète and is desperate to flee from Hercule. Déjanire agrees to protect her and to flee with her. She gives orders for their departure.

No. 2 The women sing an enchanting song about Hercule's night rage, but Déjanire is ready to confront him.

No. 2bis The music turns darker as he enters. She feigns defeat and says goodbye, but Hercule is suspicious. Iole enters, veiled, to her meek music. Hercule seizes her and threatens to have Philoctète put to death if she rejects him again. She is forced to give in, so preparations for the wedding are put in hand.

When Déjanire comes to take Iole away, the latter refuses, having now promised, under threats, to wed Hercule. Philoctète comes in, at once understanding the price she has paid to save his life. Déjanire sends Phénice to fetch the box containing a tunic dipped in Nessus's blood, which she then holds up with its decoration of jewels and precious stones. She instructs Iole to give it to Hercules who, on wearing it, they suppose, will rediscover his love for Déjanire.

No. 2ter After a noisy 'Gloire au Dieux' sung by the men offstage, the women and the female coryphée sing a *Hymne à Éros* (**No. 3**), urging the god of love to do his work with an enthusiasm and appealing vigour that should set young Cupid to work at once.

ACT IV

Prélude et Cortège The nuptial pyre is ready and the palace is decorated for the ceremony. The stage fills with the various groups who take their places across the wide space of the arena. The music is 'white-note' modal, seemingly in D minor or A minor, but perhaps neither, with episodes in D major and D minor, and a final triumphant entry for Hercule to a full orchestral version of his theme, ex. 11.5. Déjanire, Phénice and Philoctète are watching from the crowd. Hercule addresses the people and invites them to share in his joy.

No. 1 The tenor coryphée sings an *Épithalame* to a harp accompaniment, with more of the character of a salon piece than an address to ten thousand spectators. Iole steps forward with the box containing the tunic. She acknowledges some gifts from Hercule and tells him that her gift promises marvellous results for lovers. They retire to their respective palaces to prepare for the ceremony.

Nos. 2, 3 There follows the *divertissement*, as in an opera, made up of a *Chœur dansé*, a *Pantomime* and a *Prière*. The sixty dancers now have their main moment, with the chorus singing and striking cymbals. The *Chœur dansé* is a lively movement with a strong climax, which must have been an impressive spectacle. The *Pantomime* is an austere unison line as Hercule, wearing the magic tunic, and Iole share the ceremonial libations. The tunic's magic will take effect when it is exposed to the sun, so Déjanire is watching closely. Throughout the *Prière*, in which the chorus remain on a chord of A♭ major throughout, Hercule is showing signs of distress as the fire of the tunic begins to devour him. He rushes into the crowd and collapses on the steps of the palace. Everyone is transfixed by terror and the dissonances bite hard. Déjanire realises that she was misled by the centaur and, while Hercule seizes torches to light the nuptial pyre and then leaps into the flames invoking Jupiter, she draws a dagger and kills herself.

As the smoke and flames clear, Hercule is seen standing in a triumphant apotheosis. Hercule is invincible, the chorus sing; even though he dies he rises up again immortal. Full chorus, orchestra and military bands conclude the spectacle with a noisy din that could be heard for miles.

* * * * *

This story is perhaps a surprising choice for its purpose, burdened as it is with tight personal hostility and passion. Is it possible to portray character in detail on such a huge canvas? Hercule himself is one-dimensional, accustomed always to defeating his opponents (and killing them) and taking mistresses freely, so the situation here shows him in the only light he is ever seen in, even when Déjanire and Iole oppose his wishes. He must be a man of heroic bearing and stentorian voice, and no doubt Georges Dorival fitted the part, having played a number of classical roles including Britannicus and Oedipus. He had played Frédéri in Daudet's *L'Arlésienne*, and he lived to make a great number of films, as late as 1938.

From the women something more subtle is required, since both Iole and Déjanire are confronted with agonising choices, and Déjanire must all the time be seen to be in love with Hercule. Her suicide would be an operatic necessity whether Hercule survived or not, and in addition we imagine an element of cruelty in the gift of Nessus's tunic, in parallel with Medea's horrific murder of Jason with a poisoned garment. The anointed garment was to be kept hidden from the light. But she had by mistake allowed a shred of wool with which she was weaving the garment to fall into the sunlight, and it had burned fiercely. Despite her misgivings as to whether the charm would do good or harm, her horror when she finally sees how it destroys Hercule is real. The part was played at Béziers by Cora Laparcerie, a strikingly beautiful twenty-two-year-old actress from the Odéon with big black eyes, who had recently turned down an engagement in St Petersburg and who had a distinguished later career in the theatre. Iole was played by the twenty-nine-year-old Caroline Segond-Weber, also from the Odéon, whose portraits show a somewhat grim-faced character and whose career was built on classical roles.

There are opportunities for grand processional scenes and dancing, especially in the last act, and it must be imagined that the chorus and dancers filled the central area. The musicians were placed with the conductor on the right-hand side of the arena. If the two military bands were on opposite sides they would have needed sub-conductors, who were normally employed in choral works anyway, so perhaps Saint-Saëns had as many as three assistant conductors, which would not in itself call for comment.

The event was repeated the following year with two more performances on 27 and 29 August 1899, with Fauré helping out as conductor. Open-air performances without amplification are now no more than a memory, so it is hard to judge how successful these performances of *Déjanire* were. At performances of opera in Roman arenas today in France and Italy (where amplification is often in place) the acoustics are often found to be surprisingly clear, yet the declamation of verse would be hard to sustain in a big arena such as Béziers, where the building would have been more helpful if it had been complete. Yet the Montpellier *Éclair* reported: 'The acoustics are so perfect that the slightest vocal inflexions could be heard anywhere in the auditorium.'[15] Public declamation was part of an actor's training, yet few actors can have expected to face a situation of this kind. Their success is all the more creditable. Even orchestral music can sound weak in the open air, which persuaded Saint-Saëns to include as many wind instruments as possible in his ensemble.

The Paris press was exhilarated by a trip to the sun and profoundly impressed by the successful management of so many participants. In the main, too, they admired Saint-Saëns's balance of grand and intimate, formal and free. Some critics attempted to portray Béziers as a French response to Bayreuth, although nothing could have been further from the minds of Saint-Saëns or Castelbon de Beauxhostes. Ironically, the more turbulent, disturbed music of *Déjanire* sounds more Wagnerian than anything he

---

[15] Quoted in the programme for the 1899 performances.

Figure 11.3 *Déjanire* at Béziers, 1898
L'Univers illustré, August 1898

had written before. The event was above all local and popular, not national and exclusive, and although Saint-Saëns was seen as its leader by the public, there was no hint of a shrine or a cult to be attached to his name.

One of the most interesting responses came from the writer Emile Baumann, who published a long essay on the work in the *Nouvelle Revue* two years later.[16] For once Saint-Saëns was being appraised by an intelligent critic with real musical competence and no inclination to take sides.

> The simplicity of *Déjanire* is no fantasy by a dilettante musician. Beyond a certain point music cannot deny its accomplishments without denying itself. It is folly to want to be primitive. Greek music will never inject new blood into art, despite the wealth of its modes. Scholars are deluded on this point.[17] An inspired composer like Saint-Saëns can see all too clearly that Greek melody, with its ties to the ancient orient, will never prevail over polyphonic melody and its infinite range of expression. He himself made a fine judgment of this music of antiquity in his preface to *Antigone*: 'It is line drawing, enlivened by plain colours whose extreme simplicity supplies all the charm.'

---

[16] *La Nouvelle Revue*, 1 August 1900, pp. 432–46, published as a separate brochure by Durand.
[17] Baumann here points a finger at Gevaert and Bourgault-Ducoudray in a footnote.

His idea in writing *Déjanire* was not to revive classical art. Where he is close to psalmody he is imagining some precise effect because drama is more strongly enlivened by it. The *Prière* to Jupiter, at the end, is made up entirely of the chord of A♭ repeated by the chorus without expression. But that is how Hercules's tragic illusion in thinking he has found permanent peace is brought out.

There is no trace of floating rhythm, like plainchant, such as is found in the *Hymne de Delphes*.[18] The truthfulness of the realisation is ideal, symbolic, and spontaneous. That is why Saint-Saëns was able to bring it to life with the natural resources of art. Turbulent polyphony conveys the demoniacal grimness of the incantations of 'Ô terrible nuit, pleine de fantômes'; the *Hymne à Éros* enjoys the full splendour of tonal harmony. The *Épithalame* is beautifully graceful, with a melody as alive as a fine human body, supple and strong, with sudden movements, offering its bareness as the pure essence of its being.

Baumann went on to publish a full enthusiastic study of Saint-Saëns's music in 1905,[19] before devoting himself to the cause of the Catholic revival and to writing novels.

If Saint-Saëns did not include more unison singing and monodic lines in the score of *Déjanire*, following the example of *Antigone* – for there is much in this version of *Déjanire* that could be found in a modern opera designed for a house of modest size – he was all the while thinking, no doubt, that an alternative version of the play, in a conventional theatre, would work equally well even without the spectacular sets and ample stage space of the arena. In a reduced form, scored for a normal orchestra, the work was played six times in November 1898 at the Odéon, Paris. The same actors were engaged (who must have been relieved not to have to fill the larger space) and there was still a chorus of good size, with some choreography in Act IV. The conductor was Édouard Colonne. The score was modified in certain details and a chorus added, which Saint-Saëns called 'mystérieux et fantastique'.[20] The regret was uttered that Déjanire did not make her entrance in a chariot.

This indoor version of *Déjanire* had a life of its own for a few years, being revived in Montpellier in 1900 and 1902, in Toulouse in 1901 and in Bordeaux in 1902. At the back of Saint-Saëns's mind there was perhaps the thought that all that declamation could be adapted into a conventional opera by having the principals sing. This idea was to be realised nearly ten years later.

The Odéon performances in November 1898 were overshadowed by the death, a few weeks before, of Louis Gallet, Saint-Saëns's faithful collaborator for twenty-six years as the librettist of *La Princesse jaune*, *Étienne Marcel*, *Proserpine*, *Ascanio* and *Déjanire*. An unbroken correspondence between the two men ranged over the whole

---

[18] The reference is to a Greek melody reconstructed by the antiquarian Théodore Reinach with help from Saint-Saëns and Fauré.
[19] BAUMANN 1905.
[20] Letter of 14 September 1898 to Gallet, RATNER 2012, p. 385. Since neither libretto nor vocal score were published until 1899, it is hard to know what modifications were made for the Odéon performances.

world of music and literature, with a core of solid friendship between them expressed in lengthy correspondence adorned with drawings and jokes. There was barely a composer with whom Gallet had not collaborated, for, despite his full-time job as a hospital administrator, he was immensely productive and active, and was liked and admired by all. He was unusual at the time in working on his own in a genre, the libretto, which had for years normally been the product of at least two writers.

If Saint-Saëns lost a good friend in Gallet, he acquired one in Castelbon de Beauxhostes, with whom he sustained a warm correspondence for the rest of his life. Saint-Saëns remained the chief musical adviser for the Béziers festival, overseeing Fauré's *Prometheus* in 1900 and composing his own *Parysatis* in 1902.

12 | Lola, Les Barbares

Leaving Paris after the November 1898 performances of *Déjanire* at the Odéon, Saint-Saëns headed once again for his winter quarters in the Canary Islands. This was his longest absence ever from France, for he remained there until May 1899 and then went on directly to Brazil, where he gave a series of chamber and orchestral concerts. He was not back until August 1st, when he landed at Bordeaux. The main work he wrote during this period was the String Quartet in E minor, op. 112, completed in April and first performed in Rio de Janeiro in May. Surprisingly for a composer of such classical sympathies, this was Saint-Saëns's first string quartet, composed at the age of sixty-three, to be followed by a second in 1918.

He was also occupied putting together his next book, *Portraits et souvenirs*, which appeared in January 1900. Everything in it except its preface had appeared before, so it was not a new statement of artistic principles; his views had become more and more familiar to his readers, and the essay 'L'Illusion wagnérienne' might be seen as Saint-Saëns's definitive position about Wagner. Most of the book was devoted to affectionate portraits of men he greatly admired: Berlioz, Liszt, Gounod, Rubinstein, Bizet and Gallet. But as the nineteenth century came to an end, he could not help recording his alarm about the fate of the art he treasured, seeing deviation from the true path in composers who pursued advanced harmony for its own sake or who ignored the principles of classical form. He made no secret of his conservative instincts, or of his admiration for Mozart, and he was ever more irritated by critics who laid down the new rules than by composers who broke the old ones:

> Along with Gounod and Ambroise Thomas and all those who are not uncontrollably infatuated with wrong harmony, Victor Massé is now classed as one of the 'pompiers' by the flock of starlings that has taken hold of music criticism in the last few years. One of these gentlemen has compared the fresh and teasing tinkle of bells that opens [Massé's] *Noces de Jeannette* with the solemn tolling of bells in *Parsifal*. You can imagine the sneer.[1]

Saint-Saëns seems to have decided to play this role to the full, prepared to stand up against the abandonment of hallowed principles of musical beauty, even though he recognised the inevitability of artistic change. His intelligence was to some extent at war with his ears, since he truly disliked the sound of parallel chords in Debussy and Satie, yet could not declare such things to be contrary to historical or natural forces. His

---

[1] SAINT-SAËNS 1899, pp. 139–40.

own introduction of 'Greek' melody and prosody had, after all, stepped outside the conventional boundaries of classical and romantic musical language. At least he had no plan to give up composing, and his own music had all the resources he needed without reaching out for idioms and textures he personally disliked.

On returning to France in August 1899, Saint-Saëns went to Dieppe, then Paris, then Toulouse. His first formal engagement was the second Béziers festival, with a revival of the open-air *Déjanire*. Two performances were given on 27 and 29 August with the same cast as the year before. Saint-Saëns had invited Gabriel Fauré to conduct since he, Fauré, had on Saint-Saëns's recommendation been commissioned to write a new work for the 1900 festival. For the present season Saint-Saëns had to dissuade Castelbon de Beauxhostes from adding a short piece as a warm-up. If there was a short play for the actors' understudies to put on, that was allowable, but nothing that needed music. 'Remember that putting on *Déjanire* in the arena was almost impossible; don't go any further!' he told him.[2]

Whatever was done previously to present the apotheosis of Hercules at the end, rising triumphant from the flames in which he has just perished, Saint-Saëns and Castelbon put some thought into how to improve it. Saint-Saëns suggested a gigantic statue of Hercules, but then reflected that statues of Hercules are always nude, so putting clothes on it would not do. Perhaps a colossal two-dimensional gold image, he thought, rising from behind the fixed set and lit by electric light. 'He could then fly away in a hydrogen balloon,' he went on, 'but I don't recommend that.' Whether or not any vast image of Hercules was actually made, Saint-Saëns enjoyed the performances and was in good spirits, but at the same time he was privately depressed by the absence of Louis Gallet. 'It was for him I wrote the music of *Déjanire*,' he wrote, 'and without him it all leaves me cold.'[3]

His next concern was the Paris premiere of *Javotte* at the Opéra-Comique and a revival of *Proserpine* at the same theatre a few weeks later. His failure to dissuade the director Albert Carré from casting Jean in *Javotte* as a female dancer has been mentioned in the previous chapter, but it was a battle he knew he could win in the provinces, if not in Paris. He even admitted that it was not a work that he was prepared to get too worked up about and that he was particularly happy for his young collaborator, Jean-Louis Croze, who wrote the scenario, to see his work staged in Paris.

He had to bear in mind, too, that it was going to be harder to get a revival of *Proserpine* right.[4] The revised version of the opera had been played in Toulouse in 1894 and this was adopted in Paris also. It was successful enough to get seventeen performances between November 1899 and May 1900, and at one point Saint-Saëns even

---

[2] Letter to Castelbon de Beauxhostes, 16 April 1899, RATNER 2012, p. 386.
[3] Letter to Auguste Durand, 20 August 1899, RATNER 2012, p. 386,
[4] See Chapter 7, pp. 182–85.

imagined that, in addition to *Javotte* and *Proserpine*, the theatre could revive the two works which had originated there, *La Princesse jaune* and *Phryné*. *Samson et Dalila* was in repertoire at the Opéra and *Henry VIII* had recently been seen at Covent Garden, so that if he had accepted a proposal from Gailhard, director of the Opéra, to revive *Ascanio* at this time, this would all have added up to a Saint-Saëns festival and put him at the head of French opera composers. But he rejected Gailhard's offer, for reasons unknown. Bonnerot simply and enigmatically said it was 'un mauvais moment'. Massenet's standing was not to be dislodged, especially after the recent premiere of *Cendrillon* at the Opéra-Comique.

Once again he headed to the Canaries for the winter with the promise to write a piece for Colonne and another for the Paris Exhibition to be held in the summer of the new year 1900. Colonne's piece was called *La Nuit*, a mild, beautiful piece for soprano, female chorus and orchestra, and the Exhibition cantata was a more ambitious choral work, *Le Feu céleste*, on a poem by Armand Silvestre, celebrating the miracle of electricity. It requires a 'récitant' declaiming in gaps between the music, a soprano solo and a chorus, and it lapses inevitably into banality, not so much when the exciting luminosity of electricity is evoked by massed harps, organ and brass, but when nature is seen to be mastered by the ingenuity of man, and in the orchestral passages that intervene at undue length.

Saint-Saëns returned to Paris in May for the first performance of this piece and to discuss a new project which belied any promises he had been making in the previous eight years not to write any more operas. Perhaps the profusion of revivals of his existing operas encouraged him to write another. At all events he was prepared to listen to a plan which came from the successful playwright Victorien Sardou. Having already written over sixty plays, including some opera librettos, Sardou was recognised as the doyen of his profession, although few would class him among the great playwrights of the nineteenth century. In this respect he follows in the footsteps of the even more prolific Eugène Scribe, whose deft plotting and formulaic approach he admired and imitated. Today he is best known for Puccini's *Tosca*, based on a play written for Sarah Bernhardt in 1887. He had supplied librettos for Offenbach, Paladilhe, Bizet and a number of other composers, although he preferred, since librettos normally had to be in verse, to leave the versification to a collaborator.

With Pierre-Barthélemy Gheusi, Gallet's successor as editor of the *Nouvelle Revue*, as his chosen partner, he proposed an opera to be set in the Roman period and more particularly to be set in the Roman city of Orange, where the spectacular remains of a Roman theatre and amphitheatre are still to be marvelled at. The theatre had for some years been mounting plays and operas, and its present director, Paul Mariéton, favoured works either of ancient origin or on subjects from antiquity. He had the support of Paris politicians anxious to decentralise French culture, many of whom were ready to claim that Orange rather than Béziers should be promoted as the French rival to Bayreuth. Sophocles's *Antigone*, with Saint-Saëns's music, was performed there in 1894, and his *Hymne à Pallas-Athéné* for soprano and orchestra, premiered there in 1894, was repeated in August 1899. The appeal of outdoor theatricals in this period was enhanced by the survival of many theatres and arenas from ancient times, by the modern taste for large-scale performances involving chorus singers and orchestral players to be numbered in hundreds, and by the Mediterranean climate. With Gluck's *Iphigénie en Tauride* scheduled for 1900, the Sardou–Saint-Saëns opera would be intended for August 1901.

Their proposal reached Saint-Saëns in Las Palmas in March 1900. He had earlier discussed the possibility of performing in the Roman theatre in Orange with Gallet and they had come to the conclusion that nothing would work unless the immense stone stage set (essentially a tall back wall with wings) could be modified and that that would cost too much. In any case the acoustics were poor if there was any suspicion of wind. Even though the commission had the backing of the Ministry of the Interior and the Opéra, he declined, explaining at length why he found the proposal unworkable. To Durand he reported that there was another reason, 'which I will whisper in your ear'. Perhaps his earlier renunciations of opera still held; perhaps he feared that either Sardou or Gheusi (or both) would be uncongenial to work with.

In any event his carefully argued refusal was soon overcome by concessions from all parties. The money required to adapt the theatre to his needs and to engage the best singers and orchestra from Paris would be made available, and the Opéra promised to stage the work after the Orange performances. The three collaborators worked together in Paris in the summer months and the opera took shape. It told a story of love, war and betrayal in the classic grand opera tradition, although the historical background was still not settled in September 1900, when Saint-Saëns reported that it concerned the conflict between the Romans and barbarians identified as Goths, Visigoths and Ostrogoths, which places it no earlier than the fifth century CE. The eventual opera was set at a historical moment, 105 BCE, when the Romans controlled the southern part of Gaul, present-day Provence. The Battle of Arausio (present-day Orange) in that year was a resounding defeat for the Roman army at the hands of two tribes, the Cimbri and the Teutons. The opera was to be called *Les Barbares*.

* * * * *

At the Béziers festival in 1900 the main work was by Gabriel Fauré, entitled *Prométhée*. Without Gallet to supply a drama, the text, which required declamation and singing as before, was by André-Ferdinand Hérold, grandson of the composer of *Zampa*, and the aesthete playwright Jean Lorrain. Marcel Jambon was again engaged as designer, and his set this year was an immense mountain landscape that towered above the stage area and the spaces filled with musicians. The play recounts Prometheus's theft of fire from the gods, his punishment chained to a rock, and finally his rescue by Hercules. Saint-

Saëns is always acknowledged as Fauré's guide and mentor in this enterprise, but not always as the composer of a *Prologue* that was performed at the beginning of the show.[5] A vocal score of *Prométhée* was published by Hamelle, but it did not include Saint-Saëns's contribution, which is a fully scored background to the declamation of a poem by Sylva Sicard, deputy mayor of Béziers, a practising doctor and a poet. His verses rather charmingly evoke Gallet, mentioning some of his librettos: *Le Rêve* (Bruneau), *Thaïs* and *Le Mage* (Massenet), and *Étienne Marcel* and *Ascanio* by Saint-Saëns himself. Since Saint-Saëns conducted the *Prologue* himself, it was clearly not meant to be part of *Prométhée* in any sense, but a tribute to the festival and an assertion of its permanence. Fauré's music and the spectacle were both very well received. In Castelbon de Beauxhostes's mind at least, if not in Saint-Saëns's, the plan for what eventually became *Parysatis*, the 1901 production at Béziers, was born.

After the two performances of *Prométhée*, the first of which had to be postponed for twenty-four hours because of a torrential storm, Saint-Saëns went to Spain. One of his reasons was to prepare himself for composing a little musical drama in the Spanish style. 'I had just got back from Spain,' he later wrote, 'and was totally obsessed with that Andalusian music, which I imitated as best I could. What came out of it was not banal.'[6]

Lola

(Ratner 329)

Scène dramatique in verse

Libretto by Stéphane Bordèse

First performance: Salon du *Figaro*, Paris, 21 January 1901

Lola, jeune bohémienne Gitana	soprano
Don Bénites, jeune seigneur	comédien

Accompanied by piano, or:

Orchestra: 2 flutes, 2 oboes, 2 clarinets, 2 bassoons, 4 horns, 2 trumpets, 3 trombones, timpani, cymbals, tambourine, castanets, harp, strings.

What came out of it was *Lola*, a 'dramatic scene in verse for two characters' composed in late September 1900 with verse by the poet Stéphan Bordèse (1847–1919), who worked for Saint-Saëns's publisher Durand and was a favourite provider of lyrics for salon songs. Saint-Saëns had set one himself, *Présage de la croix*, in 1891. The two characters are Lola, a Spanish gypsy who has to speak, sing and dance, and Don

---

[5] RATNER 2012, p. 507. The manuscript of the *Prologue* is at F-Pn MS 771.
[6] Letter to Marguerite Herleroy, 14 January 1916, RATNER 2012, p. 462.

Bénites, a young Spanish nobleman who only has to speak, and the accompaniment was a piano. It adds up to a miniature opéra-comique with an overture and four numbers interspersed with extensive dialogue in alexandrines.

Dialogue After a short overture which gives a foretaste of the 'Conclusion' and a snatch of the first of three numbers, the gypsy Lola is found lying exhausted after escaping from an oppressive master who has ill-treated her for three years.

Le Songe She has had a dream in which she was wandering in a field of flowers ('Le Songe'); the flowers told her that a white-winged angel would lead her to happiness. She woke from her dream lying in a field of poppies, the colour of blood. The accompaniment of her first song consists of a single Spanish formula, ex. 12.1:

Example 12.1 *Lola*, 'Le Songe'

This is repeated constantly over a series of shifting tonics and beneath a melodic line of great character. A middle section moves to the major without deviating from the essential rhythm of ex. 12.1.

Dialogue She is continuing to muse about white angels and red poppies when footsteps alarm her. Could it be her tormentor in pursuit? It is instead Don Bénites whom, as a nobleman, she treats with respect, explaining that she is in search of her freedom. He offers her a roof for the night, since he is the lord there, and when she insists on leaving he forces her to stay. He will let her go only if she will first sing one of her gypsy songs to him.

Le Rossignol So the second number is 'Le Rossignol', a set-piece song again in Spanish style. Wielding castanets, she sings the tale of a nightingale that having sung all night is captured and caged by a child. Alas the nightingale sings no more. Then one bright morning the child releases the nightingale and thereafter the bird sings at the child's window every morning at dawn. Every nuance of this little drama is caught by the music, a perfect showpiece for a versatile soprano.

Dialogue Lola has won her liberty by singing, so now she wants to leave. But Don Bénites has fallen in love with her and does not want to let her go. If she would now dance, he will always have a memory of her.

Tango So she dances, and her dance is a tango, not the South American type familiar today, but the Andalusian tango, whose accompaniment we would label a Habanera.

The music conforms to all the clichés of the genre, and keeps its haunting pulse going for 147 bars.

Dialogue Lola's dancing, like her singing, so bewitches Don Bénites that he reaches for her hand and asks for a kiss. It develops into a struggle. This is not the kind of freedom he had promised, so she draws a stiletto and lunges at his heart. He parries the blow with his arm. Remembering the red poppies of her dream she runs off, leaving him to mop the blood with his handkerchief and console himself with the line 'On se blesse parfois en touchant à la rose'. Some strong Spanish phrases supply the musical 'Conclusion'.

Lola is a charming work, whose neglect is readily explained by the lack of sung music for Don Bénites and by the soprano's obligation also to speak and dance. As usual with Saint-Saëns, each number is polished to a perfect shine, and the Spanish tone is maintained throughout, circling around E minor and E major. The feisty, independent Lola has inevitably been compared to Carmen, although her Don is an aristocrat, not a sergeant.

Lola was performed in the salon of *Le Figaro* in January 1901 with Marguerite van Gelder, a student at the Conservatoire, as Lola, and Henri-Louis Ravet of the Comédie-Française as Don Bénites. *Le Figaro* commended Saint-Saëns's permanently youthful touch and his inspiration 'both powerful and delicate, both tender and cheerful'. It being January, Saint-Saëns himself was not there, but he heard reports from Durand, who suggested orchestrating it. Reluctant to do this himself, being deep into the composition of *Les Barbares*, Saint-Saëns suggested Henri Rabaud, who declined. So did Fauré, who then recommended Charles Koechlin, who had recently scored Fauré's *Pelléas et Mélisande* and who was given the job. It was performed twice more, now with orchestra and the same principals, on 7 March 1901 by the Concerts Colonne and on 14 May 1901 at the Théâtre de la Renaissance conducted by Oscar de Lagoanère.

* * * * *

Saint-Saëns moved out of the city to St-Germain-en-Laye in September 1900 to work on *Les Barbares*, although the libretto was not yet ready and Sardou was kept busy by other work. At least he had the first act to work on. He did not receive a complete draft until the end of October. Towards the end of the year he moved south, first to Montpellier, where *Déjanire* was being revived, then to Lyon, then, at the end of December, to Annaba, on the north-east tip of Algeria, then known as Bône, where the first draft of the opera was completed at the beginning of February 1901. 'I was too well known in Algiers to be left in peace there, so I chose Bône where I knew no one. I took an apartment facing the sea, furnished it in oriental style, and resumed work corresponding with Sardou every day by telegraph or by post.'[7] A draft of the whole opera was ready by the beginning of February, and this was sent back to Durand who was having Georges Marty prepare the vocal score for printing.

---

[7] Document at F-Po, RATNER 2012, p. 265.

The authorities in Orange were simultaneously admitting that there was too little money for the adaptation of the theatre and (by implication) for the engagement of personnel from the Opéra in Paris. Almost everyone was relieved to abandon the idea of staging the opera in the Roman theatre, so a premiere at the Opéra in the autumn was agreed. This gave the authors more flexibility with the option of more than one background set and of more stage exits than the two sides, and it gave Saint-Saëns more time to devote to the orchestration and relieved his mind about the acoustics. In addition there was no longer the constraint of finishing before 10.30 p.m. to allow the audience to catch the last train back to Avignon. Since full-length operas in Paris would normally finish around midnight, Saint-Saëns even suggested to Sardou that a short item precede the opera, so that those who dined at eight would not have to miss any part of it.

The three-sided collaboration between Sardou, Gheusi and the composer was uneven since Saint-Saëns found Sardou extremely congenial, if dilatory, to work with but Gheusi abominable. 'I gained the incomparable benefit of getting to know Sardou extremely well, and of drinking at that unceasing spring of wit, erudition and good humour which cannot be described and whose abundance recalled those sacred streams blessed by nature.'[8] In fact Sardou found Saint-Saëns a difficult partner. When the composer reported that he had made some cuts in the main duet in Act II, Gheusi complained to Sardou, who wrote: 'I'll write to calm him down. I don't know what he means with this duo. I don't know a note of it but I'm sure he has cut everything of interest in it. It's not a collaboration, it's a battle!'[9]

Gheusi as versifier fell far short of what Saint-Saëns expected, always ready to compare him to Gallet in his mind. He had to rewrite many of his lines himself. He wrote to Durand in February 1901: 'I have finally received the Prologue. Like everything Gheusi has done it's execrable and I'll be forced to rewrite it. I could do without this. The fellow is really no good for anything except to be lackey to Sir Pedro de la Gailhardière and to cause embarrassment.'[10]

Saint-Saëns returned to Paris in April 1901, since he had duties to perform at the Académie des Beaux-Arts and concerts to give in Brussels and London. He completed the orchestration of *Les Barbares* on June 15th, while the vocal score and choral scores were issued by Durand in May to enable rehearsals to begin at the Opéra. He had agreed with Castelbon de Beauxhostes to compose a ballet for the 1901 Béziers festival to accompany a revival of Fauré's *Prométhée*, but his preoccupation with *Les Barbares* and a severe cold in May forced him to pass the job to the young composer Max d'Ollone, who had won the Prix de Rome in 1897. D'Ollone's ballet *Bacchus mystifié* opened the festival, which Saint-Saëns attended once again.

---

[8] Ibid.   [9] Marie-Gabrielle Soret, 'Luttes d'influence', BARBARES 2014, p. 34.
[10] RATNER 2012, p. 260.

Les Barbares opened at the Opéra on 23 October 1901 and was well received, proof that Saint-Saëns was now so well established as a composer of opera that his new works were treated with respect in the press. The press displayed the usual variety of trivial complaints and the usual incompetence in judging the music, while many critics were honest admirers of the composer's work without venturing into much detail.[11] There was barely any comment on the anti-German slant of the story. The opera provoked neither gales of applause nor open hostility. None of the singers were world-class, but Saint-Saëns was content with them for the most part, and with the conductor, Paul Taffanel. He was very impressed by Jeanne Hatto (Floria) and Albert Vaguet (Marcomir) in their big duet in Act II, although a pair of different singers seven years later in Barcelona made him realise that his original singers never achieved the warmth that is in the music. Marcel Jambon was once again responsible for the dramatic sets depicting Roman Orange. There were twenty-eight performances between October 1901 and December 1902.

* * * * *

Les Barbares
(Ratner 294)

Tragédie-lyrique in three acts and a prologue

Libretto by Victorien Sardou and P.-B. Gheusi

First performance: Opéra, Paris, 23 October 1901

Marcomir	ténor
Scaurus	basse
Le Récitant	basse
Le Veilleur	ténor
Hildibrath	baryton
Floria	soprano
Livie	contralto

Germains, légionnaires, Romains, habitants d'Orange,
Vestales, femmes et enfants Gallo-Romains

The action takes place in Orange, one century BCE at the time of the Teutonic invasions.

Orchestra: 3 flutes (incl.piccolo), 2 oboes, cor anglais, 2 clarinets, bass clarinet, 2 bassoons, contrabassoon, 4 horns, 4 trumpets, 3 trombones, tuba, timpani, bass drum, cymbals, triangle, castanets, 2 harps, strings.

Offstage: 2 trumpets, 4 trombones, 2 soprano saxhorns, 2 alto saxhorns, timpani, bass drum, cymbals.

---

[11] The notices of *Les Barbares* are collected in DOUCHE 2005 and summarised by Sylvie Douche as 'La réception des *Barbares* dans la presse parisienne', in BARBARES 2014, pp. 42–46.

Saint-Saëns called *Les Barbares* a 'tragédie lyrique' but without any serious intention of emulating Lully or Gluck. It has an extended Prologue and a full set of ballets in the last act, but it complies rather with traditional grand opera in its historical setting, its tribal conflict (Romans versus Germanic tribes), its scenes of grandeur, bloodshed and religious ceremony, and a love story across battle lines. Marcomir, the barbarian warrior, falls in love with Floria, the Vestal Virgin, who breaks her vow of chastity in order to save the lives of her people, only to see her lover Marcomir killed by her sister Livie,[12] whose husband he had killed in battle. Sardou was celebrated for his broad strokes and powerful situations in dramatic plotting, but here the essential relationships are simple and there are no subsidiary elements in the plot. Both Floria and Marcomir undergo profound changes of heart in the course of the action, while Livie is driven throughout by her desire for revenge.

The action was moved from the late Roman Empire to 105 BCE in order to locate it in the city of Orange, where a famous battle was fought in that year. The names Marcomir and Hildibrath belong to the later period, but all the characters (except possibly the consul Scaurus) are entirely fictional. It was also pointed out at an early stage that the theatre in Orange had not been built at the earlier date and that the action is centred on the temple of Vesta, not the theatre. It was undoubtedly Saint-Saëns's intention that the 2000-year-old conflict represented in the opera should be seen as relevant to the present day, when the cultural conflict between France and Germany, which had been gathering steam since 1870, could be interpreted as a battle between civilisation and barbarism. Today we find such blatant cultural stereotyping offensive, which effectively banishes *Les Barbares* from the modern stage, but our political sensitivity would have been considered pusillanimous by France's right-wing activists at that time, when the difference between the races was a proper subject for wide quasi-scientific speculation. The Dreyfus case had sharpened French hostility to Germany, and the clamour for revenge for the humiliation of 1871 and the loss of Alsace and Lorraine was daily getting louder. Saint-Saëns had himself become more and more outspoken against the invasion of 'nordic' and 'Germanic' culture, to which French culture, with its roots in Greek and Roman antiquity, offered a defiant alternative. He was always careful not to condemn German music itself, not even Wagner, because he admired it profoundly; his target was instead those critics and composers who imitated, or who applauded the imitation of, modern German music and turned their backs on what he considered the true path of French music. There was a physical dimension to this, since he associated the north with cold and cold with all the ailments he had suffered since childhood; the Mediterranean offered him better health and a sense of a civilisation going back many centuries. After the row over *Harmonie et Mélodie* in 1886,[13]

---

[12] Livie is not identified in any of the cast lists as Floria's sister, but Floria addresses her once at the beginning of Act II as 'noble sœur'.
[13] See Chapter 7, p. 165.

it is remarkable that he went back to Germany at all, but even as late as 1913 he was in Berlin, attempting to bridge a tragically widening abyss.

Apart from the opera's title, it might be considered provocative that in the 'Argument' printed at the front of the libretto and of the vocal score and in the libretto itself the Romans' adversaries are are identified as 'barbares' and 'hordes germaniques', not Cimbri or Teutons, the actual names of those tribes.

Prologue Knowing that the opera itself with only three acts was relatively short, Saint-Saëns wrote a long Prologue in order to set the tone of the opera and introduce some of its themes. He also has a Récitant (bass) appear in the course of the movement to set the scene. If the opera had been performed in the Roman theatre in Orange, as originally intended, the Récitant would have simply stepped forward to sing, but in the indoor theatre he enters through the curtain, and we do not see the first set until the Prologue is over.

The Prologue is in five sections. Unrelentingly dark in the opening section, with the bass clarinet prominent, the music succeeds in conveying the permanent state of danger and alarm that the citizens of Orange would have experienced in those warlike years. A prominent trumpet call heightens the tension, which finally recedes for the entry of the Récitant. Saint-Saëns must have had Berlioz's *L'Enfance du Christ* in mind for this convenient device of taking us directly to the time and place of the action. Three hundred thousand 'Germains' have been pressing south, driving the Gauls into the forests. To much calmer music, including ex. 12.7B and D, his 'Venus' themes, he then reveals the essentials of the plot: a young Vestal Virgin gives herself to the enemy in order to save the town: Cypris ('Vénus' would have been more helpful) outbids Vesta, who then takes revenge 'in the conqueror's blood', as ex. 12.15 is heard for the first time.

The third section is a melodious Andantino, based on the duet for Floria and Livie in Scene 1 of Act II (ex. 12.7) with a solo violin to take the melody. Fanfares proclaiming the conqueror Marcomir (ex. 12.6) open the fourth section, followed by a fast and furious Allegro to represent battle. In this part of the Prologue a number of themes are prominent that are not heard again in the opera, ex. 12.2:

Example 12.2 *Les Barbares*, Prologue

The imitative choral passage from Act III (ex. 12.12) and the last part of the love duet from Act II are also heard. With little change of tempo a trumpet supported by brass brings back ex. 12.16, the theme of Livie's vengeance for the death of her husband Euryale. After some dark echoes of *Parsifal*, the fifth and final section recapitulates the fourth section and drives forward to a close. The Prologue obviously serves as the opera's overture and could perhaps be played as a concert item by omitting the Récitant's entry. Of Saint-Saëns's previous operas only *Le Timbre d'argent* and *La Princesse jaune* had overtures as opposed to preludes, so *Les Barbares* can be added to that number, with perhaps *Frédégonde*, as viable movements on their own.

ACT I

Scene 1 The set is the Roman Theatre in Orange with its heavy stone back wall. It has been adapted to represent the temple of Vesta with its sacred flame burning on the altar. Floria (soprano), High Priestess of Vesta, is seen surrounded by the Vestal Virgins and various women and children. They watch the flame anxiously in fear that it should go out.

Highly unsettled music continues throughout the first scene, in which the women pray for deliverance from the barbarian yoke and warlike men's voices are heard in the distance. Example 12.3 is a prominent figure:

Example 12.3 *Les Barbares*, Act I, Scene 1

Only Floria is calm, and she attempts to reassure the crowd. A watchman (tenor), the equivalent of the Messenger in Greek tragedy, reports from the ramparts with news that one of the consuls, Euryale, has been driven back to the walls. Livie (mezzo-soprano), Euryale's wife, is confident that the enemy will be driven back.

Floria leads the Vestals in a prayer, calmly certain that Vesta will protect them while her flame burns. The battle still rages beyond the walls, reported by the watchman, who can see the two consuls, Scaurus and Euryale, the latter recognisable in his purple coat. The sacred flame suddenly flickers; the purple coat is down! As the offstage band adds to the clamour, Livie would rush out to aid her husband if Floria and the Vestals did not bar her way.

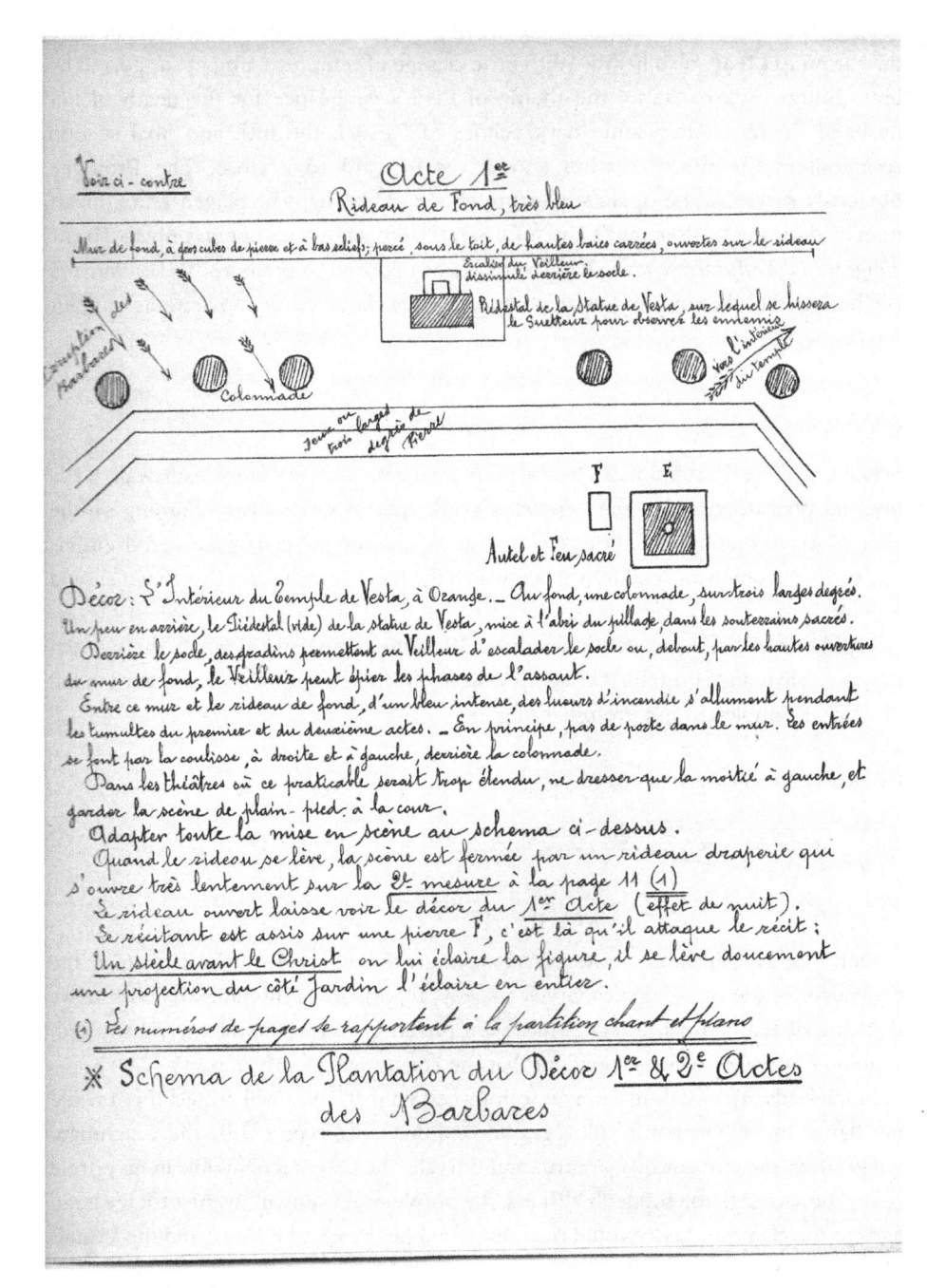

Figure 12.1 *Les Barbares*, mise-en-scène, Act I
Hugh Macdonald Collection, Norwich

Scene 2 Scaurus (bass) appears with a group of soldiers bearing Euryale's body and urges everyone to flee to the woods, since the enemy cannot be stopped. Euryale is recalled throughout the opera with the brief figure ex. 12.4:

Example 12.4 *Les Barbares*, Act I, Scene 2

Desperate for vengenace, Livie wants to know who killed Euryale, and the fury subsides briefly while she pays solemn tribute to him. Floria still begs the women to stay (ex. 12.3), confident that Vesta will protect them, but it is too late, since the watchman reports that Scaurus has fled and that the barbarian hordes are entering the city. The hordes have a motif, ex. 12.5:

Example 12.5 *Les Barbares*, Act I, Scene 2

Scene 3 The orchestra is in full throat as the barbarians pour in, led by Hildibrath (baritone) breathing fire and slaughter and invoking Thor and Odin. A trumpet call (ex. 12.6) announces the arrival of the Teuton chief Marcomir (tenor), with drawn sword and a commanding presence.

Example 12.6 *Les Barbares*, Act I, Scene 3

He issues the brutal command to his men either to sell the women into slavery or kill them. 'Death!' is the unanimous reponse. As the music suddenly opens grandly into C major, Floria waves to the Vestal flame, which shoots up. Hildibrath attributes this to the god Thor, and a second spurt makes Marcomir take note. 'Who are you?' he asks Floria, impressed. 'My name is Floria. I am priestess of Vesta, goddess of the flame!' Over ex. 12.6 in the bass, Marcomir pays homage to her beauty, stepping towards her. For a third time the flame spurts up, while she affirms her dedication to the goddess.

Hildibrath and the men are impatient to condemn this impudent woman, but Marcomir turns on them in fury and orders them to go and collect booty. The temple is off limits. He will decide the women's fate later. He cannot take his eyes off Floria, and she too cannot look away. Example 12.6 closes the act in a mood of peace and benevolence.

ACT II

Prélude Act II begins with a reminder of the ferocious music that brought the barbarians on stage in the previous act (ex. 12.5) and, as before, this gives place to Marcomir's theme (ex. 12.6) on offstage trumpets, echoed by horns in the orchestra.

Scene 1 The curtain rises on the same location as before, but now seen from the side, so that part of the amphitheatre seating is seen at the back. The only light comes from a fading moon (libretto) or a blood-red sunset (score). Women and children are asleep here and there.

Livie is awake, plaintively sorrowing over the loss of so many soldiers and heroes. The light scoring with divided strings is beautifully expressive here, with a shifting time-signature that recalls Queen Catherine's lament at the end of *Henry VIII*. With a reminder of ex. 12.4, she cries out to Euryale to return to their aid. She gets rapidly more agitated, waking Floria with her vengeful outburst. Floria suggests she should be calm and offer thanks to Vesta, to which Livie shrewdly replies that it was Venus, not Vesta, that softened Marcomir's heart when he set eyes on her, all sung over a steady scale on violins and harp that ascends through three octaves and down again.

There follows a duet in E major 12/8 for the two women, which opens with a long, beautifully shaped cantilena for Livie, ex. 12.7, parts of which, marked A to D, recur as motifs throughout the opera, usually in reference to Venus and the power of love:

Example 12.7 *Les Barbares*, Act II, Scene 1

The scoring of section B is particularly expressive. Livie reminds her sister that Venus has extraordinary powers, but Floria insists that it is Vesta she serves, otherwise the flame on the altar would go out. Livie then repeats her music verbatim, with Floria occasionally adding an upper voice. Here is an opportunity missed, for the duet could have developed musically into something much more penetrating, with equal shares for both sisters. As it stands, Livie pays no attention to Floria but simply repeats what she sang before, lovely though that is.

Scene 2 Creeping through the shadows Scaurus comes in with a breathless plan to lead them all to safety and rejoin the Roman army. Floria firmly resists, and so does Livie, and the women all accept Floria's decision to stay. Behind Livie's refusal are two sinister chords played by four low trumpets, ex. 12.8, which we shall hear again:

Example 12.8 *Les Barbares*, Act II, Scene 2

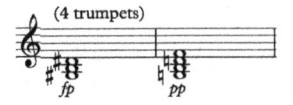

So Scaurus stays too.

The watchman arrives to fetch Livie to attend the funeral pyre of Euryale (ex. 12.4). A new broad theme is heard as she once again swears to avenge his death. He leads her solemnly away, with some of the women.

Scene 3 With the usual tumult (ex. 12.5), Hildibrath and a troop of barbarians barge in looking for Scaurus. Floria claims the sanctuary of the temple for the fugitive, but Scaurus steps forward and gives himself up. Hildibrath is ready to despatch him on the spot, but Floria and the Vestals call out for Marcomir.

Scene 4 Marcomir obediently enters. Scaurus is determined to die 'like a true Roman' and although Marcomir's arrival replaces furiously active music with the tranquillity of ex. 12.7B, Scaurus defies Floria's attempt to save him. Nonetheless Marcomir insists that he be spared, which draws praise of Vesta's powers from the women and sullen suspicion from Scaurus in an all-too-short ensemble. Marcomir orders everyone to leave, calling only Floria back, while a group of woodwind quietly lowers the temperature.

Scene 5 The final scene of the act, like the duet in Act II of *Samson et Dalila*, is crucial, dramatically and musically, and it presents a similarly ambiguous 'love scene' between two people who are sworn enemies subject to forces that happen to bring them together in 'une immense volupté'. In Marcomir's case the force is chemical, the attraction of a vigorous man for a beautiful woman intensified by his power over life and death and her vow of chastity; in Floria's case she is forced to yield by the threat of massacre only to find herself drawn by an attraction to this ruthless man with a vein of tenderness in his harsh soul. Perhaps he does love her, as he insists. She does not love him, but having cast aside her vow, she allows herself to fall under the spell of Venus.

The scene is full of musical ideas, some of them short-lived, others drawn from the motifs we have already heard, always sensitively scored. Saint-Saëns is more mobile in his harmonic shifts than before, rarely remaining longer than a couple of bars without slipping into another key using fluent intermediate chromatics. The procedure is Wagnerian without sounding like Wagner.

Once alone with Floria, as Marcomir wonders how he spared Scaurus's life in order to please Floria, we hear again the three-octave scale representing Venus from the first scene of the act. Again she has to remind him that Vesta is her guardian, not Venus (ex. 12.9):

Example 12.9 *Les Barbares*, Act II, Scene 5

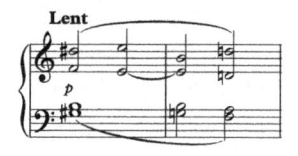

He finds this incomprehensible and explains that the coldness which these austere chords suggest excites his wrath and draws out of him threats to the temple, the altar and the Vestals themselves. His men will soon be drunk and fired up for rape and carnage (ex. 12.5). A new theme on trombones is more menacing, but still unavailing.

Marcomir then resorts to endearments, borrowing the music with which Livie addressed Floria earlier (ex. 12.7). But declarations of love are received only with 'Killer!' and 'Barbarian!' from Floria. What finally tips the scale is the sound of drunken men offstage invoking Odin and Thor and swearing death to the Romans. 'Save them!' she cries in a sudden change of heart. Marcomir immediately gives orders to Hildibrath to hold the men off, and their shouts recede into the distance.

The printed libretto is a good deal more extended here than the printed scores. The offstage invocation of gods in that text also includes appeals to Freia, Erda, Asgard, Donar, Ymer and the three Norns. Did Saint-Saëns see this as encroaching too far into Wagnerian territory? And Floria's volte-face, effected in the music sources with a cry and the single line 'Qu'ai-je dit ? Pardonne-moi . . . j'ai peur . . . sauve-les !' ('What have I said? Forgive me . . . I'm frightened . . . save them !') runs on in the libretto text as follows:

>   FLORIA
>   A curse on my foolish pride!
>   You see me begging and weeping!
>   Pain confuses my senses!
>   Enslaved, I must die by a powerless altar!
>
>   MARCOMIR
>   I understand nothing; I want you and I love you!
>
>   FLORIA, in despair
>   O, if you loved me without blaspheming
>   And if your heart had pity on my feelings,
>   You would want to let me be mistress of myself
>   And get nothing from me but myself.
>   I do not hate you. Be more magnanimous;
>   In our view, alas, force is a crime!

Saint-Saëns wisely chose to manage this moment in the briefest possible way, which imposes on the staging and the acting an obligation to make its crucial importance clear.

Example 12.7B on four cellos beautifully expresses the pain in Floria's heart. She now has the opportunity to explore the conflicting feelings of guilt and gratitude within her. She is nervous of succumbing to Venus; she is frightened of his gaze, his voice, even his silence. His ardour increases, with a lover's traditional promises of bliss, and the next stage of her downfall – yielding to the lure of love – is carried on a phrase repeated a semitone lower in each bar, and her voice reaches all the way down to low B as she falls into Marcomir's arms. A sombre chord on harp, bass drum and low woodwind signals the extinction of the Vestal flame.

Having abandoned Vesta, she is now in the power of Venus. With further reminders of Livie's music from the start of the act, Marcomir urges her to give herself up to the ecstasy of love, and the remaining moments of the act finally offer a compact love duet, which includes ex. 12.10, gentle, understated and laden with sensuousness:

Example 12.10 *Les Barbares*, Act II, Scene 5

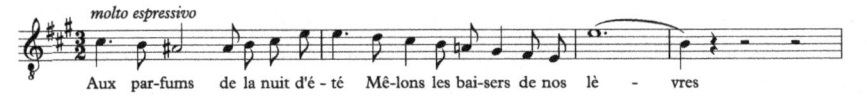

Aux par-fums de la nuit d'é-té Mê-lons les bai-sers de nos lè - vres

ACT III

Prélude An interlude that represented Floria in Marcomir's arms would never be to Saint-Saëns's taste, nor does he depict war and devastation. Instead he wrote a simple Prelude of a positive, open-air character, perfectly formed of course, and delightful, and probably intended to convey the joyous mood of the citizens of Orange.

Scene 1 The setting is a square close to the city wall with a half-dismantled gate showing open country and a river beyond. The Temple of Vesta is at the side. Watched by the delighted inhabitants, the barbarians, under the command of Hildibrath on horseback, are loading booty on to waggons in preparation for departure.

This provides an opportunity for a choral scene that the opera has until now noticeably lacked. Example 12.11 offers an ideal background for conversational choral exchanges, with individual citizens sharing thoughts on their deliverance:

Example 12.11 *Les Barbares*, Act III, Scene 1

The watchman reminds them to make due ritual sacrifices to their gods. Some of the women bewail their loss of money and jewellery, which prompts Scaurus to point out that thanks to the gods no women were raped and no men sent into slavery. From the ramparts the watchman reports that the enemy army has disappeared over the horizon in a cloud of dust. The chorus even indulge in some imitative polyphony, because they can (ex. 12.12):

Example 12.12 *Les Barbares*, Act III, Scene 1

Di - v - ni - tés li-bé-ra-tri - ce

A celebration is called for. The watchman and Scaurus lead the people in a hymn to Apollo, the sun-god whose rising has seen the enemy's departure. Its Handelian character is appropriate, and it prepares us for the *divertissement*.

Entrée A group of young people playing flutes appear, standing on one leg. Their piece is strongly ethnic, with a drone bass and an ornamented dance tune above it. Castanets and triangle mark the stamping rhythm. A solemn procession of priests then passes through, to the accompaniment of harps and strings, bearing the instruments and victims of ritual sacrifice to the temple. The Vestal Virgins then sprinkle lustral water on whatever has been fouled by the barbarian presence.

Ballet The first *Air de Ballet* is (except at the end) delicately scored and charmingly tuneful. The second section (in A major, following an E♭ major movement!) has a particularly neat melody, passed every eight bars from one section of the orchestra to another. The third section, in F major, is a playground of shifting phrase-lengths, with a predominance of five-bar phrases constantly alternating with three- and four-bar phrases. It may be this movement that Saint-Saëns referred to in his letter of 7 February 1902 to René Thorel: 'These sketches are rhythmic studies for ballet which on an impulse I constructed using the metres of Latin verse. It amused me a lot, but it remains to be seen if it amuses anyone else.'[14] In its tunefulness and lightness of touch, the whole of this ballet is unmistakably in the tradition of French ballet music, a match for anything by Bizet or Delibes.

No praise can be high enough for the 2ème *Air de Ballet*, so effortlessly melodious, so perfectly shaped and executed that if an orchestra were ever to play this as a three-minute concert encore, any audience would be astonished that they had never heard it before and beg to know who could have composed it. Combining his two subsidiary

---

[14] RATNER 2012, p. 260.

themes at the end is a crowning touch. In this sphere at least, old Saint-Saëns had lost not a grain of his natural inventiveness and musicality.

Invocation et Farandole The Chief Priest emerges from the temple to announce that the omens are good. This triggers a general dance in and out of the streets and colonnades, and the dance is the *farandole*, a traditional provençal dance, here represented by a four-bar bass line, ex. 12.13, repeated twenty-four times before moving to the upper voices for eighteen repetitions (in the manner of Glinka's *Kamarinskaya* and Tchaikovsky's Second Symphony). The last few iterations move through strange keys to reach an animated coda which should fill the stage with colour and movement in a wild dance of joy.

Example 12.13 *Les Barbares*, Act III, *Farandole*

Scene 2 Floria, Livie and the Vestals appear at the entrance to the temple suppported by ex. 12.14, a perfect example of a scene-motif, used here but not elsewhere in the opera:

Example 12.14 *Les Barbares*, Act III, Scene 2

Floria is admired for her beauty and happy smile and addressed as priestess of Vesta. Now she has to confess that she is no longer a priestess, she is Marcomir's wife. The noisy consternation this news provokes is quietened by Scaurus, who explains that she sacrificed her virginity in order to save the city from massacre. Public reaction is now quite different, with the chorus building to a broad homage.

'I do not deserve this', protests Floria. 'For submitting to your conqueror without love?' objects Livie. Floria explains that it was not without love. She bought their lives with her free and grateful love for Marcomir. 'His country is my country, and his gods are my gods', she declares. The crowd murmurs nervously in awe.

Scene 3 Marcomir enters on horseback, according to the score. In fact Sardou insisted on a chariot drawn by two oxen brought in from the suburbs for each performance. All bow low. He has to demand a price for the ransom of the city and has only to take Floria's

Figure 12.2 *Les Barbares*, oxen waiting in the wings at the Opéra
José Pons Collection, Paris

hand to show that she will be his prize and the city will be free. Scaurus and the chorus offer thanks and praise: 'Marcomir, O noble German, you deserve to be a Roman!'

To ex. 12.7 Marcomir invites Floria to choose those whom she would like to accompany her to her new home. Every Vestal wants to be chosen, but Floria insists that they stay in the land of their forefathers so that she can take up her new home alone.

At this point Livie steps forward, and the key moves to C minor. From here to the end of the opera the march-like pulse and dark tonality – C minor at first, later F minor – combine to generate an overwhelming sense of tragedy. As it becomes clear that Livie's desire for vengenace will overturn the happy conclusion that the ballets have celebrated, there is an overarching structure that betrays the hand of a master dramatist. The first two acts had scarcely hinted at the tension that was to seize the musical action at the end.

Euryale's motif (ex. 12.4) tells us what is above all in Livie's mind when she asks Floria if she could go with her to her new life. She has nothing to live for where she is. Example 12.8, sounding more and more like a glimpse of *Rheingold*, represents her desire for vengeance, for which she will have to go to barbarian country. First she has to attend to Euryale's funeral ceremony. The timpani set up a sombre pattern of beats and a magnificent web of counterpoint colours the steady minims of the march. With F minor established, the timpani continue to underscore Euryale's funeral music, as heard in Act I (ex. 12.15), alternating with ex. 12.8:

Example 12.15 *Les Barbares*, Act III, Scene 3

[musical example: Livia — "Ô noble é-poux___ Qu'a tra-hi la for-tu-ne con-trai - re,"]

The march builds to a climax before Marcomir casually asks who is being so honoured.

'Euryale,' Floria replies.

'Euryale, the consul?'

'Yes. Struck down by someone on your side.'

'Don't tell . . . It was I who killed him.'

Livie does not hear this exchange, but she stands there grasping a broken spear taken from her husband's body and her chosen weapon of vengeance. Alarmed, Floria implores Livie not to leave with them, but to stay and care for Euryale's tomb. As tension mounts in the orchestra, Livie more and more suspects Floria's motives, especially when she urges Marcomir to remount his horse. When Livie cries out 'It was him!', Floria is grimly silent. Livie confronts Marcomir and accuses him of striking Euryale in the back. 'You lie!' he replies, 'it was in the heart!'

'In the heart, then!' is Livie's response as she thrusts the spear into Marcomir's chest. A broad restatement of ex. 12.15 brings down the curtain. In the words of the *Argument* at the head of the score, 'Marcomir's death at one stroke avenges both the death of Euryale and Venus's outrage against Vesta.'

* * * * *

Sardou's lack of experience in large-scale opera is evident from the treatment of the chorus, who only participate strongly in the last act. In the first, when the city of Orange is overwhelmed by the invading hordes, only the Vestal Virgins on one side and the yells of the invaders on the other are heard. The citizens themselves take no part. Similarly there is an opportunity for choral reaction in Act II, Scene 4, when Marcomir unexpectedly spares Scaurus's life. The Vestals say only 'Prodige! Vesta se révèle!', when there was no need to hurry on with the action. They are entitled to a little more expression of wonder than that.

The failure to elaborate the duet for Floria and Livie in Scene 1 of Act II must be attributed equally to librettist and composer, who several times expressed concerns that the opera was too short. The last act is the most successful in operatic terms, forcing the inevitability of tragedy in both the action and the music. Both Floria and Marcomir have satisfying leading roles, but Livie is not given an extended solo or any motive more complicated than revenge. Saint-Saëns is elsewhere generous to the mezzo voice, but he and his librettists saw no need to elaborate her role in this opera. He was aware that Scaurus and Hildibrath were minor players and did his best to fill the roles out.

Saint-Saëns's musical invention is as prodigal as ever, and his harmonic adventurousness more pronounced than before. Marcomir and the barbarians have distinct motifs, and Livie's single-minded quest for vengeance is represented in a strong musical theme, but Floria is curiously sparsely painted. A short bland figure represents her in Act I, but it conveys no more than her unsullied record as a Vestal Virgin. Her capacity for amorous involvement is not revealed until the end of Act II and this is the doing of Venus, embodied in the extended melody of ex. 12.7, as if Floria was the victim of the goddess, not responsible for her lapse. More important is Floria's self-sacrifice in order to save the city from destruction, a gesture of nobility that has no equivalent in the music. Breaking her vow saved the city, but it was falling genuinely in love with Marcomir that led to tragedy, since she insisted on leaving the city with him, leaving Livie behind and thus giving away her knowledge of the truth about Euryale's slaying.

Saint-Saëns is at his best when building up the crisis that precipitates the tragedy. He would have been equally proud of his ballet music, for which modern critics have less patience. He was certainly proud of this work, and of its freedom from systematic models. 'The music is moulded on the drama, with complete freedom', he wrote in October 1901.[15] 'It's a magnificent work', was his comment after seeing it in Vichy in 1913.[16]

Performances of *Les Barbares* continued at the Opéra until December 1902. In 1901 Charles Rousselière, who played the part of the watchman, obligingly recorded part of

---

[15] Letter of 26 October 1901, RATNER 2012, p. 263.
[16] Letter of 4 July 1913 to Jacques Durand, RATNER 2012, p. 267.

his scene in Act III. Meanwhile there were performances also in Lyon, in February 1902, and in Algiers in the same month. After his hibernation in Cairo, Saint-Saëns conducted the Prologue in a concert in London on 3 May 1902. It was very successfully staged in December 1908 in Barcelona, where Saint-Saëns was acclaimed by the orchestra as well as by the public, a success marred by the recent deaths of two of his original collaborators, Sardou and Taffanel. *Les Barbares* was also revived in Lyon at that time, and there were three more stagings before the outbreak of war: Vichy in July 1913; Monte Carlo in March 1914; and Dijon also in March 1914. One last revival gave Saint-Saëns extreme pleasure a year before his death: in Bordeaux in November 1920.

Les Barbares has never been played in Belgium, Italy, Germany, England or the United States. But luckier than some, it has been revived recently and recorded. The performance took place at the St-Étienne Festival in February 2014, and the admirable recording of this performance was issued by Palazzetto Bru Zane in their series of recordings of forgotten French operas, in the same year.

13 | *Parysatis, Botriocéphale, Andromaque, Le Roi Apépi, Hélène*

The Comédie-Française marked the centenary of the birth of Victor Hugo with a revival of his 1843 play *Les Burgraves*, opening on 26 February 1902. Saint-Saëns was invited to compose music for this many months in advance, and he had begun to do so by the summer of 1901, when he observed that the considerable publicity already building up never mentioned his name. On June 10th he wrote to Jules Claretie, the director, renouncing 'the honour of writing the musical part of *Les Burgraves*'.[1] What he had already written consists of settings of two songs from the first act of the play, and perhaps these were performed, since the manuscripts ended up in the theatre's archive.

The first is sung offstage by a baritone, with a chorus, at the rise of the curtain; the second is a carefree song about love sung by the young Lupus, Count of Mons. An important revival of this kind with Mounet-Sully in the leading role would have required much more music than this, and it is possible that Saint-Saëns wrote more. Otherwise some other composer (equally uncredited) must have filled the gap.

In any case Saint-Saëns was far away when the play opened, spending the winter of 1901–02 in Egypt. He had an ambitious undertaking in mind, since he had promised Castelbon de Beauxhostes a new work for the 1902 Béziers festival and had been discussing it for some time. This was to be *Parysatis*, the origin of which was a novel by Jane Dieulafoy (1851–1916), published in 1890. With her husband Marcel, Jane Dieulafoy spent several years exploring the Middle East, especially Persia, and her two books of travel notes earned her the Légion d'Honneur. In order to move freely in those countries she dressed as a man and passed herself off as her husband's son. She adopted this as her permanent dress and (like the painter Rosa Bonheur) was granted official *permission de travestissement* in France.

With his interest in the Middle East, Saint-Saëns would have known her travel books and was subsequently so impressed with her novel that he approached her with his plan for a large-scale dramatic work for outdoor performance on the pattern of *Déjanire*. They got on very well. Despite her inexperience in the theatre, she agreed to write the libretto, the bulk of which was done by the summer of 1901. Saint-Saëns was able to tell Castelbon de Beauxhostes that it would be 'splendid, for the staging and the costumes, very dramatic and varied, with a ballet too. We will be able to revive the arrangements

---

[1] Letter of 10 June 1901, RATNER 2012, p. 422.

for *Déjanire*, with the singers and chorus moving around in the main area and the orchestra set to one side.'[2]

Having reached Alexandria on 8 January 1902, he began work, having allowed the text and the subject to ferment in his mind for six months. Saint-Saëns found he had to refashion Dieulafoy's verse a good deal, and he felt a little nervous in attempting to use Persian modes and rhythms. He found himself working slowly, with a good deal of sketching and revision, like Beethoven, he reminded himself, ruing the fluency with which he once wrote orchestral scores (presumably the symphonic poems) without any sketches at all. At least, he said with relief, he did not yet need to use a piano when composing.[3]

By the end of January he had moved to Cairo, where Mohammed Ali Pasha, the Khedive's brother, lent him a villa on Rhoda Island in the centre of the city. He was 'surrounded by the waters of the sacred river Nile, dreaming beneath the gilded ceiling of an immense salon, all decorated in the style of the Alhambra in Granada, with palm trees, fig trees and thousands of roses for neighbours.'[4] He would have gone to Persia if it were not so cold there. He composed the first scene of Act II first, then Act I, without its Prologue, all the time aware that he was taking more trouble with this music than usual, especially over the exotic elements, even if that did not guarantee a better work. The first two acts were finished by February 19th. Composition of the third act was done quickly, since he had to meet the deadline for composing a march commissioned for the coronation of Edward VII, due to take place in London in June. Both were done by the end of March, at which point he wrote the piano reduction of *Parysatis*, normally a straightforward task, but here unusually tricky because of the exotic orchestration and the loss of special colouristic effects.

Once done, the piano reduction was sent to Paris to be printed. Then he purchased a quantity of Arabic finger cymbals to be held and played by the dancers, and set off for Béziers to play the music through to Castelbon de Beauxhostes on the piano. From there he returned to Paris to give a similar performance for the Dieulafoys and to sign up actors and singers for the production. The hot topic of those months was Debussy's *Pelléas et Mélisande*, which opened at the Opéra-Comique on April 30th. Saint-Saëns called it a 'strange' work and was unable to conceal his conviction that it was wrong to transfer the melody in opera from the voice to the orchestra. He also felt that the erosion of functional harmony was bound to weaken formal control, as indeed Debussy himself found in his later

---

[2] Letter of 9 June 1901, RATNER 2012, p. 399.
[3] Letter to Auguste Durand, 20 January 1902, RATNER 2012, p. 400.
[4] BONNEROT 1922, pp. 176–77.

works. Each composer had a rather narrow circle of close friends which overlapped only in Durand's publishing office.

There were two trips abroad to undertake before returning to Béziers, one to Weimar to attend the inauguration of a statue of Liszt, to whom he felt eternal gratitude, the second to London to take part in the last concert of the London Musical Festival, sharing the podium with Henry Wood, and for the coronation. This was postponed when the king developed peritonitis, so Saint-Saëns could not stay, being needed back in Paris to rehearse *Parysatis*. But he did have time to be received at Buckingham Palace by Queen Alexandra in company with the Dutch cellist Joseph Hollmann, who had been asking him to write a cello concerto for him for as much as two years. This time Saint-Saëns saw an opening ahead and gave the cellist something close to a promise.

At the beginning of August he returned to Béziers to bring together, once again, a vast army of actors, singers, scene-painters, dancers and musicians, not to mention chariots, dogs and horses. Charles Eustace was once again charged with the heavy task of orchestrating all the music for military bands. The stage set was again designed by the brilliant Marcel Jambon, who worked from Dieulafoy's archaeological finds in the city of Susa and on mosaics and bas-reliefs from Persepolis in the Louvre. There were some new covered boxes for the audience facing the stage, and two government ministers attended, but otherwise the event lacked the novelty that attended *Déjanire* in 1898. It was still well supported locally and once again managed with unflagging energy by Castelbon de Beauxhostes. Fauré joined Saint-Saëns to provide musical and moral support. Jane Dieulafoy was there of course, dashing about in rehearsals with the actors. 'She is neither man nor woman,' Saint-Saëns wrote, 'she's a flame!'[5]

Parysatis opened on 17 August 1902, with a second performance two days later. Saint-Saëns felt it surpassed anything they had yet done in Béziers. A fair report was sent by Fauré to his wife. After the dress rehearsal: 'From the point of view of drama I find the work more and more banal. But there'll be processions, horses, dogs, hunting horns, and a ballet, in other words a sauce that will make the fish appetising, especially for the public who basically prefer the sauce.' Two days later, after the first performance:

> Saint-Saëns had a great ovation yesterday. The weather, which was dreadful in the morning, brightened up around one o'clock, and was superb at five [when the show started]. As the performance went on the sky became even more beautiful. The work was a great success. But clearly it has its detractors and it doesn't satisfy everyone. Someone said to me that *Prométhée* made an Olympian impression, but *Parysatis* was just Olympic.[6]

* * * * *

[5] Letter to Jacques Durand, no date, RATNER 2012, p. 403.
[6] FAURÉ 1951, pp. 67–68; RATNER 2012, p. 403.

Parysatis
(Ratner 312)

Drama in a prologue and three acts

Libretto by Jane Dieulafoy

First performance: Les Arènes, Béziers, 17 August 1902

Spoken roles:
    Parysatis, queen of Persia, mother of Artaxerxès
    Aspasie, a young Greek woman
    Phédyme, Parysatis's nurse
    Atossa, maid of honour
    Andria, maid of honour
    Artaxerxès, king of Persia
    Darius, son of Artaxerxès
    Orontès, a sorcerer
    Keeper of the royal seal
    A Greek captive

Sung roles:
Choryphée	soprano
Choryphée	ténor
Choryphée	baryton

Chœurs

60 Danseuses

The action takes place in Susa between 401 BCE and 394 BCE.

Orchestra:
    2 military bands
    string orchestra
    20 harps
    25 trumpets
    17 hunting horns

piccolo, 2 flutes, 2 oboes, cor anglais, 2 clarinets, bass clarinet, 3 bassoons, contrabassoon, 4 horns, 4 trumpets, 3 trombones, tuba, timpani, cymbals, bass drum, side drum, triangle, tambourine, tamtam, 4 harps, strings.

Of her part in the proceedings Jane Dieulafoy wrote:

I felt that history has the same rights as heroic and divine legend and that the drama would lose nothing by being represented as human. Justly proud of their surprising defeat of the Persians, the Greeks called on all the arts to celebrate: artists, musicians and poets went to work, but they saw everything from the European point of view. It was interesting to see it from the Asian side. My decision was to select the period between the battle of Cunaxa and the battle in which the Persians took revenge for Salamis in the waters of Cnidos.[7]

The events to which she refers are the Battle of Salamis, 480 BCE, in which the Greek fleet soundly defeated the invading Persian fleet; the Battle of Cunaxa, 401 BCE, fought near the river Euphrates north of Babylon, in which Cyrus's army defeated the army of his brother Artaxerxes but in which Cyrus was himself killed; and the Battle of Cnidos, in the Aegean, 394 BCE, in which a combined Greek and Persian fleet defeated the Spartan fleet.

Like Flaubert's *Salammbô*, Dieulafoy's novel evokes an ancient world steeped in cruelty and superstition, full of exotic religious practices and evocative vocabulary, all developed from the narratives of Xenophon and Plutarch and her own archaeological researches. Her story places Parysatis, mother of Cyrus and Artaxerxes, at the centre, a formidable woman brave enough to face up to a tyrant on behalf of her son. If this reminded Saint-Saëns of his own mother, he did not say so. For the purposes of the Béziers pageant, Dieulafoy reduced the novel to its bare essentials, removing secondary characters and allowing for plenty of ceremonial, processions and dancing. Singing is heard only from the chorus and from three *choryphées*, two sopranos and a tenor, while the principal characters declaim their verses in speech.

Anxious to convey the flavour of ancient Persian music, Saint-Saëns could rely on little authentic source material beyond reliefs of the period showing harps, flutes and some percussion instruments. There was no known source that could help him with melody or mode beyond the speculations of Fétis, Ambros and others. In his *Histoire générale de la musique depuis les temps les plus anciens jusqu'à nos jours*, published in 1869, Fétis devoted twenty pages to ancient Persian music, which he believed to be based on small divisions of the scale, which Saint-Saëns made no attempt to reproduce. So he fell back, as in *Déjanire*, on the mediaeval modes applied in plain textures and stark rhythms and on augmented seconds to stand for the Middle East. This is interleaved with music in the modern style, chromatic and expressive, especially for moments of strong personal interaction.

Prologue The action begins half way through the novel, with the news of Artaxerxes's defeat of his brother Cyrus and his Greek mercenaries at Cunaxa. The two orchestras lay down the despair of the defeated army, using ex. 13.1 in various transformations. Cyrus, Parysatis's favourite son, is dead.

Example 13.1 *Parysatis*, Prologue

---

[7] *L'Art du théâtre*, 22 (October 1902).

Act I
On the Persian side, victory is celebrated with a hymn to their god Ormazd and praise of their king Artaxerxes. A break in the jubilation is caused by the entrance of Parysatis, the king's mother, to a stark, solemn theme in E♭ minor. Her lament over the body of Cyrus provokes a warning from the priest Orontès that she should not enflame the wrath of her other son. She makes a slow dignified exit as the triumphalism resumes.

Like the Philistines in *Samson et Dalila*, the Persians in *Parysatis* betray their crude culture in music of nugatory sophistication, loud and mostly unharmonised. Among the Greek captives is Aspasie, Cyrus's mistress, anxious to conceal her identity, like Aida in similar circumstances. Her fellow captives beg her to intercede for them.

Parysatis returns with Darius, Artaxerxes's son (played by a female actor), who has his eye on Aspasie, and who persuades the captives to renounce their religion in favour of the Persian cult of Mazda, thus sparing Aspasie from Artaxerxes's revenge. The sopranos of the chorus sing an enchanting song in praise of Anaïta, the goddess of the mountains, and the act ends in noisy acclaim of the king.

Act II In the first part of the act Darius woos Aspasie, who responds with warmth, even though both know that Artaxerxes wants her for himself. The second part is mostly *divertissement*, with Parysatis and Artaxerxes watching a series of four ballets, the second of which is a ravishing vocalise for coloratura soprano entitled 'Le Rossignol et la Rose'. This is quite well known and has been recorded many times. The orchestral ballet movements have been recorded too, displaying Saint-Saëns's customary skill and resourcefulness in such pieces.

A Hunters' Chorus celebrates Darius successfully killing a leopard, a feat that wins Aspasie's heart and alerts Parysatis to danger. The final women's chorus 'Le bonheur a-t-il fui de ces lieux' is full of dissonance and foreboding, with ex. 13.1 appearing in the bass.

Act III The priests welcome peace and the men's chorus celebrate the might of Artaxerxes's kingdom. The King moves down 'followed by twenty-four girls playing the harp'. The final scene shows Aspasie formally acknowledging her new faith but also confessing her love for Darius. In a fury, Artaxerxes orders both Darius and Aspasie to be seized. Once again, Parysatis steps forward, now calmly supported by intertwining strings and a trumpet spelling out the opening theme of the Prologue.

In the novel Darius makes a wild attack on the king and is himself killed by one of the bodyguards. Aspasie is despatched by Parysatis to the Mazdean equivalent of a nunnery. This ending was replaced in the drama by Artaxerxes so enraged by Parysatis's intervention that he orders the immediate execution of Aspasie. 'Frappez !' he shouts. She expires over richly scored strings. He then orders Darius and Parysatis to be led separately away, but before she has gone far she turns and unloads on Artaxerxes a mother's most murderous curse, punctuated by heavy unisons from the brass. The guards who approach her are compelled to kneel before her powerful presence. A series of thunderbolts respond to the curse, striking down Artaxerxes in the dust. The full chorus call upon the gods to restore peace to humankind.

Like *Déjanire*, there can be little prospect of ever reviving *Parysatis* with the elaboration it received at Béziers in 1902. Its musical interest is decidedly weaker than that of *Déjanire* and the drama amounts to little more than that of two men vying for the love of the same woman, with a powerful mother controlling the outcome. The ballets can be extracted and played as orchestral pieces, but there are really no choruses that deserve to be salvaged. The problem is that Saint-Saëns's concern to conjure up an antique sound led to a texture nearly always thin and sometimes reduced to bare unisons. There was some compensation in the orchestration, featuring harps, flutes and such percussion as crotales, not to mention the weight of two military bands for marches and processions. At all events, the public enjoyed the two performances in 1902 enough to justify two more performances at Béziers in 1903, conducted by Paul Viardot. Some choruses and ballets were performed in Paris in March 1903, leading Debussy to remark that the choruses were charming in a concert setting, though they should not have been, having been intended for the open air.[8] But there was not enough substance in *Parysatis* to adapt it as a conventional opera, as was proposed, without outcome, in 1906.[9] *Déjanire*, as we shall see in Chapter 15, was much more suitable for that treatment, being reincarnated as an opera in 1911.

* * * * *

Botriocéphale

Bouffonnerie antique in three scenes

First performance: Béziers, August 1902

| Botriocéphale | Faune |
| Alecton | Furie |

As a diversion during the Béziers festivals, it was customary for one of Saint-Saëns's plays to be put on in the town theatre. In previous years it had been *La Crampe des écrivains*, and in 1902 it was *Botriocéphale*, a ten-minute *bouffonnerie* for two actors, which turns the story of Beauty and the Beast on its head. Botriocéphale (which Saint-Saëns must have taken to mean 'grape-head') is a faun of appalling ugliness, while Alecton is one of Pluto's Furies who has been allowed to become a beautiful faun provided that she never allow anyone

---

[8] *Gil Blas*, 16 March 1903.   [9] BONNEROT 1922, p. 177.

to kiss her. Though shy, Botriocéphale is enamoured of her at once and eventually agrees to dance for her. She falls in love with him, allowing him to kiss her. Instead of the Beast becoming beautiful, Beauty is snatched back to the realm of Pluto as a Fury.

* * * * *

Andromaque
(Ratner 320)

Tragédie in five acts
by
Jean-Baptiste Racine

Incidental music

First performance: Théâtre Sarah-Bernhardt, Paris, 7 February 1903

Orchestra: 2 flutes (incl. piccolo), 2 oboes, 2 clarinets, 2 bassoons, 2 horns, 2 trumpets, 3 trombones, timpani, cymbals, triangle, strings.

In London that June (1902), Saint-Saëns crossed paths with the great Sarah Bernhardt, whose celebrity as an actor at that time had no rivals in Europe. Tirelessly touring both within and beyond France, she was also manager of the Théâtre des Nations at the Châtelet, which in 1899 she renamed the Théâtre-Sarah-Bernhardt, the name it retains today. She was planning a production of Racine's *Andromaque* for which Saint-Saëns agreed to compose the music, and on his return from Béziers he settled into the task. It occupied him in September and October, and in November he was able to compose the cello concerto, his second, which he had promised for Joseph Hollmann when he was in London. He played through the *Andromaque* music to Sarah Bernhardt at the beginning of December, then handed over the responsibility for performing it to Édouard Colonne, whose orchestra were to be playing in the theatre. Saint-Saëns himself was in the usual hurry to leave Paris for the winter, heading again for Egypt. He was thus absent from Berlin for the premiere of the Second Cello Concerto in January 1903 and from Paris for the performances of *Andromaque*, which opened on February 7th.

Major theatres at this time employed a full orchestra in the pit, so Saint-Saëns was able to supply fully scored music for *Andromaque* with an overture and a number of entr'actes. When composing music for Racine's *Phèdre* at the Odéon two years earlier, Massenet composed an overture and four entr'actes (or rather added the entr'actes to an overture he had composed in 1873). Often there was also the option of songs in the text, as in Shakespeare (though not in Racine), or music to cover silent action such as processions, or as *mélodrame* to be played under speech. For *Andromaque* Saint-Saëns wrote seventeen pieces of music, some as short as ten bars or less, others longer:

a substantial overture, preludes for Acts II, III, IV and V, postludes for Acts I, II and IV, and eight more pieces to connect scenes or to cover exits and entrances. There was one *mélodrame*, in Act III. Nothing was sung. The use of postlude and prelude is helpful in removing the ambiguity with entr'actes, since it is not always clear whether they belong to the act that precedes or follows, or whether they are there to cover scene changes while the audience remains in place.

The overture is conventional in passing from a few pages of slow music to an Allegro that takes up the rest of the piece, but is unconventional in musical language. Saint-Saëns remarked that it passes from sharps to flats with 'deplorable facility' and is full of 'bizarre things',[10] by which he means juxtaposition of unrelated chords and some wandering harmony. Although F♯ minor is its principal key, the score is frequently without key signature in the face of persistent modulations. Saint-Saëns would not have attempted to represent the play in any narrative way in the overture, but a tone of tragedy is pervasive, and the themes may safely be linked to the leading characters, since they recur in later scenes.

The opening passage, hesitant and fragmentary, for example, must represent Andromaque, since it recurs for her entry in Act I, Scene 4 and again for the postlude to Act I, which closes on her dilemma in being forced to save her son by yielding to her captor Pyrrhus. A second theme, signalled by violent violin tremolos, will set the scene for Orestes's rage at the start of Act I, and a third theme (ex. 13.2), heard soon after the start of the Allegro section on violas and cellos with a feverishly restless accompaniment, may represent Pyrrhus's position caught between Hermione's passion for him, which he does not return, and his equally unrequited passion for Andromaque:

Example 13.2 *Andromaque*, Overture

This theme will be heard in Act III after Pyrrhus has left Andromaque with undisguised threats, and after Act IV when he has been similarly threatened by Hermione. The fiery final pages of the overture match the music for Hermione's rage in Act V (it was Hermione that Bernhardt played in this production, not Andromaque).

The *mélodrame* in Act III, Scene 8 was probably intended to cover Andromaque's speech beginning 'Ah ! de quel souvenir viens-tu frapper mon âme !', as she recalls her husband Hector going out to meet Achilles on the field of battle and bidding farewell to his son.

---

[10] Letters to Auguste Durand, September 1902, RATNER 2012, p. 428.

There were fifteen performances of *Andromaque*. The reviews once again exemplified the poverty of professional criticism at this time, for if opera critics had little knowledge of music, drama critics had even less. 'If anything were needed to show how unmusical we are in France,' Saint-Saëns wrote, 'it would be the articles against the music for *Andromaque*. Of course the play can do without music, but an overture and some entr'actes can only enhance and complement the impression it makes, and the public don't complain.'[11] *Le Temps* sent both drama and music critics to see the play, and while the former, Fernand Nozière, reported that the audience was wildly enthusiastic, he thought the music interrupted the flow of an 'ardent and rapid' drama. Their music critic, Pierre Lalo, the composer's son, whose only musical qualification was his parentage, wrote a sustained attack on Saint-Saëns for the sacrilege of composing music for Racine, which was always pointless, he said, and always harmful. Saint-Saëns 'seems to have taken care not to have any ideas that are too striking, which would draw attention to themselves at the expense of Racine's verse, and he has succeeded. His score consists mostly of entr'actes and preludes, none of which, save perhaps that to Act IV, are of the slightest interest.'[12]

Durand published scores of the Overture and the Prelude to Act IV, but there are other pieces which, if this music is ever to be heard again, could be incorporated in an orchestral suite, notably the Preludes to Acts II and V and the Marche at the beginning of Act I. The overture has been recorded by David Robertson and the Orchestre Philharmonique de Monte Carlo.

* * * * *

En route to Egypt, Saint-Saëns spent a few days in December 1902 in Monte Carlo. In 1879 the Principality of Monaco opened a magnificent new opera house designed, like the new Paris Opéra, by Charles Garnier, and intended to be home to a splendid new tradition of opera. This did not come about at once, but in 1892 the theatre was put in the charge of Raoul Gunsbourg, an adventurous figure of French-Romanian Jewish origin, who fought on the Russian side in the Russo-Turkish War of 1877 and was partly trained as a doctor and partly as an actor. After playing with a French theatre company in Bucharest, he came briefly to Paris in 1879, and moved directly on to Moscow, where he found himself mounting operettas in a small theatre. Before long he was working directly for the Tsar on mysterious missions to the Pope, to China and to the President of France, through whose influence he became, still under thirty years of age, director of the Grand Theatre in Lille.

These fantastic wanderings came to an end in 1892 when he was appointed director of the Monte Carlo theatre, a post which he held, unbelievably, until 1951. He was a man of exceptional gifts, without doubt, for in the twenty-two years leading up to the First World War, Monte Carlo was one of the leading opera centres in Europe.

---

[11] Letter to Auguste Durand, 18 February 1903, RATNER 2012, p. 428.
[12] *Le Temps*, 9 and 10 February 1903.

Gunsbourg commissioned a steady flow of new works and engaged the greatest singers of the age; Patti, Chaliapin, Melba are some of the names who appeared regularly on his *affiches*, a luxury made possible by the profits of the casino and by the keen support of Prince Albert I and his Princess, Alice, an American who devoted much of her energy to opera and ballet, especially after separation from her husband in 1902. After the war she gave Diaghilev's ballet company a home in Monte Carlo.

Both Massenet and Saint-Saëns came to see Monte Carlo as the most welcoming of European opera houses. *Manon* and *Werther* had been played there before Massenet was commissioned to compose *Le Jongleur de Notre-Dame*, which opened in February 1902. No less than five more of his operas would open in Monte Carlo in the remaining years before the war. Saint-Saëns, similarly, had had *Samson et Dalila* played there in three seasons before he was asked to compose a new opera for the company. Once his *Hélène* was played there in February 1904, others followed: *L'Ancêtre* in February 1906; *La Foi* in April 1909; and the revised *Déjanire* in March 1911, along with revivals of *Le Timbre d'argent*, *Henry VIII*, *Proserpine* and *Les Barbares*.

Gunsbourg also brought to life operas which their composers had not lived to see: Bizet's *Don Procopio*, Lalo's *La Jacquerie* and Franck's two operas *Hulda* and *Ghiselle*. Of French composers other than the big two, he was a gallant patron. The following all had operas performed in Monte Carlo: De Lara, Desjoyeux, d'Harcourt, Trémisot, Bruneau, Leroux and Bellenot. Never Fauré or Debussy.

Saint-Saëns's discussions with Gunsbourg in December 1902 were evidently not the first the two had shared.[13] No doubt Gunsbourg asked him for an opera when he was busy with other things or disinclined to write any opera at all. In 1901, after all, he had said, '*Parysatis* will be my last folly.'[14] This time Saint-Saëns yielded, since he had long been thinking about Helen of Troy, and a scenario had taken shape in his mind, which, as we have seen, had been almost exclusively concentrated, as far as the stage was concerned, on antiquity, especially the Greek myths. The plan was for an opera in one act, to be staged early in 1904. Without Gallet he was at a loss for a librettist, but quite quickly decided to write his own libretto. He knew how the plot was to unfold and he knew how to write verse. Had he not published a volume of poetry ten years before? His collaborators were Homer, Theocritus, Aeschylus, Virgil and Ovid, he claimed, and felt sure that good classicists would recognise lines he had taken from those authors.

---

[13] Saint-Saëns's account of the genesis of *Hélène* appeared in *Le Figaro* on 13 January 1905, when the opera was performed in Paris at the Opéra-Comique. A shorter account appeared in *Le Figaro* on 4 June 1919, when it was performed at the Opéra. SORET 2012, pp. 612–14 and 1028–29.

[14] Letter to Auguste Durand of 26 August 1901, RATNER 2012, p. 400.

Before the end of the year he was in Alexandria to rehearse *Proserpine*, which was staged there and in Cairo in the new year, 1903. In Cairo he was again comfortably installed as the guest of Mohammed Ali Pasha and was all set to begin work on the new libretto when the Khedive decided to put on a concert of Saint-Saëns's music to raise money for Breton sailors (a strange cause, when they had apparently suffered no recent disasters). This took all his attention for a week or two and also broke the spell in Cairo. As so often before when he needed to work, he had to find tranquillity, so in February he went to Ismailia, on the Suez Canal, 'in the middle of the desert', where he had stayed in the past, and there he was able to put the libretto together in less than two weeks. Ismailia 'is the *beata solitudo*, tempered by a very civilised group of people of both sexes', he wrote. 'Employees of the Suez Canal Company and their families, it is a little select group that even has two talented poets in their number. And since these nice people are very busy, they inhabit the solitude without disturbing it.'[15] Before leaving Cairo he composed a *Valse langoureuse* as a gift for Mohammed Ali.

There was no question of staying longer in Egypt to compose the music of *Hélène* since a revival of *Henry VIII* at the Opéra was scheduled for April and he intended to supervise it. In the middle of March, with the libretto drafted, he went to Monte Carlo to read it through to Gunsbourg and to discuss staging and casting. The months in Paris were filled with everything other than composing, including a memorial concert for Augusta Holmès, who died in January at the age of fifty-five. In his twenties Saint-Saëns had proposed to her, according to legend, and they had certainly been close friends.

In search of the right spot that summer, Saint-Saëns spent a week in Biarritz, then a week in Cannes, and a quick visit to Monte Carlo to meet the Prince before heading to a refuge in the mountains east of Aix-les-Bains, Mont Revard, reached by a rack railway with a hotel at an altitude of 1500 metres. Here, in July 1903, the music of *Hélène* was drafted, all but the final scene. He hoped to finish it before he was needed back in Paris to rehearse the singers for Béziers, whose festival in mid August this year presented both of Saint-Saëns's pageants *Déjanire* and *Parysatis* with two performances of each, beginning on August 9th and concluding on August 18th. The second performance of *Parysatis* was poorly attended, precipitating a change of direction for Castelbon de Beauxhostes, whose friendship with Saint-Saëns was not impaired even though the festival continued until 1926 with no more revivals of his music except *Antigone* played in 1921 and *Déjanire* played in 1924.

---

[15] SORET 2012, p. 613.

> *Le Roi Apépi*
>
> Comedy in four acts and five tableaux
>
> after a story by Victor Cherbuliez
>
> First performance: Béziers, August 1903
>
> > Le Marquis de Miraval
> > Horace
> > Monsieur Navet
> > François
> > Jean
> > Le Portier de l'Hôtel
> > Madame Véretz
> > Hortense
> > Sidonie
> > Madame Navet
> > Annette

This year, 1903, he had a new play, *Le Roi Apépi* ('King Apépi'), a comedy in four acts based on a story by Victor Cherbuliez. It concerns a young man so boring about his passion for Egyptology that his fiancée, whom he believes to be interested in it too, walks out. In the Geneva hotel where this all takes place, however, he meets a young girl who refuses to return to Paris with her parents, especially when she gets the offer of a trip . . . to Egypt. Saint-Saëns is disarmingly making fun of his own passion for Egypt and his insatiable curiosity about its history and archaeology. Perhaps he, too, had sent his listeners to sleep recounting the history of the Pharaohs.

Being busy at Béziers, Saint-Saëns was unable to attend the celebrations in Grenoble on August 16th and 17th marking the centenary of the birth of Berlioz. With his renewed poetic impulse he wrote a passionate *Ode* which was recited in the interval of the second concert, in his absence, by a local dignitary.[16] A week later a small Berlioz Museum was opened in the Salle des Lions in the Château Louis XI at La Côte-St-André, the town where Berlioz was born, but again Saint-Saëns was unable to attend. He wrote a speech, which was read by the mayor, upholding the integrity and greatness of *Les Troyens* and including an account of his painful last meeting with Berlioz on his deathbed.[17]

He preferred to return to Paris to complete the draft of *Hélène* and then make the piano reduction, which had to be sent for engraving in time for rehearsals. This was done by early September and the job of orchestrating the opera followed, being

---

[16] Published in *Le Monde musical*, 30 August 1903; SORET 2012, pp. 575–76.

[17] The speech was published in the *Livre d'Or du Centenaire d'Hector Berlioz*, Paris, Georges Petit, and Grenoble, Allier Frères, 1903, pp. 174–75. Only the last part of it is included in SORET 2012, p. 577.

completed in October. Before he could escape for his African hibernation, he had some concerts to give in Germany, including a ceremony inaugurating a statue of Wagner in Berlin which, rather surprisingly, he attended. Then in early December he left once again for Egypt. This time, it seems, he took a break from composition.

Saint-Saëns arrived in Monte Carlo on 21 January 1904 with a month to go before the opening of *Hélène* and he stayed at the Hôtel de Paris. There was much work to be done correcting the parts, and the set was delivered very late. A persistent tradition holds that the title role in the opera was written for the great Australian soprano Nellie Melba, but although she did indeed sing it, both in Monte Carlo and in London four months later, there is no evidence that this is so. She probably put the idea into circulation herself.[18] She had sung Gounod's Juliette in Monte Carlo in the 1890 season, Rosina in *Il barbiere di Siviglia* in 1900, and Mimi in *La Bohème* in 1902, so she was a familiar member of Gunsbourg's troupe, but she was engaged by Gunsbourg for *Hélène* without reference to Saint-Saëns, who had apparently heard her before somewhere. He had known from the start that the contralto Meyriane Héglon would be singing Pallas Athene, with her rich low range. The other members of the cast were Louise Blot, a high soprano singing Vénus and new to Monte Carlo, and the tenor Albert Alvarez as Pâris. Alvarez's fame exceeded that of Melba at the time, since he had sung the major French tenor roles such as Faust, Roméo and Samson as well as Rhadames in *Aida* and some Wagner too. He was the original Nicias in Massenet's *Thaïs*. Alvarez and Héglon were the leading singers in *Samson et Dalila* which Gunsbourg courteously revived as a tribute to Saint-Saëns ten days before the opening of *Hélène*, and Alvarez also sang Araquil in Massenet's *La Navarraise*, which was coupled with *Hélène* as a double bill. This was a part he had sung at the opera's premiere in London in 1894. Saint-Saëns hoped that *La Princesse jaune* could be the other work in the programme, but Gunsbourg would not go that far. The conductor was Léon Jehin, resident conductor of the theatre.

The three performances of *Hélène* on 18, 20 and 23 February 1904 gave Saint-Saëns enormous satisfaction. The long account Saint-Saëns sent to his friend, the composer Charles Lecocq, finds praise for all the singers, the chorus, the staging, the lighting, the conductor and the audience.[19] His only complaint was that the set was not Greek enough for him, and the costumes were supplied from wardrobe, not copied from Greek vases, as he would have liked. He thought the nymphs looked too much like the flower maidens in *Parsifal*.

> We have nothing like Madame Melba in Paris, it must be admitted. She has gained a warmth which she didn't have before and a grand sense of style, which is rare. She can sing a phrase quite simply, without frills, and with true feeling. [. . .] Alvarez is especially good in moments of force and passion, and he sang the phrase 'des astres de la nuit tes yeux ont la clarté' to perfection, with soft, exquisite expression. [. . .] Mme Héglon was perfect, once I'd taught her

---

[18] See MURPHY 2015.   [19] Letter of 4 and 5 March 1904, RATNER 2012, pp. 277–80.

to drop the slides which would have spoilt the character. Her low F rang out like a bell. [...] Mlle Blot is pretty as a rose and as clumsy as a goose. She has a lovely voice which she doesn't use to the best advantage, and she would have been even more admirable if she didn't keep slowing the tempo.

* * * * *

Hélène
(Ratner 296)

Poème lyrique in one act

Libretto by the composer

First performance: Théâtre de Monte-Carlo, 18 February 1904

Hélène	soprano
Vénus	soprano
Pallas	contralto
Pâris	ténor

Spartiates, nymphes, Troyens et Troyennes

Orchestra: 3 flutes (incl. piccolo), 2 oboes, cor anglais, 2 clarinets (incl. alto clarinet), bass clarinet, contrabass clarinet, 2 bassoons, 4 horns, 4 trumpets, 3 trombones, tuba, timpani, bass drum, cymbals, triangle, 2 harps, strings.

Offstage: 2 recorders or piccolos, oboe, clarinet, trumpet, tambourine, harp, organ, military band.

The myths surrounding Helen of Troy were already abundant in classical literature before European artists, dramatists and musicians took up her story. The best-known part of it tells how Helen, although married to King Menelaus of Sparta, was abducted or seduced by Paris, one of the sons of Priam, King of Troy, thus initiating the ten-year Trojan War and all that flowed from that great conflict. As background, it was told that Paris had been invited by Zeus, because he was a young man of sagacity and honesty, to award the Golden Apple to whichever of the three goddesses Juno, Minerva or Venus (known in Greek as Hera, Pallas Athena and Aphrodite) was the most beautiful. Each tried to sway his judgment, Juno with the promise of a kingdom, Minerva with military glory, and Venus with the fairest woman in the world. He awarded the prize to Venus, which seemed fair, since she was herself the goddess of beauty.

To find the fairest woman in the world Paris went to Sparta, since Helen, a daughter of Zeus, was acknowledged to hold that trophy. While Menelaus was away, Paris took Helen away to Troy, whether by force or persuasion being a question the ancients disagreed upon. In Saint-Saëns's conception Helen is torn between her love for Paris and her obligation to Menelaus, an operatic conflict of conscience which is played out in scenes where the two goddesses Pallas and Venus represent, as if in court, the arguments for and against. Pallas was said to have held a deep grudge against Paris for not awarding her the prize of beauty, but Saint-Saëns presents her more as the voice of respectability and duty, as well as a siren prophetess of the carnage that will ensue if Helen leaves for Troy. Venus's arguments are the simpler enticements of love and sexual ecstasy.

'A long time ago,' he wrote, 'I had this vision of Helen fleeing in the night, exhausted, at the sea's edge, far from her palace, followed by Paris. A scene of passion, her resistance eventually overcome, and the final flight of the lovers after a desperate battle of conscience ... I could never see Helen simply as a woman in love. She is the slave of Destiny, the victim of Venus, the price of the Golden Apple.'[20]

Saint-Saëns knew *Paride ed Elena* (1770), the last opera Gluck wrote with Calzabigi as librettist, at least he knew that Gluck had recycled parts of it for later scores. It was not included in the series of Gluck scores edited by Saint-Saëns and not revived on stage until 1901, in Prague. The opera was based on Ovid's *Heroides*, of which two sections recreate letters, the first from Paris to Helen, full of passion, although he had not yet met her, the second from Helen to Paris, cautious and hesitant but ultimately admitting her love for Paris. Calzabigi has Helen merely betrothed to Menelaus, which greatly weakens the dramatic tension, and although he has appearances from Venus and Pallas, the latter only appears in Act V, in a cloud, with dire warnings of the future (of which Paris and Helen take no notice, having had Venus coaxing them on stage almost throughout).

Saint-Saëns also knew – but no doubt wished he didn't – Offenbach's highly successful *La Belle Hélène* (1864), with a libretto by Meilhac and Halévy that Saint-Saëns found offensive for its vulgarity and for its wilful distortion of one of the great episodes of antiquity.

Saint-Saëns's own libretto is arranged as seven scenes, running continuously. The opera lasts an hour. At the beginning Paris is welcomed at Menelaus's court. Scene 2 is the scene Saint-Saëns described as his vision, with Helen running from the palace. In Scene 3 Venus, with a group of nymphs, entices Helen. In Scene 4 Paris himself adds persuasion. Scene 5 is the crucial confrontation with Pallas, and Scene 6 develops into a passionate love duet, Helen's resistance finally giving way. Scene 7 is the apotheosis as they sail away to their destiny.

* * * * *

With the resources of the Monte Carlo orchestra at his disposal Saint-Saëns was able to score *Hélène* with unusual richness. He was particularly intrigued to learn that they had a contrabass clarinet, so he set up a quartet of clarinets of four different sizes, which

---

[20] *Le Figaro*, 13 January 1905; SORET 2012, p. 612.

give a distinct colour to certain scenes. He was also able to call on offstage instruments and a military band, which are used, along with offstage chorus, for particularly powerful effect. The chorus sing offstage in Scenes 1 and 5 and are seen as nymphs in Scene 3. The particular attention to lighting effects in the libretto reflects the advanced technical know-how of the Monte Carlo stage crew.

Introduction A brief Introduction before the curtain rises is a vigorous piece of mood-setting in E major, with two contrasting sections within it. The first presents a shadowy form of the motif for Hélène's love (ex. 13.3):

Example 13.3 *Hélène*, Introduction

The second (ex. 13.4) is to be heard later in Scene 4, when Hélène proudly declares that she is the daughter of a god:

Example 13.4 *Hélène*, Introduction

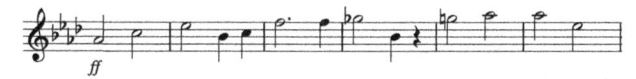

Scene 1 The first scene is boldly set mostly out of vision. Festivities are going on in Ménélas's palace, accompanied by an offstage band (which includes two recorders or piccolos), but we see only the outside of the building from which can be heard voices raised in acclamation of Pâris, the 'charming hero', to which Pâris responds with a toast to King Ménélas and, naturally, a toast to the noble queen 'Hélène of the fair arms'. Then the scene changes to a clifftop, with the sea in the distance. Dawn is breaking.

Scene 2 If the first scene was simple operatic scene-setting, the second scene takes us right to the heart of the drama with a superb solo scene for a despairing Hélène. The benefits of being his own librettist are fully on display, as Saint-Saëns matches every line with music that has no settled key and no settled themes but which is dramatic to the very core. We are reminded of Cassandre and Sieglinde in this portrait of a woman disturbed to the point of suicide, and the structure of the scene is perfectly contrived to give her passionate pleas to the gods the balance of memories of a once peaceful life. In the background is the steady rise and fall of the sea.

Recalling Pâris's invitation to flee with him, to a series of mysterious chords, ex. 13.3 is heard, again low on the clarinet, followed by a delicately scored passage that carries the critically vulnerable side of her heart (ex. 13.5):

Example 13.5 *Hélène*, Scene 2

[musical score: Hélène, solo violin, harp — "Ah! pour-quoi l'ai-je vu-e, Cet-te tê-te char-man-te!"]

The scene rises to a great storm of passion as she approaches the clifftop and prepares to cast herself into the sea.

Scene 3 Vénus suddenly appears in a glowing light above the sea, and gradually she is seen to be set in a charming landscape surrounded by nymphs and cupids. She has strong arguments for deterring Hélène from leaping off the cliff. As a goddess she knows that Destiny has a different future in mind for her; and secondly, she had promised her to Pâris in gratitude for the Golden Apple. She knows, or at least senses, that Hélène loves him, despite her denial. 'I hate him,' says Hélène, 'Never will I go with him!' Fear, not virtue, causes you to say that, replies Vénus, and the rest of the scene is taken over by her and her escort of nymphs who charm Hélène (and us) with some coloratura and sensual, feminine music that might belong to *Les Pêcheurs de perles* or *Lakmé*, harps always prominent. As the scene fades, the support comes from offstage instruments.

Scene 4 Pâris comes in, breathlessly searching for Hélène. 'How can you run away when you love me?' he wonders. 'Let me go, I hate you!' is the reply, to the defiant rhythm ex. 13.6 in the orchestra:

Example 13.6 *Hélène*, Scene 4

[musical score fragment, marked f]

Flattery and passionate admiration do not seem to move her, so he tries a calmer approach, first in 3/4 in D, then at the words:

> Naguère avant de voir
> Ta beauté, j'ignorais quel était son pouvoir !
>
> Once, before I saw
> Your beauty, I had no idea of its power!

in 4/4 in A♭, with gorgeous string underpinning. Still unmoved, Hélène protests that she is loyal to Ménélas, and the hollow tread of ex. 13.4 is heard in the brass. Pâris compares Sparta's, yes, spartan surroundings with the rich harvests and glittering palaces of Troy, but still with the protection of ex. 13.6 she insists that she will remain. At her mention of Ménélas's love he interrupts her with the accusation that she only thinks she loves him. Over long pauses she repeats 'Je crois aimer !', and then in a flood of rapture breaks down, the helpless victim of the goddess of love. Her lies and hypocrisy she can sustain no longer, she admits; she loves Pâris, to an ecstatic ex. 13.7, over a relentlessly rising bass line:

Example 13.7 *Hélène*, Scene 4

While Pâris can think only of their elopement, Hélène turns to her father Zeus with a great invocation and prayer, 'Preserve me from myself!'

Scene 5 A highly chromatic orchestral interlude, mostly obscure rumbling over thunder and lightning effects, covers the gradual appearance of Pallas 'glowing in the dark'. The scene that follows is coloured by some remarkable orchestration, with contrabass clarinet and contrabassoon in the main orchestra and an offstage orchestra of unspecified wind instruments full enough to provide backing for a full chorus, also offstage.

Pallas brings the reply of their father, Zeus, to Hélène's prayer. Let Pâris abandon his plan and he will be spared his cruel destiny, she solemnly intones, with a descent to low F. Pâris defiantly rejects such an idea, which prompts Pallas to call up a vision of Troy, seen first as a dim red light, then growing to a full view of the city in flames. Her picture of blood and carnage gets more and more lurid, and the cries of the offstage chorus get more and more desperate.

The vision fades and Pallas addresses Pâris squarely (her quarrel is not with Hélène). 'Defy Zeus at your peril! Leave Greece, and leave alone!' Pâris is as unmoved as the bass line in the broad phrase heard now, ex. 13.8:

Example 13.8 *Hélène*, Scene 5

Pallas yields to his determined passion. 'Va vers l'amour ! Va vers la mort !' 'Go find love! Go find death!'

Scene 6 Day gradually breaks, with three solo strings initiating what feels like a delicious movement of chamber music, all too short. All that remains is for Hélène and Pâris to pour out the duet that opera demands, and here Saint-Saëns does not fail us. For the control of pace and temper is masterly as they confess their separate passions and gradually unite. Holding back the tempo to start with, Hélène declares her willingness to run the trials their crime will bring, abandoning husband and home, and yielding entirely to love. Pâris likewise is restrained at first, marvelling at Vénus's conquest. The duet proper begins with Pâris building on ex. 13.3, which leads directly into ex. 13.5. One phrase climbs over another until the two voices are finally united in a huge Puccinian unison for the first time.

They rush off together as the orchestra seizes ex. 13.7 at top speed. Other themes are recalled from Scene 4, including ex. 13.4, leading directly into:

Scene 7 Example 13.3 thunders out in the full orchestra as the stage reveals the open sea. On it a ship passes with Hélène and Pâris seen in a passionate embrace. Their duet ends with more unison accompanied by an organ and a harp offstage, and the main orchestra brings down the final curtain.

* * * * *

Hélène is surely one of Saint-Saëns's finest operas. The invention is, as always, fresh, never banal. The motifs are reminders, not labels. The intensely dramatic scenes for the two lovers, Scenes 2, 4 and 6, are partitioned by the very different scenes (3 and 5) for the two goddesses, each with special theatrical support in the form of chorus and lighting effects, so that they seem to appear from unearthly space and return there afterwards. Hélène's emotional dilemma is intensely human and believable and sustained right to the point where her abandonment to love is inevitable. The orchestration is modern and highly inventive, eschewing the brass noisiness that we hear in Strauss, but more concerned with delicacy and clarity. And since Saint-Saëns would never forget the necessity for well-crafted form, the three scenes of passion (involving Hélène and Pâris only) reach a climax in each that seems to grow at precisely the pace of the scene itself. Massenet also had this gift of pacing scenes carefully so that they are whole and satisfying, yet an intrinsic part of the act or of the whole opera.

Being a one-act opera, *Hélène* can no longer expect to be staged as frequently as it was in Saint-Saëns's lifetime. Even *Pagliacci* and *Dido and Aeneas* struggle for a place in an operatic culture where one-act operas are scorned by managements and public. It should be paired with Massenet's one-act operas (*Le Portrait de Manon*, *La Navarraise*) or Bizet's *Djamileh*, or any of the great legacy of nineteenth-century short operas. Or if it were played on its own – it lasts one hour – it would provide a truly satisfying evening.

The Monte Carlo performances in 1904 were very successful and it was quickly taken up in other cities. Covent Garden, London, was the first, opening on 20 June 1904 with Melba again singing Hélène. The English translation was by Hermann Klein and the conductor was Messager, who now had the benefit of printed score and parts. Saint-Saëns was deeply impressed by Melba's singing, and the two got on well. She told him she would be glad to sing it at the Opéra-Comique in Paris, but in the event the role was sung by Mary Garden on 18 January 1905 with dreadful French. Saint-Saëns hated Albert Carré's direction of the opera and discouraged revivals there.

It was played in Frankfurt in January 1905 also. Meanwhile it had been sung at the Teatro Lirico, Milan, on 26 November 1904, a performance that delighted the composer, and the city of Genoa took it up in March 1905 at the same time as its revival in Monte Carlo. Melba was replaced by the soprano Félia Litvinne, who had sung Catherine in *Henry VIII* at the Opéra. Later Monte Carlo revivals took place on 13 February 1909 (Litvinne again) and 12 March 1916 (Marthe Davelli).

In New York in 1906 Saint-Saëns read in the newspapers that Oscar Hammerstein I was planning to open a new opera house in rivalry with the Metropolitan. It was announced that *Hélène* would be included in the repertoire, with Melba singing the main role. Saint-Saëns then received a telegram in February 1907 to confirm this news.[21] But although many French operas were performed in the few years of the company's existence, some of them with Melba singing, it appears that *Hélène* was not one of them.

The last performance in Saint-Saëns's lifetime was given at the Opéra on 20 June 1919 with Marcelle Demougeot as Hélène. The next hearing was apparently a performance at the Paris Conservatoire in the 1950s, for which scant details are available. In modern times the opera's fate has been turned around by the Prague State Opera, which mounted it on 13 February 2008 in a concert performance conducted by Guillaume Tourniaire. From this followed the superb recording (Melba records) in 2008 with Tourniaire conducting an Australian cast led by Rosamund Illing as Hélène.

---

[21] Letters to the Durands, 22 November 1906 and 1 February 1907; RATNER 2012, pp. 281–82.

14 | L'Ancêtre, La Foi

With *Hélène* launched in Monte Carlo in February 1904 and cities elsewhere queuing up to stage it, Saint-Saëns resumed his habitual travels, taking in performances of his latest opera where he could. He went first to Naples to compose a piece for violin and orchestra which he had been promising to write for the Dutch violinist Johannes Wolff for fifteen years. This is the *Caprice andalous*, based on Andalusian melodies he had heard in Cadiz many years before. He was back in Paris for two concerts given in his honour by the Société des Concerts at the end of April. In these he appeared as pianist (in Mozart's D minor Concerto), organist (in his own Third Symphony) and as conductor (in *Le Déluge*). Next he was in Edinburgh to give a trio concert on June 4th with two young musicians: Jacques Thibaud (violin) and Josef Hasselmans (cello). Four days later he was in London to play the *Africa* fantasy at the Queen's Hall under Henry Wood and to rehearse *Hélène* at Covent Garden. Whether he was there for the first night on June 20th is unclear, since the following day he took possession of a ground-floor apartment in the Rue de Longchamp in Paris, his first residence there for some years.

On June 26th Saint-Saëns made his first recording. Introduced to a recording of Caruso and to the English Gramophone and Typewriting Company by Nellie Melba, he worked in the studio in Paris with the pioneer of recording engineering, Fred Gaisberg. On his own he played a group of piano solos, then he accompanied Meyrianne Héglon (his Pallas in Monte Carlo) in extracts from *Samson et Dalila* and *Ascanio* and some songs.[1] She would have liked another session to re-record her pieces, but Saint-Saëns had to leave next day for Genoa where a berth awaited him on the *Città di Milano* to take him to South America. He spent two months giving concerts in Buenos Aires, Montevideo and Rio de Janeiro, and returned in September.

The year had still more travel ahead: to Milan in November for the Italian premiere of *Hélène* and to Cologne in December for a revival of *Le Timbre d'argent*. In 1904 he was at the same time actively writing on many different subjects for the press, and he read a paper on mirages on the Red Sea to the Astronomical Society. His writing that year culminated in the lengthy essay 'Causerie sur l'art du théâtre', which appeared as the preface to the annual publication *Annales du théâtre et de la musique* at the start of 1905. To his thoughts on Greek theatre, on Wagner and on French operatic tradition we shall return in the final chapter, since, as he approached his seventieth birthday and looked

---

[1] These recordings have been reissued as *The Piano G & Ts*, volume 3 (APR 5533).

back on his manifestly successful career, he found the leisure to reflect on the fundamental issues of opera and to set out his (mostly) long-held beliefs on the subject.

Saint-Saëns was accompanied in Milan by Raoul Gunsbourg, both men anxious to see how 'their' opera would fare sung in Italian under the direction of Sonzogno at the Teatro Lirico. The performance was excellent and the audience enthusiastic. Having already decided to revive *Hélène* in 1905, Gunsbourg took the opportunity to press the composer for a new opera for his 1906 season. Saint-Saëns replied that he was in discussion about a new work for the Opéra, but that he would much prefer to have his new work performed in Monte Carlo. It was decided that an exchange of letters between Saint-Saëns and the Prince should be published, asserting that an agreement had already been reached with Monte Carlo, effectively curtailing any negotiations with the Opéra. These letters were published in the *Journal de Monaco* on 25 April 1905 with the announcement that the title of Saint-Saëns's new opera would be *L'Ancêtre*,[2] that the librettist would be Lucien Augé de Lassus, and that following its Monte Carlo premiere it would be given at the Opéra-Comique.[3]

Saint-Saëns's letter to the Prince, written from Algiers on 1 February 1905, opens with what seems like a refusal: 'The theatre no longer appeals to me, and I felt with *Hélène* that that was my goodbye.' But he went on to affirm that he would do his very best.[4] All this leaves unclear the nature of his discussions with the Opéra and the process by which librettist and subject were arrived at. After collaborating on *Phryné* in 1893, Augé de Lassus remained friendly with the composer and had no doubt offered him ideas for operas, just as Gallet used to do. A disinclination to write more operas would no doubt have been his normal response, and his own satisfactory experience as a librettist with *Hélène* might have convinced him that he did not need librettists at all. Unfortunately neither Saint-Saëns nor Augé de Lassus in his memoir about the composer gave any details about the early genesis of *L'Ancêtre*, unlike the colourful history of *Phryné*, which we have partially recounted in Chapter 9. The latter only revealed that the strong contrast in setting and character between *Phryné* and *L'Ancêtre* appealed greatly to both of them. Saint-Saëns was perhaps glad to be dragged out of the ancient world.

Having stayed in Paris until mid January in order to oversee rehearsals of *Hélène* at the Opéra-Comique, Saint-Saëns left for Algeria with a plan to ruminate upon. He wrote on February 28th from Biskra, having moved inland from Algiers to avoid the cold:

> I am much preoccupied with my new work. The first act ends with a grand superhuman scene which rests entirely on the leading female role. I originally thought I would assign this to a contralto, but I see that's impossible and that it can only be done with a proper dramatic

---

[2] 'Ancêtre' has no feminine form in French, so the translation is 'The Ancestress'.
[3] WALSH 1975, pp. 195–96, with the date May 23; REES 1999, p. 363, gives the correct date.
[4] Letter of 1 February 1905, RATNER 2012, p. 293.

soprano. I regard Mme Litvinne as the only possible one. Only she has the voice and authority for such a role and such a scene.[5]

Meanwhile *Hélène* was being revived in Monte Carlo on March 18th and 21st. An entirely new cast was led by Litvinne as Hélène. Saint-Saëns told the Prince that he 'almost' went to see it but felt obliged to stick to the task he had assigned him. In fact he was composing a second cello sonata, a full four-movement work, followed by a setting for male-voice chorus of a Horace Ode he had translated himself. 'The ease with which I composed this little work seems to me to bode well for *L'Ancêtre*, a bigger bite to swallow! As always when I have to broach something new, I get into a blind terror.'[6] Before composing any music for the opera he needed to absorb its locale.

The island of Corsica enjoyed a certain aura in France as the birthplace of Napoleon, but it was notable in nineteenth-century French literature more for the institution of the *vendetta*. Two novellas exploited this with particular success: Mérimée's *Colomba* in 1840 (set as an opera by Alexander Mackenzie in 1883); and Dumas's *Les Frères corses* in 1844. Augé de Lassus had been to Corsica, enjoying the food, fraternising with the men 'who sometimes kill but never steal', and listening to their stories. He was walking one day on a quiet road near Ajaccio when he saw two rifles pointing at him from the bushes. After a while the men ran off and disappeared into the woods.[7] This gave him the idea for *L'Ancêtre* of a story of two families split by a *vendetta* and – inevitably for an opera – the son of one family in love with the daughter of the other. Tébaldo, of the Néra family, is in love with Margarita, of the Fabiani family, but Nunciata, the ancestress of the Fabiani, upholds the *vendetta* against the Neri, leading inevitably to tragedy when Nunciata's granddaughter is killed instead.

Having embarked on this plan, Saint-Saëns naturally wanted to visit Corsica too, but he had first to conduct his Third Symphony in Marseille on April 2nd and give an organ recital there. On May 4th he played the solo part in Beethoven's Emperor Concerto at the Société des Concerts in Paris. After that he was free to visit Corsica. 'He explored it, or rather he listened to it, he breathed it; thus there passed into the music something of the harsh scents that fill that tragic yet so delightful island.'[8] The summer was set aside for composing the score, a more substantial score than anything he had written for five years. As in 1903, for *Hélène*, he sought a tranquil spot where he could be undisturbed. The first stop was Pallanza, on Lake Maggiore in northern Italy, where he stayed under his old pseudonym Charles Sannois. He began work on June 20th and had finished a draft of the first tableau by July 2nd. Correspondence about details with Augé de Lassus shows him to be getting to grips with the text: 'You really do have an aversion to

---

[5] Letter of 28 February 1905 to Prince Albert, RATNER 2012, pp. 293–94.
[6] Letter of 23 May 1905 to Auguste Durand, RATNER 2012, p. 294.
[7] This story is told not by Augé de Lassus himself but by BONNEROT 1922, p. 182.
[8] AUGÉ DE LASSUS 1914, p. 203.

clarity,' he told his librettist, 'which is both strange and troubling. It's as if you thought it was a humiliation to dot one's i's.'[9] To his publisher he observed: 'It's neither a grand opera nor an opéra-comique. O how we miss the Théâtre-Lyrique! I don't see what we will be able to do with this opera after Monte Carlo.'[10]

After a couple of weeks in Paris, he resumed his incognito and settled this time for a month at the Hotel Freienhof in Thun, Switzerland, a resort also favoured by Brahms, who spent his summer holidays there in 1886–88.[11] A week later he had to dash back to Paris just for a single day. Nonetheless he made good progress with the second tableau, and soon after his return Augé de Lassus arrived with his wife for a brief visit. They decided to cast the opera in three acts, so that the second tableau became the second act. His visitors were treated to the pleasure of watching the portly composer 'swimming like a Triton' in the icy waters of the Aar, after which he led them back to the hotel to play his unfinished score on the hotel's feeble piano, 'more of a kitchen utensil than a musical instrument'.[12] Their friendly relations did not prevent Saint-Saëns inspecting every line with care and making suggestions for improvements, like Verdi with his collaborators. At one point in the third act he was held up waiting for Augé de Lassus to send him some revisions, so he had to fill time by making the piano reduction, a job that needed to be done in good time so that the singers could learn their roles.

By the second week of August it was time to return to Paris. The draft was complete save for the final bars with the death of Vanina. These were composed at the railway station at Pontarlier just across the border into France while waiting for his connection. There remained the two tasks of writing the piano reduction for the vocal score and orchestrating the whole piece. Saint-Saëns did not need isolation or quiet for these, so he remained in Paris for the next three months, with occasional visits to Dieppe. The vocal score was done by September 12th and the orchestral score by October 26th. He had a meeting with Gunsbourg in Paris, more discussion with Augé de Lassus and a careful exchange about the decor with Visconti, Gunsbourg's resident set designer. The most important interruption for Saint-Saëns was a trip to Burgos in northern Spain on August 30th to watch a total eclipse of the sun.

In November he went to Cannes with plenty of proofs to read, and from there to Monte Carlo to confer with Visconti and look over the sets. In Genoa he saw Oscar Wilde's *Salome* and was appalled at its bad taste. Better than platitudes, he agreed, but still unacceptable. News of Strauss's opera came in that month from Dresden, and he assumed, with heavy sarcasm, it would soon be staged at the Opéra-Comique. Then he sailed via Naples for Egypt, and he remained in Cairo until it was time to present himself in Monte Carlo for rehearsals of *L'Ancêtre*.

---

[9] Letter of 25 June 1905, RATNER 2012, p. 294. [10] Letter of 25 June 1905, RATNER 2012, p. 294.
[11] The author stayed in the same hotel in 2009, unaware that Saint-Saëns had been a guest earlier. His incognito was still secure.
[12] AUGÉ DE LASSUS 1914, p. 206.

He arrived in Monte Carlo at the beginning of February 1906 and stayed at the Hôtel de Paris for a day or two before moving into the royal palace as a guest of the Prince. Fellow-guests were Massenet and his wife, attending a revival of his 1877 opera *Le Roi de Lahore*. Despite the evident desire of Saint-Saëns's biographers to see great bitterness between them, there is no reason to believe that the relationship of the two composers, France's most successful composers of opera, was anything but courteous and friendly, even though Saint-Saëns had felt some resentment at Massenet's successes in the past. His regard for Massenet, which contained plenty of admiration, was quite different from his feelings, never warm, for Franck and his disciples. He certainly admired *Le Roi de Lahore* (whose libretto was by Gallet) and would have enjoyed seeing it again.[13]

The season began with *Tannhäuser*, in which three of his singers for *L'Ancêtre* were taking part. One of them was the twenty-three-year-old American soprano Geraldine Farrar, who had already appeared for two seasons in Monte Carlo and who was now singing Elisabeth in the Wagner, Sita in the Massenet and Margarita in *L'Ancêtre*. A fourth member of his cast, Charles Rousselière, blacksmith-turned-tenor who had sung Samson and the watchman (in *Les Barbares*) at the Opéra, was in *Le Roi de Lahore*. A member of the corps de ballet for the season was, strange to relate, Mata-Hari.

L'Ancêtre opened on 24 February 1906, with four performances to follow. Félia Litvinne joined the company to sing the part of Nunciata, the ancestress. Margarita was Geraldine Farrar, Vanina was Marie Charbonnel, a new mezzo at the beginning of her career, Tébaldo was Rousselière, Maurice Renaud sang the part of the old hermit Raphaël, and Bursica, the Fabiani's servant, was Henri-Alexandre Lequien, an all-purpose bass for the company for several seasons. The sets were by Visconti. There are scenes that require a chorus, but no ballet. The conductor was again Léon Jehin.

Audience response at the first night, a benefit night for a colonial charity, was unanimously enthusiastic. Saint-Saëns was seated in the Prince's box, and after the performance the Prince gave a dinner for thirty-two guests. One of these was Fauré, who came from Paris to support his friend and mentor, also to write a review for *Le Figaro*, which must have been written before the performance since it appeared on the 25th. Fauré's report is warm and sincere, appreciative of Saint-Saëns's profound mastery of the essentials of opera. He did not proclaim a masterpiece, however, which would be rare from any critic of any opera on its first night. Pierre Lalo in *Le Temps* on February 28th was, as usual, entirely dismissive of both libretto and score, having long before persuaded himself that the composer had no talent. Saint-Saëns had a public confrontation in Monte Carlo with one of the most odious of unmusical critics, Henry Gauthier-Villars, who, under the pseudonym Willy, derided whatever target he chose.[14]

* * * * *

[13] See BRANGER 2012. [14] See SORET 2012, p. 33.

L'Ancêtre
(Ratner 297)

Drame lyrique in three acts

Libretto by Lucien Augé de Lassus

First performance: Grand Théâtre de Monte-Carlo, 24 February 1906

Raphaël, ermite	baryton
Tébaldo, de la famille des Piétra Néra	ténor
Bursica, porcher, serviteur des Fabiani	basse
Nunciata, de la famille des Fabiani	soprano
Margarita, sœur de lait de Vanina	soprano
Vanina, petite-fille de Nunciata	contralto
Léandri, petit-fils de Nunciata	personnage muet
Un coryphée	soprano

Parents, serviteurs des deux familles Piétra Néra et Fabiani

The action takes place in Corsica during the First Empire.

Orchestra: 3 flutes (incl. piccolo), 2 oboes, cor anglais, 2 clarinets, bass clarinet, 2 bassoons, 4 horns, 3 trumpets, 3 trombones, tuba, timpani, bass drum, cymbals, triangles, celesta, 2 harps, strings.

ACT I

Prélude A number of important themes are laid out in the Prelude, beginning with a calm one that represents the ancestress herself, Nunciata, whose venomous commitment to the vendetta is at the heart of the tragedy. Perhaps the unmoving bass note stands for her rigidity of purpose (ex. 14.1):

Example 14.1 *L'Ancêtre*, Act I, Prelude

Four solemn unconnected root-position triads will also recur, an idea that Britten put to marvellous effect in *A Midsummer Night's Dream*: A major in the strings, G major in the woodwind, E♭ minor in the trombones, then A major in the woodwind.

Next comes the violent music heard in Act II when Nunciata laments her dead grandson Léandri, ex. 14.2:

Example 14.2 *L'Ancêtre*, Act I, Prelude

Example 14.1 returns, then the key shifts to A major with music full of birdsong for the lifting of the curtain into the first scene.

Scene 1 The three acts are centred, roughly speaking, on three different individuals. The third act is Vanina's, the second is Nunciata's and the first belongs to the hermit Raphaël (baritone). He is on stage almost throughout and his gentle nature sets the tone. He can be fierce, as we shall see, but his love of humanity and his devotion to God are on a level with the love of his bees, which he is tending in the opening scene.

In the mountains of Corsica we see a rustic hermitage at sunrise with some beehives nearby. Beside the paths that lead into the mountains are two mortuary chapels, one inscribed FABIANI, the other PIETRA-NERA. Over a bed of gently murmuring strings and harp, Raphaël welcomes the sunrise and the morning lark with a suave cantilena. Then he turns to his bees and removes the hives' covers. Muted strings buzz merrily under a calm vocal line in praise of nature. The hermit is not afraid of being stung. Saint-Saëns had already orchestrated bees in the *Pas d'abeille* in Act I of *Le Timbre d'argent*, represented there by tremolo violas and here by three-part rapid staccato bowing – modest means for a big effect. Four solo cellos close his musings about the bees.

When Raphaël turns his thoughts to humans, the music takes on a darker tone. He would like to reconcile the Fabiani and the Piétra-Néra families but he knows that the old matriarch of the Fabiani, Nunciata, will not abandon her inveterate hatred. Example 14.1 is heard, followed by four root-position chords on clarinets and bassoons as he speaks of their 'ancient hatred'.

Scene 2 Tébaldo (tenor) comes running in. He is the only named member of the Piétra-Néra family in the opera and apart from his love for Margarita, foster-daughter of the Fabiani family, his heart is set on being a soldier and fighting for Napoleon, not on local hostilities. He is in uniform[15] and his music is military in character, hinting at the *Marseillaise*. Raphaël reminds him that he tended him as a child (a clever bass line illustrates the older man slowing his walking pace to that of the child) and that he owes a debt to God.

Scene 3 A group of people approach from the village and gather on the left of the stage. They are members of the Piétra-Néra family and their friends, called by Raphaël to talk about a truce. Over a mellifluous flow of semiquavers in the violas and cellos, Tébaldo greets them. The scene has the firmly diatonic flavour of a German folksong as set by Brahms, with a happy tune that the chorus take up with enthusiasm as they pay their respects to the old hermit, ex. 14.3. The theme serves as a motif of reconciliation.

Example 14.3 *L'Ancêtre*, Act I, Scene 3

Meanwhile a Fabiani group is approaching from the other side, including Vanina, Nunciata's granddaughter (contralto), Margarita, her foster-sister (soprano), and

[15] The libretto published in 1906 gives a few more details than the vocal score.

Bursica, their old servant (bass), who is carrying a rifle. In discreet asides Margarita and Tébaldo observe each other, and Vanina spots Tébaldo too. Over the chorus singing pianissimo, she and Margarita wonder which of them he prefers. The essential point is that Vanina is in love with Tébaldo too, a fact that the libretto fails to articulate clearly.

Raphaël blesses both families, hoping that this gathering will bring peace. Vanina laments the toll of death and firmly calls for an end to the vendetta, echoed by the chorus. Margarita adds her voice to the call, all supported by the opening bar of their happy tune. Tébaldo, with his usual dotted rhythms in support, renounces hatred too. The lone voice of objection is that of Bursica, the swineherd (and the trombones). He is proud of his reputation as a settler of accounts, owing allegiance only to Léandri, Vanina's brother and head of the Fabiani (the older males all being presumed dead), who has no taste for sermons.

The four solemn chords, in three different permutations, presage the arrival of Nunciata. As Bursica explains, she is half blind, but she can still spot an enemy when she sees one. She is led in by Léandri (a silent role), kneeling briefly as she passes the Fabiani mortuary chapel.

Scene 4 All make way for Nunciata, as ex. 14.1 is heard. Over the reconciliation theme ex. 14.3 Raphaël implores her to make an end to the killing and the grief. He launches into a solemn Adagio, backed by the chorus, 'Toi qui donnas ton fils', addressed more to the Almighty than to the ancestress. The first verse is thinly scored with the chorus responding 'Seigneur !' to each line of the hermit's prayer, while the second verse reverses the roles and adds some intensely chromatic accompaniment.

Nunciata is unmoved. In the faster ensemble that follows Raphaël, Vanina and Margarita lead the chorus in an impassioned and urgent plea. Silence follows. The violins quietly state the reconciliation theme ex. 14.3, and Raphaël once again, now gently, asks if she would vow to make peace and forget. A horrifying 'Non !' is the one word Nunciata utters in this act, following a vicious chord from the full orchestra.

Raphaël's rage now boils over. In a powerful C minor movement he pours on her the most bitter scorn his gentle nature is capable of:

> You who refused to pardon cannot expect pardon.
> Go back to the wolf in his lair! Go!
> Uncounted tears, my voice foretells,
> Will make your face burn and your eyes give out
> From the fires that your hatred has kindled!

An important new theme, ex. 14.4, emerges from this:

Example 14.4 *L'Ancêtre*, Act I, Scene 4

Va re-trou-ver le loup dans sa ta-niè-re

Led by Léandri and Vanina, Nunciata slowly moves off back to the village, while the chorus burst out in horror at the prospect of unending hostility and death. Much use is made of ex. 14.4. With an unpleasant threat, Bursica leaves too, and Raphaël goes into his hermitage.

Scene 5 When Margarita starts to go, Tébaldo holds her back. Their duet marries their smooth vocal cantilena to a feathery, skittish accompaniment, confirming that they are neither of them too troubled by the scene they have just witnessed. Nor is it a passionate duet. In alternating lines they recollect their childhood together. Margarita mentions her jealousy of Vanina, so Tébaldo has to assure her that his heart has never been shared. She then regrets that she is obliged to hate him because of their families' feud, which Tébaldo dismisses as unimportant. Eventually their voices come together with tender parting words. The music is perfect for innocent young lovers, and, as always, Saint-Saëns produces a perfectly crafted and balanced structure.

Scene 6 Knowing she is expected back, Margarita leaves. Example 14.4 on a bassoon, then bass clarinet, brings Raphaël out of his hermitage with a warning to Tébaldo to take care. Tébaldo is not inclined to take notice, so Raphaël has to call in a trumpet and some trombones to press home the danger that lurks. But Tébaldo is a soldier; he's sure he can defend himself. He strides confidently off.

Scene 7 As at the start of the act, Raphaël is once more alone, musing on the wickedness of men. The bees begin to buzz. What wonderful work they do, renewing nature. But now it's time to sleep, so he replaces their covers.

ACT II

Scene 1 A loud, swift introduction picks up ex. 14.4 and, after a climax, subsides for the quiet chords that mark the rise of the curtain. The scene is the courtyard of a simple but large house, with a carriage gateway and countryside beyond. Vanina comes out of the house since her grandmother is asleep, untroubled by the hermit's harsh words. She, on the other hand, is deeply troubled, and the intricate writing for the orchestra in her solo scene reflects the tensions and unease in her heart. She loves Tébaldo and knows that he could one day be the target of her family's vengeance. The words of this scene were written by Saint-Saëns himself, as we know from a letter to his publisher: 'I have been wrestling with a recalcitrant recitative. I managed it only by rewriting the text completely, which slowed me down. My collaborator tends to give his characters a mass of useless things to say which

Figure 14.1 *L'Ancêtre*, Act II, set by Albert Dubosq, Antwerp 1912
FelixArchief/Stadsarchief, Antwerp

do not tell the listener what he needs to know. I cannot follow him along that route.'[16]

A plain fugue begins softly in the strings. As Vanina wonders why Léandri is late coming home she hears chanting in the distance, a nine-note sequence repeated many times, ex. 14.5:

Example 14.5 *L'Ancêtre*, Act II, Scene 1

---

[16] Letter of 15 July 1905, RATNER 2012, p. 296.

She is already in a state of dread before she hears the words of the chorus, still out of sight: 'Holy Virgin Mary, receive the Christian who has departed.' The procession comes into view, lit by torches. On a litter made of branches they are carrying a body which they lay down in the middle of the stage. Unable at first to see who it is, Vanina is appalled when she finds it is her brother Léandri; she collapses on a bench.

Scene 2 The nine-note lamentation of ex. 14.5 continues on the same notes wherever the music wanders, and now for the entrance of Nunciata out of the house a good deal of chromatic intensity is needed. She, too, wants to know who has been brought in, and she cannot quite believe it is her grandson. Yet she is used to such sights and is firmly in control in her denunciation of her family's enemies. She silences the mourning and orders everyone to stand.

She has something to say and a great monologue in which to say it. Determination and rage both overflow from the music that supports her first declaration (ex. 14.2). With great shouts the chorus echo her assertion that Léandri was a man of honour and rectitude. The sinister series of four slow chords follows Nunciata throughout, and now she recites a eulogy/lament almost bare of accompaniment, and briefly revealing a tender side of her heart. Four more slow chords turn the page to the savage side as string tremolos and double-dotted rhythms (as in ex. 14.2) support her call for a worthy burial and, inevitably, vengeance. 'Guerre aux Piétra-Néras !' she cries, chillingly echoed by the full chorus at full volume.

The rest of the scene moves swiftly in 3/4 time[17] with the chorus closely echoing the ancestress's stream of hatred. It is modal, with a consistent B♭ in the key of D major. The singer is faced with the tricky task of maintaining the brisk tempo while seeming to be old and infirm, for when she turns to Vanina to charge her with the duty of taking the next life, she pleads that but for her poor eyesight and trembling hands she would do it herself. Vanina is horrified, being forced to swear publicly that she will do it. As Nunciata and the chorus leave, first ex. 14.2 is heard, then, twice more, the nine-note lament, ex. 14.5.

Scene 3 Vanina is confronted by Bursica, who enters with his characteristic motif in the cellos and basses. Until now no mention has been made of who might be responsible for killing Léandri. It is simply assumed to be one of the Piétra-Néra. But Bursica knows: it was Tébaldo.

---

[17] In the full score *Molto allegro* is modified with *(non presto)*.

ACT III

Introduction The introduction is calm and quiet. Then the music picks up the duet for Margarita and Tébaldo from Scene 5 of Act I, with clarinet and bassoon taking the vocal melody for the most part.

Scene 1 With the music playing, the curtain rises on an outdoor scene in the mountains. On the left is a fountain with a stone bench and at the back is a small chapel. The sea is visible in the distance. Margarita wanders on humming the melody of the duet, and she continues vocalising without words until the end, with a little more elaboration than when she sang it with Tébaldo, and then wanders off stage. Augé de Lassus wrote words for Margarita in this scene, but Saint-Saëns decided that it was much more 'eloquent and original' without them.[18]

Scene 2 A group of women go up to the fountain carrying pails. They chatter happily among themselves while the violins suggest the continuous ripple of water (or perhaps of chatter). One of them asks another what she thinks of the latest news, that Léandri is dead. Such a shame, they say, such a handsome boy! Raphaël the hermit comes in and tells them rather mysteriously that the field where happiness grows is marked out in narrow furrows. The women are not amused and skittishly run away rather than listen to his disturbing thoughts.

Scene 3 So much delicate, graceful music serves as a foil to the cloud that will darken the action. Tébaldo comes in to face a rebuke from Raphaël who has heard about the murder of Léandri. 'Thou shalt not kill' he reminds him. Tébaldo explains that he was lured into a trap: Léandri treacherously seized him, and Tébaldo fired in self-defence. Raphaël is ready to help Tébaldo escape, stressing urgency. Tébaldo, ever dreamy, will not think of leaving without his beloved Margarita. Raphaël is willing to help them since she can no longer expect happiness in the Fabiani family. Conveniently, she appears at that moment.

Scene 4 The scene is a trio in A major which gives each voice a few separate lines (for audibility's sake) before combining them in pairs and as a trio. An operatic convention requires fugitives to sing awhile before taking flight, usually with more urgency than we encounter here. The pace is steady (Andantino con moto) and the melody sweet, returning a couple of times like a rondo. Only in the second episode does Raphaël begin to press the lovers to stop dreaming of a happy future and to speed away to find it. The second return of the rondo, with all three singing, is in fact faster than before, but it returns to a leisurely pace and an unhurried mood to allow the lovers to leave, with Raphaël following at a distance.

Saint-Saëns's correspondence shows that he intended the three of them at the end of their trio to enter the chapel where Raphaël would marry them. This makes sense if

---

[18] Letter to Augé de Lassus, 1 August 1905, RATNER 2012, p. 297.

they then encounter Nunciata and Vanina on emerging. But the authors wanted the lovers to call out each other's name as a way of confirming for Vanina that Tébaldo was in love with Margarita. The return of the lovers is then unexplained, when Raphaël has urged them to get far away.

Scene 5 Example 14.6 coupled with the first phrase of ex. 14.2 sets the atmosphere for Vanina's entrance in understandable distress.

Example 14.6 *L'Ancêtre*, Act II, Scene 5

She has managed to put off for a week carrying out her vengeful orders (which means that Tébaldo and Margarita have delayed their flight for a week too). She too contemplates flight. But she is being pursued once again by Bursica, who is carrying a rifle. She should not be out alone unarmed, he tells her. Take mine! Disingenuously she asks what she would do with it, and equally disingenuously he says he, a mere swineherd, is not allowed to kill above his rank. He leaves.

Scene 6 The third phrase of ex. 14.2, with its associations with her grandmother, is heard as Vanina confronts the hideous duty of killing Tébaldo, whom she loves. A tender Adagio in E♭ supports her longing for the chance of happiness one day. In the distance can be heard Tébaldo calling Margarita's name. The first time is too distant, but the second time Vanina catches the name clearly, and Margarita calling out to Tébaldo confirms her worst fear: that Tébaldo loves Margarita. A strong burst of rage over ex. 14.2 and ex. 14.6 gives her the strength to pick up the gun, at which moment Nunciata appears, delighted to see Vanina ready for action.

Tébaldo and Margarita approach the chapel. Perhaps Raphaël had advised this. The sanctuary created by the proximity of the Lord's house allows for a very beautiful quartet in which Margarita and Tébaldo reprise their duet from Act I with a new accompaniment, unaware that they are being watched. As the quartet closes, the lovers move away from the chapel in the direction of Vanina and Nunciata. They pass unharmed out of sight.

Furious, Nunciata orders Vanina to shoot, but she cannot do it: she drops the gun and admits she loves him. Even more enraged, Nunciata heaps curses on her, picks up the gun herself and strides after Tébaldo. Vanina runs after her in despair.

Scene 7 Bursica comes in, thinking Tébaldo must have escaped, when a shot is heard. Nunciata returns. 'When your sight is poor, you rely on chance' she says, sending Bursica off to check. She moves away and is gone before Bursica runs into Vanina, wounded and staggering. She is happy, she says, and a few bars of her E♭ Adagio in Scene 6 tells us why: she is happy for Tébaldo. Her dying words are: 'Thinking she was killing Tébaldo, grandmother killed me.' The closing bars recall the final bars of Act I depicting the calm of nature.

The original idea was for Bursica to leave Vanina dying and go after Nunciata, which Saint-Saëns suppressed, preferring to have Nunciata still in sight in the distance for a long time, while Bursica remains with Vanina.

Nunciata hit the wrong target by mistake, we should not doubt that. But did Vanina deliberately intercept the bullet? Her last words before rushing out after Nunciata were 'No! It should be I who die!' (or, as given in the printed libretto, 'I alone must die'). Vanina is yet one more operatic heroine who dies to save someone she loves.

* * * * *

There are moments in *L'Ancêtre* when a composer with a stronger record in *verismo* than Saint-Saëns is required, for the eternal refinement of his music jars with the raw *mores* of Corsican peasants. His orchestration never screams, and his dissonances are sophisticated, not brutal. On the other hand, refinement and sophistication are unmistakable virtues in all his music, no less in *L'Ancêtre* than elsewhere, and the depiction of hard-bitten bigotry in Nunciata is powerful, especially in Act II. Such characterisation is a great challenge for a singer, which Saint-Saëns knew when he insisted on having Litvinne cast for the role. Bursica is a one-dimensional peasant. Tébaldo is a dreamy young man whose thoughts are divided between his love for Margarita and his ambition to fight for Napoleon; he never grasps the implications of being a Piétra-Néra and at the same time loving Margarita, and Margarita herself is innocent of the feud by virtue of being a foster-child and is content simply to love Tébaldo.

Vanina is the character that suffers from internal conflict, since she is fully aware of her family obligations. Here, surely, Augé de Lassus and Saint-Saëns underestimated the role, for they could have done much more to portray her conflicting feelings. She does not even have any distinct themes. Her brother, the head of the family, is killed; the man whom she loves belongs to the hated enemy family; furthermore he is in love with someone else; it falls to her to carry out the vendetta by killing the man whom she loves but whom she knows she can never have. It would surely have justified a much longer solo scene for her at the beginning of Act II, and again an extended scene of agonising self-analysis in the last act when she can no longer put off her obligation as executioner. Saint-Saëns did in fact urge Augé de Lassus to write 'a real *air*' for Vanina in Scene 5,[19] but the score as we have it cannot be so described. Saint-Saëns had shown that he could do great things with the contralto voice, in Anne Boleyn and Scozzone for example, and Vanina could have been the finest of these if he had considered her the central character. As it is, the ancestress herself takes centre stage and the title role, and when well sung and acted she would certainly leave a powerful impression.

There is no local colour in the score, no folk dancing and no 'amusing' village types. Raphaël as the old hermit is a marvellous character, railing against the vendetta, but unable to do anything about it; no wonder he finds solace in the beauty of nature and lovingly tends his bees. The chorus have a good part, with a real winner in the 'reconciliation chorus' in Act I. They blow with the wind, siding with Nunciata in Act II when she stirs them up to fury. They can only be penitents in Act III.

Bursica always has his own signature music, but motifs are not otherwise systematically employed. Example 14.5, first heard in the Prelude, is put to use in many ways when Nunciata's insistence on vengeance is the issue. The theme of vendetta may be dark, but the opera would be impossible if the music were not relieved by tenderness and warmth. The 'reconciliation chorus' in Act I, the duet for Tébaldo and Margarita in Act I and the quartet in Act III are excellent examples of numbers that lift the tone of the opera and prevent the drama from enslaving the music.

Saint-Saëns was right to wonder if *L'Ancêtre* would have a future after Monte Carlo, since it is not a big enough work (about eighty-seven minutes of music) for a big house and is an awkward fit on a double bill. In fact it was played in a variety of cities during the composer's lifetime. After the five performances in Monte Carlo, it was next played early in 1907 in Toulouse. A German translation by R. Batka was inserted in the vocal score, which enabled it to be played in Prague in German in April 1908. In July 1909 it was played in Aix-les-Bains, and in early 1911 it was played thirteen times in Paris, at the Opéra-Comique, the antagonism that formerly existed between Saint-Saëns and the theatre's director Albert Carré having been put behind them. There were evidently performances in Nantes, Geneva and perhaps other cities too.

Overseas performances began in February 1911 in Algiers and in February 1912 in Cairo. Montreal performed it in the spring of 1912, and in November 1912 Saint-Saëns went to Antwerp to see a staging there of *L'Ancêtre* coupled with Debussy's *L'Enfant prodigue*. Albert Dubosq designed new sets, which have survived to this day. The last performances were two revivals in Monte Carlo in March 1915. This is definitely a record of international success, yet since that date over a hundred years passed without a single performance, a silence that ended in March 2019 when the opera was staged in Munich by the Theaterakademie August Everding with support from Palazzetto Bru Zane.

*****

---

[19] Letter of 21 July 1905, RATNER 2012, p. 297.

The chronicle of Saint-Saëns's travels in 1906 following his weeks in Monte Carlo with *L'Ancêtre* is as extensive as ever, with the spring spent in Italy, Spain and Portugal, followed by concerts in London, Berlin and Salzburg, revivals of his operas in Bordeaux (*Henry VIII*) and Dieppe (*La Princesse jaune*), the summer festival in Béziers, culminating in his first trip to North America (New York, Philadelphia, Washington and Chicago). In America he was seriously ill with diphtheria, but he managed to complete the tour. The illness left him with a permanently damaged soft palate, which may account for his speaking voice being remembered by Jacques Vidal as like the quack of a duck.[20]

The principal compositions of the year were the cantata *La Gloire de Corneille* and a *Fantaisie* for mechanical organ written in London for an organ that worked on the same principle as the pianola. The Corneille cantata set a new poem by Sébastien-Charles Leconte as well as passages from Corneille's plays for a variety of voices and orchestra, and was commissioned by *Le Journal* to celebrate the 300th anniversary of the dramatist's birth. Saint-Saëns incorporated part of his *Scène d'Horace*, composed over forty years earlier. It was performed at the Opéra in June 1906 and in part in a 'concert monstre' given in honour of the composer's seventieth birthday (eleven months late) on September 2nd in Béziers.

After a week or two in Egypt, he was back in Monte Carlo in February 1907 to assist with a revival not of *L'Ancêtre* but of *Le Timbre d'argent*, in the version he had worked out in 1903 in expectation of a revival at the Opéra-Comique that did not happen. Marguerite Carré, wife of the Opéra-Comique's director, sang Hélène and Maggie Teyte (aged eighteen) was Rosa. He had to accept the omission of an act. He then accompanied the Monte Carlo company on a visit to Berlin on the invitation of the Kaiser. The Prince had suggested taking *Le Timbre d'argent*, but the first act of *Samson et Dalila* was done instead. Massenet was a fellow-guest with part of *Hérodiade*, and so was Grieg. He heard Strauss's *Salome*, with considerable disapproval of the subject but great admiration for Strauss's 'prodigious talent' and real astonishment at the orchestration.

The dancing role of Circé/Fiametta in *Le Timbre d'argent* was played in Monte Carlo by Carlotta Zambelli, prima ballerina at the Opéra (later to dance the title role in *Javotte* there), and the dancing master was played by Mathilde Salle, also from the Opéra. These two dancers invited Saint-Saëns to compose a ballet for them to be staged in Monte Carlo the following season, 1908, so he sketched out on the spot 'an amusing scenario' for two dancers entitled *Pierrot astronome*. His knowledge of astronomy was clearly to be put to a purpose. Since his health was still far from restored, he asked his former pupil Philippe Bellenot, choirmaster at St-Sulpice for over fifty years and a competent composer, to do the orchestration.

In fact no music was ever even sketched. Bonnerot says that Saint-Saëns took the scenario with him on all his travels until finally giving up any intention of composing it in

---

[20] Information passed to the author by David Cairns.

1920. Meanwhile it featured regularly in his correspondence between 1913 and 1915.[21] He promised it to Rachet (perhaps an impresario or dancer) for the summer of 1914, but evidently did not keep the promise. In June 1914 he agreed to compose it for the Opéra-Comique, telling Bellenot that he was now fit enough to do the orchestration himself. Once war was declared, however, he felt unable to embark on the ballet, even when Gunsbourg suggested staging it in his 1916 season. No trace of scenario or music of *Pierrot astronome* has ever been found.

Meanwhile he was already in discussion with the playwright Eugène Brieux about composing incidental music for a five-act play entitled *La Foi* ('Faith'). Brieux (1858–1932) was a productive and successful writer whose plays generally attacked social injustice or political corruption. George Bernard Shaw described him as 'incomparably the greatest writer France has produced since Molière'. As it happened, the proposal to compose music for a drama set in the Egypt of the Pharaohs reached Saint-Saëns while he was in Cairo in January 1907. Saint-Saëns's love of Egypt and of the ancient world was evidently already known to Brieux, so he needed little persuasion to accept. He was already planning to recreate an ancient musical idiom, as he had in *Antigone* and *Parysatis*.

The play was intended for the Odéon, where the director André Antoine, celebrated for his advocacy of naturalistic acting, would be in charge. By March 1907 it was Sarah Bernhardt's theatre where it was to be staged, which meant that Saint-Saëns could only compose for a small backstage orchestra, the orchestra pit being out of use. Saint-Saëns could already envisage a second version as a grand opera which could be played at the Opéra when *Aida* was not in the repertoire. 'No one can predict the future,' he rather fatuously added.[22] He was also consulting the Egyptologist Victor Loret, who had discovered a series of tombs in the Valley of the Kings.

Brieux did not deliver the text of the play until December 1907, by which time new negotiations had begun with Gabriel Astruc, one of the most prominent impresarios of the time. Astruc was already planning to build a new theatre (eventually the Théâtre des Champs-Élysées, opened in 1913) and would provisionally accept the play for performance there. But without a guarantee of performance, Saint-Saëns was not prepared to compose the score. In fact he had already begun to sketch it, having settled in Luxor for the month specifically to do so in the inspiring environment of many ancient ruins. He befriended Georges Legrain, the French Egyptologist who was in charge of rebuilding the eleven massive columns of the temple at Karnak, just outside Luxor, which had collapsed in 1899. In 1903 Legrain discovered nearly 800 stone statues there. He lent Saint-Saëns some ancient documents, 'forty centuries old', from which Saint-Saëns claimed to have 'refreshed his stock of oriental motifs'. What this means is unclear, since our knowledge of Egyptian music is derived solely from literary sources and from images of instruments; there is no hint of musical notation.

---

[21] BONNEROT 1922, p. 185; RATNER 2012, p. 369.
[22] Letter of 26 March 1907 to Jacques Durand; RATNER 2012, p. 435. What we know about the history of *La Foi* is almost entirely found in the letters printed in RATNER 2012, pp. 434–40.

By 10 January 1908 he had sketched the music for two acts, having moved back to Mohammed Ali's villa in Cairo. *Henry VIII* was being revived at the opera house there. By March, when he left Egypt for Monte Carlo for the revival there of *Henry VIII*, with Litvinne singing Catherine, the draft of four of the five acts of *La Foi* was done. There was still no theatre to stage it, but he continued, partly out of respect for Brieux, whom he liked. Perhaps, he thought, some extracts could be salvaged as concert music, since (he told Durand) 'it's ravishing'. The fifth act was drafted in Béziers in April, but he was not prepared to start the orchestration until the play had a definite future.

Rescue came in July 1908 from the Comtesse Greffuhle, the elegant wife of a wealthy Belgian banker, who devoted herself to promoting musical events in Paris, often in partnership with Astruc. She was a regular visitor to Monte Carlo and had arranged for some of their productions to be brought to Paris, including Gunsbourg's famous staging of Berlioz's *La Damnation de Faust*. She persuaded the Prince to accept a production of *La Foi* as an addendum to the opera season of 1909. With this plan in place, Saint-Saëns withdrew to his summer refuges, Pallanza on Lake Maggiore and Mont Revard near Aix-les-Bains, to do the orchestration. This was ready by the end of August.

Heading for his winter quarters, this year in Las Palmas, he oversaw yet another revival of *Henry VIII*, this time in Toulouse, then a revival of *Les Barbares* in Barcelona. He returned to Monte Carlo in the new year, 1909, but whether he was in time to see the one performance of *Hélène* on February 13th is unclear. That would have been too soon for rehearsals of *La Foi*, which opened on April 10th, with two more performances on the two following days. The actors, mostly drawn from the Odéon, included Véra Sergine, the painter Renoir's daughter-in-law, as Miéris, and the single dancer named in the cast (although none of the music is specificied for dancing) was Natalia Troukhanova, who had recently (May 1907) stood in for Emmy Destinn in Strauss's *Salome* in Paris dancing the Dance of the Seven Veils.

* * * * *

La Foi
(Ratner 321)

Play in five acts
by
Eugène Brieux

Incidental music

First performance: Théâtre de Monte-Carlo, 10 April 1909

Orchestra: 3 flutes (incl. piccolo), 2 oboes, cor anglais, 2 clarinets, 2 bassoons, 4 horns, 3 trumpets, 3 trombones, timpani, petites timbales, bass drum, cymbals, triangles, crotales, sistres, castanets, pitched gong, sacred bells, celesta, 2 harps, harmonium, strings.

Brieux's play supposes that the people of ancient Egypt during the Middle Kingdom are thrown into disarray by an individual who questions the authority of their gods. Every year, in order to ensure that the Nile inundates its flood plain to provide a harvest, a virgin is selected and sacrificed to the river. Yaouma, the young girl who has been selected, is engaged to a young man Sitna, who has spent two years travelling and has learned that other peoples have different gods. He is convinced that the gods are merely an invention of the priesthood, used by the Pharaohs to keep order and suppress the people. When a couple of apparent miracles happen, the people assume that he has divine power, but he is firm in his atheism and in his belief that morality grows out of the common interest, not from divine instruction. Saint-Saëns would surely have identified with Sitna, whose name perhaps implies a saint (or even a Saint-).[23] He is bitterly opposed by many but supported by a few enlightened souls. He is convinced that the Nile will flood every year of its own accord, and he is determined to demonstrate that the nodding head of the goddess Isis is contrived by machinery, not by divine magic. Such a scenario would be topical in any age, as Brieux intended, but the play ends not with the triumph of liberal thought but with Sitna's death at the hands of the enraged populace and with Yaouma's sacrifice to the Nile.

Each of the five acts has a prelude and innumerable short pieces of music at specific moments in the action, often with speech over music. The two principal musical sources, an autograph full score and a printed piano reduction with cues, do not exactly match either with each other or with the printed play, which is evidence that cuts or additions were made in rehearsal, especially when a long passage of speech had to be spoken over music, reaching a close or a particular moment simultaneously. Revisions were made for the London production and for the 1912 revival of the play in Paris.

Saint-Saëns was attracted to the idea of recreating Egyptian music, for which purpose he calls for a number of ethnic instruments: large and small drums, a gong, sacred bells and sistra played on stage. The harp, known to be of Egyptian origin, is naturally prominent. Saint-Saëns used what he believed to be authentic Egyptian modes, as he explained in a letter to the *Revue musicale* in 1909: 'If I used these three scales [shown as ex. 14.7] it was not simply to escape the tyranny of major and minor scales and give a vaguely oriental colour. These scales are authentic Egyptian scales.'[24]

---

[23] In a letter to Eugène Gigout of 27 April 1909 he wrote: 'In this Egyptian drama there is a reflection of my most profound convictions and of my most personal thoughts.' RATNER 2012, p. 438.

[24] *Revue musicale*, 15 November 1909; SORET 2012, p. 662.

Example 14.7 *La Foi*, scales

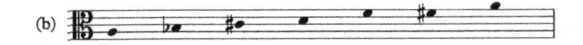

(a)

(b)

(c)

The music heard as the curtain rises, for example, is entirely built on mode (a), which includes two augmented seconds. The harp plays throughout that scene. Later in Act I Sitna's father, Pakh, intones a prayer to Ammon to protect his wife, who is fetching water from the Nile, from a crocodile he has spotted. Supported by a cor anglais and tremolo violins, he sings entirely on the notes B♭-C-D-E-F♯-G, close to mode (c), with its hints of the whole-tone scale. The exact mode (c) is used for Act I, Scene 5 in a passage not found in the autograph, probably a late addition. This is immediately followed by a rising bass on mode (b).

The Prelude to Act III calls for 'petites timbales' playing tuned pitches an octave above the normal timpani. Their two-bar rhythmic pattern is repeated throughout while the two harps have a one-bar figure repeated throughout. A solo oboe has an inflected melody of distinctly Middle Eastern flavour, recalling the *Bacchanale* from *Samson et Dalila*. Saint-Saëns doubtless knew that he could hardly write the entire score in a pseudo-Egyptian idiom, so in other movements he combines ethnic percussion and harps with normal orchestral instruments, and a great number of movements have no ethnic or Egyptian elements at all. The approach is parallel to Massenet's adoption of eighteenth-century idioms in *Manon*, casting into relief those passages in the modern style which carry a strong emotional charge.

As an example of the mixed idiom, there is in Act I of *La Foi* a scene containing a general prayer to Isis to name the chosen virgin. This is a diatonic movement in D major which flows gently over harp arpeggios while the 'petites timbales' alternate bar by bar with crotales, and the sistra shake during alternate bars. A scene in Act III, similarly addressed to Isis, is in a solid diatonic B major with plenty of harp and solemn strokes every bar on a bass drum and a 'gong musical' tuned to F♯. A harmonium sustains the harmony. The printed score has E♯ throughout where the autograph has E♮, a change perhaps made in a desire to give the movement a hypolydian modal colour.

A curious movement is the lament for the death of Pakh in Act III, Scene 7, in effect a passacaglia on a strongly modal theme centred on C♯, ex. 14.8:

Example 14.8 *La Foi*, Act III, Scene 7

No exotic instruments are involved, but the tune and some of the nine iterations it undergoes are harmonised in unorthodox ways.[25] Saint-Saëns writes unusual and surprising harmonies throughout, acting as counterparts to Brieux's rich vocabulary in describing objects of Egyptian culture and devising pseudo-Egyptian names for all the characters.

With the play being performed in the Monte Carlo opera house, there was room for a full orchestra. In the autograph full score Saint-Saëns indicates that the orchestra should play 'sur le théâtre' until Act IV, but it is hard to imagine that up to fifty musicians were playing backstage for those longer movements that require full instrumentation. One such is the imprecation to Isis in Act I, already mentioned, which builds up to a strong diminished seventh when Yaouma's name is called. The final music of the first act is also a strong piece for full orchestra, as Sitna tries to lure Yaouma away from her determined role as sacrificial victim.

The most elaborate music covers the entire Scene 7 in Act IV when the High Priest announces that the Holy of Holies in the Temple will be opened. Its motif is a heavy descending phrase for brass, ex. 14.9:

Example 14.9 *La Foi*, Act IV, Scene 7

He orders the people to pray for the poor and needy, which they do over the ravishing sound of murmuring strings and soft brass chords in A♭ minor. They pray ever more ardently to Isis to nod her head as a sign that the goddess is listening, as the orchestral intensity rises too. Sitna, who has been entrusted with the lever that nods the

---

[25] The autograph has eleven iterations, not nine. The movement was probably adjusted to fit the stage action.

head and is determined not to use it, finally gives way to the clamour and lowers the lever (ex. 14.9 *tutta forza*). The head nods and the people rejoice wildly. Sitna knows that his plan to persuade the people that the gods are false has failed.

Certain characters and concepts have recurrent motifs. Yaouma, for example, the young girl who rejoices to have been chosen for the ritual sacrifice to the Nile, is represented by ex. 14.10 scored for three solo strings:

Example 14.10 *La Foi*, Act I, Scene 1

An older woman, Miéris, is blind, and although she shares Sitna's lack of faith in the gods, she is convinced he should be able to restore her sight. In its warm form, she is represented by ex. 14.11 on a solo cello:

Example 14.11 *La Foi*, Act I, Scene 4

But at her first appearance this theme is heard in the minor mode on the oboe with agonising harmonies from two clarinets. Other themes recur from time to time.

* * * * *

It is hard to evaluate the impact this music has on the effectiveness of the play, not only because it is unlikely to be heard in that context, but also because the performance of orchestral music during spoken theatre, being one of the few applications of classical music that resolutely refuses to be revived, is impossible to judge today with any confidence. *La Foi*, though, is of considerable interest as part of Saint-Saëns's persistent attempt to reproduce, or at least to evoke, the music of the ancient world. Conservative though he was in his respect for the fundamentals of music, he felt, like most composers of the time, that the arrival of a new century needed the injection of new ideas. He could never accept either the idea of total chromaticism or the notion that chords have independence, free of functional pressure, but he was much more sympathetic to the Europe-wide interest in folksong which the Russians and Czechs had shown to be fruitful and which was cultivated with success in Scandinavia and England. With his pride in all things French, he might have pursued the study of French folksong, but in fact he was more original than that by treating ancient music as a possible source for contemporary music. In *La Foi* he finally came up against the problem of not having any original Egyptian music as a model, and even his recreations of Greek music in *Antigone* and Persian music in *Parysatis* rested on flimsy examples, or at least on imperfect scholarship. It was in that sense a vain quest. Like many modernisms of the time, it was destined to lead to nowhere in particular.

After the three very successful performances of *La Foi* in Monte Carlo in 1909, it was taken up by Sir Herbert Beerbohm Tree, manager of His Majesty's Theatre in London, and staged there in September 1909. Under the title *False Gods* and translated by J. F. Fagan, it received no less than sixty-two performances. At first Saint-Saëns was led to believe that there would be no, or almost no, music, but Sir Herbert was persuaded to allow an orchestra of fifty musicians. The next problem was that Brieux wanted to change the order of certain scenes. Being in London a month earlier, Saint-Saëns engaged his former pupil Benoit Hollander to take charge of the music and to deal with all such problems on his behalf. He was there to see it himself in October 1909, reporting to his publisher that he did not recognise the music and in lots of places did not recognise the play either. 'But what survived of the music seemed to me to be of rare quality.'[26]

The next performances were at the Théâtre de l'Odéon in Paris in May 1912, where the director was André Antoine, the director whom Brieux wanted from the beginning. Brieux made a few more adjustments and restorations, to Saint-Saëns's exasperation, since the piano score had to be held back before publication. Véra Sergine was the only member of the cast from the Monte Carlo production. Nine performances were given. Negotiations to mount the play in New York broke down.

Saint-Saëns salvaged the music for *La Foi* by fashioning three movements from the music for Acts I, III and IV, and having them published and performed as *Trois Tableaux symphoniques*. In this form he was able to restore some of the music that had been cut in the theatre. The suite offers the only available avenue to capturing the tone and flavour of *La Foi*, with its occasional touches of exoticism. Happily it has twice been recorded: by Ronald Zollman and the Basel Symphony Orchestra in 1994; and by Michel Plasson and the Orchestre National du Capitole de Toulouse in 1995, both recordings giving us a vivid hint at how substantial and how powerful this music must have seemed in the theatre.

---

[26] Letter of 21 October 1909, RATNER 2012, p. 439.

15 | L'Assassinat du Duc de Guise, Déjanire (opera), On ne badine pas avec l'amour

Many features of Saint-Saëns's music for the play La Foi resemble the intermittent technique of film music, especially when an isolated handful of bars is heard in support of an episode or entry to heighten the action. So it was a happy accident that the next dramatic music he wrote was indeed the music for a film, L'Assassinat du Duc de Guise.[1] Although planned and written after the music for La Foi, the film was first shown some five months before the first performance of the play.

No other composer of Saint-Saëns's generation wrote music for the cinema, and even composers of the next two generations, such as Strauss and Elgar, even Stravinsky, contributed little or nothing to this art form. Not until the late 1920s were scores composed for specific films, since it was normal practice in the silent era for cinema orchestras to play from a repertoire of extracts as background to standard scenes such as a fight or a chase or a love scene. Unless they improvised action music themselves, pianists and organists used the same resource. This underlines the extraordinary openness of Saint-Saëns in taking on a task for which there were no precedents, dependent on a rapidly developing technology, and likely to expose him to ridicule in the press. It is said that the American composer Nathaniel D. Mann's score for the film The Fairylogue and Radio-Plays, which mixed film and stage acting, was written four months earlier in the summer of 1908, but nevertheless the singularity of Saint-Saëns's contribution to the history of film music is by any standards remarkable. It has deservedly been given special attention by historians of the French cinema.[2]

Saint-Saëns himself left no record of how this unusual commission came about. The invention of the cinema is generally attributed to the Lumière brothers in about 1895, and at first films could do little more than show short comic or action scenes. The function of music was largely to cover the noise of the projection equipment and to discourage chatter by the audience. In 1907 a production company, Le Film d'Art, was formed in Paris by Paul Lafitte and others in order to attempt something more elevated and dramatic. Their plan was to involve experienced actors, directors and composers, sensing, rightly as it turned out, that the cinema had a future as a serious art form. They were evidently introduced to Saint-Saëns by his pupil Fernand Leborne, a minor composer, who signed the contract on his behalf and received the dedication of the score. L'Assassinat du Duc de Guise was the studio's first venture and a turning-point

---

[1] The film can be seen with its accompanying music on YouTube and other sites.
[2] See MARKS 2012.

in the history of the cinema. Henri Lavedan, a successful playwright and member of the Académie Française, wrote the scenario for the film, which was directed by André Calmettes and Charles Le Bargy. The latter played the part of King Henry III and the remaining actors were drawn from the Comédie-Française.

Unlike the standard procedure in later film-making, it appears that Saint-Saëns completed the score on 8 October 1908 before filming, shot in a studio in Neuilly, near Paris, was done. After that date there was still some doubt as to whether there would be a fifth tableau or not, causing Saint-Saëns to grumble that 'these people' keep changing their minds. It is remarkable in the circumstances that the score and the film, which lasts about nineteen minutes, are so well synchronised. We have to imagine that Saint-Saëns conducted his players while watching the film, adjusting tempos and pauses to keep in line with the film's action, a skill that later film composers found difficult even after years of experience.

The music was scored for twelve players (flute, oboe, clarinet, bassoon, horn, five strings, piano and harmonium) since space in the Salle Charras, where the film was to be shown, was limited. The first showing was on 18 November 1908, with a preview the day before.[3] If Saint-Saëns was in charge that day, he left immediately afterwards, being in Toulouse by the 21st. The film was acclaimed by the press but not shown many times. It was released in the United States without any specification of Saint-Saëns's music, and it was re-released in France a few years later, but Saint-Saëns was vague about whether his music was played and whether any royalties were due. On 4 August 1909 he wrote to Leborne: 'It was you who signed the contract and it is only you who can force Pathé to pay what they will owe in future. I have signed nothing and can only pursue them through you.'[4] In 1913 he had an enquiry from Brussels about how to synchronise the music, and in 1915 he wrote, 'I see from my royalties that my music is a presence in cinemas, which have become a boon for me.'[5] This may be a reference to the growing use of his instrumental music, such as the *Danse macabre*, to accompany silent films, yet it suggests equally that *L'Assassinat du Duc de Guise* and its original music were not quickly forgotten.

* * * * *

Henry III, last of the Valois kings, ruled France from 1574 to 1589. The end of his reign was overshadowed by the 'War of the Three Henrys', the other two being Henry of Navarre, a Protestant, and Henry, Duc de Guise, head of the Catholic League. The king feared the Duc de Guise as a rival for the throne, worried that he would claim it as a direct descendant of Charlemagne. The city of Paris supported the Duc, while the King fled to Chartres. In December 1588 the King summoned the Duc to Blois. Guise

---

[3] Bonnerot gives the 16th for the premiere, Ratner the 17th; see RATNER 2012, p. 468.
[4] RATNER 2012, p. 469. [5] Letters of 16 July 1913 and 8 October 1915; RATNER 2012, p. 469.

> **L'Assassinat du Duc de Guise**
> (Ratner 331)
>
> Film in five tableaux
>
> Scenario by Henri Lavedan
>
> Directed by André Calmettes and Charles Le Bargy
>
> First showing: Salle Charras, Paris, 18 November 1908
>
> Orchestra: flute, oboe, clarinet, bassoon, horn, five strings, piano, harmonium.

was warned that the King was not to be trusted, but he replied that Henry would not dare try anything. He spent the night with his mistress, the Marquise de Noirmoutiers (who had been the mistress of Henry of Navarre) and next morning, December 23rd, as he waited to be admitted to the King's chambers, royal guards stabbed him to death.

These events are succinctly retold in *L'Assassinat du Duc de Guise* over continuous music divided into an Introduction and five tableaux. The characters and the action have well-matched music, as, for example, in the Introduction when low-pitched rumblings vividly suggest dark conspiracy, with a strong clarinet theme to stand for the assassination and another in the strings, while the credits are shown. The first tableau shows the Marquise de Noirmoutiers in a skittish mood as she enters from her bedroom and lights some candles. A page enters and delivers a message (shown on an intertitle) warning the Marquise not to let the Duc attend the Council since the King was plotting 'un mauvais tour'. When the Duc enters, a particularly warm melody is heard (ex. 15.1):

Example 15.1 *L'Assassinat du Duc de Guise*, Tableau 1

Determined to attend the Council, the Duc writes on the note 'Il n'oserait !' before taking an affectionate farewell of his mistress, leaving her alone with ex. 15.1 on the oboe.

Tableau 2 is in the King's quarters entirely supported by conspiratorial, unsettled music as the King instructs the dozen men (not the 'forty-five' of Dumas's tale *Les Quarante-cinq*) who are to assassinate the Duc. He distributes daggers, blesses them and shows where he is intending to hide. The whole scene is acted in an exaggerated, stagey manner in the theatrical style of the time, the King mostly crouching with his legs wide apart.

Tableau 3 is in the Council Chamber, where the music matches the genial greeting the Duc receives from a group of clergy and councillors, with refreshments served. A conspirator enters to lead away the Duc, who leaves with generous expressions of devotion and good cheer.

Tableau 4, the longest, is back in the King's quarters. The conspirator leads the Duc in while the King watches from his hiding place. They pass into an adjoining room, where the full group of conspirators greet him with false amity and the music remains on tiptoe. Suddenly they turn on him, and the music that breaks out is as violent as anything Saint-Saëns ever wrote, all the more so since he had only a dozen instruments to convey it with. The conspirators drag the Duc back into the King's room, where he is finally laid low. A clarinet and a solo violin state the assassination theme, and a series of intensely chromatic harmonies are heard as the King inspects the body to make sure the Duc is dead. The final part of the tableau recycles music from the symphony 'Urbs Roma' of 1857, while the King collapses in a chair. They empty the Duc's pockets and carry the body out.

The score then includes a section entitled 'The Staircase', with a note to explain that this is only needed if the reel includes the staircase scene. Otherwise the music proceeds directly into the last tableau, set in the guardroom, where the conspirators first lay the body out on a stone chest and then, after what the music suggests is a moment of remorse, they load the body on to the fire in the fireplace. Piano arpeggios suggest flickering flames, while a frantic version of ex. 15.1 portrays the entry of the Marquise in a state of fury and despair. A swift coda beings back the assassination theme.

It was obviously a technical triumph to produce a score that so well matches the action, pace and mood of the moving images, by whatever method it was achieved. It is odd that Saint-Saëns seems to have thought little about the enterprise and showed no interest in following it up. The score is perhaps more immediately and continuously dramatic than anything in the operas. An overall balance is preserved by the recurrence of themes, but the music is otherwise wholly determined by the action, not by formal considerations of any kind, which may be why Saint-Saëns considered it to be marginal to his main work. In the years when he was writing symphonic poems he was regularly criticised for following the flag of 'programme music', a complaint which he found irksome, since he took special pains not to allow the programme to control the form of the music. Here, in *L'Assassinat du Duc de Guise*, he may have felt he had strayed too far from that worthy ideal.

* * * * *

Within days of the three performances of *La Foi* in Monte Carlo in April 1909 Saint-Saëns was planning his next opera. In the past he had sometimes needed a break from the theatre after one of his operas was staged, even though an appealing idea could take his fancy at any time. The atmosphere in Monte Carlo that year was as welcoming as ever, and the Prince remained one of his strongest supporters and patrons. This time he asked for a new work for the 1911 season, an offer Saint-Saëns could not possibly refuse. He was troubled to be in concurrence with Fauré, who had been working on his *Pénélope* (for Monte Carlo) since 1907, but that opera would not in the end be ready until 1913, largely because Fauré had taken on the arduous job of Director of the Paris Conservatoire. Meanwhile, in 1908, the directorship of the Opéra changed hands from Pedro Gailhard and Pierre Gheusi to André Messager and Leimistin Broussan, a pair more sympathetic to Saint-Saëns despite Gheusi's collaboration on *Les Barbares*. Messager was, unusually for such a post, a composer. He had helped with the orchestration of *Phryné* and had written a number of successful operas himself. He and his partner approached Saint-Saëns for a new work at the same time as the Prince, in fact probably earlier.

Still absorbed by the ancient world, Saint-Saëns had been thinking about rewriting his open-air Béziers pageant *Déjanire* of 1898 into a fully sung opera, an idea that both commissioning parties accepted. The author of the text, Gallet, being no longer alive, Saint-Saëns decided to refashion his lines, which were of varying length, himself, and to adjust them to the needs of being set to music. The actors in the original version would be replaced by singers. The structure of the opera was already in place, and so Saint-Saëns planned to spend his winter sojourn of 1909–10 in Egypt working on it.

These were the years when revivals of his operas were taking place with steady frequency all over Europe, not many of which Saint-Saëns chose to attend himself. In 1909 he had already missed *Hélène* in Monte Carlo, *Javotte* at the Opéra and *La Princesse jaune* in Stuttgart. But he went in April to London where Covent Garden was performing *Samson et Dalila* for the first time as an opera and in French; previously they had sung it as an oratorio in deference to clerical opinion. Dalila was sung by Louise Kirkby-Lunn, who made an admirable recording of her aria from Act I, 'Printemps qui commence', in 1915.

In June, after a concert appearance for Saint-Saëns in Darmstadt, *Henry VIII* was revived again at the Opéra, with something like the original version restored. In July, the theatre at Aix-les-Bains put on *L'Ancêtre* for the first time, not with Litvinne as

Nunciata, but with a little-known soprano named Magne, who proved to be excellent in the role, to Saint-Saëns's great satisfaction, especially in the second act. 'People say they are too horrified by that scene [when the body of Léandri is brought in] to be able to applaud, but I believe it will one day earn a different response, because the more I hear it, the more it seems to me that I have never done anything better.'[6] In August, *Phryné* was played at the Trianon-Lyrique, a new theatre in the XVIIIème Arrondissement in Paris; in September, *La Foi* was staged at His Majesty's Theatre in London; and in October *La Princesse jaune* was revived for the second time at the Opéra-Comique. Any composer of opera would be proud of such international popularity and be ready to add one more to his list.

Saint-Saëns's participation in Parisian music was otherwise conducted at arm's length, as it were, by means of his writings, sometimes strongly polemical, in the press. His support of Fauré and his circle carried with it an undiminished hostility to anyone from Franck's circle, notably d'Indy. He wrote a long essay on the question of history or legend as good material for opera for the *Revue de Paris* in August, and he fulfilled his functions as member of the Institut.

On his travels he was already sketching out ideas for *Déjanire*. Serious work could not begin, however, until he had finished another work for the cellist Joseph Hollmann, this time a one-movement double concerto for violin and cello, the intended violinist being Eugène Ysaÿe. He was drafting it during his autumn travels and completed it after he arrived in Egypt for the winter, spending a few days first at Luxor then at Aswan. Determined to begin *Déjanire*, he installed himself comfortably in Mohammed Ali's villa in Cairo at the very end of December. After two months there he had completed three of the four acts, and the rest was drafted in Cannes and Monte Carlo by 19 March 1910. He next made a vocal score, a job he dreaded, but it had to be done in good time so that it could be printed and given to the singers to learn. It was published in September. The full score, which came last, was completed at the beginning of August 1910. The opera then passed out of his hands to Gunsbourg, once they had agreed on the singers to be engaged. Most important was to engage Félia Litvinne as Déjanire, which was done. The tenor, for Hercule, was Lucien Muratore, a strong actor who later sang the tenor leads in *Pénélope* and in Massenet's last operas.

Otherwise the year 1910 passed much like 1909, with a great deal of travelling, constant proof correcting, voluminous correspondence, the normal administrative affairs in Paris, with less writing for the press and very little composing. The duet for violin and cello emerged with a title, *La Muse et le poète*, and was given its first performance in the Queen's Hall, London, on 7 June 1910, with Saint-Saëns at the piano, and in its full form with orchestra at the Théâtre-Sarah-Bernhardt on 20 October 1910, conducted by Fernand Leborne, the dedicatee of *L'Assassinat du Duc de Guise*. The piece is remarkable for its

---

[6] Letter to Durand of 17 July 1909, RATNER 2012, p. 305.

abundance of invention, new ideas pouring out of the score as they had always tumbled out of the composer's brain, with never a sign of banality or triteness. Indeed it might be more familiar today if it had more homogeneity and tunefulness.

Another hold-up in his work on *Déjanire* was a *pièce d'occasion* written for the inauguration of an oceanographic museum in Monaco, the brainchild of the Prince, who was as passionate about oceanography as he was about opera. The *Ouverture de fête* was rapidly composed in January 1910. 'I don't know what to call it,' he wrote to his publisher,

> it's neither a march nor an overture nor a symphonic poem, it's a bit of all three. I've included a calm sea, a storm, even deep-sea fishing for creatures which sparkle like stars when you bring them to the surface. In German, *Festouvertüre* would be fine. *Ouverture de fête* in French is boring. *Ouverture triomphale* would be too ambitious and that's not its character. *Ouverture pour l'inauguration du Musée Océanographique de Monaco* would be the true title, but imagine that on a concert programme! We can't have *Ouverture océanographique*.[7]

If only Saint-Saëns and Durand had had the courage to call it *Oceanographic Overture*! It might not have fallen into such submarine depths of neglect, for when it forgets to be a march, it is a marvellously descriptive piece, with wind and waves and, yes, a vivid description of fish sparkling in the sun as they are hauled up from the ocean.

The *Ouverture de fête* was performed at the grand opening ceremony in Monte Carlo on 29 March 1910 and again in Paris later that year, on October 9th, in a concert that celebrated Saint-Saëns's seventy-fifth birthday. The main attraction in the Monte Carlo season that year was Massenet's genial new opéra-comique *Don Quichotte* with Fyodor Chaliapin in the title role. It opened on February 19th, with four more performances to follow. Saint-Saëns arrived on or about March 1st, but did he see it? History does not relate. He was not there just to conduct the *Ouverture de fête*; *Proserpine* was the last production of the season, with three performances in March. Did Massenet see it?

Amid the constant reports of his operas being revived, Saint-Saëns had the extraordinary satisfaction of arranging a series of concerts in London in June, beginning with the first performance (*en trio*) of *La Muse et le poète*, followed by three concerts in the Bechstein Hall (now the Wigmore Hall), in which he played eleven Mozart piano concertos, mostly with his own cadenzas. Before playing K. 450 he announced to the audience that this was the work he had played at the age of six, nearly seventy years before. On his return to Paris he moved house for the last time, as it turned out, to no. 83*bis* Rue de Courcelles, close to the Parc Monceau.

On September 19th, following a return to Aix-les-Bains, this time to oversee a revival of *Proserpine*, he was in Munich with Fauré and Dukas for a mini-festival devoted to French music. In a concert of his works he conducted the Third Symphony with Widor playing the organ. Although he was reluctant to take part, he enjoyed being reminded

---

[7] Letter to Durand of 14 January 1910, RATNER 2002, p. 326.

of hearing *Das Rheingold* and *Die Walküre* there for the first time in 1869. 'I also saw there that miraculous production of *Die Meistersinger* that we will never see again. Eight months' rehearsal under the composer, costumes after Dürer, a perfect ensemble, and Hans von Bülow on the podium, the right arm of a master.'[8]

His seventy-fifth birthday fell on 9 October 1910, on which day Colonne and his orchestra gave a concert of his works in Paris, while the composer himself was in Lausanne sharing an organ recital with the blind organist Albert Harnisch. After that he stayed in Paris while preparations for *L'Ancêtre* went ahead at the Opéra-Comique, its first appearance in Paris. If these revivals (plus revivals of *Phryné* in Nîmes and of *Henry VIII* in London) seem to confirm the widespread international acceptance of Saint-Saëns as a leading composer of opera, the climax must have been the revival in quick succession of *Samson et Dalila*, *Henry VIII*, *Phryné*, *Javotte* and *L'Ancêtre* in the municipal opera house in Algiers, beginning in January 1911. So he chose Algiers that year as his winter quarters.

* * * * *

Déjanire
(Ratner 298)

Tragédie lyrique in four acts

Libretto by Louis Gallet and Camille Saint-Saëns

First performance: Théâtre de Monte-Carlo, 14 March 1911

Déjanire	soprano dramatique
Iole	soprano
Phénice	contralto
Hercule	ténor
Philoctète	baryton
Lichas, chef des Héraclides	

Les Héraclides, compagnons d'Hercule – Les Œchaliennes, compagnons d'Iole
Les Étoliennes de la suite de Déjanire

Orchestra: 3 flutes (incl. piccolo), 3 oboes (incl. cor anglais), 3 clarinets (incl. bass clarinet/soprano saxophone), 2 bassoons, contrabassoon, 4 horns, 3 trumpets, bass trumpet, 3 trombones, contrabass trombone, timpani, bass drum, celesta, cymbals, triangle, tambourine, castanets, 2 harps, strings.

Offstage: 4 trumpets, alto piston trombone, 2 tenor piston trombones, piston bass trombone, alto saxhorns, tenor saxhorns, large tambourins.

---

[8] *Musica*, November 1910, p. 173; SORET 2012, p. 671.

A comparison of the new *Déjanire* with the old reveals the extent of revisions that it underwent and much of Saint-Saëns's skill in moving from open-air drama to sung opera. No doubt some of those who attended the performances in Monte Carlo in 1911 (or 1912) had seen the original presentation in Béziers in 1898 (or 1899 or 1903), but they were surely more attentive to the drama being enacted before their eyes than to any esoteric question of adaptation from one genre to another. Let us therefore treat the 1911 *Déjanire* as if it were a new work and set comparisons aside, at least until later.

Gallet's plot tells the story of Hercules's death brought about by the poisoned tunic of Nessus, a story of violent jealousy and passion drawn from two classical plays, *The Trachiniae* by Sophocles (Greek) and *Hercules Œtaeus* by Seneca (Latin). In the opera Déjanire is married to Hercule, who is now pursuing Iole, daughter of the king of Œchalia, who is in turn in love with Philoctète, Hercule's companion, a love chain that can only be resolved by violence and tragedy.

ACT I

The Prelude takes the principal theme from the symphonic poem *La Jeunesse d'Hercule* of 1877 (see ex. 11.5, p. 277) and works it into a short movement that grows to a full tutti for the opening of the curtain.

The setting of Act I is Hercule's palace in Œchalia, seen on the left, with the gynaeceum (women's quarters) on the right and a view of distant mountains in between. The chorus of Héraclides (men) sing the praises of their valiant hero in a strong unison line. Breaking into harmony they inform us that the tyrant Eurytus is dead and that his daughter Iole is Hercule's captive. The Œchalian women lament Iole's fate, having to suffer the unwanted attentions of her father's murderer. Iole (soprano) enters with her attendants and sings a bitter tirade against Hercule's cruelty and the state of her country (including the passage shown as ex. 11.6, p. 277). The women echo her feelings and move off into the gynaeceum.

Offstage trumpets announce the arrival of Hercule (tenor) and Philoctète (baritone), escorted by Lichas and guards. Puffed up with pride Hercule is proud of his conquests but regretful that the goddess Juno, out of jealousy of his mother, has filled him with the 'criminal' passion for Iole, the daughter of his defeated enemy Eurytus. So now he loves her, with a theme on bass clarinet and solo cello to express it (ex. 15.2):

Example 15.2 *Déjanire*, Act I

The pitilessness of his love distorts that theme with more tension (ex. 15.3):

Example 15.3 *Déjanire*, Act I

[musical example: Allegro, marked with (wind), (strings), (wind), (strings), (tutti)]

In an aside, Philoctète wrestles with the news, since he too loves Iole. Hercule invites, or rather orders, Philoctète to break the news to her, since she will surely take it badly from Hercule himself. He goes on to instruct Philoctète to prepare Déjanire for the news that Hercule is leaving her. He is too ashamed of his betrayal to tell her himself.

Supported by rich wind scoring and Wagnerian harmony, a venerable white-haired figure approaches with two servants behind her. This is Phénice (contralto), Déjanire's old nurse with a sorceress's visionary powers. She reports that Déjanire, tired of begging for Hercule's return, has come herself to Œchalia and awaits him in the city. With more self-pity (ex. 15.3) Hercule replies that Phénice must tell her that he is powerless in the hands of destiny and that she must return to Calydon. But Phénice is not one to take such orders. Invoking the gods she calls for vengeance, foreseeing horror and despair, tears and blood. The bass trumpet solemnly steps down a whole-tone scale as she casts an anathema on the hero and moves slowly away with her arms raised to heaven. This is a scene that leaves more than a shiver behind.

Hercule and his Héraclides go into the palace (ex. 11.5 on strings), leaving Philoctète alone and enraged. His scene is restless and powerful, set to strain any baritone, and he ends by blaming his ancestors for some unknown crime for which he is paying the price.

Iole herself then appears as two flutes in octaves give out a simple melody said to be of modern Greek origin. This is used as her motif throughout the opera. As if she can foresee what is in store for her, she begs Philoctète to protect her from her conqueror. He is spared the task of delivering unpleasant news since she is aware that Hercule loves her. When Philoctète accuses her of being ready to submit, she is enraged by his mistrust and is ready to leave. But she is held back a little longer to allow for a short but impressive love duet. They leave the stage in separate directions over a fragment of the Greek tune.

The Héraclides enter looking alarmed, and their music is agitated enough to reflect it, for Déjanire has been seen approaching. In unison they compare her fury and her tears to those of mythical figures such as the Maenads and the Hyrcanian tigress. The incessant dactylic figure in the strings effectively prepares us for the arrival of Déjanire herself (dramatic soprano) and her formidable motif, ex. 11.7 (see p. 278). Her hair and clothes are dishevelled and she is accompanied by Phénice, a group of Aetolian women and servants bearing small caskets. Her opening outburst is a scathing imprecation to Juno to help her bring down the hated Hercule, with the orchestra at its most menacing. Even when the tempo relaxes the bile is no milder. Phénice seeks to calm her down, assuring her that Juno will have her vengeance in good time. Déjanire impatiently responds by pointing out that she herself calls for vengeance too, for Hercule's heroic deeds were done in order to win her and now he is in thrall to his slave Iole. Phénice's suggestion that deep down she still loves him is met with ferocious denial: vengeance alone drives her now. Overlapping versions of ex. 11.7, with a lurid description of flames from three trumpets, return to bring the act to a frightening end.

ACT II

Even though its simplicity does less than justice as a portrait of Iole, Saint-Saëns left the Prelude unchanged from the 1898 version. Its plain modality may be intended to suggest the ancient world. The setting of Act II is the interior of the gynaeceum, leading out to the garden. Iole's solo, addressed to her waiting women, is a delightful display of classical lore, with a hint, in her mention of 'métamorphose', that Ovid has provided her with the transformations she longs to undergo in order to escape the horror of her present fate. With a sly reference to Saint-Saëns's symphonic poem *Phaéton*, she longs to be one of Phaethon's sisters, forever mourning him on the banks of the Eridanos into which his flaming chariot plunged. Why can she not be a siren, weeping eternally from the waters of Sicily, or Philomel warbling in the forests of Thrace? The lightly scored music obediently summons up images of waves and birdsong.

Déjanire enters with an abbreviated but heavy return of ex. 11.7. She now confronts Iole and Hercule in turn. She is mercilessly hard on her rival Iole, who, accompanied by three flutes, retains her dignity and declares herself blameless for Déjanire's predicament. At the sound of trumpets offstage Iole's women take fright, knowing that they announce the approach of Hercule, all the more threatening for their noisy harmonisation with five parts of a whole-tone scale. The hero orders everyone out save Déjanire, who adopts a quite different tone when confronted by this superhuman braggart. 'Who are you to challenge my authority?' he demands.

Her motif, ex. 11.7, is itself humbled by his presence. Déjanire hates and curses no more, she says, she is driven only by love. While she reminds him of his promise to love her, he reminds her of her promise to obey, commanding her to return to Calydon at once. She agrees to do so, but will take her captive, Iole, with her. His violent reaction reignites the fury of a woman scorned (Allegro molto), and the scene ends with threats and recriminations. With ex. 11.7 restored to its angular ferocity, she storms off.

Hercule summons Philoctète in order to find out how Iole is reacting to his plans of marriage, arguing with little appeal to reason or sentiment that as her father's killer he owes her a husband's support. The trumpet's reiteration only underlines his hypocrisy. Philoctète can only report that the murder is for Iole an inflexible barrier to their union.

Next to appear is Iole herself, also summoned by Hercule, who has the gall to repeat his view that marriage will compensate her for the murder, since hate cannot live for ever. Example 15.2 returns as he reaffirms his love, quickly transformed into ex. 15.3, as before. She quietly reminds him that love cannot be forced, which leads him to suspect that she loves someone else. With increasing desperation he tries to force her to name her lover, so when Philoctète appears and she gasps, he knows that it is he. They both admit their love. Enraged, Hercule orders Philoctète to be led away.

Over a hurtling orchestral presto Hercule has a final tirade against the gods, especially Juno, for allowing this betrayal in return for his great labours and triumphs. Swearing that his vengeance will astonish the world, he storms off, leaving the chorus to close the act. This is exactly what is needed at such a point, a noisy shout of alarm at what the gods are up to and what Hercule's fate might be.

Supported by the harp and a veil of string sound, the women's chorus and Iole implore Pallas to appease the vengeful hero. The men's chorus recall that Hercule is destined to die in that place, and ex. 11.5 quietly draws down the curtain.

ACT III

This act takes place on the same set as Act II, within the gynaeceum. Déjanire and Phénice enter to the same music as the latter's entry in Act I, now on muted strings and even more expressive. In her mobile contralto Phénice offers Déjanire the benefits of her sorcery which has accomplished miracles in reversing the laws of nature. The latter firmly declines the offer since she has something else in mind. She recounts once having had to cross a raging river with Hercule after his triumphant series of fights. The centaur Nessus agreed to take her across but, once there, with Hercule still on the other bank, Nessus attempted to rape her. Hercule heard her screams and shot him with deadly aim. The dying Nessus took a white tunic and dipped it in his own blood, telling her that it can guarantee a man's love. 'If your husband is unfaithful, he has only to put on the enchanted tunic. When sunlight falls on it a divine fire is lit within him, and his love will be reborn.' The narrative is illustrated by music that moves along with the story, pointing out details such as the river, the centaur's pain and the magical property of the tunic. This is some magic, represented by ex. 15.4, she is willing to try.

Example 15.4 *Déjanire*, Act III

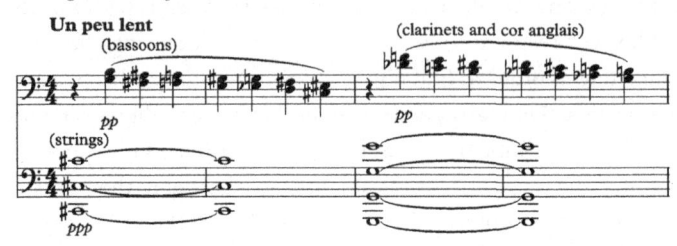

Iole runs in in great distress, followed as usual by her women. Déjanire is surprised to learn that she loves not Hercule but Philoctète, who is in chains as a result. Iole hopes that if Hercule could be persuaded to return to Déjanire, Philoctète would be freed. With a flight motif taking shape in the violins (ex. 15.5) both women are anxious to leave the city, supposing that if Hercule can be separated from Iole he will return to his wife. So Déjanire is willing to take Iole with her and drop the idea of magic. She tells Phénice to prepare for their departure.

Example 15.5 *Déjanire*, Act III

The women seize their chance to sing an appealing song describing Hercule's wild ravings, the nature of the music being more descriptive of them than of him.

Déjanire is left alone on stage to confront a pale, weary Hercule. Over a steady repetitious figure in 12/8 A major, Déjanire, all smiles, bids him farewell. If ever he has a change of mind she will be there to receive him back, but meanwhile she asks Aphrodite to look kindly on his new marriage and departs.

Hercule is polite but suspicious. Iole comes in dressed for a secret departure. In her confusion she tells him she is going to the temple. But ex. 15.5 betrays her and he knows she is preparing to flee. Declaring that no one except Déjanire may leave town, he tells Iole, Scarpia-like, that she must yield to him or Philoctète will die. The hitherto meek Iole summons all her strength in a passionate (A♭ minor!) denunciation of the heroic Hercule now behaving like a beast. His response is a complacent acknowledgement that he is vile, but he loves her. Again she plunges into A♭ minor with a plea for mercy that he has no intention of granting.

A bizarre sequence of chromatically descending chords covers Iole's defeat. With a single gesture she capitulates and collapses. Hercule's triumphalism is gross in its crudity, ordering preparations for a wedding and marching out of the gynaeceum leaving Iole prostrate.

Déjanire appears, with Phénice. Everything is ready for their departure, she whispers over ex. 15.5. Iole 'as in a dream' confesses that she has saved the life of Philoctète, has sworn to marry Hercule and cannot leave. Trumpets and trombones underline her predicament with a series of painful chords. Philoctète himself appears. He is free but furious with Iole for her 'cowardly betrayal', yielding to Hercule when he would rather die to keep their love pure – sentiments entirely in keeping with classical codes of conduct. He is prevented from leaving by Déjanire, who hints that she has plans to intervene. She orders Phénice to fetch the casket that contains the magic tunic and explains to Iole and Philoctète the power of Nessus's blood (ex. 15.4). When Phénice returns, Déjanire takes the tunic out and shows how she has embroidered it with jewels, so that the bloodstains look like flowers. Iole is to present it to Hercule as a wedding gift, thus restoring his love for Déjanire, despite Phénice's fear that its magic properties may be fatal.

On the urging of Phénice, who sees Eros as the only god who can save them, the act closes with a hymn to Eros sung by the attendant women.

ACT IV

In honour of the forthcoming nuptials the last act begins with dancing and ceremonial. The setting is the space in front of the temple of Jupiter with a raised platform at the back. The opening scene is a vigorous dance, bimodal at first, which is interrupted by a fanfare for the arrival of the Héraclides and Hercule himself in a glittering costume. A noisy working of ex. 11.5 concludes the introduction.

Hercule's opening address to the people is answered by a short loyal chorus. He then takes a lyre and sings a lyrical song to his bride, praising her beauty. Iole steps forward, holding the casket that contains the tunic. She presents it to him with demure courtesy and his presents to her are brought in. He then goes into the temple with the casket. Example 11.7 intruding into the polite music tells us that Déjanire is in the crowd, which she joins with Phénice and Philoctète. With a speeded up ex. 15.4, she gloats on the thought that the setting sun will strike the tunic and work its magic.

The *chœur dansé* is a hymn to marriage over an incessant rhythmic pattern of four notes. Saint-Saëns introduces a soprano saxophone in C into this movement, although it is heard only in unison with the full wind, not on its own.[9] The chorus are instructed

---

[9] The soprano saxophone is normally in B♭, not C, and the narrow range of notes required would be equally suited to the alto saxophone.

to strike 'grands tambourins' at certain points.[10] This is another white-note piece which Saint-Saëns intended to evoke, if not resemble, the music of ancient Greece.

Hercule now enters wearing the enchanted tunic. Déjanire watches with impatience. Unison strings and Hercule lead Iole to a throne. Then he signals for the arrival of a tripod ablaze, with jugs and cups for libations and incense. A sacrifical ram is led in and two girls are holding doves. Throwing incense on the fire, Hercule prays to his father Jupiter, solemnly echoed by the chorus.

Suddenly Hercule drops a cup and clutches his chest, tearing at the tunic. Against screaming discords he calls out for water. Déjanire immediately leaps to his aid, explaining that she had wanted to win him back by magic (ex. 15.4) but the centaur had tricked her. Hercule calls to Jupiter to strike the nuptial pyre with a thunderbolt, and the bolt duly falls. The stage catches fire and is consumed in smoke while the orchestra plays the music that had represented this very scene in the symphonic poem *La Jeunesse d'Hercule*. As the smoke clears Hercule is seen transfigured, raised to Olympus among the gods and acclaimed by the chorus over the final bars of the symphonic poem.

* * * * *

There are few significant differences in the action of *Déjanire* the pageant and *Déjanire* the opera, but the most striking alteration is that Déjanire does not kill herself. Taken in by the centaur's ambiguous words, she intended that the tunic would cause Hercule to burn with the fire of love reborn, not with real fire. She is always in love with Hercule, even when she is most enraged, and is innocent of his death, but now she has lost him forever. As for chorus and ballet, the change from large-scale outdoor performance to indoor stage performance is surprisingly straightforward, since this kind of opera needs a strong chorus and can accommodate dancing, albeit less of it than before.

The music, on the other hand, is transformed by the change of scale, since there are no more military bands and merely the theatre's harps. Offstage trumpets are still required, but fewer of them. Most of the earlier music was incorporated in some form, although adjustments were many, and a good deal of it was re-scored: Saint-Saëns was not a lazy composer. The coryphée's song with a lyre in the last act was given to Hercule to sing. The choral endings of Acts II and III were preserved and much of the ceremonial in Act IV, although the *chœur dansé* was replaced by a new one. Both versions begin and end with reference to the symphonic poem *La Jeunesse d'Hercule*.

By far the most significant change was the setting of all the dialogue for the principal characters, adding up to three-quarters of the new score. The absence of rhyme gives it a markedly modern flavour. The music sung by the two coryphées was given either to

---

[10] The 'tambourin' is correctly a long provençal drum. Since 'large' ones would be impractical for the chorus, large tambourines must be intended, even though they should properly be termed 'tambours de basque'. See p. 234, n. 16.

the chorus or to Hercule. There is no more *mélodrame*, but a series of scenes to which Saint-Saëns devoted special attention, writing some of his most powerful dramatic music and giving his characters a vitality they did not have before. Gallet's dialogue left little opportunity for ensembles, so the singers rarely sing together and there are no trios or quartets. The love duet for Iole and Philoctète is short but strong. Elsewhere Saint-Saëns shows himself master of the dramatic confrontation between two characters, so that we have superb scenes between Hercule and Phénice, between Déjanire and Iole, between Déjanire and Hercule, between Hercule and Iole, and monologues for Philoctète, Iole and Déjanire. The intricacy of the plot and the absence of any subplot give the action urgency and compactness. Among the pages of newly composed music are a number of allusory motifs, while some motifs are retained from the pageant version.

Saint-Saëns's recreation of a Greek tragedy is successful not so much because he occasionally imitates the practices of Greek theatre and adopts their musical modes, but because, like the masters of French classical theatre and the Greek tragedians themselves, he grasps the way that men and women are ultimately helpless in the hands of the gods, yet unable to escape the force of their own emotions. Obligation, loyalty, friendship and love are strong enough forces in our daily lives, but when these are toyed with by Jupiter and his sometimes cruel colleagues on Olympus, the tensions can be unbearable. *Déjanire* is a tragedy since she loses the Hercule she has always loved. She is deceived by Juno's action in making him love Iole and by Nessus's deceptive gift of the poisoned tunic. Hercule is a braggart and a murderer, but his betrayal of Déjanire is ordered by the gods, and he is rewarded for his heroic labours (and excused his murderous deeds) by being elevated to Olympus. The incomprehensible actions of the gods have no counterpart in the music, whereas the feelings and actions of the protagonists are powerfully expressed in this music, and their dilemmas and conflicts have no resolution except in bowing to the inevitable.

Saint-Saëns was now, in his seventies, in comfortable command of a musical language that had evolved gradually over his career. We do not think of him as a chromatic composer, but in fact the music shifts key constantly without losing sight of a main tonality, and his harmony is inflected with dissonance whenever he needs to be expressive. Plain, non-modulating music he reserves for ballet and formal scenes, but anything personal is painted in fluent chromatic music of surprising complexity. This is supported by a masterly and imaginative command of orchestration, and since he was never short of fresh musical ideas, the opera is intriguing and strong, never boring or banal.

The role of Hercule is a heavy one, demanding a tenor with stamina. He needs to sing lyrically too. He is also the villain of the story, behaving with cruel disregard for people's feelings but ultimately excused because of his divine origin and his obeisance to the gods. The three female roles are very different one from another, but all rewarding. Iole is young and innocent but capable of snarling like a dog; Phénice is both a sorceress and a servant, able to predict an ugly future and not afraid to spell it out; Déjanire is another of Saint-Saëns's great roles for a dramatic soprano, and his insistence that it had to be played by someone of Litvinne's calibre underlines the demands of the role and the powerful effect it can have when properly sung. With so much to commend it and so little that can be criticised as dramatically or musically weak, *Déjanire* is one of Saint-Saëns's best operas.

* * * * *

Writing from Algeria in January 1911, before the first performances of *Déjanire* in Monte Carlo, Saint-Saëns said: 'This will be my last foolishness.'[11] Ten days later he confirmed the thought: 'As for writing music, I've done enough, all I have to do is stop. *Déjanire* will be the last round in the chamber.'[12] As if to prevent the writing of any more music, he undertook to write regular articles for *L'Écho de Paris* and in the next three years he sent in sixty-seven articles on every kind of musical topic from all corners of Europe and north Africa. This was surely not to compensate for lack of inspiration, as Marie-Gabrielle Soret has suggested,[13] but to limit the flow, since he had never suffered from *la crampe des écrivains* and would continue to compose substantial works in the remaining years of his life. The year 1912 saw the composition of an oratorio about Moses, *La Terre promise*, to an English text by Hermann Klein, first performed at the Three Choirs Festival in Gloucester in 1913. He was nevertheless aware of the dangers of writing too much and of the likelihood that the public appetite for his music could not be extended indefinitely. As far as his operas were concerned, the public was currently exposed to them in many different cities at a greater rate than ever before.

It was always planned that *Déjanire* would be taken up by the Opéra after its opening spell in Monte Carlo. This came about on 22 November 1911, with sixteen more performances. The last was on 2 July 1912. The cast was almost the same as in Monte Carlo: Litvinne as Déjanire, Muratore as Hercule and Heni Dangès as Philoctète. Yvonne Dubel, as Iole, was replaced by a younger singer, Yvonne Gall, and Germaine Bailac, as Phénice, was replaced by Lyse Charny. The opera was conducted by André Messager, but the staging was dreadful, in Saint-Saëns's view, and the tempos 'stupid'.[14] 'It's clear that Messager misunderstood the character of the work', he wrote. 'He sees it as classical and solemn, thinking only of Iole's elegy at the start of Act II. It's above all a lively and passionate work, people also speak of its *nobility*. It's certainly about nobility: it's also about jealousy, rage, love in all its forms. That's how it was

---

[11] Letter to N. Bernardin, 2 January 1911, Ratner 2012, p. 327.
[12] Letter to Caroline de Serres, 10 January 1911, Vente Alde 15 April 2013.
[13] Soret 2012, p. 30.   [14] Letter to Philippe Bellenot, 21 December 1912, Ratner 2012, p. 334.

played in Marseille.'[15] Before the end of the run at the Opéra, Saint-Saëns conducted one of the performances himself, and restored some life into the tempos.

The performances in Marseille in March 1912 were the best, in the composer's view, of the many that took place that year. After Paris it was played at the Monnaie, in Brussels, in December 1911, then in Dessau (in German), Lyon, Rouen, Marseille, Bordeaux, Aix-les-Bains, Enghien and Algiers, as well as a revival in Monte Carlo. Cairo and Cannes followed in 1913. Saint-Saëns urged Durand to have an Italian translation done, but without one, it seems, the opera was not heard in Italy. The last performances on record before sinking into a century's silence took place in New York in 1914 and Chicago in 1915. A curiosity is the recording of the *Épithalame* in Act IV (Hercule's 'Viens, ô toi') by the Puerto Rican tenor Antonio Paoli made in 1911. He sings in French from the Béziers version of the vocal score, but it is not known in which, if any, performances of *Déjanire* he took part. Writing from London in May 1913, Saint-Saëns speaks of the 'stunning' success of the *Épithalame*, which had been available as a separate publication since 1899.[16]

The year 1912 was a particularly good one for revivals of his operas, in addition to *Déjanire*. *La Foi* was revived at the Odéon; *L'Ancêtre* was played in Cairo, Montreal and Antwerp; *Étienne Marcel* was revived in Bordeaux; *Samson et Dalila* was played in Sofia, St Petersburg and Cremona; *Proserpine* was played in Marseille; *Javotte* was danced in Cairo, Marseille and Trouville. The following years, 1913 and 1914, were similar, with *Samson et Dalila* reaching Johannesburg, and all the others except *Ascanio* appearing somewhere.

At the beginning of 1913 the Odéon revived a play by Émile Bergerat, originally played in 1887. This was *La Nuit florentine* based on Machiavelli's satirical comedy of 1514, *Mandragola*. Two fragments of music survive attributed to Saint-Saëns, although they are not in his hand;[17] whether he contributed these fragments (or any more) is unknown. One is a short song 'Belles qui semez le tourment', and the second is a dismal wordless chant for string quartet.

Saint-Saëns made only one further contribution to music for the stage, and that was the music he wrote for a production of Alfred de Musset's play *On ne badine pas avec l'amour* in 1917. The outbreak of war in 1914 was no boost to the spirit of someone who had been denouncing the growing influence of Germany since 1870, and he became even more outspoken in his defence of French music and, like many others, pessimistic about the outcome. His critics accused him of promoting his own music, but he continued to insist that French composers were abundant enough and talented enough to supply the needs of their country. The activity of theatres and concert halls was greatly curtailed, except those concerts in aid of the war effort in which he frequently

---

[15] Letter to Broussan, 1 January 1913, RATNER 2012, p. 335.
[16] Letter to Jacques Durand, 26 May 1913, RATNER 2012, p. 336.
[17] See RATNER 2012, pp. 441–42.

took part. In 1914–15, for the first time for many years, he spent the winter in Paris, and then, after keeping up his regular visits to Monte Carlo where *L'Ancêtre* was being played, he embarked in May 1915 for the United States. After a few days in New York he headed west and spent four weeks in San Francisco, where he made speeches and gave three concerts. These exhibited a wide selection of his music in all genres, including scenes from *La Foi* and *Henry VIII*, as well as the first performance of *Hail California!*, a large-scale cantata incorporating the *Marseillaise* and the *Star-spangled Banner* and a military band conducted by John Philip Sousa.

Back in France, concert tours in Paris and the provinces kept him on the move, and he again spent a winter, 1915–16, in France. *Phryné* was revived at the Opéra-Comique in April 1916, and before that there was a revival of *Hélène* in Monte Carlo in March. *Les Barbares* returned in September to the Opéra, which had been silent for sixteen months at the beginning of the war. In 1916 there was another transatlantic trip, this time to South America with concerts in Brazil, Argentina and Uruguay, and it was on this tour, beginning on the crossing itself, that he composed the music for *On ne badine pas avec l'amour*, commissioned by the director of the Odéon, Paul Gavault. The orchestration was done at Bourbon-l'Archambault, a small spa town in central France, where he went to convalesce after the exertions of the South American tour. The play opened at the Odéon on 8 February 1917.

* * * * *

On ne badine pas avec l'amour
(Ratner 323)

Comédie in three acts and eleven tableaux
by
Alfred de Musset

Incidental music

First performance: Théâtre de l'Odéon, Paris, 8 February 1917

Chorus

Orchestra: 2 flutes, 2 oboes, 2 clarinets, cor anglais, 2 bassoons, 4 horns, 2 trumpets, 3 trombones, timpani, harp, organ, strings.

De Musset's play *On ne badine pas avec l'amour* was written in 1834, following his famous liaison with George Sand, and published in the *Revue des deux mondes* in that year. It was not staged until 1861, after de Musset's death. It tells the story of two cousins, Perdican and Camille, son and niece respectively of the Baron, who have been brought up together and are now reunited after a separation of ten years. The Baron would like them to marry. Although Camille is deeply attached to her cousin, she has been led by her convent training to mistrust men. Perdican learns that she has done everything possible to make him dislike her and plans to remain in the convent. He then takes up with a peasant girl, Rosette. Camille out of spite and jealousy tells Rosette that Perdican is just using her and confesses her love to Perdican. When Rosette dies in despair, Camille tells Perdican a simple 'adieu'.

The play has elements of comedy and of romantic drama, and it is precisely this mixture that became a source of disagreement when Saint-Saëns's music came to be judged by the press. The composer was compelled to write to the *Courrier musical* as follows:

> Several people have expressed regret that my music was not lighter; they found it too 'serious' for de Musset's play.
>
> De Musset's play does not strike me as a light play at all. Following the principles of the romantic school, Musset mixed the comic and the tragic, but the tragic is predominant. The comic is merely an accessory, for nothing is more serious than the dialogue between Camille and Perdican in which they explore the remotest depths of the human soul. Nothing is more weighty than the struggle between human love and divine love. 'That is sad enough to die for', says Camille; and what is more tragic in the theatre than the ending, a calamity both physical and moral. What is more tragic than the death of the innocent girl, a victim of the struggle of two lovers separated for ever by that cruel ending.
>
> Light music to accompany such a drama would have struck me as a sacrilege.[18]

Saint-Saëns wrote about eighteen passages of music (which have never been published), some of them of substantial length. It is remarkable that with the war causing extreme stringencies in the daily life of the capital, the Odéon could present a play with no nationalist element and provide a full orchestra and organ for the music. Such largesse would barely survive the end of the war. As for the character of the music itself, the final piece, with strident augmented harmony and a peroration on the organ, is unmistakably serious. On the other hand, the music that introduces Maître Blazius, Perdican's tutor, at the beginning of the play is excellent comic writing; a group of men singing in chorus describe him as like 'an antique amphora' (Saint-Saëns was once again setting prose). The opening of Act I, Scene 3 is also comic in a four-square Handelian manner to describe the meeting of Maître Blazius and the equally portly curate. After Act II, Scene 4, when the Baron has heard of his niece's determination not to marry, the music is loud and strong for full orchestra, followed by lilting solos for woodwind with harp, a touching contrast full of sentiment rather than comedy.

A distorted fugue in C minor in Act III, Scene 4 would certainly strike any listener as testing, but it is appropriate for introducing the chorus who sing, 'Assuredly there is something serious going on in the château'. After Act I, Scene 3 the violins enter in fury,

---

[18] *Courrier musical*, 1 March 1917; SORET 2012, p. 968.

perfectly expressing the Baron's displeasure with Dame Pluche, Camilla's misanthropic governess. But the same passage is followed by a gorgeous Lento in which the oboe introduces a motif used later in the score as a kind of leitmotif for Perdican, ex. 15.6:

Example 15.6 *On ne badine pas avec l'amour*, Act I

It is a pity that this music should be buried beneath the corpse of nineteenth- and early twentieth-century orchestral theatre music, but there is no reason why the best of it, as with other notable examples of incidental music such as *Peer Gynt* and *L'Arlésienne*, or Saint-Saëns's own *La Foi*, should not be made into a suite of three or four movements which would represent the composer at his best.

* * * * *

When Camille closes *On ne badine pas avec l'amour* with the words 'Adieu, Perdican!', it is hard not to reflect that another Camille was saying goodbye to a long record of composing for the stage. He was now eighty-one, and although he wrote no more incidental music, no more film music and no more operas, in the remaining five years of his life the pace of composing, of concert-giving and of travel let up scarcely one iota. With a variety of choral and vocal works, he also composed his second string quartet and the three gem-like sonatas for clarinet, oboe and bassoon, each with piano, composed in the last year of his long life.

Even though his health could be intermittently troublesome, his obsessive travelling continued. In 1919, for example, he made an autumn concert tour that took in Strasbourg and Mulhouse (now regained from Germany), Le Havre, Poitiers, Lille, Bordeaux, Béziers, Arles and Marseille, all within two months before heading for Algiers. His greatest satisfaction came from a trip to Greece in May 1920, where he climbed the Acropolis, touched the Parthenon, gave three concerts, and drank in the air of ancient Greece which he had so often imagined and recreated in his mind.

His fingers never slowed down, so he was playing virtuoso works like the *Rapsodie d'Auvergne* as late as 1921. His last concert was given in the Casino in Dieppe on 6 August 1921. He died on December 16th of that year in the Oasis Hotel, Algiers.

The operas continued to enjoy revivals to his very last days. Both Monte Carlo and Bordeaux were especially devoted to them, including a revival of *Étienne Marcel* in Monte Carlo in March 1918. His friendship with Jacques Rouché, who became director of the Opéra in 1913, meant that France's premier opera house would sustain his work. *Les Barbares* was revived there in September 1916, *Henry VIII* in December 1917 and May 1919, and *Hélène* in June 1919. Saint-Saëns was able to supervise the rehearsals of most of these, even if he did not always attend the performances. Most pleasing of all was the revival of *Ascanio* at the Opéra in November 1921. This opera had had, unaccountably, only one production – in Bordeaux in 1911 – since its initial successful run at the Opéra in 1890–91, and it was now performed seven more times in a production that greatly pleased the composer. The last performance was on December 21st, within a week after his death. Who could have guessed that the steady record of revivals of the operas would then come to a complete halt? Only *Samson et Dalila* slipped through the gate.

16 | Saint-Saëns the Dramatist

Saint-Saëns's music for the stage represents a major part of his work, yet with the exception of *Samson et Dalila* most of it lies still, nearly a century after his death in 1921, in the shadows. More remarkable than today's neglect of much of Saint-Saëns's music, which is not particularly surprising, is the extraordinary contrast between the success of his music, especially the operas, during his lifetime and the almost complete silence that descended after his death.

An opera may be considered a failure when it is staged for the first time with a few performances soon after and then never again. There must be thousands of operas that have suffered this fate. With that definition of failure, none of Saint-Saëns's twelve operas were a failure. The closest to failure for Saint-Saëns was *Frédégonde*, with only eight performances in his lifetime. If you lived in Paris between 1909 and 1914 with a desire to see Saint-Saëns's operas performed, you would have been able to see all twelve operas of the main canon (i.e. excluding *Le Duc de Parme* and *Frédégonde*) without travelling further than Brussels and Bordeaux. His operas enjoyed international success rivalled only at that time among living composers by Massenet and Puccini. All his operas were published in vocal score and full score in his lifetime and performed many times. Durand issued the *Mise-en-scène* of each opera which opera directors could follow, complete with a list of props required, in order to make the production as close to the original as possible.

These are the approximate numbers of revivals (not performances) of his eight most successful operas during his lifetime: *Samson et Dalila* well over a hundred; *Henry VIII* thirty-five; *Phryné* thirty-one; *Proserpine* eighteen; *Déjanire* fifteen; *Les Barbares* eleven; *La Princesse jaune* and *Étienne Marcel* ten. That leaves *L'Ancêtre*, *Hélène*, *Le Timbre d'argent* and *Ascanio* with less than ten revivals. Strangely enough, it was *Ascanio*, in my view one of his best operas, that was least successful in Saint-Saëns's lifetime, mainly owing to the loss of its sets, being performed only in Paris and Bordeaux, with a late revival at the Opéra in the last days of the composer's life.

* * * * *

The merit of an opera can be judged, it will be argued, only when it is performed with the singers, orchestra, dancers, sets and production which its creators intended for it, which means, in essence, only in its own time. Once that time has passed, everything may have to be recreated. And while an opera may offer new insights if some of these elements are adjusted to contemporary taste, something is always subtracted. Today it is normal for musicians to interpret the scores of opera with as much exactitude as scholars and players can attain, while sets and production present an open territory disputed by those who would recreate the original style and those who wish to impose a different and original concept. To present French grand opera with the plenitude that was available in the nineteenth century now costs sums that almost no opera house can contemplate, so in most cases economies have to be made, the usual target being sets and costumes. The argument that stage direction is a fluid discipline that cannot be recreated is actually belied by the fact that in Saint-Saëns's time production manuals which record stage movement with great precision were always kept and often published, while costumes and sets invariably survive as drawings, maquettes or photographs. French provincial opera houses relied heavily on these manuals and costume designs in order to reproduce the Paris production as closely as possible. If recordings can bring the music alive, the visual record and a good imagination will provide the rest.

In studying Saint-Saëns's operas, I have kept in mind his close involvement with designers, choreographers, singers and conductors, since he and his librettists regarded the sets and stage movement as intrinsic to the identity of the opera itself. Stage direction was a by-product of the text, nominally in the control of the theatre's director, although he was principally an administrator, not a member of the creative team. Gallet, Saint-Saëns's preferred partner as librettist, invariably provided full stage directions and a detailed description of the decor he imagined for his operas, and in some cases designed it himself. As for the score, it is not a dead document, but a record of sound that can be brought to life without any mystery when played, and by well-trained ears, a little mysteriously, when read.

I maintain that these documents – the score, the libretto, the sets and the production guides – are sufficient material on which to base a critical appraisal of Saint-Saëns's operas, along with the admittedly vast range of documents in which he himself reported on the origins, genesis, performance, reception and significance of his work. Others may be persuaded that certain aspects of his personality have a bearing on the operas, but I am not convinced that, for example, his politics or his sexuality made any more than a marginal contribution to them. Politics were nonetheless of the greatest concern to him. As France's leading composer for many years, he could not escape being upheld as a symbol of national achievement, nor did he shy away from that role. His impatience, even rage, at Germany's aggrandisement after 1871 and the willingness of young Germans (and young Frenchmen) to sit cravenly at Wagner's feet, spewing out the Master's philosophy in ill-digested torrents, was an *idée fixe* of his writings, and no doubt of his conversation too, but his music is guilty of such jingoism only when he set openly patriotic texts such as *À la France !* of 1904. In his operas the music is there solely to serve the needs and realise the potential of the libretto.

Only one of the operas, *Les Barbares*, is openly political, with the Germans of 1900 being transparently represented as the barbarians of the Roman era. They are invaders, as in 1870, bringing death and distress to the people of the city of Orange. The story was deliberately placed there in order to make the political point. But Saint-Saëns did not boast about that; he was far from indifferent, but he simply went about the composition of the opera with his finest skills. The Gallo-Roman victory at the end is celebrated with a *Farandole*, a local dance, and the opera was successful in France. A modern revival, ironically, would probably have to change the location and the era to spare too many damaged sensibilities.[1]

As a lifelong republican, Saint-Saëns no doubt sided with the oppressed populace in *Étienne Marcel*, but the convoluted plot of that opera allows our sympathies to swing back and forth between the factions, and the star-crossed lovers deserve a better future (and perhaps attain it). Out of patriotism Saint-Saëns many times expressed a preference for French historical subjects, but *Étienne Marcel* displays no more political argument than *Henry VIII*. The depiction of King Henry as ruthless and tyrannical (but with a vulnerable side) is in line with the generally accepted historical record and accords with the literary sources of the libretto.

As for his sexuality, stories of Saint-Saëns's fondness for cross-dressing, for dancing with Tchaikovsky and for discreet North African retreats have led his biographers to conclude that he was gay, a term strictly to be understood within the different ethos of nineteenth-century France. At least a part of his personality fits that categorisation, even if the truth is a great deal more complex.[2] Unwilling to reveal or even discuss his private life, a composer such as Saint-Saëns might well choose to explore or explain it cryptically in his dramatic works. But there is no special admiration for youthful males such as we find in the operas of Szymanowski, Britten and Tippett, and no special sympathy for those who are outlawed by society. If he ever displayed misogyny – resistance to feminism was scarcely the exclusive attitude of homosexuals in a male-dominated society – it is hard to treat the wicked women of his operas as an expression of personal prejudice. Dalila and Proserpine bring death and mayhem down on those who love them and on themselves, like many an operatic *femme fatale*, from Handel's Cleopatra to Verdi's Lady Macbeth, but they are women of complex motivations, subject to the pressures that their very different social circumstances apply. Dalila has been brought vividly to life by a great list of famous singers. She is a scorned woman who can simulate passion in order to gain her ends, and having the only female role in the opera she leaves all the stronger impression. Déjanire is a furious female, a wronged wife who takes vengeance on her erring husband, but then kills herself in remorse (in the pageant version of the work); her character is determined by her classical myth-

---

[1] For a full analysis of the political implications of *Les Barbares*, see LETEURÉ 2014, pp. 99–110.
[2] See FAURE 1985, pp. 45–52; STUDD 1999, pp. 252–54; MORRIS 2012.

makers. The Duchesse d'Étampes, in *Ascanio*, causes nothing but trouble, but her evil designs are thwarted by Scozzone's self-sacrifice. Presumably the king likes her, having her as his mistress, but no one else does. The blackest woman in Saint-Saëns's operas is Frédégonde, an unmitigated villainess with no trace of softer emotions either in the music or in the historical record.

Looking at Saint-Saëns's stage works as a whole, we cannot fail to be struck by the immense range and variety they exhibit. He was proud of his versatility and could turn his hand to a satirical farce such as *Gabriella di Vergy* or to a film score such as *L'Assassinat du Duc de Guise* or to massive open-air pageants such as the Béziers *Déjanire* and *Parysatis*. In opera we look, among other things, for penetrating characterisation and for strong ensemble work, and we do not have to look far to find these in Saint-Saëns. Outstanding characters naturally include those wicked women, Dalila, Proserpine, the Duchesse d'Étampes and Frédégonde. But the gallery of female characters in these operas is wider than that, with each one depicted in the music according to the needs of the libretto. *L'Ancêtre*, for example, has a bigoted older woman in Nunciata, unrelenting in her attachment to old Corsican ways and inevitably the cause of the tragedy, while Vanina, her granddaughter, is caught in a terrible emotional ambush by loving the man she is ordered to destroy. These two women, the older woman with the higher voice, may be compared to Queen Catherine and Anne Boleyn in *Henry VIII*, where it is the younger woman who is a party to the tragic deposition of the older Queen. Anne is not the wretched victim of Henry VIII's cruelty, but a schemer determined to replace the legitimate queen Catherine. Saint-Saëns had originally assigned the higher voice to the younger Anne, but then exchanged these, putting Catherine much more at the centre of the action. The opera is all about her, Catherine, who should perhaps have been given the opera's title if her husband did not carry more name recognition. Floria, in *Les Barbares*, has a fine role but is less compelling, perhaps because the composer failed to give her the musical space her complex situation demands, especially in her Act II duet with Marcomir. In that opera there is an extraordinarily moving moment when Livia finds out who has killed her husband. Then in *Hélène* there is the magnificent opening monologue for Hélène as she grapples with the conflict, conventional enough, between love and duty, between the Trojan Pâris and her husband Menelaus. The title role is one of Saint-Saëns's greatest creations, since both the conception and the libretto were his. The conflict in her heart is vividly played out by interventions from Pallas and Venus, and her decision to leave Sparta for Troy concludes the opera with the superb image of love fulfilled but calamity ultimately guaranteed. Among gentler female characters, we should not overlook Hélène and Rosa in *Le Timbre d'argent*, and Léna in *La Princesse jaune*, whose touching solo (no. 3) shows the master's hand.

Another claimant for an outstanding woman's role is Scozzone in *Ascanio*, whose passion for Cellini drives her to plot to murder Cellini's new model Colombe. But when Cellini renounces Colombe because she is in love with Ascanio, Scozzone sacrifices her own life in order to save that of the innocent Colombe. Her nobility of spirit is perfectly matched by her contralto voice, a voice Saint-Saëns was fond of, probably inspired by his friendship with Pauline Viardot, whose voice famously embraced both contralto and mezzo-soprano ranges. The term 'contralto' was little used in France except in choral music, but Saint-Saëns applied it to four of his later roles: Livie (*Les Barbares*); Pallas (*Hélène*); Vanina (*L'Ancêtre*); and Phénice (*Déjanire*). Anne Boleyn is classified as a mezzo-soprano, and Scozzone as either mezzo or contralto. In the mezzo role of Frédégonde the Belgian Meyriane Héglon made a great impression, and she went on to sing the roles of Livie and Pallas and to make recordings of airs for Dalila and Scozzone, with the composer at the piano, in 1904. Saint-Saëns said she had 'the richest contralto voice ever heard at the Opéra'.[3]

There are young women subject to innocent feelings of love and attachment but who suffer from the carelessness or villainy of others. Both Hélène and Rosa in *Le Timbre d'argent* are in this group. So are Angiola in *Proserpine* and Colombe in *Ascanio*. Béatrix, in *Étienne Marcel*, is more or less powerless to do anything other than what her father or her lover demand, a source of conflict in itself, and her union with Robert is left unconfirmed at the end.

The element of comedy places the character of Phryné in a unique category in this group of operas. The harlot with a sense of fun is an appealing basis for a story, and when she punctures the self-importance of city officials we are wholly on her side. In pure comedy the peasant Javotte embodies in dance everything we expect of French ballet. Not to be forgotten is Fiametta, the alluring dancer/mime who has to play a taxing role in *Le Timbre d'argent* as Dr Spiridion's wicked sidekick.

Of the many sopranos he worked with, he particularly admired Caroline Miolan-Carvalho, for whom the part of Hélène in *Le Timbre d'argent* was written (although she never sang it); Caroline Salla, as Hélène (in *Le Timbre d'argent*) and Proserpine; Gabrielle Krauss, as Queen Catherine; the 'enchantress' Sybil Sanderson, as Phryné; and Félia Litvinne, as Queen Catherine, Hélène (in *Hélène*), Nunciata and Déjanire.

Saint-Saëns assigned men's roles without departing far from convention, so that lovers and young men are tenors, older men and villains are baritones, kings and priests are basses. The twenty-year-old Dauphin in *Étienne Marcel* is to be sung by a contralto, and the young slave Lampito, in *Phryné*, is sung by a soprano. Samson is the mightiest of the tenor heroes, if only because he pulls down the temple pillars. He must have the voice to match the muscle. In Samson, strength is pitted against weakness, a weakness ruthlessly exploited by Dalila and the Philistines, and from the beginning he has the charisma and vision to deliver the Hebrews from oppression. Other strong-arm tenors are Mérowig (in *Frédégonde*), Marcomir (in *Les Barbares*) and Hercule (in *Déjanire*).

---

[3] Saint-Saëns, 'Les Déesses : les trois Carolines', *L'Écho de Paris*, 1 March 1914; SORET 2012, p. 884.

Hercule has few redeeming features in this episode in his life, but Marcomir overcomes the presumption that he is a cruel barbarian by falling for Floria, the Vestal Virgin, and by helping her compatriots, although it cannot save him from a victim's revenge. The category of constant tenor lovers includes Robert (in *Étienne Marcel*), Don Gomez (in *Henry VIII*), Ascanio (in *Ascanio*) and Pâris (in *Hélène*). Sabatino (in *Proserpine*) is faithful to Angiola, but only because Proserpine refuses him.

Other tenor lovers prove wayward if not actually unfaithful. Each one is a victim of the power of art. Conrad (in *Le Timbre d'argent*) treats his fiancée Rosa badly out of obsession with his painting of the model Fiametta and his spineless yielding to the lure of the mad doctor Spiridion. Kornélis (in *La Princesse jaune*) is equally heartless to his fiancée Léna, bewitched like Conrad by a painting, in his case a painting of the Japanese beauty Ming. Benvenuto Cellini (in *Ascanio*), actually a baritone, is incapable of truly loving either Colombe or Scozzone since his true mistress is his art.

A successful piece of character casting, probably to be credited to Guiraud, is the poet Fortunatus in *Frédégonde* as a tenor. Other character parts include Raphaël, the baritone hermit in *L'Ancêtre*, with his attachment to bees, and Eustache, in *Étienne Marcel*, the unlikely traitor who sings a folksy song to amuse the company in Act I.

The most substantial baritone roles are Henry VIII and Benvenuto Cellini, calling for singers of the highest artistry, while Spiridion (in *Le Timbre d'argent*) is a splendid baritone part for a fine character actor, clever in disguises and artfully persuasive at all times. Henry VIII and the High Priest in *Samson et Dalila*, both baritones, confound the tradition of casting kings and priests as basses, while the other kings, François I and Charles V (in *Ascanio*), and the holy men Campeggio and Cranmer (in *Henry VIII*) and Prétextat (in *Frédégonde*) are true to tradition as basses.

Le Carnaval des animaux and *Les Odeurs de Paris* can leave no doubt that Saint-Saëns possessed a strong sense of humour, resulting in comic operas of which at least two are truly comic, not merely 'comiques'. *Gabriella di Vergy* in 1885 and *Phryné* in 1893 make fun, in turn, of Italian opera and the pomposity of officials, both relatively easy targets. The first is obviously slight in substance and purpose, but the second offers excellent opportunities for operatic humour that are actually rare outside the field of operetta. The main target of the action is the 'archonte' Dicéphile, a superb role for a comic bass, with a supporting pair of clowns, Cynalopex and Agoragine. The French version with dialogue is much to be preferred to the Italian version with recitatives. Phryné herself must have a fine sense of comic timing as well as a brilliant voice and a Praxitelean figure.

A composer who could offer the operatic chorus such a fine participation in the action as in *Samson et Dalila* is to be rebuked, it must be said, for failing to involve them as much as they might have been in his later grand operas, especially *Les Barbares*. Even in *Henry VIII* their contribution to the action is largely formal, and in *L'Ancêtre* there is scope for a stronger contribution from the two warring families with strength of numbers behind them. Gallet's librettos, too, fail to exploit the participatory potential of the chorus. Nevertheless, the writing for chorus in all these operas is never less than expert, with some great ensemble moments in *Étienne Marcel*, *Henry VIII* and elsewhere. At the end of Act I of *Henry VIII* the procession leading Buckingham to the block is heard from the street outside, while all inside react with horror to the king's merciless treatment of his subjects. This is superbly dramatic. One of the best of these ensembles in *Henry VIII* is the Septet at the end of Act II, which was replaced by ballets before the first performance and has not been published and has probably never been performed to this day. As for Saint-Saëns's orchestration, it is so solid a part of his armoury that no criticism can penetrate it, unless it were for failing to adopt the weightiness of Wagner or Bruckner, or the crudity of Puccini or Mascagni. Refinement and sensitivity govern Saint-Saëns's choice of instrumentation at all times, with a few unusual sonorities brought in for special effect: the anvils in Cellini's workshop, the sistra in *La Foi*, the contrabass clarinet in *Henry VIII* and *Hélène*.

A word of advocacy is necessary for the ballet music in these operas, since it is an easy target for the scissors wielded by opera companies that cannot afford dancers and by audiences with little taste for the spectacle. At the Paris Opéra, opera and ballet enjoyed equal status as art forms and commanded an equally large following in the public. Large operas that included ballet satisfied all parties, since pure spectacle was an acknowledged part of the attraction. For the composer, ballet provided opportunities for virtuosity, both in orchestral playing and in resourcefulness of colour, especially if exotic lands were the setting or exotic entertainers, such as gypsies, were called in. For Saint-Saëns, the ballet music was important, not something to be left to the last moment, and he was proud of the variety and vitality of his ballet music. He once admitted that he found his knowledge of Latin verse a help in finding rhythms for dancing.[4] It is a pity that he wrote no more than the one stand-alone ballet, *Javotte*, too little appreciated today as a masterly ballet score.

Saint-Saëns liked to evoke places and things, relying on his rich orchestral imagination. The different worlds of the Hebrews and the Philistines in *Samson et Dalila* illustrate this well, for although it was hardly original to give the Hebrews a recognised church style in their lamentations, the depiction of Philistines as shallow and pagan is brilliantly achieved with music whose vulgarity is more and more pronounced as the opera proceeds. In *L'Ancêtre* the hermit Raphaël's solo at the end of Act I, addressed to his hive of bees, offered the composer a superb opportunity for buzzing music to which, of course, he did not fail to respond. In *Phryné*, as in the incidental music for *Antigone* and in *Déjanire*, Saint-Saëns attempted to recreate Greek music, relying on the work of Gevaert and Bourgault-Ducoudray. He went on to

---

[4] Letter of 8 January 1901, RATNER 2012, p. 147.

introduce what he supposed to be Persian music in *Parysatis* and Egyptian music in *La Foi*.

When it comes to inventive stagecraft, few operas come close to *Le Timbre d'argent* with its many dissolves and transformations, not to mention the underwater scene in the last act. With all this to devise, the stage staff at any theatre would have an unusual challenge. This is a remarkably ambitious opera, definitely the work of a young man keen to make an impression and who gave all the principal roles of Spiridion, Conrad and Hélène magnificent numbers in solo and in ensemble.

Theatre music for Saint-Saëns meant much more than opera. From the beginning he was writing music for plays and ballets as well as for operas, and the latter part of his career is notable for his widening delight in unorthodox combinations of music and drama. This came to the fore with the Béziers adventure starting in 1898, a large-scale open-air concept that claimed without much authority to be recreating the theatre of ancient Greece. The music for the film *L'Assassinat du Duc de Guise* has a claim to be the most dramatic music he ever wrote, and we should not overlook the dramatic force of the *Scène d'Horace* of 1860 or of many of his songs. Two settings of Hugo poems are just a glimpse of what Saint-Saëns could do in a smaller frame: *Le Pas d'armes du Roi Jean*, composed at the age of seventeen, and *La Fiancée du timbalier* of 1887, both small dramas with orchestra, both superbly effective and vivid.

What Saint-Saëns's operas do not exhibit is the unbuttoned emotion that has made Tchaikovsky's symphonies and Puccini's operas so popular. Nor do we find it in Mozart, whom Saint-Saëns regarded as the supreme model. It was simply not in his nature to move so far from his natural terrain where refinement, dignity and clarity were preponderant. He was a classicist through and through, with a formidable technique and range always kept in check by the need for balance and formal order. A number of like-minded Frenchmen understood this. Reynaldo Hahn wrote in his obituary:

> Saint-Saëns is one of the greatest musicians of all time and all countries. His immense œuvre displays an extraordinary variety and richness. The beauty of his style is not to be surpassed. No one wrote better than he did, which should be sufficient to make all artists admire him. [. . .] He has been criticised for not being a 'man of the theatre'. That arises because he devoted to his theatrical works, perhaps wrongly, the same care for form, the same intellectual control, and – this is what many regard as a crime – the same refined taste as to his chamber or concert works. A sense of proportion in the area of feeling and a careful display of expression are, it seems, forbidden to the composer of opera. [. . .] Saint-Saëns is the last great classical composer.[5]

Fauré, in his review of *L'Ancêtre*, argued that the opera displayed all Saint-Saëns's great characteristics as an opera composer, namely:

---

[5] Reynaldo Hahn, 'Saint-Saëns', *Excelsior*, 18 December 1921.

Truth, steadfastness, clarity in the depiction of character and in the presentation and development of situations; complete accuracy in expression; an infallible sense of balance and proportion; a constantly surprising sobriety and directness; an unrivalled facility and clarity in complex passages; in a word, every admirable feature of opera that his versatile and powerful genius has brought to the theatre.[6]

*****

No discussion of late nineteenth-century French opera can escape the issue of Wagner, largely because it was a central preoccupation of critics at that time and has remained a concern of writers on French opera to this day.[7] Wagner was endlessly discussed in every salon and at every dinner table, and worshipped or excoriated according to taste; yet for composers more was at stake than simple admiration or distaste. Before his death in 1883, Wagner's music was very little known in Paris and his ideas imperfectly transmitted by selective quotation and translation. Performances of the prelude to *Tristan und Isolde* in Paris in 1860 had left the impression that his new style was extremely chromatic, which was correct, and (in the general opinion) ugly. At first 'Wagnerian' was a term of abuse, but in the 1880s, when Wagnerism became a popular fad, composers were berated for not being Wagnerian enough. Chromatically advanced music such as Bizet's was dubbed 'Wagnerian', even though his style evolved naturally from the heritage of Berlioz, Chopin, Gounod, Halévy and David, perhaps Schumann, while Brahms developed a chromatic style from that of Schumann without ever being accused of stealing from Wagner. For French composers the picture was different, since they recognised that Wagner's style could not be simply grafted on to the inherited French style, even when their own explorations led inevitably to chromaticism. Franck's chromaticism, for example, is much more successful in his instrumental music than when he overtly imitates Wagner in his operas. In Saint-Saëns's operas the chromaticism is more and more marked as time goes on, in a gradual progression, and occasionally chords or sequences sound like Wagner, but it was never imitation or theft.

The other elements that were widely understood to be Wagnerian were the use of leitmotifs, a continuous action from scene to scene, and a faith in mythology as the only fit material for opera. None of these were truly Wagner's invention, and the first two were products of the natural historical development of opera away from the aria-dominated aesthetic of baroque opera. They are part of the maturation process in Verdi, to cite only one contemporary composer, and they occur naturally in Saint-Saëns as part of his growth as a composer for the stage.

[6] Gabriel Fauré, 'L'Ancêtre', Le Figaro, 25 February 1906.
[7] Note, for example, the subtitle of Steven Huebner's valuable and far-ranging study, *French Opera at the Fin de Siècle: Wagnerism, Nationalism, and Style*, Oxford, 1999.

On the subject of leitmotifs he wrote to Camille Bellaigue in 1910: 'I have used leitmotifs generously in all my operas, not out of caprice but on principle. But while Wagner makes a strong feature of them, I put them in the background, with the vocal part, treated *vocally*, in the foreground as far as the stage circumstances allow.'[8] It may have been out of concern not to be too Wagnerian that many of the leitmotifs in Saint-Saëns's operas are not prominent enough, or at least not used to make a dramatic point as much as they could. Many of them are in any case orchestral rather than vocal. It has been my purpose in this book to identify leitmotifs which the listener might miss, since their employment is sometimes short-lived and needlessly subtle in their application. Rarely, if ever, does Saint-Saëns use a motif as a jolt to the memory at moments of dramatic intensity, as does Thomas, for example, at the end of Ophélie's dying solo, when 'Doute la lumière' drifts into her failing brain with gripping effect.

More confessions of faith came in an open letter concerning the opera *Proserpine* in 1887:

> I believe that drama tends towards a synthesis of different styles: singing, declamation, orchestral music in a balance that allows the creator to use all the resources of his art, and the listener to be satisfied in his legitimate appetites. That's the balance I seek, and which others will certainly achieve. My nature and my thinking both drive me in this direction and I would not know how to do otherwise. This is why I am rejected on the one hand by the Wagnerians who despise a melodic style and the art of singing, and on the other by reactionaries who are stuck with the opposite view and regard declamation and symphonic music as superfluous. [...] You have only to divide your work into scenes and not into traditional numbers to be told that you are doing exactly what Wagner does. But baroque French opera was divided into scenes. There is nothing new under the sun.[9]

In mentioning reactionaries who despise declamation and symphonic music, Saint-Saëns is referring to the old school of *bel canto* which still had its advocates in 1887. It is hard to believe that he felt any sting from their opinions.

At no time did Saint-Saëns set out to imitate or borrow from Wagner, despite the fact that he deeply admired Wagner's music, knowing that he himself could never challenge him on his own territory. It was the idolatry of Wagner's followers that aroused his anger, not Wagner's music and not the Wagner he knew before the events of 1870 turned him against the author of *Eine Kapitulation*. He had impressed Wagner playing the piano for him in 1860 and he had attended the opening of the Bayreuth Festspielhaus in 1876, with long articles to describe the event and the music, so it was his own choice not to imitate that music except when he needed to, and not to subscribe to the philosophy in which Wagner's work was encased. Yet the critics raised the issue of Wagner every time he wrote a new opera. Like Verdi, Bizet and Massenet,

---

[8] Letter of 18 November 1910; RATNER 2012, p. 181.
[9] '*Proserpine* : une lettre de M. Camille Saint-Saëns', *Le Ménestrel*, 17 April 1887; SORET 2012, p. 377.

Saint-Saëns sometimes needed to write chromatic music, sometimes needed to weld one scene to another in a continuous flow, and sometimes needed to apply motifs to identify characters or ideas in an opera. None of these techniques were Wagner's monopoly.

* * * * *

In formulating his views on the nature of opera, Saint-Saëns held firm to a number of common-sense principles based on his respect for the classics, for the traditions of grand opera and opéra-comique that had been in place in France since early in the century, and for his leading predecessors, notably Berlioz and Gounod. He accepted the role of ballet in grand opera and the function of dialogue in opéra-comique, both of these resisted by opera houses and audiences today. He was versatile by instinct. He could write like Offenbach or he could write like Meyerbeer. He was instinctively averse to modernism for its own sake. He had a deep respect for art and a lively sense of humour. He cared greatly about matching his music to particular voices and finding the right singer for particular roles. His political views changed over the years, and although he felt less and less comfortable in Paris he was always a patriot. His plan for a series of operas on historical French subjects produced three works, *Étienne Marcel*, *Ascanio* and *Les Barbares* (not forgetting *L'Assassinat du Duc de Guise*), with *Henry VIII* proving the vitality of a non-French historical setting in the tradition of Meyerbeer. His librettist and close friend Louis Gallet proposed subjects from both history and myth with some regularity, and after *Phryné* in 1893 and the adventure of *Déjanire* at Béziers in 1898, he showed a preference for the mythologies of ancient Greece and the Middle East, partly as a response to Wagner's absorption in Nordic mythology. *Hélène*, with its story from the Trojan War recounting the intervention of the gods, is treated in the spirit of historical narrative, exploring the real cause of those great events. He rejected the semi-historical subject of *Frédégonde* when it was proposed to him by Gallet, but he nonetheless later completed the score that Guiraud was working on when he died, out of respect for its composer, and he was wounded by the opera's failure.

In 1909, in response to a debate about the place of history and legend in opera, Saint-Saëns wrote a long article for the *Revue de Paris* to argue that both backgrounds had their place in opera, and that history and legend constantly overlapped. What he questioned was the argument that the timeless element of legend forced the listener to contemplate the inner meaning of the action. Historical events, he argued, can carry equal significance and meaning that the music can enhance. Lully, he pointed out, drew his material from mythology because it was ideal for spectacle, not because there was much to learn from the feelings of the participants. His summary is clear:

> So let composers choose their subjects for opera and the form of their operas as they wish and in line with their temperament. How many young talents in our own time have lost their

way because instead of following their own instincts they felt they had to toe the line. All great artists, with the illustrious Richard the most obvious of all, have defied the critics. Like the miller in the fable, they have pleased themselves, and been wise.[10]

In an article of 1879 Saint-Saëns expressed some further thoughts on dramatic music:

> In relation to the theatre my principles are quite simply those of common sense. I find they have been admirably formulated by M. César Cui of St Petersburg. I could not express them better myself: 'Dramatic music must be in perfect alliance with the words. It must always have intrinsic worth, independent of the text. The structure of scenes in opera must depend entirely on the relationship between the characters, as well as on the general progress of the action.'[11]

Saint-Saëns's comment on this is: 'These principles are similar to those of Richard Wagner; they are not identical. If these principles are mine, it does not follow that I am an admirer of the young Russian school. Principles are one thing, the way you put them into practice is another.'

Cui's mention of the words is a reminder that in Saint-Saëns's vocal music, both opera and *mélodie*, his declamation is exemplary, with the French language placed perfectly in terms of stress and accent. Singers have much to thank him for in this respect. This is a quality he shares with Massenet, but without Massenet's extremely fussy directions to singers. In contrast, neither Halévy nor his pupil Bizet showed much respect for correct declamation, which in Bizet's case allowed him to appropriate an earlier piece of music set to different words, a practice Saint-Saëns would never sanction. Fertility was never Saint-Saëns's problem, so that although there are cases of self-borrowing in his music, these are all confined to instrumental music.[12] Borrowings in his operas involve only ballet movements or instrumental sections transferred from one context to another, for example a theme from the finale of *Le Duc de Parme* recycled as a ballet in *Henry VIII*, never to vocal music.

In 1917, towards the end of his life, he wrote a note to introduce a revival of *Henry VIII* at the Opéra:

> As long as I have been writing for the stage my method has not changed. I find that singers are there to sing and the orchestra to support them and not stifle them. [. . .]
> The voice being the most beautiful of instruments, with the superiority over instruments that living creatures have over inanimate objects, I find that it, not the orchestra, should be

---

[10] Saint-Saëns, 'L'Histoire et la Légende dans le drame lyrique', *La Revue de Paris*, 15 August 1909; SORET 2012, p. 655. The reference is to La Fontaine, *Fables*, Book III, no. 1, 'The Miller, his Son and Ass', translated by R. Thomson, 1884:
> 'Whate'er I seem in other people's eyes,
> I'll please myself.' He did so, and was wise.

[11] Saint-Saëns, 'Causerie musicale', *La Nouvelle Revue*, October–November 1879; SORET 2012, p. 236.

[12] See RATNER 1997.

the main vehicle for the melody. That does not prevent the orchestra from commenting on the action, or illustrating the hidden drama, or expressing the inexpressible. Is there anyone, in a hundred listeners, who understands this orchestral language? I lost many illusions about this the day I was sitting next to a well-known Wagnerian lady at a performance of one of the god's works, and I heard her explain to me the meaning of the music by saying exactly the opposite of what the composer was trying to express. So why would I employ that method? Because of the immense resources it offers for the development of music, and then, if I may say so, for pleasure. For the composer's greatest joys are in the conception and working out of his work much more than in its performance. Yet the pleasure is great when the work is performed as it was at the beginning, as *Henry VIII* will be tomorrow.[13]

Two points raised in this passage need comment. In saying that his method of composing had not changed since he began as a composer, Saint-Saëns acknowledges his isolated position in the face of twentieth-century modernism, whose arrival distressed him greatly. There is steady development of his style over the years, with an increased chromaticism in the operas after *Phryné*, in *Les Barbares* and *Hélène* especially, reaching a furthest point in the operatic version of *Déjanire*, while he furiously resisted the move away from tonality represented by Debussy's exploration of parallel rather than functional chordal movement. His exploration of the music of the ancient world was enough of a deviation from his previous path to qualify as one of the many modernist quests that sprang up around 1900, even if he was almost its only exponent.

The second point is that Saint-Saëns was right to say that the composer's pleasure lay in the creation of a work, not in its performance, for he evidently did not much enjoy hearing his own music. Everyone was astonished that he was not there in Rouen in March 1890 when *Samson et Dalila* was staged for the first time in France, and he was not in Paris a few weeks later for the premiere of *Ascanio*, not even for the period of rehearsal. In later years, when his operas were being revived with great frequency all over Europe, he rarely attended. When *Proserpine* was revived in Toulouse in 1894 in a new version that considerably altered the last two acts, he went there when rehearsals started, but was away in north Africa before opening night.

There are other important writings by Saint-Saëns on the nature of dramatic music, too extensive to quote here, for example: 'Drame lyrique et drame musical' in 1889;[14] and 'À propos du drame lyrique' in 1897.[15] His voluminous writings reveal a constant concern for the nature of dramatic music, as even a cursory sampling of the collected *Écrits* will reveal.

* * * * *

---

[13] 'Henry VIII', *Le Figaro*, 30 November 1917; SORET 2012, pp. 977–78.
[14] Published in *L'Artiste*, November 1889, pp. 395–404; SORET 2012, pp. 416–22.
[15] Published in the *Revue politique et littéraire : Revue bleue*, 3 July 1897; SORET 2012, p. 529.

So what happened to this magnificent body of music after 1921? It should never be said that Saint-Saëns lived too long, since he retained his faculties to the end and wrote excellent music in his eighties. But it was his misfortune to live into the post-war world which was determined to turn its back not only on Romanticism and Wagner but on Debussyist impressionism too. 'Son rôle cessa avec sa vie', wrote André Cœuroy of Saint-Saëns in 1956.[16] Nothing could be further from 1920s taste than heroic grand opera and any suggestion of romantic sentiment as found in the operas of Saint-Saëns and Massenet, and although the latter clung to the side of the sinking ship with *Manon* and *Werther*, the former took a serious plunge, the survival of *Samson et Dalila* notwithstanding. As its contribution to the centennial of Saint-Saëns's birth in 1935, in what should have been a celebration, the *Revue musicale* published an assessment by Robert Bernard which essentially denied him any greatness at all: 'Who would hesitate to sacrifice Saint-Saëns's entire *œuvre* for a single page of the *St Matthew Passion*, of *Don Giovanni*, of any Beethoven quartet, of *Dichterliebe*, or of *Boris Godunov*?'[17]

Part of the blame may go back to Saint-Saëns's decision in 1871 to replace his publisher Georges Hartmann with Auguste Durand. Hartmann was tireless in promoting young French composers, chief among them Massenet, whose career took off brilliantly in the 1870s under Hartmann's care, while Saint-Saëns was having difficulty getting anyone to stage his works. The house of Durand has never been much concerned with opera, in strong contrast with Choudens, Hartmann and Heugel, all of whom pestered opera houses and critics on behalf of their composers, while Durand, and later his son Jacques, saw his business in terms of selling printed music without stepping far beyond no. 4 Place de la Madeleine. With Saint-Saëns himself constantly away from Paris, it was often left to Gallet or other friends to take on the public relations needed to promote large works like operas. The fact that Saint-Saëns's operas still did well in the years leading up to the First World War suggests that with strong representation they would have done even better. Since his death, Saint-Saëns has had no spokesman to work on his behalf in this sphere.

No composer as versatile and as productive as Saint-Saëns can expect to see his works sustained in the repertoire indefinitely. There is simply too much of it, and it is represented in every genre: symphonies, symphonic poems, choral music, songs, chamber music, piano music, organ music, opera, ballet, and even film. Two obvious parallel cases are provided by Tchaikovsky and Dvořák, both born within a few years of Saint-Saëns, both unceasingly productive all their lives, both prepared to write in every genre, both leaving about a dozen operas of which just one stands out in popularity: Tchaikovsky's *Eugene Onegin* and Dvořák's *Rusalka* (with the *Queen of Spades* coming close in the former case). Saint-Saëns also shared with Tchaikovsky a compulsion to travel, never staying in one place for long. Versatility in a composer is seen to come at

---

[16] Cœuroy 1956, p. 346.   [17] *La Revue musicale*, XVI/160 (November 1935), p. 243.

a price, while single-mindedness toward opera gave us Wagner, Verdi, and Puccini, who dominate the repertoire, while Saint-Saëns, Tchaikovsky and Dvořák retain their modest hold. Only Mozart has escaped paying the price for his versatility.

The good news is that in the last few years things have improved. For a list of recordings, see Discography. The list of performances of Saint-Saëns's operas since 1921 is short, but it shows a marked increase since 2000:

Staged Performances since 1921 (excluding *Samson et Dalila*)

1935	*La Princesse jaune*	Paris, Opéra-Comique
1938	*Phryné*	Cairo
1946	*La Princesse jaune*	Paris, Opéra-Comique
1983	*Henry VIII*	San Diego
1991	*Henry VIII*	Compiègne
2002	*Henry VIII*	Barcelona
2004	*La Princesse jaune*	Paris, Opéra-Comique
	La Princesse jaune	Lucca
2005	*La Princesse jaune*	Berlin
2008	*La Princesse jaune*	Zwolle
2010	*La Princesse jaune*	Siena
2013	*La Princesse jaune*	Buxton
2017	*La Princesse jaune*	Melbourne
	Le Timbre d'argent	Paris, Opéra-Comique
	Frédégonde	Ho Chi Minh City
2019	*L'Ancêtre*	Munich

Concert Performances since 1921 (excluding *Samson et Dalila*)

1960	*Phryné*	Paris, ORTF
1989	*Henry VIII*	Montpellier
1994	*Étienne Marcel*	Montpellier
2001	*La Princesse jaune*	New York
2004	*La Princesse jaune*	London
2008	*Hélène*	Prague
2012	*Henry VIII*	Bard College, New York
2014	*Les Barbares*	St-Étienne
2016	*Proserpine*	Munich
	Proserpine	Versailles
2017	*Ascanio*	Geneva

Staged performances are still a rarety, with *La Princesse jaune, Le Timbre d'argent* and *Frédégonde* revived in 2017 and *L'Ancêtre* in 2019. In concert the later operas have been more fortunate, with performances of *Henry VIII* and *Étienne Marcel* at the Montpellier Festival, and *Proserpine, Ascanio, Hélène* and *Les Barbares* all revived without staging elsewhere.

Most of these concert performances are available as CDs. A recording of *Phryné* given by French Radio in 1960 was issued as a CD in 2013. *Henry VIII* was revived at Compiègne in 1991 and *Étienne Marcel* was revived at Montpellier in 1994, and both performances were recorded, *Henry VIII* as a DVD. *Hélène* was revived in concert in Prague in 2008 and recorded, with a disc of Saint-Saëns ballet music from the same conductor. The best news comes from the foundation Palazzetto Bru Zane, which has issued a recording of *Les Barbares* from the concert performance in St-Étienne in 2014, a recording of *Proserpine* from performances in Munich and Versailles in 2016, and another of *Le Timbre d'argent* following its revival at the Opéra-Comique in June 2017. The concert performance of *Ascanio* in Geneva was issued as a CD in 2018. The operas that still remain to be recorded are *Le Duc de Parme*, *Parysatis* and both versions of *Déjanire*.

The revival of these forgotten operas on the stage is a risky proposition in the contemporary climate of stage direction which favours familiar works in unexpected settings rather than unfamiliar works with traditional settings. Few directors can be trusted to take a Saint-Saëns opera seriously. Much more effective would be a campaign to see that all the stage works are recorded, and recorded well, so that reliable assessments of their theatrical viability can be made and their abundant musical riches can be heard at last.

BIBLIOGRAPHY

1. Scores and Librettos, with Approximate Timings
2. Libraries and Archives
3. Main Reference Works
4. Saint-Saëns's Writings on Music
5. Letters
6. General Bibliography

1. SCORES AND LIBRETTOS, WITH APPROXIMATE TIMINGS

(* = may be consulted on Gallica)
(† = may be consulted on IMSLP)
All publications in Paris unless otherwise indicated

L'Ancêtre 1 h 27 m
Main autograph: F-Pn MS 2450
Full score: Durand, 1906, 338 p.*†
Vocal score: Durand, 1906, 221 p.*†
Libretto: Calmann-Lévy, 1906, 34 p.

Andromaque
Main autograph: F-Pn MS 518
Full score: Durand, 1903, 112 p.*
Vocal score: none
Libretto: Racine, *Andromaque*

Antigone
Main autograph: F-Pn MS 517
Full score: Durand, 1909, 95 p.*
Vocal score: Durand, 1893, 64 p.*†
Libretto: Calmann-Lévy, n.d.

Ascanio 3 h 15 m
Main autograph: F-Pn MS 480–481*
Full score: Durand, 1893, 446 p. *†
Vocal score: Durand Schœnewerk, 1890, 391 p.†
Durand, 1893, 363 p.
Libretto: Calmann-Lévy, 1890, 92 p.*†
Calmann-Lévy, n.d., 88 p.

L'Assassinat du
Duc de Guise 19 m
Main autograph: lost
Full score: Durand, 1908 (orchestral parts)†
Piano score: Durand, 1908, 35 p.*†
Libretto: none

Les Barbares 1 h 58 m
Main autograph: F-Pn MS 556
Full score: Durand, 1901, 414 p.*†
Vocal score: Durand, 1901, 291 p.†
Libretto: Calmann-Lévy, 1901, 39 p.

Déjanire (I)
Main autograph: F-Pn MS 510
Full score: Durand, 1898, 29 p. (*Prélude et Cortège*)*†
Vocal score: Durand, 1898, 115 p.†
Libretto: Calmann-Lévy, 1899, 42 p.*

Déjanire (II) 1 h 42 m
Main autograph: F-Pn MS 509*†
Full score: Durand, 1911, 414 p.*†
Vocal score: Durand, 1910, 213 p.†
 Durand, 1911, 160 p. (with German translation)†
Libretto: Calmann-Lévy, 1910, 34 p.

Le Duc de Parme
Main autograph: F-Pn MS 2494
Full score: none
Vocal score: none
Libretto: lost

Étienne Marcel 2 h 28 m
Main autograph: F-Pn MS 551
Full score: Durand Schœncwerk, 1880, 651 p.*†
Vocal score: Durand Schœnewerk, 1879, 365 p.*†
 Durand Schœnewerk, 1885, 357 p.
 Durand Schœnewerk, n.d., 343 p.
Libretto: Calmann-Lévy, 1879, 67 p.*

La Foi
Main autograph: F-Pn MS 2448*
Full score: Durand, 1909 (*3 Tableaux symphoniques*)*†
Vocal score: Durand, 1912, 73 p.*†
Libretto: P.-V. Stock, 1909

Frédégonde
Main autograph:	F-Po E Rés 669a
Full score:	none
Vocal score:	Dupont, 1895, 322 p.*
Libretto:	Michel Lévy Frères, 1895, 49 p.

Gabriella di Vergy
Main autograph:	Collection Durand-Texte
Full score:	none
Vocal score:	none
Libretto:	Édition de la Trompette, 1883.*

Hélène   1 h 1 m
Main autograph:	F-Pn MS 2452*†
Full score:	Durand, 1904, 202 p.*†
Vocal score:	Durand, 1904, 132 p.†
Libretto:	Calmann-Lévy, 1903, 22 p.

Henry VIII   3 h 17 m
Main autograph:	F-Po A.640a*
Full score:	Durand Schœnewerk, 1883, 651 + 9 p.†
Vocal score:	Durand Schœnewerk, 1883, 444 p.†
	Durand Schœnewerk, n.d., 390 p.
	Durand Schœnewerk,, n.d., 384 p. (with German translation)*
	Durand Schœnewerk, n.d., 343 p. (with Italian translation)
Libretto:	Tresse, 1883, 57 p.
	Tresse et Stock, 1883, 49 p.
	Leipzig, 1887
	Tresse et Stock, 1889, 49 p.
	Calmann-Lévy, 1903, 49 p.
	P.-V. Stock, 1907, 49 p.

Javotte   59 m
Main autograph:	F-Pn MS 513*
Full score:	Durand, 1896, 244 p.*
Piano score:	Durand, 1896, 127 p.*†
Libretto:	Calmann-Lévy, 1899

Lola
Main autograph:	F-Pn MS 819
Full score:	none
Vocal score:	Durand, 1900, 25 p.*†
Libretto:	Calmann-Lévy, 1901, 23 p.

Le Martyre de Vivia
Main autograph: F-Pn MS 875 (j)
Full score: none
Vocal score: none
Libretto: Garnier Frères, 1850

Nina Zombi
Main autograph: F-Pn MS 875(q)
Full score: none
Vocal score: none
Libretto: none

On ne badine pas avec l'amour
Main autograph: F-Pn MS 2446
Full score: none
Vocal score: none
Libretto: Alfred de Musset play

Parysatis
Main autograph: F-Pn MS 519
Full score: Durand, 1902, 56 p. (*Airs de ballet*)*
Vocal score: Durand, 1902, 151 p.*†
Libretto: Félix Juven, 1902, 60 p.

Phryné 49 m + dialogue
Main autograph: F-Pn MS 516
Full score: Durand, 1893, 175 p.*†
Vocal score: Durand, 1893, 145 p.*†
Durand, 1896, 197 p. (with Italian translation)
Durand, 1909, 147 p. (with German translation)
Libretto: Ollendorff, 1893, 64 p.

La Princesse jaune 44 m + dialogue
Main autograph: F-Pn MS 532*
Full score: Durand Schœnewerk, 1880 (*Ouverture* only)*†
Vocal score: Hartmann, 1872, 71 p.†
Durand, 1885, 71 p.
Durand, 1906, 88p.†
Eroïca, 88 p., n.d., with dialogue
Libretto: Michel Lévy frères, 1872
Calmann-Lévy, 1912

Proserpine	1 h 24 m
Main autograph:	F-Pn MS 539–543
Full score:	Durand, 1895, 297 p.†
Vocal score:	Durand Schœnewerk, 1887, 245 p.
	Durand, 1892, 234 p.†
	Durand, 1900, 234 p. (with Italian translation)
Libretto:	Michel Lévy frères, 1887, 51 p.
	Calmann-Lévy, 1899, 48 p.

Samson et Dalila	1 h 58 m
Main autograph:	F-Pn MS 544*
Full score:	Durand Schœnewerk, 1883, 494 p.
	Durand, 1900, 497 p.†
	Durand, 1930, 497 p. (miniature score)
	Kalmus, n.d., 497 p.
	Dover, Mineola, 1998, 512 p.
Vocal score:	Durand Schœnewerk, 1876, 264 p. (with German translation)†
	Durand, 1892, 268 p.*
	Schirmer, New York, 1892, 222 p. (with English translation)†
	Durand, 1891, 266 p. (with Italian translation)
	Durand, 1894, 224 p. (with English translation)
	Durand, 1900, 285 p.†
	Durand, 1907, 274 p. (with German translation)†
	Gutheil, Moscow, n.d., 261 p. (with Russian translation)
Libretto:	Hoftheater, Weimar, 1877
	Calmann-Lévy, 1892, 44 p.
	Ditson, Boston, 1895, 26 p.
	Rullman, New York, c. 1935, 21p.

Le Timbre d'argent	2 h 33 m + dialogue
Main autograph:	Fonds Choudens
Full score:	Choudens, 1902, 419 p.
Vocal score:	Choudens, 1877, 304 p.*
	Choudens, 1879, 271 p.†
	Choudens, 1903, 285 p.
	Choudens, 1903, 252 p. (with German translation)
	Choudens, 1913, 318 p.*
Libretto:	Michaelis, 1877, 77 p.
	Choudens, 1902, 71 p.
	Choudens, 1913, 69 p.

2. LIBRARIES AND ARCHIVES

F-DI	Dieppe, Médiathèque Jean-Renoir
F-Po	Paris, Bibliothèque-Musée de l'Opéra
F-Pn	Paris, Bibliothèque nationale de France, Département de la Musique
GB-Lbl	London, British Library
US-NYpm	New York, Pierpont Morgan Library

3. MAIN REFERENCE WORKS

RATNER 2012   RATNER, Sabina Teller. *Camille Saint-Saëns 1835–1921: A Thematic Catalogue of his Complete Works*, Vol. II, *The Dramatic Works*, Oxford University Press, 2012.

SORET 2012   SORET, Marie-Gabrielle (ed.). *Camille Saint-Saëns : Écrits sur la Musique et les Musiciens 1870–1921*, Vrin, 2012.

4. SAINT-SAËNS'S WRITINGS ON MUSIC (COLLECTED IN SORET 2012)

SAINT-SAËNS 1885   SAINT-SAËNS, Camille. *Harmonie et Mélodie*, Paris, Calmann-Lévy, [1885].

SAINT-SAËNS 1894A   SAINT-SAËNS, Camille. *Problèmes et Mystères*, Paris, Flammarion, 1894.

SAINT-SAËNS 1894B   SAINT-SAËNS, Camille. *Charles Gounod et le Don Juan de Mozart*, Paris, Ollendorff, 1894.

SAINT-SAËNS 1899   SAINT-SAËNS, Camille. *Portraits et Souvenirs*, Paris, Calmann-Lévy, 1899, ²1909.

SAINT-SAËNS 1913   SAINT-SAËNS, Camille. *L'École buissonnière. Notes et souvenirs*, Paris, Pierre Lafitte, [1913].

SAINT-SAËNS 1914   SAINT-SAËNS, Camille. *Au Courant de la vie*, Paris, Dorbon-Aîné, [1914].

SAINT-SAËNS 1919   SAINT-SAËNS, Camille. *Musical Memories*, translated by Edwin Gile Rich, Boston, MA, Small, Maynard & Co., 1919.

SAINT-SAËNS 1990   SAINT-SAËNS, Camille. *Regards sur mes contemporains*, ed. Yves Gérard, Arles, Bernard Coutaz, 1990.

SAINT-SAËNS 2008   SAINT-SAËNS, Camille. *Camille Saint-Saëns on Music and Musicians*, ed. Roger Nichols, Oxford University Press, 2008.

5. LETTERS

Nectoux, Jean-Michel (ed.). *Camille Saint-Saëns et Gabriel Fauré : Correspondance*, Paris, Heugel, 1973.

Bondeville, Emmanuel (ed.). *Camille Saint-Saëns 1835–1921. Correspondance inédite*, Paris, La Revue Musicale, 1983.

Jousse, Eurydice et Gérard, Yves (ed.). *Lettres de compositeurs à Camille Saint-Saëns*, Lyon, Symétrie, 2009.

Soret, Marie-Gabrielle (ed.). *Camille Saint-Saëns Jacques Rouché Correspondance (1913–1921)*, Actes Sud, 2016.

Soret, Marie-Gabrielle et Herlin, Denis (eds.). Camille Saint-Saëns : Correspondance avec Auguste et Jacques Durand, forthcoming.

6. GENERAL BIBLIOGRAPHY

AGUÉTANT 1938	AGUÉTANT, Pierre. *Saint-Saëns par lui-même d'après des lettres reçues et commentées*, Paris, Alsatia, [1938].
AUGÉ DE LASSUS 1894	AUGÉ DE LASSUS, Lucien. *Les Grands Maîtres mis en petites comédies*, Paris, Ollendorf, 1894.
AUGÉ DE LASSUS 1914	AUGÉ DE LASSUS, Lucien. *Saint-Saëns*, Paris, Delagrave, 1914.
AVANT-SCÈNE 1978	SAINT-SAËNS, Camille. *Samson et Dalila*, L'Avant-Scène Opéra, no. 15, May–June 1978.
BARBARES 2014	SAINT-SAËNS, Camille. *Les Barbares*, CD-book, Venice, Palazzetto Bru Zane, 2014.
BARD 2012	*Saint-Saëns and his World*, Bard Festival programme book, 2012.
BARTOLI 1996	BARTOLI, Jean-Pierre. 'À la recherche d'une représentation sonore de l'Égypte antique : l'égyptomanie musicale en France de Rossini à Debussy', in *L'Égyptomanie à l'épreuve de l'archéologie*, Paris, Musée du Louvre, 1996.
BAUMANN 1905	BAUMANN, Emile. *Les Grandes Formes de la musique: l'œuvre de Camille Saint-Saëns*, Paris: Ollendorff, 1905, with a second edition in 1923.
BELLAIGUE 1890	BELLAIGUE, Camille. *L'Année musicale octobre 1889 à octobre 1890*, Paris: Delagrave, 1890.
BERLIOZ 1852	BERLIOZ, Hector. *Les Soirées de l'orchestre*, Paris, Michel Lévy Frères, 1852.
BERLIOZ 1975	BERLIOZ, Hector. *Correspondance générale*, Vol. II, ed. Frédéric Robert. Paris, Flammarion, 1975.
BERLIOZ 2001	BERLIOZ, Hector. *Correspondance générale*, Vol. VII, ed. Hugh Macdonald, Paris, Flammarion, 2001.
BÉZIERS 1989	*L'Opéra dans l'arène, ou l'aventure de Fernand Castelbon mécène à Béziers*, Béziers, Conseil Général de l'Hérault, 1989.
BIZET 1867	BIZET, Georges. 'Causerie musicale', *La Revue nationale et étrangère*, 3 August 1867.
BONNAURE 2010	BONNAURE, Jacques. *Saint-Saëns*, Arles, Actes Sud, 2010.
BONNEROT 1914	BONNEROT, Jean. *C. Saint-Saëns. Sa Vie et son œuvre*, Paris, Durand, 1914.
BONNEROT 1922	BONNEROT, Jean. *C. Saint-Saëns (1835–1921). Sa Vie et son œuvre*, nouvelle édition, Paris, Durand, 1922.
BRANGER 2012	BRANGER, Jean-Christophe. 'Rivals and Friends: Saint-Saëns, Massenet, and Thaïs', in PASLER 2012, p. 33–47.
BRANGER 2017	BRANGER, Jean-Christophe and LARDIC, Sabine Teulon (eds.). *Provence et Languedoc à l'opéra en France au XIXe siècle: cultures et représentations*, Publications de l'Université de Saint-Étienne, 2017, p. 333–51.

BROOKS 2008	BROOKS, Erin. '« Une culture classique supérieure » : Saint-Saëns et l'esthétique antique', in *Figures de l'Antiquité dans l'opéra français : des Troyens de Berlioz à Œdipe d'Enesco*, Actes du Colloque du IXe Festival Massenet, Saint-Étienne, 9 et 10 novembre 2007, ed. Jean-Christophe Branger and Vincent Giroud, Publications de l'Université de Saint-Étienne, 2008, pp. 235–58.
BÜLOW 1907	BÜLOW, Hans von. *Briefe*, VI. Band, Leipzig, 1907.
CHABRIER 1994	CHABRIER, Emmanuel. *Correspondance*, ed. Roger Delage and Frans Durif, Paris, Klincksieck, 1994.
CHANTAVOINE 1921	CHANTAVOINE, Jean. *L'Œuvre dramatique de Camille Saint-Saëns*, Paris, 1921.
CHANTAVOINE 1947	CHANTAVOINE, Jean. *Camille Saint-Saëns*, Paris, Richard Masse, 1947.
CHARLTON 2003	CHARLTON, David (ed.). *The Cambridge Companion to Grand Opera*, Cambridge University Press, 2003.
CŒUROY 1956	CŒUROY, André. *Dictionnaire critique de la musique ancienne et moderne*, Paris, Payot, 1956.
COLLET 1922	COLLET, Henri. *Samson et Dalila de C. Saint-Saëns : étude historique et critique, analyse musicale*, Paris, Librairie Delaplane, 1922.
CONDÉ 2009	CONDÉ, Gérard. *Charles Gounod*, Paris, Fayard, 2009.
DANDELOT 1930	DANDELOT, Arthur. *La Vie et l'œuvre de Saint-Saëns*, Paris, Éditions Dandelot, 1930.
DAVID 1922	DAVID, Marc. *L'œuvre dramatique de Camille Saint-Saëns*, Guide de Concert, 3 (1922), 31–32.
DEBUSSY 1987	DEBUSSY, Claude. *Monsieur Croche et autres écrits*, ed. François Lesure, Paris, Gallimard, 1987.
DESTRANGES 1895	DESTRANGES, Étienne. *Une Partition méconnue : Proserpine de Camille Saint-Saëns : étude analytique*, Paris, Fischbacher, 1895,
DIEPPE 2003	*Camille Saint-Saëns et l'Algérie*, Dieppe, Château-Musée de Dieppe, 2003.
DOUCHE 2005	DOUCHE, Sylvie, ed. *Camille Saint-Saëns, 'Les Barbares' : dossier de presse parisienne (1901)*, Weinsberg, Musik-Edition Lucie Galland, 2005.
DUKAS 1948	DUKAS, Paul. *Les Écrits de Paul Dukas sur la musique*, ed. G. Samazeuilh, Paris, Société d'éditions françaises et internationales, 1948.
FAURE 1985	FAURE, Michel. *Musique et Société, du Second Empire aux années vingt*, Paris, Flammarion, 1985.
FAURÉ 1951	FAURÉ, Gabriel. *Lettres intimes*, ed. Philippe Fauré-Fremiet, Paris, Éditions du vieux Colombier, 1951.
FAUSER 2005	FAUSER, Annegret. *Musical Encounters at the 1889 Paris World's Fair*, University of Rochester Press, 2005.
FULCHER 1987	FULCHER, Jane. *The Nation's Image: French Grand Opera as Politics and Politicized Art*, Cambridge University Press, 1987.
GALLOIS 2004	GALLOIS, Jean. *Charles-Camille Saint-Saëns*, Sprimont, Mardaga, 2004.
GERHARD 1998	GERHARD, Anselm. *The Urbanization of Opera: Music Theater in Paris in the Nineteenth Century*, University of Chicago Press, 1998.

GILCHER 2005	GILCHER, Dagmar. *Studien zum Opernschaffen von Camille Saint-Saëns*, Kaiserslautern, Reinhold Gondrom Verlag, 2005
GIRDLESTONE 1969	GIRDLESTONE, Cuthbert. *Jean-Philippe Rameau: His Life and Work*, New York, Dover, 1969.
GOLDBECK 2015	GOLDBECK, Melanie von (ed.). *Lettres de Charles Gounod à Pauline Viardot*, Arles, Actes Sud, 2015.
GOUNOD 1896	GOUNOD, Charles. *Mémoires d'un artiste*, Paris, Calmann-Lévy, 1896.
HARDING 1965	HARDING, James. *Saint-Saëns and his Circle*, London, Chapman & Hall, 1965.
HERVEY 1921	HERVEY, Arthur. *Saint-Saëns*, London, John Lane, 1921.
HIPPEAU 1883	HIPPEAU, Edmond. *Henry VIII et l'opéra français*, Paris, La Renaissance musicale, 1883.
HUEBNER 1999	HUEBNER, Steven. *French Opera at the Fin de Siècle: Wagnerism, Nationalism, and Style*, Oxford University Press, 1999.
JOHNSON 1995	JOHNSON, James H. *Listening in Paris*, Berkeley, CA, University of California Press, 1995.
LACOMBE 1997	LACOMBE, Hervé. *Les Voies de l'opéra français au XIXe siècle*, Paris, Fayard, 1997.
LETEURÉ 2014	LETEURÉ, Stéphane. *Camille Saint-Saëns et le Politique de 1870 à 1921 : le Drapeau et la Lyre*, Paris, Vrin, 2014.
LETEURÉ 2017	LETEURÉ, Stéphane. *Camille Saint-Saëns, le compositeur globe-trotter (1857–1921)*, Arles, Actes Sud, 2017.
LOCKE 1991	LOCKE, Ralph. 'Constructing the Oriental "Other": Saint-Saëns's *Samson et Dalila*', *Cambridge Opera Journal* 3 (1991), 261–302.
LOCKE 2009	LOCKE, Ralph P. *Musical Exoticism: Images and Reflections*. Cambridge University Press, 2009.
LYLE 1923	LYLE, Watson. *Camille Saint-Saëns: His Life and Art*, London, Kegan Paul, Trench, Trubner & Co, 1923.
MACDONALD 1993	MACDONALD, Hugh. 'Dr. Mephistopheles: Doctors and Devils in the Librettos of Barbier and Carré', *Journal of Musicological Research*, 13 (1993), 67–78.
MACDONALD 2014	MACDONALD, Hugh. 'Lost Legacy', *Opera News*, 78/11 (May 2014), 32–35.
MARKS 2012	MARKS, Martin. 'Saint-Saëns and Silent Film / Sound Film and Saint-Saëns', in PASLER 2012, pp. 357–69.
MASSENET 1992	MASSENET, Jules. *Mes Souvenirs*, ed. Gérard Condé, Paris, Plume, 1992.
MASSENET 2001	MASSENET, Anne. *Jules Massenet en toutes lettres*, Paris, Éditions de Fallois, 2001.
MONTARGIS 1919	MONTARGIS, Jean. *Camille Saint-Saëns. L'œuvre – l'artiste*, Paris, La Renaissance du Livre, 1919.
MORRIS 2012	MORRIS, Mitchell. 'Saint-Saëns in (Semi) Private', in PASLER 2012, pp. 2–7.
MORTIER 1878	MORTIER, Arnold. *Les Soirées parisiennes de 1877 par un monsieur de l'orchestre*, Paris, St Germain, 1878.

MURPHY 2015	MURPHY, Kerry. 'Saint-Saëns' poème lyrique Hélène, Nellie Melba and Beyond', *Musicology Australia*, 37(2) (2015), 122–34.
NECTOUX 1991	NECTOUX, Jean-Michel. 'Notes sur les spectacles musicaux aux Arènes de Béziers 1898–1910', in *150 Ans de musique française*, Lyon, Actes Sud, 1991, pp. 151–61.
NECTOUX 2008	NECTOUX, Jean-Michel. *Gabriel Fauré : les voix du clair-obscur*, 2nd edn, Paris, Fayard, 2008.
NEITZEL 1899	NEITZEL, Otto. *Camille Saint-Saëns*, Berlin, Harmonie, 1899.
PASLER 2009	PASLER, Jann. *Composing the Citizen: Music as Public Utility in Third Republic France*, Berkeley, CA, University of California Press, 2009.
PASLER 2012	PASLER, Jann, ed. *Camille Saint-Saëns and his World*, Princeton University Press, 2012.
PONS 2014	PONS, José. 'Albert Vizentini, an Enlightened Theatre Director', in *Dimitri*, CD-book, Venice, Palazzetto Bru Zane, Ediciones Singulares, 2014, pp. 69–74.
PROSERPINE 2016	SAINT-SAËNS, Camille. *Proserpine*, CD-book, Venice, Palazzetto Bru Zane, 2016.
RATNER 1997	RATNER, Sabina Teller. 'Saint-Saëns's Self-Borrowings', *Échos de France & d'Italie*, Paris, Buchet/Castel, 1997.
RATNER 2002	RATNER, Sabina Teller. *Camille Saint-Saëns 1835–1921: A Thematic Catalogue of his Complete Works*, vol. I, *The Instrumental Works*, Oxford University Press, 2002.
REES 1999	REES, Brian. *Camille Saint-Saëns: A Life*, London, Faber & Faber, 1999.
SERVIÈRES 1923	SERVIÈRES, Georges. *Saint-Saëns*, Paris, Félix Alcan, 1923.
SHAW 1932	SHAW, George Bernard. *Music in London 1890–94*, London, Constable, 3 vols., 1932.
SORET 2017	SORET, Marie-Gabriel. 'Dans les coulisses des Barbares (1901), « tragédie lyrique » de Saint-Saëns', in *Provence et Languedoc à l'opéra en France au XIXe siècle : cultures et représentations*, ed. Jean-Christophe Branger and Sabine Teulon Lardic, Publications de l'Université de Saint-Étienne, 2017, pp. 177–98.
SOUBIES, 1893	SOUBIES, Albert and MALHERBE, Charles. *Histoire de l'Opéra-Comique. La Seconde Salle Favart 1860–1887*, Paris, Flammarion, 1893.
STEGEMANN 1984	STEGEMANN, Michael. Camille Saint-Saëns und das französische Solokonzert von 1850 bis 1920, Mainz, Schott, 1984. In English as *Camille Saint-Saëns and the French Solo Concerto from 1850 to 1920*, Portland, Amadeus Press, 1991.
STEGEMANN 1988	STEGEMANN, Michael. *Camille Saint-Saëns*, Reinbek, Rowohlt, 1988.
STUDD 1999	STUDD, Stephen. *Saint-Saëns: A Critical Biography*, London, Cygnus Arts, 1999.
THOREL 1903	THOREL, René. 'La genèse d'*Henry VIII* racontée par Ch. Gounod, Camille Saint-Saëns et Armand Silvestre', *Le Gaulois*, 17 May 1903, 1–2.
WAGNER 1911	WAGNER, Richard. *My Life*, 2 vols., London, Constable, 1911.

WALSH 1975   WALSH, T. J. *Monte Carlo Opera 1879–1909*, Dublin, Gill and Macmillan, 1975.

WALSH 1981   WALSH, T. J. *Second Empire Opera. The Théâtre Lyrique, Paris, 1851–1870*, London, Calder, 1981.

WILD 1997   WILD, Nicole. 'Eugène Lacoste et la création de *Henry VIII* à l'Opéra de Paris en 1883', in *Échos de France & d'Italie : Liber amicorum Yves Gérard*, ed. Mongrédien and Nectoux Mussat, Paris, Buchet/Castel, 1997, pp. 213–32.

YON 2007   YON, Jean-Claude. 'Lucien Augé de Lassus (1841–1914) : passeur culturel ou simple vulgarisateur ?', in *Pitres et pantins : transformations du masque comique : de l'Antiquité au théâtre d'ombres*, ed. Sophie Basch and Pierre Chuvin, Paris, Presses de l'Université Paris-Sorbonne, 2007, pp. 193–210.

For a record of all performances at the Paris Opéra, see http://chronopera3.free.fr/#accueil_questce.

DISCOGRAPHY

Andromaque

Ouverture

Prélude to Act IV
1 Orchestre Philharmonique de Monte Carlo, conducted by David Robertson, Auvidis-Valois, 1994.

Ascanio

Complete

Cellini	Jean-François Lapointe
Ascanio	Bernard Richter
Scozzone	Ève-Maud Hubeaux
La Duchesse d'Étampes	Karina Gauvin
Colombe	Clémence Tilquin
conductor	Guillaume Tourniaire

Chœur du Grand Théâtre de Genève.
Chœur et Orchestre de la Haute école de musique de Genéve.
B-Records LBM 013, recorded November 2017.

'Enfants, je ne vous en veux pas'
1 Jean Lassalle (1847–1909), 1902.
2 Marcel Journet (1867–1933), 16 May 1922.
3 Louis Morturier (1888–?1969).

'La, la, la'
1 Méyriane Héglon, with Saint-Saëns, piano, recorded 26 June 1904.
2 Régine Crespin, Orchestre de la Suisse Romande, cond. Lombard.

Ballets nos. 1–12
1 Orchestra Victoria, conducted by Guillaume Tourniaire. Melba Records, 2011.

Ballet no. 9, arranged for flute by Taffanel
1 Philippe Gaubert, 1919.
2 Jean-Jacques Kantorow, violin and orchestra.
3 Robert Aitken, flute, and Elisabeth Westenholz, piano, 1980.

L'Assassinat du Duc de Guise

1 Ensemble Musique Oblique, recorded in 1994.

Les Barbares

Complete

Floria	Catherine Hunold
Livie	Julia Gertseva
Marcomir	Edgaras Montvidas
Scaurus	Jean Teitgen
conductor	Laurent Campellone

Chœur Lyrique et Orchestre Symphonique Saint-Étienne Loire.
Ediciones Singulares ES 1017.
Palazzetto Bru Zane, recorded October 2014.

'N'oublions pas les sacrifices'
Charles Rousselière (1875–1950), with piano, 1901. On YouTube.

Prologue, Act III Prélude, Air de Ballet, Farandole
1 Orchestra Victoria, conducted by Guillaume Tourniaire. Melba Records, 2011.

Déjanire

'Viens ô toi dont le clair visage'
Antonio Paoli (1871–1946), ensemble conducted by Carlo Sabajno, recorded in 1911. On YouTube.

Étienne Marcel

Complete

Étienne Marcel	Alain Fondary
Béatrix	Michèle Lagrange
Robert de Loris	Daniel Galvez-Vallejo
Eustache	Frank Ferrari
Le Dauphin	Alexandra Papadjiakou
Jehan Maillard	Philippe Fourcade
conductor	Hubert Soudant

Orchestre de Radio France, Chœurs des opéras du Rhin et de Montpellier.
Broadcast 11 July 1994. House of Opera CD 598.

'O beaux rêves évanouis'
Joan Hammond (1912–1996), Philharmonia Orchestra, conducted by Walter Susskind, recorded 25 March 1953.

Ballets 1–6
Orchestra Victoria, conducted by Guillaume Tourniaire. Melba Records, 2011.

Ballet, arr. Debussy
Daniel Blumenthal and Robert Groslot, two pianos, recorded 18 to 20 March 1991.

La Foi

Trois Tableaux symphoniques, op. 130
1 Basel Symphony Orchestra, conducted by Ronald Zollman, recorded in 1994.
2 Orchestre National du Capitole de Toulouse, conducted by Michel Plasson, recorded in 1995.

Hélène

Complete

Hélène	Rosamund Illing
Pâris	Steve Davislim
Vénus	Leanne Kenneally
Pallas	Zan McKendree-Wright
conductor	Guillaume Tourniaire

Orchestra Victoria, the Belle Époque Chorus.
Melba Records, recorded October 2007, MR 30114-2.

Henry VIII

Complete
1

Henry VIII	Sherrill Milnes
Catherine of Aragon	Cristina Deutekom
Anne Boleyn	Brenda Boozer
Don Gomez de Feria	Jacques Trussel
Papal Legate	Kenneth Cox
Duke of Norfolk	Kevin Langan
Earl of Surrey	Robert Schmoor
conductor	Antonio Tauriello

Orchestra and chorus of San Diego Opera.
Legendary Recordings, 1984, sung in English.

2

Henry VIII	Alain Fondary
Catherine of Aragon	Françoise Pollet
Anne Boleyn	Magali Chalbeau-Damonte
Don Gomez de Feria	Christian Lara
Papal Legate	Gérard Sekoyan
Duke of Norfolk	Patrick Meroni
Earl of Surrey	Daniel Gomez Vallejo
conductor	Sir John Pritchard

Orchestre et Chœur National de Lyon.
Broadcast from Montpellier, 18 July 1989.

3 (Video)

Henry VIII	Phillippe Rouillon
Catherine of Aragon	Michèle Command
Anne Boleyn	Lucile Vignon
Don Gomez de Feria	André Gabriel
Papal Legate	Gérard Serkoyan
Duke of Norfolk	Philippe Bohée
Earl of Surrey	Alexandre Laiter
conductor	Alain Guingal

Orchestre Lyrique Français, Chœurs de Théâtre des Arts de Rouen.
Recorded in the Théâtre Impérial de Compiègne, 1991.

4

Henry VIII	Simon Estes
Catherine of Aragon	Montserrat Caballé
Anne Boleyn	Nomeda Kazlaus
Don Gomez de Feria	Charles Workman
Papal Legate	Paolo Pecchioli
Duke of Norfolk	Hans Voschesang
Earl of Surrey	Claude Pia
conductor	José M. Collado

Orchestra and chorus of the Gran Teatro del Liceo, Barcelona.
Premiere Opera Ltd, 2002.

'Reine ! Je serai reine !'
1 Elina Garanca, 2016.

Ballet Music
1 Rasumovsky Sinfonia, Mogrelia, 27 March 1995.

Gypsy Dance
1 Boston Pops.
2 Ed Colonne, 1906.

Gypsy Dance and Fête du Houblon
1 Orchestra Victoria, conducted by Guillaume Tourniaire. Melba Records, 2011.

Gypsy Dance and Finale
1 Bournemouth Municipal Orchestra, Dan Godfrey, n.d., on 78s.

'Qui donc commande'
1 Louis Lestelly (1877–1936).
2 Jean Noté (1859–1922).
3 Paul Lantéri, on 78s.

'O cruel souvenir'
1 Françoise Pollett, 1989.
2 Véronique Gens, with Les Talens Lyriques, conducted by Cristophe Rousset. Les Héroïnes Romantiques, Tragédiennes 3, from Erato, 2011.

'Chère Anne que j'adore – La reine alors n'est plus la reine'
1 Daniel Vigneau (1881–1970), on 78.

Javotte

Complete
Queensland Theatre Orchestra, conducted by Andrew Mogrelia, Marco Polo 8223612, recorded March 2004.

Fantaisie for orchestra
Orchestre Philharmonique de Monte Carlo, conducted by David Robertson Auvidis-Valois, 1994.

Parysatis

Ballets Entrée, A, C, D
1 Geoffrey Simon, London Philharmonic Orchestra, recorded 14 to 19 January 2014. Cala Records. On YouTube.

Ballets Entrée A, C, arranged for two pianos by Saint-Saëns
1 Tetsu and Masaki. On YouTube.

Ballet B 'Le Rossignol et la Rose'
1 Evelyn Scotney (1886–1967), on HMV 481.
2 Lily Pons (1898–1976), Odeon 188645. On YouTube.
3 Mado Robin, with piano. On YouTube.
4 Marilyn Dale with Julius Drake, piano, BBC broadcast 4 May 1987.
5 Eva Leoni, Columbia, L. 1988.
6 Elisabeth Vidal, with Susan Manoff, piano, 1994 on Naive V 5396.
7 Chen Reiss, with Charles Spencer, piano, on Onyx Classics.

Phryné

Complete

Phryné	Denise Duval
Nicias	Michel Hamel
Dicephile	André Vessières
Lampito	Nadine Sutereau
Agoragine	Georges Alès
Cynalopex	Jean Mollien
conductor	Jules Gressier

Orchestra and Chorus of Radio Lyrique of RTF, recorded 1960.
Bismark Beane MRF 194. Issued as a CD in 2013.

La Princesse jaune

Complete

1

Léna	Nadine Sautereau
Kornélis	Jean Mollien
conductor	Tony Aubin

Orchestre et Chorale Lyrique de l'ORTF.
Black Disc – Bismark Beane MRTF 194, recorded in 1957.

2

Léna	Maria Costanza Nocentini
Kornélis	Carlo Allemano
conductor	Francis Travis

Orchestra della Svizzera Italiana and Cantemus.
Chandos CHAN 9837, recorded in 2000.

3

Léna	Janis Kelly
Kornélis	John Graham-Hall
conductor	Peter Robinson

BBC Broadcast 13 May 1999, sung in English.

Overture

1 Opéra-Comique Orchestra, conducted by Albert Wolff.
2 Société des Concerts, conducted by André Cluytens.
3 Boston Symphony Orchestra, conducted by Charles Munch. RCA Victor, 1951.
4 Ulster Orchestra, conducted by Hilary Davan Wetton, BBC Radio 3, 4 December 1985.
5 Royal Scottish National Orchestra, conducted by Neeme Järvi. Chandos 2012.
6 London Philharmonic Orchestra, conducted by Geoffrey Simon. CALA, 1993.
7 Berlin Philharmonic Orchestra, conducted by Alain Mulichar.

Selections

Odeon Orchester, cond. Paul Minssart, 2 sides of a 78.

Proserpine

Complete

Proserpine	Véronique Gens
Angiola	Marie-Adeline Henry
Sabatino	Frédéric Antoun
Squarocca	Andrew Foster-Williams
Renzo	Jean Teitgen
conductor	Ulf Schirmer

Münchner Rundfunkorchester and the Flemish Radio Choir.
Ediciones Singulares.
Palazzetto Bru Zane, 2017.

Samson et Dalila (complete recordings only)

Many of the recordings listed below originated as radio or television broadcasts, sometimes issued later as CDs or DVDs. Only one reference is given to the issuing company, since the recordings have frequently passed from one company to another.

Recordings of *Samson et Dalila* have been surveyed in the following publications: *Opera on Record 2*, p. 208; Rodolfo Celletti, *Il Teatro d'Opera in Disco*, 1988, p. 755; *Opera on CD*, pp. 85, 94, 105; *L'Avant Scène Opéra* 15, p. 92; *The Metropolitan Opera Guide to Recorded Opera*, 1993, p. 495; *The Metropolitan Guide to Opera on Video*, 1997, p. 299; *The Penguin Guide to Opera on Compact Discs*, 1993, p. 376; *Opera on Video*, p. 145; Elvio Giudici, *L'Opera in CD e Video*, 1995, pp. 758, 1248; *American Record Guide*, May/June 1996, vol. 59 no. 3, p. 67; *International Opera Collector*, Spring 1998, No. 7, p. 30; *Opera Magazine*, No. 29, May 2008, p. 28.

Date. Conductor, orchestra and chorus. Samson, Dalila, Grand-Prêtre, Abimélech. Label

1936. Maurice Abravanel, Metropolitan Opera. René Maison, Gertrud Pålson-Wettergren, Ezio Pinza, John Gurney. Guild. Broadcast 26 December 1936.

1941. Wilfrid Pelletier, Metropolitan Opera. René Maison, Risë Stevens, Leonard Warren, Norman Cordon. Omega. Broadcast 13 December 1941.

1946. Alexandere Melik-Pasheyev, Bolshoi Theatre. Nikander Khanayev, Maria Maksakova. Melodiya. In Russian.

1946. Louis Fourestier, Paris Opéra. José Luccioni, Hélène Bouvier, Paul Cabanel, Charles Cambon. Pathé.

1948. Eugène Bigot, Grand Théâtre de Genève. José Luccioni, Susanne Lefort, Pierre Nougaro, Ernest Mestrallet. Malibran Music.

1948. Hans Altman, Bayerische Rundfunk. Lorenz Fehenberger, Res Fischer, Fred Destal, Max Eibel. Walhall. In German.

1949. Emil Cooper, Metropolitan Opera. Ramón Vinay, Risë Stevens, Robert Merill, Osie Hawkins. Omega. Broadcast 26 November 1949.

1953. Fausto Cleva, Metropolitan Opera. Ramón Vinay, Risë Stevens, Sigurd Björling, Norman Scott. Broadcast 14 March 1953.

1954. Leopold Stokowski, NBC SO. Jan Peerce, Risë Stevens, Robert Merrill. RCA Victor.

1954. Robert Shaw, NBC. Jan Peerce, Risë Stevens, Robert Merrill. RCA Victor.

1955. Fritz Rieger, San Carlo Opera, Naples. Ramón Vinay, Ebe Stignani, Antonio Manca-Serra, Giovanni Amodeo. Bongiovanni. In Italian.

1956. Herbert Sandberg, Royal Swedish Opera. Set Svanholm, Blanche Thebom, Sigurd Björling. Caprice. In French and Swedish.

1958. Sir Thomas Beecham, Teatro Colón, Buenos Aires. Ramón Vinay, Blanche Thebom, Giuseppoe Taddei, Fernando Corena. Melodram.

1958. Fausto Cleva, Metropolitan Opera, New York. Mario del Monaco, Risë Stevens, Martial Singher, Norman Scott. CLS MD.

1959. Francesco Molinari-Pradelli, Teatro di San Carlo, Naples. Mario del Monaco, Jean Madeira, Lino Puglisi, Plinio Clabassi. Melodram.

1960. Renato Cellini, New Orleans Opera. Ramón Vinay, Risë Stevens, Joseph Mordino, Arthur Cosenza. VAI.

1963. Georges Prêtre, Paris Opéra. Jon Vickers, Rita Gorr, Ernest Blanc, Anton Diakov. EMI Classics.

1963. Pierre Dervaux, Tearo Colón, Buenos Aires. Jon Vickers, Biserka Cvejic, Angelo Marriello, Carlos Feller. The Opera Lovers SAMD.

1963. Georges Prêtre, San Francisco Opera. James McCracken, Sandra Warfield, Julien Haas, Joshua Hecht. Premiere Opeera Ltd.

1964. Georges Prêtre, Metropolitan Opera, New York. Jess Thomas, Irene Dalis, Gabriel Bacquier, Justino Díaz. The Opera Lovers SAMD.

1964. Jean Fournet, Netherlands Radio. Jon Vickers, Oralia Dominguez, Ernest Blanc, Henk Driessen. Opera D'oro.

1965. Jean Fournet, Chicago Lyric Opera. Jon Vickers, Grace Bumbry, Sesto Bruscantini, Morley Meredith. Omega Opera Archive.

1965. Fausto Cleva, Metropolitan Opera, New York. Jon Vickers, Giulietta Simionato, Norman Mittelman, Justino Díaz. The Opera Lovers SAMD.

1969. Kurt Adler, Rumanian Radiotelevision. Ludovico Spiess, Elena Cernei, Dan Jordachescu, Constantin Dumitru. Electrecord.

1970. Georges Prêtre, Teatro alla Scala, Milan. Richard Cassily, Shirley Verrett, Robert Massard, Giovanni Foiani. Opera D'oro.

1971. Serge Baudo, Metropolitan Opera, New York. Richard Tucker, Grace Bumbry, Gabriel Bacquier, Paul Plishka. The Opera Lovers SAMD.

1971. Carlo Moresco, Philadelphia Grand Opera. Richard Tucker, Mignon Dunn, Seymour Schwartzman, Irwin Densen. Live Opera.

1971. Thomas Schippers. Teatro Colón, Buenos Aires. James King, Regina Farfaty, Jean C. Gebelin, Levon Boghossian. Opera Depot.

1972. Serge Baudo, Metropolitan Opera, New York. James McCracken, Grace Bumbry, Gabriel Becquier, Paul Plishka. The Opera Lovers SAMD.

1972. Serge Baudo, Metropolitan Opera, New York. Jon Vickers, Grace Bumbry, Gabriel Becquier, Paul Plishka. The Opera Lovers SAMD.

1972. Argeo Quadri, Radio Symphonieorchestre, Vienna. Ludovic Spiess, Christa Ludwig, Kostas Paskalis, Tugomir Franc.

1972. Kurt Adler, Rumanian Radiotelevision. Ludovico Spiess, Elena Cernei, Dan Jordachescu, Constantin Dumitru. Electrecord.

1973. Giuseppe Patané, Orchestre de la Suisse Romande. Guy Chauvet, Tatiana Troyanos, Henri Peyrotte, Michel Bouvier. Premiere Opera.

1973. Giuseppe Patané, Bayerische Rundfunk. James King, Christa Ludwig, Bernd Weikl, Alexander Malta. Eurodisc, BMG.

1974. Peter Maag, Arena di Verona. Gilbert Py, Fiorenza Cossotto, Silvano Carroli, Ivo Vinco. Omega Opera Archive.

1975. Georges Prêtre, Opéra, Paris. Guy Chauvet, Fiorenza Cossotto, Robert Massard, Joseph Rouleau. Bella Voce.

1977. Sixtgen Ehrling, Metropolitan Opera, New York. Guy Chauvet, Fiorenza Cossotto, William Walker, Justino Díaz. Bensar.

1978. Daniel Barenboim, Orchestre de Paris. Plácido Domingo, Elena Obraztsova, Renato Ruson, Pierre Thau. Deutsche Grammophon.

1981 (DVD). Julius Rudel, San Francisco Opera. Plácido Domingo, Shirley Verrett, Wolfgang Brendel, Arnold Voketaitis. Kultur Video.

1981. Michel Plasson, Chicago Lyric Opera. Carlos Cossutta, Yvonne Minton, Tom Krause, Dimitri Kavrakos. The Opera Lovers SAMD.

1982 (DVD). Colin Davis, Royal Opera House. Jon Vickers, Shirley Verrett, Jonathan Summers, John Tomlinson. Kultur Video.

1984 (DVD). Michelangelo Veltri, Santiago Philharmonic Orchestra. Gilbert Py, Ann Howard, Ernest Blanc, Mario Solomonoff. Live Opera Heaven.

1985. Colin Davis, Royal Opera House, London. Plácido Domingo, Agnes Baltsa, Jonathan Summers, Roderick Earle. House of Opera.

1985. Georges Prêtre, Opéra de Nice. Plácido Domingo, Waltraud Meier, Ernest Blanc, Jacques Mars. House of Opera.

1987. Jean Fournet, Metropolitan Opera, New York. Jon Vickers, Marilyn Horne, Louis Quilico, Terry Cook. The Opera Lovers SAMD.

1988. Sylvain Cambreling, Volksoper, Vienna. Carlos Cossutta, Marjana Lipovsek, Alain Fonday, Yves Bisson. Koch Schwann.

1989. Jacques Delacôte, Gran Teatro del Liceo, Barcelona. Plácido Domingo, Agnes Baltsa, Alain Fondary, Ismael Pons. House of Opera.

1989. Colin Davis, Bayerische Rundfunk. José Carreras, Agnes Baltsa, Jonathan Summers, Simon Estes. Philips.

1990. Georges Prêtre, Staatsoper, Vienna. Plácido Domingo, Agnes Baltsa, Alain Fondary, Claudio Otelli. Lyric Distribution.

1991. Myung-whun Chung, Bastille. Plácido Domingo, Waltraud Meier, Alain Fondary, Jean-Philippe Courtois. EMI Classics.

1993. Imre Pallo, Vlaamse Opera, Antwerp. Vladimir Popov, Florence Quivar, Jean-Philippe Lafont. Premiere Opera.

1995 (DVD). Jacques Delacôte, Orchestre Philharmonique, Nice. José Carreras, Luciana D'Intino, Wolfgang Brendel, Riccardo Ferrari. Legato Classics.

1996. Jacques Delacôte, Teatro Bellini, Catania. Heikki Siukola, Olga Borodina, Silvano Carroli, Carlo de Bortoli. Legato Classics.

1998 (DVD). James Levine, Metropolitan. Plácido Domingo, Olga Borodina, Sergei Leiferkus, Richard Paul Fink. Deutsche Grammophon.

1998. Leonard Slatkin, Metropolitan Opera, New York. Plácido Domingo, Denyce Graves, Sergei Leiferkus, Alan Held. Celestial Audio.

1998. Colin Davis, London Symphony Orchestra. José Carreras, Olga Borodina, Jean-Philippe Lafont, Egils Siliņš. Erato.

1999 (DVD). Luis Antonio García-Navarro, Orquesta Sinfónica, Madrid. Plácido Domingo, Carolyn Sebron, Alain Fondary, Jean-Philippe Courtis. Premiere Opera.

1999. Isaac Karabtchevsky, La Fenice, Venice. Kristjan Johannsson, Hadja Michael, Carlo Guelfci, Philippe Kahn. Mondo Musica.

2002 (DVD). Gary Bertini, La Scala, Milan. Plácido Domingo, Olga Borodina, Jean-Philippe Lafont, Ildar Abdrazakov. Premiere Opera.

2005. Bertrand De Billy, Metropolitan Opera, New York. José Cura, Denyce Graves, Jean-Philippe Lafont, James Courtney. Celestial Audio.

2006. Emmanuel Villaume, Metropolitan Opera, New York. Clifton Forbis, Olga Borodina, Jean-Philippe Lafont, James Courtney. House of Opera.

2007 (DVD). David Levi, Aukso Orchestra, Poland. Charles Alves da Cruz, Klara Uleman, Peter Michailov, Charlotte Besijn. Opera Spanga.

2007. Karen Keltner, San Diego Symphony Orchestra. Clifton Forbis, Denyce Graves, Greer Grimsley, Philip Skinner. Premiere Opera Ltd.

2007. Kazuchi Ono, La Monnaie, Brussels. Carl Tanner, Olga Borodina, Jean-Philippe Lafont, Federico Sacchi. Celestial Audio.

2009. Tomás Netopil, Vlaamse Opera, Antwerp. Yorsten Keri, Mariana Tarasova, Nikola Mijailovic, Milcho Borovinov. Premiere Opera.

Recorded extracts up to 1978 are fully listed in *L'Avant-Scène Opéra*, no. 15 (June 1978), pp. 92–95.

Le Timbre d'argent

'Bonheur est chose légère'

Ninon Vallin (1886–1961) with R. Barthalay (violin) and Madeleine D'Aleman (piano). Recorded between 1927 and 1932. Odeon 123 583.

A complete recording of *Le Timbre d'argent* is to be issued in 2019.

INDEX

About, Edmond
   Guillery, 164
Achard, Léon, 25
Adam, Adolphe, 89
   Giselle, 267
   Poupée de Nuremberg, La, 43
   Toréador, Le, 8
Adini, Ada, 191, 192
Aeschylus, 321
   Oresteia, 278
Aix-en-Provence, 240
Aix-les-Bains, 159, 185, 224, 240, 267, 322, 347, 350, 360, 362, 373
Ajaccio, 334
Albert I, Prince, 321, 322, 333, 334, 336, 360
Albertini, Raphaël-Diaz, 165
Alboni, Marietta, 134
Alexander the Great, 125
Alexandra, Queen, 313
Alexandria, 185, 322
Algiers, 73, 93, 122, 160, 190, 192, 217, 218, 223, 227, 236, 240, 241, 244, 265, 292, 310, 333, 347, 363, 373, 376
Ali Pasha, Mohammed, 312, 322, 350, 361
Alice, Princess, 321
Allemano, Carlo, 90
Altès, Ernest, 131
Alvarez, Albert, 251, 324
Amable, 251
Amadis the Gaul, 253
Amelineau, Émile, 266
Amsterdam, 73, 121, 122
Angers, 89
Annaba, 292
Anthology of Ten Thousand Leaves, The, 82
Antoine, André, 349, 355
Antwerp, 73, 159, 241, 273, 347, 373
Arbeau, Thoinot
   Orchésographie, 211

Arles, 376
Arthur, King, 253
Artiste, L', 193
Astruc, Gabriel, 349, 350
Aswan, 265
Athenaeus of Naucratis, 230
Athens, 376
Attaingnant, Pierre, 211
Auber, Daniel, 9, 22, 23, 44
   Ambassadrice, L', 8
   Fra Diavolo, 231
   Muette de Portici, La, 43
Aubin, Tony, 90
Aubrecicourt, Eustache d', 117
Auer, Leopold
   My Long Life in Music, 25
Augé de Lassus, Lucien, 225–29, 241–43, 333–37, 346–47
   Amour vengé, L', 225
   Ancêtre, L', 225–347
   Chez le Bey de Tunis, 225
   Didon, 225
   Endymion, 225
   Forum, Le, 225
   Phryné, 225–43
   Routes et Étapes, 225
   Saint-Saëns, 225
   Spectacles antiques, Les, 225
   Thèbes, Hymne et Chanson, 225
   Voyage aux Sept Merveilles du Monde, 225
Auguez, Numa, 54, 121
Avignon, 293

Bach, Johann Sebastian, 2, 54, 266
   St Matthew Passion, 391
Baden-Baden, 125
Bagier, Prosper, 26
Bailac, Germaine, 372
Baillet, Jean, 99

Bailly, 251
Balzac, Honoré de
   Peau de chagrin, Le, 43
Barbier, Jules, 14, 20–28, 43–46, 88, 108, 161
   Contes d'Hoffmann, Les, 20, 28, 45, 46
   Marionnettes du docteur, Les, 21, 46
Barcelona, 73, 159, 160, 241, 273, 275, 294, 310, 350
Bard Festival, xiii, xiv, 159
Batka, R., 347
Baumann, Émile, 283, 284
Bayreuth, 12, 95, 165, 166, 282, 289, 387
Bazin, François, 22
Beatrice, Princess, 121
Beauplan, Arthur de, 43
Beerbohm Tree, Sir Herbert, 355
Beethoven, Ludwig van, 2, 5, 12, 53, 164, 166, 312, 391
   Fidelio, 75
   Piano Concerto no. 3, 14
   Piano Concerto no. 5, 334
   Symphony no. 5, 1
Bellaigue, Camille, 232, 387
Bellenot, Philippe, 321, 348
Bellini, Vincenzo
   Straniera, La, 189
Bergerat, Émile
   Nuit florentine, La, 373
Berlin, 47, 90, 130, 131, 165, 185, 246, 273, 296, 318, 324, 348
Berlioz, Hector, 1, 4, 5, 7, 9, 10, 11, 22, 23, 44, 58, 65, 66, 166, 263, 286, 323, 386, 388
   Benvenuto Cellini, 5, 189, 191, 197, 218
   Damnation de Faust, La, 6, 10, 102, 180, 350
   Enfance du Christ, L', 10, 52, 105, 140, 296
   Grande Messe des morts, 10
   Grand Traité d'instrumentation, 14, 58, 234
   Lélio, 10, 14
   Mémoires, 23
   Roméo et Juliette, 1, 10
   Symphonie fantastique, 60
   Troyens, Les, 6, 22, 150, 217, 234, 237, 323, 327
Bernard, Robert, 391
Bernhardt, Sarah, 227, 288, 318, 319
Bertin, Louise
   Esmeralda, 13, 163
Bertrand, Paul, 250

Bevin, Elway, 130
Béziers, xiii, 194, 248, 273–76, 282–284, 287–290, 311–314, 317, 322, 323, 348, 350, 364, 376, 381, 385, 388
Bianchini, Charles, 195
Biarritz, 322
Birmingham, 125
Bizet, Georges, 6, 10, 19, 20, 24, 27, 44, 76, 77, 79, 89, 125, 223, 231, 244, 253, 286, 288, 305, 386, 387, 389
   Arlésienne, L', 253, 281, 376
   Carmen, 6, 24, 80, 91, 162, 174, 187, 244, 253, 292
   Coupe du Roi de Thulé, La, 24, 77
   Djamileh, 77, 79, 80, 89, 331
   Don Procopio, 321
   Grisélidis, 77, 244
   Ivan IV, 6, 25
   Jolie Fille de Perth, La, 24, 45, 73
   Pêcheurs de perles, Les, 6, 19, 22, 45, 328
   Symphony no. 2, 166
   Vasco de Gama, 223
Blanc, Raymond, 89
Blanpied, Caroline, 262
Blau, Édouard, 77
Blaze de Bury, Henri, 6, 18
Blida, 227
Bloch, Rosine, 73, 127, 222
Blot, Louise, 324, 325
Blum, Ernest, 27
Boccaccio, Giovanni, 244
Boëly, Alexandre, 7
Boieldieu, François-Adrien
   Dame blanche, La, 80
Boisselot, Xavier, 21
Boito, Arrigo, 245
Boleyn, Anne, 133, 134
Boleyn, Thomas, 133
Bologhine, 53
Bône, 292
Bonheur, Rosa, 311
Bonnerot, Jean, 13, 17, 21, 51, 54, 125, 162, 163, 164, 192, 226, 288, 348
Bordeaux, 10, 16, 73, 122, 159, 217, 224, 240, 284, 286, 310, 348, 373, 376, 377, 378
Bordèse, Stéphan, 290
Borodin, Alexander Porfiryevich, 244
   Prince Igor, 213

Bosman, Rosa, 192, 195
Bouhy, Jacques, 73, 222
Boulanger, Ernest, 22
Boulogne-sur-mer, 90
Bourgault-Ducoudray, Louis-Albert, 247, 384
   Michel Columb, 164
   Thamara, 224
Brach, Coralie, 24
Brahms, Johannes, 167, 245, 335, 339, 386
   Requiem, 72
   symphonies, 1
Bréval, Lucienne, 248, 251
Bréville, Pierre de, 244
Brieux, Eugène, 349–55
Britten, Benjamin, 380
   Midsummer Night's Dream, A, 337
   Owen Wingrave, 43
Brooks, Erin, 232
Broussan, Leimistin, 360
Bruant, Emilia, 55
Bruch, Max, 130, 245
   Scottish Fantasy, 148
Bruckner, Anton, 384
Bruneau, Alfred, 321
   Rêve, Le, 290
Bruneau, Louis, 163
Brunet-Lafleur, Madame, 72
Brunhilda, 252, 253
Brussels, 18, 45–48, 70, 90, 121, 122, 160, 164, 185, 189, 193, 224, 227, 241, 247, 267, 273, 293, 357, 373, 378
   Monnaie, Théâtre de la, 45, 48, 72, 94
Bucharest, 320
Buckingham, Duke of, 133, 134
Budapest, 55
Buenos Aires, 73, 332
Bülow, Hans von, 12, 55, 72, 363
Burgos, 335
Bussine, Romain, 52, 55, 76
Buxton, 90
Byrd, William, 129
   Carman's Whistle, 153

Cadiz, 72, 194, 273, 332
Caesar, Julius, 105, 125
Cain, Henri

Vivandière, La, 245
Cairo, 73, 159, 185, 194, 241, 265, 310, 312, 322, 335, 347, 349, 350, 361, 373
Caisso, Victor, 55
Calderón de la Barca, Pedro
   Cisma de Inglaterra, La, 126, 132–34
Calmann-Lévy, 97, 165
Calmettes, André, 357
Calonne, Ernest de, 15
Calvé, Emma, 191, 227
Calzabigi, Raniero, 326
Cambridge, 245
Camões, Luiz Vaz de
   Lusiadas, Os, 127
Campagne, Daniel, 228
Campeggio, Cardinal, 133
Canary Islands, 72
Cannes, 240, 322, 335, 361, 373
Capoul, Victor, 126
Carcano, Giulio, 17
Carl Alexander, Grand Duke, 55, 56
Carpezat, 132, 251
Carré, Albert, 185, 240, 273, 287, 331, 347
Carré, Marguerite, 47, 348
Carré, Michel, 14, 20–28, 43–46, 88, 108, 185
   Contes d'Hoffmann, Les, 20, 28, 45, 46
   Faust et Marguerite, 20
   Marionnettes du docteur, Les, 21, 46
Caruso, Enrico, 332
Carvalho, Caroline Miolan-, 23, 25, 45, 382
Carvalho, Léon, 6, 22, 23, 24, 25, 164, 167, 168, 182, 185, 226, 240, 244, 273
Castelbon de Beauxhostes, Fernand, 274–75, 282, 285, 287, 290, 293, 311, 312, 322
Castillon, Alexis de, 92
Catherine, Queen, 132
Cavaillé-Coll, 93
Cazalis, Henri, 93
Celestine III, Pope, 189
Cellini, Benvenuto
   Vita, 189, 191, 197, 200, 218
Chabrier, Emmanuel, 73, 95, 167
Chaliapin, Fyodor Ivanovich, 321, 362
Chaperon, Philippe, 80, 132, 228, 251
Charbonnel, Marie, 336
Charlemagne, 357

Charles of Navarre, 99
Charles the Bad, King, 99
Charles I, King, 132
Charles V, King, 133, 218
Charles VI, King, 98, 99, 100
Charny, Lyse, 218, 372
Charpentier, Gustave
   Didon, 225
   Louise, 273
Charpentier, Marc-Antoine
   Malade imaginaire, Le, 223
Charton-Demeur, Anne, 18
Chaucer, Geoffrey, 244
Chausson, Ernest, 95, 244, 262
Cherbuliez, Victor, 323
Chicago, 348, 373
Chollet, Jean-Baptiste, 80
Chopin, Frédéric, 2, 386
   Préludes, 1
Choudens, Antoine, 24, 45, 47, 48, 192, 244, 391
Chronique de Paris, 27
Chronique musicale, 55
Claretie, Jules, 311
Clement VII, Pope, 132
Clermont, Maréchal de, 99
Clermont, Robert de, 100
Clothar, King, 253
Cœuroy, André, 391
Cohen, Henri, 55
Cohen, Jules, 195
Collet, Henri, 50
Cologne, 47, 185, 332
Colonne, Édouard, 53, 55, 72, 193, 224, 284, 288, 318, 363
Combarieu, Jules, 50
Comettant, Oscar, 6
Compiègne, 160, 393
Condé, Gérard, 9
Constantin, Charles, 22
Coppée, François, 80
Coquard, Arthur, 224, 244
Corneille, Pierre, 348
   Horace, 17, 348
Corti brothers, 163
Cortot, Alfred, 89
Cossira, Émile, 195

Cosyn, Benjamin, 129
Côte-St-André, La, 323
Cottinet, Edmond, 245
   Vercingétorix, 245
Courrier musical, 375
Cranmer, Thomas, 133
Cremona, 373
Cromwell, Thomas, 133
Croze, Jean-Louis, 267, 287
Cui, César, 389
Cusins, William G., 128

Damiani, Elisa, 267
Danbé, Jules, 27, 167, 168, 228
Dangès, Henri, 372
Danhauser, Adolphe-Léopold, 22
Darmstadt, 360
Daudet, Alphonse
   Arlésienne, L', 281
Davelli, Marthe, 331
David, Félicien, 386
   Désert, Le, 223
   Ode-symphonies, 52
De Lara, Isidore, 321
Deauville, 240
Debussy, Claude, 95, 122, 193, 224, 248, 253, 286, 321, 390, 391
   Enfant prodigue, L', 347
   Pelléas et Mélisande, 207, 238, 273, 312
   Symphony, 166
Deffès, Louis
   Café du Roi, Le, 80
Delibes, Léo, 19, 27, 92, 212, 244, 305
   Coppélia, 267
   Jardinier et son seigneur, Le, 19
   Kassya, 244
   Lakmé, 162, 328
   Roi l'a dit, Le, 136
   Roi s'amuse, Le, 136
   Source, La, 19
   Sylvia, 267
Deloffre, Adolphe, 80
Delrat, Michel, 97
Demougeot, Marcelle, 218, 331
Dereims, Étienne, 131
Deschamps, Blanche, 216

Desjoyeux, Noël, 321
Dessau, 373
Destinn, Emmy, 350
Destranges, Étienne, 186
Détroyat, Léonce, 125–35, 163, 225, 227, 228
    Inès de Castro, 127
Détroyat, Mme, 126, 127, 130, 225
Diaghilev, Sergei, 321
Diaz, Eugène
    Benvenuto Cellini, 163
    Coupe du Roi de Thulé, La, 77
Diaz, Narcisse, 77
Dickens, Charles
    A Tale of Two Cities, 220
Diémer, Louis, 89, 164
Dieppe, xiv, 17, 90, 194, 273, 287, 335, 348, 376
Dieulafoy, Jane, 311–14
Dieulafoy, Marcel, 311
Dijon, 73, 224, 310
Donizetti, Gaetano, 134
    Anna Bolena, 134
    Gabriella di Vergy, 161, 162
    Gemma di Vergy, 161
    Roberto Devereux, 127
Dorival, Georges, 281
Doucet, Camille, 22
Dresden, 165, 335
Dreyfus, Alfred, 250, 295
du Locle, Camille, 25, 26, 53, 76, 79
Dubel, Yvonne, 372
Dubois, Théodore, 76, 249
    Aben Hamet, 163
    Farandole, La, 267
Dubosq, Albert, 347
Ducasse, Alice, 80
Dukas, Paul, 251, 362
Dumas, Alexandre, 163, 169, 218
    Ascanio, 197
    Frères corses, Les, 334
    Hamlet, 17
    Orestie, 189
    Quarante-cinq, Les, 359
Duparc, Henri, 76, 92
Dupont, Paul, 262
Duprato, Jules, 22
Duprez, Gilbert

    Samson, 58
Durand, Auguste, 55, 57, 74, 90, 94, 97, 120, 131, 168, 182, 191, 192, 195, 211, 215, 225, 229, 241, 262, 263, 289, 290, 292, 292, 313, 320, 378, 391
Durand, Jacques, 94, 121, 131, 350, 362, 373, 391
Dürer, Albrecht, 363
Duval, Denise, 241
Dvořák, Antonín, 391, 392
    Rusalka, 391

Eames, Emma, 193, 195
Écho de Paris, L', 372
Edinburgh, 332
Edward VII, King, 130, 132, 312, 313
Edward, the Black Prince, 98
Egypt, 122
Elberfeld, 47, 241
Elgar, Sir Edward, 356
Elwart, Antoine, 22
Enghien, 373
Erard et Cie, 2
Erard, Pierre, 194
Escudier, Léon, 95, 96
Estafette, L', 95, 126
Étampes, Mme d', 197
Euripides, 247
    Iphigenia, 278
    Trojan Women, The, 247
Eustace, Charles, 275, 313

Fagan, J. F., 355
Falguière, Alexandre, 230
Farrar, Geraldine, 336
Fauré, Gabriel, 55, 56, 73, 76, 89, 93, 263, 282, 292, 313, 321, 336, 361, 362, 385
    Pelléas et Mélisande, 292
    Pénélope, 360, 361
    Prométhée, 285, 287, 289, 290, 293, 313
    Symphony, 166
Faure, Jean-Baptiste, 25, 126
Ferenczy, Franz, 55
Fétis, François-Joseph, 315
    Histoire générale de la musique depuis les temps les plus anciens jusqu'à nos jours, 315
Figaro, Le, 24, 228, 246, 292, 336
Flaubert, Gustave

Salammbô, 315
Florence, 73, 166
Fondary, Alain, 123
Fontainebleau, 191
Forgues, Mme, 16
Forster, Will, 129
Fortunatus, Venantius, 252
Fourcaud, Louis de, 168
France, La, 168, 192
Franck, César, 76, 92, 167, 183, 262, 336, 361, 386
    Ghiselle, 244, 321
    Hulda, 321
    Rédemption, 52
    Symphony, 166, 193
François I, King, 190, 197, 218
Frankfurt, 159, 331
Froissart, Jean, 99
Fugère, Lucien, 228

Gabrieli, Giovanni, 136
Gailhard, Pierre, 158, 188, 190, 194, 195, 288, 293
Gaisberg, Fred, 332
Galand, 182
Gall, Yvonne, 372
Gallet, Louis, 20, 53, 77–81, 84, 88–99, 117–120, 163, 164, 166–71, 182–87, 189–98, 203, 206, 209, 213, 218, 224, 225, 244, 249–52, 267, 274–76, 281–87, 289, 290, 293, 321, 333, 336, 360, 364, 379, 384, 388, 391
    Coupe du Roi de Thulé, La, 24, 77
    Notes d'un librettiste, 79
Galli, Amintore, 241
Galli-Marié, Célestine, 24, 80
Gallois, Jean, 100
Garcin, Jules, 193
Garden, Mary, 331
Garnier, Charles, 124, 320
Garnier, Gustave, 121
Gaulois, Le, 132, 168
Gauthier-Villars, Henry (Willy), 6, 336
Gautier, Théophile, 19
Gavault, Paul, 374
Gaveau-Sabatier, Mme, 14
Gay, Sophie, 126
Gelder, Marguerite van, 292
Geneva, xiv, 73, 221, 223, 224, 241, 323, 347

Genivet, Jean-Baptiste, 97
Genoa, 331, 332, 335
Gérôme, Jean-Léon, 230
Gevaert, François-Auguste, 246, 247, 384
    Histoire et théorie de la musique de l'Antiquité, 247
Ghent, 159, 241
Gheusi, Pierre-Barthélemy, 90, 293, 360
Gimel, Comtesse de, 241
Girardin, Émile de, 126
Glazunov, Alexander Konstantinovich, 33, 244
Glinka, Mikhail Ivanovich
    Kamarinskaya, 306
Gloucester, 372
Gluck, Christoph Willibald, 4, 7, 295
    Alceste, 264
    Écho et Narcisse, 264
    Iphigénie en Tauride, 58, 289
    Orphée, 18, 264
    Paride ed Elena, 326
Godard, Benjamin, 76
    Pedro de Zalamea, 127
    Vivandière, La, 245
Goethe, Johann Wolfgang von
    Faust, 20, 43
Goldbeck, Melanie von, 25
Gounod, Charles, 4, 5, 9, 10, 11, 22, 44, 65, 92, 126, 168, 196, 229, 249, 262, 286, 386, 388
    Faust, 20, 23, 24, 36, 40, 68, 74, 97, 110, 188, 324
    Médecin malgré lui, Le, 80
    Mireille, 23
    Nonne sanglante, La, 9
    Polyeucte, 68, 96, 126, 127
    Reine de Saba, La, 20, 70, 198
    Roméo et Juliette, 20, 23, 24, 27, 191, 193, 195, 324
    Sapho, 9, 13, 237
    Tribut de Zamora, Le, 121, 126, 127, 131
    Ulysse, 9
Goupil & Cie, 230
Gouzien, Armand, 55
Graham-Hall, John, 90
Granada, 194, 312
Graupner, Christoph, 57
    Simson, 57
Greffuhl, Comtesse, 350
Gregory of Tours, 252

Grenoble, 323
Gressier, Jules, 241
Grieg, Edvard, 245, 348
   Peer Gynt, 376
Groot, Adolphe de, 197
Gros, Aimé, 93, 96, 97
Guiraud, Ernest, 76, 194, 195, 224, 244, 251, 383, 388
   Frédégonde, xi, xiv, 78, 189, 224, 227, 249–62
   Kobold, Le, 25, 77
Guise, Henry Duc de, 357
Gunsbourg, Raoul, 217, 322, 333, 335, 349, 350, 361
Gye, Ernest, 121

Hague, The, 159, 167, 241
Hahn, Reynaldo, 6, 187, 218, 221, 385
Halanzier, Hyacinthe, 54, 94, 96, 121, 124, 126
Halévy, Fromental, 14, 20, 21, 22, 44, 94, 110, 386, 389
   Fée des Roses, La, 8
   Juive, La, 103, 112, 150, 193
   Noé, 244
Halévy, Ludovic, 326
Hamburg, 72, 130
Hamelle, Julien, 290
Hamilton, Newburgh, 57
Hammerstein Oscar, I, 331
Handel, George Frideric, 59, 233, 266, 305, 375
   Giulio Cesare, 380
   Hercules, 274
   Samson, 52, 57
Hansen, Joseph, 195
Hanslick, Eduard
   Vom musikalische Schön, 1
Harcourt, Eugène d', 321
Harding, Jane, 241
Harnisch, Albert, 363
Hartmann, Georges, 80, 92, 94, 192, 391
Hasselmans, Josef, 332
Hatto, Jeanne, 294
Haussmann, Baron, 11
Héglon, Meyrianne, 251, 324, 324, 332, 382
Heine, Heinrich, 2
Henry of Navarre, 357
Henry III, King, 357
Henry VIII, King, 126, 133

Hérold, André-Ferdinand, 289
Hérold, Louis-Joseph-Ferdinand, 89
   Zampa, 80, 289
Hervé, Louis-Auguste-Florimond
   Chilpéric, 253
Heugel, Henri, 192, 391
Heuzey, Léon, 228
Hilpéric, King, 253
Hippeau, Edmond, 132
Ho Chi Minh City, xiv, 250, 262, 392
Hoffmann, Dr, 9
Hoffmann, E. T. A., 20
Hollander, Benoit, 355
Hollmann, Joseph, 313, 318
Holmès, Augusta, 52, 53, 193, 322
   Ôde triomphale en l'honneur du centenaire de 1789, 193
   Montagne noire, La, 251
Homer, 321
Horace, 334
Huebner, Steven, 118
Hugo, Victor, 125, 163, 164, 169, 188, 385
   Burgraves, Les, 311
   Légende des siècles, La, 222
   Lucrèce Borgia, 43
   Notre-Dame de Paris, 163
   Roi s'amuse, Le, 169
Hummel, Johann Nepomuk, 266
Hyperides, 230

Illing, Rosamund, 331
Indépendance belge, 56
Indy, Vincent d', 89, 167, 244, 264
   Symphonie sur un chant montagnard français, 166
Ingres, Jean-Dominique, 13
Innocent III, Pope, 189
Ismailia, 194, 322

Jacquet, Louis, 250
Jambon, Marcel, 251, 275, 289, 294, 313
Japan, 79
Jauner, Franz, 55
Jean II, King, 98
Jehin, Léon, 324, 336
Johannesburg, 373
Joncières, Victorin, 6, 126, 134, 263

Chevalier Jean, Le, 163
Dimitri, 26
Journal des débats, 168
Journal, Le, 249, 348
Journet, Marcel, 218
Jullien, Adolphe, 6, 80
Justament, Henri, 27

Kalkbrenner, Frédéric, 266
Kassel, 165
Kastner, Georges, 22
    Manuel général de musique militaire, 234
Kelly, Janis, 90
Khedive of Egypt, 322
Kirkby-Lunn, Louise, 360
Klein, Hermann, 331, 372
Koechlin, Charles, 187, 292
Krauss, Gabrielle, 127, 131, 147, 159, 382

La Fontaine, Jean de, 267
Lacoste, Eugène, 132
Lafargue, Marie, 251
Lafitte, Paul, 356
Lagoanère, Oscar de, 292
Lalo, Édouard, 6, 76, 92, 224
    Fiesque, 6
    Jacquerie, La, 224, 244, 321
    Roi d'Ys, Le, 6, 125, 216
    Symphony, 166
Lalo, Pierre, 320, 336
Lamoureux, Charles, 72, 92
Lamy, Marcel, 97
Laparcerie, Cora, 282
Lassalle, Albert de, 80
Lassalle, Jean-Louis, 131, 140, 191, 192, 195, 196, 216
Lassen, Eduard, 55
Lausanne, 363
Lauzières, Achille de, 6
Lavastre, J.-B. and aîné, 132, 167
Lavedan, Henri, 357
Le Bargy, Charles, 357
Le Havre, 376
Le Tréport, 130
Leborne, Fernand, 356, 357, 361

Lecocq, Charles, 324
Leconte, Sébastien-Charles, 348
Lecoq, Robert, 99, 100
Lefèbvre, Charles, 22
Legoux, Eugénie
    Joël, 163
Legrain, Georges, 349
Leipzig, 130, 264
Lelièvre, Stéphane, 43
Lemaire, Fernand, 50, 51, 52, 57, 58, 60, 125
Lemotte, 182
Leoncavallo, Ruggero
    Pagliacci, 240, 331
Lequien, Henri-Alexandre, 336
Leroux, Xavier, 321
Leschetizky, Theodor, 6
Lhérie, Paul, 80
Liberté, La, 126
Liège, 72
Lille, 130, 320, 376
Lisbon, 73, 185
Liszt, Franz, 7, 12, 53, 55, 56, 57, 72, 159, 166, 286, 313
    Legend of St Elizabeth, The, 166
Litolff, Henri, 21
Litvinne, Félia, 159, 265, 331, 334, 336, 346, 350, 360, 372, 382
Loën, A. von, 89
London, 70, 73, 90, 97, 121, 125, 128, 159, 160, 163, 165, 166, 188, 196, 216, 217, 227, 227, 241, 245, 275, 293, 310, 312, 313, 324, 331, 332, 348, 351, 355, 360, 361, 361, 363
Loret, Victor, 349
Loris, Robert de, 100
Lorrain, Jean, 289
Loti, Pierre, 90
    Madama Butterfly, 90
Louis X, King, 99
Louis XIV, King, 2, 267
Lubert, Albert, 167
Lucca, 90
Luigini, Alexandre, 97
Lully, Jean-Baptiste, 223, 276, 295
Lumière brothers, 356
Luther, Martin, 134
Luxor, 265, 349, 361

Lyon, 72, 93, 94, 96, 97, 120, 122, 124, 159, 182, 185, 224, 240, 248, 267, 273, 275, 292, 310, 373

Mackenzie, Alexander, 334
MacMahon, Patrice de, 100
Mâcon, Josseran de, 100
Madrid, 125, 126, 159, 273
Magne, 361
Mahler, Gustav, 1
Maillard, Jean, 99, 100
Malaga, 194
Malherbe, Charles, 196, 264
Mann, Nathaniel D., 356
Manoury, Théophile-Adolphe, 55
Marc, Perrin, 99
Marcel, Étienne, 98, 99, 100, 122
Marcel, Marguerite, 100
María, Infanta, 132
Marie, Gabriel, 73, 222
Marié, Irma, 24
Mariéton, Paul, 288
Mariquita, Madame, 267
Marmontel, Antoine-François, 253
Marseille, 159, 185, 224, 240, 250, 334, 373, 376
Marsick, Martin, 164
Martapoura, Jean, 192
Marty, Georges, 292
Mary, Queen, 133
Mascagni, Pietro, 384
Massé, Victor, 44, 286
    Galathée, 14, 21, 43
    Noces de Jeannette, Les, 14, 286
    Paul et Virginie, 26
Massenet, Jules, xii, 10, 19, 65, 76, 77, 89, 96, 211, 249, 273, 321, 331, 336, 348, 361, 362, 387, 389, 391
    Cendrillon, 288
    Cid, Le, 78, 164, 188, 193
    Coupe du Roi de Thulé, La, 24, 77
    Don César de Bazan, 89
    Don Quichotte, 362
    Esclarmonde, 192, 228
    Ève, 52, 78, 93
    Grisélidis, 244
    Hérodiade, 130, 142, 164, 216, 224, 348
    Jongleur de Notre-Dame, Le, 321
    Mage, Le, 224, 251, 290
    Manon, 91, 118, 164, 167, 227, 321, 352, 391
    Marie-Magdeleine, 52, 78, 93
    Navarraise, La, 324, 331
    Phèdre, 318
    Portrait de Manon, Le, 250, 331
    Roi de Lahore, Le, 55, 74, 77, 78, 89, 93, 94, 121, 224, 336
    Thaïs, 78, 228, 241, 249, 251, 266, 274, 290, 324
    Werther, 224, 321, 391
Masson, Charlotte, 7
Mata-Hari, 336
Maupassant, Guy de
    Une Soirée, 132
Maupéou, Léon de
    Amour vengé, L', 225
Maurel, Victor, 163
Maximilian, Emperor, 125
Mayer-Marix, 39
Méhul, Étienne
    Joseph, 70
Meilhac, Henri, 326
Melba, Nellie, 193, 241, 321, 324, 331, 332
Melbourne, 90
Melchissédec, Léon, 27, 45, 95
Mélingue, Étienne, 189
Mendelssohn-Bartholdy, Felix
    Antigone, 246
Ménestrel, Le, 24, 168, 192, 194, 241
Méranie, Agnès de, 189
Mérante, Louis, 131
Mérante, Zina, 24
Mérimée, Prosper
    Colomba, 334
Messager, André, 89, 97, 227, 228, 241, 331, 372
    Madame Chrysanthème, 90, 227
    Symphony, 166
Metternich, Princess Pauline, 17
Meulan, Jean de, 99
Meurice, Paul, 164, 191, 198, 200, 203, 218, 246, 249
    Benvenuto Cellini, 189, 197
    Hamlet, 17
Meyendorff, Olga von, 55
Meyerbeer, Giacomo, 4, 20, 58, 94, 110, 118, 216, 388
    Africaine, L', 193
    Huguenots, Les, 100, 143, 193

Prophète, Le, 8, 10, 150, 193
Mézeray, Louis, 97
Mézeray, Reine, 97
Milan, 73, 124, 147, 159, 159, 163, 185, 195, 231, 241, 265, 266, 273, 331, 332, 333
'Miller of Dee, The', 148
Milton, John, 70
   Samson Agonistes, 57
Minkus, Léon, 19
Mirbeau, Octave, 27
Molière (Poquelin, Jean-Baptiste)
   Sicilien, Le, 223
Mollien, Jean, 90
Montagné, 217
Monte Carlo, 47, 73, 122, 159, 185, 217, 224, 240, 310, 320, 322, 324, 332, 360, 361, 362, 364, 373, 374, 376
Montéclair, Michel Pignolet de
   Jephté, 70
Montevideo, 332
Montpellier, 73, 122, 160, 224, 275, 284, 292, 392, 393
Montreal, 73, 347, 373
Mortier, Arnold
   Soirées parisiennes de 1877, Les, 21
Moscow, 73, 147, 159, 320
Mounet-Sully, Jean, 248, 311
Mozart, Wolfgang Amadeus, 5, 7, 188, 286, 385, 392
   Così fan tutte, 58
   Don Giovanni, 7, 8, 188, 391
   Nozze di Figaro, Le, 5, 15, 18
   Piano Concerto K. 450, 14, 266, 362
   Piano Concerto K. 466, 332
   piano concertos, 7
   Zauberflöte, Die, 176
Mulhouse, 130, 376
Müller, Augusta von, 55
Munich, 185, 362, 393
Muratet, Antoine, 192
Muratore, Lucien, 361
Musset, Alfred de
   Namouna, 77
   On ne badine pas avec l'amour, 373, 374
Mussorgsky, Modest Petrovich, 244
   Boris Godunov, 391

Nantes, 73, 185, 224, 347
Naples, 161, 265, 332, 335
Napoleon Bonaparte, 2, 4, 334
Neitzel, Otto, xii
New Orleans, 73, 241
New York, 73, 90, 97, 160, 216, 227, 331, 348, 355, 373, 374
Nice, 217, 224, 240
Nicot, Charles-Auguste, 54
Nieuwerkerke, Comte de, 11
Nilsson, Christine, 24
Nîmes, 240, 248, 363
Nocentini, Maria Costanza, 90
Norfolk, Duke of, 133
Nouvelle Revue, La, 283, 288
Noverre, Jean-Georges, 267
Nozière, Fernand, 320

Offenbach, Jacques, 26, 45, 166, 228, 231, 235, 242, 244, 253, 288, 388
   Belle Hélène, La, 326
   Contes d'Hoffmann, Les, 20, 27, 43, 162, 227, 244
   Fantasio, 76
Ollone, Max d'
   Bacchus mystifié, 293
Orange, 248, 267, 274, 288, 289, 293, 295, 380
Ordre, L', 27
Ovid, 321, 366
   Heroides, 326
   Metamorphoses, 21

Paderewski, Ignacy Jan, 6
Pagès, Alphonse, 222
Paladilhe, Émile, 22, 77, 80, 288
   Mandolinata, La, 79
   Passant, Le, 79, 80, 89
   Patrie, 188, 193
Palazzetto Bru Zane, xiii, 49, 185, 310, 393
Palestrina, Giovanni Pierluigi da
   Alla riva del Tebro, 205
Pallanza, 334, 350
Palmas, Las, 194, 249, 275, 289, 350
Paoli, Antonio, 373
Paris
   Académie des Beaux-Arts, 293

Paris (cont.)
   Bibliothèque nationale de France, 46, 191, 211
   Bibliothèque-Musée de l'Opéra, 46
   Cercle Volney, 96
   Champs-Élysées, Théâtre des, 349
   Chat Noir, Le, 231
   Château d'Eau, 118
   Châtelet, Théâtre du, 26, 55, 72, 124, 168, 192
   Cirque Napoléon, 11
   Comédie-Française, 246, 248, 311, 357
   Commune, 25, 54, 76, 124
   Concert National, 53, 55
   Concerts Colonne, 92, 292
   Concerts Danbé, 92
   Concerts Populaires, 11, 92, 125
   Conservatoire, 2, 8, 10, 11, 63, 97, 125, 249, 331, 360
   École Niedermeyer, 17
   École Polytechnique, 100
   Eden, Théâtre de l', 73, 195, 222, 223, 253
   Exposition Universelle 1867, 24, 79
   Exposition Universelle 1878, 95
   Exposition Universelle 1889, 168, 188, 190, 192, 193
   Exposition Universelle 1900, 288
   Gaîté, Théâtre de la, 26, 95, 240
   Gymnase, 231
   Hôtel de Ville, 11, 100
   Institut, 96
   Louvre, Musée du, 11, 80, 218, 313
   Madeleine, Église de la, 6, 9, 51, 76, 92, 249
   Nations, Théâtre des, 318
   Odéon, Théâtre de l', 13, 21, 194, 245, 275, 282, 284, 286, 318, 349, 355, 373, 374, 375
   Opéra, 2, 3, 6, 8, 9, 13, 19, 22, 24, 25, 54, 55, 68, 70, 72, 73, 74, 76, 89, 92, 93, 94, 96, 97, 100, 121, 122, 124, 130, 159, 162, 164, 165, 182, 188, 189, 191, 192, 193, 210, 216, 217, 222, 223, 224, 229, 250, 262, 263, 273, 288, 289, 293, 309, 320, 322, 331, 333, 348, 360, 372, 374, 376, 378, 384
   Opéra Populaire, 26
   Opéra-Comique, xiv, 4, 6, 8, 13, 15, 22, 25, 26, 46, 47, 49, 53, 54, 72, 76, 79, 80, 89, 90, 92, 162, 164, 167, 168, 170, 182, 185, 188, 191, 192, 193, 217, 225, 227, 227, 239, 240, 241, 244, 245, 250, 273, 287, 312, 331, 333, 335, 347, 348, 361, 363, 374, 392, 393
   Opéra-National, 43
   Opéra-National-Lyrique, 26, 95
   Orphéon, 92
   ORTF, 241
   Palais de l'Industrie, 193
   Porte-St-Martin, Théâtre de la, 189, 197
   Renaissance, Théâtre de la, 225, 227, 228, 292
   Saint-Merry, Église de, 9, 99
   Salle Charras, 357
   Salle Érard, 125
   Salle Pleyel, 14, 125, 266
   Salle Ventadour, 24, 26, 95, 124
   Sarah-Bernhardt, Théâtre, 318, 349, 361
   Second Théâtre-Français, 246
   Société des Concerts, 11, 13, 92, 93, 193, 251, 332, 334
   Société des Concerts du Conservatoire, 92, 93
   Société des Jeunes Artistes, 11
   Société Nationale de Musique, 7, 26, 53, 76, 79, 89, 92, 125, 166, 167, 224
   Société Ste-Cécile, 10, 11
   Théâtre de la Renaissance, 24
   Théâtre-Italien, 4, 6, 8, 24, 26, 124, 163, 164
   Théâtre-Lyrique, 5, 19, 22, 23, 25, 26, 51, 80, 95, 191, 240, 335
   Théâtre-Lyrique-Populaire, 121
   Théâtre-Marigny, 267
   Théâtre-National-Lyrique, 47
   Trianon-Lyrique, 185, 240, 361
   Trocadéro, 125, 163
   Troisième Théâtre-Lyrique Français, 26
   Trompette, La, 161, 166, 250
Pasdeloup, Jules-Étienne, 9, 11, 18, 92
Patti, Adelina, 191, 195, 321
Perrault, Charles, 244
Perrens, F.-T.
   Etienne Marcel, prévot des Marchands, 100
Perrin, Émile, 25, 46, 76
Persepolis, 313
Petipa, Marius, 33
Petit, Jules, 18
Philadelphia, 348
Philipp, Isidore, 250
Philippe-Auguste, King, 189
Pindar, 247
Plançon, Pol, 97, 195

Plasson, Michel, 355
Pleyel et Cie, 2
Ploux, Edith, 121
Plutarch, 315
Pohl, Richard, 55, 57
Poitiers, 376
Pompeii, 225, 234
Ponchard, Charles, 167
Poniatowski, Prince Joseph, 22
Ponsard, François
    Agnès de Mélanie, 189
Pougin, Arthur, 6, 80
Pourtalès, Comtesse de, 17
Prague, 120, 122, 130, 159, 165, 166, 326, 331, 347, 393
Praxiteles
    Aphrodite, 230
Prétextat, Bishop, 253
Prévost, Antoine-François, 167
    Manon Lescaut, 167
Priola, Margaret, 80
Prix de Rome, 8, 9, 14, 19, 22, 52, 76, 79, 225, 293
Puccini, Giacomo, 273, 330, 378, 384, 385, 392
    Bohème, La, 324
    Madama Butterfly, 88, 90, 227
    Tosca, 288
Purcell, Henry
    Dido and Aeneas, 331
Puget, Jules, 24

Quinault, Philippe, 57

Rabaud, Henri, 292
Rachet, 349
Racine, Jean, 320
    Andromaque, 318
    Phèdre, 318
Raff, Joachim
    Samson, 57
Rameau, Jean-Philippe, 7, 211, 263
    Dardanus, 264
    Hippolyte et Aricie, 264
    Pièces de Clavecin, 264
    Samson, 50, 57
    Zaïs, 264
Rappel, Le, 193
Ratner, Sabina Teller, 161, 257

Ravel, Maurice
    Boléro, 266
Ravet, Henri-Louis, 292
Reber, Henri, 127
Reboul, Jean, 13
Regnault, Henri, 52, 94
Régnier de la Brière, François-Joseph, 127, 131
Reinach, Theodore, 284
Renaissance littéraire et artistique, La, 92
Renaissance musicale, 132
Renaud, Armand, 222
Renaud, Maurice, 217, 336
Reszke, Jean de, 191, 195
Revue de Paris, La, 361, 388
Revue des deux mondes, La, 18, 192, 374
Revue et gazette musicale, 53
Revue musicale, La, 351, 391
Reyer, Ernest, 6, 10, 80, 168
    Salammbo, 224
    Sigurd, 188, 189, 251
Ribadeneyra, Pedro de
    Historia eclesiástica del cisma del reino de Inglaterra, 133
Richard, Renée, 131, 191, 192, 193, 195
Richault, Simon, 10
Ricordi, Giuseppe, 124
Rimsky-Korsakov, Nicolay Andreyevich, 44, 148, 193, 244
Rio de Janeiro, 73, 286, 332
Ritt, Eugène, 158, 188, 190, 194, 216
Robertson, David, 320
Robinson, Peter, 90
Roch, Madeleine, 249
Roger, Gustave, 8, 80
Rolland, Romain, 274
Rome, 8
Roqueplan, Nestor, 15
Rosa, Carl, 163
Rossini, Gioacchino, 2, 6, 7, 9, 10–11, 134
    Barbiere di Siviglia, Il, 228, 324
    Guillaume Tell, 193, 269, 272
    Moïse, 70
    Otello, 63
Roth, François-Xavier, 49
Rouché, Jacques, 217, 376
Rouen, 73, 121, 195, 222, 224, 240, 253, 373, 390

Rouen (cont.)
    Théâtre des Arts, 72
Rouget de Lisle
    Marseillaise, La, 339, 374
Rousseau, Armand, 250
Rousseau, Samuel, 244
    Merowig, 253
Rousselière, Charles, 309, 336
Rubé, Auguste, 80, 132, 228
Rubinstein, Anton, 6, 50, 51, 286

Saigon, 250
St-Étienne, 310
St-Germain-en-Laye, 292
St Petersburg, 47, 73, 241, 273, 282, 373
Saint-Saëns, André, 96
Saint-Saëns, Camille
    À la France!, 379
    Africa, 222, 332
    Ancêtre, L', 34, 321, 332–47, 360, 363, 363, 373, 374, 378, 381, 382, 383, 384, 385, 393
    Andromaque, 318
    Antigone, 246–49, 267, 274, 283, 284, 289, 322, 349, 355, 384
    Antony and Cleopatra, 17
    Ascanio, xiv, 41, 72, 73, 78, 97, 128, 131, 188–221, 223, 224, 242, 246, 273, 284, 288, 290, 332, 347, 377, 378, 381, 382, 383, 384, 388, 390, 392, 393
    Assassinat du Duc de Guise, L', 356–57, 360, 361, 381, 385, 388
    Barbares, Les, xiii, 90, 288–310, 321, 336, 350, 360, 374, 376, 378, 380, 381, 382, 383, 388, 390, 392, 393
    Botriocéphale, 194, 317–18
    Brunhilda. See Frédégonde
    Cantiques, 52
    Caprice andalous, 332
    Caprice arabe, 249
    Carnaval des animaux, Le, xi, 7, 166, 383
    Causerie sur l'art du théâtre, 332
    Cello Concerto no. 1, 53, 76, 93
    Cello Concerto no. 2, 318
    Cello Sonata no. 1, 93
    Château de la Roche-Cardon, 17
    Crampe des Écrivains, La, 223, 317
    Cygnes, Les, 223

Danse macabre, xi, 53, 76, 93, 166, 235, 357
Déjanire 1, 78, 274–87, 292, 311, 313, 315, 317, 322, 380, 381, 382, 384, 388, 393
Déjanire 2, 78, 284, 321, 360–73, 378, 380, 382, 384, 390, 393
Déluge, Le, 78, 89, 94, 164, 332
Désir de l'Orient, 83
Duc de Parme, Le, 15, 16, 148, 378, 389, 393
Étienne Marcel, 26, 53, 72, 73, 78, 92–123, 124, 125, 126, 127, 136, 162, 163, 164, 173, 180, 203, 222, 274, 284, 290, 373, 376, 378, 380, 382, 383, 384, 388, 392, 393
Fantaisie, 348
Feu céleste, Le, 288
Feuille du peuplier, 16
Fiancée du timbalier, La, 188, 385
Foi, La, 321, 349–55, 360, 361, 373, 374, 376, 384, 385
Frédégonde, 78, 189, 249–63, 265, 297, 378, 381, 382, 383, 388, 392
Fuite, La, 223
Gabriella di Vergy, 161, 162, 381, 383
Gavotte op. 23, 26
Gloire de Corneille, La, 348
Guerriers, Les, 188
Hail California!, 374
Hamlet, 17
Harmonie et Mélodie, 165, 295
Hélène, xiii, 91, 238, 242, 321–34, 350, 360, 374, 376, 378, 381, 382, 383, 384, 388, 390, 392, 393
Henry VIII, xiii, 15, 16, 72, 121, 124–65, 167, 188, 189, 191, 193, 195, 200, 211, 217, 218, 220, 223, 251, 265, 273, 275, 288, 300, 321, 322, 331, 347, 348, 350, 360, 363, 374, 376, 378, 380, 381, 382, 383, 384, 388, 389, 390, 392, 393
Hymne à Pallas-Athéné, 248, 267, 289
Hymne à Victor Hugo, 128, 163, 164
Imogine, 14
Javotte, xiii, 267–73, 287, 288, 348, 360, 363, 373, 384
Jeunesse d'Hercule, La, 243, 277, 364, 370
Jota Aragonese, 125
Lola, 290–92
Lyre et la Harpe, La, 125
Macbeth, 16
Marche du Couronnement, 130
Marche héroïque, 53, 94
Martyre de Vivia, Le, 13–14

Mélodies persanes, 222
Morceau de Concert, 188
Mort de Thaïs, La, 266
Muse et le poète, La, 361, 362
Nina Zombi, 96
Noces de Prométhée, Les, 24
Notes sur les décors de théâtre dans l'antiquité romaine, 225
Nuit, La, 288
Nuit à Lisbonne, Une, 125
Nuit florentine, La, 373
Nuit persane, 222
Ode, 323
Odeurs de Paris, Les, 383
Offertoire, 130
On ne badine pas avec l'amour, 374–76
Ouverture de fête, 362
Parysatis, 285, 290, 311–17, 321, 322, 349, 355, 381, 385, 393
Pas d'armes du Roi Jean, Le, 385
Phaëton, 53, 93, 243, 366
Phryné, 91, 217, 225–46, 249, 273, 288, 333, 360, 361, 363, 363, 374, 378, 382, 383, 384, 388, 390, 393
Piano Concerto no. 1, 94
Piano Concerto no. 2, xi, 11, 51, 94, 245
Piano Concerto no. 4, 94
Piano Concerto no. 5, 266, 269
Piano Quartet, 9
Piano Quintet, 9
Piano Trio no. 2, 223
Pierrot astronome, 348, 349
Portraits et souvenirs, 286
Près de ces charmilles, 14
Présage de la croix, 290
Princesse jaune, La, 26, 53, 76–94, 124, 164, 170, 240, 242, 284, 288, 297, 324, 348, 360, 361, 378, 381, 383
Problèmes et Mystères, 249
Prologue to Prométhée, 290
Proserpine, xiii, 72, 77, 78, 162–89, 193, 227, 246, 250, 267, 273, 284, 287, 288, 321, 322, 362, 362, 373, 378, 380, 381, 382, 383, 387, 390, 392, 393
Psalm 17, 52
Rapsodie d'Auvergne, 164, 376
Rimes familières, 79, 194
Roi Apépi, Le, 323

Roméo et Juliette, 17
Rouet d'Omphale, Le, 53, 76, 79, 93, 243, 245
Samson et Dalila, xi, xii, xiii, 10, 24, 26, 50–75, 76, 90, 92, 93, 94, 95, 97, 121, 124, 125, 130, 131, 145, 148, 159, 164, 182, 187, 195, 204, 216, 217, 220, 222, 223, 224, 240, 242, 245, 251, 273, 275, 288, 316, 321, 324, 332, 336, 348, 352, 360, 363, 373, 377, 378, 380, 381, 382, 383, 384, 390, 391
Scène d'Horace, 17, 348, 385
Scherzo, 194
Soldats de Gédéon, Les, 78
Souvenir d'Ismaïlia, 250
Souvenirs de Frédégonde, 262
String Quartet no. 1, 286
String Quartet no. 2, 286
Suite algérienne, 125, 227
Symphony 'Urbs Roma', 11, 16
Symphony no. 1, 9, 10, 11, 14
Symphony no. 2, 11
Symphony no. 3, xi, 104, 166, 193, 332, 334, 362
Tarantelle op. 6, 11
Terre promise, La, 372
Thème varié, 249
Three Preludes and Fugues, 249
Timbre d'argent, Le, xiii, 20–49, 51, 53, 55, 57, 76, 77, 83, 88, 91, 92, 94, 95, 97, 124, 161, 164, 167, 185, 212, 242, 267, 297, 321, 332, 339, 348, 378, 381, 382, 383, 385, 392, 393
Toilette de la Marquise de Présalé, 16
Trois Tableaux symphoniques, 355
Valse langoureuse, 322
Variations on a Theme of Beethoven, 94
Vercingétorix, 249
Violin Sonata no. 1, 164
Violin Sonata no. 2, 265
Saint-Saëns, Clémence, 9, 13, 97, 128, 189, 192, 194, 315
Saint-Saëns, Jacques-Joseph-Victor, 264
Saint-Saëns, Jean-François, 96
Saint-Saëns, Marie-Laure (née Truffot), 128
Salla, Caroline, 27, 45, 167, 382
Salle, Mathilde, 348
Salomon, Marius, 96
Salvayre, Gaston
   Richard III, 163
Salzburg, 348

Sammarco, Mario, 265
San Diego, 160
San Francisco, 160, 374
Sand, George, 374
Sanderson, Sybil, 192, 227, 228, 231, 241, 249, 382
Sannois, Charles, 194, 222, 334
Saratov, 73
Sardou, Victorien, 288, 289, 292, 293, 295, 309, 310
   Grisélidis, 244
Satie, Erik, 248, 286
Sautereau, Nadine, 90
Schindler, Anton, 1
Schroeder, Marie, 24
Schubert, Franz, 166
   Erlkönig, Der, 10
Schumann, Robert, 1, 7, 386
   Dichterliebe, 391
   Symphonies, 12
Scott, Sir Walter
   Kenilworth, 17
Scribe, Eugène, 288
Scudo, Paul, 6
Seghers, François, 9, 10, 11, 12
Seneca
   Hercules Œtaeus, 274, 364
Sergine, Véra, 350, 355
Seymour, Jane, 134
Shakespeare, William, 133, 134, 318
   Henry VIII, 127, 133, 136
Shaw, George Bernard, 60, 349
Sheffield, 93
Sicard, Sylva, 290
Sieg, Charles-Victor, 22
Siena, 90
Sigibert, King, 252, 253
Silvestre, Armand, 126, 127, 130, 134, 244, 288
Simonnet, Cécile, 167
Singapore, 250
Socrates, 127
Sofia, 373
Sonzogno, Edoardo, 333
Sophocles
   Antigone, 246, 289
   Œdipus Rex, 248
   Trachiniae, The, 274, 364
Soret, Marie-Gabrielle, xiv, 92

Soubies, Albert, 15
Soudant, Hubert, 123
Soulié, Frédéric
   Mémoires du Diable, Les, 43
   Sathaniel, 189
Sousa, John Philip, 374
Stamaty, Camille, 7
Stanford, Charles Villiers, 245
Star-spangled Banner, The, 374
Stéphanne, Théodore, 97
Stockholm, 241
Stoumon, Oscar, 94
Strasbourg, 130, 376
Strauss, Richard, 1, 356
   Salome, 75, 335, 348, 350
Stravinsky, Igor, 356
   Œdipus Rex, 248
Stuttgart, 89, 360
Subra, Mlle, 148
Suffolk, Duke of, 133
Sullivan, Sir Arthur
   Mikado, The, 88
   Ruddigore, 43
Surrey, Earl of, 133
Susa, 313
Szymanowski, Karol, 380

Taffanel, Paul, 251, 266, 294, 310
Talazac, Alexandre, 73, 222
Tallis, Thomas
   Dorian Service, 130
Tardieu, Charles, 55
Taskin, Émile-Alexandre, 167, 168
Tchaikovsky, Modest Ilyich, 242
Tchaikovsky, Pyotr Ilyich, 111, 118, 157, 242, 245,
   267, 380, 385, 391, 392
   Eugene Onegin, 391
   Queen of Spades, The, 391
   Symphony no. 2, 306
   Symphony no. 4, 1, 245
Temps, Le, 320
Téqui, 195
Teyte, Maggie, 47, 348
Theocritus, 321
Théodore, Adeline, 45
Thibaud, Jacques, 332

Thierry, Augustin
   Récits des temps mérovingiens, 252
Thomas, Ambroise, 4, 92, 97, 286
   Caïd, Le, 8
   Françoise de Rimini, 96, 121
   Hamlet, 20, 24, 25, 68, 94, 108, 110, 147, 387
   Mignon, 20, 91, 168
   Psyché, 21, 43
   Songe d'une nuit d'été, Le, 8, 134
   Tempête, La, 193
Thomas, Théodore, 228
Thorel, René, 305
Thun, 335
Tippett, Michael, 380
Titian, 218
Tolbecque, Auguste, 93
Toulon, 192
Toulouse, 73, 122, 159, 182, 185, 191, 216, 224, 250, 274, 284, 287, 347, 350, 355, 357, 390
Tourniaire, Guillaume, 123, 221, 331
Travis, Francis, 90
Trémisot, Édouard, 321
Troukhanova, Natalia, 350
Trouville, 373
Troy, Eugène-Louis, 24
Truffot, Marie-Laure, 96
Tuczek, Vincenz
   Samson, 57
Tudor, Arthur, 133

Vacquerie, Auguste, 163, 164, 166, 169, 170, 182, 185, 186, 193, 246, 249
   Mes premières années de Paris, 163
Vaguet, Albert, 294
Valence, 274
Vasseur, Léon
   La Timbale d'argent,, 26
Vaucorbeil, Emmanuel, 70, 121, 124, 125, 126, 127, 130, 131, 156, 188
Vega, Lope de, 127
Verdhurt, Henri, 72, 73, 195, 222
Verdi, Giuseppe, 7, 58, 75, 114, 126, 127, 135, 157, 178, 245, 265, 335, 386, 387, 392
   Aida, 64, 75, 103, 121, 124, 150, 193, 194, 224, 251, 261, 324, 349
   Don Carlos, 25, 150

Falstaff, 204, 231, 235, 250
Macbeth, 380
Otello, 251
Rigoletto, 74, 134, 169, 193, 218
Simon Boccanegra, 118
Traviata, La, 34
Vêpres siciliennes, Les, 118
Vergnet, Edmond, 54
Verona, 73
Versailles, 93, 393
Vianesi, Augusto, 195
Viardot, Paul, 317
Viardot, Pauline, 9, 10, 54, 161, 166, 382
Vichy, 160, 240, 309, 310
Victoria, Queen, 121, 163
Vidal, Jacques, 348
Vidal, Paul, 245
Vie contemporaine, La, 249
Vienna, 55, 68, 122, 166, 224
Villot, François, 80
Virgil, 321
Visconti, 335, 336
Vizentini, Albert, 26, 27, 45, 47, 95, 267, 272
Voltaire (Arouet, François-Marie)
   Orphelin de la Chine, Un, 126
   Samson, 50, 57, 58
Voltaire, Le, 125

Wagner, Richard, 5, 7, 12, 13, 44, 67, 72, 74, 75, 78, 95, 111, 118, 132, 137, 157, 165, 166, 167, 186, 196, 220, 229, 253, 262, 286, 295, 302, 324, 332, 365, 379, 384, 388, 389, 391, 392
   Fliegende Holländer, Der, 67
   Kapitulation, Eine, 387
   Lohengrin, 5, 55, 165, 194, 224, 262
   Meistersinger, Die, 113, 165, 204, 250, 363
   Parsifal, 286, 297, 324
   Rheingold, Das, 12, 308, 363
   Ring des Nibelungen, Der, 1, 12, 95, 125, 189, 251
   Tannhäuser, 150, 165, 224, 336
   Tristan und Isolde, 12, 63, 386
   Walküre, Die, 67, 74, 168, 195, 229, 248, 327, 363
Warlock, Peter
   Capriol Suite, 211

Warot, Victor, 27
Washington, 348
Weber, Carl Maria von
   Euryanthe, 262
   Freischütz, Der, 18, 26
   Oberon, 18
Weimar, 53, 55, 57, 70, 95, 97, 121, 130, 194, 313
Wertheimber, Palmyre, 25
Wiesbaden, 72
Wilde, Oscar
   Picture of Dorian Grey, The, 43
   Salome, 75, 335
Wilhelm II, Kaiser, 348

Willy, 6, 336
Windsor, 121
Wolff, Albert, 90
Wolff, Johannes, 332
Wolsey, Thomas, 133, 134
Wood, Sir Henry, 313, 332

Xanilef, Nedje, 222
Xenophon, 315

Zambelli, Carlotta, 348
Zanardini, Angelo, 124
Zollman, Ronald, 355

Made in the USA
Columbia, SC
30 December 2024